EYEWITNESS TRAVEL GUIDES

GERMANY

Mr. & Mrs. R. H. Whitlock
426 Dean Drive Cedarcoft
Kennett Square, PA 19348

Rostock

MECKLENBURG-
LOWER
POMERANIA

Schwerin

BRANDENBURG

Berlin

Potsdam

Magdeburg

ONY-ANHALT

EASTERN
GERMANY

Leipzig

Dresden

SAXONY

rt

INGIA

Nürnberg

BAVARIA

Munich

SAXONY-ANHALT
Pages 132–147

**MECKLENBURG-
LOWER POMERANIA**
Pages 452–467

BERLIN
Pages 58–109

BRANDENBURG
Pages 118–131

THÜRINGIA
Pages 172–187

SAXONY
Pages 148–171

MUNICH
Pages196–223

BAVARIA
Pages 224–273

GERMANY

Main contributor: JOANNA EGERT-ROMANOWSKA
AND MAŁGORZATA OMILANOWSKA

DK

LONDON, NEW YORK,
MELBOURNE, MUNICH AND DELHI

Produced by Wydwnictwo Wiedza i Życie, Warsaw
CONTRIBUTORS Małgorzata Omilanowska, Marek Stańczyk,
Tomasz Torbus, Hanna Köster, Teresa Czerniewicz-Umer
CARTOGRAPHERS Kartographie Huber (Munich),
Magdalena Polak, Dariusz Romanowski
PHOTOGRAPHERS Adam Hajder, Dorota and Mariusz Jarymowiczowie,
Wojciech Mędrzak, Tomasz Myśluk, Paweł Wójcik
ILLUSTRATORS Lena Maminajszwili, Paweł Marczak,
Andrzej Wielgosz, Bohdan Wróblewski, Magdalena Żmudzińska
DTP DESIGNERS Paweł Pasternak, Paweł Kamiński
EDITORS Teresa Czerniewicz-Umer, Joanna Egert-Romanowska
PRODUCTION Anna Kożurno-Królikowska
DESIGNERS Ewa Roguska, Piotr Kiedrowski

Dorling Kindersley Limited
EDITORS Sylvia Goulding, Irene Lyford
TRANSLATORS Magda Hannay, Ian Wisniewski
DTP DESIGNERS Jason Little, Conrad Van Dyke
PRODUCTION Marie Ingledew

Printed and bound by South China Printing Co. Ltd., China

First American Edition 2001
04 05 10 9 8 7 6 5 4 3

Published in the United States by DK Publishing, Inc.,
375 Hudson Street, New York, New York 10014

Reprinted with revisions 2003, 2004

Copyright © 2001, 2004 Dorling Kindersley Limited, London

Published in Great Britain by Dorling Kindersley Limited.

ISSN 1542-1554
ISBN 0-7894-9427-2

THROUGHOUT THIS BOOK, FLOORS ARE REFERRED TO IN ACCORDANCE WITH
EUROPEAN USAGE, I.E., THE "FIRST FLOOR" IS THE FLOOR ABOVE GROUND LEVEL.

◁ **Church in Bavaria nestled at the foothills of the Alps**

CONTENTS

**Renaissance doorway of the
Rathaus (town hall) in Gotha**

Picturesque landscape in Mecklenburg

Statue of a dancing figure, Stadtmuseum in Munich *(see p204)*

Mainz Cathedral *(see pp336–7)*

HOW TO USE THIS GUIDE

HIS GUIDE will help you to get the most out of a visit to Germany, providing expert recommendations as well as thoroughly researched practical information. The first section, *Introducing Germany*, locates the country geographically and provides an invaluable historical and cultural context. Succeeding sections describe the main sights and attractions of the different regions and major cities. Feature spreads, with maps and photographs, focus on important sights. Information on accommodation and restaurants is provided in *Travellers' Needs*, while the *Survival Guide* has useful tips on everything you need to know from money to getting around.

BERLIN

This section is divided into two parts: East and West. Sights outside the centre are described in the section *Around Berlin*. All sights are numbered and plotted on a map of the region. Detailed information for each sight is given in numerical order to make it easy to locate within the chapter.

Sights at a Glance describes, by category, buildings in a particular area: Historic Streets and Buildings, Museums and Galleries, Churches, Parks and Gardens.

2 Street-by-Street Map gives a bird's-eye view of each sightseeing area described in the section.

Stars indicate the sights that no visitor should miss.

Pages marked with red refer to Berlin.

A locator map shows where you are in relation to the city plan.

1 Area Map
For easy reference the sights in each area are numbered.

A suggested route for a walk is marked with a broken red line.

3 Detailed Information
All the sights of Berlin are described individually. Addresses, telephone numbers, opening hours, admission charges and information on how to get there are given for each sight. The key to symbols is shown on the back flap.

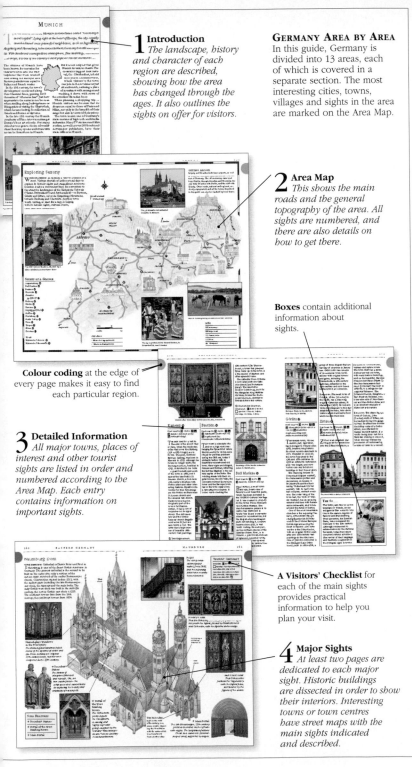

1 Introduction
The landscape, history and character of each region are described, showing how the area has changed through the ages. It also outlines the sights on offer for visitors.

GERMANY AREA BY AREA
In this guide, Germany is divided into 13 areas, each of which is covered in a separate section. The most interesting cities, towns, villages and sights in the area are marked on the Area Map.

2 Area Map
This shows the main roads and the general topography of the area. All sights are numbered, and there are also details on how to get there.

Boxes contain additional information about sights.

Colour coding at the edge of every page makes it easy to find each particular region.

3 Detailed Information
All major towns, places of interest and other tourist sights are listed in order and numbered according to the Area Map. Each entry contains information on important sights.

A Visitors' Checklist for each of the main sights provides practical information to help you plan your visit.

4 Major Sights
At least two pages are dedicated to each major sight. Historic buildings are dissected in order to show their interiors. Interesting towns or town centres have street maps with the main sights indicated and described.

INTRODUCING
GERMANY

Putting Germany on the Map

LOCATED in the centre of Europe, between the North and
Baltic Seas and the Alps, Germany covers an area of
nearly 360,000 sq km (139,000 sq miles). Its neighbouring
countries are Poland and the Czech Republic to the east,
Austria and Switzerland to the south, France, Belgium,
Luxembourg and Holland to the west, and
Denmark to the north. The capital is
Berlin. Its largest river is the
Rhine. Germany is
inhabited by over 81
million people.

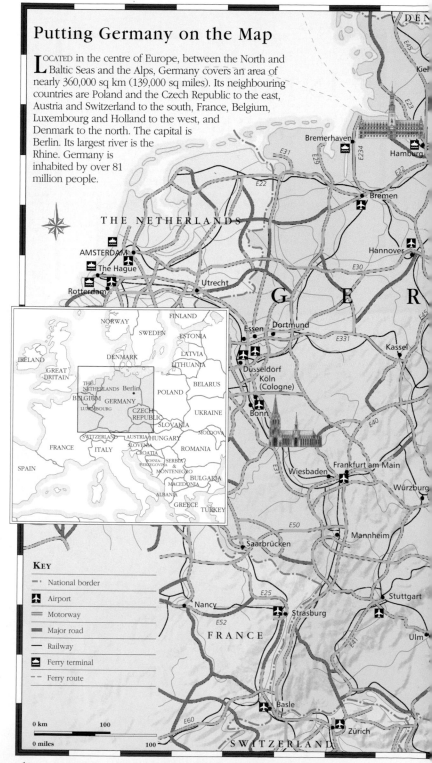

KEY

–·–·	National border
✈	Airport
═══	Motorway
━━━	Major road
───	Railway
⛴	Ferry terminal
– – –	Ferry route

0 km   100

0 miles   100

◁ **Grapevines stretching as far as the eye can see in the North Rhine-Palatinate**

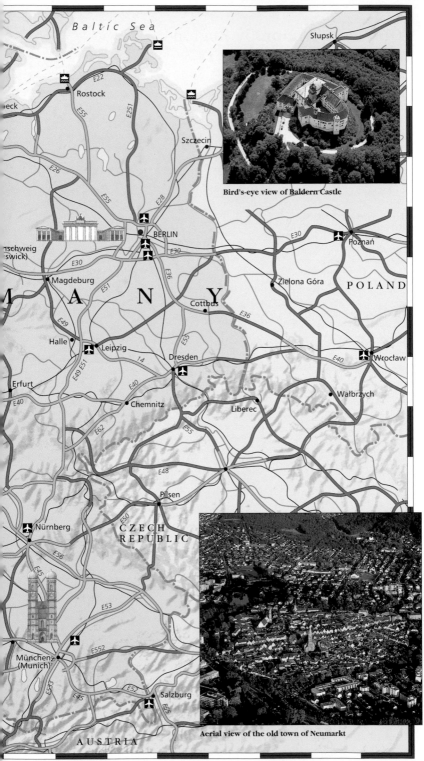

Baltic Sea

Słupsk

E22

Rostock

eck

E55

E251

E55

E26

Szczecin

Bird's-eye view of Baldern Castle

E55

E28

BERLIN

E30

E30

Poznań

nschweig
(swick)

E30

Magdeburg

E51

M   A   N   Y

Zielona Góra

P O L A N D

E49

Cottbus

E36

Halle

Leipzig

E55

Dresden

Wrocław

E49 E51

14

E40

E40

Wałbrzych

Erfurt

E40

Chemnitz

Liberec

E62

E55

E48

Pilsen

E50

C Z E C H
R E P U B L I C

Nürnberg

E56

E45

München
(Munich)

E53

E552

Salzburg

E593

E52

E55

A U S T R I A

Aerial view of the old town of Neumarkt

Germany: Region by Region

The federal republic of germany is made up of 16 states. Bremen is the smallest state, with around 700,000 inhabitants; North Rhine-Westphalia is the most densely populated state, with 18 million inhabitants. The largest state, Bavaria, covers an area of 70,531 sq km (27,232 sq miles). Berlin, Bremen and Hamburg are self-governing city-states.

How to Get There

Germany has an excellent transport system. There are 14 international airports with flights to all parts of the world; a comprehensive network of toll-free motorways that make travelling by car easy and fast; and an efficient railway system, with high-speed InterCity Express (ICE) link between major cities.

Key

✈ Airport

🚆 Railway

━━ Motorway

━━ Major road

0 km		100

0 miles		100

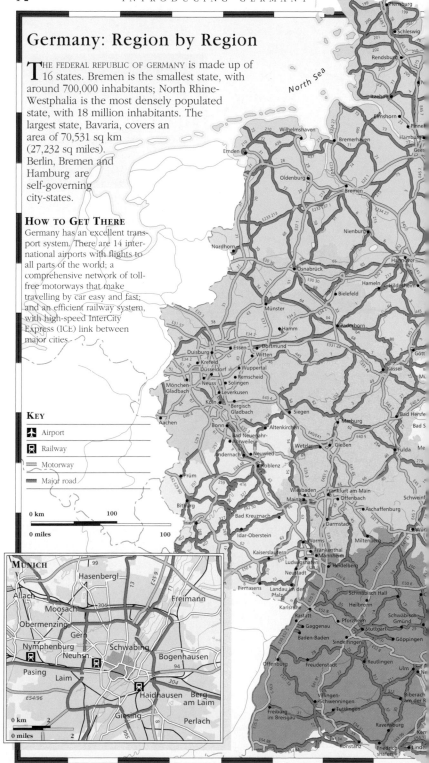

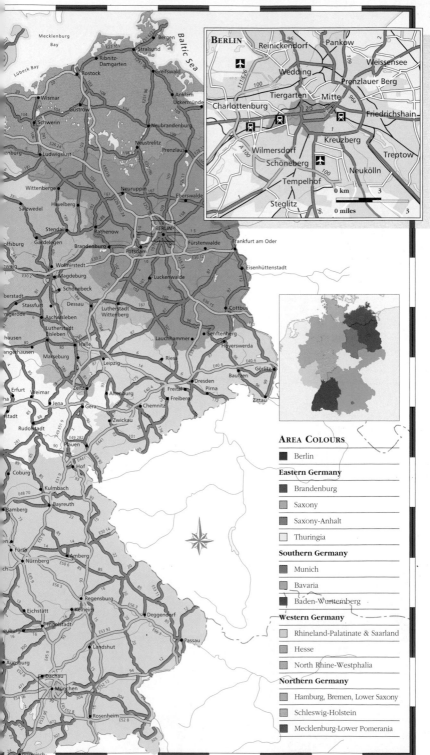

BERLIN

Reinickendorf
Pankow
Weissensee
Wedding
Prenzlauer Berg
Tiergarten
Mitte
Charlottenburg
Friedrichshain
Wilmersdorf
Kreuzberg
Schöneberg
Treptow
Tempelhof
Neukölln
Steglitz

0 km 3
0 miles 3

AREA COLOURS

Berlin

Eastern Germany

Brandenburg

Saxony

Saxony-Anhalt

Thuringia

Southern Germany

Munich

Bavaria

Baden-Württemberg

Western Germany

Rhineland-Palatinate & Saarland

Hesse

North Rhine-Westphalia

Northern Germany

Hamburg, Bremen, Lower Saxony

Schleswig-Holstein

Mecklenburg-Lower Pomerania

A PORTRAIT OF GERMANY

ERMANY IS A WEALTHY COUNTRY, *whose people are generally regarded as hard-working, determined and efficient. This view stems from the country's industrial might and the smooth functioning of its economy, but it overlooks other important aspects of Germany. These include its important contributions to art and culture, its breathtaking scenery and excellent tourist facilities.*

Contemporary Germany is far removed from the traditional, stereotyped view of the country. In the last 50 years, it has developed into a multi-ethnic, multi-cultural melting pot. Over 7 million of Germany's inhabitants are immigrants; the majority of these are Turks, with more recent guest workers arriv-ing from the former Yugoslavia, Italy and Greece. In the city of Stuttgart, every third inhabitant is a foreigner; in Frankfurt it is one in four. Hamburg has more mosques than any other city in Europe and, in some schools in Berlin, German children are in the minority. Almost every town has a selection of Italian, Chinese, Greek and Turkish restaurants and cafés, testifying to the multi-ethnicity of its population.

The colourful Bavarian coat of arms

HISTORY AND ROMANCE

For many, the river Rhine epitomizes tourist Germany, particularly the romantic stretch between Mainz and Cologne. The country has far more than this to offer in the way of scenery, however. There is the ever-changing Baltic coastline, the sandy islands of the North Sea, the lakes of Mecklenburg, lonely castles perched on crags in Baden and Thu-ringia, mountain ranges including the Alps, the vast Bodensee lake, medieval cities and fairy-tale villages. Not all of the latter are original, as countless towns were destroyed by bombs during World War II, but many have been meticu-lously rebuilt to the original plans, and now it is difficult to tell the difference between the old and the new.

Verdant Alpine meadow against a backdrop of majestic, snowy peaks

◁ **Alter Flecken – Freudenberg's quarter of traditional-style houses**

Procession during the Plärrer Fest, a beer festival in Augsburg

TRADITIONS

Today's German nation has evolved over the past thousand years, mainly from various Germanic tribes, notably the Franks, Saxons, Swabians and Bavarians. Traditions and dialects have developed within regional ethnic groups that emerged as a result of historical alliances. There is no such thing as a single German tradition. Even the assumption that Germany is a country of beer-drinkers is belied by the large numbers of wine-lovers. These groups, along with consumers of stronger beverages, have given Germany a high position in the world league table for alcohol use. Nevertheless, drunks are rarely seen in Germany.

Various ethnic groups in the country are ascribed different characteristics. The people of Mecklenburg, for example, are seen as introspective, while Swabians are regarded as thrifty; the Saxons are seen as disciplined and cunning, while Bavarians are typified as a people bound by rustic traditions, quick to quarrel and fight. Indeed, one of the most pop-

-S HUBERTUS

Bavarian scene on a beer glass

A Bavarian dressed in regional costume

ular Bavarian men's folk-dances ends with them slapping each other in the face. Bavaria, of course, is home to the traditional Oktoberfest, a beer festival that brings millions of people to Munich every year from virtually all over the world.

The people of the Rhineland have a reputation for enjoying life. Their favourite season is the Carnival period, and they spend practically the entire year preparing for this week-long event. It begins on the last Thursday before Lent, with "town soldiers", helped by the huge crowds, storming the town hall. The town councillors surrender and power passes to the masked revellers. On the Monday, the Carnival proceeds through the thronged streets of the towns on the Rhine, and the pubs are busy until the end of Shrovetide.

Carnival is rooted in ancient rituals marking the banishment of winter. This custom was most common in the south of Germany, but it also reached the Rhineland, the Palatinate and Hessen. There is a special enthusiasm for the festival among the inhabitants of the former East Germany, where Carnival used to be banned, as it had been during the Third Reich.

ART AND CULTURE

Germany is a land of sagas and legends that tell of woodland spirits, beautiful

princesses, magicians and sirens such as the Lorelei. These legends have had a strong influence on German art. An example is the German epic poem, the *Nibelungenlied*, which was written around 1200 on the basis of old legends. This poem was the inspiration for Richard Wagner's cycle of operas, *The Ring of the Nibelungen*, as well as for a trilogy of plays by Christian Friedrich Hebbel and a film by Fritz Lang.

Germans have won eight Nobel Prizes for Literature. The most recent prizewinner was Günter Grass, whose *Tin Drum* brought him world renown. More recently a film adaptation of the book was made by Volker Schlöndorff, which won the Golden Palm at the Cannes Film Festival. After a relatively stagnant period, the German film industry became revitalized around 1995 with a number of hits, albeit only at the national level. German cinemas are now always full and traditional cinemas are increasingly being replaced by multiplexes.

Germans read widely, even in today's age of television and the internet. Every year 70,000 new books are published in Germany and eight times that many titles are on sale. Germany is second only to the United States in the number of books published annually, while the number of bookshops per square kilometre is the highest in the world. The same applies to museums and art galleries.

Germany has over 2,000 national, provincial and local history museums,

The historical Frohnauer hammer forge near Annaberg in Saxony

as well as numerous church museums, folk museums and former royal palaces. This variety and choice owes much to the fact that, in the past, local dukes acquired collections of art in order to impress others and to demonstrate their wealth. The Bavarian dukes also built up extensive collections of machines, artisans' tools, musical instruments and minerals. As early as the 16th century, Munich was an international centre of the arts and the Grünes Gewölbe in 17th-century Dresden was one of the largest treasuries for storing fine art in Europe. Of the many art galleries to be found throughout Germany, the finest are in Cologne, Frankfurt, Stuttgart, Munich and Berlin.

Lorelei overlooking the Rhine

Music also flourishes in Germany. Most large cities have their own symphony orchestra and opera company and every year some 100 regional and local music festivals take place. Musical comedies are especially popular.

The imposing Schönburg Castle, near Oberwesel on the Rhine

SOCIETY AND POLITICS

The scars of World War II are more evident in Eastern Germany, although they are gradually disappearing there, too. Görlitz, Bautzen, Leipzig and Weimar have now acquired a splendour that was previously hidden behind the grim façade of East Germany. The mental, social and political scars of the war and subsequent division of Germany have, however, left deeper scars. Although reunification took place on 3 October 1990, unity among the people themselves has been longer in

The *Bundestag* in session in the old Reichstag building

coming. East Germans are the poor relations: the region has high unemployment rates and its people tend to regard their western counterparts as arrogant and self-assured. The latter, for their part, claim that the inhabitants of the "new states" are jealous and ungrateful despite the billions of marks that have been poured into the region to equalize living standards.

Germany has almost always been divided regionally into states with fluctuating borders. The present-day states were, for the most part, created after 1945 while those in East Germany were not created until forty years later. In all cases, old territorial and historical ties were taken into account. That is the reason for their evocative names, such as the "Free State of Bavaria" or the "Free State of Saxony".

There are now 16 federal states, or provinces. North Rhine-Westphalia, Baden-Wurttemberg and Bavaria are the largest and are like economically powerful countries. At the other end of the scale, the tiny province of Saarland has only 1.1 million inhabitants, while the Free Hanseatic City of Bremen has fewer than 700,000. The former East German states are also relatively small but all play an important role in the *Bundesrat*, or Federal Council, where they are instrumental in enacting legislation. All laws, apart from those relating to the Federation as a whole, such as defence or foreign policy, require the agreement of the *Bundesrat*, which is made up from current local governments. Depending on the number of inhabitants, each federal state has from four to six votes.

The skyline of Frankfurt am Main, reminiscent of New York

A government with a majority in the *Bundestag* (parliament) cannot always count on support in the *Bundesrat*, even if it has a majority there. Each state looks after its own interests and often makes alliances with other states to achieve its own aims, without regard for party loyalty. The complex working of German federalism is based on the compromises that this system makes necessary.

Bathers on the sandy beaches of Norddeich

DAILY LIFE

The traditional image of German women used to be summed up in the "three Ks": *Küche, Kinder, Kirche* (kitchen, children, church). As in other Western European countries, however, this stereotype no longer holds true. Although cookery is fashionable and there are countless TV cookery programmes starring celebrity chefs, for everyday meals, ready-prepared dishes are eaten, either at the work canteen or from the supermarket. The German birthrate is declining, while the anti-authoritarian model of education that was introduced in the 1960s has to some extent relieved parents of many of the more onerous duties of child-rearing. As a result, many young people show little respect for their elders. The churches, for their part, are usually empty. Although the largest churches (Catholic and Protestant) have many adherents, the vast majority are not practising believers and limit themselves to the payment of church dues.

Participant in a parade marking the Reunification celebrations

Germans speak of themselves as a high-performance society *(Leistungsgesellschaft)*, which gives the highest rewards to those who devote almost all their energies to their careers. As a result, stress is often a factor in people's lives, from schooldays onwards. In Germany today there are increasing numbers of people who live alone.

Single-person households are most common in the cities and even young people regard their careers as of paramount importance. Increasingly large numbers say that they are not interested in having a family.

Nevertheless, Germans enjoy mass events such as public holidays and popular festivals. The country has the highest number of public holidays in Europe and German workers have the longest annual holidays. Its citizens are Europe's most enthusiastic travellers, each year spending over DM 70 million on foreign holidays. When they return there is a tendency to long for the southern climes they have just visited – perhaps this explains why restaurants offering Mediterranean food are so popular.

The Bodensee, a popular tourist destination

Flora and Fauna

Black-headed gull

GERMANY IS A VAST country whose varied geography has given rise to a great diversity of flora and fauna. It is famous for its forests, many of mixed deciduous trees, including oak, beech and birch. Around 31 per cent of the country is forested. The Alpine regions have a rich variety of wild flowers, with meadow species a particular feature in spring and summer. On the northern peat moors, heaths and heathers are common. Germany is home to a wide range of wildlife, including wild boar, lynx and marmots. Many valuable wildlife areas have now been placed under protection.

GERMAN WILDLIFE

The fauna of Germany is typical of central Europe, with a variety of woodland, wetland and Alpine birds. Of the larger mammals, visitors are most likely to see deer, squirrels and foxes. Small populations of rarer species such as lynx and European beaver exist, but these are threatened with extinction.

Alpine raven

COASTAL REGIONS

Germany's coasts vary considerably: the North Sea coast is predominantly flat with drained land, dikes and islands; the Baltic Sea coast is hillier with sandy inlets and cliffs. Together with differences in tides and temperature, these variations determine the variety of species found along coastal regions.

Cross-leaved heath *is a species of heath that is commonly found growing on the moors and peat bogs and in the damp coastal forests of northern Germany.*

Sea lavender *is one of the salt-tolerant species that grow along Germany's North Sea coast.*

Sea holly *is a beautiful thistle-like plant with an amethyst hue. It is commonly found growing in sand dunes.*

LAKES

Most of Germany's lakes are grouped in the northern part of the country, mainly in the Mecklenburg region, where they are divided from the south by the mountain ranges, rifts and valleys of the Central Uplands. However, the largest lake in Germany – the Bodensee (Lake Constance) – is situated in the south, on the border with Austria and Switzerland.

Yellow floating heart *grows in shallow, fertile water. Its habitats are disappearing but it still survives in the Rhine basin and on the lower Elbe.*

The white water lily, *with its elegant floating flowers and lush foliage, adorns lakes and reservoirs.*

Yellow flag *is a protected species of iris that is found amongst reeds and in damp woodlands, particularly in older, mixed species forests.*

Wild boars are mammals of the pig family, living in boggy forests. They feed mainly on acorns, beechnuts and the small animals that live in the ground cover of the forest.

Deer live in leafy and mixed forests and are one of the most common mammals seen in Germany.

Marmots live on vegetation growing in the high Alpine meadows. Rodents of the squirrel family, they sleep in burrows at night and whistle loudly when anxious.

Lynx are distinguished by small tufts of hair on the tips of their ears. These mammals are becoming ever rarer.

UPLANDS

Upland landscapes dominate the southern part of Germany, including Bavaria. Here, the climate is mild, and forests cover nearly a third of the region. In this picturesque and popular part of the country, winter-sports centres and spa resorts are common.

MOUNTAINS

Mountain ranges in Germany vary both in age and in height above sea level. Older, not very high mountains covered with forests predominate. The Bavarian Alps are higher and more recent. Here sub-alpine plants grow, with alpine plants at higher altitudes.

Beech is one of the commonest trees found in Germany's forests of mixed deciduous species.

Gentian, with its intensely blue trumpet-like flowers, is one of the most impressive plants to be seen in the Alps. It is pollinated by bumblebees.

Holly, the symbol of Christmas with its glossy leaves and scarlet berries, is found in forests of beech or beech and fir in the west of the country.

Edelweiss is a small flowering plant with flat, white flowers and grey-green woolly leaves. It grows high up in the Alps.

Hepatica is a protected plant in Germany. It blooms in early spring and the seeds of the blue, star-like flowers are distributed by ants.

Rhododendron hirsutum is a low, dense variety of rhododendron, one of a group of plants that grow at sub-Alpine levels.

German Literature

THE FIRST KNOWN examples of written German date from the 8th century. German literature flourished in the Renaissance, although it was mainly later writers who entered the world's canon of great literature. Goethe and Schiller, who wrote many of their most famous works in the *Sturm und Drang* (Storm and Stress) era, in the late 18th century, count among the greatest. Germany also produced many dramatists, poets and novelists in the 19th and 20th centuries. German writers have won eight Nobel Prizes for literature, awarded to Nelly Sachs, Thomas Mann, Heinrich Böll and Günter Grass among others.

Schleswig-Holstein

Gotthold Ephraim Lessing
(1729–81), the most famous German writer of the Age of Enlightenment, wrote dramas such as Nathan the Wise, *reviews of plays performed in Hamburg as well as essays on literary and cultural theory.*

Lower Saxony, Hamburg, Bremen

North Rhine-Westphalia

Erich Maria Remarque
(1898–1970) emigrated from Germany in 1931. His pacifist writings, including All Quiet on the Western Front *and* L'Arc de Triomphe, *brought him acclaim around the world.*

Hesse

The Brothers Grimm,
Jacob Ludwig Karl (1785–1863) and Wilhelm Karl (1786–1859), were university professors and philologists, but better known as writers of some of the world's favourite fairy-tales.

Rhineland-Palatinate & Saarland

Baden-Württemberg

Friedrich Schiller
(1759–1805) wrote about the concept of individual freedom in his great dramas, such as The Robbers *and* Wallenstein. *He also wrote ballads and songs, including* Ode to Joy.

0 km   75

0 miles   75

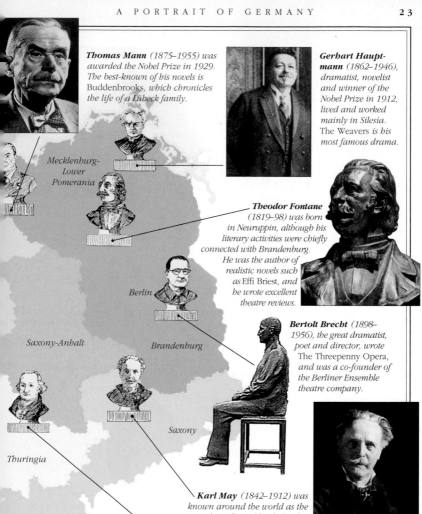

Thomas Mann *(1875–1955) was awarded the Nobel Prize in 1929. The best-known of his novels is* Buddenbrooks, *which chronicles the life of a Lübeck family.*

Gerhart Hauptmann *(1862–1946), dramatist, novelist and winner of the Nobel Prize in 1912, lived and worked mainly in Silesia.* The Weavers *is his most famous drama.*

Mecklenburg-Lower Pomerania

Theodor Fontane *(1819–98) was born in Neuruppin, although his literary activities were chiefly connected with Brandenburg. He was the author of realistic novels such as* Effi Briest, *and he wrote excellent theatre reviews.*

Berlin

Saxony-Anhalt

Brandenburg

Bertolt Brecht *(1898–1956), the great dramatist, poet and director, wrote* The Threepenny Opera, *and was a co-founder of the Berliner Ensemble theatre company.*

Saxony

Thuringia

Karl May *(1842–1912) was known around the world as the author of travel books but his great popularity stems from a cycle of stories featuring the Indian chief* Winnetou, *which he wrote in Radebeul.*

Bavaria

Johann Wolfgang von Goethe *(1749–1832) was the most highly acclaimed German poet and writer of the* Sturm und Drang *period. Born in Frankfurt, he spent most of his life in Weimar. His most famous work is* Faust.

Munich

Lion Feuchtwanger *(1884–1958) lived in Munich until his opposition to the National Socialists forced him to emigrate in 1933. He wrote in exile, alluding to contemporary events in his historical novels.*

Music in Germany

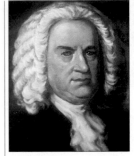

GERMAN COMPOSERS have made an enormous contribution to the world's cultural heritage. Many great musical geniuses were born and worked here, including Johann Sebastian Bach and Ludwig van Beethoven. Today their work, and that of other German composers, continues to be performed to enthusiastic new generations of music-lovers in concert halls and opera houses around the world. In Germany, their work is celebrated regularly at hugely popular music festivals.

Richard Strauss

Renowned composer, Johann Sebastian Bach (1685–1750)

EARLY MUSIC

DURING THE EARLY Middle Ages, music evolved in the courts and monasteries of Europe. The basis of sacred music was the Gregorian chant, which was introduced by Pope Gregory I in the late 6th century. An influential role in medieval court music was played by roving poets (*Minnesänger*), who sang love verses to a lute accompaniment. From the 14th century, German singing guilds known as *Meistersinger* emerged. Unlike the *Minnesänger*, these artistes adopted a settled lifestyle. In the succeeding centuries, both vocal and instrumental music continued to evolve, with many new forms appearing.

In the second half of the 17th century, interest in organ music developed and organ schools were established in many towns. One of the best

was in Nuremberg. This was directed by Johann Pachelbel (c.1653–1706), who worked in Vienna, Stuttgart, Erfurt and Nuremberg as a church organist. He is best known for his organ work *Canon*, a set of variations on a theme.

The first German opera, *Dafne*, was composed by Heinrich Schütz (1585–1672). Completed in 1627, the opera has unfortunately been lost.

THE 18TH CENTURY

A HUGE FLOWERING of musical talent took place in Germany during the 18th century, when divisions both in German politics and religion led to the development of several important artistic and cultural centres. The most

Georg Friedrich Händel (1685–1759)

renowned figure in German music in the 18th century was undoubtedly Johann Sebastian Bach who, until 1717, was associated with the Weimar court. From 1723 until his death, he was associated with Leipzig, where he was the choir master at the church of St Thomas. Bach's output as a composer is vast and embraces most of the musical forms known at that time. His Passions are today performed in many countries during Holy Week, and his Brandenburg Concertos are among his most frequently performed works. His sons – Wilhelm Friedemann, Carl Philipp Emanuel, Johann Christoph Friedrich and Johann Christian – also became acclaimed composers and made significant contributions to German classical music.

Georg Friedrich Händel was another great composer of late Baroque music. Before forging a prestigious career in England, he began as the cathedral organist in Halle, from where he transferred to the opera house in Hamburg. A friend of Händel and another important composer, Georg Philipp Telemann (1681–1767) was employed as conductor at many German courts. His work includes chamber music, operas and church music.

MUSIC FESTIVALS

Germany is a country of musical festivals, which are usually held in the summer and early autumn. Among the most popular are the festivals dedicated to the works of a single composer, such as Wagner in Bayreuth, Bach in various cities of Thuringia, Handel in Halle and Beethoven in Bonn. Apart from these specialized festivals, opera festivals with a broader repertoire are also popular. These include the outdoor opera festival in Berlin and the Sommerfestspiele in Xanten.

The Bach festival in Leipzig's Church of St Thomas

Son of a court musician and arguably the greatest figure in classical music, Ludwig van Beethoven (1770–1827) was born in Bonn, although he worked mainly in Vienna. Among his best-known works are his nine symphonies, as well as piano and violin concertos, two masses, various chamber works and the opera *Fidelio*.

The life of this great composer, is shrouded in legend. Succeeding generations have been fascinated not just by his music, but also by the fact that he began to lose his hearing at the age of 30. During his final years, when totally deaf, he composed from memory.

Statue of Ludwig van Beethoven

THE 19TH CENTURY

ROMANTICISM brought about the flowering of opera in Germany. One of the leading creators in this tradition was the composer Ernst Theodor Amadeus Hoffmann (1776–1822), whose opera *Undine* was staged for the first time in 1816 in Berlin. Carl Maria von Weber (1786–1826) rose to prominence following the success of his opera *Der Freischütz*. which was the first opera in the German Romantic tradition. Another

Composer Felix Mendelssohn-Bartholdy (1809–47)

major figure from this time was Felix Mendelssohn-Bartholdy, whose "Wedding March" from *A Midsummer Night's Dream* accompanies wedding celebrations around the world. As well as this famous piece of music, however, Mendelssohn left a legacy that includes five symphonies, piano music, chamber music and oratorios. In 1843, Mendelssohn founded Germany's first musical conservatory, in Leipzig.

The master of chamber music was Robert Schumann (1810–56), a poet and composer whose miniature works for piano, violin sonatas and song cycles all remain popular. The Hungarian composer Franz Liszt, who worked in Weimar from 1848 to 1861, also made a significant contribution to the evolution of German music.

In the second half of the 19th century, Richard Wagner was the major influence on German opera. During his early years, he composed traditional operas such as *Tannhäuser*. He later developed his own creative synthesis, integrating lyrics with the music. This found its finest expression in his Ring cycle, which was based on medieval sagas. Wagner's ideas about musical theatre, including his use of *leitmotifs* (recurring phrases), were adopted by Richard Strauss (1864–1949), who composed many operas, symphonies and songs. The first bars of his symphonic poem *Zarathustra* became a guiding musical motif in Stanley Kubrick's 1968 film *2001: A Space Odyssey*. Johannes Brahms (1833–97) composed in traditional forms and was

Richard Wagner (1813–83)

Composer and pianist Johannes Brahms (1833–97)

unsympathetic to the progressive ideas of Wagner and Liszt. From 1872 to 1875, Brahms was the musical director of the *Gesellschaft der Musikfreunde* (Society of Friends of Music).

THE 20TH CENTURY

DURING THE 20th century, many contemporary composers continued the traditions of the earlier masters. One renowned figure was Paul Hindemith (1895–1963), whose work includes opera, ballet and concertos. His music was banned by the Nazis in 1933 and Hindemith emigrated to the USA in 1939.

Another important figure in German musical life was Carl Orff (1895–1982) whose best-known work is the oratorio *Carmina Burana*, based on 13th-century Latin and German poems found in a Benedictine monastery in Bavaria. The Austrian composer Arnold Schönberg (1874–1951) lived in Berlin during the 1920s and exerted great influence on German music.

Among the most important composers living and working in Germany today, mention should be made of Hans Werner Henze, Paul-Heinz Ditrich, Dieter Schnebel, Helmut Lachenmann and Georg Katzer.

German Painting

THE DIVERSITY IN German painting has its roots in the political and religious divisions that existed in the country in the past. The Old Masters working in the north, for example, were more likely to be influenced by the Netherlandish school, while artists working in the south leaned towards Italian styles. German art reached the peak of its individuality during the late-Gothic, late-Baroque and Expressionist periods – all periods when one of the chief characteristics of artistic style was strength of expression.

Emil Nolde (1867–1956), one of Germany's foremost Expressionists, painted landscapes of his native region. Pictured above is his North Friesian Landscape.

Schlesw Holstei

Master Francke (14th–15th century) was the leading representative of the North German Late-Gothic style, working in Hamburg c.1410–24. He painted religious scenes and his works include St Thomas's Altar, *of which this is a detail.*

Bremen, Hamburg and Lower Saxony

North Rhine-Westphalia

Hesse

Rhineland-Palatinate and Saarland

Peter von Cornelius (1783–1867) joined the Nazarenes during the anti-academic rebellion. He later became director of the academy in Dusseldorf and others. He painted the picture The Wise and Foolish Maidens *at that time.*

Baden-Wurttemburg

Adam Elsheimer (1578–1610) was born in Frankfurt am Main but spent most of his life in Rome. His poignant landscapes, such as The Flight to Egypt *shown here, greatly influenced the development of 17th-century painting.*

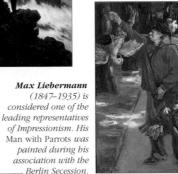

Caspar David Friedrich
(1774–1840) was one of the most prominent exponents of Romanticism. He created poignant images, such as this Traveller above the Sea of Clouds, *in which Man contemplates the power of Nature as created by God.*

Mecklenburg-Lower Pomerania

Max Liebermann
(1847–1935) is considered one of the leading representatives of Impressionism. His Man with Parrots *was painted during his association with the Berlin Secession.*

Berlin

Saxony-Anhalt

Brandenburg

Lionel Feininger
(1871–1956) was born in the USA but spent much of his life in Germany. He lectured at the Bauhaus and painted Cubist-inspired scenes of architectural subjects, such as this Gelmeroda IX.

Saxony

Thuringia

Albrecht Dürer *(1471–1528) is one of the best-known German painters. This great master of the Renaissance period was also an outstanding engraver and art-historian. His* Paumgärtners' Altar *was made for St Catherine's Church in Nuremberg.*

Bavaria

Munich

Wilhelm Leibl *(1844–1900) painted this scene of women praying in a village church in Bavaria,* Three Women in a Church, *which is regarded as one of the outstanding works of German Realism.*

0 kilometres 80

0 miles 80

Castles in Germany

IN A NUMBER OF GERMAN regions, medieval castles are among the most characteristic features of the landscape. Some have survived only in the form of picturesque ruins, but many others, refurbished and modernized over the years, continue to be the main residence for the families for whom they were built. The most impressive grouping of great fortresses is to be found along the banks of the Mosel and the central Rhine, while, in the Münster area, you will see the most beautiful moated castles to have survived in the lowlands.

Crest from the castle portal in Gotha

The Great Knights' Hall, where knights ate, drank and entertained, was a feature of every castle.

The 15th-century Michaels-kapelle

Marburg Castle *is one of the best-preserved fortresses in Hesse. At its core is a 12th-century building, but the castle's current appearance is the result of work carried out between the 14th and 16th centuries* (see p355).

The Royal Room was an apartment specially designated for the use of important guests.

The Wartburg *in Eisenach is one of the most important monuments in Thuringia, not only because of its excellently preserved architecture but also for its association with Martin Luther* (see pp176–7).

Heidelberg Castle *has survived as a picturesque ruin. A Gothic-Renaissance structure of imposing proportions, it continues to captivate with its commanding position and fascinating architecture* (see pp284–5).

Gardens were laid out in the 19th century in an area between the castle walls and the site of the farm buildings.

Raesfeld *is one of the most beautiful castles in Münsterland, a region of Westphalia that is renowned for its historic moated castles. The castle was extended in the mid-17th century for Alexandra II von Velen (see p374).*

19TH-CENTURY CASTLES

In the 19th century, many ruined castles in Germany were rebuilt in a wave of nostalgia for the Middle Ages. A number of completely new castles were built, which were modelled on medieval designs.

The Schwerin castle, *built on an island, has a 16th-century chapel, but the rest, dating from 1843–57, was inspired by the French castles along the river Loire (see p456).*

Lichtenstein castle
owes its fame to the novel Lichtenstein *by Wilhelm Hauff and its beauty to the Romantic-style remodelling that was carried out in 1840–41 (see p301).*

Evangelical Chapel

The main entrance to the castle leads through a gate house – here in the form of a tower.

Wernigerode's *castle dominates the entire city. Despite later extensions, it has retained a late-Gothic tower, a beautiful staircase dating from 1495 and some valuable furnishings (see p136).*

BURG HOHENZOLLERN

The family seat of the Hohenzollern family, Burg Hohenzollern in Hechingen, is set on a clifftop in the Swabian Jura. The first building was established here in the 13th century and rebuilt many times over the years. The current medieval appearance is the result of work that was carried out in 1850–67 in the spirit of romantic historicism *(see p300).*

Burg Eltz, *set high above the Mosel, is one of the most beautiful castles in Germany. Built between the 12th and 16th centuries, it has survived with very few alterations (see p331).*

German Scientists and Inventors

GERMANY IS POPULARLY regarded as a nation of practical people, so it is hardly surprising that the history books abound with the names of Germans who have made important contributions to technological progress and the development of science. They include Johann Gutenberg (c.1400–68), who invented printing with movable type, and Karl Benz (1844–1929) and Gottlieb Daimler (1834–1900) who developed the first petrol-driven car. In terms of Nobel Prize winners alone (and not counting those who received the prize for achievements in other fields), there is currently a total of 69 Germans. One of the most illustrious of these is physicist Albert Einstein (1879–1955).

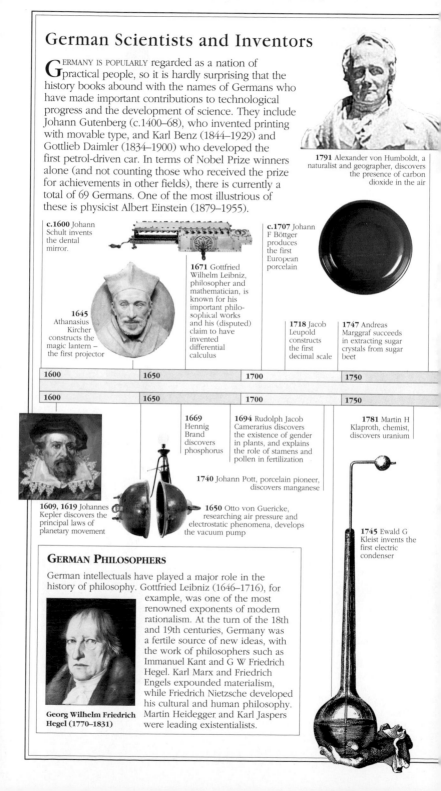

1791 Alexander von Humboldt, a naturalist and geographer, discovers the presence of carbon dioxide in the air

c.1600 Johann Schult invents the dental mirror.

1671 Gottfried Wilhelm Leibniz, philosopher and mathematician, is known for his important philosophical works and his (disputed) claim to have invented differential calculus

c.1707 Johann F Böttger produces the first European porcelain

1645 Athanasius Kircher constructs the magic lantern – the first projector

1718 Jacob Leupold constructs the first decimal scale

1747 Andreas Marggraf succeeds in extracting sugar crystals from sugar beet

1600	1650	1700	1750

1600	1650	1700	1750

1669 Hennig Brand discovers phosphorus

1694 Rudolph Jacob Camerarius discovers the existence of gender in plants, and explains the role of stamens and pollen in fertilization

1781 Martin H Klaproth, chemist, discovers uranium

1740 Johann Pott, porcelain pioneer, discovers manganese

1609, 1619 Johannes Kepler discovers the principal laws of planetary movement

1650 Otto von Guericke, researching air pressure and electrostatic phenomena, develops the vacuum pump

1745 Ewald G Kleist invents the first electric condenser

GERMAN PHILOSOPHERS

German intellectuals have played a major role in the history of philosophy. Gottfried Leibniz (1646–1716), for example, was one of the most renowned exponents of modern rationalism. At the turn of the 18th and 19th centuries, Germany was a fertile source of new ideas, with the work of philosophers such as Immanuel Kant and G W Friedrich Hegel. Karl Marx and Friedrich Engels expounded materialism, while Friedrich Nietzsche developed his cultural and human philosophy. Martin Heidegger and Karl Jaspers were leading existentialists.

Georg Wilhelm Friedrich Hegel (1770–1831)

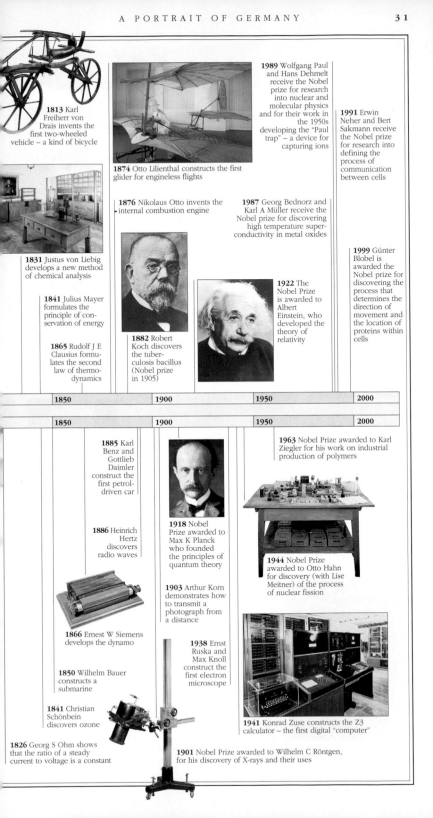

1813 Karl Freiherr von Drais invents the first two-wheeled vehicle – a kind of bicycle

1989 Wolfgang Paul and Hans Dehmelt receive the Nobel prize for research into nuclear and molecular physics and for their work in the 1950s developing the "Paul trap" – a device for capturing ions

1991 Erwin Neher and Bert Sakmann receive the Nobel prize for research into defining the process of communication between cells

1874 Otto Lilienthal constructs the first glider for engineless flights

1876 Nikolaus Otto invents the internal combustion engine

1987 Georg Bednorz and Karl A Müller receive the Nobel prize for discovering high temperature super-conductivity in metal oxides

1831 Justus von Liebig develops a new method of chemical analysis

1841 Julius Mayer formulates the principle of con-servation of energy

1865 Rudolf J E Clausius formu-lates the second law of thermo-dynamics

1882 Robert Koch discovers the tuber-culosis bacillus (Nobel prize in 1905)

1922 The Nobel Prize is awarded to Albert Einstein, who developed the theory of relativity

1999 Günter Blobel is awarded the Nobel prize for discovering the process that determines the direction of movement and the location of proteins within cells

| 1850 | 1900 | 1950 | 2000 |

| 1850 | 1900 | 1950 | 2000 |

1885 Karl Benz and Gottlieb Daimler construct the first petrol-driven car

1963 Nobel Prize awarded to Karl Ziegler for his work on industrial production of polymers

1886 Heinrich Hertz discovers radio waves

1918 Nobel Prize awarded to Max K Planck who founded the principles of quantum theory

1903 Arthur Korn demonstrates how to transmit a photograph from a distance

1944 Nobel Prize awarded to Otto Hahn for discovery (with Lise Meitner) of the process of nuclear fission

1866 Ernest W Siemens develops the dynamo

1938 Ernst Ruska and Max Knoll construct the first electron microscope

1850 Wilhelm Bauer constructs a submarine

1841 Christian Schönbein discovers ozone

1826 Georg S Ohm shows that the ratio of a steady current to voltage is a constant

1941 Konrad Zuse constructs the Z3 calculator – the first digital "computer"

1901 Nobel Prize awarded to Wilhelm C Röntgen, for his discovery of X-rays and their uses

German Beer

ALTHOUGH FINE WINES are produced in Germany, beer is unquestionably the country's favourite alcoholic drink. Germans drink an average of 140 litres of beer annually and Bavarians lead the world in consumption, drinking an average of 240 litres each per annum. Beer is drunk on every occasion, but it tastes best in the summer when it is poured straight from a barrel at one of the numerous festivals or public holidays.

Hop flower cones

The **mass** *is a tankard that is used to serve beer in Bavaria. It holds a litre, but waitresses are used to carrying eight or nine such tankards at a time.*

Historic brewing facilities in Freising (see p251)

GERMAN BREWERIES

IN GERMANY most towns and the larger villages have a brewery. The country's oldest brewery, established in 1040, is the Weihenstephan Benedictine monastery in Freising, which is believed to be the oldest working brewery in the world. Many large breweries and consortiums produce beer that is known throughout the world, but beers produced by small operators, which are available only in a few regional pubs, are in no way inferior. When visiting Germany, do try the produce of small local breweries as well as the beer produced by the giants, such as Paulaner and Löwenbrau.

Logo of the famous Munich brewery, Paulaner

STYLES OF BEER

ONE OF THE MOST POPULAR STYLES of beer is *Pils* (short for *Pilsener*) a light, bottom-fermented beer of the lager type. Of the seasonal beers, it is worth trying spring beers such as *Maibock* or *Doppelbock*, and in autumn the strong beer that is brewed especially for the Oktoberfest. In the lower Rhine valley, *Altbier* is still produced; this is a top-fermented beer, prepared by traditional methods. In the south, *Weizenbier*, a wheat beer, is also produced. The Berlin version, *Berliner Weisse* (white beer), is served with fruit juice. Dark beers, such as *Dunkel* and *Schwarzbier*, also enjoy great popularity. Breweries have their own specialities. In Bamberg, they produce *Rauchbier*, which has a light smokiness; in Kulmbach it is *Eisbock*, which gains its thicker consistency through a freezing process.

Wheat beer, Berliner Weisse

Seasonal autumn beer, Bock

The largest pub in the world, created during the Oktoberfest

DRINKING BEER

IN GERMANY, BEER is served with a head. Pouring lager from a barrel is supposed to take about 10 minutes, so the head sinks to the regulation level and has a thick consistency. A small beer is normally 0.3 litre, a large one 0.5 litre. In Bavaria, however, a large beer is served in a *Mass*, a tankard holding 1 litre. When travelling in Germany, order the brew of the local brewery, ideally in a *Bierkeller* or *Bierstube* (pub) and, in summer, in a *Biergarten* (beer garden). The largest gardens are in Bavaria – Munich's *Hirschgarten* caters for 8,000 beer drinkers. The Oktoberfest, which is celebrated each year in Munich (see p217), is the largest beer festival in the world.

How Beer is Brewed

The method of brewing beer that is now virtually standard dates from the 19th century, when Czech brewers first produced bottom-fermented beers at lower temperatures. The method was perfected by Gabriel Sedlmayr. Each brewery has its secrets, but the initial stages of production are the same.

A climbing plant, hops are trained to grow up special supports

Mashing vat

Barley and hops

1 The main ingredients in the production of beer are barley, hops and crystal-clear water. Other grains, including wheat and rice, can also be used – for example Weizenbier is made from wheat rather than barley. The first stage of brewing is malting, when the grains are soaked and left to germinate. After a few days, these are dried and then milled.

2 The milled barley is mixed with warm water and placed in a copper mashing vat. During the mashing process, the starches in the grain turn into fermentable sugars. The mash is then filtered to separate out a liquid, known as the wort, from the mash.

3 The wort is put into a copper vessel with the hops and then cooked. Depending on the amount of hops added, the beer will be more or less bitter. Traditionally the hops are added to the vessel by hand, in carefully measured proportions. Sometimes, however, they are added, as required, during the cooking process.

4 The wort is filtered again, cooled and combined with yeast. Fermentation then takes place. At temperatures above 20° C (68° F), the liquid reaches "top fermentation", which takes 3–5 days. "Bottom fermentation", where the temperature is below 12° C (54° F), takes 7–10 days.

5 The young beer produced by fermentation is left to rest in special containers that enable a higher pressure to be maintained. During this resting stage, which can last from a couple of weeks to a year or even longer, the beer matures. The effect of resting the beer is to make it stronger. Resting takes place in metal or traditional wooden barrels.

6 The mature beer, which is ready to be sold, is then transferred to bottles or cans and pasteurized. This process removes micro-organisms that threaten the quality of the beer.

Traditional wooden barrels containing resting beer

Sport in Germany

SPORT HAS LONG enjoyed a significant role in German life both for active participants and spectators. The country regularly produces world champions in a variety of activities, including football, tennis and motor racing. Excellent facilities exist throughout the country for taking part in sporting activities, including sailing, swimming, climbing and skiing as well as in field- or track-based events. Southern Germany plays host to a variety of winter sports and competitions.

The German Open in Hamburger Rothenbaum

FOOTBALL

THE LARGEST SPORTS organi-zation in the country, the German Football Association has over 6 million registered members in some 25,000 clubs. The national team has won the World Cup three times – in 1954, 1974 and 1990 – and the European Cup in 1972, 1980 and 1996.

One of the outstanding figures in German football is Franz Beckenbauer, who was a member of the team that won the European Cup in 1972 and the World Cup in 1974. He trained the team that took second place in the 1986 World Cup and first place in 1990. Beckenbauer was twice named the best footballer in Europe.

The best-known club is Bayern München, which has won the German Cup a record 16 times. Matches between teams in the elite *Bundesliga* enjoy a great following. League matches are held on Saturday afternoons while European Cup games are usually held on Wednesday evenings. The club teams include a

significant number of professionals from abroad. The 2006 World Cup will be held in Germany.

Competing in Hamburg's annual Deutsches Spring Derby

SHOW-JUMPING AND EQUESTRIAN EVENTS

SHOW-JUMPING is another sport at which Germany excels. Since it was intro-duced to the Olympic Games in 1912, German riders have won 32 gold, 18 silver and 21 bronze medals. Major equestrian events are held in Hamburg and Aachen in June. Hamburg's Derby Week is popular with racing fans.

LAWN TENNIS

THE GERMAN TENNIS Assoc-iation is the largest in the world with over 2 million members, belonging to some 10,200 clubs. From the mid-1980s, Germany became one of the world's most success-ful tennis nations thanks to some outstanding players. In 1985, aged 18, Boris Becker was the youngest player to win the Wimbledon champ-ionships. He repeated his achievement in 1986 and 1989 and was runner-up to fellow-German Michael Stich in 1991. From 1987–91 Steffi Graf was ranked number one among the world's female tennis players.

ATHLETICS

DURING THE COLD WAR period, East and West German athletes competed against each other for the glory of their rival political systems as much as for the love of their sport. The extra-ordinary achievements of the East German athletes during that time have since been tarnished by revelations of systematic drug abuse. Since reunification, some athletes have managed to maintain their reputations, but the majority have not.

Germany's most important event, the International Stadionfest (ISTAF), is held each year in Berlin, as the climax of the season.

Bundesliga **football match (Hertha BSC Berlin v FC Bayern München)**

FORMULA ONE

BACK IN THE 1930s, motor-racing was dominated by the famous "Silver Arrows", made by Mercedes-Benz. Formula One has been a decidedly German discipline since its beginnings in 1950. In all the events there have always been at least three German drivers taking part. The German Formula One Grand Prix is held each July at the Hockenheim-Ring, near Heidelberg. In most years there is a second Grand Prix at the Nürburgring circuit close to the Belgian border. This is dubbed the European Grand Prix or the Luxembourg Grand Prix.

Germany's leading Formula One driver, Michael Schumacher, won the World Championship in 1994, 1995 and 2000. He has also twice achieved second place and been twice in third place.

The Hockenheim race track near Heidelberg

Markus Eberle during the slalom in Ofterschwang in the Allgäu

SKIING

SINCE 1953, the last week of December and the first week of January have been dominated by the Four Ski Jumps Championship for ski jumpers. This classic event, which is held in Oberstdorf and Garmisch-Partenkirchen in Germany, as well as in Innsbruck and Bischofshofen in Austria, attracts several thousand spectators and millions of television viewers. German athletes have gained first place in this competition 15 times over the years.

As well as in the German Alps, which have the most popular ski resorts, excellent conditions exist for downhill and cross-country skiing in the less glamorous and less expensive Black Forest and the Harz Mountains.

CYCLING

CYCLING ENJOYS a great following in Germany. The Tour de France is broadcast simultaneously by two television stations, and ever-increasing numbers of people are taking part in the sport, both for pleasure and competitively. Success on the cycle track has long been a German tradition, but Jan Ullrich exceeded all expectations when he won gold in the long distance and silver in a time trial at the Sydney Olympics in 2000.

SAILING

KIELER WOCHE is the most important regatta in the world, according to Paul Henderson, the President of the International Sailing Federation. On 1 September 1881, five officers of the Emperor's navy held a yachting race in the Bay of Kiel, as it was then called. The following year 20 yachts competed while thousands of spectators watched from the shore. The championship went on to become an international event, which gained in prestige as the Emperor took part in each race from 1894 until 1914.

Today it is traditional for the president of the German Federal Republic to formally open the regatta (in the last week of June) in which thousands of yachts from many countries take part.

SWIMMING

SWIMMING, more than any other sport in Germany, has seen a decline in success since reunification and the subsequent cessation of competition between East and West. At the 1988 Olympics in Seoul, for example, Kristin Otto won 6 gold medals. In 2000, the reunified German team returned from Sydney having gained only three bronze medals. Two figures who rose to the top in the past are Michael Gross, who was a member of the West German team, and Franziska van Almsick, a member of the East German team.

Franziska von Almsick during the German Swimming Championships

GERMANY THROUGH THE YEAR

ERMANS LOVE to have fun and this is evident from the huge number of light-hearted events that are held throughout the year. Virtually every town has a calendar of festivals and fairs. These include folk festivals connected with local traditions – for example celebrating the asparagus or grape harvest.

A festival mascot

Many towns preserve the tradition of an annual fair – or *Jahrmarkt* – known in Westphalia as *Kirmes* and in Bavaria as *Dult*. Germany is also known for its music and film festivals, which attract an international audience, as well as for organizing major international trade fairs, such as the annual Frankfurt Book Fair.

Witches participating in the Walpurgisnacht celebrations in Thale

SPRING

SPRING IS an idyllic time to arrive in Germany. In the high mountains, conditions are still ideal for skiing, while in the valleys everything is already in bloom. In April and May the first spring fairs and festivals are held. Spring is also time for the traditional solemn observance of Easter and its associated celebrations. May Day, which is also International Labour Day, is marked both by traditional festivities and, in some cities, by demonstrations.

MARCH

Sommergewinn *(3 weekends before Easter)* Eisenach. The largest folk festival in Thuringia, linked with a fair.
CeBIT *(end of March)* Hanover. International trade fairs dedicated to information technology, telecommunications and automation.
Easter During Holy Week, Passion concerts are held throughout the country and colourful church services take place, particularly in

rural Catholic areas. On Easter Sunday, in cities in the Luzyce region, horse races and a gala take place.
Leipziger Buchmesse *(end of March)* Leipzig. International book fair, with antiquarian books.
Thüringer Bach-Wochen Celebration of the life and works of Johann Sebastian Bach with concerts and lectures: held in Arnstadt, Eisenach, Erfurt, Gotha, Mühlhausen and Weimar.

APRIL

Kurzfilmtage Oberhausen. The International Festival of Short Films has been held here since 1955.

The International Dixieland Festival, held annually in Dresden in May

Hannover Messe *(2nd half of April)* Hanover. International industrial trade fairs.
Hamburger Dom *(April, August and November)* Hamburg. The largest folk festival in northern Germany, held three times a year.
Walpurgisnacht *(30 April/ 1 May)* On the witches' sabbath, witches gather on Brocken Mountain and in several other places in the Harz mountains.

MAY

Maibaumaufstellen *(1 May)*. In Bavarian villages, maypoles are decorated with highly ornamental wreaths.
Rhein in Flammen *(1st Saturday in May)*. Festival with firework displays, in towns in the Rhine Valley.
Hafengeburtstag *(7 May)* Hamburg. A huge festival with fireworks, regatta and a parade of sailing boats.
Ruhrfestspiele *(May–July)* Recklinghausen. Cultural festival with a number of concerts, performances and exhibitions.
International Dixieland Festival *(2nd week of May)* Dresden. A traditional jazz festival has been held here since 1971.
Blutritt *(Friday after Ascension)* Weingarten. A horseback procession carrying religious relics around the town – held here for 450 years,
Leineweber Markt *(end of May)* Bielefeld. Street theatre, jazz and folk concerts.

SUMMER

IN GERMANY the summer is a time of great open-air festivals and other outdoor events and activities. Nearly every town and village has its festival with a parade, street shows, concerts and fairs. In many places there are colourful illuminations and firework displays. Banquets and knights' tournaments are held in historic castles, while concert series are organized in palaces and castles with the tourist particularly in mind. In June, a number of classical music festivals take place, while July is a popular month for wine and beer festivals.

Yacht race during the annual Kieler Woche regatta in Kiel

JUNE

Spreewaldfest *(June)* Spreewald. Folk festivals are held throughout the summer in Lübbenau and other villages in Spreewald.
Fronleichnam. Observed in states with a Catholic majority. Magnificent processions take place in towns in Bavaria and in Cologne.
Christopher Street Day *(mid-June)*. Gay and lesbian parades held in many cities, including Berlin and Köln.
Kieler Woche *(3rd week in June)* Kiel. Huge yachting regatta with concerts and street fairs.
Open-Air-Saison *(4th week in June, beginning of July)* Berlin. Opera festival held on outdoor stages and in squares in the city.

A wedding couple during the Landshuter Hochzeit festival

Schützenfest *(June)* marks the traditional start of the hunting season. Celebrated in many north German cities.

JULY

Landshuter Hochzeit *(every 4th summer: 2005; 2009)* Landshut. Re-enactment of the wedding feast of Georg, son of Duke Ludwig the Rich and Polish Princess Jadwiga. Costumed wedding procession and medieval tournament.
Love Parade *(2nd Saturday)* Berlin. A parade for fans of techno music, who dance throughout the day and night in all the city's discos and around vehicles equipped with sound systems.

Internationaler Johann-Sebastian-Bach Wettbewerb Leipzig. International music competition dedicated to Johann Sebastian Bach.
Schwörmontag *(penultimate Monday)* Ulm. Folk festival with a parade by the Danube.
Kinderzeche *(3rd Monday)* Dinkelsbühl. Ten-day folk festival commemorating the events of the Thirty Years' War (1618–48).
Richard-Wagner-Festspiele *(last week July/August)* Bayreuth. Festival dedicated to the works of Richard Wagner.

AUGUST

Zissel *(beginning of August)* Kassel. Picturesque folk festival with parades, markets and concerts.
Mainfest. Frankfurt am Main. Feast of the river Main.
Gäubodenfest *(mid-August)* Straubing. Folk festival with a market and beer tasting.
Rhein in Flammen *(2nd Saturday)* Koblenz. Huge firework display on the Rhine and a flotilla of illuminated passenger ships.
Wikingerfest *(even years)* Schleswig. Historical festival with costumed participants, tournaments and regattas.
Weindorf *(end August)* Stuttgart. Huge wine festival with wines served along with typical Swabian cuisine.

Performance of *Tannhäuser* at Richard-Wagner-Festspiele, Bayreuth

AUTUMN

AUTUMN IS a popular time for tourism in Germany, especially September and early October when many cities, including Berlin and Munich, organize cultural events and important festivals. The autumn is also the time when the most significant trade fairs and great sporting events take place. At this time, also, conditions in the mountains and countryside continue to be ideal for outdoor activities such as walking and cycling.

SEPTEMBER

Berliner Festwochen, Berlin. Lasting all month, this is a major series of cultural events, opera performances, exhibitions and various literary events.
Beethovenfestival, Bonn. A musical festival of the works of Beethoven in the city where he was born.
Heilbronner Herbst *(1st Saturday)* Heilbronn. Wine festival, including parades and firework displays.
Berlin-Marathon *(1st or 2nd Sunday)* Berlin. Marathon through the streets of the city centre, with runners in various age groups and the participation of the disabled in wheelchairs.
Oktoberfest *(last Saturday)* Munich. Beer festival held

Pumpkin race during Dorffest

over 16 days, beginning with a parade through the city's streets. Ceremonial removal of the bung from a new barrel of beer brewed for the festival.
Plärrer *(May and September)* Augsburg. Festival held twice a year, considered one of the most important in Swabia.
Dorffest im Spreewald *(end)* Lehde. Folk festival.
Cannstatter Wasen *(end September/beginning October)* Stuttgart. The second largest beer festival in the world.
Internationales Stadionfest (ISTAF), Berlin. The largest athletics event at the end of the season.

The International Book Fair in Frankfurt am Main

OCTOBER

Tag der Deutschen Einheit *(3 October)*. National holiday, established after re-unification. Concerts, parades and meetings.
Frankfurter Buchmesse *(2nd week in October)* Frankfurt am Main. The world's largest book fair, which attracts publishers from around the world.
Freimarkt *(mid-October)* Bremen. Two-week folk festival beginning with a procession.
Liszt-Tage Weimar. Celebration of the life and work of Franz Liszt, with concerts at which world-class musicians are invited to perform.
Ost-West Jazz Festival *(end October)* Nuremberg. International jazz folk festival.
Colmansfest *(2nd Sunday)* Schwangau. Religious festival featuring hundreds of horses and decorated carriages.

NOVEMBER

St Leonard's Day *(1st Sunday in November)*. Folk festival in Bavaria, which is held in conjunction with horse parades.
Kasseler Musiktage *(beginning of November)* Kassel. One of Europe's longest-established classical music festivals.
Weinfest *(1st weekend in November)* Cochem. Festival celebrating the removal of the bung from the first barrel of young Mosel wine.
Martinsfest *(11 November)*. St Martin's Day is celebrated in northern Baden and the Rhineland with fairs and the essential roast goose. In the Rhine Valley, St Martin's Day signifies the beginning of the Carnival season.
Internationales Film-festival *(2nd week in November)* Mannheim-Heidelberg. Annual festival of short, documentary and educational films.

A major film gala held during Berlinale in Berlin

WINTER

DECEMBER IS synonymous with Christmas festivities. Every city has fairs where you can buy Christmas-tree decorations, delicacies and presents. In December, shops have longer opening hours and the skiing season begins in the Alps. January and February are a time for parties and balls (the Carnival season), with enjoyment reaching a peak in the last few days of the season. Then the fun continues all weekend from Thursday, reaching a height on *Rosenmontag* then diminishing on the last Tuesday of Carnival.

DECEMBER

Christkindelsmarkt and **Weihnachtsmarkt**. Christmas fairs are held from

The famous Christmas market in the city of Nuremberg

the beginning of the month until Christmas Eve. The most beautiful are in Baden-Wurttemberg and in Bavaria, while the most renowned is held in Nuremberg.
Christmas *(25/26 December)*. Traditionally celebrated throughout Germany. A Christmas tree is considered essential, together with presents and delicacies.
New Year's Eve *(31 December)*. The New Year is greeted at balls, opera galas, in restaurants, clubs, private houses and in the streets and squares of city centres.

JANUARY

Four Ski Jumps Tournament *(begins 1 January)*. Renowned tournament for ski-jumping held annually in Garmisch-Partenkirchen.
Sechs-Tage-Rennen *(begins 1 January)* Berlin. Spectacular cycle races with associated events, held in Berlin Velodrome.
Grüne Woche *(last week)* Berlin. International trade fairs dedicated to agriculture, animal breeding and the food processing industry. Producers from all over the world offer specialities from their own national cuisines.

FEBRUARY

Berlinale–Internationale Filmfestspiele *(2nd and 3rd weeks)* Berlin. International film festival in which major stars participate.

Fastnacht, also known as **Fasnet**, **Fasching** or **Karneval** (Shrovetide). Carnival is celebrated enthusiastically in virtually every region of Germany. The most interesting events are held in the Rhine Valley, and particularly in Cologne. *Karneval am Rhein*, which marks the lasts three days of the Carnival, begins on the Thursday of the week before Ash Wednesday with a women's parade, known as *Weiberfastnacht*. On the Monday there is a superb costume parade, known as *Rosenmontagsumzug*.

Costumed revellers on the streets of Cologne during Carnival

The German Climate

GERMANY LIES in a temperate climatic zone. In the north of the country, with marine influences predominating, summers tend to be quite cold and winters mild, with relatively high rainfall. In the eastern part of the country, however, the climate is more continental and this produces harsher winters and hotter summers. Germany's highest rainfall and the lowest temperatures are recorded in the Alps.

SCHLESWIG-HOLSTEIN

Average daily maximum temperature

Average daily minimum temperature

Average daily amount of sunshine

Average monthly rainfall

°C			
2.2	10.5 / 3	20 / 12	13 / 7
-2			

☼	1.3 hrs	5.5 hrs	7 hrs	3 hrs
☂	80 mm	55 mm	92 mm	90 mm
Month	Jan	Apr	Jul	Oct

BREMEN, HAMBURG, LOWER SAXONY

°C			
3.2	12.5 / 3.5	22 / 12	14 / 6
-2			

☼	1.3 hrs	5 hrs	6 hrs	3 hrs
☂	56 mm	48 mm	69 mm	55 mm
Month	Jan	Apr	Jul	Oct

NORTH RHINE-WESTPHALIA

°C			
4.5	14 / 3.6	23 / 12.5	15 / 6
-1			

☼	1.5 hrs	5 hrs	6.5 hrs	3.7 hrs
☂	62 mm	54 mm	84 mm	55 mm
Month	Jan	Apr	Jul	Oct

HESSE

°C			
3	14 / 4	24 / 13	14 / 6
-2			

☼	1.3 hrs	5 hrs	7.4 hrs	3.3 hrs
☂	44 mm	51 mm	63 mm	50 mm
Month	Jan	Apr	Jul	Oct

RHINELAND-PALATINATE, SAARLAND

°C			
3	13 / 4	23 / 12	14 / 7
-1.5			

☼	1.3 hrs	5 hrs	7 hrs	3 hrs
☂	60 mm	53 mm	69 mm	65 mm
Month	Jan	Apr	Jul	Oct

BADEN WÜRTTEMBERG

°C			
4	14 / 5	23 / 13	15 / 7
-1			

☼	1.7 hrs	5 hrs	8 hrs	4 hrs
☂	60 mm	80 mm	95 mm	66 mm
Month	Jan	Apr	Jul	Oct

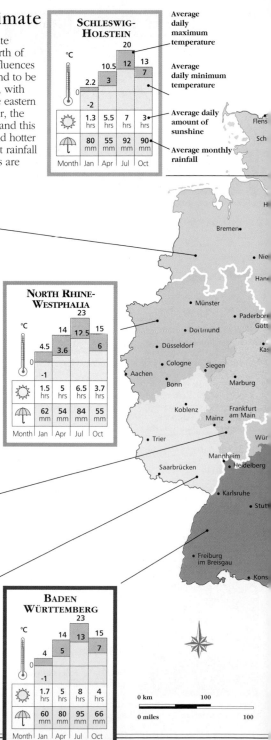

Flens
Sch
H
Bremen
Nie
Hane
Münster
Paderborn
Gott
Dortmund
Düsseldorf
Kas
Cologne
Siegen
Aachen
Bonn
Marburg
Koblenz
Frankfurt am Main
Mainz
Trier
Wür
Mannheim
Saarbrücken
Heidelberg
Karlsruhe
Stut
Freiburg im Breisgau
Kons

0 km 100
0 miles 100

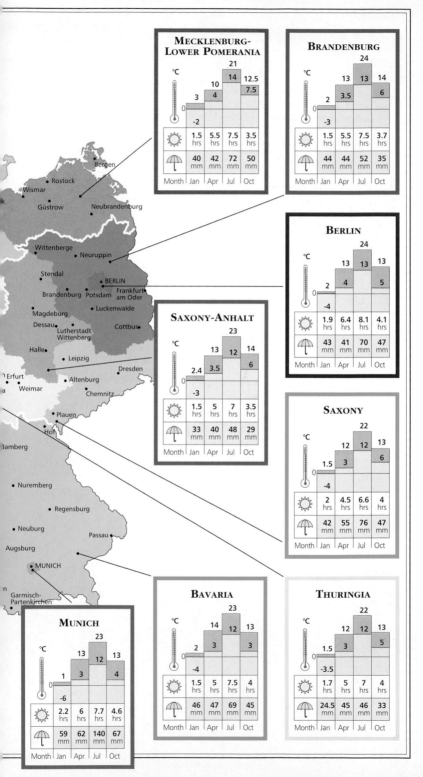

MECKLENBURG-LOWER POMERANIA

°C				
	3	10	21	12.5
		4	14	7.5
0				
	-2			

☀	1.5 hrs	5.5 hrs	7.5 hrs	3.5 hrs
☂	40 mm	42 mm	72 mm	50 mm
Month	Jan	Apr	Jul	Oct

BRANDENBURG

°C				
	2	13	24	14
		3.5	13	6
0				
	-3			

☀	1.5 hrs	5.5 hrs	7.5 hrs	3.7 hrs
☂	44 mm	44 mm	52 mm	35 mm
Month	Jan	Apr	Jul	Oct

BERLIN

°C				
	2	13	24	13
		4	13	5
0				
	-4			

☀	1.9 hrs	6.4 hrs	8.1 hrs	4.1 hrs
☂	43 mm	41 mm	70 mm	47 mm
Month	Jan	Apr	Jul	Oct

SAXONY-ANHALT

°C				
	2.4	13	23	14
		3.5	12	6
0				
	-3			

☀	1.5 hrs	5 hrs	7 hrs	3.5 hrs
☂	33 mm	40 mm	48 mm	29 mm
Month	Jan	Apr	Jul	Oct

SAXONY

°C				
	1.5	12	22	13
		3	12	6
0				
	-4			

☀	2 hrs	4.5 hrs	6.6 hrs	4 hrs
☂	42 mm	55 mm	76 mm	47 mm
Month	Jan	Apr	Jul	Oct

MUNICH

°C				
	1	13	23	13
		3	12	4
0				
	-6			

☀	2.2 hrs	6 hrs	7.7 hrs	4.6 hrs
☂	59 mm	62 mm	140 mm	67 mm
Month	Jan	Apr	Jul	Oct

BAVARIA

°C				
	2	14	23	13
		3	12	3
0				
	-4			

☀	1.5 hrs	5 hrs	7.5 hrs	4 hrs
☂	46 mm	47 mm	69 mm	45 mm
Month	Jan	Apr	Jul	Oct

THURINGIA

°C				
	1.5	12	22	13
		3	12	5
0				
	-3.5			

☀	1.7 hrs	5 hrs	7 hrs	4 hrs
☂	24.5 mm	45 mm	46 mm	33 mm
Month	Jan	Apr	Jul	Oct

Map labels: Bergen, Rostock, Wismar, Güstrow, Neubrandenburg, Wittenberge, Neuruppin, Stendal, BERLIN, Brandenburg, Potsdam, Frankfurt am Oder, Magdeburg, Luckenwalde, Dessau, Lutherstadt Wittenberg, Cottbus, Halle, Leipzig, Dresden, Erfurt, Altenburg, Weimar, Chemnitz, Plauen, Hof, Bamberg, Nuremberg, Regensburg, Neuburg, Passau, Augsburg, MUNICH, Garmisch-Partenkirchen

THE HISTORY OF GERMANY

GERMANY IS *a country of cultural and religious contrasts. Regional differences in culture, language and traditions arose from the historical division of the country into many small states. Such differences have been further accentuated by the recent experience of generations of Germans who, until 1990, grew up under two conflicting social systems: capitalism and communism.*

EARLY HISTORY

In the 1st millennium BC, the basins of the Rhine, Danube and Main rivers were settled by Celts, who had been largely displaced by Germanic tribes by the 2nd century BC. In the 1st century BC the Roman legions waged wars with the Germans, and conquered the territories west of the Rhine. The settlements they

Heinrich I, from the house of Liudolf

founded there later developed into towns like Trier, Mainz, Cologne and Xanten. The Romans made numerous attempts to conquer the eastern regions between the Rhine and the Elbe rivers. They eventually reached the Elbe at the end of the 1st century BC, but the Germans, under the leadership of Arminius, also known as Germanus, defeated the Roman armies in the Teutoburg Forest in AD 9, and so ended their presence in this region. A system of fortifications, or *limes,* built in the 2nd century along the course of the Danube and the Rhine, divided the region into two: *Germania Romana*, the Roman province, and *Germania Libra*, free Germany. The free German tribes,

notably the Goths, often entered into alliances with the Romans. In the 5th century, however, they took advantage of Rome's weakness to appropriate parts of the empire for themselves.

EARLY MIDDLE AGES

After the collapse of the Roman Empire, the area between the Rhine and the Elbe was ruled by the Franks, who gradually converted to Christianity from the 6th century. One of the most important figures in this process was the 8th-century missionary, St Boniface. When Charlemagne was crowned Emperor in 800, the territory of present-day Germany became part of the Frankish Empire. The Empire was partitioned by the Treaty of Verdun in 843, with the eastern part going to Ludwig the German. In the 10th century the kingdom, which was made up of numerous tribal states, passed to the house of Liudolf. Otto I, son of Heinrich I and the first king from this Saxon family, was crowned Emperor in 962 after several political and military victories, in particular his defeat of the Magyars.

TIMELINE

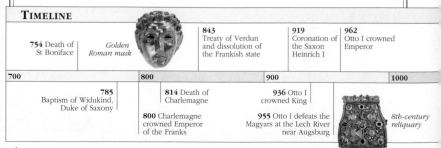

| | | **843** Treaty of Verdun and dissolution of the Frankish state | **919** Coronation of the Saxon Heinrich I | **962** Otto I crowned Emperor |

754 Death of St Boniface

Golden Roman mask

700 | **800** | **900** | **1000**

785 Baptism of Widukind, Duke of Saxony

814 Death of Charlemagne

800 Charlemagne crowned Emperor of the Franks

936 Otto I crowned King

955 Otto I defeats the Magyars at the Lech River near Augsburg

8th-century reliquary

◁ *Germany's Awakening,* **a patriotic 19th-century work by Christian Köhler**

Consolidating Power

With Otto being crowned emperor, the dynasty of the Saxon house of Liudolf acceded to power. It gave the country three further rulers – Otto II, Otto III and Heinrich II. In the year 925 Otto I annexed Lotharingia (present-day Lorraine). On the eastern frontier he created two "marks", the Nordmark and the Ostmark, as buffer states designed to subjugate the Slav-populated regions east of the Oder River. After Heinrich II's death, the house of the Salian Franks took the imperial throne and used their authority to limit the power of the local feudal dukes.

Stained-glass window in Augsburg cathedral

The Investiture Controversy

In the 11th century the empire came into conflict with the papacy. Matters came to a head in the so-called "investiture controversy". Pope Gregory VII asserted the church's right to appoint bishops. Emperor Heinrich IV meanwhile, who had been relying on the support of the clergy he had appointed, called his bishops together and asked the Pope to step down. Pope Gregory VII excommunicated Heinrich.

The dukes of Saxony used the opportunity to appoint a king in opposition to Heinrich, and the Pope attempted to intervene in the dispute. Heinrich IV saw himself forced to march to Canossa in Italy, where the Pope had sought refuge, in order to stop his empire from falling apart. Doing penance in this way forced the Pope to withdraw his excommunication. However, the dispute did not end there, but continued for several years, finally ending with the Signing of the Concordat of Worms in 1122.

Enamelled Romanesque medallion, dating from c.1150

Hohenstaufens and Welfs

After the Salian dynasty died out in 1125 and the brief reign of Lothar III of the Saxon dynasty, another long drawn-out conflict broke out, between the houses of Hohenstaufen and Welf (known in Italian as Ghibellines and Guelphs). Imperial power went to the Hohenstaufens, while the greatest political victories were scored by Friedrich I Barbarossa (meaning "red beard"). He intended gradually to break up his subject principalities and to rule them under a feudal system. The 12th century also saw further expansion eastwards and northwards into areas inhabited by the northwestern Slavic tribes. From the start of the 13th

12th-century reliquary from the Welf family vaults

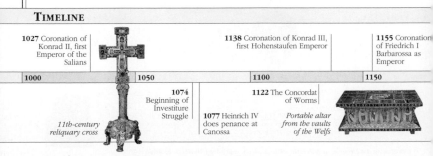

TIMELINE

1027 Coronation of Konrad II, first Emperor of the Salians

1138 Coronation of Konrad III, first Hohenstaufen Emperor

1155 Coronation of Friedrich I Barbarossa as Emperor

1000	1050	1100	1150

11th-century reliquary cross

1074 Beginning of Investiture Struggle

1077 Heinrich IV does penance at Canossa

1122 The Concordat of Worms

Portable altar from the vaults of the Welfs

century Barbarossa also conquered territories occupied by the Baltic peoples and the Estonians, which involved armed expeditions by the North German cities and orders of knights.

Friedrich II, crowned Emperor in 1220, was also King of Sicily and his Italian interests brought further conflict with the papacy. Ultimately his policies brought about the collapse of imperial power. After his death in 1250, his successor was unable to find any support, which led to the period known as the Great Interregnum.

Emperor Rudolf I of Habsburg

THE INTERREGNUM

The fall of the Hohenstaufens marked the end of the old imperial system. The absence of an overall ruler led to a breakdown in law and order, and resulted in the rise of the *Raubritter* (robber-barons). To protect their common interests, the trading cities set up alliances. The collapse of imperial power, and the decline in the power of the dukes thus gradually led to an increase in the power of the German cities.

From the beginning the imperial throne had been elective, with dukes electing the emperor from the male members of the dynasty. There was also no capital city, as the emperors moved from one city to another, thus spreading the costs of maintaining the imperial court among different duchies. In the

13th century a system evolved by which only seven elector-dukes had the right to elect the emperor. These were the Margrave of Brandenburg, the Elector of Palatine (or the Bavarian dukes), the Duke of Saxony, the King of Bohemia and the Archbishops of Trier, Cologne and Mainz. Starting with Rudolf I of Habsburg, who was elected king of Germany in 1273, until 1438 the kings came from the rival houses of Habsburg, Wittelsbach and Luxemburg. After 1312, the same houses also competed for the title of Emperor. The most outstanding of the 14th-century rulers of Germany was Karl IV of Luxemburg, who resided permanently in Prague. In 1338 the electors had rejected the requirement for the Pope to confirm election results. In 1356 Karl IV issued the "Golden Bull" which underlined the federal nature of the state, and clarified the rules for electing its leader.

A "Minneteppich" – part of a medieval tapestry, depicting a variety of human traits and a griffin, the mythical beast

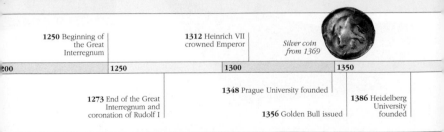

1250 Beginning of the Great Interregnum

1312 Heinrich VII crowned Emperor

Silver coin from 1369

200 | 1250 | 1300 | 1350

1273 End of the Great Interregnum and coronation of Rudolf I

1348 Prague University founded

1356 Golden Bull issued

1386 Heidelberg University founded

The Hanseatic League

THE GERMAN Hanseatic League, or Hanse, was only one of many guilds of traders or cities that existed in the Middle Ages, but its important historical role made it one of the best known. Established in the 13th century, it reached its peak in the 14th century and declined again in the 16th century. Over 160 cities, primarily the trading cities of northern Germany, but also including Baltic ports as far afield as Visby, Riga and Tallinn, joined the League. It exercised total control over trade from the Baltic in the east to England in the west. The Hanseatic cities were among the wealthiest in Europe, and crafts and the arts flourished there.

Madonna of the Roses
15th-century painting by Stefan Lochner of the Cologne School.

The Wise and Foolish Maidens
The flowering of art in the Hanseatic cities brought about works such as this portal of Magdeburg Cathedral.

Hanse ships, loaded with merchandise, entering the harbour

Revenue officials awaiting the cargo

Crucifix in Lübeck Cathedral
This crucifix is one of only few painted wood-carvings made by Bernt Notke of Lübeck that have survived until today.

Round wooden cranes with swivelling arms were used to unload ships. One example still survives in Lüneburg.

Cogs
Cogs – heavy, flat-bottomed sailing ships with limited manoeuvrability – were fishermen's and merchants' boats or navy vessels in the North Sea and the Baltic from the 12th to the 14th centuries.

Panoramic view of Lübeck
The vast port town of Lübeck was the largest Hanseatic city. This 15th-century woodcut shows a view of the city with its numerous church spires.

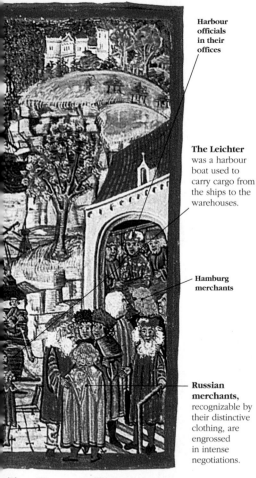

Harbour officials in their offices

The Leichter was a harbour boat used to carry cargo from the ships to the warehouses.

Hamburg merchants

Russian merchants, recognizable by their distinctive clothing, are engrossed in intense negotiations.

THE PORT OF HAMBURG

Hamburg, along with Bremen, Lübeck and Gdansk, was one of the leading Hanseatic cities. In the 14th century, it was the main centre for trade between the North Sea and the Baltic. This miniature, showing the port of Hamburg, dates from the 15th century.

THE HANSEATIC CITIES

In the major Hanseatic cities, the most prominent buildings grew up around the *Markt* (market square) and along the streets that led to the port. The market square would contain the *Rathaus* (town hall), with its multi-functional interiors, and the equally splendid banqueting halls and ballrooms, such as the Gürzenich in Cologne. The main cathedrals in the cities were dedicated either to St Mary or St Nicholas. The gabled residential houses had narrow façades with distinctive portals. The townscape of the port areas was dominated by granaries, warehouses and numerous cranes. The cities were all enclosed and protected by solid fortifications.

The town hall in Brunswick, with its open upper arcades and statues of the Welfs, is one of the finest surviving Hanseatic secular buildings.

The Kröpeliner Tor in Rostock (see p462) *is one of 22 towers on the defensive walls around the medieval city centre.*

Jan Hus being burned at the stake

THE HUSSITE WARS AND THE HABSBURG DYNASTY

The last king and emperor of the house of Luxemburg, Sigismund, brought an end to the "Great Schism" in the Western church that had persisted since 1378. The Council of Constance, which he called in 1414, led to the election of a single, rather than two rival popes. However, new religious controversy was provoked by the death sentence for heresy passed in 1415 on Jan Hus, a religious reformer from Bohemia. The ensuing Hussite Wars ravaged the northern and western regions of Germany.

From 1482 the imperial crown went to the Habsburgs, who retained it

Title page of the first German edition of the Bible

until 1740. Attempts at political reform in the second half of the 15th century failed. The most ambitious reformer was Maximilian I. He called an Imperial Tribunal in 1495 which set about transferring part of the king's authority to the judiciary; however, it did not result in any great practical changes, although it gave slightly more power to the *Reichstag*, the imperial parliament.

THE REFORMATION

Germany entered the 16th century as a country simmering with social conflict, gradually becoming steeped in the ideas of humanism, thanks to the writings of Erasmus of Rotterdam and others. The rise of Martin Luther, who in 1517 nailed his 95 Theses to the door of the Castle Church in Wittenberg, and who opposed the trade in

Lion-shaped water jug (1540)

indulgences conducted by the clergy, set the Reformation in motion *(see pp116–17)*. The idea of ecclesiastical reform propounded by Luther gained a growing following. His supporters included princes who hoped to profit from the secularization of church property, as well as other social classes that simply saw an opportunity to improve their lot. In 1519 Maximilian I died, and Karl V was elected to succeed him. Karl's interests were focused on Spain and the Netherlands, and he was unable to prevent the spread of Lutheranism.

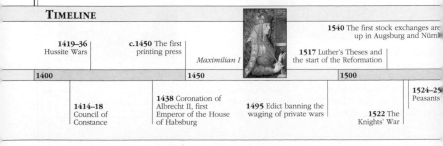

TIMELINE

1419–36 Hussite Wars

c.1450 The first printing press

Maximilian I

1540 The first stock exchanges are up in Augsburg and Nürnb

1517 Luther's Theses and the start of the Reformation

1400   **1450**   **1500**

1414–18 Council of Constance

1438 Coronation of Albrecht II, first Emperor of the House of Habsburg

1495 Edict banning the waging of private wars

1522 The Knights' War

1524–25 Peasants

Urban life in Germany in the early 16th century, in a painting by Jörg Breu the Elder (c.1475–1537)

The unrest led to rebellions such as the Knights' War of 1522 and the Peasants' War of 1524, and these were followed by continuous religious conflict. In 1530 the Protestants set up the League of Schmalkalden, which was finally broken up by the Emperor in the war of 1546–7. These basically religious clashes ultimately led to the division of Germany into a northern Protestant part and a Catholic south, a situation that was sanctioned in 1555 by the Peace of Augsburg. This established the principle of *cuius regio, eius religio*, which meant that each ruler had the right to decide on the faith of the region, and the only option left for anyone of a different persuasion was to move elsewhere.

THE THIRTY YEARS' WAR

The second half of the 16th century was relatively stable for Germany, despite the religious conflicts. However, the influence of the Counter-Reformation in the early 17th century ended this stability. The Protestant Union and Catholic League were established in 1608 and 1609 respectively. Unrest in Prague, where the states with a Protestant majority opposed the election of the Catholic Ferdinand II as king of Bohemia, began the Thirty Years' War. This religious war quickly spread throughout Germany, and also drew in Denmark, Spain, Sweden and France. Much of the country and many towns were laid waste, and vast numbers of people died. Finally, in 1648, the German states, France and Sweden signed the Peace of Westphalia in Münster, resulting in major losses of territory for Germany, mainly in the north. A new political system emerged, with the German princes enjoying complete political independence, under a weakened emperor and pope. The second half of the 17th century was marked by the rebuilding of towns and the hard work of restoring the ruined economic infrastructure.

A scene in the Thirty Years' War, in a painting by Wilhelm von Diez

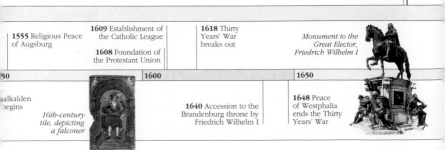

Goethe in the Roman Campagna by Johann H. W. Tischbein (1787)

ABSOLUTISM AND THE RISE OF PRUSSIA

In the second half of the 17th century and throughout the 18th century, Germany was a loose federation of small, politically weak states in the west, and much more powerful states in the east and the south – Saxony, which was ruled by the house of Wettin, and Bavaria, ruled by the Wittelsbachs. However, the rising star was the state of Brandenburg, ruled by the house of Hohenzollern, which from 1657 also ruled Prussia. In 1701 the Elector Friedrich III crowned himself King of Prussia (as Friedrich I), and subsequently the name "Prussia" was applied to all areas ruled by the house of Hohenzollern. During the 18th century Prussia became the greatest rival to Habsburg Austria. In 1740, Friedrich II, also known as Frederick the Great,

Portrait of Frederick the Great as successor to the throne

was crowned King of Prussia. Under his rule, Berlin became a major European city and a centre of the Enlightenment. In 1740–42, in the Seven Years' War, Frederick the Great took Silesia from the Habsburgs without major losses. In 1772 he took part in the first partition of Poland.

In the second half of the 18th century Germany produced a succession of great poets and playwrights – figures such as Gotthold Ephraim Lessing, Friedrich Schiller and Johann Wolfgang von Goethe.

THE NAPOLEONIC WARS, RESTORATION AND REVOLUTION

From 1793 onwards the German states were involved in the Napoleonic Wars. After France's occupation of the lands west of the Rhine, a territorial reform was carried out by the Reichsdeputations Hauptschluss in 1803. This resulted in the secularization of most church property, and the total of 289 states and free cities was reduced to 112 larger states. States that gained from this supported Napoleon in his defeat of Austria in the war of 1805–7. In 1806 the Holy Roman Empire of German Nations was dissolved, and Bavaria, Saxony and Wurttemberg were given the status of kingdoms. Napoleon defeated Prussia at Jena and the country was occupied by France.

TIMELINE

1701 The first king of Prussia is crowned

1702–14 Germany joins the War of Spanish Succession

1740–42 The Silesian War

Leopold Hermann von Boyen, Prussian army general

1813 Battle the Natio at Leipz

1700	1730	1760	1790

1710 Meißen porcelain factory opened

1700 Academy of Sciences founded in Berlin

1756–63 The Seven Years' War

1740 Frederick the Great crowned King of Prussia

1803 Territorial reform of the German states

1806 Dissolution of the Empire

1814–15 The Congress of Vie

The tide turned for Germany at the Battle of Leipzig in 1813, when Russia, Austria and Prussia defeated the French. After Napoleon's final defeat at Waterloo in 1815, the Congress of Vienna established a German Confederation under Austrian control. Its supreme body was the Bundestag (federal parliament), which met at Frankfurt am Main.

Victory Report at the Battle of Leipzig by Johann Peter Krafft (1839)

The wars of liberation against Napoleon had led to a growth in nationalism and democratic awareness, as well as a desire for unification. In 1848 the March Revolution broke out in Berlin. Its main driving force was the urban middle class, but the revolt was finally put down by Prussian troops in 1849.

In the 1820s and 1830s, Germany underwent rapid industrialization, and the establishment of the Zollverein (customs union) in 1834 marked the first step towards a united Germany. Uniting Germany was the main goal of the Prussian premier Otto von Bismarck. Prussia's victories over Austria in 1866 and France in 1871 resulted in the proclamation of a German Empire on 18 January 1871.

Vase with portrait of Kaiser Wilhelm II

THE SECOND REICH

The Second Reich was a federation of 25 states, and its first Chancellor was Otto von Bismarck. The unification of Germany led to a widespread confrontation between the state and the Catholic Church (known as the "Kulturkampf"). The economy, however, flourished, due to the boom in industry, in particular mining, metallurgy, electrical and chemical engineering. This led to the rise of a workers' movement, inspired by the ideas of Karl Marx. In 1875 the workers' parties united and formed the Social Democratic Party of Germany (SPD). Although the party was banned between 1878 and 1890, it rapidly gained support, and a system of social welfare for workers was gradually introduced.

At the beginning of the 20th century, Germany was a powerful state with overseas colonies. Imperialist tendencies grew, and increased tensions in European politics, particularly in the Balkans, led inevitably to war.

Fighting on the Barricades in May 1848, a fanciful picture of the revolution in Berlin by Julius Scholz

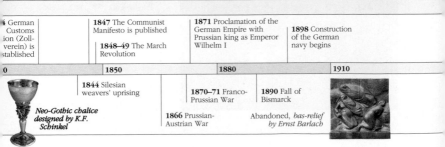

...4 German Customs ...ion (Zoll-verein) is ...stablished	**1847** The Communist Manifesto is published	**1871** Proclamation of the German Empire with Prussian king as Emperor Wilhelm I	**1898** Construction of the German navy begins
	1848–49 The March Revolution		
0	1850	1880	1910
	1844 Silesian weavers' uprising	**1870–71** Franco-Prussian War	**1890** Fall of Bismarck
Neo-Gothic chalice designed by K.F. Schinkel		**1866** Prussian-Austrian War	Abandoned, *bas-relief by Ernst Barlach*

Bismarck's Germany

THE ESTABLISHMENT of a Reich headed by the King of Prussia on 18 January 1871 ensured Prussia's prominent role over the following decades. The Chancellor was the Prussian Prime Minister Otto von Bismarck. Thanks to large reparations paid by France and a favourable economic situation, the economy flourished throughout the Reich. This in turn fostered the development of science and culture. The cities grew rapidly, and the housing shortage led to the development of huge *Miets-kasernen*, blocks of apartments for renting.

GERMANY IN 1871

■ *The Second German Reich*

Kaiser Wilhelm I
Mosaics, depicting a procession of members of the house of Hohenzollern, decorate the vestibule of the Kaiser-Wilhelm Gedächtnichskirche (memorial church) in Berlin.

The Kaiser's Family Taking a Walk in Sanssouci Park
"Happy family" portraits such as this one were often painted for propaganda purposes.

The Reichstag
The monumental Reichstag (parliament building), was built in the centre of the capital, Berlin, by the architect Paul Wallot.

Members of Parliament

Heads of the federal states

A Steel Mill in Königshütte
Germany's economic progress was achieved through a high degree of industrialization. Adolf von Menzel's painting depicts a steel mill in Königshütte, Upper Silesia.

Officer's helmet
The characteristic spiked helmet worn by German soldiers was known as a Pickelhaube.

Ludwig II of Bavaria
The federal states, which made up the Reich, enjoyed complete autonomy. Their rulers, however, for instance King Ludwig II of Bavaria, patron of Richard Wagner and builder of "fantastic" castles and palaces, had little real political influence.

The Kaiser's wife, Augusta Victoria

Wilhelm, the heir to the throne

Mourning dress
was worn by the women and black ribbons by the men as a mark of respect for the two previous Kaisers who had died in 1888 – the father and grandfather of Wilhelm II.

The Diplomatic Corps

Otto von Bismarck

Kaiser Wilhelm II

INAUGURATION OF THE REICHSTAG

This vast canvas by Anton von Werner (1893) shows the opening ceremony for the Reichstag after the coronation of Kaiser Wilhelm II on 25 June 1888 in the Kaiser's Palace in Berlin. The painter depicts the moment when the Kaiser delivers his speech.

Otto von Bismarck
Originating from a Pomeranian family of Junkers, the Prussian Premier and Chancellor of the Reich was one of the most prominent political figures of his time.

BISMARCK

WORLD WAR I

When Germany entered World War I in 1914, the Kaiser's generals hoped for a quick victory, but their invasion of France was halted on the Marne. The war dragged on for the next four years, devastating much of Europe, and ending in Germany's defeat. The Allied offensive in the summer of 1918 forced Germany to the negotiating table – it also led to the November revolution in Germany. Within days the state monarchs were toppled from power, Kaiser Wilhelm II abdicated, and on 9 November 1918 a republic was proclaimed. The form of government had not been decided, and at first the political advantage was held by the socialists. But the Workers' Uprising in Berlin in 1919 was defeated.

Ein Volk, ein Reich, ein Führer!

Propaganda poster for
Adolf Hitler

THE WEIMAR REPUBLIC

The Treaty of Versailles of 1919 imposed many unfavourable conditions on Germany. The country lost a great deal of her territory, mainly to Poland, France and Lithuania, and she was obliged to pay huge reparations, undergo partial demilitarization and limit arms production.

During the Weimar Republic, Germany was riddled with instability. The economy collapsed under the heavy burden of reparation payments and the onset of hyperinflation. Constant changes of government failed to stabilize the political situation, which led to the rise both of left-wing revolutionaries and of right-wing nationalists, and to a general dissatisfaction with the country's status after the humiliating Treaty of Versailles. It is perhaps remarkable that at this time German culture flourished.

DURCH LICHT ZUR NACHT

Cover of a Socialist
magazine attacking
the book-burning

However, this was not sufficient to stave off the political disaster that led to the rise of the Nazi Party (the NSDAP or National Socialist German Workers' Party).

A Berlin synagogue burning during Kristallnacht, 1938

THE THIRD REICH

Adolf Hitler was appointed Chancellor by President Hindenburg on 30 January 1933 and immediately started to get rid of potential opponents. A fire that burned down the Reichstag served as a pretext for persecuting the communists,

TIMELINE

1914 World War I breaks out	**1919** Signing of the Treaty of Versailles	**1926** Germany accepted in League of Nations
	1921 Adolf Hitler becomes leader of the NSDAP	
1915	**1920**	**1925**
		1926 Hitler Youth set up
Poster of Marlene Dietrich	**9 Nov 1918** Declaration of the Republic **1923** Hitler's Putsch in Munich	**1925** Hitler writes *Mein Kampf*

THE BLONDE VENUS

while in April 1933 a boycott of Jewish businesses began. Trade unions were banned, as were all parties apart from the Nazis. Books by "impure" authors were burned, and the work of "degenerate" artists was exhibited as a warning, marking the start of the persecution of artists and scientists, many of whom decided to emigrate. At the same time, Hitler attempted to present to the world a face of openness and success, particularly with the Berlin Olympics of 1936. Germany broke almost all the demilitarization conditions of the Versailles Treaty. The growth in arms production brought with it an improved economic situation, increasing Hitler's popularity. All his opponents who had not managed to emigrate were either killed or sent to concentration camps.

The centre of Dresden after Allied carpet-bombing

In 1935 the Nuremberg Laws were passed, which officially sanctioned the persecution of Jews. During the *Kristallnacht* (crystal night) of 9 November 1938, synagogues throughout Germany were burned and Jewish shops and homes were looted, resulting in streets littered with broken glass. Hitler's plans to conquer Europe were realized in March 1938, with the "Anschluss" (annexation) of Austria, then in 1939 German forces occupied Czechoslovakia. After obtaining peace guarantees from the USSR, Germany invaded Poland on 1 September 1939, thus starting World War II.

Pieta, sculpture by Käthe Kollwitz (1937–8)

WORLD WAR II

The first two years of World War II were marked by one victory after another for the German Army, which managed to occupy half of Europe. Great Britain was the only country that succeeded in fending off Hitler. In 1941 the Wehrmacht occupied large swathes of the Soviet Union. Terror and genocide were instigated in all occupied territories. The decision to exterminate all Jews in Europe was taken at the Wannsee Conference in Berlin in January 1942. Attempts to oppose Hitler in Germany were crushed. The course of the war did not change until 1943, when on 31 January Germany suffered a major defeat in the Battle of Stalingrad.

The Allied landings in Normandy and the creation of the second front helped bring the war to an end. When Soviet forces reached Berlin in 1945 the city lay in ruins and the populace was starving. During five and a half years, 55 million people had lost their lives.

1935 Enactment of law to build up army

30 Jan 1933 Hitler appointed Chancellor of the Reich

1938 Anschluss with Austria; occupation of Czechoslovakia
9/10 Nov 1938 "Kristallnacht"

1 Sep 1939 German invasion of Poland; the beginning of World War II

The Enigma Code machine

'30 | **1935** | **1940** | **1945**

Poster for the Berlin Olympics in 1936

1936 Berlin Olympics

1935 November laws sanction persecution of Jews

22 Jun 1941 Germany invades USSR

20 Jan 1942 Wannsee conference

30 Apr 1945 Hitler commits suicide as Soviet troops enter Berlin

Nazi war criminals on trial at Nuremberg

THE AFTERMATH OF WORLD WAR II

Germany's unconditional surrender was signed on 8 May 1945, ending the bloodiest war in human history. Peace negotiations began which were to shape the new face of Europe for decades to come. In fact, discussions on Germany's future had already taken place at the Tehran and Yalta Conferences, where the leaders of the Big Three Powers met. But it was not

The Berlin Airlift in 1948–9

until the Potsdam Conference that the terms were finally agreed.

Germany lost large parts of its territory to the east, displacing the German population there. It was decided to demilitarize Germany. The four Allied powers – the USA, the USSR, Britain and France – divided Germany into zones of occupation which they would rule until democratic structures were in place. The main perpetrators of war crimes were tried in Nuremberg and sentenced to death. Unfortunately, tensions increased between the Western powers and the Soviet Union, rapidly escalating in the "Cold War", which was largely played out in occupied Germany. In

1948 the three western zones introduced a new currency, which led the Soviets to blockade the western part of Berlin. Thanks to the Berlin Airlift, which supplied the population with food and fuel, the blockade was abandoned. On 23 May 1949 the Federal Republic (Bundesrepublik) of Germany was established in the three western zones, and on 7 October 1949 the German Democratic Republic (DDR) was set up in the Soviet zone. West Berlin, as it was then known, became an enclave inside East Germany.

GERMANY 1949–90

■ *Federal Republic*

□ *DDR*

GERMANY DIVIDED

The German Democratic Republic was democratic only in name. It became one of the satellites of the Soviet Union, and as the westernmost outpost of the Eastern Bloc it was subject

Graffiti-covered section of the Berlin Wall

TIMELINE

24 Jun 1948 Blockade of West Berlin starts

1949 Federal Republic and DDR established

1955 Federal Republic and German Democratic Republic gain sovereignty

1968 Student riots

1973 West and E Germany accep into

1945	1950	1955	1960	1965	1970

4–11 Feb 1945 Yalta Conference
8 May Germany capitulates

Konrad Adenauer

7 Jun 1953 Workers' uprising in East Berlin

13 Aug 1961 Building of the Berlin Wall

1972 Official relations established between East and West Germany; Munich Olympics

Reunification ceremony outside the Reichstag in Berlin in 1990

to great restrictions. Attempted protests, such as the Workers' Uprising of 17 June 1953 in Berlin, were ruthlessly suppressed. For many people the only solution was to leave the country. As the exodus of skilled workers to the West continued, on 13 August 1961 a wall with barbed wire was built to contain them. Many attempts to cross the frontier between the two Germanies ended in death. A highly efficient apparatus was set up in East Germany to watch over citizens' activities by the infamous Stasi secret police.

The first Chancellor of the Federal Republic of Germany, Konrad Adenauer, had Germany's integration into Western Europe as his main objective. Thanks to aid under the Marshall Plan, the economy rapidly recovered. Willy Brandt, first elected as Chancellor in 1969, pursued a policy of openness to the East, and recognized the German Democratic Republic.

REUNIFICATION

German reunification was made possible by a number of political events, in particular those going on in Eastern Europe. The Soviet premier Gorbachev's policy of *glasnost* led to the loosening of political constraints throughout the Eastern Bloc. Democratic changes in Poland set off a chain reaction. In 1989, people started to flee the German Democratic Republic en masse via its embassy in Prague and across the Austro-Hungarian border. Then, on 9 November 1989, the Berlin Wall fell and East Germans were free to leave. When, only three weeks later, Chancellor Helmut Kohl presented a ten-point plan for German reunification, few believed that it would happen, but the country was officially reunified on 3 October 1990. Since then, Germany has been undergoing a process of integration.

Crowds visiting the giant Expo 2000 exhibition in Hannover

1982 Helmut Kohl becomes German Chancellor

Helmut Kohl and Richard von Weizsäcker at the reunification ceremony

8 Nov 1989 Fall of the Berlin Wall

2002 Floods cause havoc across Germany

75 | 1980 | 1985 | 1990 | 1995 | 2000

3 Oct 1990 Reunification of Germany

The Trabant, a trademark of East German industry

1994 Withdrawal of last Russian military units from Berlin

1998 Gerhard Schröder becomes Chancellor

2000 Expo 2000 World Fair in Hannover

BERLIN
AREA BY AREA

Berlin at a Glance

Sᴵɴᴄᴇ ᴛʜᴇ ʀᴇᴜɴɪꜰɪᴄᴀᴛɪᴏɴ of Germany in 1990, Berlin has become an increasingly popular destination for visitors. The following pages provide a useful guide to places of interest both in the town centre and the outskirts, including historic monuments such as Nikolaikirche *(see p76)*, museums, modern developments, such as the Potsdamer Platz, as well as places of recreation and amusement, such as the Botanical Gardens *(see p100)*. In the guide, we have divided central Berlin into two parts (east and west); these, however, do not correspond with the city's former partition into East and West Berlin.

Lᴏᴄᴀᴛᴏʀ Mᴀᴘ

Wᴇꜱᴛᴇʀɴ Cᴇɴᴛʀᴇ

The Tiergarten *was once a royal hunting estate but, after 1818, it was converted into a landscaped park by Peter Joseph Lenné* (see p83) *with lakes and streams.*

The Gemäldegalerie (see pp86–7) *houses an exceptional collection of European masters, including Hans Holbein's* Portrait of George Gisze *(1532).*

The Kaiser-Wilhelm-Gedächtnis-Kirche *was almost totally destroyed by bombs during World War II. However it was rebuilt in 1963 to a design by Egon Eiermann* (see p82).

The Reichstag is a vast, Neo-Renaissance building, designed in 1884 by Paul Wallot. It now features an elliptical dome, which was designed in the 1990s by Sir Norman Foster (see p89).

The Pergamonmuseum owes its name to the magnificent Zeus Altar from Pergamon, which stands in the main hall. Built between 1912 and 1930, the museum houses rich collections of Greek, Roman and Asian art (see pp72–3).

```
0 m            400

0 yards        400
```

EASTERN CENTRE

The imposing *Neo-Classical Brandenburg Gate stands at the end of Unter den Linden. It is crowned with a 6-m (20-ft) high sculpture of the Roman Quadriga driven by Victoria, the goddess of victory (see p65).*

The Jüdisches Museum (Jewish Museum) is housed in a building designed by Daniel Libeskind. It features a symbolic projection of a broken Star of David (see p76).

EASTERN CENTRE

THIS PART of Berlin is the historic centre of the city, and includes the Mitte district and parts of Kreuzberg. Its beginnings date back to the 13th century when two settlements were established on the banks of the river Spree. One was the former Cölln, situated on an island, and the other its twin settlement, Berlin. Berlin's first church, the Nikolaikirche, survives to this day.

Relief on Schadow-Haus

This part of the city features most of its historic buildings, which are located mainly along Unter den Linden. It also includes Museumsinsel, the location of the vast Berliner Dom as well as of the impressive collection of museums that gives the island its name. These include the Pergamonmuseum.

During the city's partition, Mitte belonged to East Berlin while Kreuzberg was in West Berlin.

SIGHTS AT A GLANCE

Museums and Galleries
Alte Nationalgalerie ⑰
Altes Museum ⑮
Bodemuseum ⑲
Checkpoint Charlie ㉖
Deutsches Technikmuseum Berlin ㉙
Jüdisches Museum ㉗
Märkisches Museum ㉕
Neues Museum ⑯
Pergamonmuseum ⑱
Topographie des Terrors ㉘
Zeughaus ⑦

Streets and Squares
Alexanderplatz ㉒
Bebelplatz ②
Nikolaiviertel ㉔
Schlossplatz ⑬
Unter den Linden ④

Churches
Berliner Dom ⑭
Deutscher Dom ⑪
Französischer Dom ⑨
Friedrichswerdersche Kirche ⑧
Marienkirche ⑳
St Hedwigs-Kathedrale ③

Historic Buildings and Monuments
Brandenburger Tor ①

Fernsehturm ㉓
Humboldt-Universität ⑤
Konzerthaus ⑩
Neue Wache ⑥
Rotes Rathaus ㉑
Schlossbrücke ⑫

GETTING THERE
This part of Berlin is served by S-Bahn 1, 2, 3, 5, 7, 9, 75 and U-Bahn 2, 5 & 9. Bus 100 runs along Unter den Linden and Karl-Liebknecht-Strasse.

KEY

▓	Street-by-Street map *See pp64–5*
▓	Street-by-Street map *See pp70–1*
🚉	Railway station
Ⓢ	S-Bahn station
Ⓤ	U-Bahn station
🅿	Parking

0 m   400
0 yards   400

◁ **Personification of History** adorning the monument of Friedrich Schiller

Street-by-Street: Around Bebelplatz

Eagle from Altes Palais

THE SECTION of Unter den Linden between Schlossbrücke and Friedrichstrasse is one of the most attractive areas in central Berlin. As well as some magnificent Baroque and Neo-Classical buildings, many of them designed by famous architects, there are also some restored palaces that are now used as public buildings. Of particular interest is the beautiful Baroque building of the Zeughaus (the former Arsenal), which now houses the German History Museum.

Neue Wache
Now serving as a memorial to all victims of war and dictatorship, this monument was designed by Karl Friedrich Schinkel **6**

Humboldt University
The university courtyard teems with life all year round. Second-hand booksellers set up their stalls in front of the gate **5**

0 metres   100
0 yards   100

UNIVERSITÄTSSTRASSE

CHARLOTTENSTRASSE

UNTER DEN LINDEN

BEBEL– PLATZ

BEHRENSTRASSE

Unter den Linden
Replanted with four rows of lime trees in 1946, this is one of the most famous streets in Berlin **4**

Branden- burg Gate

Altes Palais

Staatsbibliothek
Designed by Ernst von Ihne and constructed between 1903 and 1914, this impressive building houses part of the State Library collection.

KEY

– – –   Suggested route

★ Zeughaus (Deutsches Historisches Museum)
Minerva, goddess of wisdom, decorates this beautiful Baroque building ❼

LOCATOR MAP
See Street Finder, maps 1, 4 & 5

WESTERN CENTRE

EASTERN CENTRE

Staatsoper Unter den Linden

★ Friedrichs-werdersche Kirche
In this Neo-Gothic church, designed by Karl Friedrich Schinkel, is a museum devoted to the great architect ❽

HINTER DER KATH. KIRCHE

Rotes Rathaus

Kronprinzenpalais
A magnificent portal from the dismantled Bauakademie building can be found the rear of the palace.

St-Hedwigs-Kathedrale
Bas-reliefs (1837) by Theodore Wilhelm Achtermann adorn the cathedral's supports ❸

STAR SIGHTS

★ Friedrichswerdersche Kirche

★ Zeughaus

Brandenburger Tor ❶

BRANDENBURG GATE

Pariser Platz. **Map** 4 A2, 15 A3.
Ⓢ *Unter den Linden.* 🚌 *100.*

THE BRANDENBURG GATE is the quintessential symbol of Berlin. A magnificent Neo-Classical structure, modelled on the Athenian Propylaea (the entrance to the Acropolis), it was constructed between 1788 and 1791. Its sculptured decorations were completed in 1795. A pair of pavilions, once used by guards and customs officers, frames its powerful Doric colonnade and entab-lature. The bas-reliefs depict scenes from Greek mythology and the whole structure is crowned by Johann Gottfried Schadow's famous sculpture, *Quadriga*. In 1806, during the French occupation, the sculpture was dismantled, on Napoleon's orders, and taken to Paris. On its triumphal re-turn in 1814, it was declared a symbol of victory, and the goddess received a staff bearing the Prussian eagle and an iron cross adorned with a laurel wreath.

Throughout its history, the Brandenburg Gate has borne witness to many of Berlin's important events. Located in East Berlin, the gate was restored between 1956 and 1958, when the damaged *Quadriga* was rebuilt in West Berlin. Over the next 40 years it stood watch over the divided city, until 1989, when the first section of the Berlin Wall came down.

Frieze and sculpture, *Quadriga,* **on the Brandenburg Gate**

Bebelplatz ❷

Map 4 C2. Ⓢ & Ⓤ *Friedrichstraße.*
🚌 *100, 157, 348.*

O NCE NAMED Opernplatz (Opera Square), Bebelplatz was intended to be the focal point of the Forum Fridericianum – an area designed to mirror the grandeur of ancient Rome. Although the plans were only partly implemented, many important buildings were eventually erected here.

On 10 May 1933, the square was the scene of the infamous book-burning act organized by the Nazi propaganda machine. Some 25,000 books, written by authors considered to be enemies of the Third Reich, were burned.

Today, a monument in the square commemorates this dramatic event. A translucent panel inserted into the road surface provides a glimpse of a room filled with empty bookshelves, while a plaque bears the tragically prophetic words of the poet Heinrich Heine, written in 1820: "Where books are burned, in the end people will burn."

Relief on the façade of the Staatsoper (Opera House), Bebelplatz

St-Hedwigs-Kathedrale ❸
ST HEDWIG'S CATHEDRAL

Bebelplatz. **Map** 4 C2. Ⓢ & Ⓤ
Friedrichstraße. 🚌 *100, 157, 348.* ☐
*10am–5pm Mon–Fri, 10am–4:30pm
Sat, 1pm–5pm Sun & holy days.*

T HIS HUGE CHURCH, set back from the road and crowned with a dome, is the Catholic Cathedral of the Roman Archdiocese of Berlin.

The façade of St-Hedwigs-Kathedrale, with beautiful bas-relief sculptures

It was built to serve the Catholics of Silesia (part of present-day Poland), which became part of the kingdom of Prussia in 1742 following defeat in the Silesian Wars.

The initial design, by Georg Wenzeslaus von Knobelsdorff, was similar to the Roman Pantheon. Construction began in 1747 and the cathedral was consecrated in 1773, although work continued on and off until 1778. Later work was carried out from 1886 to 1887. The cathedral was damaged during World War II and subsequently rebuilt between 1952 and 1963. The building received a reinforced concrete dome and its interior was refurbished in a modern style.

The crypt holds the tombs of many of the bishops of Berlin. It also contains a 16th-century Madonna and a Pietà dating from 1420.

Unter den Linden ❹

Map 1 C4, 4 A2, B2, C2, 5 D2.
Ⓢ *Unter den Linden.* 🚌 *100, 157, 348.*

O NE OF THE MOST FAMOUS streets in Berlin, Unter den Linden starts at Schlossplatz and runs down to Pariser Platz and the Brandenburg Gate. It was once the route to the royal hunting grounds, which were later transformed into the Tiergarten.

In the 17th century, the street was planted with lime trees, to which it owes its name. Although the original trees were removed around 1658, four rows of limes were planted in 1820.

During the 18th century, Unter den Linden became the main street of the westward-growing city and gradually came to be lined with

WILHELM AND ALEXANDER VON HUMBOLDT

The Humboldt brothers rank among the most distinguished Berlin citizens. Wilhelm (1767–1835) was a lawyer and politician on whose initiative the Berlin University (later renamed Humboldt University) was founded in 1810. At the university, he conducted studies in comparative and historical linguistics. His brother Alexander (1769–1859), a professor at the university, researched natural science, including meteorology, oceanography and agricultural science.

Alexander von Humboldt

prestigious buildings, which have been restored in the years following World War II.

Since the reunification of Germany in 1990, Unter den Linden has acquired several cafés and restaurants, as well as many smart new shops. The street has also become the venue for interesting outdoor events. It is usually crowded with tourists and students browsing the book-stalls around the Humboldt Universität and the Staats-bibliothek (State Library).

Humboldt Universität ➎
HUMBOLDT UNIVERSITY

Unter den Linden 6. **Map** 4 C2. Ⓢ & Ⓤ *Friedrichstraße.* 🚌 *100, 157, 348.*

THE UNIVERSITY BUILDING was constructed in 1753 for Prince Heinrich of Prussia. The overall design of the palace, with its main block and the courtyard enclosed within two wings, has been extended many times. Two marble statues by Paul Otto (1883) stand at the entrance; these represent Wilhelm and Alexander von Humboldt.

Many famous scientists have worked at the university, in-cluding physicians Rudolf Virchow and Robert Koch and physicists Max Planck and Albert Einstein. Among its graduates are Heinrich Heine, Karl Marx and Friedrich Engels.

After World War II, the university was in the Russian sector and the difficulties encountered by the students of the western zone led to the establishment in 1948 of the Freie Universität.

Neue Wache ➏

Unter den Linden 4. **Map** 7 A3, 16 E2. Ⓢ *Hackescher Markt.* 🚌 *100, 157, 348.* ☐ *10am–6pm daily.*

DESIGNED BY Karl Friedrich Schinkel and built between 1816 and 1818, this monument is considered to be one of the finest examples of Neo-Classical architecture in Berlin. The front of the

monument is dominated by a huge Doric portico with a frieze made up of bas-reliefs depicting goddesses of victory.

In 1930–31 the building was turned into a monument to soldiers killed in World War I. Following its restoration in 1960, Neue Wache became the Memorial to the Victims of Fascism and Militarism. It was rededicated in 1993 to the memory of all victims of war and dictatorship. Inside is an eternal flame and a granite slab over the ashes of an unknown soldier, a resistance fighter and a concentration camp prisoner. In the roof opening is a copy of the sculpture *Mother with her Dead Son*, by Berlin artist Käthe Kollwitz.

Zeughaus ➐

Unter den Linden 2. **Map** 5 D2. 🅒 *20 30 40.* Ⓢ *Hackescher Markt.* 🚌 *100, 157, 348.* **New wing** ☐ *10am–6pm daily.*

THIS FORMER arsenal was built in the Baroque style in 1706 under the guidance of Johann Arnold Nering, Martin Grünberg, Andreas Schlüter and Jean de Bodt. A magnificent structure, its wings surround an inner courtyard. Its exterior is decorated with Schlüter's sculptures, which include masks of dying warriors.

Princesses Luise and Friederike in the Schinkel-Museum

Since 1952, the building has housed the German History Museum. It is currently being refurbished by the Japanese-American architect I M Pei, with the addition of a modern new wing and a glass canopy over the inner courtyard. The museum will reopen in 2004.

Friedrichswerder-sche Kirche (Schin-kel-Museum) ➑

Werderstraße. **Map** 5 D2. 🅒 *(030) 2090 55 55.* Ⓤ & Ⓢ *Friedrich-strasse.* 🚌 *100, 147, 157, 257, 348.* ☐ *10am– 6pm Tue–Sun.* 🈂 🚻

THE FIRST Neo-Gothic church to be built in Berlin, this small single-nave structure with its twin-tower façade was designed by Karl Friedrich Schinkel and built between 1824 and 1830.

Schinkel's original interior was largely destroyed in World War II. Following its reconstruction, the church was con-verted to a museum. It currently houses the Nationalgalerie's permanent sculpture exhibi-tion. Highlights include a model of the famous sculpture by Johann Gottfried Schadow, depicting the princesses Fried-erike and Luise (later Queen of Prussia).

Part of the façade of the Zeughaus on Unter den Linden

Side elevation of the Französischer Dom, built for Huguenot refugees

Französischer Dom ⑨

FRENCH CATHEDRAL

Gendarmenmarkt 6. **Map** 4 C2.
(*(030) 204 15 07.* **U** *Stadtmitte or Französische Straße.* **Museum**
○ *noon–5pm Tue–Sat, 9am–7pm daily.* 🏛 **Viewing Platform** ○ *9am–7pm daily.* 🏛 **Church** ○ *Sep–May: 10am–10pm Tue, 10am–6pm Wed–Sun; Jun–Aug: 10am–10pm Tue, 10am–7pm Wed–Sun.* ✝ *Sun 10am.*

ALTHOUGH THE TWO churches standing on opposite sides of Schauspielhaus seem identical, their only common feature is their matching front towers. The French cathedral was built for the Huguenot community, who found refuge in protestant Berlin following their expulsion from France after the revocation of the Edict of Nantes. The modest church, built between 1701 and 1705 by Louis Cayart and Abraham Quesnay, was modelled on the Huguenot church in Charenton, France, which was destroyed in 1688. The interior features a late-Baroque organ from 1754.

The structure is dominated by a massive, cylindrical tower, which is encircled by Corinthian porticos at its base. The tower and porticos were designed by Carl von Gontard and added around 1785. It houses the Huguenot Museum, which charts the history of the Huguenot community in France and Brandenburg.

There is a smart restaurant on the upper floor. The 60-bell carillon in the tower can be heard every day at noon, 3pm and 7pm.

Konzerthaus ⑩

CONCERT HALL

Gendarmenmarkt 2. **Map** 4 C2.
(*(030) 203 09 21 01.* **U** *Stadtmitte.*

A LATE NEO-CLASSICAL jewel, this magnificent theatre building, known until recently as the Schauspielhaus, is one of the greatest achievements of Berlin's best-known architect, Karl Friedrich Schinkel. It was built between 1818 and 1821 around the ruins of Langhan's National Theatre, destroyed by fire in 1817. The portico columns were retained in the new design. Following bomb damage in World War II, it was reconstructed as a concert hall and the exterior was restored to its former glory. The Konzerthaus is now home to the Berlin Symphony Orchestra.

The whole building is decorated with sculptures alluding to drama and music. The façade, which includes a huge Ionic portico with a set of stairs, is crowned with a sculpture of Apollo riding a chariot pulled by griffins.

In front of the theatre stands a shining white marble statue of Friedrich Schiller, which was sculpted by Reinhold Begas and erected in 1869. Removed by the Nazis during the 1930s, the monument was returned

Interior of the Konzerthaus, formerly the Schauspielhaus

to its rightful place in 1988. The statue is mounted on a high pedestal surrounded by allegorical figures representing Lyric Poetry, Drama, Philosophy and History.

Deutscher Dom ⑪

GERMAN CATHEDRAL

Gendarmenmarkt 1. **Map** 4 C3.
(*(030) 227 30431.* **U** *Stadtmitte or Französische Straße.* **Exhibition**
○ *10am–10pm Tue, 10am–6pm Wed–Sun (Jun–Aug 10am–7pm).*

THE CATHEDRAL at the southern end of the square is an old German Protestant-Reformed church. Based on a five-petal shape, it was designed by Martin Grünberg and built in 1708 by Giovanni Simonetti. In 1785 it acquired a dome-covered tower identical to that of the French cathedral.

Burned down in 1945, it was rebuilt in 1993, with its interior adapted as exhibition space. On display is the popular "Fragen an die Deutsche Geschichte" ("Questions on German History"),

Sculpture from Deutscher Dom

which was formerly on show in the Reichstag building.

Schlossbrücke ⑫

Map 5 D2. ⑤ *Hackescher Markt.*
🚌 *100, 157, 348.*

THIS IS ONE of the city's most beautiful bridges, connecting Schlossplatz with Unter den Linden. It was built in 1824 to a design by Karl Friedrich Schinkel. Statues were added to the top of the bridge's sparkling red-granite pillars in 1853. These figures, made of white Carrara marble, were also created by Schinkel. The statues depict tableaux from Greek mythology, such as Iris, Nike and Athena, training and looking after their favourite young warriors. The elaborate wrought-iron balustrade is decorated with intertwined sea creatures.

The surviving Stadtschloss portal fronting a government building

Schlossplatz ⓑ

Map 5 D2. Ⓢ *Hackescher Markt.* 🚋 *100, 157, 348.*

THIS SQUARE was once the site of a huge residential complex known as Stadt-schloss (City Castle). Built in 1451, it served as the main residence of the Brandenburg Electors. It was transformed from a castle to a palace in the mid-16th century when Elector Friedrich III (later King Friedrich I) ordered its reconstruction in the Baroque style. The building works, which lasted from 1698 until 1716, were overseen initially by Andreas Schlüter and then by Johann von Göthe and Martin Heinrich Böhme.

The three-storey residence, designed around two court-yards, was the main seat of the Hohenzollern family for almost 500 years until the end of the monarchy. The palace was partly burned during World War II but, after 1945, it was provisionally restored and used as a museum.

In 1950–51, despite protests, the palace was demolished and the square was renamed Marx-Engels-Platz under the GDR.

Now all that remains of the palace is the triumphal-arch portal that once adorned the façade on the Lustgarten side. This is now incorporated into the wall of the government building, the Staatsratgebäude, which was erected in 1964 on the square's south side. The building's decor features the remaining original sculptures, including the magnificent atlantes by the famous Dresden sculptor, Balthasar Permoser. Their inclusion was not due to their artistic merit, but rather to their propaganda value: it was from the balcony of the portal that in 1918 Karl Liebknecht proclaimed the birth of the Socialist Republic.

In 1989 the square reverted to its original name. In 1993, a spectacular model of the palace was made out of cloth stretched over a scaffolding frame. After much debate, it has been decided not to rebuild the palace instead to incorporate the remaining elements into a new museum.

Berliner Dom ⓭

Am Lustgarten. **Map** 5 D1. 📞 *(030) 20 26 91 19.* Ⓢ *Hackescher Markt.* 🚋 *100, 157, 348.* ⭕ *Oct–Mar: 9am–7pm; Apr–Sep: 9am–8pm daily (from noon Sun).* 🎧 ✝ *10am, 6pm Sun.*

THE ORIGINAL Berliner Dom was based on a modest Baroque design by Johann Boumann. Built between 1747 and 1750 on the site of an old Dominican church, the cathedral included the original crypt of the Hohenzollern family, one of the largest of its kind in Europe. The present Neo-Baroque structure is the work of Julius Raschdorff and dates from 1894 to 1905. The central copper dome is 98 m (321 ft) high. Following severe World War II damage, the cathedral has been restored in a simplified form. The Hohenzollern memorial chapel, which originally adjoined the northern walls of the cathedral, has been dismantled.

The Neo-Baroque interior of the Berliner Dom

BERLIN'S BRIDGES

Despite wartime damage, Berlin's bridges are still well worth seeing. The Spree river and the city's canals have some fine, exemplary architecture on their banks, while many of the bridges were designed and decorated by famous architects and sculptors. Probably the most renowned bridge is the Schlossbrücke designed by Karl Friedrich Schinkel. Further south along the Kupfergrabenkanal, the Schleusenbrücke, dating from c.1914, is decorated with reliefs of the early history of the city's bridges and sluices. The next bridge, heading south, is the Jungfernbrücke (1798), which is the last drawbridge in Berlin. The next bridge along is the Gertraudenbrücke. Where Friedrichstrasse crosses the Spree river is the Weidendammer Brücke, built originally in 1695–7 and subsequently rebuilt in 1923, with an eagle motif adorning its balustrade. On the Spree near the Regierungsviertel is the magnificent Moltkebrücke (1886–91). The bridge is guarded by a huge griffin wielding a shield adorned with the Prussian eagle, while cherubs dressed in a military fashion hold up lamps. On the arches of the bridges are portraits of leaders, designed by Karl Begas.

Ornamental feature of a bear on the Liebknechtbrücke

Street-by-Street: Museum Island

T HE LONG ISLAND that nestles in the tributaries of the
Spree river is the cradle of Berlin's history. It was here
that the first settlements appeared at the beginning of the
13th century: Cölln is mentioned in documents dating
back to 1237, and its twin settlement, Berlin, is mentioned
a few years later, in 1244. The island's character was
transformed by the construction of the Brandenburg
Electors' palace, which served as their residence from
1470. Although it was razed to the ground in 1950, some
interesting buildings on the north side of the island have·
survived, including the Berliner Dom (Berlin Cathedral)
and the impressive collection of
museums that give the
island its name,
Museuminsel.

LOCATOR MAP
See Street Finder, maps 4 & 5

Bode Museum
*A rounded corner of the
building, crowned with
a dome, provides a
magnificent end-piece to
the tip of the island* ⑲

AM KUPFER-GRABEN

Neues Museum
*Currently undergoing
reconstruction, this
museum will house an
impressive Egyptian
collection when it
reopens in 2005* ⑯

Alte Nationalgalerie
*The equestrian statue of
King Friedrich Wilhelm IV
in front of the building is
the work of Alexander
Calandrelli* ⑰

★ **Pergamonmuseum**
*The museum is famous
for its reconstruction of
fragments of ancient
towns, as well as the
original friezes from
the Pergamon altar* ⑱

KEY

– – – Suggested route

★ **Altes Museum**
The corners of the central building feature the figures of Castor and Pollux, heroes of Greek mythology ⑮

0 metres 400
0 yards 400

Lustgarten
A 70-ton granite bowl, the biggest in the world, was placed in the garden in 1828 ⑤

LUSTGARTEN

STAR SIGHTS

★ **Pergamonmuseum**

★ **Altes Museum**

Altes Museum ⑮

Am Lustgarten (Bodestraße 1–3).
Map 5 D1. (030) 20 90 55 55.
Hackescher Markt. 100, 157, 348. 10am–6pm Tue–Sun.

DESIGNED BY Karl Friedrich Schinkel, this museum building is one of the world's most beautiful Neo-Classical structures, with an impressive 87-m (285-ft) high portico supported by 18 Ionic columns. Officially opened in 1830, the museum was purpose-built to house the royal collection of art and antiquities.

In the years that followed World War II, the museum building was used only to display temporary exhibitions. Since 1998, however, it has housed the Antikensammlung, with a magnificent collection of Greek and Roman antiquities. **Pericles' Head**

Neues Museum ⑯
NEW MUSEUM

Bodestraße 1–3. **Map** 5 D1.
Hackescher Markt or Friedrichstraße.
100, 147, 257, 348. 1, 2, 3, 4, 5, 13, 53, 58. until 2005.

THE NEUES MUSEUM was built on Museum Island between 1841 and 1855 to a design by Friedrich August Stüler. Until World War II, it housed a collection of antiquities, mainly ancient Egyptian art. The rooms in the museum building were decorated to complement the exhibitions

they contained, while wall paintings by Wilhelm von Kaulbach depicted key events in world history.

The building was damaged in 1945 and reconstruction work has only recently started. When complete, it will house the collection of Egyptian art once again as well as the Museum of Early History. It will also serve as a venue for exhibitions.

Alte Nationalgalerie ⑰
OLD NATIONAL GALLERY

Bodestraße 1–3. **Map** 5 D1. (030) 20 90 55 55. Hackescher Markt or Friedrichstraße. 100, 147, 257, 348. 1, 2, 3, 4, 5, 13, 53, 58. 10am–6pm Tue–Sun, 10am–10pm Thu.

THE NATIONALGALERIE building, designed by Friedrich August Stüler, was erected between 1866 and 1876. It was originally intended to house the collection of modern art that had been on display in the Akademie der Künste (Art Academy). After World War II, however, the collection was split up and part of it was shown in West Berlin, where the Neue Nationalgalerie was erected for this purpose (see p84). This building was then renamed Alte Nationalgalerie.

Following the reunification of Germany, the modern art collections were merged again. Two new exhibition halls now show paintings from the German Romantic era, including work by Caspar David Friedrich and Karl Friedrich Schinkels.

Arnold Böcklin's *The Island of the Dead* (1883), Alte Nationalgalerie

Pergamonmuseum ⑱

The PERGAMONMUSEUM WAS BUILT between 1912 and 1930 to a design by Alfred Messels and Ludwig Hoffmann. It houses one of the most famous collections of antiquities in Europe and owes its name to the famous Pergamon Altar, which takes pride of place in the main hall. The three independent collections – the Museum of Antiquities (Greek and Roman), the Museum of Near Eastern Antiquities and the Museum of Islamic Art – are the result of intensive archaeological excavations by German expeditions to the Near and Middle East at the end of the 19th and beginning of the 20th century.

★ **Pergamon Altar** *(170 BC)*
This scene, featuring the goddess Athena, appears on the large frieze illustrating a battle between the gods and the giants.

Roman Mosaic
(3rd or 4th century AD)
This ancient mosaic was found at Jerash, Jordan. A second part of it is in the collection of the Stark Museum of Art, Texas.

Non-exhibition rooms

First floor

The Goddesss Athena
This enchanting Hellenistic sculpture of the goddess Athena is one of many displayed in the museum.

Ground floor

Main entrance

Assyrian Palace
Parts of this beautifully reconstructed palace interior, from the ancient kingdom of Assyria, date from the 12th century BC.

Aleppo Zimmer
(c.1603)
This magnificent panelled room comes from a merchant's house in the Syrian city of Aleppo.

GALLERY GUIDE
The central section of the ground floor houses reconstructions of ancient monumental structures, while the left wing is devoted to the Antiquities of Greece and Rome. The right wing houses the Museum of Near Eastern Antiquities; the first floor of the right wing houses the Museum of Islamic Art.

Façade of the Mshatta Palace *(AD 744)*
This fragment is from the southern façade of the Jordanian Mshatta Palace, presented to Wilhelm II by Sultan Abdul Hamid of Ottoman in 1903.

★ **Market Gate from Miletus** *(c.120 AD)*
Measuring over 16 m (52 ft) in height, this gate opened onto the southern market of Miletus, a Roman town in Asia Minor.

★ **Ishtar Gate from Babylon**
(6th century BC)
Original glazed bricks decorate both the huge Ishtar gate and the impressive Processional Way that leads up to it.

STAR EXHIBITS

★ **Ishtar Gate from Babylon**

★ **Market Gate from Miletus**

★ **Pergamon Altar**

KEY

◻ Antiquities (Antikensammlung)

◼ Near Eastern antiquities (Vorderasiatisches Museum)

◻ Islamic art (Museum für Islamische Kunst)

◻ Non-exhibition rooms

The Bodemuseum designed by Ernst von Ihne

Bodemuseum ⑲

Monbijoubrücke (Bodestraße 1–3).
Map 4 C1. ☏ *(030) 20 90 55 55.*
Ⓢ *Hackescher Markt or Friedrichstraße.*
🚌 *100, 147, 257, 348.* 🚊 *1, 2, 3, 4, 5, 13, 53, 58.* ● *until 2006.*

THE FOURTH MUSEUM building on Museuminsel was constructed between 1897 and 1904. It was designed by Ernst von Ihne to fit the wedge-shaped northwestern end of the island. The interior was designed with the help of an art historian, Wilhelm von Bode, who was the director of the Berlin state museums at the time.

The museum displayed a rather mixed collection that included some old masters. Its original name, Kaiser Friedrich Museum, was changed after World War II. Following the reassembling of the Berlin collections, all the paintings were rehoused in the Kultur-forum *(see pp80–81)*, while the Egyptian art and the papyrus collection were moved to the Ägyptisches Museum (Egyptian Museum) at Charlottenburg *(see p92)*.

Following its current refurbishment, the building will once again house its collection of coins, medals and Byzantine art. It will also be home to the reassembled collection of sculptures, which includes the works of Tilman Riemenschneider, Donatello, Gianlorenzo Bernini and Antonio Canova. A copy of the magnificent equestrian statue of the Great Elector, Friedrich Wilhelm, by Andreas Schlüter, will once again take its place in the old hall.

Marienkirche ⑳

Karl-Liebknecht-Straße. **Map** 5 E1.
Ⓢ *Hackescher Markt.* 🚌 *100, 157.*
◻ *10am–4pm Mon–Thu, noon-4pm Sat -Sun.* 📷 *1pm Mon & Tue.*
✝ *10:30am Sun.*

ST MARY'S CHURCH, or the Marienkirche, was first established as a parish church in the second half of the 13th century. Started around 1280, construction was completed early in the 14th century. During reconstruction works in 1380, following a fire, the church was altered slightly, but its overall shape changed only in the 15th century when it acquired the front tower. In 1790, the tower was crowned with a dome, designed by Carl Gotthard Langhans, which includes both Baroque and Neo-Gothic elements.

The Marienkirche was once hemmed in by buildings, but today it stands alone in the shadow of the Fernsehturm (Television Tower). The early Gothic hall design and the

Baroque altar in the Marienkirche, designed by Andreas Krüger

lavish decorative touches make this church one of the most interesting in Berlin. An exquisitely carved alabaster pulpit by Andreas Schlüter, dating from 1703, is decorated with bas-reliefs of St John the Baptist and the personifi-cations of the Virtues.

The Baroque main altar was designed by Andreas Krüger around 1762. The paintings with which it is adorned include three works by Christian Bernhard Rode.

A Gothic font, dating from 1437, is supported by three black dragons and decorated with the figures of Jesus Christ, Mary and the Apostles.

Rotes Rathaus ㉑
RED TOWN HALL

Rathausstraße 15. **Map** 5 E2.
Ⓤ & Ⓢ *Alexanderplatz.* Ⓤ *Kloster-straße,* 🚌 *100, 142, 157, 257, 348.*

THIS IMPRESSIVE structure is Berlin's main town hall. Its predecessor was a much more modest structure that, by the end of the 19th century, was inadequate to meet the needs of the growing metropolis.

The present building was designed by Hermann Friedrich Waesemann, and the construction works went on from 1861 until 1869. The architect took his main inspir-ation from Italian Renaissance municipal buildings, but the tower is reminiscent of Laon cathedral in France. The walls are made from red brick and it was this, rather than the political orientation of the mayors, that gave the town hall its name.

The whole building has a continuous frieze known as the "stone chronicle", which was added in 1879. The frieze features scenes and figures from the city's history and traces the development of its economy and science.

The Rotes Rathaus was severely damaged during World War II but, following its reconstruction between 1951 and 1958, it became the seat of the East Berlin authorities. The West Berlin magistrate was housed in the

Fernsehturm ㉓

THE TELEVISION TOWER, called by the locals *Telespargel*, or toothpick, remains to this day the city's tallest structure at 365 m (1,197 ft). It is also the second-tallest structure in Europe. The tower was built in 1969 to a design by a team of architects including Fritz Dieter and Günter Franke, with the help of Swedish experts. However, the idea for the tower originated much earlier from Hermann Henselmann (creator of the Karl-Marx-Allee development) in the Socialist-Realist style.

The television antenna is visible all over Berlin.

Transmitter aerial

The metal sphere is covered with steel cladding.

View from the Tower
On a clear day the viewing platform offers a full view of Berlin. Visibility can reach up to 40 km (25 miles).

Concrete structure rising to 250 m (820 ft)

The concrete shaft contains two elevators that carry passengers to the café and viewing platform.

Tele-Café
One of the attractions of the tower is the revolving café. A full rotation takes about half an hour, so it is possible to get a bird's-eye view of the whole city while sipping a cup of coffee.

The monumental, red-brick town hall, known as the Rotes Rathaus

Schöneberg town hall *(see p99)*. Following the reunification of Germany in 1990, the Rotes Rathaus became the centre of authority, housing the offices of the mayor and the Berlin cabinet.

The forecourt sculptures by Fritz Kremer, which depict Berliners helping to rebuild the city, were added in 1958.

Alexanderplatz ㉒

Map 5 E1, F1. Ⓤ & Ⓢ *Alexanderplatz.* 🚌 100, 142, 157, 257.

ALEXANDERPLATZ, or "Alex" as it is called locally, has a long history, although it would be hard now to find any visible traces of the past. Once known as Ochsenmarkt (oxen market), it was the site of a cattle and wool market. It was later renamed after Tsar Alexander I who visited Berlin in 1805. At that time, the square boasted a magnificent monumental colonnade, which was designed by Carl von Gontard.

In time, houses and shops sprang up around the square and a market hall and urban train line were built nearby.

"Alex" became one of the city's busiest spots. Its frenzied atmosphere was captured by Alfred Döblin (1878–1957) in his novel *Berlin Alexanderplatz*.

In 1929, attempts were made to develop the square, though only two office buildings were added – the Alexanderhaus and the Berolinahaus, both by Peter Behrens.

World War II erased most of the square's buildings and it is now surrounded by characterless 1960s edifices, including the Forum Hotel (formerly Hotel Stadt Berlin) and the Fernsehturm. Now Alexanderplatz awaits its next transformation, to be based on the winning design chosen from a competition for the square's redevelopment.

Riverside buildings of the Nikolaiviertel

Nikolaiviertel ㉔

Map 5 E2. **U** & **S** Alexanderplatz. **U** Klosterstraße. 🚌 100, 142, 157, 257, 348.

THIS SMALL AREA on the bank of the Spree is a favourite place for both Berliners and tourists. Some of Berlin's oldest houses stood here until they were destroyed in World War II. The redevelopment of the area, which was carried out by the GDR government between 1979 and 1987, was an interesting attempt to recreate a medieval village. Now, with the exception of one or two restored buildings, the Nikolaiviertel consists entirely of newly built replicas of historic buildings.

The **Nikolaikirche** was destroyed by bombing in 1945 and rebuilt in 1987. All that remains of the original structure, which was probably built around 1230, is the base of the two-tower façade of the present church, which dates from around 1300.

The only Baroque building in Nikolaiviertel to escape damage during World War II was the **Knoblauchhaus**, a small townhouse built in 1759 for the Knoblauch family. The current appearance of the building is the result of work carried out in 1835 when the façade was given a Neo-Classical look.

Ephraim-Palais was built in 1766 for Nathan Veitel Heinrich Ephraim, Frederick the Great's mint master and court jeweller. Parts of the original structure, which were saved from demolition, were used in the reconstruction.

Märkisches Museum ㉕

Am Köllnischen Park 5. **Map** 5 F2. 📞 (030) 30 86 60. **U** Märkisches Museum. **S** Jannowitzbrücke. 🚌 147, 240, 265. ⬜ 10am–6pm Tue–Sun. 🎷 (free Wed). Presentation of mechanical instruments 3pm Sun.

BUILT between 1901 and 1908, this complex of red brick buildings was inspired by the brick-Gothic style popular in the Brandenburg region. The museum, founded in 1874, is dedicated to the cultural history of Berlin from the first settlements to today. The department "Berliner Kunst" (art), for example, presents a remarkable collection of paintings, sculpture, textiles, faiences, glass and porcelain. The main hall features the original Gothic portal from the sculpture *Quadriga*, which once crowned the Brandenburg Gate *(see p65)*. A further collection is devoted to the Berlin theatre during the period 1730 to 1933. One of the galleries houses some charming old-time mechanical musical instruments.

Surrounding the museum is the Köllnischer Park. The park is home to three brown bears – the official city mascots.

Checkpoint Charlie ㉖

Friedrichstrasse 43–45. **Map** 4 C4. 📞 (030) 253 72 50. **U** Kochstrasse. 🚌 129. **Haus am Checkpoint Charlie** ⬜ 9am–10pm daily. 🎷

THE NAME OF THIS notorious border crossing between the American and Soviet sectors comes from the word that signifies the letter C in the international phonetic alphabet: Alpha, Bravo, Charlie.

Between 1961 and 1990, Checkpoint Charlie was the only crossing for foreigners between East and West Berlin. It came to represent a symbol of both freedom and separation for the many East Germans trying to escape Soviet communism.

Today, a single watchtower is all that remains, and this houses a museum – **Haus am Checkpoint Charlie**. Its rich collection details the years of the Cold War in Berlin.

Jüdisches Museum ㉗

Lindenstraße 14. **Map** 4 C5. 📞 (030) 25 99 33. **U** Hallesches Tor or Kochstraße. 🚌 129, 240, 341. ⬜ 10am–10pm Mon, 10am–8pm Tue–Sun.

THE BUILDING housing the city's recently opened Jewish Museum is an exciting and imaginative example of 20th century architecture. Designed by a Polish-Jewish architect based in the United States, Daniel Libeskind, the plan,

The exterior of the Märkisches Museum, echoing a medieval monastery

shape, style, and interior and exterior arrangement of the building are part of a profoundly complicated philosophical programme. The museum's architecture itself is intended to convey something of the tragic history of the millions of Jews who perished in the Holocaust. For example, the zig-zag layout recalls a torn Star of David.

The interior arrangement is dominated by a gigantic empty crack, which cuts a swathe through the building. Several corridors lead to a windowless Holocaust tower.

The collection focuses on Jewish history and art. Also on display are artifacts that were once part of everyday Jewish life in Berlin.

The new museum is accessible only through an underground passageway in the former Berlin-Museum building next door.

The austere, steel-clad walls of the Jüdisches Museum

Topographie des Terrors ㉘

Stresemannstraße 110 (enter on Niederkirchner Straße). **Map** 4 B4.
📞 *(030) 25 48 67 03.* Ⓢ &
Ⓤ *Potsdamer Platz.* 🚌 *129, 248, 341.* 🕐 *Oct–Apr: 10am–6pm daily; May–Sep: 10am–8pm daily.* 🖼

D URING the Third Reich, Prinz-Albrecht-Straße was probably the most frightening address in Berlin: here, three of the most terrifying Nazi political departments had their headquarters. The Neo-Classical Prinz-Albrecht palace,

which stands at Wilhelmstraße No. 102, became the headquarters of Reinhard Heydrich and the Third Reich's security service. The school of arts and crafts at Prinz-Albrecht-Straße No. 8 was occupied by the head of the Gestapo, Heinrich Müller, while the Hotel Prinz Albrecht at No. 9 became the headquarters of the Schutzstaffel or SS.

After World War II, the buildings were pulled down. In 1987, however, in cellars that were once torture cells, an exhibition documenting Nazi crimes was mounted.

A new museum building, designed by Peter Zumthor, has been under construction on the site since 1998.

Deutsches Technikmuseum Berlin ㉙

Trebbiner Straße 9. **Map** 4 A5.
📞 *(030) 90 25 40.* Ⓤ *Gleisdreieck.*
🚌 *129.* 🕐 *9am–5:30pm Tue–Fri, 10am–6pm Sat–Sun.* ♿ 🖼

T HE TECHNICAL MUSEUM was first established in 1982 with the intention of grouping more than 100 smaller, specialized collections under one roof. The current collection is arranged on the site of the former trade hall, the size of which allows many of the

Exhibition documenting Nazi crimes at the Topographie des Terrors

museum's exhibits, such as locomotives, water towers and storerooms, to be displayed full-size and in their original condition.

Of particular interest in the collection are the dozens of locomotives and railway carriages from different eras, as well as vintage cars. There are also exhibitions dedicated to flying, the history of paper manufacture, printing, weaving, electro-technology and computer technology. There are also two windmills, a brewery and an old forge. The section called Spectrum is especially popular with children as it allows them to try the "hands-on" experiments. A new hall for aircraft and engines will open at the end of 2003.

A special attraction of the Technical Museum is the Historical Brewery, which opened in 1995. The building was once used by the brewery Tucker Bräu for storing beer, but it was destroyed in World War II. Decades later, the brewery was rebuilt on four levels. Some visitors claim they can smell roasted malt.

One of dozens of locomotives displayed in the Deutsches Technikmuseum

WESTERN CENTRE

THIS PART OF BERLIN includes the areas of Tiergarten, Charlottenburg and parts of Kreuzberg, as well as a small section of Mitte, which used to belong to East Berlin.

Tiergarten, which was once a royal hunting estate, became a park in the 18th century. It survives as a park to this day, although in an altered form.

To the south of Tiergarten is the Kulturforum – a large centre of museums and other cultural establishments, which was created after World War II. The neighbouring Potsdamer Platz is now an ultra-modern development, built in recent years on the wasteland that formerly divided East and West Berlin. Although the eastern part of Charlottenburg does not feature a great number of historic buildings, it is one of the city's most attractive districts, which, after World War II, became the commercial and cultural centre of West Berlin. Kreuzberg is a lively area that is now populated by immigrants, artists and affluent young professionals.

Detail from Theater des Westens façade

SIGHTS AT A GLANCE

Museums and Galleries
Bauhaus-Archiv ❼
Bendlerblock ❽
Gemäldegalerie ❾
Hamburger Bahnhof ❿
Käthe-Kollwitz-Museum ❸
Kunstgewerbemuseum ⓬
Kupferstichkabinett und Kunstbibliothek ❿
Museum für Naturkunde ⓲
Musikinstrumenten-Museum ⓮
Neue Nationalgalerie ⓫

Streets and Squares
Kurfürstendamm (Ku'damm) ❷
Potsdamer Platz ⓯

Tiergarten ❺
Zoologischer Garten ❹

Churches
Kaiser-Wilhelm-Gedächtniskirche ❶

Historic Buildings and Monuments
Philharmonie ⓭
Reichstag ⓰
Siegessäule ❻

GETTING THERE
This part of town is served by S-Bahn lines 3, 5, 7, 9, 75 and by U-Bahn lines 1, 2, 9, 15.

KEY

	Street-by-Street map *See pp80–81*
🚉	Railway station
Ⓢ	S-Bahn station
Ⓤ	U-Bahn station
🅿	Parking

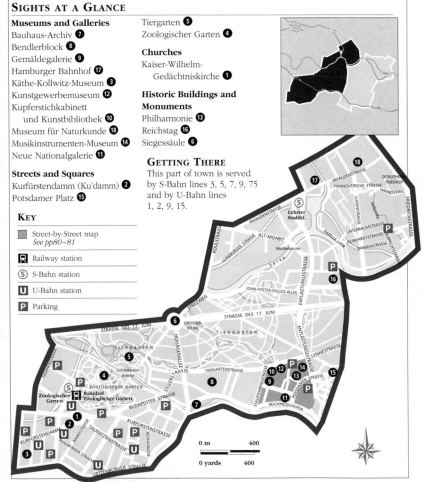

◁ **Mosaic in Kaiser-Wilhelm-Gedächtniskirche depicting a herald bearing the Prussian royal insignia**

Street-by-Street: Kulturforum

Sculpture by Henry Moore

THE IDEA OF CREATING a new cultural centre in West Berlin was first mooted in 1956. The first building to go up was the Berlin Philharmonic concert hall, built to an innovative design by Hans Scharoun in 1961. Most other elements of the Kultur-forum were realized between 1961 and 1987, and came from such famous architects as Ludwig Mies van der Rohe. The area is now a major cultural centre that attracts millions of visitors every year.

★ **Kunstgewerbe-museum**
Among the collection at the Museum of Arts and Crafts you can see this intricately carved silver and ivory tankard, made in an Augsburg workshop around 1640 ⑫

Kupferstichkabinett
The large collection of prints and drawings owned by this gallery includes this portrait of Albrecht Dürer's mother ⑩

★ **Gemäldegalerie**
Among the most important works of the old masters exhibited in this gallery of fine art is this Madonna in Church *by Jan van Eyck (c.1425)* ⑨

Kunstbibliothek
The Art Library boasts a rich collection of books, graphic art and drawings.

REICHPIETSCHUFER

LANDWEHRKANAL

STAR SIGHTS

★ **Gemäldegalerie**

★ **Kunstgewerbe-museum**

★ **Philharmonie**

KEY

– – – Suggested route

Neue Nationalgalerie
Sculptures by Henry Moore and Alexander Calder stand outside this streamlined building, designed by Ludwig Mies van der Rohe ⑪

★ Philharmonie
Its exterior covered in a layer of golden aluminium, the Berlin Philharmonic concert hall is known all over the world for its superb acoustics **⑬**

LOCATOR MAP
See Street Finder maps 1 & 3

Musikinstrumenten-Museum
This clavichord is part of a collection of musical instruments dating from the 16th to the 20th century **⑭**

SCHAROUNSTRASSE

POTSDAMER STRASSE

MATTHÄIKIRCH PLATZ

SMUNDSTRASSE

POTSDAMER STRASSE

St-Matthäus-Kirche
This picturesque 19th-century church stands out among the modern buildings of the Kulturforum.

0 metres 50
0 yards 50

Staatsbibliothek
Hans Scharoun designed this public lending and research library built in 1978.

Kaiser-Wilhelm-Gedächtnis-Kirche ❶

T HIS CHURCH-MONUMENT is one of Berlin's most famous landmarks. The vast Neo-Romanesque church was designed by Franz Schwechten. It was consecrated in 1895 and destroyed by bombs in 1943. After the war the ruins were removed, leaving only the front tower, at the base of which the Gedenkhalle (Memorial Hall) is situated. This hall documents the church's history and contains some original ceiling mosaics, marble reliefs and liturgical objects. In 1963, Egon Eiermann designed a new octagonal church in blue glass and a new freestanding bell tower.

VISITORS' CHECKLIST

Breitscheidplatz. **Map** 2 B4.
C *(030) 218 50 23.*
S & **U** *Zoologischer Garten* or **U** *Kurfürstenstraße.* 🚌 *100, 119, 129, 146, X-9.* 🔲 **Church** *9am–7pm daily.* **Gedenkhalle** *10am–4pm Mon–Sat.* 🎵 *10am & 6pm Sun. In English, Jul–Aug: 9am Sun.* 🈺

Tower Ruins
The damaged roof of the former church has become one of the best-known symbols of Berlin.

Tower Clock

★ **Kaiser's Mosaic**
Kaiser Heinrich I, seated on his throne, is depicted in this elaborate mosaic.

Main entrance

Figure of Christ
This vast sculpture by Hermann Schaper once decorated the church altar. It survived World War II damage.

Main Altar
The massive figure of Christ on the Cross is the work of Karl Hemmeter.

STAR SIGHTS

★ **Kaiser's Mosaic**

Ku'damm ②

Plan 2 A5, 2 B4. **U** *Kurfürsten-damm.* 🚌 *109, 119, 129, 219.*

THE EASTERN AREA of the Charlottenburg region, around the boulevard known as Kurfürstendamm (the Ku'damm), was developed in the 19th century. Luxurious buildings were constructed along the Ku'damm, while the areas of Breitscheidplatz and Wittenbergplatz filled up with hotels and department stores. After World War II, with the old centre (Mitte) situated in East Berlin, Charlottenburg became the centre of West Berlin. Traces of wartime destruction were removed very quickly and the area was transformed into the heart of West Berlin, with dozens of new company headquarters and trade centres being built.

Mother and Child, from the Käthe-Kollwitz-Museum

Käthe-Kollwitz-Museum ③

Fasanenstraße 24. **Map** 2 A5. **C** *(030) 882 52 10.* **U** *Uhland-straße or Kurfürstendamm.* 🚌 *109, 119, 129, 219, 249.* ⏰ *11am–6pm Wed–Mon* 📷 🔊

THIS SMALL private museum provides a unique opportunity to become acquainted with the work of Käthe Kollwitz (1867–1945). Born in Königsberg, the artist settled in Berlin where she married a doctor who worked in Prenzlauer Berg, a working-class district. Her drawings and sculptures portrayed the social

A tranquil area within the Tiergarten

problems of the poor, as well as human tragedy and suffering. She frequently took up the theme of motherhood and war after losing a son and grandson in World Wars I and II.

This museum displays the work of Käthe Kollwitz and includes posters, drawings and sculptures as well as documents, such as letters and photographs.

Zoologischer Garten ④

ZOOLOGICAL GARDEN

Hardenbergplatz 8 / Budapester Str. 34. **Map** 2 B3, C3, 2 B4, C4. **C** *(030) 25 40 10.* **S** & **U** *Zoologischer Garten.* 🚌 *100, 109, 145, 146, 149, 245, 249.* ⏰ *Apr–Sep: 9am–6:30pm daily; Oct–Mar: 9am–5pm daily.* 📷

THE ZOOLOGICAL garden is actually part of the Tier-garten and dates from 1844, making this one of the oldest zoos in Germany. It offers a number of attractions, including the monkey house, which contains a family of gorillas, and a specially darkened pavilion for observing nocturnal animals. A glazed wall in the hippopotamus pool enables visitors to observe these enormous animals moving through the water. The large aquarium contains sharks, piranhas and unusual animals from coral reefs. There is also a huge terrarium with an overgrown jungle that is home to a group of crocodiles. One of the best loved animals at the zoo is the giant panda named Bao-Bao.

Tiergarten ⑤

Map 2 C3, 3 D3, E3, F3. **S** *Tiergarten or Bellevue.* 🚌 *100, 187, 341.*

ONCE A FOREST used as the Elector's hunting reserve, the Tiergarten was transformed into a landscaped park by Peter Joseph Lenné in the 1830s. A Triumphal Avenue, lined with statues of the country's rulers and statesmen, was built in the eastern section at the end of the 19th century. World War II inflicted huge damage, but replanting has now restored the Tiergarten and its avenues are bordered with statues of figures such as Johann Wolfgang von Goethe and Richard Wagner.

Near the lake and the Land-wehrkanal are memorials to Karl Liebknecht and Rosa Luxemburg, the leaders of the Spartakus movement who were assassinated in 1918.

Siegessäule ⑥

TRIUMPHAL COLUMN

Großer Stern. **Map** 3 D2. **S** *Bellevue.* 🚌 *100, 187, 341.* ⏰ *Apr–Oct: 8:30am–6:30pm daily; Nov–Mar: 8:30am–5:30pm daily.*

THE TRIUMPHAL column, based on a design by Johann Heinrich Strack, was built to commemorate victory in the Prusso-Danish war of 1864. After further Prussian victories in wars against Austria (1866) and France (1871), a gilded figure representing Victory, known as the "Goldelse", was added to the top of the column. It originally stood in front of the Reichstag building but was moved to its present location by the Nazi government in 1938. The base is decorated with bas-reliefs commemorating battles, while higher up a mosaic frieze depicts the founding of the German Empire in 1871. An observation terrace at the top offers magnificent vistas over Berlin.

Siegessäule (Triumphal Column)

The captivating, streamlined buildings of the Bauhaus-Archiv

Bauhaus-Archiv ❼

Klingelhöferstraße 14. **Map** 3 D4, E4.
🛈 *(030) 254 00 20.* Ⓤ *Nollendorf-platz.* 🚌 *100, 129, 187, 341, 1, X-9.*
◯ *10am–5pm Wed–Mon.* 🎨 *(free Mon.)* ♿

THE BAUHAUS school of art, started by Walter Gropius in 1919, was one of the most influential art institutions of the 20th century. Originally based in Weimar, it inspired many artists and architects. Staff and students included Mies van der Rohe, Paul Klee and Wassily Kandinsky. The school moved to Berlin in 1932 from Dessau, but was closed by the Nazis in 1933.

After the war, the Bauhaus-Archiv was relocated to Darmstadt. In 1964 Walter Gropius designed a building to house the collection but, in 1971, the archive was moved to Berlin and the design was adapted to the new site. As Gropius had died in 1969, Alexander Cvijanovic took over the project. Built between 1976 and 1979 the gleaming white building with its glass-panelled gables houses the archive, library and exhibition halls.

Bendlerblock (Gedenkstätte Deutscher Widerstand) ❽

Stauffenbergstraße 13–14.
Map 3 E4, F4. 🛈 *(030) 26 99 50 00.*
Ⓤ *Mendelssohn-Bartholdy-Park.*
🚌 *129, 142, 148, 341.*
◯ *9am–6pm Mon–Wed, 9am–8pm Thu, 10–6pm Sat–Sun.* ● *1 Jan, 24, 25 & 31 Dec.* 🎨

THE COLLECTION of buildings known as the Bendlerblock was built during the Third Reich as an extension to the German State Naval Offices. During World War II they were the headquarters of the Wehrmacht (German Army). It was here that a group of officers planned their assassination attempt on Hitler on 20 July 1944. When the attempt led by Claus Schenk von Stauffenberg failed, he and his fellow conspirators were arrested and death sentences passed. Stauffenberg, Friedrich Olbricht, Werner von Haeften, and Ritter Mertz von Quirnheim were shot in the Bendler-block courtyard. A monument commemorating this event, designed by Richard Scheibe in 1953, stands where the executions were carried out.

On the upper floor of the building there is an exhibition documenting the history of the German anti-Nazi movements.

Gemäldegalerie ❾

See pp86–7.

Kupferstichkabinett und Kunstbibliothek ❿

Matthäikirchplatz 6. **Map** 3 F3.
🛈 *(030) 20 90 55 55.* Ⓢ *&* Ⓤ
Potsdamer Platz or Ⓤ *Mendelssohn-Bartholdy-Park.* 🚌 *129, 142, 148, 248, 348.* **Kupferstichkabinett: Exhibitions** *10am–6pm Tue–Fri, 11am–6pm Sat–Sun.* **Studio gallery** *9am–4pm Tue–Fri.* **Kunstbibliothek: Exhibits** *10–6pm Tue–Fri, 11am–6pm Sat–Sun.* **Library** *2–8pm Mon, 9am–8pm Tue–Fri.* 🎨 ♿ 🚫

THE PRINT COLLECTIONS of galleries in the former East and West Berlin were united in 1994 in the Kupferstich-kabinett (Print Gallery), whose collection includes around 2,000 engraver's plates, over 520,000 prints and 80,000 drawings and watercolours.

The **Kunstbibliothek** (Art Library) is not only a library with a range of publications about the arts; it is also a museum with an extensive collection of posters, advertisements and other practical forms of design.

Munch's lithograph *Girl on a Beach*, Kupferstichkabinett

Neue Nationalgalerie ⓫

Potsdamer Straße 50. **Map** 3 F4.
🛈 *(030) 20 90 55 55.* Ⓤ *&* Ⓢ
Potsdamer Platz or Ⓤ *Mendelssohn-Bartholdy-Park.* 🚌 *129, 142, 148, 200, 248, 341, 348.* ◯ *10am–6pm Tue, Wed, Fri, 10am–10pm Thu, 11am–6pm Sat & Sun.* 🎨 ♿

AFTER WORLD WAR II, when this magnificent collection of modern art ended up in West Berlin, the commission to design a suitable building to house it was given to Mies van der Rohe. The result is a striking building with a flat steel roof over a glass hall, which is supported only by six slender interior struts.

The collection comprises largely 20th-century art, but begins with artists of the late 19th century, such as Edvard Munch. German art is well represented: as well as the Bauhaus movement, the gallery shows works by exponents of a crass realism, such

Karl Schmidt-Rottluff's *Farm in Daugart* (1910), Neue Nationalgalerie

as Otto Dix. The most celebrated artists of other European countries are included, as are examples of post-World War II art.

Kunstgewerbe-museum ⓬

Matthäikirchplatz. **Map** 3 F3. 📞 *(030) 20 90 55 55.* Ⓢ *Potsdamer Platz.* Ⓤ *Potsdamer Platz or Mendelssohn-Bartholdy-Park.* 🚌 *129, 142, 148, 248, 341, 348.* ⏰ *10am–6pm Tue–Fri, 11am–6pm Sat & Sun.* 📅 *Tue after Easter, Whitsun, 1 Oct, 24, 25 & 31 Dec.* 🎧 ♿ ⌀

THIS MUSEUM holds a rich collection embracing many genres of craft and decorative art, from the early Middle Ages to the modern day. Goldwork is especially well represented, as are metal items from the Middle Ages. Among the most valuable exhibits is a collection of medieval goldwork from the church treasures of Enger and the Guelph

treasury from Brunswick. The museum also takes great pride in its collection of late Gothic and Renaissance silver from the civic treasury in the town of Lüneberg. In addition, there are fine examples of Italian majolica, and 18th- and 19th-century German, French and Italian glass, porcelain and furniture.

Philharmonie ⓭

PHILHARMONIC AND CHAMBER MUSIC HALL

Herbert-von-Karajan-Straße 1. **Map** 3 F3. 📞 *(030) 25 48 80.* Ⓢ & Ⓤ *Potsdamer Platz or* Ⓤ *Mendelssohn-Bartholdy-Park.* 🚌 *129, 142, 148, 248, 348.*

HOME TO ONE of the most renowned orchestras in Europe, this unusual building is among the finest postwar architectural achievements in

Europe. Built between 1960 and 1963 to a design by Hans Scharoun, the Philharmonie pioneered a new concept for concert hall interiors, with a podium occupying the central section of the pentagonal hall, around which are galleries for the public. The exterior is reminiscent of a circus tent. The gilded exterior was added between 1978 and 1981.

Between the years 1984 to 1987 the Kammermusiksaal, which was designed by Edgar Wisniewski on the basis of sketches by Scharoun, was added to the Philharmonie. This building consolidates the aesthetics of the earlier structure by featuring a central multi-sided space covered by a fanciful tent-like roof.

Musikinstrumenten-Museum ⓮

Tiergartenstraße 1. **Map** 1 A5. 📞 *(030) 25 48 11 78.* Ⓢ & Ⓤ *Potsdamer Platz or* Ⓤ *Mendelssohn-Bartholdy-Park.* 🚌 *129, 142, 148, 248, 348.* ⏰ *9am–5pm Tue–Fri, 10am–5pm Sat–Sun.* **Wurlitzer Organ demonstration** *noon, first Sat of the month.* 🎧 ♿

BEHIND the Philharmonie, in a small building designed by Edgar Wisniewski and Hans Scharoun between 1979 and 1984, the fascinating Museum of Musical Instruments houses a collection dating from 1888. Intriguing displays trace each instrument's development from the 16th century to the present day. Most spectacular of all is a working Wurlitzer cinema organ dating from 1929. Saturday demonstrations of its impressive sounds attract enthusiastic crowds. There is also an archive and a library.

The tent-like gilded exterior of the Philharmonie and Kammermusiksaal

Gemäldegalerie ⑨

Woman in a Bonnet **by Rogier van der Weyden**

THE GEMÄLDEGALERIE collection is exceptional in the consistently high quality of its paintings. Unlike those in other collections, they were chosen by specialists who, from the end of the 18th century, systematically acquired pictures to represent all the major European schools. Originally part of the Altes Museum collection *(see p71)*, the paintings achieved independent status in 1904 when they were moved to what is now the Bodemuseum *(see p74)*. After the division of Berlin in 1945, part of the collection was kept in the Bodemuseum, while the majority ended up in the Dahlem Museum *(see p100)*. Following reunification, and with the building of a new home as part of the Kulturforum development, this unique collection has finally been united again.

★ **Cupid Victorious** (1602)
Inspired by Virgil's Omnia vincit Amor, *Caravaggio depicted a playful god trampling over the symbols of Culture, Fame, Knowledge and Power.*

Madonna with Child (c.1477)
A frequent subject of Sandro Botticelli, the Madonna and Child are depicted here, surrounded by singing angels holding lilies to symbolize purity.

Circular lobby leading to the galleries

Birth of Christ (c.1480)
This beautiful religious painting is one of the few surviving paintings on panels by Martin Schongauer.

Portrait of Hieronymus Holzschuher (1529)
Albrecht Dürer painted this affectionate portrait of his friend, who was the mayor of Nuremberg.

Main entrance

The Glass of Wine
(c.1658–61)
Jan Vermeer's carefully composed picture of a young woman drinking wine with a young man gently hints at the relationship developing between them.

Love in the French Theatre
This picture has a companion piece called Love in the Italian Theatre. *Both by French painter, Jean-Antoine Watteau (1684–1721).*

★ Portrait of Hendrickje Stoffels (1656–57)
Rembrandt's portrait of his lover, Hendrickje Stoffels, is typical of his work in the way it focuses on the subject and ignores the background.

KEY

- ☐ 13th–16th-century German painting
- ☐ 14th–16th-century Dutch and French painting
- ☐ 17th-century Flemish and Dutch painting
- ☐ 18th-century French, English and German painting
- ☐ 17th–18th-century Italian painting, 17th-century German, French and Spanish painting
- ☐ 13th–16th-century Italian painting
- ☐ 16th–18th-century miniatures
- ☐ Digital gallery

GALLERY GUIDE
The main gallery contains over 900 masterpieces grouped by period and country of origin. These are complemented by around 400 works in the educational gallery on the lower floor and by a computerized digital gallery.

STAR EXHIBITS

★ **Cupid Victorious**

★ **Dutch Proverbs**

★ **Portrait of Hendrickje Stoffels**

★ Dutch Proverbs (1559)
Pieter Brueghel managed to illustrate more than 100 proverbs in this painting.

Potsdamer Platz ⑮

IN THE SHORT SPACE of a few years a new financial and business district has sprung up on what was the vast wasteland surrounding the Potsdamer Platz. It boasts splendid constructions designed by Renzo Piano, Arata Isozaki and Helmut Jahn. As well as office blocks, the area has many public buildings, including cinemas and a theatre, as well as a huge shopping centre (the Arkaden) plus a luxury hotel, restaurants and several bars.

***The Sony Tower**, designed by Helmut Jahn, is the tallest building in Potsdamer Platz and is curved on one side and flat on the other.*

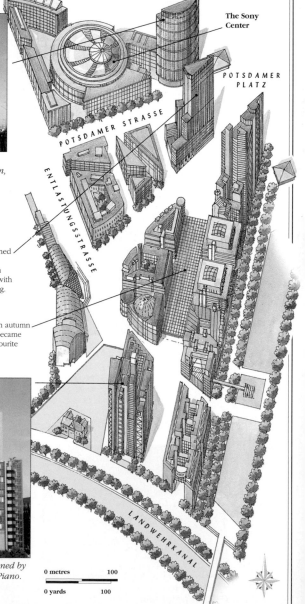

The Sony Center

POTSDAMER PLATZ

POTSDAMER STRASSE

ENTLASTUNGSSTRASSE

LANDWEHRKANAL

This office building, designed by Kollhoff & Timmermann Partnership, alludes to North German building traditions with its clinker brick wall cladding.

Arkaden, opened in autumn 1998, immediately became one of the city's favourite shopping centres.

***The Debis House** designed by Italian architect Renzo Piano.*

0 metres		100

0 yards		100

The Reichstag, crowned by a dome designed by Sir Norman Foster

Reichstag ⓰

Platz der Republik. **Map** 1 B4, 4 A1, A2. 🛈 *(030) 22 73 21 52.* Ⓢ *Unter den Linden.* 🚌 *100, 248, 257.*
Dome ◯ *8am–midnight daily.*
Assembly Hall ◯ *9am–5pm Mon–Fri, 10am–4pm Sat–Sun, holidays by appointment only.* 🎟 *noon Tue (in English).* ● *1 Jan, 24–26 & 31 Dec.*

BUILT TO HOUSE the German Parliament, the Reichstag was constructed between 1884 and 1894 to a New-Renaissance design by Paul Wallot. Capturing the prevailing spirit of German optimism, it became a potent symbol to the populace.

In 1918, from the Reichstag, Philipp Scheidemann declared the formation of the Weimar Republic. The next time the world heard about the building was in February 1933, when a fire destroyed the main hall. The Communists were blamed, accelerating a political witch-hunt driven by the Nazis, who then came to power.

With the onset of World War II, the building was not rebuilt, yet its significance reson-ated beyond Germany, as shown by a photograph of the Soviet flag flying from the Reichstag in May 1945, which became a symbol of the German defeat.

Following rebuilding work between 1957 and 1972, the Reichstag provided a meeting-place for the lower house of the German Parliament as well as a spectacular backdrop for festivals and rock concerts. After German reunification in 1990, the Reichstag was the first meeting place of a newly elected Bundestag. The latest rebuilding project, to a design by Sir Norman Foster, transformed the Reichstag into a modern meeting hall in which the first parliamentary meeting took place on 19 April 1999.

Hamburger Bahnhof ⓱

Invalidenstraße 50/51. **Map** 1 A2, B2. 🛈 *(030) 20 90 55 55.* Ⓢ *Lehrter Stadtbahnhof.* 🚌 *245, 340.* ◯ *10am–6pm Tue–Sun.* ● *1 Jan, Tue following Easter and Whitsun, 24, 25 & 31 Dec.* ♿ 🚫 📷

THIS MUSEUM is situated in a Neo-Renaissance building, formerly the Hamburg Railway station, which dates from 1847. The building stood vacant after World War II but, following refurbishment by Josef Paul Kleihues, it was opened to the public in 1996. The neon installation surrounding the façade is the work of Dan Flavin. The museum houses a magnificent collection of contemporary art, including the work of Erich Marx and, from 2004, the world-renowned Flick collection. The result is one of the best modern art museums to be found in Europe, which features not only art, but also film, video, music and design.

***Jeff and Ilona* (1991), Hamburger Bahnhof**

Museum für Naturkunde ⓲

NATURAL HISTORY MUSEUM

Invalidenstraße 43. **Map** 1 E2. 🛈 *(030) 20 93 85 91.* Ⓤ *Zinnowitzer straße.* 🚌 *157, 245, 340.* 🚊 *6, 8.* ◯ *9:30am–5pm Tue–Fri, 10am–6pm Sat–Sun.* 📷

OCCUPYING A purpose-built Neo-Renaissance building constructed between 1883 and 1889, this is one of the biggest natural history museums in the world, with a collection containing over 60 million exhibits. Although it has undergone several periods of extension and renovation, it has maintained its unique old-fashioned atmosphere.

The highlight of the museum is the world's largest dinosaur skeleton, which is housed in the glass-covered courtyard. The colossal brachiosaurus measures 23 m (75 ft) long and 12 m (39 ft) high. It was discovered in Tanzania, in 1909, by a German fossil-hunting expedition.

The adjacent rooms feature collections of colourful shells and butterflies, as well as stuffed birds and mammals. A favourite with children is Bobby the Gorilla, who lived in Berlin Zoo from 1928 until 1935. The museum also boasts an impressive collection of minerals and meteorites.

Brachiosaurus skeleton in the Museum für Naturkunde

FURTHER AFIELD

BERLIN is a huge city with a unique character that has been shaped by the events in its history. Until 1920 the city consisted only of the districts that now comprise mainly Mitte, Tiergarten, Wedding, Prenzlauer Berg, Friedrichshain and Kreuzberg. At that time the city was surrounded by satellite towns and villages that had been evolving independently over many centuries.

In 1920, as part of great administrative reform, seven towns, 59 parishes and 27 country estates were incorpo-

Detail from Schloss Charlottenburg

rated into the city, thus creating an entirely new city covering nearly 900 sq km (350 sq miles), with a population of 3.8 million. This metropolis extended to small towns of medieval origin, such as Spandau, as well as to private manor houses and palaces, towns and smart suburban districts. Although the 20th century has changed the face of many of these places, their unique characters have remained undiminished. Because of this diversity, a trip to Berlin is like exploring many different towns simultaneously.

SIGHTS AT A GLANCE

Museums and Galleries
Ägyptisches Museum ❸
Brecht-Haus ⓫
Bröhan-Museum ❶
Brücke-Museum ㉔
Gedenkstätte Berlin-
    Hohenschönhausen ⓯
Gedenkstätte Plötzensee ❾
Sammlung Berggruen ❷
Stasi-Museum ⓰

Places of Interest
Flughafen Tempelhof ⓳
Klein Glienicke ㉘
Köpenick ⓱
Muzeumszentrum Dahlem ㉒
Nikolskoe ㉗

Olympia-Stadion ❼
Pfaueninsel ㉖
Prenzlauer Berg ⓭
Strandbad Wannsee ㉕

Streets, Squares and Parks
Karl-Marx-Allee ⓮
Schlosspark ❹
Treptower Park ⓲
Victoriapark ⓴

Historic Buildings and Monuments
Jagdschloss Grunewald ㉓
Messegelände ❻

0 metres   400

0 yards   400

Neue Synagoge ⓬
Rathaus Schöneberg ㉑
Schloss Charlottenburg ❺
Schloss Tegel ❿
Zitadelle Spandau ❽

KEY

▨	Central Berlin
▢	Outskirts of Berlin
✈	Airport
▬	Motorway
▬	Main road
=	Secondary road
—	Railway line

MAP OF GREATER BERLIN

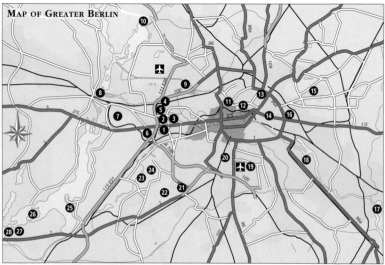

◁ Façade of Schloss Charlottenburg

Pablo Picasso's *Woman in a Hat* (1939), Sammlung Berggruen

Bröhan-Museum ❶

Schlossstraße 1a. [(030) 32 69 06 00. U Richard-Wagner-Platz & Sophie-Charlotte-Platz. S Westend. 🚌 109, 110, 145, 1, X-21, X-26. ◯ 10am–6pm Tue–Sun. ● 24 & 31 Dec. ♿

LOCATED IN A late-Neo-Classical building is this interesting, small museum. The collection was amassed by Karl H Bröhan who, from 1966, collected works of art from the Art Nouveau (Jugendstil or Secessionist) and Art Deco styles. The paintings of artists who were particularly connected with the Berlin Secessionist movement are especially well represented. Alongside the paintings are fine examples of other media and crafts including furniture, ceramics, glassware, silverwork and textiles.

Each of the main halls features an individual artist, often using an array of media. There is also a display of furniture by Hector Guimard, Eugène Gaillard, Henri van de Velde and Joseph Hoffmann, glasswork by Emile Gallé, and porcelain from the best European manufacturers.

Sammlung Berggruen ❷

Schlossstraße 1. [(030) 326 95 80. U Richard-Wagner-Platz & Sophie-Charlotte-Platz. S Westend. 🚌 109, 110, 145, X-21, X-26. ◯ 10am–8pm Tue–Sun. 🗓 (free first Sun of the month.) 🅿 ♿

HEINZ BERGGRUEN assembled this tasteful collection of art dating from the late 19th and first half of the 20th century. Born and educated in Berlin, he emigrated to the US in 1936, spent most of his life in Paris, but finally entrusted his collection "Picasso and his Time" to the city of his birth.

The museum opened in 1996, in what was once the west pavilion of the barracks, using space freed up by moving the Antikensammlung to Museum Island (see p70). The exhibition halls were modified according to the designs of Hilmer and Sattler, who also designed the layout of the Gemäldegalerie.

The Sammlung Berggruen is well known for its large collection of paintings, drawings and gouaches by Pablo Picasso. In addition to these, the museum displays more than 20 works by Paul Klee and paintings by other major artists – Van Gogh, Braque and Cézanne. The exhibition is supplemented by some excellent sculptures, particularly those of Henri Laurens and Alberto Giacometti.

Ägyptisches Museum ❸

EGYPTIAN MUSEUM

Schlossstraße 70. [(030) 343 57 30. U Richard-Wagner-Platz & Sophie-Charlotte-Platz. S Westend. 🚌 109, 110, 145, 1, X-21, X-26. ◯ 10am–6pm Tue–Sun.

THE TWO PAVILIONS on either side of Schlossstraße were built between 1851 and 1859 by Friedrich August Stüler, inspired by a design by King Friedrich Wilhelm IV. The eastern pavilion now houses the collection of the Egyptian Museum. Many sculptures, sarcophagi, murals and architectural fragments of various eras are on display. The greatest attraction is the fascinating collection from 19th-century archaeological digs by Richard Lepsius and Johann Ludwig Burckhardt in Tell al-Amarna. This was the capital of Egypt during the reign of Amenhotep IV (also called Akhenaten), a pharaoh in the 14th century BC. He revolutionized Egyptian religion and also brought about a radical change in the basic principles of representative arts. In a break from tradition he and his wife, Nefertiti, are shown more naturalistically with broad hips and swollen stomachs. The pharaoh is plainly depicted, but the queen is beautiful, as can be seen from other displays in the museum.

Figure from Ägyptische Museum (c.660 BC)

Schlosspark ❹

PALACE PARK

Luisenplatz (Schloss Charlottenburg).
🆄 *Richard-Wagner-Platz & Sophie-Charlotte-Platz.* Ⓢ *Westend.*
🚌 *109, 110, 145, X-21, X-26.*
Neuer Pavillon ☎ *(030) 32 09 14 43.* 🗂 *year-round: 10am–5pm Tue–Sun.* **Mausoleum** 🗂 *Apr–Oct: 10am–5pm Tue–Sun.* **Belvedere** ☎ *(030) 32 09 14 46.* 🗂 *Apr–Oct: 10am–5pm Tue–Sun; Nov–Mar: noon–4pm Tue–Fri, noon–5pm Sat & Sun.*

THIS EXTENSIVE royal park surrounding Schloss Charlottenburg is a favourite place for Berliners to stroll. The park is largely the result of work carried out after World War II, when 18th-century prints were used to help reconstruct the layout of the original grounds. Just behind Schloss Charlottenburg is a French-style Baroque garden, constructed to a strict geometrical design with a vibrant patchwork of flower beds, carefully trimmed shrubs and ornate fountains adorned with replicas of antique sculptures. Beyond the curved carp lake is a less formal English-style landscaped park, the original layout of which was created between 1819 and 1828 under the direction of the renowned royal gardener, Peter Joseph Lenné.

Designed by Karl Friedrich Schinkel and completed in 1825, the Neo-Classical **Neuer Pavillon** is a charming two-storey building with rooms ranged around a central staircase. A cast-iron balcony encircles the entire structure.

The **Mausoleum** in which Queen Luise, wife of Friedrich Wilhelm III, was laid to rest, was designed by Karl Friedrich Schinkel in the style of a Doric portico-fronted temple. After the death of the king in 1840, the mausoleum was refurbished to create room for his tomb. The tombs of the king's second wife and those of Kaiser Wilhelm I and his wife were added later.

Built as a summerhouse for Friedrich Wilhelm II, with a mixture of Baroque and Neo-Classical elements, the **Belvedere** now houses the Royal Porcelain Workshop, with pieces ranging from the Rococo period up to late Biedermeier.

Schloss Charlottenburg ❺

See pp94–5.

The Funkturm (radio tower) in Berlin's Messegelände

Messegelände ❻

Hammarskjöldplatz. Ⓢ *Witzleben.* 🆄 *Kaiserdamm.* 🚌 *104, 149, 204, 219.*

THE PAVILIONS of the vast exhibition and trade halls south of Hammarskjöldplatz cover more than 160,000 sq m (1,700,000 sq ft). The original exhibition halls were built before World War I, but nothing of these buildings remains. The oldest part is the Funkturm and the pavilions surrounding it. The building at the front (Ehrenhalle) was built in 1936 to a design by Richard Ermisch, and is one of the few surviving buildings in Berlin designed in a Fascist architectural style.

The straight motorway at the rear of the halls is the famous Avus, the first German autobahn, built in 1921. At one point adapted as a car-racing track, it now it forms part of the autobahn system.

Olympia-Stadion ❼

Olympischer Platz. Ⓢ & 🆄 *Olympia-Stadion.* 🚌 *218.*

OLYMPIA-STADION, originally known as Reichssportfeld, was built for the 1936 Olympic Games in Berlin. It was designed by Werner March in the Nazi architectural style and was inspired by the architecture of ancient Rome. To the west of the stadium lie the Maifeld and what is now called the Waldbühne. The former is an enormous assembly ground surrounded by grandstands and fronted by the Glockenturm, a 77 m (250 ft) tower, while the latter is an open-air amphitheatre. Stretching north is a group of sports grounds and swimming pools. The entire complex provided the infrastructure for Berlin to hold the Olympics. However, it also provided Hitler plenty of opportunities to use it for his own propagandist purposes.

French-style garden in the Schloss Charlottenburg park

Schloss Charlottenburg ❺

THE PALACE IN CHARLOTTENBURG was intended as a summer home for Sophie Charlotte, the wife of Elector Friedrich III. Construction began in 1695 to a design by Johann Arnold Nering. Johann Eosander von Göthe enlarged the palace between 1701 and 1713, adding the orangery wing. Further extensions were undertaken between 1740 and 1746 by Frederick the Great (Friedrich II) who added the east wing.

Detail from the main gate

The palace was restored to its former elegance after World War II and its richly decorated interiors are unequalled in Berlin.

GALLERY GUIDE
The ground floor of the main building can only be visited by guided tour. The upper floor and the Neuer Flügel can be visited independently.

First floor

Ground floor

Museum für Vor- und Frühgeschichte
The museum is housed in a pavilion that served formerly as the court theatre, designed by Carl Gotthard Langhans.

★ Porzellankabinett
This exquisite mirrored gallery has walls lined from top to bottom with a fine display of Japanese and Chinese porcelain.

Main entrance

Monument to the Great Elector

Schlosskapelle
Only the pulpit in the court chapel is original. All the remaining furniture and fittings, including the splendid royal box, are reconstructions.

Palace Façade
The central section of the palace is the oldest part of the building. It is the work of Johann Arnold Nering.

Fortuna
A new sculpture by Richard Scheibe crowns the palace, replacing the original statue destroyed during World War II.

Eichengalerie
This long gallery, lined with huge oil paintings and decorated with oak-panelling, was completed in 1713.

VISITORS' CHECKLIST

Luisenplatz. **Altes Schloss (Nering-Eosanderbau)**
[📞] (030) 32 09 14 40.
[U] Richard-Wagner-Platz & Sophie-Charlotte-Platz.
[S] Westend. [🚌] 109, 110, 145, X-26. [◯] 9am– 5pm Tue–Fri, 10am–5pm Sat & Sun.
[📷] (compulsory on ground floor only). [♿] **Neuer Flügel (Knobelsdorff-Flügel)**
[📞] (030) 32 09 14 42.
[◯] 10am–6pm Tue–Fri, 11am–6pm Sat & Sun. [♿]

KEY

- [ ] Official reception rooms
- [ ] Sophie-Charlotte's apartments
- [ ] Neuer Flügel or Knobelsdorff-Flügel exhibition space
- [ ] Friedrich Wilhelm II's apartments
- [ ] Mecklenburg apartments
- [ ] Friedrich Wilhelm IV's apartments
- [ ] Friedrich Wilhelm II's apartments
- [ ] Frederick the Great's apartments
- [ ] Non-exhibition space

Weisser Saal

Goldene Galerie

Frederick the Great's Apartments
Located in the new wing, these elegant living quarters feature the king's exquisite furniture.

★ Gersaint's Shop Sign (1720)
An avid collector of French painting, Frederick the Great bought this and seven other fine canvases by Antoine Watteau for his collection.

Hohenzollern coat of arms above the main gate of Spandau's citadel

Spandau **8**

Zitadelle Spandau Am Juliusturm.
((030) 354 94 42 00. **U** Zitadelle.
○ 9am–5pm Tue–Fri, 10am–5pm Sat
& Sun. 🖼

SPANDAU IS ONE of the oldest
towns within the area of
greater Berlin, and it has
managed to retain its own
distinctive character. Although
the town of Spandau was only
granted a charter in 1232,
evidence of the earliest
settlement here dates back to
the 8th century.

The area was spared the
worst of the World War II
bombing, so there are still
some interesting sights to visit.
The heart of the town is a
network of medieval streets
with a picturesque market
square and a number of the
original timber-framed houses.
In the north of Spandau,
sections of the town wall
dating from the 15th century
are still standing.

In the centre of town is the
magnificent Gothic St-Nikolai-
Kirche, dating from the 15th
century. The church holds
many valuable ecclesiastical
furnishings, such as a
splendid Renaissance stone
altar from the end of the 16th
century, a Baroque pulpit
from around 1700 that came
from a royal palace in Potsdam, a Gothic baptismal font
and many epitaphs.

A castle was first built on
the site of the Zitadelle
Spandau (citadel) in the 12th
century, but today only the
36 m (120 ft) Juliusturm
(tower) remains. In 1560 the
building of a fort was begun

here, to a design by Francesco
Chiaramella da Gandino. It
took 30 years to complete and
most of the work was super-
vised by architect Rochus Graf
von Lynar. Although the
citadel had a jail, the town's
most infamous resident,
Rudolf Hess, was incarcerated
a short distance away in a
military prison after the 1946
Nuremberg trials. In 1987,
when the former deputy
leader of the Nazi party died,
the prison was torn down.

Gedenkstätte Plötzensee **9**

PLÖTZENSEE MEMORIAL

Hüttigpfad. **(** (030) 344 32 26.
U Jakob-Kaiser-Platz, then 🚌 123,
126. **○** Mar–Sep: 9am–5pm;
Nov–Feb 9am–4pm.

A NARROW street leads from
Saatwinkler Damm to the
site where nearly 2,500 people
convicted of crimes against

Memorial to concentration camp
victims at Gedenkstätte Plötzensee

the Third Reich were hanged.
The Gedenkstätte Plötzensee
is a simple memorial in a
brick hut, which still retains
the iron hooks from which
the victims were suspended.

Claus Schenk von Stauffenberg and the other main
figures in the assassination
attempt against Hitler on 20
July 1944 were executed in
the Bendlerblock (see p84),
but the rest of the conspirators were executed here
at the Plötzensee prison.

Count Helmut James von
Moltke, one of the leaders of
the German resistance movement, was also killed here.
He was responsible for organizing the Kreisauer Kreis –
a political movement that
gathered and united German
opposition to Hitler.

Schloss Tegel **10**

Adelheidallee 19–21. **(** (030) 434
31 56. **U** Alt Tegel. 🚌 124, 133,
222. **○** May–Sep: 10am–noon &
3–4pm Mon. 📷 compulsory.

SCHLOSS TEGEL is one of the
most interesting palace
complexes in Berlin. The site
was occupied in the 16th
century by a manor house. In
the second half of the 17th
century, this was rebuilt into a
hunting lodge for the Elector
Friedrich Wilhelm. In 1766
the ownership of the property
passed to the Humboldt
family and, between 1820 and
1824, Karl Friedrich Schinkel
thoroughly rebuilt the palace,
giving it its current style.

Decorating the elevations
on the top floor of the towers
are tiled bas-reliefs designed
by Christian Daniel Rauch,
depicting the ancient wind
gods. Some of Schinkel's
marvellous interiors have
survived, along with several
items from what was once a
large collection of sculptures.
The palace is still privately
owned by descendants of the
Humboldt family, but guided
tours are offered on Mondays.

It is also worth visiting the
park in which the palace
stands. On the western limits
of the park lies the Humboldt
family tomb, also designed by
Schinkel. The tomb contains a

The elegant Neo-Classical façade of Schloss Tegel

copy of a splendid sculpture by Bertel Thorwaldsen. The original piece stands inside the Schloss Tegel.

Bertolt Brecht's study in his former apartment

Brecht-Weigel-Gedenkstätte **⑪**

BRECHT-WEIGEL MEMORIAL

Chausseestraße 125. **【** (030) 283 05 70 44. **Ⓤ** Zinnowitzer Straße or Oranienburger Tor. **🚌** 157. **🚋** 13. **◯** 10am–noon Tue–Fri, also 5–7pm Thu, 9:30am–noon, 12:30–2pm Sat, 11am–6pm Sun. **🎟** compulsory. Every half hour (every hour on Sun). **⬤** Mon, public holidays. **📷**

Pₗₐᵧwᵣᵢgₕₜ Bertolt Brecht was associated with Berlin from 1920, but emigrated in 1933. After the war, his left-wing views made him an attractive potential resident of the newly created German socialist state. Lured by the promise of his own theatre, he returned to Berlin in 1948 with his wife, the actress Helene Weigel.

In 1953, Brecht moved into Chausseestraße 125 and lived there until his death in 1956. His wife founded an archive of his work, which is located on the second floor.

Neue Synagoge **⑫**

NEW SYNAGOGUE

Oranienburger Straße 30. **【** (030) 880 28 451. **Ⓢ** Oranienburger Straße. **🚋** 1, 13. **🚌** 157. **◯** May–Sep: 10am–8pm Sun & Mon, 10am–6pm Tue–Thu, 10am–5pm Fri; Oct–Apr: 10am–6pm Sun–Thu, 10am–2pm Fri. **📷 Ⓞ**

Cₒₙₛₜᵣᵤₜₜᵢₒₙ of the New Synagogue was begun in 1859 by architect Eduard Knoblauch, and completed in 1866. The design was a highly sophisticated response to the asymmetrical shape of the plot of land, with a narrow façade flanked by a pair of towers and crowned with a dome containing a round vestibule. A series of small rooms opened off the vestibule, including an anteroom and two prayer rooms – one large and one small. The two towers opened onto a staircase leading to the galleries, while the main hall had space for around 3,000 worshippers.

The Neue Synagoge with its splendidly reconstructed dome

An innovative use of iron in the construction of the roof and galleries put the synagogue at the forefront of 19th-century civil engineering.

With its gilded dome, this was Berlin's largest synagogue, until 9 November 1938 when it was partially destroyed during the infamous *Kristall-nacht*. The building was damaged further by Allied bombing in 1943 and was eventually demolished in 1958 by government authorities.

Reconstruction began in 1988 and was completed in 1995. Public exhibitions by the Centrum Judaicum are held in the front of the building.

Prenzlauer Berg **⑬**

Sammlung Industrielle Gestaltung Kulturbrauerei entrance, Knaack-straße 97. **【** (030) 443 17868. **Ⓢ** Senefelderplatz or Eberswalderstraße. **◯** 1pm–8pm Wed–Sun.

Tₒwₐᵣᵈₛ ₜₕₑ ₑₙᵈ of the 19th century this was one of the most impoverished, densely populated districts of Berlin, which became a centre for anti-Communist opposition.

After 1989, however, artists, journalists and students began to gather here from all parts of Berlin, creating a colourful, vibrant community.

Schönhauser Allee is the main thoroughfare of Prenzlauer Berg. A former old brewery was transformed into the "Kulturbrauerei", a centre for cultural events. It also houses a museum – **Sammlung Industrielle Gestaltung** – with a collection of industrial designs from East Germany.

Heading along Sredzkistraße you reach Husemannstraße. At No. 12 was the former Museum Berliner Arbeiter-leben; its collection of period interiors has been transferred recently to the Märkisches Museum *(see p76)*. Amid the greenery around Belforter Straße is a water tower built in the mid-19th century. Near-by, on Schönhauser Allee, there is an old Jewish cemetery dating from 1827. Among those buried here is the renowned painter Max Liebermann.

Fragment of Socialist Realist decoration from Karl-Marx-Allee

Karl-Marx-Allee ⓮

Map 5 F1. **U** *Strausberger Platz or Weberwiese.*

THE SECTION OF Karl-Marx-Allee between Strausberger Platz and Frankfurter Tor is effectively a huge open-air museum of Socialist Realist architecture. The route to the east was named Stalinallee in 1949 and chosen as the site for the showpiece of the new German Democratic Republic. The avenue was widened to 90 m (300 ft) and, in the course of the next ten years, huge residential tower blocks and a row of shops were built. The designers, led by Hermann Henselmann, succeeded in combining three sets of architectural guidelines. They used the style known in the Soviet Union as "pastry chef" according to the precept: "nationalistic in form but socialist in content", and linked the whole work to Berlin's own traditions. Hence there are motifs taken from famous Berlin architects Schinkel and Gontard, as well as from the renowned Meissen porcelain.

The buildings on this street, renamed Karl-Marx-Allee in 1961, are now considered historic monuments.

Gedenkstätte Berlin-Hohen-schönhausen ⓯

Genslerstraße 66. **C** *(030) 982 42 19.* **S** *Landsberger Allee, then* 🚊 *5, 6, 7, 15, 17.* 🚌 *256.* ✦ *11am & 1pm Mon–Fri, 11am, 1pm & 3pm Sat–Sun.* ✦

THIS MUSEUM was established in 1995 within the former custody building of the Stasi.

The building was part of a huge complex built in 1938. In May 1945, the occupying Russian authorities created a special transit camp here, in which they interned war criminals and anyone under political suspicion. From 1946 the buildings were refashioned into the custody area for the KGB; in 1951, it was given over to the Stasi.

The prisoners' cells and interrogation rooms are on view, two of which have no windows and are lined with rubber. Housed in the cellars was the "submarine" – a series of cells without daylight to which the most "dangerous" suspects were brought.

Forschungs-und Gedenkstätte Normannenstraße (Stasi-Museum) ⓰

Ruschestraße 103 (Haus 1). **C** *(030) 553 68 54.* **U** *Magdalenenstraße.* ✦ *11am–6pm Mon–Fri, 2–6pm Sat–Sun.* ✦

UNDER THE German Democratic Republic, this huge complex of buildings at Ruschestrasse housed the Ministry of the Interior. It was here that the infamous Stasi (GDR secret service) had its

Office of the infamous Stasi chief Erich Mielke at the Stasi Museum

headquarters. The Stasi's "achievements" in infiltrating its own community were without equal in the Eastern block.

Since 1990 one of the buildings has housed a museum that displays photographs and documents depicting the activities of the Stasi. Here, you can see a model of the headquarters, and equipment that was used for bugging and spying on citizens suspected of holding unfavourable political views. You can also walk around the office of infamous Stasi chief Erich Mielke.

Köpenick ⓱

S *Spindlersfeld, then* 🚌 *167 or* **S** *Köpenick, then* 🚌 *269, 360.* 🚢 *26, 60, 62, 67, 68.* **Kunstgewerbemuseum** *Schloss Köpenick, Schlossinsel.* **C** *(030) 20 90 55 55.* ✦ *ring for times.*

KÖPENICK IS MUCH older than Berlin. In the 9th century AD, this island contained a fortified settlement known as Kopanica. In about 1240 a castle was built on the island, around which a town began to evolve. Craftsmen settled here and, after 1685, a large colony of Huguenots also settled.

In the 19th century Köpenick recreated itself as an industrial town. Despite wartime devastation it has retained its historic character and, though there are no longer any 13th century churches, it is worth strolling around the old town. By the old market square and in the neighbouring streets, modest houses have survived that recall the 18th century, alongside buildings from the end of the 19th century.

At Alt Köpenick No. 21 is a vast brick town hall built in the style of the Brandenburg Neo-Renaissance. In 1906, a famous swindle took place here and the event became the inspiration for a popular comedy by Carl Zuckmayer, *The Captain from Köpenick.*

Köpenick's greatest attraction is a three-storey Baroque palace, built between 1677 and

A reconstructed drawing room from 1548 in the Kunstgewerbemuseum

1681 for the heir to the throne Friedrich (later King Friedrich I), to a design by the Dutch architect Rutger van Langfield. In 2003, the **Kunstgewerbemuseum** (*see p85*) opened a suite of Renaissance and Baroque rooms to the public in the Köpenick Palace.

Gigantic wreath commemorating the Red Army in Treptower Park

Treptower Park ⑱

Archenhold-Sternwarte, Alt-Treptow.
Ⓢ *Treptower Park.* 🚍 *166, 167, 177, 265.* **Archenhold Sternwarte** ⒸⒽ *(030) 534 80 80.* 📷 *compulsory: Sternwarte 8pm Thu, 3pm Sat–Sun; astronomical museum 2pm–4:30pm Wed–Sun; astronomical observations Oct–Mar: 8pm Fri; sun observations Jul–Aug: 3pm Wed.*

THE VAST PARK in Treptow was laid out in the 1860s on the initiative and design of Johann Gustav Meyer. In 1919 it was where revolutionaries Karl Liebknecht, Wilhelm Pieck and Rosa Luxemburg assembled 150,000 striking workers.

The park is best known for the colossal monument to the Red Army. Built between 1946 and 1949, it stands on the grave of 5,000 Soviet soldiers killed in the battle for Berlin in 1945. The gateway, which leads to the mausoleum, is marked by a vast granite sculpture of a grieving Russian Motherland surrounded by statues of Red Army soldiers.

In the farthest section of the park is the astronomical observatory, **Archenhold Sternwarte**, built for a decorative arts exhibition in 1896. Given a permanent site in 1909, the observatory was used by Albert Einstein for a lecture on the Theory of Relativity in 1915. It is also home to the longest reflecting telescope in the world (21 m or 70 ft), and a small planetarium.

Beyond Treptower Park lies another park, Plänterwald.

Flughafen Tempelhof ⑲

Platz der Luftbrücke. Ⓤ *Platz der Luftbrücke.* 🚍 *104, 119, 184, 341.*

SITUATED BEYOND Kreuzberg, the Tempelhof was once Germany's largest airport. Built in 1923, the structure is typical of Third Reich architecture. The additions to the original structure were completed in 1939.

In 1951, a monument was added in front of the airport. Designed by Edward Ludwig, it commemorates the airlifts of the Berlin Blockade. The names of those who lost their lives during the Blockade appear on the plinth.

Viktoriapark ⑳

Ⓤ *Platz der Luftbrücke.*
🚍 *119, 140.*

THIS RAMBLING PARK, with several artificial waterfalls, short trails and a small hill, was designed by Hermann Mächtig and built between 1884 and 1894. The Neo-Gothic Memorial to the Wars of Liberation at the summit of the hill is the work of Karl Friedrich Schinkel and was constructed between 1817 and 1821. The monument commemorates the Prussian victory against Napoleon's army in the Wars of Liberation. The monument's cast-iron tower is well ornamented.

In the niches of the lower section are 12 allegorical figures by Christian Daniel Rauch, Friedrich Tieck and Ludwig Wichmann. Each figure symbolizes a battle and is linked to a historic figure – either a military leader or a member of the royal family.

Rathaus Schöneberg ㉑

SCHÖNEBERG TOWN HALL

John-F-Kennedy-Platz.
Ⓤ *Rathaus Schöneberg.*

THE SCHÖNEBERG town hall is a gigantic building with an imposing tower, which was built between 1911 and 1914. From 1948 to 1990 it was used as the main town hall of West Berlin, and it was outside here, on 26 June 1963, that US President John F Kennedy gave his famous speech. More than 300,000 Berliners assembled to hear the young president say "*Ich bin ein Berliner*" – "I am a Berliner", intended as an expression of solidarity from the democratic world to a city defending its right to freedom.

While Kennedy's meaning was undoubtedly clear, pedants were quick to point out that what he actually said was "I am a small doughnut".

Japanese woodcut from the Museum für Ostasiatische Kunst

Museumszentrum Dahlem ㉒

Lansstraße 8, Dahlem. 📞 (030) 20 90 55 55. Ⓤ Dahlem Dorf. 🚌 110, 183, X-11. **Museum für Indische Kunst. Museum für Ostasiatische Kunst, Ethnologisches Museum (formerly Museum für Völker-kunde), Museum für Kunst Afrikas & Nordamerika Ausstellung** ☐ 10am–6pm Tue–Fri, 11am–6pm Sat & Sun. 🎧

DAHLEM'S FIRST museums were built between 1914 and 1923, but the district was confirmed as a major cultural and education centre after World War II with the establishment of the Freie Universität and completion of the museum complex. With many of Berlin's collections fragmented, a miscellany of art and artifacts was put on display here. In the 1960s the museums were extended and the new Museumszentrum was created to rival East Berlin's Museum Island.

German reunification in 1990 meant that the collections could be reunited and reorgan-ized. Paintings were moved to the Kulturforum (see pp80–81), and sculptures to the Bode-museum (see p74).

Five museums are now housed at Dahlem: the Ethnologisches Museum (Museum of Mankind); the Museum für Indische Kunst (Museum of Indian Art); the Museum für Ostasiatische Kunst (Museum of Far

Eastern Art); the Museum für Kunst Afrikas (Museum for African Art) and the Nord-amerika Ausstellung (Exhibition of Native North American Cultures).

Highlights include bronzes from Benin at the Museum of African Art, gold Inca jewellery at the Museum of Mankind, and Japanese woodcuts from Chinese Turkestan at the Museum of Far Eastern Art. The Exhibition of Native North American Cultures, opened in 1999, includes a collection of 600 ceremonial objects.

Jagdschloss Grunewald ㉓

Am Grunewaldsee 29. 📞 (030) 813 35 97. 🍽 for renovation work until 2004 due to fire damage. 🎧

JAGDSCHLOSS GRUNEWALD is one of the oldest surviving civic buildings in Berlin. Built for the Elector Joachim II in 1542, it was rebuilt around 1700 in a Baroque style.

In this small palace on the edge of the Grunewaldsee is Berlin's only surviving Renaissance hall, which currently houses a collection of paintings that includes canvases by Rubens and van Dyck, among others.

In the east wing is the small Waldmuseum, which has illustrations depicting forest life and the history of forestry. Opposite the Jagdschloss, a hunting museum (Jagdmuseum) houses a collection of historic weapons and equipment.

Brücke-Museum ㉔

Bussardsteig 9, Dahlem. 📞 (030) 831 20 29. 🚌 115. ☐ 11am–5pm Wed–Mon.

THIS ELEGANT Functionalist building hosts a collection of German Expressionist painting linked to the Die Brücke group. It is based on almost 80 works by Schmidt-Rottluff bequeathed to the town of Dahlem in 1964. In addition to other works of art contemporary to Die Brücke, there are paintings from the later creative periods of these artists, as well as works of other closely associated artists. Nearby lie the foundation's headquarters, established in the former studio of the sculptor Bernhard Heliger.

Strandbad Wannsee ㉕

Wannseebadweg. Ⓢ Nikolassee. 🚌 513.

THE VAST lake Wannsee, on the edge of Grunewald, is a popular destination for Berliners seeking recreation. The most developed part is the southeastern corner where there are yachting marinas and harbours. Further north is one of the largest inland beaches in Europe, Strandbad Wannsee, which was devel-oped between 1929 and 1930 by the construction of shops, cafés and changing rooms on man-made terraces. It is also pleasant to walk around Schwanenwerder island, with its many elegant villas.

Boarding point for lake cruises on the Wannsee

The Schloss Pfaueninsel designed by Johann Brendel

Pfaueninsel ㉖

Pfaueninsel. **[** (030) 80 58 68 30. **Ⓢ** Wannsee, then take **A16, 316.** **Schloss Pfaueninsel.** **◯** Apr–Oct: 10am–5pm Tue–Sun.

THIS PICTURESQUE island, named for the peacocks that inhabit it, is now a nature reserve, reached by ferry across the Havel river. It was laid out in 1795 according to a design by Johann August Eyserbeck. Its final form, which you see today, is the work of the landscape architect Peter Joseph Lenné.

One of the most interesting sights on the island is the small romantic palace of **Schloss Pfaueninsel**. Dating from 1794, it was designed by Johann Gottlieb Brendel for Friedrich Wilhelm II and his mistress Wilhelmine Encke (the future Countess Lichtenau). The palace was built of wood, with a façade fashioned in the form of a ruined medieval castle. The cast-iron bridge that links the towers was built in 1807. The palace is open to the public in the summer months, when you can see the 18th- and 19th-century furnishings.

Other sights worth visiting include **James's Well**, which was built to resemble an ancient ruin. Towards the northeast corner of the island is the **Luisentempel** in the form of a Greek temple. Its sandstone portico was relocated to the island from the mausoleum in Schloss-park Charlottenburg *(see pp94–5)* in 1829. Nearby is a stone commemorating Johannes Kunckel, an alchemist who lived on

Pfaueninsel in the 17th century. During his quest to discover how to make gold, he discovered a method of producing ruby-coloured glass. Near the **Aviary**, home to multicoloured parrots and pheasants, is a tall fountain that was designed by Martin Friedrich Rabe in 1824.

Nikolskoe ㉗

Nikolskoer Weg. **Ⓢ** Wannsee, then take **A16 or 316.

ACROSS THE RIVER from Pfaueninsel (Peacock Island) is Nikolskoe. Here you'll find the Blockhaus Nikolskoe, a Russian-style *dacha* (country house) that was built in 1819 for the future Tsar Nicholas I and his wife, the daughter of King Friedrich Wilhelm III.

The house was built by the German military architect Captain Snethlage, who was responsible for the Alexandrowka estate in Potsdam *(see p124)*. Following a fire in 1985, the *dacha* was reconstructed. It currently houses a restaurant.

Guests on the terrace of the Blockhaus Nikolskoe in summer

Close by is the church of St Peter and Paul, which was built between 1834 and 1837, to a design by Friedrich August Stüler. The body of the church is completed by a tower crowned by an onion-shaped dome, reflecting the style of Russian Orthodox sacral architecture.

Klein Glienicke ㉘

■ 116. **[** (030) 805 30 41. **◯** mid-May– mid-Oct: 10am–5pm Sat–Sun.

THE PALACE in the palace-park of Klein Glienicke was built in 1825 according to a design by Karl Friedrich Schinkel for Prince Karl of Prussia. The charming park in which it is located was created by Peter Joseph Lenné. Beyond the Neo-Classical palace extends an irregular cluster of buildings, grouped around a courtyard, including a pergola and staff cottages. Passing by the palace, you approach the **Coach House**, also designed by Schinkel and now housing a restaurant. Nearby are an orangery and greenhouses designed by Ludwig Persius. Also by Persius is the **Klosterhof**, a mock monastery with pavilions, on whose walls are many Byzantine and Romanesque architectural elements from Italy. Towards the lake is the **Grosse Neugierde**, a circular pavilion based on the Athenian monument to Lysikrates from the 4th century BC. From here there are beautiful views across the Havel river and **Glienicker Brücke** (known under the East German regime as the bridge of unity). The border with West Berlin ran across this bridge where, during the Cold War, the exchange of spies was conducted.

Karl Friedrich Schinkel's Neo-Classical Schloss Klein Glienicke

ENTERTAINMENT IN BERLIN

WITH SO MUCH entertainment on offer, from classical drama and cabaret to variety theatre and an eclectic nightclub scene, it is possible to indulge just about any taste in Berlin. During the summer, many bars and restaurants set up outdoor tables, and the areas around Unter den Linden, Ku'damm and the whole of Kreuzberg and Prenzlauer Berg turn into one large social arena. The city really comes into its own at night, when its cocktail

Flute player

bars, cafés and bars are open all night and dancing goes on until dawn. The city has many nightlife centres, each with a slightly different character. The younger generation favours Kreuzberg and Prenzlauer Berg, while Friedrichshain is more exclusive and Kreuzberg has a vibrant gay scene. The Mitte district offers a true mixture, with its opera house and classical theatre surrounded by lively bars.

PRACTICAL INFORMATION

THERE ARE SO many things going on in Berlin that it can be difficult to find what you're looking for. Tourist Information Centres offer basic information, but the most comprehensive guides are the listings magazines *Tipp* and *Zipp*, which are published every other Wednesday. The daily *Berliner Morgenpost* publishes its supplement *bm Live* on Fridays, while *Ticket* comes out on Wednesdays, together with the *Tagesspiegel*. *Cinemataz*, the Thursday supplement to *Taz*, gives weekly cinema programmes. *Berlin Program* gives monthly lists of events, while *Berlin Magazin*, published by Berlin Tourismus Marketing GmbH, gives quarterly information. The most comprehensive information can be found in

the monthly *Kunstkalender*. It is also worth checking the free pamphlets and music publications that are on display in bars, cafés and by the entrances to public toilets.

TICKETS

THEATRE AND concert tickets can usually be booked up to two weeks in advance, and can be bought directly at the box offices or by telephone. Reserved tickets must be picked up and paid for at least half an hour before the performance. You can also pre-book tickets at special outlets all over Berlin: the best one in the city centre is the **Fullhouse Service**.

One agency that specializes in last-minute ticket purchase is **Hekticket Theaterkassen** on Hardenbergerstrasse, where you can get tickets on the day, even an hour before a show.

Cinema Zoo Palast, where many cinema festivals are held

These tickets are usually sold at a 50 per cent discount.

Students, seniors and the disabled are entitled to a 50 per cent discount on tickets, for which they must present proof of status.

THEATRES AND CINEMAS

BERLIN IS one of the most important towns on the theatrical map of Germany. One of its most famous theatres, the magnificent **Berliner Ensemble**, was once managed by Bertold Brecht. The **Deutsches Theater** offers an ambitious programme, while **Volks-bühne** stages works by young playwrights.

Berlin has many multiplex cinemas, offering a good selection of the latest films. The biggest, with 19 screens, is **CinemaxX** in Potsdamer Platz. Some of the films there

Prokofiev's *The Love of Three Oranges* staged at the Komische Oper

Whitsun Karneval der Kulturen in the streets of Kreuzberg

are shown in the original language. Next door is the ultra-modern **Imax** cinema whose huge curved screen is 27m (89ft) in diameter.

MUSIC AND DANCE

BERLIN HAS one of the finest orchestras in the world — the Berlin Philharmonic Orchestra, whose home, the **Philharmonie**, is also one of the world's most beautiful concert halls. The city boasts three opera houses: the **Staatsoper Unter den Linden** and the **Komische**

Oper are in the eastern part of city, while the **Deutsche Oper Berlin** is in the west. The three opera houses have ballet programmes built into their repertoires and these are performed largely by resident dance companies.

Apart from regular concerts, the city stages many festivals, such as Musik-Biennale and the Open Air Festival, as well as many concerts organized in churches and public parks.

ROCK, JAZZ AND POP

BERLIN IS always a popular destination for world-famous musicians, whose concerts are often held in the **Waldbühne**. Numerous music clubs offer daily opportunities to hear good music: favourite venues are **Quasimodo** in the western part of the city centre, **Schlot** in Prenzlauer Berg and **Junction Bar** in Kreuzberg. Good traditional jazz can be heard during the annual Jazzfest Berlin, and modern experimental work at the Total Music Meeting.

CHILDREN

THE CHOICE of entertainment for children and teenagers is huge. Special attractions include circuses, zoological gardens, Deusches Technik-museum (see p77), **Museumsdorf Düppel** and **Kindermuseum Labyrinth**. An ascent to the rotating café at the top of the Fernsehturm (television tower) (see p75) is a great treat and always popular. Many restaurants provide play areas for children.

A glimpse of medieval life at the Museumsdorf Düppel

DIRECTORY

TICKET AGENTS

Hekticket Theaterkassen
Hardenbergerstr. 29d.
Map 2 B4.
📞 (030) 230 99 30.

Karl-Liebknecht-Str. 12/ZDF-Shop.
Map 5 D2.
📞 (030) 24 31 24 31.

Fullhouse Service
Unter den Linden.
Map 4 B2.
📞 (030) 30 87 85 685.

THEATRES

Berliner Ensemble
Bertold-Brecht-Platz 1.
Map 1 C3.
📞 (030) 28 40 81 55.

Deutsches Theater
Schumannstr. 13a.
Map 1 C3.
📞 (030) 28 44 12 25.

Hebbel Theater
Stresemannstr. 29.
Map 4 B5.
📞 (030) 25 90 04 27.

Volksbühne am Rosa-Luxemburg-Platz
Rosa-Luxemburg-Platz.
📞 (030) 247 67 72.

CINEMAS

CinemaxX
Potsdamer Platz
Potsdamer Str. 1–19.
Map 4 A3.
📞 (030) 524 63 62 99.

Imax
Marlene-Dietrich-Platz 4.
📞 (030) 26 06 62.

MUSIC AND DANCE

Philharmonie
Herbert-von-Karajan-Str. 1.
Map 3 F3.
📞 (030) 25 48 80.

Deutsche Oper Berlin
Bismarckstr. 34–37.
📞 (030) 341 02 49.

Komische Oper
Behrenstr. 55–57.
Map 4 B2.
📞 (030) 47 99 74 00.

Staatsoper Unter den Linden
Unter den Linden 7.
Map 4 C2.
📞 (030) 20 35 45 55.

ROCK, JAZZ, AND POP

Junction Bar
Gneisenaustr. 18.
📞 (030) 694 66 02.

Schlot
Kastanienallee 29
📞 (030) 448 21 60.

Quasimodo
Katzlerstr. 12a.
📞 (030) 312 80 86.

Waldbühne
Glockenturmstr. 1.
📞 (030) 81 07 50.

CHILDREN

Museumsdorf Düppel
Clauertstr. 11.
📞 (030) 802 66 71.
⏰ Apr–Oct:3–6pm Thu, 10am–4pm Sun and hols.

Kindermuseum Labyrinth
Osloer Str. 12.
📞 (030) 494 53 48.
⏰ 2–4pm Tue, 1–6pm Wed & Sat, 2–6pm Thu & Fri, 11am–6pm Sun.

Tierpark Berlin
Am Tierpark 125.
📞 (030) 51 53 10.

BERLIN STREET FINDER

MAP REFERENCES given for historic buildings, hotels, restaurants, bars, shops and entertainment venues refer to the maps included in this section of the guidebook. The key map below shows the area of Berlin covered by the Street Finder. The maps include all major sightseeing areas, historic attractions, railway stations, bus stations, U-Bahn stations and the suburban stations of the S-Bahn. The names of the streets and squares in the index and maps are given in German. The word *Straße* (or *STRASSE, Str*) indicates a street, *Allee* an avenue, *Platz* a square, *Brücke* a bridge and *Bahnhof* a railway station.

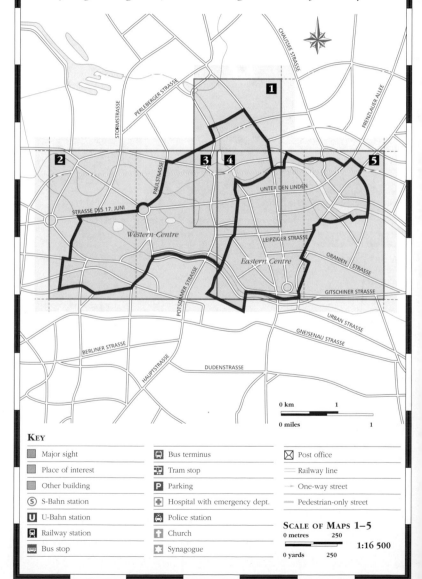

KEY

▨	Major sight	🚌	Bus terminus	⊠	Post office
▨	Place of interest	🚃	Tram stop		Railway line
▨	Other building	Ⓟ	Parking	→	One-way street
Ⓢ	S-Bahn station	✚	Hospital with emergency dept.		Pedestrian-only street
Ⓤ	U-Bahn station	🚓	Police station		
🚆	Railway station	✝	Church		
🚌	Bus stop	✡	Synagogue		

SCALE OF MAPS 1–5

0 metres   250

0 yards   250

1:16 500

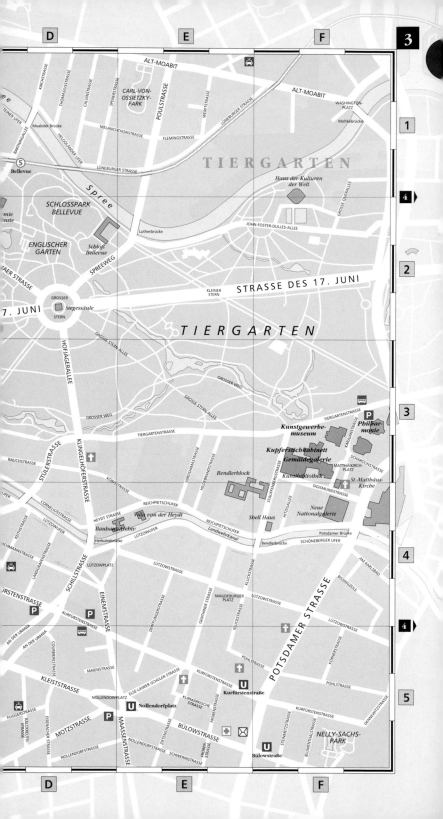

EASTERN
GERMANY

Eastern Germany at a Glance

THE EASTERN region of Germany is immensely rich in tourist attractions. The imposing valley of the Elbe River, the beautiful lake district of Lower Brandenburg, attractive trails in the Harz Mountains of Saxony-Anhalt, the Thuringian Forest as well as the Erzgebirge and the Lusatian Mountains in Saxony all invite the visitor with their dramatic scenery and excellent recreational facilities.

Eastern Germany is rich in historic sights, too, ranging from the Baroque residences of Potsdam in Brandenburg to the grand architecture of Dresden and Leipzig in Saxony and the important cultural centre of Weimar in Thuringia. The most rewarding destinations in the region are featured here.

The Magdeburg Reiter, in the market square, is the copy of one of Thuringia's most famous sights. The identity of the rider is not certain.

Naumburg Dom is a huge, well preserved Gothic cathedral (see pp140–141), one of Germany's greatest buildings. Splendid statues of its founders, Ekkehart and Uta, adorn the walls of the presbytery.

Erfurt Dom dominates the townscape. A massive Gothic structure, the cathedral's three towers were built on the Romanesque foundations of an earlier church.

SAXONY-ANHALT
(see pp132–4)

THURINGIA
(see pp170–87)

Weimar, with its picturesque market square (see pp184-5) and historic buildings, was an important cultural centre for many centuries. Friedrich Schiller, Johann Wolfgang von Goethe and Johann Sebastian Bach all lived here.

Sanssouci in Potsdam (see pp126–7), *the enchanting Baroque summer residence built for Prussia's King Frederick the Great, stands on the site of former gardens and vineyards.*

0 km   20

0 miles   20

LOCATOR MAP

Schloss Wörlitz is surrounded by a romantic landscaped park (see pp146–7) criss-crossed by a network of waterways open to pleasure boats.

BRANDENBURG
(see pp118–31)

The Völkerschlachtdenkmal in Leipzig (see pp152–3) *was erected to celebrate the centenary of the battle fought by Prussia, Austria, Russia and Sweden against Napoleon's army in 1813.*

SAXONY
(see pp148–69)

The Zwinger in Dresden (see pp164–5), *Saxony's glorious palace and a Baroque jewel, was immaculately restored to its original glory after World War II destruction.*

Meißen Porcelain

Until the early 18th century the only porcelain known in Europe was that imported from the Far East, and the Chinese jealously guarded the secrets of its production. Finally, in 1707, Johann Friedrich Böttger and Ehrenfried Walther von Tschirnhaus succeeded in developing a recipe which made it possible to produce genuine

Figurine by J. J. Kändler

porcelain. A factory was set up in Meißen, and from 1713 it began to export its products to the entire European continent. Its first famous designers were Johann Joachim Kändler and Johann Gregor Höroldt.

The Porcelain Museum, opened in 1906, holds exhibitions and demonstrations illustrating the various stages in the manufacture of porcelain. The museum also runs courses on porcelain-making.

BÖTTGER STONEWARE

Johann Friedrich Böttger's first success in recreating Chinese ceramics came in 1707 when, with the assistance of Ehrenfried Walther von Tschirnhaus, he managed to produce stoneware almost identical to that produced in Yi Hsing. The stoneware was dark, varying in colour from red to brown.

These plates and bowls are typical examples of Böttger stoneware; its plain and simple lines were modelled on Far-Eastern designs.

The dark colour of the dishes is due to the use of red clays.

The "Yellow Lion" design, dating from c.1728, was used to decorate the first Meißen service.

Imari tree

The "Yellow Lion" was in reality a tiger.

FAR-EASTERN MOTIFS

Until the 17th century the only porcelain known in Europe came from the Far East, and the first items made from Saxon hard porcelain were initially strongly influenced by the Asian products. In Meißen, Chinese figurines and dishes were copied, adapting "European" shapes, but using Japanese or Chinese motifs for decoration. Special designs were created to adorn the services intended for the royal court. The oldest among these include the "Yellow Lion" and the "Red Dragon". New designs, inspired by European art, began to appear after 1738, and gradually replaced the Asian patterns.

PRODUCTION PROCESS

The process of porcelain production has not changed significantly over the centuries. The formula for "hard-paste" porcelain contains kaolin, quartz and feldspar. Each product is dried and fired, with glazed products being fired twice. The decoration can be applied before or after the glazing process. Hand-painted and gilded items are the most expensive.

Demonstration of the intricate art of hand-painting porcelain at the Meißen factory

TABLEWARE

In the second half of the 18th and in the 19th centuries, porcelain manufacturers developed their own designs. This proved so popular that some remain in production to this day. The best-known Meißen designs are the "vine-leaves" and the "onion" patterns, first introduced in the 18th century. Customers can thus still replace items in the services which have graced their family tables for generations.

This coffee pot and cup is decorated with the cobalt "onion" pattern, depicting stylized pomegranate fruits.

FINE-ART MOTIFS

A new type of decoration, which became popular in the second half of the 18th century, involved the accurate copying of famous paintings or etchings onto a vase, a pot or a plate. This type of decoration proved particularly popular during the Classicist period.

Decorator copying an etching onto a vessel

Vase decorated with a miniature of a painting by Antoine Watteau

SERVICES AND FIGURINES

Several outstanding sculptors and painters were employed in the Meißen porcelain manufacture to design unique services and figurines for the royal courts. The most famous among them are the services designed by Johann Joachim Kändler. He also created sets of figurines to adorn dining tables, vases and censers (containers for burning incense) for decorating the home, and large religious compositions for churches.

Figurine of August III

"Swan" Service Tureen

Europa, a figure from the "Four Continents" series, designed by J. J. Kändler

MARKS ON MEISSEN PORCELAIN

All porcelain manufacturers mark their products with their own symbols. The symbols are generally applied under the glaze, at the bottom of the piece. The Meißen factory initially used marks that imitated Japanese or Chinese writing; later, for a short time, letters were used, and from 1724 blue trademarks in the shape of crossed swords became the standard mark. The last three symbols below identify the respective court for which each piece of porcelain was produced.

K.P.F.

Königliche Porzellan-Fabrik, trademark used in 1723

K.P.M.

Königliche Porzellan-Manufaktur, trademark used in 1723–4

Trademarks used from 1724

R

***Augustus Rex**, the initials of King August*

K.H.K

Königliche Hof-Küche

K.H.C.W.

Königliche Hof-Conditorei Warschau

Luther and the Reformation

Coat of arms

IN 1517, on the eve of All Souls' Day (31 October), Martin Luther nailed his 95 "theses" to the doors of the castle church in Wittenberg, condemning the practice of indulgences. His subsequent pronouncements, in which he criticized many aspects of the Church's teaching, made him the "father" of the Reformation movement in Germany and other countries. Luther's teaching gained the support of many of the princes, who in 1531 formed the Schmalkalden Union and started to introduce a new administration to the Church. This led to religious wars which finally ended with the Augsburg Peace Treaty, signed in 1555, which confirmed the religious division of Germany.

The Bible, *translated into German by Luther, was first published in one volume in 1534. One year later an illustrated, two-volume luxury version was published in Augsburg.*

The Schlosskapelle *in Hartenfels Castle, in Torgau (see p154), was built in 1543–4 and consecrated by Martin Luther. It is generally considered to be the first church built specifically for the Lutheran community.*

The baptism of a child is performed by Philipp Melanchthon.

The Last Supper, at the centre of the altar, stresses the importance attached by Lutherans to the sacrament of communion. The figures of the Apostles are portraits of the main church reformers.

Martin Luther, *the great theologian and religious reformer, initiator of Church reform and founder of Lutheranism, is depicted in this portrait by Lucas Cranach the Elder (1520).*

This group of faithful, listening to the sermon, includes members of Luther's family.

Luther's Room (Lutherstube), *shown here, is part of Luther's House in Wittenberg* (see p144). *The famous reformer lived here with his wife and family.*

Cup Bearer Serving at the Table is the title of a portrait by Lucas Cranach the Younger.

Philipp Melanchthon, *an associate of Luther's and the co-founder of Lutheranism, initiated a great educational reform. He was also known as* praeceptor Germaniae, *Germany's teacher.*

REFORMATION ALTAR

The main altar of St Mary's Church in Wittenberg *(see pp144–5)* is one of the most important works of art of the Reformation period. The central picture was painted by Lucas Cranach the Elder (c.1539), the wings by his son, Lucas Cranach the Younger, before 1547.

Protestant confession is taken by Johannes Bugenhagen.

Sermon preached by Martin Luther, who points to the figure of the crucified Christ.

Katharina von Bora, *a former nun, became Martin Luther's wife in 1525. She lies buried in the Marienkirche in Torgau* (see p154), *in a tomb which survives to this day.*

BRANDENBURG

THE PROVINCE *of Brandenburg is a lowland region criss-crossed by a dense network of rivers, canals and lakes. Quiet in part, it is also crossed by some of the main tourist routes to Berlin. Its most popular attractions are the historic sights of its capital city, Potsdam, and the Spreewald, where all day can be spent boating on the waterways of the Lusatian forests and villages.*

In early medieval times, the area that was to become present-day Brandenburg was the scene of violent conflict between various Germanic tribes. The latter conquered the region, and in 1157 created the margravate of Brandenburg. Its first ruler was Albrecht der Bär (Albert the Bear), from the house of Ascan. From 1415, Brandenburg was ruled by the Hohenzollern dynasty. It was quick to embrace the Reformation, which was officially adopted here as early as 1538. In 1618, Brandenburg merged with the duchy of Prussia through personal union. The region became entangled in the Thirty Years' War and suffered devastating losses; depopulated and plundered, it took Brandenburg many years to rise from the ashes. In 1701, the Great Elector, Frederick III, crowned himself King Frederick I, and the whole region now assumed the name of Prussia.

While Berlin remained the seat of power and a strong industrial and cultural centre, 18th-century Potsdam also played an important role: it was, after all, the favourite haunt of Frederick the Great. Other towns in the region were less significant – Brandenburg was, and still is, a fairly rural region. Reunification in 1990, however, has opened up the newly created land to Berliners and tourists alike.

Travellers in Brandenburg will encounter ancient tree-lined avenues that stretch to the horizon. The Spreewald, Brandenburg's lake district, is an oasis of tranquillity, ideal for boating and cycling. Brandenburg also has grand castles in Oranienburg, Branitz just outside Cottbus and Rheinsberg, Gothic churches and monasteries in Lehnin and Chorin and the towns of Brandenburg/Havel and Potsdam.

Baroque palace in Rheinsberg, on the shores of the Grienericksee

◁ A picturesque corner in the Babelsberg Palace in Potsdam

Exploring Brandenburg

BRANDENBURG is ideally suited for gentle exploration by bicycle or car, and its proximity to Berlin allows the visitor to make a one-day excursion to the capital. A whole day should be allocated for visiting Potsdam and the castle of Sanssouci, and another day for a boat trip in the Spreewald. A visit to Cottbus can be combined with an excursion to Frankfurt an der Oder. The best time for a visit to Chorin is the summer when concerts are held there in the ruined monastery.

SEE ALSO:

- *Where to Stay* pp476–7
- *Where to Eat* pp505–6

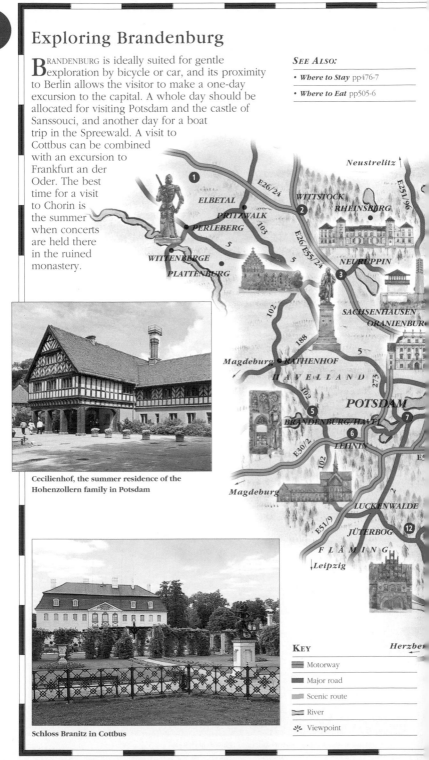

Cecilienhof, the summer residence of the Hohenzollern family in Potsdam

Schloss Branitz in Cottbus

KEY

▬	Motorway
▬	Major road
▬	Scenic route
～	River
✢	Viewpoint

Tourist boats on the Spreewald canals, near Lehde

GETTING AROUND

There are many flights to Berlin. Brandenburg has an extensive network of motorways – the circular Berliner Ring joins with the motorways A11 from Stettin, A24 from Hamburg, Schwerin and Rostock, A2 from Hanover, A9 from Munich and Nuremberg, A12 from Frankfurt an der Oder and A13 from Cottbus and Dresden. Local roads and country lanes in Brandenburg are often narrow and twisting. The outskirts of Berlin are well served by the local train network, which provides frequent links with many small towns. There are also numerous local bus services.

```
0 kilometres      20

0 miles           20
```

SIGHTS AT A GLANCE

Berlin pp58–109
Brandenburg/Havel ⑤
Chorin ⑧
Cottbus ⑩
Elbetal ①
Frankfurt an der Oder ⑨
Jüterbog ⑫
Lehnin ⑥
Neuruppin ③
Oranienburg ④
Potsdam pp124–9 ⑦
Spreewald ⑪
Wittstock ②

Elbetal ❶

Road map D2. 🚉 *to Wittenberge or Bad Wilsnack.* 🛈 *Am Markt 5, Bad Wilsnack (038791-26 20).* 🌐 www.städtenetz.prignitz.de.

THE ELBE valley in the western part of Prignitz is an area of gentle rolling hills and unspoiled nature. Storks, increasingly rare in Germany, nest here to this day. When travelling around this parkland it is worth stopping at **Pritzwalk** to admire the late-Gothic Nikolaikirche (St Nicholas church). Another place of interest is **Perleberg** with its picturesque market square featuring an original 1515 timber-frame building, a sandstone statue of the French knight Roland (1546), now standing by the 1850 Town Hall, and the town's star attraction – the 15th-century Gothic Jakobskirche (church of St Jacob).

Bad Wilsnack owes its fame to the discovery of the therapeutic properties of the iron oxide-rich mud found in the surrounding marshes. Already known in medieval times, the town was an important place of pilgrimage. After a church fire, in 1384, three hosts displaying the blood of Christ were found untouched on the altar. The Gothic **Nikolaikirche** (church of St Nicholas), which survives to this day, was built soon after for the pilgrims.

Plattenburg Castle, in a scenic situation on an island, is also worth a visit. Combining late-Gothic and Renaissance architecture, it is used as a venue for concerts.

Chapel of the Holy Sepulchre in Heiligengrabe, near Wittstock

Wittstock ❷

Road map E2. 🏠 *13,700.* 🚌 🛈 *Markt 1, Wittstock/Dosse (03394-43 34 42).* 🌐 www.wittstock.de.

THE SMALL town of Wittstock was first awarded its municipal status in 1284. From the 13th century to the Reformation, Wittstock was the see of the Havelberg bishops. Although much of the town was destroyed, the original city walls remained almost completely intact, with one surviving gate – the **Gröper Tor**. All that remains of the former bishop's castle is the gate tower, which now houses a small museum. The town's star attraction is the Gothic **Marienkirche** with its late-Gothic reredos depicting the crowning of St Mary. It originated in the wood carving workshop of Claus Berg, probably after 1532. Other interesting features include the 1516 sacrarium and the late-Renaissance pulpit, dating from 1608.

ENVIRONS: Ten km (6 miles) to the west lies **Heiligengrabe**, with its Gothic Cistercian Abbey. One of its many highlights is the 1512 **Chapel of the Holy Sepulchre** with an intricately sculpted gable and some charming timber-frame cloister buildings.

Neuruppin ❸

Road map E2. 🏠 *27,300.* 🚌 🛈 *Karl-Marx-Str. 1 (03391-454 60).* 🌐 www.neuruppin.de.

THE TOWN of Neuruppin, in a scenic location on the shores of a large lake, the Ruppiner See, is mainly Neo-Classical in style, having been rebuilt to the design of Bernhard Matthias Brasch after the great fire of 1787. The only older buildings are the Gothic post-Dominican church and two small hospital chapels. Neuruppin is the birthplace of the architect **Karl Friedrich Schinkel** and the novelist **Theodor Fontane** *(see p23).*

ENVIRONS: The beautiful, albeit neglected palace of **Rheinsberg**, 25 km (16 miles) to the north, was converted from 16th-century Renaissance castle in 1734–7. In 1734–40 it was the residence of the Crown Prince, who later became Frederick the Great, King of Prussia. Some 30 km (19 miles) northeast of Rheinsberg is the National Socialist concentration camp **Ravensbrück**, for women and children. It is now a place of remembrance.

Schinkel monument

Oranienburg ❹

Road map E3. 🏠 *30,000.* 🚉 🚌 🛈 *Bernauer Str. 52 (033 01-70 48 33);* 🌐 www.tourismus-or.de.

THE STAR attraction of the town is **Schloss Oranienburg,** the Baroque residence built for Louisa Henrietta von

The Gothic-Renaissance Plattenburg Castle, in the Elbetal

Nassau-Oranien, wife of the Great Elector Friedrich Wilhelm. Designed by Johann Gregor Memhardt and Michael Matthias Smids, it was built in 1651–5 and later extended to reach its present H-shape.

🏛 **Schloss Oranienburg**
Schlossplatz 1. 📞 *(03301) 38 63.*
⭘ *Apr–Oct: 10am–6pm; Nov–Mar: 10am–5pm.*

ENVIRONS: Sachsenhausen, which is located northeast of Oranienburg, is now a place of remembrance and a museum. Opened in 1936 by the National Socialists, this concentration camp claimed the lives of 100,000 inmates.

🏛 **Sachsenhausen**
📞 *(03301) 20 00.* ⭘ *Apr–Aug: 8:30am–5:30pm Tue–Sun; Sep–Mar: 8:30am–4pm Tue–Sun.*

Brandenburg/ Havel ❺

Road map E3. 🏠 *87,700.* 🚉 🚌
ℹ *Steinstrasse 66–67 (03381-58 58 58).* 🎭 *Havelfestspiele (Jun).* 🌐 *www. städt-brandenburg.de*

BRANDENBURG is the oldest town of the region. It was settled by Slavs as early as the 6th century, and a mission episcopate was established here in 948. Scenically sited on the Havel River, it has preserved historic centres on three islands, despite wartime destruction. The oldest island is the **Dominsel**, with its Romanesque **Dom St Peter und St Paul**. This cathedral was

Early-Renaissance palace in Caputh, north of Lehnin

constructed from 1165 to the mid-13th century. In the 14th century it was raised and given new vaultings. It contains numerous valuable Gothic objects, including the **"Czech" altar** (c.1375), the present main altar (from Lehnin, 1518) and the sacrarium of the same year. The most valuable treasures are on display in the **Dommuseum**.

Other sights worth visiting are the huge, 15th-century **Katharinenkirche** built by Hinrich Brunsberg, the **Gotthardkirche**, in the Altstadt ("old town"), with its Romanesque façade and Gothic interior, the Gothic **Rathaus** (Town Hall), with a statue of Roland from 1474, and the **Stadtmuseum**, a museum of local history and toy manufacture.

🏛 **Dommuseum**
Burghof 9. 📞 *(03381) 20 03 25.*
🌐 *www.brandenburg-dom.de.*
⭘ *Jun–Sep: 10am–5pm Thu–Tue, 10am–noon Wed; winter: 10am–4pm daily (can vary, phone to check).* 📷

🏛 **Stadtmuseum**
Ritterstr. 96. 📞 *(03381) 52 20 48.*
⭘ *9am–5pm Tue–Fri, 10am–5pm Sat & Sun.* 📷

Lehnin ❻

Road map E3. 🏠 *3,100.* 🚌
ℹ *Friedensstraße 13 (03382-76 50).*

VISITORS TO THIS small town mainly come to see the huge **Klosterkirche** (abbey) founded for the Cistercian order of Otto I, son of Albert the Bear. The church was built from the late 12th to the late 13th century, originally in Romanesque, then in early-Gothic style. Following the dissolution of the monastery, in 1542, the buildings fell into disrepair, but much of the abbey has survived.

⛪ **Klosterkirche**
Klosterkirchplatz. 📞 *(03382) 76 86 10.* ⭘ *9am–noon, 1pm–4pm Mon–Fri, 11am–noon, 1–5pm Sat (Nov–Mar: 1–4pm), 11:30am–noon, 1–5pm Sun (Nov–Mar: 1–4pm).*

ENVIRONS: Caputh, situated 23 km (14 miles) to the north, has an early-Baroque **Palace** built during the second half of the 17th century, as summer residence for the wives of the Great Electors. The interior has many fascinating original features.

The Gothic "Czech" altar in the Dom St Peter und St Paul in Brandenburg

Potsdam 🐧

AN INDEPENDENT city close to Berlin, Potsdam, with almost 138,000 inhabitants, is also the capital of Brandenburg. The first documented reference to Potsdam dates back to AD 993; it was later granted municipal rights in 1317. The town blossomed during the times of the Great Electors and then again in the 18th century. Potsdam suffered very badly during World War II, particularly on the night of 14–15 April 1945 when Allied planes bombed the town centre.

A sculpture on display in Park Sanssouci

Sightseeing in Potsdam

Potsdam remains one of Germany's most attractive towns. Tourists flock to see the magnificent royal summer residence, Schloss Sanssouci, to stroll around Neuer Garten (new garden) with its Marmorpalais (marble palace) and Cecilienhof, to visit the old city centre and the Russian colony of Alexandrowka, to be entertained in the film studios of Babelsberg and to take a walk around the parks of Schloss Babelsberg.

♣ Cecilienhof

Am Neuen Garten (Neuer Garten).
(*(0331) 969 42 44.* 🚌 *695.*
🕐 *Apr–Oct: 9am–5pm Tue–Sun; Nov–Mar: 9am–4pm Tue–Sun.*
The Cecilienhof residence played a brief but important role in history, when it served as the venue for the 1945

Potsdam Conference *(see p129).* Built between 1914 and 1917, the palace is the most recent of all Hohenzollern dynasty buildings. Designed by Paul Schultze-Naumburg in the style of an English country manor, Cecilienhof is a sprawling, asymmetrical, timber-frame building with inner courtyards and irregular breaks.

The palace remained a residence of the Hohenzollern family after they had lost the crown – the family stayed in Potsdam until February 1945. Today the palace is a hotel, where visitors interested in history are able to relax amid green shrubs. The large, scenic park

remains open to the public even when the rooms used during the Potsdam Conference are closed to visitors.

♣ Marmorpalais

Am Neuen Garten (Neuer Garten).
(*(0331) 969 42 46.* 🚌 *695.*
🕐 *15 May–15 Oct: 10am–5pm Tue–Sun; 16 Oct–14 May: 10am–4pm Sat & Sun (only with guide).*
This small palace, situated on the edge of the lake, is a beautiful example of early Neo-Classical architecture. The palace is named after the Silesian marble used on its façade. The main part of it was built between 1787 and 1791 by Carl von Gontard to a design and under the direction of Carl Gotthard Langhans, on the initiative of King Friedrich Wilhelm II.

🚋 Alexandrowka

Russische Kolonie Allee/ Puschkinallee.
🚋 *92, 95.* 🚌 *138, 604, 609, 650, 692, 697.*
A visit to Alexandrowka takes the visitor into the world of Pushkin's fairy tales. Wooden log cabins with intricate carvings, set in their own gardens, create a charming residential estate. They were constructed in 1826 under the direction of the German architect Snethlage, for twelve singers of a Russian choir that was established in 1812.

🚋 Holländisches Viertel

Friedrich-Ebert-Str , Kurfürstenstr., Hebbelstr., Gutenbergstr. 🚌 *138, 601–604, 606–612, 614, 631, 632, 650.* 🚋 *92, 95.*
Just as amazing as the Russian colony of Alexandrowka is the Holländisches Viertel (Dutch quarter), part of a Baroque town built in the middle of Germany. Dutch workers arrived in Potsdam in

A view of the Baroque Dutch district known as Holländisches Viertel

the early 18th century and, between 1733 and 1742, a settlement was built for them on the orders of Friedrich Wilhelm I to plans by Johann Boumann the Elder. It comprised 134 gabled houses arranged in four groups. The houses were built from small red bricks and finished with stone and plaster details.

🔒 Nikolaikirche

Alter Markt. 🚌 *601, 603, 692, 694, 91, 92, 93, 95, 96, 98.*
🕐 *2–5pm Mon–Fri, 10am–5pm Sat, 11:30am–5pm Sun.*

This imposing church built in the late Neo-Classical style, is indisputably the most beauti-

The Nikolaikirche, with its dome resting on a colonnaded wall

ful church in Potsdam. It was built on the site of an earlier, Baroque church, which burned down in 1795. It was designed during 1828–30 by Karl Friedrich Schinkel and the building work was supervised by Ludwig Persius. The interior decoration and furnishings of the church date from the 1850s, but were mostly based on the earlier designs by Schinkel.

🐎 Marstall

Alter Markt. 📞 *(0331) 271 81 12.*
🕐 *10am–6pm daily.* 🎫 🚌 *601, 603, 692, 694.* 🚊 *91, 92, 93, 95, 96, 98.*

This long Baroque pavilion, once used as royal stables, is the only remaining building of a royal residence. It was constructed in 1714 and currently houses a film museum devoted to the history and work of the nearby Babelsberg Film Studio.

🏛 Bildergalerie

Zur Historischen Mühle. 📞 *(0331) 969 41 81.* 🚌 *612, 614, 695.*
🕐 *15 May–15 Oct: 10am–5pm Tue–Sun.* 🎫

Baroque paintings once owned by Frederick the Great, including Caravaggio's

VISITORS' CHECKLIST

Road map E3 📞 *(0331) 14 30 00.* 🚉 *Lange Brücke* ℹ️ *Friedrich-Ebert-Str. 5; Brandenburger Str. 18 (01805–99 66 33)* 📠 *(0331) 27 55 829* 🎵 *Hofkonzerte (May–Sep); Musikfestspiele Sanssouci (Jun).* 🌐 *www.potsdam.de*

Doubting Thomas, Guido Reni's *Cleopatra's Death*, as well as paintings by Rubens and van Dyck, are on show in the picture gallery situated next to Schloss Sanssouci.

Caravaggio's *Doubting Thomas*, on show in the Bildergalerie

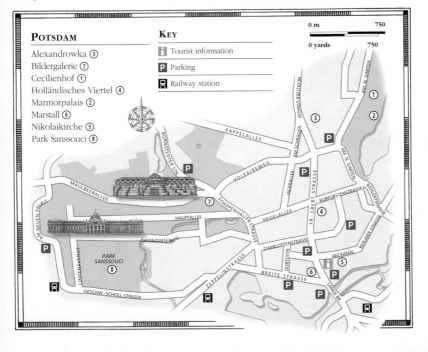

POTSDAM

Alexandrowka ③
Bildergalerie ⑦
Cecilienhof ①
Holländisches Viertel ④
Marmorpalais ②
Marstall ⑥
Nikolaikirche ⑤
Park Sanssouci ⑧

KEY

ℹ️ Tourist information
🅿️ Parking
🚉 Railway station

Park Sanssouci

Flower-filled urn, Park Sanssouci

T̄HE ENORMOUS Park Sanssouci, which occupies an area of 287 hectares (700 acres), is one of the most beautiful palace complexes in Europe. The first building to be constructed on the site was Schloss Sanssouci, built as the summer palace of Frederick the Great. It was erected in 1747, on the site of a former orchard. Over the years, Park Sanssouci was expanded considerably and other palaces and pavilions added. To enjoy the park fully, allow at least a whole day.

Communs
Situated next to a pretty courtyard, this building has an unusually elegant character. It is now used to house palace staff.

★ Neues Palais
Constructed between 1763 and 1769, the monumental building of the Neues Palais is crowned by a massive dome.

Römische Bäder
Shaded by pergolas over-grown with greenery, the Roman baths include a Renaissance-style villa.

| 0 metres | 200 |
| 0 yards | 200 |

STAR SIGHTS

★ Neues Palais

★ Schloss Sanssouci

Schloss Charlottenhof
This Neo-Classical palace gained its name from Charlotte von Gentzkow, the former owner of the land on which the palace was built.

Lustgarten
The extensive park-land is made up of several gardens. The Lustgarten (pleasure garden) is nearest to the Orangerie.

VISITORS' CHECKLIST

Am Neuen Palais. (0331) 969
42 02. 606, 695. Mid-May–
mid-Oct: 9am–5pm; mid-Oct–mid-
May: 9am–4pm (in wintertime, visit
possible only with guided tour).
Fri. (free access to park).

Orangerie
This large Neo-Renaissance palace was built in the mid-19th century to house foreign royalty and other guests.

Neue Kammern
Once the orangerie of the Sanssouci Palace, this Rococo pavilion was later rebuilt as a guest house.

★ **Schloss Sanssouci**
A beautifully terraced vineyard creates a grand approach to Schloss Sanssouci, the oldest building in the complex.

Bildergalerie
Built between 1755 and 1764, this is Germany's oldest purpose-built museum building. The Baroque pavilion houses an art gallery.

Chinesisches Teehaus
An exhibition of exquisite Oriental porcelain is housed in the small, Rococo-style Chinese Tea House.

Friedenskirche
The Neo-Romanesque Church of Peace is modelled on the Basilica of San Clemente in Rome.

Paintings in the music room, in Schloss Sanssouci

♣ Schloss Sanssouci

Zur Historischen Mühle. **[** (0331) 969 41 90. **⏲** Apr–Oct: 9am–5pm; Nov–Mar: 9am–4pm. **Damenflügel & Schlossküche:** 15 May–15 Oct: 10am–12:30pm & 1–5pm Sat & Sun.

This Rococo palace was built in 1745–7 by Georg Wenzeslaus von Knobelsdorff to sketches by Frederick the Great. Knobelsdorff and Johann August Nahl designed the interior. *Sanssouci* ("carefree") was the perfect name for the enchanting castle. The Damenflügel, the castle's west wing which was added in 1840 to house ladies and gentlemen of the court, and the Schlossküche (castle kitchen) can also be visited.

♣ Schloss Neue Kammern

Zur Historischen Mühle (Lustgarten). **[** (0331) 969 42 06. **⏲** 1 Apr–14 May 10am–5pm Sat & Sun; 15 May–15 Oct 10am–5pm Tue–Sun. **[** obligatory.

The Neue Kammern (new chambers) adjoin Schloss Sanssouci in the west, like the Bildergalerie in the east. As part of this ensemble it was originally built in 1747 as an orangery, to a design by Georg Wenzeslaus von Knobelsdorff who gave it its elegant Baroque forms. The building has an attractive roof with sloping ends and sides. In 1777 Frederick the Great ordered the building to be transformed into guest accommodation. The architect, Georg Christian Unger, left the exterior of the orangery largely untouched but converted the interior into

sumptuous suites and four elegant halls. The Rococo décor has been maintained, similar to that of other palaces and pavilions of Sanssouci.

♔ Orangerieschloss

Maulbeerallee. (Nordischer Garten). **[** (0331) 969 42 80. **⏲** 15 May–15 Oct: 10am–5pm Tue–Sun; **viewing terrace** **⏲** 1 Apr–14 May: 10am–5pm Sat & Sun; 15 May–15 Oct 10am–5pm Tue–Sun.

Above the park towers the Orangerie, designed in Italian Renaissance style and crowned by a colonnade. It was built to house guests, not plants, and served as guest residence for Tsar Nicolas and his wife, King Friedrich Wilhelm IV's sister. The Orangerie was constructed in 1852–60 for the king by Friedrich August Stüler, with the final design partly based on plans by Ludwig Persius. Modelled on the Regia Hall in the Vatican, the rooms were grouped around the Raphael Hall and decorated with replicas of this great Italian master's works. The observation terrace offers a good view over Potsdam.

♔ Chinesisches Teehaus

Ökonomieweg (Rehgarten). **[** (0331) 969 42 22. **⏲** 15 May–15 Oct: 10am–5pm Tue–Sun.

The lustrous, gilded pavilion that can be seen glistening between the trees from a

Figure on the roof of Chinesisches Teehaus

distance is the Chinese Teahouse. Chinese art was very popular during the Rococo period – people wore Chinese silk, wallpapered their rooms with Chinese designs, lacquered their furniture, drank tea from Chinese porcelain and built Chinese pavilions in their gardens. The one in Sanssouci was built in 1754–56 to a design by Johann Gottfried Büring. Circular in shape, it has a centrally located main hall surrounded by three studies. Between these are pretty *trompe l'oeil* porticos. The structure is covered with a tent roof and topped with a lantern. Gilded ornaments, columns and Chinese figures surround the pavilion. Originally a tea room and summer dining house, it houses today a collection of 18th-century porcelain.

♔ Römische Bäder

Lenné-Str. (Park Charlottenhof). **[** (0331) 969 42 24. **🚌** 606. **🚋** 91, 94, 96, 98. **⏲** 15 May–15 Oct: 10am–5pm Tue–Sun.

The Roman baths, situated by the edge of a lake, form a picturesque group of pavilions which served as accommodation for the king's guests. They were designed in 1829–40 by Karl Friedrich Schinkel, with the help of Ludwig Persius. The gardener's house at the front stands next to a low, asymmetrical tower, built in the style of an Italian Renaissance villa. In the background, to the left, extends the former bathing pavilion, which is currently used for temporary exhibitions. The pavilions are grouped around a garden planted with colourful shrubs and vegetables.

♣ Schloss Charlottenhof

Geschwister-Scholl-Str. (Park Charlottenhof). **[** (0331) 969 42 28. **⏲** 15 May–15 Oct: 10am–5pm Tue–Sun. **[** obligatory.

This small Neo-Classical palace stands at the southern end of Park Sanssouci, known as Park Charlottenhof. Built in

1826–9 for the heir to the throne, the future King Friedrich Wilhelm IV, this small, single-storey building was designed by Karl Friedrich Schinkel in the style of a Roman villa. Some of the wall paintings, designed by Schinkel in the so-called Pompeiian style, are still in place. There is also a collection of Italian engravings. The most interesting part of the interior is the Humboldt Room. The palace is surrounded by a landscaped park designed by Peter Joseph Lenné.

♣ Neues Palais

Am Neuen Palais. 【 *(0331) 969 42 55*. ☐ *Apr–Oct 9am–5pm Sat–Thu; Nov–Mar 9am–4pm Sat–Thu*. 📷 🎫 *obligatory*.

One of Germany's most beautiful palaces, this imposing Baroque structure, on the main avenue in Park Sanssouci, was built for Frederick the Great to initial plans by Georg Wenzeslaus von Knobelsdorff in 1750. Its construction, to designs by Johan Gottfried Büring, Jean Laurent Le Geay and Carl von Gontard, was delayed until 1763–9, after the Seven Years' War. The vast, three-wing structure comprises over 200 richly adorned rooms and has many interesting sculptures. The south wing houses the kings' quarters.

The impressive Marble Hall in the Baroque Neues Palais

THE POTSDAM CONFERENCE

Towards the end of World War II, the leaders of the Allies – Winston Churchill, Franklin Roosevelt, and Joseph Stalin – met in Schloss Cecilienhof in Potsdam. The aim of this conference, which lasted from 17 July until 2 August 1945, was to resolve the problems arising at the end of the war. The main participants changed, however, before it was concluded. Churchill was replaced by newly-elected Clement Attlee, and Harry S. Truman took over after President Roosevelt died. The conference set up the occupation zones, the demilitarization and monitoring of Germany, the punishment of war criminals and the reparations. It also revised the German borders. These decisions established the political balance of power in Europe, which continued for 45 years.

Attlee, Truman and Stalin in Potsdam

♣ Schloss Babelsberg

Im Park Babelsberg. 【 *(0331) 969 42 50*. ☐ *Apr–Oct:10am–5pm Tue–Sun*. 📷

Built in 1833–5 for Prince Wilhelm (Kaiser Wilhelm I), by Karl Friedrich Schinkel, this extravagant castle ranks as one of his finest works. An irregular building with many towers and bay windows, built in the spirit of English Neo-Gothic, with allusions to Windsor Castle and Tudor style, it now holds the Museum of Pre-History.

⊞ Filmpark Babelsberg

Großbeerenstr. 【 *(0331) 721 27 55*. ☐ *17 Mar–3 Nov 10am–6pm daily*. 📷

This amazing film park was laid out on the site where Germany's first films were produced in 1912. From 1917 the studio belonged to Universum-Film-AG (UFA), which produced some of the most famous films of the silent era, including Fritz Lang's *Metropolis* and some films with Greta Garbo. The *Blue Angel*, with Marlene Dietrich, was also shot at Babelsberg, but subsequently, the studios were used to film propaganda for the Nazis. The studio is still operational today, and the public can admire some of the old sets, the creation of special effects and stuntmen in action.

⊞ Einsteinturm

Albert-Einstein-Str. ☐ *once every month, by arrangement with the Urania Society (0331-288 23 33)*. 🚌 *694*.

This tower, built in 1920–21 by Erich Mendelssohn, is one of the finest examples of German Expressionist architecture. Its fantasy forms were to demonstrate the qualities of reinforced concrete to spectacular effect. However, the cost of formwork, assembled by boat builders, limited the use of the material to the first storey, while the upper floors are plastered brickwork.

Chorin  8

Road map E2. 510. Kloster
Chorin, Amt 11A. (033366)
703 77. Apr–Oct: 9am–6pm
daily; Nov–Mar: 9am–4pm daily.
Choriner Musiksommer.

ON THE EDGE OF the vast
Schorfheide heathland,
which has been listed as a
World Biosphere Reserve by
UNESCO, stands one of Brandenburg's most beautiful
Gothic buildings – the
Cistercian **Kloster** (abbey) of
Chorin. The Cistercians arrived here in 1258, but work
on the present Gothic abbey
did not start until 1270. The
church is a triple-nave, transeptial basilica, with a magnificent façade. Preserved to
this day are two wings of the
monastic quarters plus several
domestic buildings. Following
the dissolution of the monastery in 1542, the entire
complex fell into disrepair.
Today the church, deprived
of its traditional furnishings, is
used as a venue for classical
concerts. The park established
by Peter Joseph Lenné is con-
ducive to pleasant strolls.

ENVIRONS: For visitors to Nie-
derfinow, the giant **Schiffshebewerk** (barge-lift) is a
definite must. This wonder of
technology was designed for
lifting and lowering ships
from one canal to another.
Commissioned in 1934, it is
60 m (197 ft) tall and capable
of lifting barges laden with
1,000 tonnes or more.

**Portal of the St Marienkirche in
Frankfurt an der Oder**

Frankfurt
an der Oder 9

Road map F3. 87,900.
Karl-Marx-Str. 9. (0335-32 52 16).
Frankfurter Musikfesttage (Mar);
Hansefest (Aug–Sep); Kleist-Tage
(Jun–Jul).

FRANKFURT, on the banks of
the river Oder, was granted
municipal rights in 1253, prospered in the 13th century and
joined the Hanseatic league in
1368. In 1945, the right bank
was ceded to Poland and is
now known as Słubice.
Viadrin University, founded in 1506, was reopened in
1991 and now educates both
German and Polish students.
The town's most famous resident was the playwright and
writer Heinrich von Kleist

who was born here in 1777.
The Gothic **Rathaus** (town
hall) in the centre escaped
destruction in World War II
and now houses an art gallery. The main church,
Marienkirche (church of St
Mary), is a vast, five-nave
Gothic hall which has stood
in ruins since 1945. Some of
the Gothic furnishings were
rescued and can now be seen
in **St Gertraud** (church of St
Gertrude) which dates back
to 1368. The main altar from
1489 and the huge, 5m- (16ft)
-tall candelabrum from 1376
are particularly valuable. Another Gothic church, originally built for the Franciscans
in 1270, has been transformed
into the **C.P.E. Bach Konzert-
halle** (concert hall), named
after Carl Philipp Emmanuel
Bach, son of Johann Sebastian.

ENVIRONS: Neuzelle, 36 km
(23 miles) to the south, has a
magnificent former Cistercian
Abbey, with an impressive
Baroque relief façade.

Cottbus 10

Road map F3. 121,000.
Bahnhofstr. Berliner Platz 6.
(0355-754 20); W www.cottbus.de.
Karnevalsumzug (Feb); Cottbuser
Musik-Herbst (Oct).

TOURISTS RARELY visit Cottbus, despite the many at-
tractions offered by the town.
Its enchanting town square is
surrounded by impressive
Baroque buildings. The house
at No. 24 is the quaint Löwen-

The Baroque Schloss Branitz in Cottbus

apotheke (lion's pharmacy), which now houses a small pharmaceutical museum, the **Niederlausitzer Apotheken-museum**, with displays of historical interiors. Nearby, the Gothic **Oberkirche St Niko-lai** features an unusual original late-Gothic mesh vaulting. Another interesting Gothic structure, the **Wendenkirche** (Sorbian church), is a former Franciscan church, from the 14th–15th centuries.

Other attractions of the town include the remains of the medieval city walls with three preserved towers. Perhaps the most attractive building in Cottbus is the **Staats-theater** (state theatre) designed in Jugendstil (Art Nouveau style) by Bernhard Sehring and built in 1908.

The **Wendisches Museum** is devoted to the culture of the Sorbs which is experiencing a revival (see p171).

Schloss Branitz is a late-Baroque palace, originally built in the 18th century, at the southeastern edge of town. It became the residence of Prince Hermann von Pückler-Muskau in 1845, who had its interior redesigned by Gottfried Semper. Today, the palace houses the **Fürst-Pückler-Museum**, which exhibits paintings by Karl Blechen, a local artist from Cottbus. The star attraction of the palace is its **Park**, which was designed by Prince Pückler-Muskau himself. This vast landscaped garden includes a lake with an island on which stands a grass-covered mock-Egyptian earth pyramid containing the tomb of the extravagant and eccentric Prince.

🏛 **Schloss Branitz and Fürst-Pückler-Museum**
Kastanienalle 11. ☎ (0355) 751 50. ◌ Apr–Oct: 10am–6pm daily, Nov–Mar: 10am–5pm; Tue–Sun. ♿
🏛 **Wendisches Museum**
Mühlenstr. 12. ☎ (0355) 79 49 30. ◌ 8:30am–6pm Tue–Fri, 2–6pm Sat–Sun and bank holidays.
🏛 **Niederlausitzer Apothekenmuseum**
Altmark 24. ☎ (0355) 239 97. ◌ 10am–5pm Tue–Fri; 2 & 3pm Sat–Sun. ♿

Boats and canoes in the Spreewald, near Lübben

Spreewald ⑪

Road map F3. 🚉 Lübben. ℹ Raddusch, Lindenstr. 1 (035433-722 99), Lübbenau, Ehm-Welk-Str. 15 (03542-36 68). 🚉 🎉 Spreewaldfest in Lübbenau (Jul) and Lübben (Sep). 🌐 www.spreewald.de

Designated as one of the World Biosphere Reserves, this marshy region, criss-crossed by hundreds of small rivers and canals, attracts large numbers of tourists each year. An all-day trip by **Kahn** (boat) or canoe, which is best started in **Lübben** or **Lübbenau**, can prove to be an unforgettable experience. The splendour of nature, numerous water birds and the endless chain of small restaurants which serve meals straight from the jetty, ensure an exciting day for the visitor. Do not miss the local speciality, pickled gherkins.

Lübben has an original Gothic church and a Baroque palace, rebuilt in the 19th century. Lübbenau features a small Baroque church and the Neo-Classical house of the von Lynar family. In **Lehde** the small open-air museum and the private collection of the **Bauernhaus- und Gurkenmuseum** – the only gherkin museum in Germany – are highly recommended.

ENVIRONS: Luckau, 18 km (11 miles) west of Lübben, has a lovely town square, surrounded by attractive Baroque houses with stucco façades, and the ornamented, 14th-century Gothic Nikolaikirche.

Statue on Jüterbog town hall

Jüterbog ⑫

Road map E3. 🚶 13,000. 🚉 🚌 ℹ Markt 21 (03372-46 31 13).

Jüterbog is a small, picturesque town featuring many Gothic structures including some well-preserved sections of three city walls with gates and towers, dating back to the 15th century. It also boasts a beautiful town hall with arcades and three churches. **Nikolaikirche** (church of St Nicholas), the largest of them, is a magnificent hall church, with a twin-tower façade, built in several stages. The so-called New Sacristy features a set of medieval wall paintings, while the naves contain many Gothic furnishings.

ENVIRONS: Five km (3 miles) to the north of Jüterbog stands **Kloster Zinna**, a former Cistercian Abbey with an early-Gothic stone church. It features 16th-century stained-glass windows depicting the saints Bernhard and Benedikt.

The early-Gothic ex-Cistercian Kloster Zinna, near Jüterbog

SAXONY-ANHALT

THE SCENIC HARZ *mountains, a popular recreation area with fascinating rock formations and pleasant walks, are the best known attraction of Saxony-Anhalt. Yet this state also boasts a number of interesting towns, such as Lutherstadt Wittenberg and Magdeburg, steeped in history and blessed with magnificent historic remains, which range from Romanesque churches and abbeys to medieval castles.*

This province consists of the areas of the former Duchy of Anhalt and the Prussian province of Saxony, that part of the Kingdom of Saxony which was incorporated into Prussia after the Congress of Vienna (1815) as punishment for supporting Napoleon.

The landscape in this region is highly varied. Its northern part, the Altmark, is a largely flat area of farmland and heath. The gentle hills of the Harz Mountains in the southwest, although not especially high (their highest peak, the Brocken, rises to only 1142 m/3747 ft), are picturesque and fairly well provided with tourist facilities. The eastern, flat part of the region is more industrialized. It also includes two very important towns: the small town of Wittenberg, where Martin Luther proclaimed his theses in 1517, thus launching the Reformation, and Dessau, the former capital of the Duchy of Anhalt and from 1925 to 1932 the seat of the Bauhaus Art School. The southern part of the province, with its interesting and varied landscape, features one of the land's most impressive historic buildings – the gigantic Naumburg Cathedral.

After World War II Saxony-Anhalt was occupied by the Soviets, and in 1949 it was incorporated into the GDR. It underwent major industrial development, mainly due to lignite mining. The state of Saxony-Anhalt was first created in 1947, only to be abolished five years later. It was finally re-established as a federal state in 1990, with Magdeburg as its capital.

Timber-frame houses in Quedlinburg

◁ **Rousseau Island, in the landscaped gardens of Wörlitz**

Exploring Saxony-Anhalt

TOURING Saxony-Anhalt can be an unforgettable experience, especially for admirers of Romanesque art, as this region abounds in churches and abbeys of that period. A visit to Wörlitz provides the opportunity to see one of Germany's most beautiful landscaped gardens. Nature lovers, hill-walkers and, in the winter, cross-country skiers should include a few days in the romantic Harz Mountains in their schedule. An added attraction here is a ride on the narrow-gauge railway drawn by a steam engine which, today as in years gone by, still links some of the most interesting places of the region.

Interior of the Gothic cathedral in Havelberg

Zoo-Park in Dessau

SALZWEDEL

ALTMA

GARDELEGEN

E30/2

WOLMIRSTE

MAGDEBURG

MAGDEBURGER BÖRDE

HALBERSTADT

WERNIGERODE

QUEDLINBURG

BERNB

ASCHERSLEBI

THE HARZ MOUNTAIN TRAIL

SANGERHAUSEN

LUTHERSTA EISLEBEN

QUERFURT

KEY

▬	Motorway
▬	Major road
▬	Scenic route
➤	River
✵	Viewpoint

Listening to a summer water concert, in Wörlitz Park

GETTING AROUND

The A2 motorway from Hanover to Berlin runs through Magdeburg to the northern part of the region. Another motorway, the A9 which links Berlin and Munich, provides easy access to Dessau and Halle, which is also served by the recently constructed A14 motorway from Leipzig to Magdeburg. Other major and minor roads, well signposted, provide access to smaller towns and villages. Larger towns are easily accessed by rail or local bus services. In the Harz Mountains the narrow-gauge train is an alternative form of transport.

| 0 km | 15 |
| 0 miles | 15 |

SEE ALSO

- **Where to Stay** pp477–8
- **Where to Eat** pp506–7

SIGHTS AT A GLANCE

Interior of the Gothic Cathedral of Halberstadt

Halberstadt ❶

Road map D3. 🏘 *42,000.* 🚉 🚌
ℹ️ *Hinter dem Rathaus 6 (03941-55 18 15).* W www.halberstadt.de

HALBERSTADT enjoys a picturesque location in the foothills of the Harz Mountains. Its history goes back to the 9th century, when it became a seat of a mission episcopate. Once an important town, Halberstadt had 80 per cent of its buildings destroyed during World War II. Fortunately, many of its beautiful historic buildings have now been restored to their former glory.

The vast **St Stephans Dom** is the fourth successive church built on the same site. Construction began in the 13th century and the church was consecrated in 1491. The two-tower transeptial basilica ranks as one of the most beautiful pure Gothic forms in Germany. Its oldest part is the 12th-century font. Also notable are the Romanesque Crucifixion group (c.1220), set above the choir screen, and several examples of Gothic sculpture. Stained-glass windows from around 1330 have survived in the Marian Chapel, and 15th-century windows can be found along the cloisters and in the presbytery.

Romanesque Crucifixion group in the Dom, Halberstadt

The adjoining chapter buildings contain one of Germany's richest cathedral treasures – the **Domschatz**, with precious 12th-century tapestries, numerous sculptures and liturgical vessels.

Other interesting churches to have survived in the old town district include the Romanesque 12th-century **Liebfrauenkirche** and the Gothic **Marktkirche St. Martini** with a statue of Roland, symbolizing the freedom of the city. Remaining timber-frame houses can be seen in Gröper- and Taubenstrasse.

🏛 Domschatz
📞 *03941 24237.*
⏰ *call for times.*
📷 *obligatory.*

ENVIRONS: An original 12th-century Benedictine church stands in Huysburg, 11 km (7 miles) to the northwest.

Wernigerode ❷

Road map D3. 🏘 *36,000.* 🚉 🚌
ℹ️ *Nicolaiplatz 1 (03943-63 30 35).*
🎭 *Rathausfest (Jun); Schlossfestspiele (Jul & Aug).* W www.wernigerode.de

WERNIGERODE is attractively situated at a confluence of two rivers. Timber-frame houses lean across its steep, winding streets, and a massive castle rises above the

town. The **Harzquerbahn**, a narrow-gauge railway which links the small towns and villages in the Harz Mountains, between Wernigerode and Nordhausen, provides another popular tourist attraction. The Brockenbahn runs between Wernigerode and the Brocken mountain.

Strolling around the Old Town it is well worth stepping into St John's Church, featuring a Romanesque west tower. It contains some late-Gothic features, including the font and the altar. The variety of ornaments adorning the houses in Wernigerode is truly staggering. Particularly interesting are the houses along **Breite Straße**, the town's main shopping street which is closed to traffic.

♣ Schloss Wernigerode
Am Schloss 1. 📞 *03943-55 30 30.*
⏰ *May–Oct: 10am–6pm; Nov–Apr: 10am–4pm Tue–Fri; 10am–6pm Sat & Sun.* 🅿
The fairy-tale castle, spiked with towers, was created during the years 1861–83 on the site of an older fortress. Now a museum, it houses the Stolberg-Wernigerode family art collection. The castle ramparts afford a fantastic view of the town and the nearby Harz mountains.

ENVIRONS: The small town of **Osterwieck**, 22 km (14 miles) to the north, has over 400 timber-frame buildings, dating mainly from the 16th and 17th centuries.

The romantic façade of Schloss Wernigerode, now a museum

The Harz Mountain Trail ❸

THE TOURIST trail across the Harz Mountains leads through charming historic towns and villages, as well as past the other attractions of the region including some fascinating caves and unusual rock formations.

Blankenburg ②
This charming mountain town is overlooked by an 18th-century castle. The Teufels-mauer, a spectacular 4-km (2-mile) long sandstone cliff, attracts many climbers.

The Rübeland Caves ①
Rübeland's main attractions are the Hermannshöhle and Baumannshöhle, two caves with amazing stalactites and stalagmites.

Thale ③
Many mountain walks start in Thale, including one to the Hexentanzplatz, a platform suspended above a cliff, from where witches fly to Sabbath celebrations in the Walpurgis Night.

Wernigerode

Elbingerode

Quedlinburg   Hoym

Ermsleben

BODETA

RAMBERG

Hasselfelde

Güntersberge

STIEGE

Kurort Stolberg

Harzgerode ⑦
The town has charming timber-frame houses in the Old Town, and a 16th-century castle.

Gernrode ④
The star attraction in this town is the 10th-century church of St Cyriacus. Its interior is devoid of ornaments, yet enchantingly pure in form.

Burg Falkenstein ⑥
This huge castle, built in the 12th century and extended many times, is now a museum. From the castle, the visitor can enjoy a splendid view over the surrounding Harz Mountains.

Ballenstedt ⑤
The former home of the von Anhalt-Bemburg family enchants visitors to this day with its imaginative design, including the Baroque castle set in a park.

| 0 km | | 2 |
| 0 miles | | 2 |

KEY

■ Tour route
— Other road
■ Scenic route
✼ Viewpoint

**The Renaissance portal of
Quedlinburg Schloss**

Quedlinburg ❹

Road map D3. 🏚 *26,000.* 🚊 🚌
🛈 *Markt 2 (03946-90 56 24 and
90 56 25).*

THE RISE OF the small town
of Quedlinburg was close-
ly connected with its convent,
established in 936 by Emperor
Otto I and his mother, St
Mathilde. On the hill above
the town stands the vast
Romanesque structure of the
Stiftskirche St Servatius
(Collegiate Church of St
Servatius), built between 1017
and 1129. Its old crypt, the
Huysburg, which belonged to
the previous church, features
Romanesque wall paintings
and contains tombs of the
prioresses and of the Emperor
Henry and his wife Mathilde.

An exhibition of treasures is
shown in the arms of the
transept, including the
Romanesque reliquary of St
Servatius and the remaining
fragments of the 12th-century
Knüpfteppich (tapestry). The
Quedlinburg Schloss,
a Renaissance palace sur-
rounded by gardens, occupies
the other side of the hill.

Both Old and New Town of
Quedlinburg have valuable
examples of timber-frame
architecture. The buildings
date from various times – the
modest house at **Wordgasse
3**, from around 1400, is the
oldest surviving timber-frame
building in Germany. Also
noteworthy are the numerous
churches, including the 10th-
century **Norbertinenkirche**,
the **Wippertikirche** with its
early-Romanesque crypt, and
the 15th century, late-Gothic
Marktkirche St Benedicti.

Bernburg ❺

Road map D4. 🏚 *36,000.* 🚊 🚌
🛈 *Lindeplatz 9 (03471-62 60 96).*
🎭 *Stadt-und Rosenfest (May/Jun).*

ONCE THE CAPITAL of one of
Anhalt's Duchies, Bern-
burg enjoys a picturesque
location on the banks of the
Saale River. It has a **Berg-
stadt** (upper town) and a
Talstadt (lower town), and its
attractions include the Gothic

parish churches and the town
square with its Baroque buildings. The most important
historic building is the **Bernburg Schloss**, a castle built
on a rock. It owes its present
appearance to refurbishments
(1540–70), yet many features
of this multi-wing structure
are much older, including the
12th-century Romanesque
chapels and Gothic towers.

**Burg Giebichenstein, in Halle,
with the Arts and Crafts College**

Halle ❻

Road map D4. 🏚 *232,300.* 🚊 🚌
🛈 *Grosse Ulrichstrasse 60 (0345-
47 23 30).* 🎭 *Händel-Festspiele (Jun);
Hallesche Musiktage (Nov).*

HALLE IS AN old town with a
rich history in commerce
and trade, its wealth founded
on the production and sale of
salt. Later, the town was
turned into a centre for the

The impressive Bernburg Schloss, built on a rock

Renaissance residence in Merseburg

chemical industry. Halle has preserved most of its historic heritage. On the **Marktplatz** (town square) stands an interesting church, **Unser Lieben Frauen** (Our Dear Lady), whose late-Gothic main body (1530–54) was positioned between two pairs of towers that had remained intact from previous Romanesque churches. Nearby is the **Roter Turm** (Red Tower), an 84-m (276 ft) tall belfry, built in 1418–1506. The house at Nikolaistraße 5, the birthplace of Georg Friedrich Händel, now houses a small museum, the **Händel-Haus**. In Domplatz stands the early-Gothic **Dom**, built in 1280–1331 by the Dominicans and restored between 1525 and 1530 in Renaissance style, and elevated to the rank of cathedral. Inside there is an interesting pulpit dating from 1525, and the statues of saints situated by Peter Schroh's pillars.

Halle has some other medieval churches, including the late-Gothic **Moritzkirche** built in the latter part of the 14th century. It is also worth visiting the **Staatliche Galerie,** housed in the refurbished Citadel building known as **Moritzburg** and built during 1484-1503. On the outskirts of town stands **Burg Giebichenstein**, the former castle residence of the Magdeburg bishops. The upper part of the castle remains in ruins, while the lower part houses an Arts & Crafts College.

🏛 **Staatliche Galerie**
Friedemann-Bach-Platz 5. 【 (0345) 21 25 90. ◯ 11am–8:30pm Tue, 10am–6pm Wed–Sun & public holidays.

Merseburg ❼

Road map D4. 🏯 40,000. 🚉 🚌
ℹ Burgstr. 5 (03461-21 41 70).

THE FIRST sight visitors see as they arrive in Merseburg is the **Domburg** – a vast complex of buildings spiked with towers, consisting of a cathedral and residential premises. The cathedral is not uniform in style; it includes some Romanesque elements (the eastern section and twin towers in the west) erected in the 11th and 12th centuries, and the late-Gothic triplenave main body, which was built in 1510–17. All that remains of the older, early-Romanesque structure is the crypt, underneath the presbytery. The cathedral contains remarkable Gothic and Renaissance features, as well as numerous sarcophagi of bishops, such as that of Thilo von Troth (1470). The chapter buildings house a library with precious manuscripts, including the **Merseburg Bible** (c. 1200). Adjacent to the cathedral is a three-wing Renaissance-style **Schloss**. Magnificent portals and an attractive oriel in the castle's west wing are noteworthy.

Querfurt ❽

Road map D4. 🏯 11,000. 🚌
ℹ Markt 14 (034771-237 99).

THE NARROW streets of Querfurt are crammed with timber-frame houses, and the giant **Schloss** towers over the town square with its Renaissance town hall. The castle's present form is the result of Renaissance refurbishments, but it maintains many Romanesque features, such as the 11th-century donjon (keep), known as **Dicker Heinrich** (Fat Henry) and a 12th-century church. Also worth seeing is the burial chapel, the Baroque **Fürstenhaus** (ducal house) and a small museum, situated in the former armoury and granary.

Naumburg ❾

Road map D4. 🏯 30,500. 🚉 🚌
ℹ Markt 6 (03445-20 16 14).
ⓦ www.naumburg.de 🎭 Hussiten-Kirsch-Fest (Jun).

THE TOWN's star attraction is the **Dom** (cathedral of Saints Peter and Paul see pp140–41). There is a late-Gothic **Rathaus** (town hall), restored in Renaissance style, and the main square is surrounded by quaint houses. Further attractions include the **Marientor** gate (1455–6) with the puppet theatre, and the Gothic **Stadtkirche St. Wenzel** (Church of St Wenceslas). The latter has two paintings by Lucas Cranach the Elder as well as the 18th-century organ that Johann Sebastian Bach played on. Friedrich Nietzsche, the philosopher, spent his childhood at No. 18 Weingarten, now a small museum.

Gothic stone retable of the main altar in Naumburg Dom

Naumburg Dom

THE IMPRESSIVE Cathedral of Saints Peter and Paul in Naumburg is one of the finest Gothic structures in Germany. The present cathedral is the second to be built on the same site; only a section of the eastern crypt survived of the earlier Romanesque church. Construction started before 1213, with the earliest parts including the late-Romanesque east choir, the transept and the main body. The early-Gothic west choir was built in the mid-13th century, the newer Gothic east choir c.1330. The northeast towers date from the 15th century, the southwest towers from 1894.

West choir

Stained-glass Windows in the Presbytery
The stained-glass windows depict scenes of the apostles of virtue and sin. Some sections are original 13th-century work, but two were completed in the 19th century.

★ Founders' Statues
The statues of Margrave Ekkehard and his wife, Uta, are true masterpieces – the artist succeeded marvellously in capturing the beauty and sensitivity of his subjects.

★ Portal of the West Reading Room
The Gothic twin portal depicts the Crucifixion, a moving and highly expressive group sculpture by the brilliant "Naumburger Meister" whose identity remains unknown.

STAR FEATURES

★ Founders' Statues

★ Portal of the West Reading Room

★ Main Portal

Pulpit

The richly ornamented pulpit basket, from 1466, and the adjoining stairs have recently been renovated.

VISITORS' CHECKLIST

Domplatz 16–17. **C** *(03445) 23 01 10.* ◯ *Apr–Sep: 9am–6pm Mon–Sat, noon–6pm Sun; Mar & Oct: 9am–5pm Mon–Sat, noon– 5pm Sun; Nov–Feb: 9am–4pm Mon–Sat, noon–4pm Sun.* 🖼

St Mary's Altar

This late-Gothic triptych (c.1510) depicts the Virgin Mary with the Infant, framed by Saints Barbara and Catherine, with the Apostles in the wings.

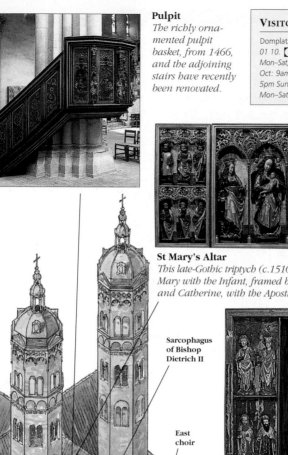

Sarcophagus of Bishop Dietrich II

East choir

East Choir Altar

This Gothic altar features the Virgin Mary with the Infant Jesus, surrounded by the figures of the saints.

The Main Altar, built in the mid-14th-century, is a stone retable depicting the Crucifixion with the saints which was transferred from another altar.

★ Main Portal

The late-Romanesque, 13th-century portal is decorated on the left side with eagles. The tympanum features Christ in a mandorla (almond-shaped area) supported by angels.

Interior of the Gothic presbytery in the Magdeburg Dom

Magdeburg ⑩

Road map D3. 🏰 *235,000.* 🚃 🚌
ℹ️ *Ernst-Reuter-Allee 10 (0391-54 04 903).* 🎭 *Ballettfestival (Jun), Ballonfahrertreffen (Jul/Aug).* Ⓦ *www.magdeburg-tourist.de*

THE LARGE-SCALE development of Magdeburg, today the capital of Saxony-Anhalt and a port on the river Elbe, began in the 10th century when Emperor Otto I established his main residence here. In medieval times the town became a political and cultural centre. Following the abolition of the archbishopric and the destruction wrought by the Thirty Years' War, it lost its political importance. About 80 per cent was destroyed during World War II, making it much less attractive, but it is still worth a visit. Many historic buildings have been reconstructed in the Old Town.

🏛 Dom St Mauritius und St Katharina
Domplatz. ⏰ *daily.*
The vast Magdeburg cathedral is one of the most important Gothic churches in Germany. Its construction, which started in 1209 on the site of an earlier Romanesque church, was completed in 1520, although much of it was built by the mid-14th century. The result is a lofty, aisled basilica with transept, cloisters, a ring of chapels surrounding the presbytery and a vast twin-tower façade. The cathedral has several magnificent, original sculptures. Other notable features include the tomb of Emperor Otto I, as well as the 12th-century bronze tomb plaques of archbishops Friedrich von Wettin and Wichmann. The memorial for the dead of World War I is the work of Ernst Barlach, dating from 1929. Visitors to the cathedral may notice several elements that were preserved from ancient structures and have been incorporated into the walls or used as ornaments inside the building.

🏛 Kulturhistorisches Museum
Otto-von-Guericke-Str. 68–73.
📞 *(0391) 540 35 01.* ⏰ *10am–5pm Tue–Sun.* 🖼
This museum contains works of art, archaeological finds and historic documents of the town. Its most valuable exhibit is the Magdeburger Reiter (Magdeburg Rider), a sculpture dating from around 1240, depicting an unknown ruler riding on a horse (probably Otto I).

⛪ Kloster Unser Lieben Frauen
Regierungsstr. 4–6.
Kunstmuseum 📞 *(0391) 56 50 20.* ⏰ *10am–5pm Tue–Sun.* 🖼
This austere Romanesque church, Magdeburg's oldest building, was built for the Norbertine order during the second half of the 11th and the early 12th centuries. Stripped of all its ornaments, it now serves as a concert hall. The adjacent Romanesque abbey is a museum with medieval and modern sculptures (Barlach, Rodin).

⛪ Halle an der Buttergasse
Alter Markt. Weinkeller Buttergasse.
The basement of a late-Romanesque market hall from c.1200 was rediscovered in 1948, and is used today as a wine cellar.

🏛 Rathaus
Alter Markt.
The present Baroque town hall, built in 1691–8 on the site of an earlier, late-Romanesque town hall, was restored after World War II.

⛪ Pfarrkirche St Johannis
Am Johannisberg 1.
Viewing tower
📞 *(0391) 540 21 26.* ⏰ *10am–7pm Tue–Sun.* 🖼
The ruins of this church, near the market square, are the remains of the Gothic church of St John, which was destroyed during World War II. In 1524 Martin Luther preached here.

Kloster Unser Lieben Frauen in Magdeburg

Stendal ⓫

Road map D3. 🏘 *39,600.*
🚉 🚌 ⓘ *Kornmarkt 8
(03931-65 11 90).*

IN MEDIEVAL times Stendal
was one of the richest
towns of the Brandenburg
margravate, and its most
valuable historical remains
date from that period. The
late-Gothic **St Nikolai**
cathedral was built in
1423–67, on the foundations
of a Romanesque Augustinian
church. Its star attractions are
15th-century stained-glass
windows in the presbytery
and the transept.

The late-Gothic, 15th-cen-
tury church **St Marien** (St
Mary) has some original
Gothic elements, and the
oldest parts of the **Rathaus**
(town hall) date back to the
14th century. Other attractions
include the remains of the
town walls, with a beautiful
tower, **Uenglinger Torturm**.

**Gothic traceries of the cloisters in
the Dom, Havelberg**

Havelberg ⓬

Road map D3. 🏘 *7,000.* 🚌 ⓘ
Uferstr. 1. (039387-79 091).

HAVELBERG played an im-
portant role in the Christ-
ianization of this region, with
a mission episcopate established here as early as the
mid-10th century. The present
cathedral – **Dom St Marien** –
was built in 1150–70, and
although redesigned in the
early 14th century, it nevertheless maintained its Romanesque character. Its most
interesting features include

**Back of the Gothic Rathaus in the
market square in Tangermünde**

huge stone candelabra taken
from the former reading
room, dating back to around
1300, and the present reading
room, which is decorated
with reliefs carved in the
workshop of the Parler
Family, in Prague, between
1396 and 1411.

Tangermünde ⓭

Road map D3. 🏘 *10,000.* 🚉 🚌
ⓘ *Marktstr. 13 (039322-37 10 and
43 750).*

SITUATED at the confluence
of the Tanger and Elbe
rivers, this town grew rapidly
during medieval times. For
centuries it remained the seat
of the Brandenburg mar-
graves, and King Charles IV
chose it as his second residence. The town joined the
Hanseatic League, and
grew in status thanks to
its trade links.

The present **Rathaus**
(town hall) has lovely
timber-frame architec-
ture. Today it houses
the municipal museum.

The only remains of
the old castle are its
main tower and the
Kanzlei (chancellery).
In 1377, King Charles IV
brought the Augustinian
monks to town and had
the **St Stephanskirche**
(church of St Stephen)
built for them. Con-
struction continued until
the end of the 15th
century. This magnifi-
cent, late-Gothic hall
church with transept
and cloister contains

interesting features: a 1624
organ made in the Hamburg
workshop of Hans Scherer
the Younger, the 1619 pulpit
created by Christopher Dehne
and a font dating from 1508,
the work of Heinrich Mente.

The east wing of the beautiful Gothic **Rathaus** (town
hall) dates back to 1430
and is the work of Heinrich
Brunsberg, its richly ornamented spire being typical of his
work. The west wing with its
arcades was added around
1480, and the external stairs
date from the 19th century.

Tangermünde has retained
some remains of the city
walls, dating from around
1300 and including a magnificent late-Gothic gate, the
Neustädter Tor, whose tall,
cylindrical tower has intricate,
lacy ceramic ornaments.

🏛 **Rathaus (Stadtge-
schichtliches Museum)**
Markt. 📞 *(039322) 42 153.* ⏱ *15
Feb–Nov 10am–5pm Tue–Sun*

ENVIRONS: A Romanesque
Klosterkirche (abbey) in
Jerichow, 10 km (6 miles)
north of Tangermünde, is the
earliest brick structure of the
region. It was built in the
1150s, for Norbertine monks.
The west towers were com-
pleted during the 15th century. Its austere, triple-nave
vaulted interior is impressive.
There are also many remains
of the former abbey.

**Interior of the former Norbertinenkirche,
in Jerichow, north of Tangermünde**

Dessau

Road map E3. 🐎 *84,400.* ▦ ➔
ℹ️ *Zerbster Str. 2c (0340-204 14 42).*
🎭 *Mosigkauer Konzertsommer.*
ⓦ *www.dessau.de*

DESSAU, ONCE A magnificent city and the capital of the duchy of Anhalt-Dessau, is less attractive today, yet it has some excellent historic sights. In the town centre are some interesting Baroque churches and the **Johannbau**, the remains of a Renaissance ducal residence.

Dessau is also known for the **Bauhaus** complex. Built in 1925 to a design by Walter Gropius, it is the home of the famous art school, which moved here from Weimar. The **Bauhausmuseum** is housed in one of its wings. Nearby, in Friedrich-Ebert-Allee, five of the so-called **Meisterhäuser** – master houses for the Art College professors – have survived World War II. The houses of Lyonel Feininger and Paul Klee are open to the public. Wassily Kandinsky was also a former resident. The **Kornhaus**, on Elballee, restored in 1996, contains a restaurant, café and dance hall.

Many splendid residences set in landscaped gardens were built in 18th- and 19th-century Dessau. In the town centre stands a Neo-Classical palace, **Schloss Georgium**, built in 1780 to a design by Friedrich Wilhelm von Erdmannsdorff. Today it houses a collection of old masters, including works by Rubens, Hals and Cranach.

🏛 **Bauhausmuseum**
Gropiusallee 38. 📞 *(0340) 65 08 250.* ◯ *10am–6pm daily.* 📷

♠ **Schloss Georgium**
Puschkinallee 100. 📞 *(0340) 61 38 74.* ◯ *10am–5pm Tue–Sun.* 📷

ENVIRONS: **Haldeburg**, which is situated on the outskirts of Dessau, has a Neo-Gothic hunting lodge built in 1782–3, and Mosigkau boasts **Schloss Mosigkau**, Princess Anna Wilhelmina's Baroque residence, designed by Christian Friedrich Damm. It contains some excellent examples of 17th-century painting.

In **Oranienbaum**, 12 km (7 miles) east of Dessau, stands a late-17th-century, early-Baroque palace that was built for Princess Henrietta Katharine of Orange by the Dutch architect Cornelius Ryckwaert.

♠ **Schloss Mosigkau**
Knobelsdorfallee 3. 📞 *(0340) 52 11 39.* ◯ *Apr: 10am–5pm Tue–Sun; May–Sep: 10am–6pm Tue–Sun; Oct & 4 Nov: 10am–5pm Tue–Sun.* ● *Dec–Mar.* 📷 📷

Lutherstadt Wittenberg ⓯

Road map E3. 🐎 *55,000.* ▦ ➔
ℹ️ *Schlossplatz 2 (03491-41 48 48).*
🎭 *Wittenberger Stadtfest & Luthers Hochzeit (Jun).*
ⓦ *www.wittenberg.de*

THIS SMALL town, named after its most famous resident, Martin Luther, enjoys a scenic position on the banks of the Elbe River. Its main development took place during the 16th century, under the Great Elector, Frederick the Wise. Wittenberg became the capital of the Reformation thanks to the work of Martin Luther and Philipp Melanchthon, and as such it attracts many visitors. Another famous resident of that period was the painter Lucas Cranach the Elder.

♠ **Schloss Wittenberg**
Schlossplatz. **Museum für Naturkunde und Völkerkunde** (Museum of Natural History and Ethnography) 📞 *(03491) 43 34 920.* ◯ *9am–5pm Tue–Sun.* 📷
Built for Frederick the Wise in 1489–1525, the castle was greatly altered during reconstruction following fire and wartime damage. A museum is housed in the west wing.

The tomb of Frederick the Wise, in Schlosskirche

🔒 **Schlosskirche**
Schlossplatz. 📞 *(03491) 40 25 85.* ◯ *May–Oct: 10am–5pm Mon–Sat, 11:30–5pm Sun; Nov–Apr: 10am–4pm Mon–Sat, 11:30am–4pm Sun.*
Built after 1497, this church was made famous by Martin Luther, who allegedly posted his theses on its door in 1517. The original door no longer exists, but the church contains many interesting tombs, including that of Frederick the Wise, created in 1527 in the workshop of Hans Vischer, as well as modest tombs of Martin Luther and Melanchthon.

Schloss Georgium in Dessau

The market square with Baroque fountain, in Lutherstadt Wittenberg

Luther was married to Katharina von Bora in this church where he also preached, and six of their children were baptised. Inside there is a magnificent Reformation altar (constructed in 1547), the work of father and son Cranach, as well as interesting tombs and epitaphs.

☷ Cranachhaus

Markt 4. ◐ *until further notice.*
This beautiful, early 16th-century Renaissance house once belonged to Lucas Cranach the Elder and was the birthplace of his son, Lucas Cranach the Younger. His studio was located at No. 1 Schlossstraße.

☷ Rathaus

Markt 26. ◐ *until further notice.*
The Renaissance town hall was built in 1523–35, and later twice extended in the 16th century. In its forecourt are two 19th-century monuments: to Martin Luther by Gottfried Schadow and to Philipp Melanchthon by Friedrich Drake.

⛪ Marienkirche

Kirchplatz. 【 *(3491) 40 32 01.*
◐ *May–Oct: 10am–5pm daily;*
Nov–Apr: 10am–4pm daily.
The Gothic church of St Mary with its twin-tower façade was built in stages, between the 13th and 15th centuries.

☷ Melanchthonhaus

Collegienstr. 60. 【 *(03491) 40 32 79.* ◐ *Apr–Oct: 10am–6pm daily; Nov–Mar: 10am–5pm daily.*
This museum is devoted to Luther's closest ally, Philipp Schwarzerd, generally known as Melanchthon.

☷ Lutherhalle

Collegienstr. 54. 【 *(03491) 42 030.*
◐ *same as Melanchthonhaus.*
The museum, which is in the former residence of Martin Luther and his family, also chronicles the work of Lucas Cranach the Elder. It has a large number of documents relating to the Reformation and Luther's translation of the Bible.

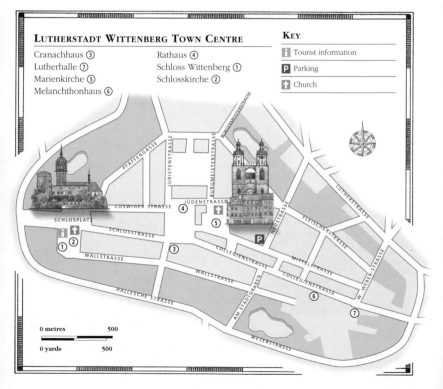

LUTHERSTADT WITTENBERG TOWN CENTRE

Cranachhaus ③
Lutherhalle ⑦
Marienkirche ⑤
Melanchthonhaus ⑥
Rathaus ④
Schloss Wittenberg ①
Schlosskirche ②

KEY

🛈 Tourist information

🅿 Parking

⛪ Church

0 metres   500
0 yards   500

Wörlitz Park ⑯

Wörlitz is a charming, English-style landscaped garden, the first of its kind in continental Europe. It was established in stages, commencing in 1764, for Prince Leopold III, Frederick Franz of Anhalt-Dessau. Many famous gardeners worked in Wörlitz, including Johann Friedrich Eyserbeck and Johann Leopold Ludwig Schoch, as well as the architect Friedrich Wilhelm von Erdmannsdorff. In its centre stands a Neo-Classical palace, holding a collection of paintings. Another interesting collection, including stained-glass paintings, can be admired in the Gotisches Haus.

Floratempel
Modelled on an ancient temple with columns, this Neo-Classical temple served as a music pavilion.

★ **Gotisches Haus**
This pavilion, built in stages, is one of the earliest examples of German Neo-Gothic style. It now houses a collection of stained-glass paintings.

Rousseau-Insel, lined with poplars, was modelled on Ermenonville, the island where the French philosopher was first buried.

Map labels: SCHOCHS GARTEN · Kleines Walloch · Floratempel · Palmebaus · SCHOCHS GARTEN · Gotisches Haus · Nymp... · Rosennsel · Wörlitzer See · Rousseau-Insel · NAUMARKS-GARTEN · Schloss · SCHLOSS-GARTEN · Galerie · Kirche · Pre... · Friedericken-brücke

Rosen-Insel
Rose island was created as one of several artificial islands in the part of the garden designed by Johann Christian Neumark.

Gondolas on the Lake
Romantic gondolas wait by the jetties to take tourists across the lake and to the islands.

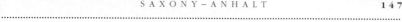

VISITORS' CHECKLIST

📧 🚏 ℹ️ *Neuer Wall 103 (0349 05-202 16); www.woerlitz-information.de* **Schloss** ◯ *Mar & 6 Nov–1 Dec: 10am–4pm Wed–Sun; Apr & Oct–3 Nov: 10am–4:30pm Tue–Sun; May–Sep: 10am–5:30pm Tue–Sun.* 🚫 ♿

Boat Concert
Classical concerts are held on Wörlitz Lake in the evening during the summer season. The audience, just like the orchestra, are all afloat in boats.

Amalien-Insel
In keeping with the fashion of the day, this artificial island, on Großes Walloch lake, has a grotto, which provides a cool resting place.

The Pantheon, built in 1795–6, houses a collection of antique sculptures.

| 0 metres | 500 |
| 0 yards | 500 |

Pantheon

WEIDEN-HEGER

Harderinsel   Großes Walloch   *Amalien-Insel*

NEUE ANLAGEN

oge

Wörlitzer See
The largest of the four lakes, which are all joined by canals, this is prettiest when the water lilies are in bloom.

Stein, a working artificial volcano modelled on Mount Vesuvius in Italy, is currently being renovated.

Stein

★ Synagogue
Built in 1790 and modelled on the Vesta Temple in Rome, the synagogue was gutted by the National Socialists in 1938. It has since been reconstructed.

STAR FEATURES

★ Gotisches Haus

★ Synagogue

SAXONY

....

SAXONY *has a long history and is rich in historic sites. Its capital city, Dresden, ranks among the most beautiful and interesting towns in Germany, despite the devastation it suffered during World War II. The region also boasts the enchanting Erzgebirge Mountains and the glorious scenery of "Saxon Switzerland", where the mighty Elbe river runs amid fantastic rock formations.*

In the 10th century, Emperor Otto I created an eastern border province (margravate) in the area presently known as Saxony. It quickly grew in size as it expanded into neighbouring territories inhabited by the Polabian Slavs. It was divided and part became the Meißen Margravate, ruled by the powerful house of Wettin from 1089. This dynasty's political power increased when it acquired the Saxon Electorate in 1423; subsequently the entire region under their rule became known as "Saxony".

From 1697 until 1763 Saxony was united with Poland, and the Saxon Great Electors, Frederick Augustus the Strong and his son Frederick Augustus II, were also kings of Poland. During this period Saxony flourished, and Dresden became a major centre of the arts and culture until the Seven Years' War (1756–63) put an end to the region's prosperity. In 1806, Saxony declared itself on the side of Napoleon, and the Great Elector acquired the title of King. But Saxony paid a heavy price for supporting Napoleon – following the Congress of Vienna (1815), the kingdom lost the northern half of its territory to Prussia, and in 1871 it was incorporated into the German Empire.

At the end of World War II Saxony was in the Soviet-occupied zone and became part of the GDR in 1949. Since 1990 it has been a state in the Federal Republic of Germany. Saxony is densely populated and in some parts heavily industrialized, but it also has many interesting and unspoiled towns.

The scenic Bastei rocks in Saxon Switzerland

◁ **Kriebstein Castle, overlooking the Zschopau river**

Exploring Saxony

WHEN TRAVELLING in Saxony, a visit to Dresden is a must. Visitors should set aside several days to explore its historic sights and magnificent museums. Dresden is also a convenient base for excursions to the attractive landscapes of the Sächsische Schweiz ("Saxon Switzerland") and further afield – to Bautzen, Görlitz and Zittau, or to the Erzgebirge Mountains, towards Freiberg and Chemnitz. Another town worth visiting, at least for a day, is Leipzig with its historic sights, cultural events, trade fairs and exhibitions.

The Old Town of Bautzen, situated high above the banks of the Spree River

SIGHTS AT A GLANCE

SEE ALSO

• **Where to Stay** pp000-000

• **Where to Eat** pp000-000

0 km   75

0 miles   75

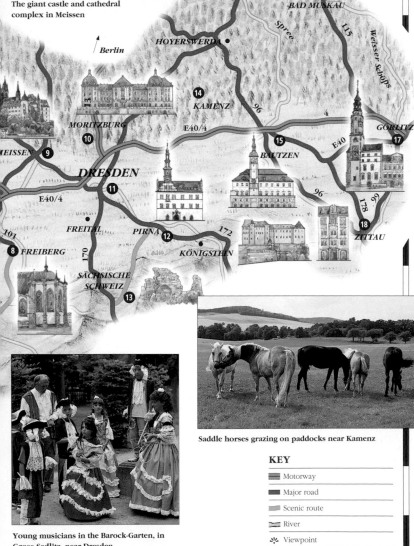

GETTING AROUND

Leipzig and Dresden both have airports, as well as excellent train and road connections with the rest of Germany. The A6 motorway runs west from Görlitz, through Dresden and Chemnitz; the A13 links Dresden with Berlin, and the A14 with Leipzig. Other roads, national and regional, are clearly sign-posted, and all the towns described in this guide can also be reached by local buses.

The giant castle and cathedral complex in Meissen

Saddle horses grazing on paddocks near Kamenz

Young musicians in the Barock-Garten, in Gross-Sedlitz, near Dresden

KEY

▬▬	Motorway
▬▬	Major road
▬▬	Scenic route
➤	River
❀	Viewpoint

Leipzig ❶

GRANTED TOWN STATUS in 1165, Leipzig is not only one of Germany's leading commercial towns, but also a centre of culture and learning, with a university founded in 1409. An important centre for the German publishing and book trade, it is the home of the Deutsche Bücherei, the German national library established in 1912. During the Leipziger Messe (autumn and spring trade fairs), it receives a great number of visitors, and it has much to offer in terms of entertainment, including concerts by the renowned Gewandhaus symphony orchestra and the Thomanerchor boys' choir, which boasts Johann Sebastian Bach as a past choirmaster.

Lofty interior of the Neo-Classical Nikolaikirche

Exploring Leipzig

Most of the interesting sights can be found in the old town encircled by the Ring road, which includes Europe's biggest railway station, the **Hauptbahnhof**, built in 1902–15 to a design by William Lossow and Max Kühne. The heart of musical Leipzig beats in the eastern part of the old town, around Augustusplatz. Here stands the **Neues Gewandhaus** (built 1977–81) and the **Opernhaus** (built 1959–60). The University Tower nearby is being redesigned.

In Nikolaikirchhof stands the **Nikolaikirche** (church of St Nicholas). The present church was built during the 16th century, although the lower sections of its north tower date from the 12th century. It has Neo-Classical furnishings. The **Alte Handelsbörse** (old stock exchange) in Naschmarkt is

an early-Baroque building, designed by Johann Georg Starcke. Built in 1678–87 and reconstructed almost from the ground after World War II, it is now a concert hall. In front of the building stands a monument (1903) to Goethe showing him as a student.

In the market square, near the beautiful Renaissance town hall, is the **Alte Waage**, the old municipal weighhouse, a Renaissance work by Hieronymus Lotter. It was built in 1555 and reconstructed in 1964 following damage in World War II.

The area to the south of the town square is taken up by a block of trade fair buildings. The most interesting are the beautifully restored **Specks Hof** (Reichestraße/Nikohinstraße), the oldest arcade in Leipzig with three enclosed courts built between 1908 and 1929, and **Mädlerpassage**, built in 1912–14, a Modernist commercial building with a three-tier passageway connecting Grimmaische Straße and Naschmarkt. Beneath it is the **Auerbachs Keller**, magnificent, 16th-century vaults, immortalized by Goethe in *Faust* and featuring a room bearing his name. The **Commerzbank** (Klostergasse/Grimmaische Straße) and the **Riquet Café**, a fine Viennese-style coffee house, are attractive Art Nouveau buildings.

Lovers of Johann Sebastian Bach's music will wish to visit **Thomaskirche**, the magnificent late-Gothic

church of St Thomas, built in 1482–96, where Bach was the choirmaster from 1723. It now contains the composer's tomb. Worth noting are the beautiful Renaissance galleries built by Hieronymus Lotter, in 1570. The famous Thomanerchor choir still sings at services on Friday evenings and Saturday afternoons, and organ concerts are held in the churches of St Thomas and St Nicholas during the summer months. Bach is also commemorated with a monument in front of the church (1908). Nearby, the **Bosehaus**, a Baroque 17th-century building, is the home of the Bachmuseum, devoted to the composer.

🏛 **Grassimuseum**
Johannisplatz 5–11. ● *until 2004. Interim Building for* **Museum für Völkerkunde, Museum für Kunsthandwerk** *and* **Musikinstrumentenmuseum** Newmarkt 20. ☎ *(0341) 213 37 19.* 🖥 *www.grassimuseum.de* ⬜ *Library and museum shop with workshops and lectures. Exhibitions 10am–6pm Tue–Sun, 10am–8pm Wed.*
The Grassimuseum complex is being renovated and is currently housed in an Interim Building. Eventually, it will open with three museums: the Museum für Völkerkunde (ethnography) with exhibits from around the world; the Musikinstrumentemuseum (musical instruments) with a magnificent collection, including the world's oldest surviving clavichord, and the Museum für Kunsthandwerk (decorative arts) with its stunning gold and ivory ornaments, as well as the valuable town treasury.

The early-Baroque pavilion of the Alte Handelsbörse, the old stock exchange

The Russische Kirche, a pastiche of the churches in Novgorod

🏛 Deutsches Buch- und Schriftmuseum

Deutscher Platz 1. 📞 *(0341) 227 13 24.* 🕐 *9am–4pm Mon–Sat.*
This museum is devoted to the history of German literature. It contains rare manuscripts and old prints as well as a splendid collection of small printed items such as leaflets.

🏛 Museum der Bildenden Künste

Grimmaische Str. 1–7 until end 2003, then Katharinenstr. (Sachsenplatz). 📞 *(0341) 216 99 14.* 🕐 *10am–6pm Tue & Thu–Sun, 1–9:30pm Wed.*
The Leipzig fine art museum has an excellent collection of German masters, including Lucas Cranach the Elder, Martin Schongauer and Caspar David Friedrich, as well as other magnificent European paintings. There are canvases by Jan van Eyck, Rubens, Frans Hals, Tintoretto and sculptures by Balthasar Permoser, Antonio Canova, Auguste Rodin and others. A room is devoted to the work of Max Klinger.

✝ Russische Kirche

Philipp-Rosenthal-Str. 📞 *(0341) 878 14 53.*
The Russian Orthodox Church of St Alexius was built in 1912–13 to commemorate the 22,000 Russian soldiers who died in 1813, in the Battle of the Nations. The architect, Vladimir Pokrowski, based his design on the churches of Novgorod in Russia.

🏛 Völkerschlachtdenkmal

Prager Str. 📞 *(0341) 878 04 71.* 🕐 *Apr–Oct: 10am–6pm daily, Nov–Mar: 10am–4pm daily.* 🏛
This giant, Teutonic-style monument is the work of Bruno Schmitz. Completed for the centenary of the 1813 Battle of the Nations, which pitched the combined Prussian, Austrian and Russian armies against Napoleon, it now houses a museum.

VISITORS' CHECKLIST

Road map E4. 🏙 *493,000.* ✈ *Flughafen Leipzig–Halle.* 🚆 *Willy-Brandt-Platz.* 📞 *(0341) 224 11 55 & 22 40.* ℹ *Richard-Wagner-Str. 1 (0341-710 42 60).* 🎭 *Leipziger Buchmesse (Mar); Leipziger Orgelsommer (Jul–Aug); Internationaler Johann-Sebastian-Bach Wettbewerb (Jul); Leipziger Jazztage (Oct).* 🌐 *www.leipzig.de*

🏛 Altes Rathaus

Markt 1. 📞 *(0341) 96 51 30.*
Museum für Geschichte der Stadt Leipzig 🕐 *10am–6pm Tue–Sun.*
The grand Renaissance town hall, built in 1556 to a design by Hieronymus Lotter, is now the home of the municipal museum. One room is devoted to Felix Mendelssohn-Bartholdy, who conducted the symphony orchestra from 1835 until his death in 1847.

🏛 Bacharchive und Bachmuseum

Thomaskirchhof 15–16. 📞 *(0341) 913 72 00.* 🕐 *10am–5pm daily.*
This museum houses archives and documents relating to the life and works of the composer, J. S. Bach, as well as a fine collection of musical instruments from his day.

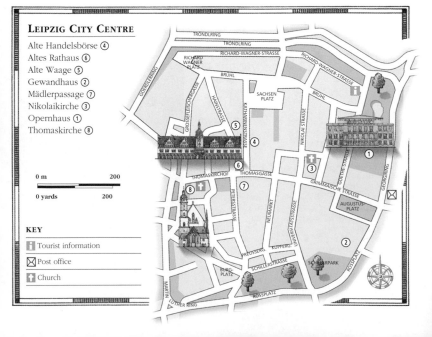

LEIPZIG CITY CENTRE

Alte Handelsbörse ④
Altes Rathaus ⑥
Alte Waage ⑤
Gewandhaus ②
Mädlerpassage ⑦
Nikolaikirche ③
Opernhaus ①
Thomaskirche ⑧

0 m   200
0 yards   200

KEY

ℹ Tourist information
☒ Post office
✝ Church

Doorway of Schloss Hartenfels, with its coat of arms, in Torgau

Torgau ❷

Road map E3. 🏰 *23,000.* 🚉 🚌
ℹ️ *Schlossstr. 11 (03421-71 25 71).*
🎭 *Torgauer Auszugsfest (Jun).*

THIS SMALL town, with its scenic location on the Elbe, was once the favourite residence of the Saxon Electors. Its main square is surrounded by attractive houses of various styles, in particular Renaissance. The Renaissance **Rathaus** (town hall), built in 1561–77, has a lovely semicircular oriel. Other old town attractions include the **Marienkirche**, a late-Gothic church with an extended Romanesque west section. The interior has many original features, including a painting by Lucas Cranach the Elder, *The Fourteen Helpers*, and the tomb of Luther's wife, Katharina von Bora, who died in Torgau.

The main historic building in Torgau is the Renaissance **Schloss Hartenfels**, built on the site of a 10th-century castle. Its courtyard is surrounded by clusters of residential wings, including the late-Gothic Albrechtspalast built in 1470–85, the Johann-Friedrich-Bau (1533–6) with its beautiful external spiral staircase and the early-Baroque west wing (1616–23). The **Schlosskapelle** (castle chapel), which was consecrated by Martin Luther in 1544, is considered to be one of the oldest churches built for Protestants.

Muldetal ❸

Road map E4.

SEVERAL magnificent old castles nestle in the scenic hills at the confluence of two rivers – the Zwickauer Mulde and the Freiberger Mulde. In the small town of **Colditz**, with its timber-frame houses, lovely Renaissance town hall and Gothic church of St Egidien, stands a huge Gothic castle built in 1578–91 on the site of an 11th-century castle. During World War II it was a famous prisoner-of-war camp known as Oflag IVC.

In **Rochlitz**, 11 km (7 miles) south of Colditz, stands another large castle, built in stages from the 12th to the 16th centuries. Travelling further south you will encounter other castles: the **Wechselburg**, a reconstructed Baroque castle featuring a late-Romanesque collegiate church, as well as the Renaissance castle in **Rochsburg**. In the neighbouring Zschopau valley stands the magnificent, oval **Burg Kriebstein**, built in stages and completed in the late 14th century. This fortress houses a small museum and concert hall, and medieval music concerts are held here during the summer.

Zwickau ❹

Road map E4. 🏰
120,000. 🚉 🚌
ℹ️ *Hauptstr. 6 (0375-194 33).* 🎭 *Robert-Schumann-Tage (Jun); TrabiTreffen (Jun).*

AN OLD commercial town, Zwickau flourished in the 15th and 16th centuries. Today it is known for the Trabant cars that were produced here during the GDR era. Almost all the town's attractions can be found in the old town, on the banks of the

Zwickauer Mulde river and encircled by the Ring road. The most important historic building in the town is the **Dom St Marien** (cathedral of St Mary), a magnificent late-Gothic hall-church built 1453–1537. Preserved to this day are its original main altar dating from 1479, the work of Michael Wohlgemut, the grand architectural Holy Tomb of Michael Heuffner, dating from 1507, as well as a Renaissance font and a pulpit of 1538, both by Paul Speck.

Also worth visiting in the old town are the **Old Pharmacy**, the **Schumann-Haus**, the composer's birthplace (1810), and the Renaissance **Gewandhaus** (cloth house), once the seat of the Drapers' Guild and now a theatre.

Chemnitz ❺

Road map E4. 🏰 *260,000.* 🚉
Georgstr. 🚌 *Markt.* ℹ️ *Markt 1 (0371-19 433).*

AFTER WORLD WAR II, when 90 per cent of its buildings had been reduced to rubble, the town was rebuilt in the

Gate of the Renaissance pulpit in the Dom St Marien, in Zwickau

Lew Kerbel's monument to Karl Marx at the Stadthalle in Chemnitz

Socialist-Realist style and renamed Karl-Marx-Stadt. Only a handful of historic buildings escaped destruction. The most interesting among these is the **Schlosskirche**, the former Benedictine abbey church St Maria, on the edge of a lake, built at the turn of the 15th and 16th centuries.

Sights in the town centre include the reconstructed **Altes Rathaus** (old town hall), the Gothic **Roter Turm** (red tower) and remains of fortifications. In the main square is the reconstructed Baroque **Siegertsches Haus,** originally built in 1737– 41 to a design by Johann Christoph Naumann. The new town centre is dominated by the vast **Stadthalle** (city hall) with Lew Kerbel's 1971 monument to Karl Marx. The **König-Albert-Museumsbau** has a museum of natural history and a fine arts collection, including works by Karl Schmidt-Rottluff.

🏛 **König-Albert-Museumsbau**
Theaterplatz 1. ◯ noon–7pm Tue–Sun. 🖾

Augustusburg ❻

Road map E4. 🏠 5,000 🚍
🛈 Marienberger Str. 29b (037291-395 50). **Schloss** ◯ Apr–Oct: 9am–6pm daily, Nov–Mar: 10am–5pm daily.

THE SMALL town is insignificant compared with the vast palace complex bearing the same name. The best way to get there is by cable car, from Erdmannsdorf. This Renaissance hunting palace was built for the Great Elector, Augustus, in 1567–72, on the site of the former Schloss Schellenberg, which had been destroyed by fire. Constructed under Hieronymus Lotter and Erhard van der Meer, it is a symmetrical, square building with towered pavilions at each corner, joined by galleries, gates and a chapel to the east, with an altar by Lucas Cranach the Younger. Today the palace houses several museums devoted to motorcycles, coaches and hunting.

Sächsische Silberstraße ❼

See pp156–7.

Freiberg ❽

Road map E4. 🏠 45,000. 🚉 🚍
🛈 Burgstr. 1 (03731-236 02).
🎪 Bergstadtfest (Jun).

DEVELOPMENT of this mining town was due to the discovery of silver deposits, and Freiberg was granted town status in 1186. It escaped World War II with remarkably little damage.

Today its attractions include the reconstructed old town and many historic buildings, the gem among them being the **Dom St Marien** (cathedral). This late-Gothic hall-church, erected at the end of the 15th century, features a magnificent main portal, the Goldene Pforte, dating from 1225–30. Inside are many original items, such as a tulip-shaped pulpit (1505), two Baroque organs by Gottfried Silbermann and many sculptures and epitaphs.

When visiting nearby Untermarkt, it is worth going to the **Stadt-und Bergbaumuseum** (municipal and mining museum) which explains the history of mining in the area, as well as the collection of minerals at the **Mineralien-und Lagerstättensammlung der Bergakademie**. A stroll along the winding streets will take the visitor to **Obermarkt**, where the 15th-century Gothic town hall, a fountain with the statue of the town's founder and attractive houses can be seen.

Otto of Meißen, founder of Freiberg

🏛 **Dom St Marien**
Untermarkt. **Goldene Pforte**
📞 (03731) 225 98. 🗓 May–Oct: 10 & 11am, 2, 3 & 4pm daily; Nov–Apr 11am, 2 & 3pm daily.
Organ presentation 11:30am Sun.
🏛 **Stadt-und Bergbaumuseum**
Am Dom 1. 📞 (03731) 202 50.
◯ 10am–5pm Tue–Sun. 🖾
🏛 **Mineralien-und Lagerstättensammlung der Bergakademie**
Brennhausgasse 14. 📞 (03731) 39 22 64. ◯ 9am–noon & 1–4pm Wed–Fri, 9am–4pm Sat.

Façade of the Renaissance Schloss Augustusburg

Sächsische Silberstraße ❼

T HE SAXON silver route, through the Erzgebirge
(mineral ore mountains), takes the visitor to
some of the most interesting and scenic places of
the region. Silver was mined here from the 12th
century, and mining traditions have been preserved to this day. Small towns entice visitors with
their interesting parish churches, former mining
settlements, museums and disused mines.

Schneeberg ①
A small mining town, which to this day cultivates
its art and crafts traditions, Schneeberg is also
famous for the St Wolfgangkirche, with an altar
masterpiece by Lucas Cranach the Elder.

Oberwiesenthal ②
This important wintersports resort, close
to the Czech border and at the foot of
the Fichtelberg, offers a ski-jump,
downhill ski runs and toboggan runs.

Annaberg-Buchholz ③
Although the town enjoyed
only a brief spell of prosperity
in the 16th century, its church
from that period, St Annen,
ranks among the most beautiful examples of late-Gothic
architecture in Saxony.

0 km   5

0 miles   5

Wolkenstein

Ehrenfriedersdorf

Olbernhau

Aue

Lauter

Schwarzenberg

Marienberg ⑥
This small town, with its
wonderful Renaissance town
hall, is known mainly for the
production of furniture.

KEY

▬ Suggested route

— Other road

▬ Scenic route

—·· State boundary

❄ Viewpoint

Greifensteine ⑤
Fantastic, craggy rock formations in the north of the
region, shaped like an
amphitheatre, attract rock-
climbers and hill-walkers.

Frohnau ④
The biggest attraction of
this town is its old forge,
featuring the Frohnauer
Hammer, a huge original
hammer that remained in
use until 1904.

TIPS FOR DRIVERS

Length of the route: *55 km
(34 miles).*
Stopping points: *inns and
restaurants in every town.*

Meißen ❾

Road map 4E. 🏞 *36,000.* 🚉 🚌
ℹ *Markt 3 (03521-419 40).*
🎭 *Stadt- und Weinfest (Sep).*
🌐 www.meissen.de

MEISSEN is famous for its porcelain manufacture. Its history began in 929, when Henry I made it the bridge-head for his expansion to the east, into Slav territories. In 966 Meißen became the capital of the newly established Meißen Margravate, and in 968 a bishopric.

This town has retained much of its charm. In the town square is the late-Gothic **Rathaus** (town hall), built in 1472–8, some beautiful Renaissance houses and the **Frauenkirche**, a late-Gothic, 15th-century church boasting the world's oldest porcelain carillon, which was hung here in 1929. It is also worth taking a stroll to St Afra's church, built in the 13th century for the Augustian monks.

⛪ Albrechtsburg

Domplatz 1. 📞 *(03521) 47 070.*
⭕ *Mar–Oct: 10am–6pm daily,*
Nov–Feb: 10am–5pm daily.
⭕ *10–31 Jan.* 🏞

The Albrechtsburg is a vast, fortified hilltop complex with a cathedral and an Elector's palace. The latter was built in 1471–89 for the Wettin brothers, Ernst and Albrecht. Designed by Arnold von Westfalen, its special feature is the magnificent external spiral staircase. From 1710 the palace was used as a porcelain factory. It was restored to its

The Baroque hunting lodge in Moritzburg

former glory in 1864. Huge wall paintings of this period, showing historical scenes, are the work of Wilhelm Römann. The cathedral church of St John the Evangelist and St Donat, built from the mid-13th century to the early 15th century, has some splendid early-Gothic sculptures, an altar by Lucas Cranach the Elder in the Georgskapelle and ducal tombs in the Fürstenkapelle.

🏺 Staatliche Porzellan-Manufaktur

Talstraße 3. 📞 *(03521) 46 87 00.*
⭕ *May–Oct: 9am–6pm daily;*
Nov–Apr: 9am–5pm daily.

The first porcelain factory in Europe was set up in 1710 in the castle and moved to its present premises in 1865. Documents relating to the history of the factory and many interesting examples of its products are on display in the exhibition rooms. Guided tours and demonstrations take the visitor through all the stages of the porcelain manufacturing process.

Moritzburg ❿

Road map 4E. 🚉 ℹ *Schlossallee 3b (035207-85 410).* 🎭 *Kammermusik-festival (Aug); Fischzug (Oct).*

THE FIRST hunting lodge in this marshy region was built in the mid-16th century, for Moritz of Saxony. The present **Schloss Moritzburg** is the result of extensive alterations ordered by Augustus the Strong, directed by Matthäus Daniel Pöppelmann, and carried out in 1723–26. The result is a square building, with four cylindrical corner towers. Much of the interior has survived, including period furnishings and hunting trophies.

Also open to visitors is the 17th-century castle chapel decorated with splendid stucco ornaments. Augustus the Strong ordered the marshes to be drained, and the newly available land to be transformed into landscaped gardens and lakes. The **Fasanenschlösschen** (little pheasant castle) in the eastern part of the gardens features several interesting Rococo interiors, and also houses a zoological exhibition.

At the end of World War II, the German artist Käthe Kollwitz spent the last years of her life in Moritzburg. The house in which she lived and worked is now the **Käthe-Kollwitz-Gedenkstätte**.

⛪ Schloss Moritzburg

📞 *(035207) 8730.* ⭕ *Apr–Oct: 10am–5pm daily; Nov–Mar: 10am–4pm Tue–Sun.* 🏞

⛪ Fasanenschlösschen

⭕ *Closed for renovation.*

The late-Gothic Rathaus in Meißen

Dresden ⑪

ONE OF GERMANY's most beautiful cities, Dresden first gained its pre-eminence in the year 1485, when the Albertine Wettins decided to establish their residence here. The town blossomed during the 18th century when it became a cultural centre and acquired many magnificent buildings. Almost all of these, however, were completely destroyed during the night of 13/14 February 1945, when British and American air forces mounted a vast carpet-bombing raid on the city. Today, meticulous restoration work is in progress to return the historic city centre to its former glory, now with renewed effort because of the damage caused by flooding in 2002.

Front tower of the Baroque Hofkirche

Statue of the Saxon King Johann, in front of the Sächsische Staatsoper

🏛 Sächsische Staatsoper

Theaterplatz 2. 📞 (0351) 49 110. **Tours** 📞 (0351) 491 14 96.

The imposing, Neo-Renaissance building of the Saxon state opera is one of Dresden's landmarks. It is also known as Semperoper after its creator, the famous architect Gottfried Semper, who designed it twice: the first building, erected in 1838–41, burned down in 1869, the second one was completed in 1878. Reconstruction after World War II dragged on until 1985. The opera house was the venue for many world premieres, including *Tannhäuser* and *The Flying Dutchman* by Richard Wagner, as well as many works by Richard Strauss.

In front of the opera, in Theaterplatz, is a monument to the Saxon King Johann, by Johannes Schilling.

🏛 Schinkelwache

Theaterplatz. **Box office** 🚻 📞 (0351) 491 17 05. ◑ 10am–6pm Mon–Fri, 10am–1pm Sat.

This small Neo-Classical building, with its sophisticated lines and its immaculate

proportions, is the work of the famous Berlin architect, Karl Friedrich Schinkel. It was built between 1830 and 1832.

🔒 Hofkirche

Theaterplatz. (Entrance on Schlossplatz). ◑ daily.

This monumental Baroque royal church, with its open-work tower visible from afar, has served as the Catholic Dom (cathedral church) of the Dresden-Meißen Diocese since 1980. The presence of this Catholic church in staunchly Protestant Saxony was dictated by political necessity: in his struggle for the Polish crown, the Elector, Augustus the Strong, was forced to convert to Catholicism. The church was designed by an Italian architect, Gaetano Chiaveri, and built in 1738–51.

The church's interior has two-tier passageways which run from the main nave to the side naves. Rebuilt after damage in World War II, it features a magnificent Rococo pulpit by Balthasar Permoser, a painting by Anton Raphael Mengus entitled *Assumption*

in the main altar, and the vast organ – the last work of Gottfried Silbermann.

🏛 Residenzschloss

Schlossplatz. **Temporary exhibitions** 📞 (0351) 491 46 01. ◑ 10am–6pm Tue–Sun. **Hausmannsturm** ◑ Apr–Oct: 10am–6pm Tue–Sun.

This former residence of the Wettin family was built in stages from the late 15th to the 17th centuries. The most recent extensions were added in 1889 and 1901. A vast, irregular, multi-wing complex of buildings, the castle is not yet fully restored. The wings which have been completed are now used for temporary exhibitions. The Hausmannsturm, a tall tower, affords a great view of Dresden.

Façade of a wing of the Residenzschloss, with *sgraffito* decoration

🚩 Fürstenzug
Augustusstr.

Langer Gang (long walk) is a long building, erected in 1586–91, which connects the castle with the Johanneum. The elegant façade facing the courtyard is decorated with *sgraffito* and has shady arcades supported by slim columns. It provided an excellent backdrop for tournaments and parades. The wall facing the street features the so-called Fürstenzug (procession of dukes) – a vast, 102 m (111 yd)-long frieze depicting the procession of many Saxon rulers. Originally created by Wilhelm Walther in 1872–6

using the *sgraffito* technique, it was replaced in 1907 by 24,000 Meißen porcelain tiles.

🏛 Verkehrsmuseum (Johanneum)
Augustusstr. 1. 📞 (0351) 86 440. ◯ 10am–5pm Tue–Sun.

This late 16th-century Renaissance building, originally designed as royal stables by Paul Buchner, was refurbished in the mid-18th century and housed first a gallery of paintings, later an armoury and a porcelain collection. Since 1956 it has been a museum of transport, with old trams, locomotives and an interesting collection of vintage cars.

Fragment of the Fürstenzug, outside Langer Gang

VISITORS' CHECKLIST

Road map E4 👥 480,000. ✈ Dresden-Klotzsche 15 km (9 miles) from centre. 🚉 Hauptbahnhof, Wiener Platz (0351-461 37 10). 🛈 Prager Str. 10–11 (0351-49 19 20); Schinkelwache, Theaterplatz. 🗾 www.dresden.de. 🚢 Sächsische Dampfschifffahrt, Radebeul, Hertha-Lindner-Str. 10. (0351) 86 60 90. 🚩 Flotten-parade der Sächs. Dampfschiff-fahrt (May); Elbhangfest; Stadtfest (Aug); Weihnachtsmarkt.

⛪ Frauenkirche
An der Frauenkirche.

This giant church, designed by Georg Bähr and built in 1726–43, used to dominate Dresden's skyline, the bold design of its grand hall, topped by a giant dome, enchanting visitors. Burned out in 1945, its shell seemed to have survived intact, only to collapse two days later. Reconstruction work started in 1993; the crypt has been open since 1996. In front of it is a monument to Martin Luther, built in 1885 by Ernst Rietschel.

DRESDEN CITY CENTRE

Albertinum ⑩
Altstädter Wache ③
Brühlsche Terrasse ⑨
Frauenkirche ⑧
Fürstenzug ⑥
Goldener Reiter ⑮
Hofkirche ④
Japanisches Palais ⑯
Johanneum ⑦
Kreuzkirche ⑫
Museum f. Sächs. Volkskunst ⑭
Neues Rathaus ⑬
Residenzschloss ⑤
Sächsische Staatsoper ②
Stadtmuseum Dresden ⑪
Zwinger ①

0 m   100
0 yards   100

KEY

🛈 Tourist information

⊠ Post office

🅿 Parking

⛪ Church

⊞ Brühlsche Terrasse

Brühlsche Terrasse.
Once part of the town's fortifications, this attractive terrace
subsequently lost its military
importance and was trans-
formed into magnificent gardens by Heinrich von Brühl
after whom it is named.
Offering splendid views over
the River Elbe, it was known
as "the balcony of Europe".
There are several great buildings on the terraces – the first
one, seen from Schlossplatz, is
the Neo-Renaissance **Landtag**
(parliament building); next to
it is a small Neo-Baroque building, the **Secundogenitur**
library built for the second
generation of Brühls, now a
popular café; this is followed
by the **Kunstakademie** (art
academy), known as Zitronen-
presse (lemon squeezer)
because of its ribbed glass
dome. Among the statues and
monuments on the terrace arc
works by the sculptor Ernst
Rietschel, the architect Gottfried Semper and the painter
Caspar David Friedrich.

⊞ Albertinum

Brühlsche Terrasse. ▪ (0351) 491 45
90. Gemäldegalerie Neue Meister &
Skulpturensammlung. ◷ 10am–6pm
Fri–Wed.
Originally a royal arsenal, the
Albertinum was rebuilt in its
current Neo-Renaissance style
in the 1880s by Carl Adolf
Canzler. Forty years earlier,
Bernhard von Lindenau had
donated his considerable
fortune to the city to set up a
collection of contemporary
art, which was then housed in
the Albertinum. Today, the
building houses a number of
magnificent collections. That
of the **Gemäldegalerie Neue
Meister**, which was
established in the mid-19th
century, contains paintings

Two Women on Tahiti, Paul Gauguin, 1892, in the Albertinum

from the 19th and 20th
centuries, including works by
the German Impressionists
Lovis Corinth and Max Liebermann, landscapes by Caspar
David Friedrich, canvases by
the Nazarine group of painters and works by European
masters such as Edgar Degas,
Paul Gauguin, Vincent van
Gogh, Édouard Manet and
Claude Monet. The **Skulpturensammlung** is a small
collection of sculptures,
including remarkable
works by Balthasar
Permoser. The most
famous of the
collections is the
Grünes Gewölbe
(green vaults), a
vast collection
of royal
jewels and
other precious items.
This is currently
closed while it is being moved
to the Residenzschloss *(see
p158),* and will reopen in 2005.

♦ Kreuzkirche

An der Kreuzkirche.
▪ (0351) 439 39 20. ◷ Summer:
10am–6pm Mon–Fri; winter: 10am–
4pm Mon–Fri. **Tower** 10am–5pm
Mon–Sat.
The present
Baroque/Neo-
Classical church was
built in 1764–92 to a
design by Johann
Georg Schmidt. To
commemorate the
shelling in World
War II, the interior
has not been fully
restored. The Cross
of Nails from the

ruins of Coventry Cathedral in
England creates a powerful
symbolic link between the
two countries.

⊞ Goldener Reiter

Neustädter Markt.
The **Neustadt** (new town),
on the right bank of the Elbe,
lost much of its former glory
through destruction in World
War II. Visitors may
therefore be sur-
prised to come
across this
glistening,
gilded eques-
trian statue of
Augustus the
Strong in the
middle of a
square, at the end of
the plane tree-lined
Hauptstraße. The
monument, which is
the work of Jean
Joseph Vinache, was erected
in 1736.

**The Goldener Reiter
in the new town**

⊞ Neues Rathaus

Dr.-Külz-Ring.
The giant Neo-Renaissance
new town hall, in the southwest of the old town, was
erected in 1905–1910. Its
round tower (70 m/230 ft),
crowned with a gilded statue
of Hercules, offers the best
view of the old city centre. In
the foyer is a large model of
the city as planned for 2015.

🏛 Museum für Sächsische Volkskunst (Jägerhof)

Köpckestr. 1. ▪ (0351) 803 05 17.
◷ 10am–6pm Tue–Sun.
This Renaissance hunting
lodge on the north bank of

Secundogenitur library on Brühlsche Terrasse

the Elbe was built between 1568 and 1613. Its west wing – the only part that escaped destruction – now houses a museum of ethnography with collections of Saxon culture and traditions, especially from the Erzgebirge Mountains.

🏛 Japanisches Palais

Palaisplatz. **[** (0351) 81 44 50. **Museum für Völkerkunde** (Museum of Ethnography) **○** 10am–5pm Tue & Thu–Sun, 3–8pm Wed. **Landesmuseum für Vorgeschichte** (State Museum of Prehistory) **○** 10am–6pm daily. **Staatliche Naturhistorische Satitilingen Dresden ○** 10am–6pm Tue–Sun.

Originally the Dutch Palais, this three-wing structure was built in 1715. It was extended in 1729–31, by Zacharias Longuelune, for Augustus the Strong's Japanese porcelain collection, at which time the palace changed its name. The porcelain was never actually housed here, however, and for years the palace served as a library.

🚻 Pfunds Molkerei

Bautzner Str. 79. **[** (0351) 80 80 80. **○** 10am–6pm Mon–Thu, Sat, 10am–3pm Fri, Sun.

In the 19th-century part of the Neustadt, with its many bars, galleries, pubs and fringe theatres, stands this old dairy founded by Paul Pfund. Its interior is lined with dazzling, multi-coloured tiles, showing Neo-Renaissance motifs relating to the dairy's products. Today there is a shop which offers hundreds of dairy products, as well as a small bar, where visitors can sample the specialities.

🏛 Kraszewski-Museum

Nordstr. 28. **[** (0351) 804 44 50. **○** 10am–6pm Wed–Sun.

This small museum is devoted to the life of the Polish writer

The Baroque Schloss Pillnitz, Augustus the Strong's summer residence

Józef Ignacy Kraszewski who, having escaped arrest in Warsaw, settled in Dresden in 1853. Inspired by the town's history, several of his novels (for example *Hrabina Cosel*, *Brühl*) are set during the time of Augustus the Strong.

🌿 Großer Garten

City centre.

The history of this great garden goes back to the 17th century, although it has been redesigned several times since. At the park's centre stands an early Baroque palace built in 1678–83 to a design by Johann Georg Starcke. A miniature railway takes visitors to Carolasee, a boating lake. It also stops at the botanical gardens in the northwest section of the park, and at the zoo. The Mosaikbrunnen (mosaic fountain) nearby was designed by Hans Poelzig and built in 1926.

🚻 Blaues Wunder

Loschwitz/Blasewitzer Brücke.

The suspension bridge which spans the River Elbe in the eastern part of the town is painted blue and nicknamed "blue wonder". Built in 1891–3, its main span is 141.5 m (464 ft) long. The bridge leads to Loschwitz, a neighbourhood in a picturesque location amidst hills, which has many attractive villas and small palaces built in the 19th century.

🚻 Schloss Pillnitz

[(0351) 261 30. **Kunstgewerbemuseum Bergpalais ○** May–Oct: 10am–6pm Tue–Sun. **Wasserpalais ○** May–Oct: 10am–6pm Wed–Mon.

This charming summer residence, on the banks of the Elbe, was built in 1720–23 by Augustus the Strong and designed by Matthäus Daniel Pöppelmann. There are two parallel palaces: the Bergpalais (mountain palace) and the Wasserpalais (water palace); the latter can be reached by stairs directly from the river jetty. Between 1818 and 1826 the two palaces were joined by a third one, the Neues Palais. Today the Bergpalais houses a fascinating crafts museum. The main attraction, however, is the large park, laid out in English and Chinese styles, with an orangery and pavilions.

🏛 Karl-May-Museum

Radebeul. Karl-May-Str. 5. **[** (0351) 837 30 10. **○** Mar–Oct: 9am–6pm; Nov–Feb: 10am–4pm Tue–Sun. **●** 24, 25, 31 Dec, 1 Jan.

Radebeul, 5 km (3 miles) northwest of Dresden, is much visited by the fans of Winnteou, a fictional Indian chief, and his friend Old Shatterhon. A museum is devoted to the life and work of the author, Karl May, who lived and died in Radebeul. It also displays May's large collection of Native American costumes and other items.

The suspension bridge across the Elbe River, nicknamed "Blaues Wunder"

The Zwinger

THE MOST FAMOUS building in Dresden is the Zwinger, a beautiful Baroque structure. Its name means 'intermural', and it was built in the space between the former town fortifications. Commissioned by Augustus the Strong, it was constructed in 1709–32 to a design by Matthäus Daniel Pöppelmann, with the help of the sculptor Balthasar Permoser. Its spacious courtyard, once used to stage tournaments, festivals and firework displays, is completely surrounded by galleries into which are set pavilions and gates. Today it houses several art collections.

Mathematisch-Physikalischer Salon
A valuable collection of scientific instruments from different ages, this also features clocks, sextants and globes, including a priceless 13th-century Arabic globe of the sky.

Kronentor
This gate owes its name (crown gate) to the crown positioned on top of its dome.

Main entrance

Allegorical figures crown the balustrades.

★ Porzellansammlung
The porcelain collection holds Japanese and Chinese pieces but its centrepiece is a collection of Meißen porcelain, including parts of the stunning Swan Service made for Heinrich Brühl, to a design by Joachim Kändler.

Glockenspielpavillon
Once known as Stadtpavillon (town pavilion), the name of this building was changed to carillon pavilion when it acquired a carillon with Meißen porcelain bells, in 1924–36 .

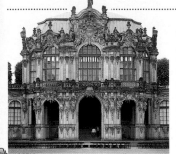

Wallpavillon
A stunning marriage of architecture and sculpture, this Baroque masterpiece is crowned by a statue of Hercules, symbolizing the Elector, Augustus the Strong.

VISITORS' CHECKLIST

Sophienstraße/Ostra-Allee/Theaterplatz. **Porzellansammlung** 🄲 (0351) 491 46 22. ◯ 10am–6pm Tue–Sun. **Mathematisch-Physikalischer Salon** 🄲 491 46 12. ◯ 10am–6pm Tue–Sun. **Rüstkammer** 🄲 491 46 22. ◯ 10am–6pm Tue–Sun. 🄫

★ **Nymphenbad**
This fountain features tritons and nymphs, sculptures, and grottoes, which were popular in the Baroque era.

Courtyard

Gemäldegalerie Alte Meister
This gallery of old masters occupies the wing which was added by Gottfried Semper (see pp166–7).

★ **Rüstkammer**
Exhibited in the armoury are magnificent arms, with the best examples dating from the 16th century, including a suit of armour made for Erik XIV by Eliseus Libaerts in 1562–4.

STAR FEATURES

★ **Nymphenbad**

★ **Porzellansammlung**

★ **Rüstkammer**

Gemäldegalerie Alte Meister

THE DRESDEN gallery of old masters contains what is considered to be one of Europe's finest art collections. Its core consists of the canvases collected by the Wettin family from the 16th century, but the majority of exhibits were purchased at the order of King Augustus II the Strong and his son Augustus III. It was during that time that the gallery was moved to its own premises – first to the Johanneum and later to its present home in the Zwinger, built by Gottfried Semper in 1847–54.

2nd floor

1st floor

Feast of Love (c.1717)
The so-called fête galante *is one of many splendid paintings by Antoine Watteau, depicting a flirtatious group in a park.*

Ground floor

Madonna and Infant Triptych (1437)
This superb small triptych depicting the Virgin Mary with the Holy Infant, St Catherine and the Archangel St Michael, is one of very few works signed by its creator, Jan van Eyck.

Girl Reading a Letter
(c.1659) *This exquisite painting, of a lone woman by the window reading a letter, is among the finest works by Jan Vermeer van Delft.*

Main entrance

★ **Self-Portrait with Saskia**
(c.1635) *This magnificent painting depicting Rembrandt with his wife, Saskia, is considered by some to be a representation of the Prodigal Son of the Bible.*

GALLERY GUIDE

The ground floor has works by Canaletto; the 1st floor has German paintings and 15th to 18th-century European works, and the 2nd floor has 18th-century and Spanish pastels, paintings and miniatures.

Portrait of a Man (c.1635)
This highly expressive portrait, by Diego Rodríguez de Silva y Velázquez, remained unfinished, yet it still captivates with its powerful imagery.

VISITORS' CHECKLIST

Georgtreuplatz 2. 📞 *(0351) 491 46 19.* 🕙 *10am–6pm Tue–Sun.*
🅿 🏩 🚻 ♿ 📷

Tribute Money (c.1516)
Titian depicts the theme of this popular New Testament parable in an unusual way, zooming in on the figures of Christ and a Pharisee who shows Him a coin.

Dresden landscapes and portraits

Miniatures

Sleeping Venus (c.1508–10)
This famous nude was probably painted by Giorgione, but recently experts have come to believe that it was the work of his pupil – Titian.

KEY

- 15th–17th-century Italian painting
- 15th–16th-century German painting
- Canaletto and scenes of Dresden
- 17th-century Dutch and Flemish painting
- 17th-century French painting
- Spanish painting
- 18th-century Italian and French painting
- German, Czech, Austrian, English and Swiss painting
- Non-exhibition space

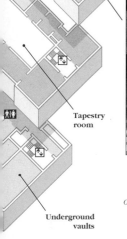

Tapestry room

Underground vaults

★ **Sistine Madonna** (c.1513)
This enchanting picture of the Madonna and Child by Raphael owes its name to St Sixtus's church in Piacenza, for which Pope Julius II had commissioned it.

STAR EXHIBITS

★ **Self-Portrait with Saskia**

★ **Sistine Madonna**

Market square with Renaissance Rathaus (town hall) in Pirna

Pirna ⑫

Road map F4. 🏃 *38,000.* 🚉 🚌
ℹ️ *Am Markt 7 (03501-465 70).*
🔲 *www.touristservice-pirna.de.*
🎭 *Stadtfest (Jun).*

IN THE old town, on the banks of the River Elbe, Pirna has preserved an amazingly regular, chequerboard pattern of streets. Time has been kind to the many historic buildings in this town. Its greatest attraction is the **Marienkirche**, a late-Gothic hall-church with fanciful vaulting designed by Peter Ulrich von Pirna and painted by Jobst Dorndorff, in 1545–6. Inside, an original late-Gothic font and a Renaissance main altar can be seen.

Other interesting buildings are the mid-16th century **Rathaus** (town hall) with its Gothic portals, the beautiful houses in the town square and the ex-Dominican, Gothic church of St Heinrich. **Schloss Sonnenstein**, extended during the 17th and 18th centuries, towers above the old town.

ENVIRONS: 10 km (6 miles) southwest of Pirna is the picturesque **Schloss Weesenstein**, much altered from its Gothic origins until the 19th century. It houses a small museum with an interesting collection of wallpapers.

⛪ Museum Schloss Weesenstein
Müglitztal, Am Schlossberg 1.
📞 *(035027) 54 26.* ⬜ *Apr–Sep: 9am–6pm; Oct–Mar: 9am–5pm.*

Sächsische Schweiz ⑬

SAXON SWITZERLAND, the wonderfully wild region around the gorge cut into the Lusatian mountains by the River Elbe, features stunningly bizarre rock formations and several formidable castles. The best way to explore the area is on foot as many places are inaccessible to cars. Alternatively you can admire the spectacular scenery from a boat, on the Elbe.

Großsedlitz ①
This vast Baroque park, established after 1719 to a design by Johann Christoph Knöffel, continues to delight visitors to this day with its flower beds and numerous sculptures.

Stolpen ⑦
The 35-year old Countess Cosel, one of Augustus II the Strong's mistresses, was imprisoned in this castle, built on rock.

Bastei ⑥
The "bastion" comprises so-called inselbergs – bizarre, tall rock formations that rise abruptly. Connected by footbridges, they offer splendid views.

Weissig

Heidenau   *Pirna*

Teplice

Festung Königstein ②
This powerful fortress was built in the
second half of the 16th century on the site of
a medieval castle, and altered in subsequent
centuries. Spectacular views have made it a
popular tourist destination.

Lilienstein ③
This tall rock, which has
to be climbed on foot,
rewards the visitor with
splendid views of
Festung Königstein.

Burg Hohnstein ④
The castle, which holds
within its walls a medi-
eval building, is now a
museum and one of
Germany's largest
youth hostels.

Bad Schandau ⑤
A small spa that is popular as a
base for walking tours into the
surrounding mountains. A small
railway, the Kirnitzschtalbahn,
takes visitors to a scenic waterfall,
the Lichtenhainer Wasserfall.

Bautzen

Bischofwerda •
6

Gr. Röder

Dürröhrsdorf

Spree

LBSANDSTEIN-

GEBIRGE

7

5

6

3

72

2

4

Schmilka

SÄCHSISCHE SCHWEIZ

KEY

▬	Tour route
▬	Road
▬	Scenic route
※	Viewpoint

0 km   4

0 miles   4

TIPS FOR VISITORS

Length of tour: *41 km (25 miles).*
Stopping places: *inns and
restaurants in every town.*
Suggestions: *walk from the railway at the Lichtenhainer Waterfalls to the Kuhstall (cow stable)
and Barbarine needle rocks.*

Gothic altar from 1513 in St Annen church, in Kamenz

Kamenz ❶❹

Road map F4. 🏛 *16,800.* 🚉 🚌
ℹ *Pulsnitzer Str. 11 (03578 700 01 11).*
🎭 *Hutbergfest (May).*

THE BEST TIME for a visit to Kamenz is the end of May or June, when the rhododendrons that cover the Hutberg (294 m/965 ft high) are in flower. The poet, Gotthold Ephraim Lessing, was born in Kamenz in 1729. Although his house no longer exists, the **Lessingmuseum**, founded in 1929, is devoted to his work.

A great fire destroyed much of the town in 1842, but it spared the late-Gothic **St Marien** church, a four-nave 15th-century structure with Gothic altars and other interesting features. Equally noteworthy for their furnishings are the Gothic ex-Franciscan **St Annen** church and the unusual hall-church **Katechismuskirche**. Originally part of the town's fortification system, it has a row of loopholes on its upper storey. The old cemetery and the Gothic funereal church **Begräbniskirche St Just** are also worth a visit. As is the new **Museum der Westlausitz**, a museum of the local region.

🏛 **Lessingmuseum**
Lessingplatz 1–3. 🅲 *(03578) 380 50.* ◘ *9am–4pm Tue–Fri, 1pm–4pm Sat–Sun.*

Bautzen ❶❺

Road map F4. 🏛 *44,000.* 🚉 🚌
ℹ *Hauptmarkt 1 (03591-4 20 16).*
🎭 *Vogelhochzeit (Jan); Internationales Folklorefestival (Jun).*

THIS TOWN is scenically situated on a high rock overhanging the Spree River valley. Known mainly for its top-security jail for political prisoners during the GDR era, today it enchants visitors with its beautifully reconstructed old town. Many signs are bilingual, German and Sorbian, reflecting the fact that Bautzen is the cultural capital of the Sorbs. The winding streets with their original houses, the city walls, the curiously crooked **Reichenturm** tower and the Baroque town hall in the town square form a very attractive complex. It is also worth climbing the

Impressive Baroque entrance to the Domstift in Bautzen

15th-century **Alte Wasserkunst**, a tower that pumped Spree water up to the town. It is the symbol of Bautzen and offers splendid views.

The cathedral **Dom St Peter** is now used jointly by Catholics (choir) and Protestants (nave). The late-Gothic **Schloss Ortenburg** houses the **Sorbisches Museum**, devoted to Sorbian history and culture.

🏛 **Sorbisches Museum**
Ortenburg 3. 🅲 *(03591) 42 403.* ◘ *Apr–Oct: 10am–5pm Mon–Fri, 10am–6pm Sun; Nov–Mar: 10am–4pm Mon–Fri, 10am–5pm Sun.*

Doorway of the Neo-Renaissance palace in Bad Muskau

Bad Muskau ❶❻

Road map F4. 🏛 *4,170.* 🚌
ℹ *Schlossstr. 3 (035771-504 92).*

BAD MUSKAU, a small town and spa, boasts one of Saxony's most beautiful parks, which has been included in the UNESCO Cultural Heritage list. It was created in 1815–45 by the writer Prince Hermann von Pückler-Muskau. The Neo-Renaissance palace at its centre was destroyed in World War II and is currently closed for reconstruction, but the English-style landscaped park surrounding it, a nature reserve since 1952, is well worth visiting. Its main part, on the northern shores of the Lusatian Neisse River, is in Poland. A joint Polish-German programme, aimed at revitalizing the park, has opened the entire area to visitors from both sides of the border.

Baroque Neptune fountain in Untermarkt, in Görlitz

Görlitz ⓱

Road map F4. 👥 66,000. 🚄 🚌
🛈 Obermarkt 29 (03581-475 70 & 194 33)). 📅 Kultursommer (May–Sep); Dreiklangfestival (Jul/Aug); Straßentheaterfestival (Jul).

THIS BORDER town, whose eastern part, Zgorzelec, has belonged to Poland since 1945, boasts a long history. Its oldest records date back to 1071. Founded in 1210–20, the town flourished in the 15th and 16th centuries. In 1990 an extensive restoration plan was begun, and now visitors can see its historic buildings in their former glory.

The charming houses in **Obermarkt** (upper market), the Renaissance portals and decorations on houses in Brüderstraße and the fascinating **Untermarkt** (lower market), with its vast town hall complex, enchant everyone. The older wing of the town hall, the work of Wendel Roskopf, has an amazing external staircase with Renaissance ornaments, and winds around the statue of Justice.

One of the most remarkable churches is the imposing five-nave, 15th-century **Hauptstadtpfarrkirche St Peter und St Paul** whose Baroque furnishings are among the finest in Saxony. Also noteworthy is the **Oberkirche**, with an original Gothic main altar and 15th-century wall paintings in the side nave. One of Görlitz's curiosities is the **Heiliges Grab** (Holy tomb), built in 1481–1504, a group of three chapels that are replicas of churches in Jerusalem. Görlitz still has remains of its medieval town fortifications with original towers and gates, including the **Kaisertrutz**, a 15th-century barbican, extended in the 19th century and now home to the town's art collection.

ENVIRONS: The small town of **Ostritz**, 16 km (10 miles) to the south, has a charming original Cistercian abbey, St Marienthal (1230). Its red-and-white buildings are to this day inhabited by nuns, who show visitors around and serve food and home-brewed beer.

Zittau ⓲

Road map F4. 👥 28,000. 🚄 🚌
🛈 Markt 1 (03583-75 21 37). 📅 Klosterfest (Ascension); Fest am Dreiländereck (Jun).

ZITTAU is an excellent starting point for excursions into the Zittau Mountains, a paradise for rock-climbers, walkers and nature lovers. The town itself has a splendidly preserved old town, with many historic buildings, such as the beautiful, Baroque **Noacksches Haus** (Markt 2). The Neo-Renaissance **Rathaus** (town hall) was built in 1840–45, to a design by Carl Augustus Schramm. The **Johanniskirche**, designed by Karl Friedrich Schinkel, combines elements of Neo-Classical and Neo-Gothic styles and is an excellent example of Historicist architecture.

ENVIRONS: The charming spa town of **Oybrin**, 9 km (6 miles) south of Zittau, can be reached by narrow-gauge railway. Its attractions include the hilltop ruins of a Gothic abbey, immortalized by Caspar David Friedrich. It is worth timing your visit for a Saturday evening in summer, when you can witness the procession of torch-bearing monks or listen to a concert.

Fountain with a statue of Roland, the French knight, in Zittau

THE SORBS

The Sorbs, also known as the Lusatians or Wends, are an indigenous Slav minority who live in the eastern regions of Saxony and Brandenburg. Their ancestors, the Lusatian Slavs, were conquered by Germans in the 10th century. Although condemned to extermination by the National Socialists, today they enjoy complete cultural autonomy. The revival of their language and traditions is apparent in the bilingual signs in towns.

THURINGIA

THURINGIA *is a beautiful state, with much to entice the visitor. The Thuringian Forest, in the south of the state, is a highland area densely covered with spruce, beech and oak forests, inviting visitors to ramble along its enchanted trails, while Thuringia's medieval abbeys, castles and charming small towns are popular destinations with those who are interested in art and history.*

The Kingdom of Thuring, as it was known in the 5th century, was conquered by the Franks in the following century. The demise of the Thuringian landgraves, who had ruled here for hundreds of years, resulted in the outbreak of the Thuringian War of Secession. It ended in 1264, with most of Thuringia falling into the hands of the Wettin dynasty.

Split into several smaller principalities, the region lost its political might, but driven by the ambitions of many of its rulers, magnificent castles, churches and abbeys were built everywhere. Thanks to enlightened royal sponsors many towns became important cultural centres, such as 18th-century Weimar, whose residents at one time included Johann Wolfgang von Goethe, Friedrich Schiller, Johann Gottfried Herder and Christoph Martin Wieland.

After World War II, Thuringia was initially occupied by the US Army, but it soon passed into the Soviet sphere of influence, and in 1949 it became part of the GDR. In 1952 Thuringia lost its status as a federal state, but this was later restored in the reunited Federal Republic of Germany, in 1990.

The majority of tourist attractions can be found in the southern part of the state. The Thuringian Forest has many popular health resorts and wintersport centres, such as Oberhof. This highland area, cut with deep river gullies, is littered with medieval castles built on steep crags. Many of these are now no more than picturesque ruins, but others, such as the Wartburg, have been completely restored to their former glory, and today delight visitors with their magnificent interiors.

Schloss Belvedere, the royal summer residence in Weimar

◁ The impressive waterfall in Trusetal, in the Thuringian Forest

Exploring Thuringia

A VISIT TO Thuringia is most enjoyable in late summer, when the magnificent forests of the Thuringian Mountains are set ablaze with all the hues of red and yellow as the leaves turn colour, or in spring when verdant green cloaks the trees. Allow at least one day to explore Erfurt, the state's capital city, with a further two days in Weimar. Eisenach, with its magnificent Wartburg castle, is also a must.

Street vendor selling hand-painted Easter eggs in Erfurt

SIGHTS AT A GLANCE

Petersburg fortress in Erfurt

Wolfenbüttel

Halberstadt

NORDHAUSEN

E I C H S F E L D   80

② HEILIGENSTADT

④

Kassel

SONDERSHAUSEN

D Ü N

③ MÜHLHAUSEN

Unstrut

H A I N I C H

Gleßen

E40/4

① GOTHA ⑥

EISENACH   ERFU

FRIEDRICHRODA

Werra

BAD SALZUNGEN   ARNSTA

19   ⑦
THÜRINGER WALD
(THURINGIAN FOREST)

MEININGEN

89

HILDBURGHAUSEN

SEE ALSO

- *Where to Stay* pp479–80

- *Where to Eat* pp509–10

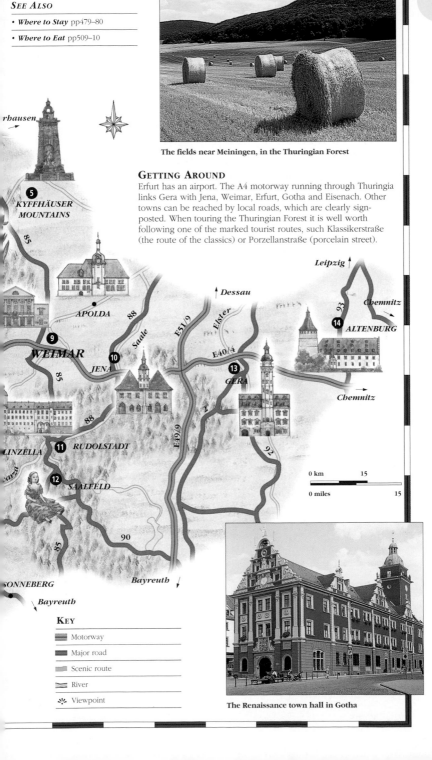

The fields near Meiningen, in the Thuringian Forest

GETTING AROUND

Erfurt has an airport. The A4 motorway running through Thuringia links Gera with Jena, Weimar, Erfurt, Gotha and Eisenach. Other towns can be reached by local roads, which are clearly signposted. When touring the Thuringian Forest it is well worth following one of the marked tourist routes, such Klassikerstraße (the route of the classics) or Porzellanstraße (porcelain street).

KYFFHÄUSER MOUNTAINS

APOLDA

WEIMAR

JENA

Saale

Elster

Dessau

Leipzig

Chemnitz

ALTENBURG

GERA

Chemnitz

RUDOLSTADT

LINZELLA

SAALFELD

SONNEBERG

Bayreuth

Bayreuth

0 km   15

0 miles   15

KEY

	Motorway
	Major road
	Scenic route
	River
	Viewpoint

The Renaissance town hall in Gotha

Eisenach – Wartburg ❶

THE MIGHTY fortress towering above the town is the legendary castle which was probably founded by Ludwig the Jumper, in the late 11th century. Reputedly, it was the setting for the singing contest immortalized by Wagner in his opera *Tannhäuser*. Between 1211 and 1228 the castle was the home of Saint Elizabeth of Thuringia, and from 4 May 1521 until March 1522 Martin Luther found refuge here while he translated the New Testament into German. Major reconstruction in the 19th century gave the castle its old-time romantic character.

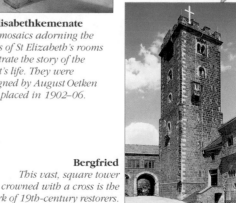

Sängersaal
The singing hall in its present form is the result of restoration work. It was allegedly the scene of the famous Minnesänger (minstrels') contest, from Wagner's opera Tannhäuser.

Landgrafenzimmer
In 1854 the landgraves' chambers in the oldest part of the castle, the Palas, were decorated with paintings depicting the castle's history, by Moritz von Schwind.

Landgrafen-zimmer

★ **Elisabethkemenate**
The mosaics adorning the walls of St Elizabeth's rooms illustrate the story of the saint's life. They were designed by August Oetken and placed in 1902–06.

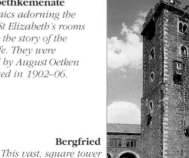

Bergfried
This vast, square tower crowned with a cross is the work of 19th-century restorers.

STAR FEATURES

★ **Elisabethkemenate**

★ **Lutherstube**

Vogtei
In 1872 this building acquired an original oriel window (c.1475), brought here from the Harsdörffersches House in Nuremberg.

VISITORS' CHECKLIST

Road map C/D4. 👥 *44,000.* 🚉
🚌 ℹ *Markt 2 (03691-67 02 60).*
📅 *Thüringer Bachwochen (Mar–Apr).* **Wartburg** 🕿 *(03691) 25 00;*
www.wartburg-eisenach.de ◯
guided tours Mar–Oct: 8:30am–5pm daily (gate closes 8pm); Nov–Feb: 9am–3:30pm daily (gate closes 5pm). 🖼 🚻 👥 🍴 📷

★ Lutherstube
The room where Martin Luther lived and worked for ten months is very plainly furnished and has simple wood-panelling on the walls.

Entrance gate

Neue Kemenate
The so-called "new chambers" were added during the mid-19th century. Today they house an art collection with beautiful sculptures from Tilman Riemenschneider's workshop.

Exploring Eisenach

The town, at the foot of the castle hill, was founded in the middle of the 12th century and played an important political role in medieval times. There are interesting remains of fortifications, dating from the late 12th century, which include a Romanesque gate, the Nikolaitor. The Nikolaikirche nearby, also Romanesque in style, once belonged to the Benedictine Sisters. In the market square is a 16th-century town hall, and in Lutherplatz stands the house where Martin Luther once lived; it is now a small museum of his work.

🔒 Predigerkirche

Predigerplatz 2. 🕿 *(03691) 78 46 78.*
◯ *9am–5pm Tue–Sun.* 🖼
This church, built in honour of Elisabeth von Thüringen shortly after she had been canonized, is part of the Thüringer Museum and has been used for changing exhibitions since 1899. It also houses a permanent exhibition, "Medieval Art in Thuringia".

🏛 Automobilbaumuseum

Rennbahn 6–8. 🕿 *(03691) 77 21 2.*
◯ *10am–5pm Tue–Sun.*
This car museum celebrates the local car manufacturing industry in Eisenach. Its collection includes old BMWs and Wartburgs.

🏛 Bachhaus

Frauenplan 21. 🕿 *(03691) 7 93 40.*
◯ *Oct–Mar: 1–4:45pm Mon, 9am–4:45pm Tue–Sun; Apr–Sep: noon–5:45pm Mon, 9am–5:45pm Tue–Sun.* 🖼
Johann Sebastian Bach, the famous composer, was born in Eisenach in 1685. His birthplace is now demolished, but this small museum nearby is devoted to his life and work.

The Bachhaus and museum, surrounded by a garden

Heiligenstadt ❷

Road map C4. 🏛 *17,500.* 🚉 🚌
ℹ *Wilhelmstr. 50 (03606-67 71 41).*

THIS PLEASANT spa and health
resort, well placed for visiting the landscaped gardens
of Eichsfeld, is worth an extended stop. Heiligenstadt is
the birthplace of Tilman Riemenschneider, an outstanding
sculptor of the Gothic era; it
is also the place where the
poet and writer Heinrich
Heine was baptized in 1825,
at the age of 28.

Heiligenstadt has several
churches worth visiting,
including the Gothic **Pfarrkirche St Marien** with its
original wall paintings dating
from around 1500. Not far
from the church stands the
Friedhofskapelle St Annen,
an octagonal Gothic cemetery
chapel. The town's most
interesting church, however,
is the **Stiftskirche St Martin**,
dating back to the 14th–15th
centuries. It has a well-preserved Romanesque crypt and
an amusing Gothic pulpit,
made in the shape of a book-holding chorister.

Mühlhausen ❸

Road map D4. 🏛 *38,000.* 🚉 🚌
ℹ *Ratsstr. 20 (03601-45 23 21).*
🎭 *Mühlhauser Stadtkirmes (Aug).*
🖥 www.muehlhausen.de

MÜHLHAUSEN is one of
Thuringia's older towns,
with its earliest records dating
back to AD 967. In medieval
times it enjoyed the status of
an imperial free town, which
could explain why it became
the centre of political activities during the 1525 Peasants'

**Part of the well-preserved town
walls surrounding Mühlhausen**

War, led by Thomas Müntzer,
a local clergyman. In 1975, on
the 450th anniversary of the
revolt, the town underwent
restoration, and it delights
visitors to this day with its
beautifully preserved old
town surrounded by **city
walls**, including gates and
towers, which have survived
almost intact.

Mühlhausen's streets are
lined with charming timber-frame houses. It is also worth
stepping into one of the six
Gothic churches in this area.
The **Pfarrkirche Divi Blasii**,
built for the Teutonic Knights,
has 14th-century stained-glass
windows in the presbytery.
The ex-Franciscan **Barfüßer-klosterkirche** (on the Korn-markt) houses a museum
devoted to the Peasants' War.
The huge five-nave 14th-century **Marienkirche**, a hall-church, is one of Thuringia's
largest sacral buildings. It has
a magnificent main portal and
late-Gothic altars. Another
interesting historic structure is
the **Rathaus** (town hall), in a
narrow street between the old
and the new town. This vast
complex was enlarged several
times, from medieval times
until the 18th century.

Sondershausen ❹

Road map D4. 🏛 *23,000.* 🚌
ℹ *Markt 9 (03632-78 81 11).*
🎭 *Tag des Bergmanns (Jun).*
🖥 www.sondershausen.de

SONDERSHAUSEN was the
capital city of the small
principality of Schwarzburg-Sondershausen. The town's
main attraction is the **Schloss**
(ducal palace), a sprawling
building, almost triangular in
shape, built in stages from the
16th to the 19th century. The
palace features some interesting original interiors. Particularly noteworthy are the
Am Wendelstein rooms,
decorated with 17th-century
stucco ornaments, as well as
the Neo-Classical Liebhaber-theater (connoisseurs' theatre,
c.1835) and the Baroque
Riesensaal (giants' hall), a
ballroom with 16 enormous
statues of ancient gods. When
strolling around the palace
gardens it is worth looking at
the **Karussell**, an octagonal
building dating from 1700.

The most interesting Neo-Classical building complex in
town can be found around
Marktplatz (market square).

ENVIRONS: In the **Hainleite**
hills, 4.5 km (3 miles) south
of Sondershausen, stands the
Jagdschloss Zum Possen, once
an 18th-century hunting lodge,
now an inn. The timber-frame
observation tower nearby,
dating from 1781, affords
beautiful views of the district.
Nordhausen, situated 20 km
(12 miles) to the north, is
worth visiting for its attractive
timber-frame houses and its
14th-century cathedral, Dom
zum Heiligen Kreuz, with a
Romanesque crypt.

The extensive façade of the ducal palace in Sondershausen

Monument to Wilhelm I in the Kyffhäuser Mountains

Kyffhäuser Mountains ❺

Road map D4. **ℹ** *Bad Franken-hausen, Anger 14 (034671-71 70).*

THIS SMALL mountain range, which runs along the border between Thuringia and Saxony-Anhalt, is not only picturesque but also shrouded in legends and associated with important historic events.

According to one legend, the Emperor Frederick I Barbarossa found his final resting place in one of the caves. Allegedly, he did not drown during the Crusades, as historic records would have us believe, but is waiting here, in the company of six knights. As soon as his beard is long enough to wind three times around the table, it is said, he will return to save Germany from oppression. On the site of the former imperial palace now stands a giant monument with a figure of Barbarossa and an equestrian statue of Emperor Wilhelm I – the work of Bruno Schmitz, erected in 1891–6.

A small health resort, **Bad Frankenhausen**, nestles at the foot of the mountains. It has a number of Gothic churches and a Renaissance palace, now home to a small museum. Nearby, on the **Schlachtberg** (slaughter mountain), the decisive battle in the Peasants' War took place. Today there is a circular pavilion with a vast panoramic picture of the battle, painted in 1971–5.

Gotha ❻

Road map D4. **🏚** *48,000.* **🚉** **🚌**
ℹ *Hauptmarkt 2 (03621-22 21 38).*
🎵 *Bachwochen (Mar).*
w www.gotha.de

FROM 1640 THE old commercial town of Gotha was the capital of Saxe-Gotha and later of Saxe-Coburg-Gotha Duchy, the dynasty from which Prince Albert, Queen Victoria's husband, descended. The vast ducal palace, **Schloss Friedenstein**, built in 1643–55, towers above the city. This mighty rectangular structure was the first Baroque building in Thuringia. Particularly noteworthy are the ballroom, the palace chapel with the ducal sarcophagi in the crypt and the court theatre, built in 1683. The palace museum houses an art collection including works by famous artists such as Peter Paul Rubens, Anton van Dyck, Frans Hals and Jan van Goyen. The palace

garden is also worth a visit. To the south of the palace stands a Neo-Renaissance building, which was purpose-built for the ducal art collection. Now it houses the **Museum der Natur**, a natural history museum. The Renaissance town hall (1567–77) in the old town is surrounded by a number of interesting houses.

Gotha played an important role in the German workers' movement: the Socialist Workers' Party (today's SPD), was founded here in 1875. The conference hall has been reconstructed and now houses the **Gedenkstätte der Deutschen Arbeiterbewegung** (memorial to the German workers' movement).

⚜ Schloss Friedenstein
📞 *03621-82 340.* **⬜** *May–Oct: 10am–5pm Tue–Sun; Nov–Apr: 10am–4pm Tue–Sun.*
🏛 Gedenkstätte der Deutschen Arbeiterbewegung
Am Tivoli 3. **📞** *(03621) 70 41 27.*
⬜ *only by prior arrangement.*

Doorway of the Renaissance town hall on the Hauptmarkt, in Gotha

Thüringer Wald (Thuringian Forest) ❼

Narrow, winding roads lead through the mountains, which are densely covered with spruce forests. Small towns, charming spas and wintersports resorts nestle in the valleys, while the ruins of once fearsome castles occupy the hilltops. This is prime walking country, and Gotha is the best starting point for a walking holiday. For a longer hike, stop in Ilmenau, and from there follow the upward trail marked G, to a hunters' shelter and a foresters' lodge.

Friedrichroda ①
The Neo-Gothic Reinhardsbrunn castle in Friedrichroda was the place where Queen Victoria met her fiancé, Prince Albert von Sachsen-Coburg-Gotha, in 1840.

Drei Gleichen ⑨
This name, meaning "three of the same", refers to three castles – Mühlburg and Burg Gleichen have stood in ruins for centuries, but the third castle, Wachsenburg, has survived and now serves as a hotel.

Arnstadt ⑧
This picturesque town, once the home of Johann Sebastian Bach, features a town hall in the Mannerist style, dating from the late 16th century. Other places of interest are an early-Gothic church and a Baroque palace which is now home to a wax museum.

Eisenach

Gotha

Bad Salzingen

Zella-Mehlis

Meiningen

Hildburghausen

Tips for Tourists

Length: *150 km (90 miles).*
Stopping places: *inns and restaurants in every town.*
Suggestions: *walk along the Goethe-Wanderweg trail, from Ilmenau. Train journey by Waftbahn, from Gotha via Friedrichroda to Tabarz.*

Schmalkalden ③
This charming little town, packed with timber-frame houses, attracts visitors to the Wilhelmsburg, its Renaissance palace, and to Neue Hütte, an interesting old smelting plant dating from 1835.

Trusetal ②
The magnificent waterfall in Trusetal, the work of human hands, was built in the mid-19th century. Another site worth visiting is the Marienglashöhle, an unusual crystal grotto.

0 km   75

0 miles   75

Oberhof ④
This is a popular winter-sports resort, with excellent ski-jumps. In the summer it is worth visiting the Rennsteiggarten, the town's botanical gardens with a vast collection of alpine plants.

Suhl ⑤
Famous from the 16th century as a centre of arms manufacture, Suhl's history can today be gleaned in the local Waffenmuseum (armaments museum).

Ilmenau ⑥
This small university town, teeming with life, is the starting point of the so-called Goethe-Wanderweg, a walking trail leading to all the places where the famous poet once stayed.

Paulinzelle ⑦
The 12th-century Romanesque abbey, now in ruins, was once a home for Benedictine monks, but it was later abandoned during the Reformation.

KEY

▮ Suggested route

═ Other road

▮ Scenic route

🌟 Viewpoint

Erfurt ❽

THE THURINGIAN capital, Erfurt, is also the oldest town in the region – its earliest historic records date from AD729, and in AD742 a bishopric was founded here. As an important trading post between east and west, the town grew quickly. Erfurt University was founded in 1392; it became a stronghold for radical thought, and Martin Luther was one of its distinguished pupils. Until the 17th century, Erfurt was famous for its red dyes extracted from the madder root; in the 18th century the town became a horticultural centre, and to this day it hosts important horticultural exhibitions.

Picturesque half-timbered houses, lining the Krämerbrücke

Exploring Erfurt
The town, on the banks of the river Gera, is dominated by two hills. On the higher one, **Petersberg**, stands a huge fortress surrounding a Romanesque church, while the lower **Domberg** has two churches, the **Dom St Marien** and the **St Severikirche**. From the Domplatz, at the foot of the hill, a row of narrow streets leads to Fischmarkt. If you cross the river here, you will get to Erfurt's old commercial district and its market square, the Anger.

🔒 Dom St Marien
Domberg. 🔲 *(0361) 646 12 65.* ⬜ *May–Oct: 2–4pm Sun, 9–11:30am & 12:30–5pm Mon–Fri, 9–11:30am & 12:30–4:30pm Sat; Nov–Apr: 10–11:30am & 12:30–4pm Mon–Sat, 2–4pm Sun.* **Maria Gloriosa** ⬤ *closed for renovation work until 2004.* 📷
The wide stairs leading from Domplatz to the main entrance of the cathedral provide a good view over the 14th-century Gothic presbytery, which is supported by a massive vaulted substructure, known as the Kavaten. The main body of the cathedral dates from the 15th century,

but its huge towers are the remains of an earlier Romanesque building. **Maria Gloriosa**, a huge bell 2.5 m (8 ft) in diameter, hangs in the centre tower. Cast by Gerhard Wou in 1497, it is one of the largest bells in the world. The church interior has well preserved Gothic decorations and rich furnishings. Particularly valuable are the 14th- and 15th-century stained-glass

Rich furnishings in the Gothic interior of Dom St Marien

windows, the Gothic stalls (c.1370) and Wolfram, a Romanesque bronze candelabra, (c.1160), shaped like a man.

🔒 St Severi-Kirche
Domberg. ⬜ *10am–12:30pm, 1:30–4pm Tue–Fri.*
This five-nave Gothic hall-church, next to the cathedral, dates from the late 13th and early 14th century. Inside it has the Gothic sarcophagus of St Severus, from about 1365, a huge font of 1467 and interesting Gothic altars.

⛪ Fischmarkt
This small market square, with its Neo-Gothic town hall (1870–74), is surrounded by houses dating from various periods, including the 16th-century Renaissance buildings **Zum Breiten Herd** (No. 13, To the Wide Hearth) and **Zum Roten Ochsen** (No. 7, To the Red Ox). On the streets off the market square are three Gothic churches: Michaeliskirche, opposite the ruins of the late-Gothic university buildings, the twin-nave Allerheiligenkirche (late 13th to early 14th century), and the ex-Dominican Predigerkirche.

⛪ Krämerbrücke
The "merchant bridge" which spans the River Gera is one of Erfurt's most interesting structures. The present stone bridge was built around 1325. It is lined by 32 houses with shops, dating mainly from the 17th to 19th centuries, which replaced its 60 original medieval houses. On its eastern viaduct stands Ägidienkirche, a 14th-century Gothic church.

🔒 Augustinerkloster– Augustinerkirche
Augustinerstr. 10. 🔲 *(0361) 576 60 10.* 📷 *Apr–Oct: 10am–noon & 2–4pm Mon–Sat; Nov–Mar: 10am–noon Tue–Sat.* 📷 *Sun after mass.* 📷
This early Gothic church was built for Augustinian monks at the end of the 13th century. Particularly noteworthy are its original Gothic stained-glass windows. In the neighbouring monastery, the reconstructed cell where Martin Luther lived as a monk can be admired.

Fischmarkt, surrounded by houses from various periods

VISITORS' CHECKLIST

Road map D4. 🏃 *200,000*.
✈ *Flughafenstraße 4
(0361-65 60)*. 🚌 *Am
Bahnhofsplatz*.
🚌 *Bürgermeister-Wagner-
Straße*. ℹ *Benediktsplatz 1
(0361-66400)*.
W *www.erfurt.de*
🎭 *Krämerbrückenfest (June),
Petersbergfest (September)*.

🏛 Stadtmuseum
Johannesstr. 169. ☎ *(0361) 655 56
50.* ◯ *10am–6pm Tue–Sun.*
Erfurt's history museum is
housed in a beautiful, late-
Renaissance building called
Zum Stockfisch (To the
Dried Cod), built in 1607.

🏮 Anger
Now pedestrianized, this is a
market square and Erfurt's
main shopping street, lined
with attractive 19th-century
mansions and commercial
premises. There are two
Gothic churches: **Kaufmanns-
kirche** and **Reglerkirche**,
with a huge Gothic altar
dating from around 1470. At
Nos. 37 and 38 there is the
Dacherödensches Haus, a
complex of beautiful Renaissance buildings.

🏛 Angermuseum
Anger 18. ☎ *(0361) 55 45 60.*
◯ *10am–6pm Tue–Sun.*
Barfüßerkirche Barfüßerstr. 20
☎ *(0361) 64 64 10 10.* ◯ *Apr–Oct:
10am–1pm & 2–6pm Tue–Sun.* 🎫
The museum, housed in a
Baroque building, has a
collection of decorative and
sacred arts including paintings
by Lucas Cranach the Elder,
and 19th- and 20th-century
German works. One of its
rooms is decorated with
Expressionist murals (1923–4)
by Erich Heckel. The
medieval section is in the
presbytery of the **Barfüßerkirche**, a former Franciscan
church that was destroyed
during World War II.

🏛 EGA and
Gartenbaumuseum
Cyriaksburg, Gothaer Str. 38.
☎ *(0361) 223 22 10.* ◯ *9am–6pm
daily.* **Museum** ☎ *(0361) 22 39 90.*
◯ *10am–6pm Tue–Sun.* 🎫
On the hill around Erfurt's
ruined castle (c.1480) are the
grounds of the International
Garden Show *(Erfurter
Gartenausstellung International)*. As well as exhibition
halls, show gardens and palm
houses, there is a museum of
horticulture and apiculture
(breeding and care of bees).

ENVIRONS: Molsdorf, 10 km
(6 miles) to the southeast, has
a lovely 16th-century Baroque
palace set in landscaped
parkland, with a museum.

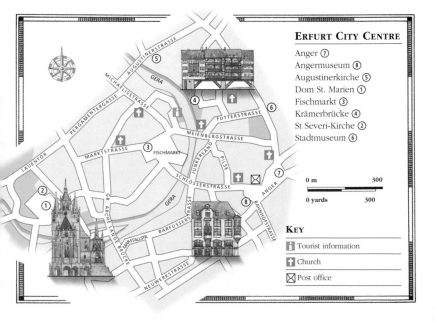

ERFURT CITY CENTRE

0 m   300
0 yards   300

KEY

ℹ Tourist information

✝ Church

☒ Post office

Weimar **9**

HAD IT NOT BEEN for the enlightened sponsorship of its rulers, Weimar would have become just another residential town in Thuringia. The town flourished, particularly under Duke Carl Augustus and his wife Anna Amalia, when Goethe, Schiller and Herder lived here. Famous 19th- and 20th-century residents included Franz Liszt, Richard Strauss, Friedrich Nietzsche and many distinguished writers and artists associated with the Bauhaus School, which was founded here in 1919. It also gave its name to the Weimar Republic, the democratic German State, lasting from World War I to 1933.

Exploring Weimar

Weimar is relatively small and most of its tourist attractions are near the town centre, on the left bank of the Ilm River. In the north of the centre are the Neues Museum and the Stadtmuseum (municipal museum). Many interesting buildings can be found around Theaterplatz, from where you proceed towards the Markt to visit the ducal palace. In the south of the centre are the former homes of Goethe and Liszt.

🏛 Neues Museum

Rathenauplatz. **(** *(03643) 54 59 63.* ◯ *Apr–Oct: 10am–6pm Tue–Sun; Nov–Mar: 10am–4:30pm Tue–Sun.*
This Neo-Renaissance building, once the Landesmuseum (regional museum), was transformed into a gallery in 1999. It displays modern art, with its central collection made up of works by Paul Maenz.

🏛 Stadtmuseum

Karl-Liebknecht-Str. 5–9. **(** *(03643) 90 38 68.* ◯ *Apr–Oct: 10am–6pm Tue–Sun; Nov–Mar: 10am–5pm Tue–Sun.*
This museum is devoted to the history of Weimar, but it also holds an interesting natural history collection. It is housed in a Neo-Classical house, built in the late 18th century for the publisher Justin Bertuch.

St Peter und St Paul, also known as the Herderkirche

▩ Deutsches Nationaltheater

Theaterplatz 2. **(** *(03643) 75 53 01.*
The present Neo-Classical building, built in 1906–7 to a design by Heilmann & Littmann, is the third theatre to stand on this site. Famous conductors who worked here include Franz Liszt and Richard Strauss, and it was also the venue for the world premiere of Wagner's *Lohengrin*. In 1919 the National Congress sat in the Nationaltheater and passed the new constitution for the Weimar Republic. In front of the theatre is a monument to Goethe (who founded the theatre) and Schiller, by the sculptor Ernst Rietschel (1857).

🏛 Bauhaus-Museum

Theaterplatz. **(** *(03643) 54 59 61.* ◯ *Apr–Oct: 10am–6pm Tue–Sun; Nov–Mar: 10am–4:30pm Tue–Sun.* ▨
This museum is devoted to the famous art school, which was founded in Weimar in 1919, moved to Dessau in 1925 *(see p144)* and later, in 1933, to Berlin *(see p84).*

🏛 Wittumspalais und Wieland-Museum

Theaterplatz. **(** *(03643) 54 53 77.* ◯ *Apr–Sep: 9am–6pm Tue–Sun; Oct–Mar: 10am–4pm Tue–Sun.* ▨
The Dowager Duchess Anna Amalia lived in this Baroque palace, designed by Johann Gottfried Schlegel and built in 1767–9. Visitors can admire fine interiors and mementoes of the Enlightenment figure Christoph-Martin Wieland.

🏛 Schillerhaus

Schillerstr. 12. **(** *(03643) 54 53 50.* ◯ *Apr–Sep: 9am–6pm Wed–Mon; Oct–Mar: 9am–4pm Wed–Mon.* ▨
The museum is in the house where Friedrich Schiller wrote *Wilhelm Tell* (1804) and spent the last years of his life.

✛ St Peter und St Paul

Herderplatz. **(** *(03643) 85 15 18.* ◯ *Easter–9 Nov: 10am–noon & 2–4pm Mon–Sat, 11am–noon & 2–3pm Sun; 10 Nov–Easter: 11am–noon & 2–3pm Mon–Sat, 2–3pm Sun.*
This late-Gothic hall-church has Baroque furnishings and an original altar painted by the Cranachs. It is also known as the Herderkirche, after the poet who preached here.

🏛 Krims-Krackow-Haus

Jakobstr. 10. **(** *(03643) 54 53 83.* ◯ *9am–6pm Tue–Sun.* ▨
This Renaissance house, which was extended in the late 18th century, is now the Herder-Museum and a literary centre.

♜ Schloss

Burgplatz 4. **Schlossmuseum** **(** *(03643) 54 59 60.* ◯ *Apr–Oct: 10am–6pm Tue–Sun; Nov–Mar: 10am–4:30pm Tue–Sun.* ▨
This vast ducal castle was rebuilt in the Neo-Classical style for Duke Carl Augustus. It has original interiors and fine paintings by the Cranachs and Peter Paul Rubens.

The Schloss in Burgplatz, with its tall Renaissance tower

Picturesque Baroque summer residence known as Schloss Belvedere

VISITORS' CHECKLIST

Road map D4. 🏠 *62,000.* 🚉 *Schopenhauerstr.* 🚌 *Washingtonstr.* ℹ️ *Markt 10 (03643-24 000).* 🌐 *www.weimar.de* 🎭 *Bach-Tage (Mar), Shakespeare-Tage (Apr), Kunstfest (Aug/Sep), Fest an Goethes Geburtstag 28 Aug), Liszt-Tage (Oct), Zwiebelmarkt (Oct).*

♣ Herzogin-Anna-Amalia Bibliothek

Platz der Demokratie 1. 📞 *(03643) 54 52 00.* ⏰ *call for times.*

This former Mannerist palace, also known as Grünes Schloss (green castle), was converted into the duchess' library, in 1761–6. Its oval Rococo interior is one of the finest of its type in Europe.

♣ Schloss Belvedere

📞 *(03643) 54 54 00.* ⏰ *Apr–mid-Oct: 10am–6pm Tue–Sun; mid-Oct–Nov: 10am–4:30pm Tue–Sun.* ♿

This ducal summer residence, which was built 1724–32 in Belvedere Park, has a fine collection of decorative art from the Rococo period, and a collection of vintage vehicles.

🏛 Goethe-Museum

Frauenplan 1. 📞 *(03643) 54 53 00.* ⏰ *as Wittumspalais opposite.* ♿

This house was presented to Goethe by the Duke Carl Augustus. It was here that the writer studied and wrote his most famous work, *Faust.* Today the museum shows items associated with Goethe and other Enlightenment poets from Weimar.

♣ Goethes Gartenhaus

Park an der Ilm. ⏰ *as Wittumspalais opposite.* ♿

Goethe's first home in Weimar, and later his summer house, this small villa stands in the pleasant park alongside the River Ilm which Goethe helped design.

🎹 Liszt-Haus

Marienstr. 17. 📞 *(03643) 54 53 88.* ⏰ *Apr–Sep: 9am–1pm & 2–6pm Tue–Sun; Oct–Mar: 10am–1pm & 2–4pm Tue–Sun.* ♿

Franz Liszt lived here in 1869–86, while he composed the *Hungarian Rhapsody.* His apartment and the room in which he worked have been preserved to this day.

ENVIRONS: Buchenwald, 8 km (5 miles) north of Weimar, was the site of a concentration camp set up by the Nazis. In 1937–45, over 54,000 people were killed here. It is now a place of remembrance, a museum and a documentation centre.

🏛 Buchenwald

📞 *(03643) 43 02 00.* ⏰ *May–Sep: 9am–6pm Tue–Sun; Oct–Apr: 8:30am–5pm Tue–Sun.*

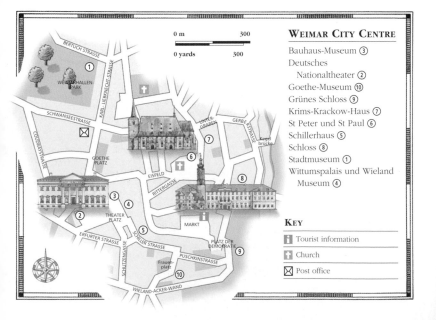

WEIMAR CITY CENTRE

KEY

ℹ️ Tourist information

✝ Church

⊠ Post office

The modest Gothic town hall on Marktplatz, in Jena

Jena ⑩

Road map D4. 🏠 *100,000.* 🚉 🚌
ℹ️ *Johannisstr. 23 (03641-80 64 00).*
🌐 *www.jena.de*

J ENA IS FAMOUS for the world-renowned Carl-Zeiss–Jena Optical Works and its university, founded in 1558. One of the most important schools in Germany, its former tutors included Schiller, Fichte and Hegel. The oldest university building is the **Collegium Jenense**. The main building was built by Theodor Fischer in 1905–8. The complex includes a 120-m (394-ft) cylindrical tower block, completed in 1972 and known as the "phallus Jenensis".

In the town's main square, Marktplatz, stands the late-Gothic **Rathaus** (town hall), dating from the early 15th century. Once every hour, a figure known as the Schnapphans tries to catch a ball, a symbol of the human soul. The Gothic church of **St. Michael** nearby was built in the 15th and the 16th centuries. The **Stadtmusem Alte Göhre** has an interesting collection of regional history. In Unterer Markt the **Romantikerhaus** is worth a visit; formerly the home of Johann Gottlieb Fichte, it now houses a museum devoted to the Romantic period.

Also worth visiting are the fascinating **Optisches Museum** on the history of the Carl Zeiss Works and the **Zeiss-Planetarium**, the world's oldest of its type. In the north is the **Goethe-Gedenkstätte**, a museum devoted to Goethe's work as poet, politician and scientist.

🏛 **Stadtmuseum Göhre**
Markt 7. 📞 *(3641) 359 80.*
◯ *10am–5pm Tue & Thu–Sun, 10am–6pm Wed.*
🏛 **Romantikerhaus**
Unterer Markt 12A. 📞 *(03641) 44 32 63.* ◯ *10am–1pm & 2–5pm Tue–Sun.*
🏛 **Optisches Museum**
Carl-Zeiss-Platz 12. 📞 *(03641) 44 31 65.* ◯ *10am–4:30pm Tue–Fri, 11am–5pm Sat.*
Historical Zeiss-Workshop 📷
11:30am Sat.

ENVIRONS: Dornburg, 12 km (8 miles) to the northeast, has three palaces: the Altes Schloss, a Gothic castle transformed in the Renaissance; the Renaissanceschloss (1539–47) and the charming Rokokoschloss (1736–41).

Rudolstadt ⑪

Road map D4. 🏠 *28,000.* 🚉 🚌
ℹ️ *Marktstr. 57 (03672-42 45 43).*
🎭 *Tanz-und Folk Fest (Jul).*

A LTHOUGH RUDOLSTADT has the Gothic-Renaissance St Andreas church, a fascinating 16th-century town hall and some historic houses in the old town, tourists come here mainly to see majestic **Schloss Heidecksburg**, a vast palace perched on a hill. Its present form is mainly the result of reconstruction work carried out in the mid-18th century by Johann Christoph Knöffel and Gottfried Heinrich Krone. Inside are some beautifully arranged Rococo

Baroque Schloss Heidecksburg towering over Rudolstadt

state rooms. The museum also holds a splendid porcelain collection (much of it locally manufactured), a gallery of paintings and the so-called Schiller's Room. From the castle there are fantastic views of the Schwarza valley.

♣ **Schloss Heidecksburg**
Schlossbezirk 1. 📞 *(03672) 42 90 22.* ◯ *10am–6pm Tue–Sun.*

Entrance gate to the 11th-century Schloss Ranis, near Saalfeld

Saalfeld ⑫

Road map D4. 🏠 *34,000.* 🚉 🚌
ℹ️ *Am Markt 6 (03671-339 50).*

S AALFELD FLOURISHED in the 14th–16th centuries. From 1680 it was the seat of the Duchy of Sachsen–Saalfeld, and the magnificent Baroque **Schloss**, built between 1676 and 1720, dates from this period. The former palace chapel, now used as a concert hall, is particularly noteworthy. Also worth visiting is the **Johanniskirche**, a late-Gothic hall-church with interesting furnishings, a valuable Gothic Holy Tomb and the sculpted life-size figure of John the Baptist, carved by Hans Gottwalt, a student of Tilman Riemenschneider.

Another interesting building in Saalfeld is the early-Renaissance **Rathaus** (town hall), built in 1529–37. The town also has remarkably well preserved medieval town fortifications with gates and towers. In the southern part of the town stands the **Hoher Schwarm**, ruins of a Gothic castle from the 13th century.

In Garnsdorf, on the outskirts of Saalfeld, are the **Feengrotten,** much-visited grottoes created by both natural and human activity. From the mid-16th century until 1846 alum slate was mined in this cave, called "Jeremiasglück" (Jeremiah's good fortune). It was finally closed due to humidity, and the dripping water has since created some astonishingly colourful stalagmites and stalactites.

♣ Feengrotten
Garnsdorf. ☐ *Dec–Feb: 10am–3:30pm daily; Mar–Oct: 9am–5pm daily; Nov: 10am–3:30pm Sat–Sun.*

ENVIRONS: From Saalfeld it is worth taking a trip to the Hohenwarte-Talsperre, an artificial lake and paradise for watersports enthusiasts. **Schloss Ranis,** a scenic hilltop castle, was probably built in the 11th century for an emperor. Later it became the seat of the Thuringian landgraves, Meißen margraves and the counts of Schwarzburg. Now it houses a museum of the region's natural history.

Gera ⑬

Road map D4. 🏙 121,000. 🚉 🚌
🛈 *Heinrich Str. 31–35 (0365-800 70 30).* 🎭 *Geraer Höhlerfest (Sep).*

T HE SECOND largest town in Thuringia, Gera is not very impressive at first sight, although it has many attractions, including a picturesque **Rathaus** (town hall) whose oldest, Renaissance part dates from 1573–6. The Geraer Elleblon, on the right-hand side of the entrance, is a unit of measurement equal to 57 cm (22 in). A short distance from the market square, in Nikolaiberg, you will find the **Salvatorkirche.** This Baroque church received its Secession-style interior in 1903, after a fire. The theatre (1900–02) was designed in the same style, by

Picturesque Altenburg Castle complex

Heinrich Seeling. The Küchengarten (kitchen garden) surrounds the ruins of **Schloss Osterstein** of which only the Baroque orangerie remains. It now houses the **Kunstsammlung,** with paintings by Lucas Cranach the Elder, Max Liebermann and others.

Otto Dix, a leading artist of the *Neue Sachlichkeit,* was born in Gera, and his birthplace has been turned into the **Otto-Dix-Haus.**

♠ Kunstsammlung
Küchengartenallee 4. 📞 *(0365) 832 21 47.* ☐ *1–8pm Tue, 10am–5pm Wed–Fri, 10am–6pm Sat & Sun.*

🏛 Otto-Dix-Haus
Mohrenplatz 4. 📞 *(0365) 832 49 27.* ☐ *1–8pm Tue, 10am–5pm Wed–Fri, 10am–6pm Sat & Sun.*

The multi-coloured Renaissance doorway of the Rathaus in Gera

Altenburg ⑭

Road map E4. 🏙 45,000. 🚉 🚌
🛈 *Moritzstr. 21 (03447-59 41 74).* 🎭 *Skatbrunnenfest (May); Musikfestival (Jun/Jul); Altstadtfest (Oct).*

I N GERMANY, Altenburg is known as "Skatstadt", the town of skat, a traditional and very popular card game. But there is more to Altenburg than the game; it also has some fascinating historic remains. The **Schloss** (ducal castle), which towers over the old town, has a 10th-century tower, reconstructed mainly in the Baroque style. Today the castle houses the **Spielkartenmuseum** (museum of playing cards). The late-Gothic castle church is also worth seeing. It has rich Baroque furnishings and an organ which was played by the composer Bach. Next to the castle gardens is the **Lindenau-Museum,** with Augustus von Lindenau's collection of 16th–20th century paintings and sculptures, including works by Simone Martini, Fra Angelico, Auguste Rodin, Ernst Barlach and Max Liebermann. The old town, at the foot of the hill, has a beautiful Renaissance town hall with an enormous octagonal tower. In Brühl Platz is a fountain and the figures of skat players, as well as the Baroque **Seckendorffsche Palais** and the Renaissance chancellery.

🏛 Schloss und Spielkartenmuseum
Schloss 2. 📞 *(03447) 31 51 93.* ☐ *10am–5pm Tue–Sun.*

🏛 Lindenau-Museum
Gabelentzstrasse 5. 📞 *(03447) 895 53.* ☐ *10am–6pm Tue–Sun.*

SOUTHERN
GERMANY

Southern Germany at a Glance

THE SOUTHERN REGIONS of Germany, with their
wealth of natural beauty, historic sights and folk
culture, are particularly attractive to tourists. This part
of the country includes two *Länder*: Bavaria, famous
for its Alps, beer and the fairytale castle of Ludwig II
at Neuschwanstein, and Baden-Württemberg, whose
highlights include the Bodensee lake, Heidelberg and
taking a trip on the scenic Schwarzwaldbahn railway
line between Offenburg and Villingen.

LOCATOR MAP

Würzburg Residenz
*Set in a magnificent park on the
eastern outskirts of the town, this
imposing bishop's palace was built
between 1720 and 1744, to a
design by Balthasar Neumann.
The palace is constructed in a
U-shape, with a central pavilion
flanked by four two-storey courts.*

BADEN-
WÜRTTEMBERG
(see pp274–313)

Heidelberg Castle *is one of Germany's
finest examples of a Gothic-Renaissance
fortress. Its origins go back to the 13th
century, but new buildings sprang up
around the inner courtyard during
the 16th century as the castle gained
importance as a royal residence.*

Maulbronn Abbey,
*founded in the heart of
the Stromberg region in
1147, is one of the best-
preserved abbeys in
Europe. It was
established by
Cistercian monks with
the bequest of a knight
named Walter von
Lomersheim and
provides a graphic
account of the austere
life led by the monks.*

Vierzehnheiligen Church, *built in 1743–72 to a design by Balthasar Neumann, is one of the most famous examples of South German Rococo. The monumental "Altar of Mercy" (Gnadenaltar) includes statues of the Fourteen Saints of the Intercession, to whom the church is dedicated.*

0 km	50
0 miles	50

BAVARIA
(See pp224–73)

Nördlingen Town Hall *was built in the 14th century, but its present form dates from the early 17th century. Prisoners used to be held in a space beneath the external stone stairway. By the wooden entrance is a wall carving of a medieval fool bearing a Latin inscription that translates as "Now there are two of us."*

Neuschwanstein Castle *is one of the three castles built for the Bavarian King Ludwig II (1845–86), involving enormous effort and expenditure. Standing on a high rock, overlooking a stream, the castle was the fulfilment of the King's vision, which was greatly inspired by the operas of Wagner.*

The Frauenkirche *in Munich was completed in 1488 and features two 99-m (325-ft) high towers crowned with copper domes. The church is one of the largest in southern Germany.*

The Baroque in Southern Germany

Because of religious conflicts and the Thirty Years' War (1618–48), the Baroque style did not flourish in Germany until the 18th century. Then it did so most lavishly in the southern, Catholic regions of the country. Here, influenced by Italian architecture, the Baroque reached new heights of flamboyance: the impressive spaciousness of religious buildings provided the setting for dynamic compositions in sculpture, fine stuccowork and vividly coloured *trompe l'oeil* paintings. Southern Germany's major artists of the 18th century included Balthasar Neumann, Francois Cuvilliés and the Asam brothers.

The main altar in Rohr, *which was created by Egid Quirin Asam in 1723, is in the form of a proscenium (stage) with wings. The sculptural group depicts the Assumption of the Virgin Mary into Heaven.*

Ceiling frescos *were a basic element of the Baroque interior. This example by Johann Baptist Zimmermann in the Wieskirche in Steingaden, presents a glowing vision of the afterlife.*

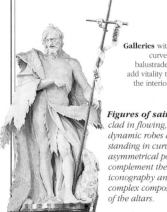

Galleries with curved balustrades add vitality to the interior.

Light plays a vital role in enlivening the interior decoration.

Figures of saints *clad in flowing, dynamic robes and standing in curving, asymmetrical poses, complement the rich iconography and complex composition of the altars.*

18th-century *monasteries in southern Germany, like this one in Ottobeuren with its imposing stairway, are reminiscent of royal residences.*

Late Baroque church façades, such as that of the Theatinerkirche in Munich, have a "rippled" design that creates an unusual effect of light and shadow.

Vaults with fine painting and exquisite stuccowork round off the architectural elements.

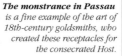

The monstrance in Passau is a fine example of the art of 18th-century goldsmiths, who created these receptacles for the consecrated Host.

BAROQUE INTERIORS

Although they may seem over-elaborate, the late Baroque interiors of southern German churches are carefully-planned compositions intended to have a powerful effect. Their magnificent combination of architecture, sculpture and painting, and often organ music, resulted in "*Gesamtkunstwerk*" – a homogenous work that combines all the arts.

The pulpit and other furnishings are designed to blend harmoniously with the decoration.

Stuccowork fills every interior space that is not decorated with paintings. Sometimes gilded, sometimes white, it may depict complex scenes or, in some cases, be adorned with ornamental designs.

BAROQUE RESIDENCES

South German Baroque was not limited solely to religious architecture. As well as the magnificent monasteries and pilgrimage churches, it was also the inspiration for the impressive residences that were built by abbots as well as by bishops. As in the rest of Europe, these were modelled on the French royal palace in Versailles with its imposing grandeur, striking interiors and breathtaking gardens.

The Baroque vestibule in the Neues Schloss in Schleissheim (see pp250–51) is decorated with exquisite stuccowork and frescos.

The Nymphenburg was a summer residence of the rulers of Bavaria. The plan includes a grand driveway and a park (see pp214–15).

Schloss Favorite is a small palace that forms part of a huge Baroque-style residence in Ludwigsburg (see pp292–3).

The German Alps

PART OF GERMANY EXTENDS into a fairly moderate section of the Alps, Europe's highest mountain range. They stretch from the Bodensee (Lake Constance) to Berchtesgaden. A section of the northern calcareous Alps belonging to the Eastern Alps of Allgäu, Bavaria and Salzburg

Alpine Chough

falls within Germany. The mountains are a holidaymaker's paradise all year round. In the summer mountain walks can be enjoyed, with well-marked trails, as well as climbing, hang-gliding and paragliding; in the winter skiing is possible in superbly equipped resorts.

Alpine meadows are rich pasture lands, providing premium quality hay. They are also home to a rich variety of wildflowers.

Mountain streams have, over the years, cut a path through the rocks to create picturesque ravines. One of the most beautiful is this one at Wimbachklamm.

Mountain peaks with their breath-taking jagged rocks.

Local architecture blends happily into the landscape.

THE ALPINE LAKES

A melting glacier created many lakes in Bavaria. Their clear, unpolluted waters attract all kinds of watersports enthusiasts, while the picturesque surroundings are equally popular with other recreational users.

The Königssee, with its crystal-clear waters, is located high in the Berchtesgaden National Park.

The Watzmann is Germany's second highest peak.

Schwarzeck

Steinplatte

Reit im Winkl

Schliers

Oberstdorf

The Zugspitze, at 2,963m (9,700 ft), is the highest peak in all of Germany.

ALPINE FLORA AND FAUNA

Alpine vegetation varies according to height above sea level. On the lower slopes are mixed deciduous forests. Higher up are Alpine forests, generally coniferous. Above the tree line, dwarf mountain pine grow and higher still are stretches of high-altitude meadows. Beyond this is bare rock. Wild goats are found above the tree line and chamois in the foothills.

The Alpine ibex lives only in the Italian and Swiss Alps. This wild goat with long, backward-curving horns is a rare sight.

The mouflon is a wild sheep with large horns. It is also found in Corsica and Sardinia

Alpine rock jasmine forms carpets of colour on the mountain slopes.

The Alpine pasqueflower is a white variant of the species that tolerates the harsh soil and climatic conditions of its Alpine habitat.

The peacock butterfly is a common Eurasian species that has adapted successfully to the harsh Alpine environment.

Alpine thrift, with its round heads of pink and purple flowers, is a delightful sight.

Tegernsee

Kochelsee is overlooked by one of the largest hydroelectric power stations in Germany.

Garmisch-Partenkirchen is one of the venues of the annual Four Ski Jumps competition.

Walchensee

Alpspitze

The Zugspitze is the highest peak in Germany.

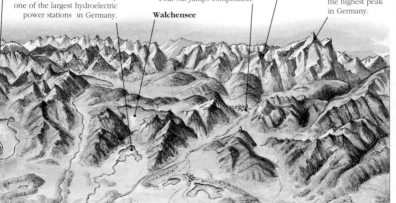

MUNICH

THE CAPITAL OF BAVARIA, *Munich is sometimes called "Germany's secret capital". Lying right at the heart of Europe, the city rapidly overshadowed once powerful neighbours, such as Ingolstadt, Augsburg and Nuremberg, to become southern Germany's main metropolis. With its vibrant cosmopolitan atmosphere, fine buildings, museums and shops, it is one of the country's most popular tourist destinations.*

The citizens of Munich have been known for centuries for their love of the arts. The masterpieces that were created here during the Baroque and Rococo periods were equal to Italian and French works.

In the 19th century, the town's development continued along Neo-Classical lines, gaining for it the name of "Athens on Isar". Just how appropriate the name is can be seen when strolling along Ludwigstrasse or Königsplatz or visiting the Glyptothek, which houses Ludwig I's collection of Greek and Roman sculptures.

In the late 19th century the Munich Academy of Fine Arts was amongst Europe's best art schools. Not many cities have as great a choice of world-class theatres, operas and museums as can be found here in Munich.

But it is not only art that gives Munich its unique charm. The country's biggest folk festival, the Oktoberfest, is held each year in Theresienwiese, where visitors to the town can join in the revelries or just sit and watch, ordering a plate of sauerkraut with sausages and washing it down with some of the excellent Bavarian beer.

When planning a shopping trip to Munich visitors can be sure that its shops are equal to those of Paris and Milan, not only in the breadth of their range but also in terms of their prices.

The town is also one of Germany's main centres of high-tech and media industries. Many TV stations and film studios, as well as over 300 book and newspaper publishers, have their main offices in Munich.

The Neo-Gothic Rathaus in Marienplatz, Munich's central square

◁ Interior of the Baroque Asamkirche, built between 1733 and 1746 by the Asam brothers

Exploring Munich

MUNICH, THE CAPITAL OF BAVARIA, is exceptionally rich in interesting museums, churches and historic sights. This urban conurbation of about 1.2 million inhabitants increasingly swallows up the neighbouring areas. Many tourist attractions are located outside the town centre but, thanks to excellent public transport, it is easy to visit them. It is worth taking a trip to Nymphenburg to visit the famous palace and gardens there. Another interesting excursion is a stroll along Leopoldstrasse or Theresienwiese, where the huge, annual Oktoberfest is held.

GETTING THERE

Munich is an important railway junction and has its own international airport. It also has motorway connections with all the major towns and cities in Germany.

The distinctive towers of Munich's skyline

STAR SIGHTS

Churches
Asamkirche ⑥
Bürgersaal ①
Dreifaltigkeitskirche ③
Frauenkirche ④
Ludwigskirche ㉑
Michaelskirche ②
Theatinerkirche (St Cajetan) ⑮

Buildings
Altes Rathaus ⑨
Bayerische Staatsbibliothek ⑳
Feldherrnhalle ⑭
Neues Rathaus ⑩
Propyläen ㉗
Residenz (pp206–7) ⑬
*Schloss Nymphenburg
 (pp214–15)* ㉙
Villa Stuck ㉝

Museums and Galleries
Alte Pinakothek (pp212–13) ㉓
Archäologische
 Staatssammlung ⑲

Bayerisches National-
 museum ⑰
Deutsches Jagd- und
 Fischereimuseum ⑤
*Deutsches Museum
 (pp218–19)* ㉜
Glyptothek ㉕
Haus der Kunst ⑯
Lenbachhaus ㉘
Neue Pinakothek ㉒
Pinakothek der Moderne ㉔
Schack-Galerie ⑱
Staatliche Antiken-
 sammlungen ㉖
Stadtmuseum ⑦
Völkerkundemuseum ⑪

Other Attractions
Bavaria-Filmstadt ㉞
Englischer Garten ㉛
Hofbräuhaus ⑫
Olympiapark ㉚
Theresienwiese ㉟
Viktualienmarkt ⑧

KEY

▮ Street-by-Street map
 pp200–201

P Parking

i Tourist information

✉ Post office

🚕 Taxi-rank

✝ Church, cathedral, chapel

Ⓢ S-Bahn

U U-Bahn

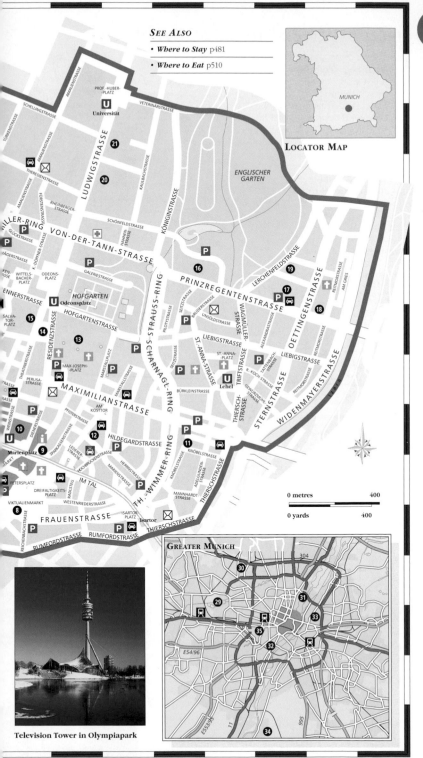

SEE ALSO
• *Where to Stay* p481
• *Where to Eat* p510

LOCATOR MAP

MUNICH

ENGLISCHER GARTEN

HOFGARTEN

Television Tower in Olympiapark

GREATER MUNICH

Street-by-Street: Around Marienplatz

IN MEDIEVAL TIMES, Marienplatz was Munich's salt- and corn-market. The origins of Munich itself lie with a handful of monks who built their abbey here, giving the place its name (from the word for 'monks') and its heraldic arms. In 1158 Welf Henry the Lion bestowed town status on Munich and 30 years later the town was allocated to the Wittelsbachs, who soon established a residence here. During the Reformation, Munich became a bastion of Catholicism and an important centre of the Counter-Reformation. Its magnificent churches, the Altes Rathaus (old town hall) and the Residenz all bear witness to that era.

HERZOG–WILHELM–STRASSE

NEUHAUSER STRASSE

Karlstor
Known as the Karl's Gate, the west entrance to the old town was part of the medieval fortifications. It was given its present name in 1791, in honour of Prince Karl Theodore.

Augustinerbräu
The oldest and most celebrated brewery in Munich was founded by Augustinian monks in 1328. It currently occupies two 19th-century houses with picturesque façades.

| 0 metres | 50 |
| 0 yards | 50 |

★ Bürgersaal
Bürgersaal was built in 1709–10 for a Marian congregation (followers of the Virgin Mary), as a place of meeting and worship. It includes an upper and lower church. Rupert Mayer, an opponent of Nazism, is buried in the crypt. He was beatified in 1987 **①**

Michaelskirche
The interior of St Michael's Church is surprisingly large. The massive barrel vaulting over the nave is the second largest after St Peter's Basilica in Rome **②**

STAR SIGHTS

- ★ **Altes Rathaus**
- ★ **Bürgersaal**
- ★ **Frauenkirche**
- ★ **Neues Rathaus**

KEY

– – – Suggested route

Deutsches Jagd- und Fischereimuseum

A huge collection of hunting and fishing exhibits is housed in the Augustinerkloster. The deconsecrated church, which has an ornate Rococo interior, once belonged to the Augustinian order ⑤

LOCATOR MAP

★ Frauenkirche

Partially demolished in 1944–45, this imposing church, with its land-mark dome-topped towers, has been rebuilt along Gothic lines ④

★ Neues Rathaus

The ornate façade of the new town hall includes figures from Bavarian legend and history. The bronze statue at the top is the "Münchner Kindl" – a character that features in the city's heraldic arms ⑩

St Mary's Column

★ Altes Rathaus

The old town hall was remodelled in its original 15th-century style in the late 19th century. It was rebuilt again after World War II. It now houses a collection of historic toys ⑨

TSTRASSE

KAUFINGERSTRASSE

ROSENSTRASSE

MARIEN PLATZ

RINDERMARKT

Isartor

Interior of the Bürgersaal, featuring original 19th-century frescos

Bürgersaal ❶

Neuhauser Straße 14. **Map** 1 F4.
U or **S** Karlsplatz. 🚋 18, 19, 20, 21, 27. **Lower church hall** ◐ 7am–7pm daily. **Upper church hall** ◐ 10.30am–noon daily.

THIS CHURCH belonging to the Marian congregation was designed by Giovanni Antonio Viscardi and built by Johann Georg Ettenhofer in 1709–10. (The Marian congregation, founded in 1563, is a Catholic organization linked to the Jesuit order.)

The church was damaged during World War II, but still features original frescos. In the oratory is a figure of the *Guardian Angel* by Ignaz Günther (1770), a fine example of south-Bavarian Rococo. Rupert Mayer, parish priest during World War II and Munich's leading opponent of Nazism, is buried in the crypt.

Michaelskirche ❷

ST MICHAEL'S CHURCH

Neuhauser Straße 52. **Map** 2 A4.
U or **S** Karlsplatz. 🚋 18, 19, 20, 21, 27. ◐ 7am–9pm daily.

THE MONUMENTAL St Michael's Church was built by Prince Wilhelm V for the Jesuits who arrived here in 1559. The foundation stone was laid in

1585 and initial building work on the first church, which was smaller than the present one, commenced in 1588. Before work had progressed very far, however, the tower in front of the presbytery collapsed, demolishing a large part of the building. A transept and new presbytery were added to the remaining part of the building and the church – which was the first Jesuit church in northern Europe – was consecrated in 1597. The interior of Michaelskirche is

Statue of St Michael at the entrance to Michaelskirche

awe-inspiring, with its wide, well-proportioned nave, three pairs of shallow chapels on either side, a short transept and an elongated presbytery. It is not certain who was the architect of the project, but it is believed that Wolfgang Müller created the main body of the church and Wendel Dietrich the Mannerist façade. Later extensions are thought to be the work of a Dutch architect, Friedrich Sustris.

In the church crypt, which is open to the public, are the tombs of many members of the Wittelsbach dynasty, including that of the famous castle-builder, King Ludwig II.

Dreifaltigkeits-kirche ❸

HOLY TRINITY CHURCH

Pacellistraße 6. **Map** 2 A3. 🚋 19.
◐ 8am–4pm Fri–Wed, noon–4pm Thu.

THE BAROQUE church of the Holy Trinity is one of the few historic buildings in the city to have avoided bomb damage during World War II. The church was built as a votive gift from the city's burghers, aristocracy and clergy in the hope of averting the dangers threatened by the War of the Spanish Succession (1702–14). The foundation stone was laid in 1711 and

the church was consecrated seven years later. The royal architect, Giovanni Antonio Viscardi, assisted by Enrico Zucalli and Georg Ettenhofer, created a building that is one of the most beautiful examples of Italian Baroque in Munich. The church's original features include the dome fresco by Cosmas Damian Asam, *The Adoration of the Trinity*.

Frauenkirche ❹

Frauenplatz 1. **Map** 2 B4. **U** *or* **S** *Karlsplatz & Marienplatz.* 🚋 *19.* **Tower** ☐ *Apr–Oct: 10am–5pm Mon–Sat.* ● *Sun & holidays.*

THE SITE OF THE Frauenkirche was originally occupied by a Marian chapel, which was built in the 13th century. Some two hundred years later, Prince Sigismund ordered a new, much bigger church to be built on the site. Its architects were Jörg von Halspach and Lukas Rottaler. The Frauenkirche was completed in 1488, though the distinctive copper onion-domes were not added to its towers until 1525. The church is one of southern Germany's biggest Gothic structures, which can accommodate a congregation of about 2,000.

A triple-nave hall with no transept features rows of side chapels, a gallery surrounding the choir and a monumental western tower. The whole huge structure measures over 100 m (330 ft) in length and almost 40 m (130 ft) wide.

The church treasures that escaped destruction during World War II include a Marian painting, dating from around 1500, by Jan Polak; the altar of St Andrew in St Sebastian's chapel, with statues by Meister von Rabenden and paintings by Jan Polak, dating from 1510; and the monumental tomb of Emperor Ludwig IV of Bavaria, the work of Hans Krumpper (1619–22).

Deutsches Jagd- und Fischerei- museum ❺

GERMAN MUSEUM OF HUNTING AND FISHING

Neuhauser Straße 2. **Map** 2 A4. **C** *(089) 22 05 22.* **U** *or* **S** *Marienplatz.* 🚋 *18, 19, 20, 21, 27.* ☐ *9:30am–5pm Tue–Wed, Fri–Sun, 9:30am–9pm Mon, Thu.* 🖼

IMMEDIATELY ADJACENT to St Michael's Church is the Augustinerkloster, the former Augustinian church, which now houses the Museum of Hunting and Fishing. The original building dates from around 1300 (the first Augustinian monks arrived here in 1294). It was rebuilt in the mid-15th century and then remodelled in the Baroque style in 1620–21. The church was deconsecrated in 1803. Since 1966, the building's ornate Rococo interior has housed a very interesting museum, with a collection of weapons dating from the Renaissance, Baroque and Rococo periods, as well as hunting trophies and related paintings, prints and

Carving on main Frauenkirche portal

dioramas. Artists represented in the museum's collection include several great names such as Rubens, Snyders and Antonio Pisanello.

Asamkirche ❻

ASAMS' CHURCH

Sendlinger Straße 32. **Map** 2 A5. **U** *Sendlinger Tor.* 🚋 *18, 20, 21, 27.* 🚌 *31, 56.* ☐ *8:30am–6pm daily.* ✝ *5pm Mon–Fri, 6pm Sat, 9am, 10:30am Sun.* 🖼 *noon Sat.*

OFFICIALLY known as St Johann-Nepomuk, this gem of Rococo architecture stands in Sendlingerstrasse and is part of a complex built by the Asam brothers in the mid-18th century. In 1729–30, the sculptor and stuccoist Egid Quirin Asam acquired two properties that he intended to convert into a family home for himself. He subsequently acquired a plot adjacent to these properties, where he wished to build a church devoted to the newly canonized St Nepomuk, a Bohemian monk who had drowned in the Danube. Above the entrance to the church is a statue of the saint.

At the same time, Cosmas Damian, the brother of Egid Quirin Asam, bought a plot on which he built the presbytery. The church building adjoins the residential house of Egid Quirin. The two buildings were joined by a corridor and from one of his bedroom windows the artist could see the main altar.

In this small but unique church, the Asam brothers achieved a rare and striking unity of style. In the church's dimly lit interior, with its rich, dynamically shaped single nave, no surface is left unembellished. Irresistibly, the eye is drawn to the altar, which features a sculpted group of the Holy Trinity.

Pulpit in the Rococo-style Asamkirche

A painting by Wilhelm von Kaulbach (1847) from the Stadtmuseum collection

Stadtmuseum ❼
TOWN MUSEUM

St Jakobsplatz 1. **Map** 2 A5.
🕿 *(089) 23 32 23 70.* **U** *or*
Ⓢ *Marienplatz.* **U** *Sendlinger Tor.*
⭕ *10am–6pm Tue–Sun.* 🈳 ▫

A FEW STEPS away from the Viktualienmarkt, on St Jakobsplatz, stands the Town Museum. Its rich collection has been housed since 1880 in the former arsenal building, which was built in 1491–93 by Lucas Rottaler. It is one of Munich's most fascinating museums, where everyone will find something to their taste, with exhibits illustrating the everyday lives of Munich's citizens of all classes throughout the centuries.

The museum's greatest treasures are the famous set of dancing Moors by Erasmus Grasser (1480). Originally this was a group of eighteen lime-wood carvings of dancing figures in highly expressive postures, surrounding the figure of a woman. Only ten of the figures, which were created originally to decorate the ballroom of the Altes Rathaus, have survived. Also on the ground floor, in the Waffenhalle, is a splendid collection of arms. Other displays include furniture (with pieces in styles ranging from Baroque to Art Deco), photographs, film, brewing equipment and musical instruments. There is also a fascinating doll collection, which is one of the largest in the world. It includes paper dolls from India and China, European mechanical dolls and a variety of original puppets. Also worth seeing is the museum's collection of paintings and prints, particularly the posters. As well as its permanent displays about the history of the city, the museum regularly stages special exhibitions.

The museum also houses a cinema, the *Filmmuseum*, which puts on nightly showings of English-language films.

Viktualienmarkt ❽

Peterplatz-Frauenstraße. **Map** 2 B5.
U *or* **Ⓢ** *Marienplatz.* 🚌 *52, 56.*

R IGHT AT THE heart of the city is the Viktualienmarkt, a large square that has been the city's main marketplace for the last two hundred years. The locals say that a tourist who fails to visit this "rustic heart" of Munich can never boast that he has seen the Bavarian capital. Apart from stalls selling vegetables and fruit brought in daily from suburban orchards or

Colourfully laden market stalls in Munich's Viktualienmarkt

village gardens, the local beer garden provides a welcome retreat for a beer or snack.

One of the features of the square is a statue of a famous Munich actor and comedian, Karl Valentin (1882–1948).

An impressive view over the market and nearby Marien-platz can be enjoyed from the tower of Peterskirche (St Peter's Church), which stands alongside the square.

Signs of the Zodiac adorning the clock face on the Altes Rathaus

Altes Rathaus ❾
OLD TOWN HALL

Marienplatz 15. **Map** 2 B4. **U** *or*
Ⓢ *Marienplatz.* ⬛ *to visitors.*
Spielzeugmuseum 🕿 *(089) 29
40 01.* ⭕ *10am–5:30pm daily.* 🈳

M UNICH's old town hall stands in the eastern part of Marienplatz, immediately next to the new town hall. The original building, which has been remodelled several times over the centuries, was built in 1470–75 by Jörg von Halspach, who also designed the Marian church.

The building's present Neo-Gothic look is the result of remodelling work carried out between 1877 and 1934, when the nearby dual carriageway ring road was being built.

The interior of the building, which was restored following World War II bomb damage, features the Dance Hall with a wooden cradle vault. It is adorned with an old frieze featuring 87 (originally 99) heraldic arms painted by Ulrich Fuetrer in 1478, and a further seven carved by Erasmus Grasser in 1477. The figures standing by the walls are copies of the famous dancing Moors, whose

originals by Erasmus Grasser (1480) are kept in the Town Museum (Stadtmuseum).

The lofty tower rising above the old city gate (Talbrucktor) was remade in 1975 based on pictures dating from 1493. Since 1983, the tower has housed the toy collection of the Spielzeugmuseum.

Neues Rathaus ⑩

NEW TOWN HALL

Marienplatz. **Map** 2 B4. ⓒ (089) 23 32 31 91. Ⓤ or Ⓢ Marienplatz. ⓞ **Town Hall and Tower:** mid-Apr–Oct festival: 9am–7pm Mon–Fri, 10am–7pm Sat & Sun; Oct festival–mid-Apr: 9am–4pm Mon–Thu, 9am–1pm Fri. ⓞ Sat, Sun. ⓗ ⓛ **Carillons:** May–Oct: 11am, noon, 5pm, 9pm daily; Nov–Apr: 11am, noon, 9pm.

THE NEO-GOTHIC new town hall standing in Marienplatz was built by Georg Hauberrisser in 1867–1909. Its 100-m (330-ft) high façade features a fascinating set of statues depicting Bavarian dukes, kings and electors, saints, mythical and allegorical figures as well as a variety of gargoyles inspired by medieval bestiaries. The central façade features an 80-m (260-ft) high clock tower, known as Glockenspiele. Each day, at 11am and 5pm, the bells ring out a carillon, while mechanical knights fight a tournament and a crowd dances. The latter is a reenactment of the first coopers' dance, which was held in 1517 to boost the morale of citizens when the town was beset by the plague. Other mechanical figures appear in the windows on the seventh floor in the evenings (9:30pm in summer, 7:30pm in winter). These are flanked by figures of the town guardsman carrying a lantern and the Guardian Angel blessing a Munich child, the *"Münchner Kindl"*.

Richly decorated entrance to the Völkerkundemuseum

Völkerkunde-museum ⑪

STATE MUSEUM OF ETHNOGRAPHY

Maximilianstraße 42. **Map** 2 D4. ⓒ (089) 210 136 100. ⓞ 9:30am–5:15pm, Tue–Sun. ⓣ 19. ⓛ

ON THE OPPOSITE side of the ring road from the Maximilianeum (the Upper Bavaria Government building) is the State Museum of Ethnography. Built in 1858–65, to a design by E. Riedel, its façade is decorated with eight figures personifying the virtues of the Bavarian people: patriotism, diligence, magnanimity, piety, loyalty, justice, courage and wisdom. Originally intended to house the Bavarian National Museum (now in Prinzregent-enstraße), the building has been home to the State Museum of Ethnography since 1925. It is the second largest (after Berlin) ethnographic museum in Germany.

The origins of the museum's collection go back to 1782, when curios taken from the treasures of various Bavarian rulers were exhibited in a gallery in the gardens of the residence. Attention began to focus on ethnography after expansion of the collection in 1868. The museum currently houses some 300,000 exhibits depicting the art and culture of non-European nations, with a particular emphasis on the Far East (China and Japan), South America and Eastern and Central Africa. The collection is presented in a series of changing exhibitions.

Hofbräuhaus ⑫

Platzl 9. **Map** 2 C4. ⓒ (089) 22 16 76. Ⓤ or Ⓢ Marienplatz. ⓞ 9am–midnight daily.

THE HOFBRÄUHAUS is the most popular beer hall in Munich and a great tourist attraction. Established as a court brewery in 1589 by Wilhelm V, it was originally housed in Alter Hof, but moved to Platzl in 1654. In 1830 permission was granted to build an inn where beer could be sold to the public.

The Neo-Renaissance form of the building dates from 1896. The Schwemme, on the ground floor, is a large hall with painted ceiling and room for about 1,000 guests. The Festall, on the first floor, has a barrel-shaped vault and can accommodate 1,300 guests.

In a courtyard, surrounded by chestnut trees, is the beer garden, which is always very popular during the summer.

Guests enjoying a drink in the beer garden of the Hofbräuhaus

Statue on façade of Neues Rathaus

Residenz ⓭

THIS FORMER residence of Bavarian kings has housed a museum since 1920. Over the years, the original Wittelsbachs' castle, which had stood on the site since the 14th century, was gradually extended. Major work in the 17th century included new surroundings for the Brunnenhof and the construction of buildings around the imperial courtyard, Hofkapelle and Reiche Kapelle. Königsbau and Festsaalbau were added in the first half of the 19th century. The Renaissance façade includes two magnificent portals and features a statue of the Holy Virgin as Patroness of Bavaria (Patrona Boiariae).

Necklace dating from 1557

Hofkapelle
This imposing chapel, dating from the early 17th century, was modelled on St Michael's Church. Vault decorations date from 1614.

Reiche Kapelle
This was the private chapel of Maximilian I. Though smaller than the Residenz's other chapel, it is richly furnished.

Grottenhof
In the eastern section of this courtyard is this grotto lined with crystal, coloured shells and tufa.

Entrance

★ Nibelungensäle
Built by Leo von Klenze, Königsbau features five Halls of the Nibelungs. The rooms owe their name to the wall paintings, which depict scenes from the famous German medieval epic Nibelungenlied.

★ Cuvilliés-Theater
Built in 1751–53, this masterpiece of theatre architecture was designed by François de Cuvilliés and his son, and is considered to be Europe's finest surviving Rococo theatre. The world premiere of Mozart's Idomeneo *was staged in the theatre on 29 January 1781.*

★ Schatzkammer V
Room V's collection includes items such as the Bavarian crown insignia and a sword belonging to Duke Christoph of Bavaria.

Entrance

Nationaltheater

Schatzkammer
Besides royal insignia, liturgical vessels and various everyday objects, the treasure house contains some unusual gold and jewellery items. The star attraction of Room III is this small equestrian statue of St George, the work (1586–97) of Friedrich Sustris.

STAR SIGHTS

★ Cuvilliés-Theater

★ Nibelungensäle

★ Schatzkammer V

Feldherrnhalle ⑭

Odeonsplatz. **Map** 2 B3.
U *Odeonsplatz.* 🚋 *19.* 🚌 *53.*
⬤ *to the public.*

UNTIL 1816, the site of this monumental building was occupied by a Gothic town gate – Schwabinger Tor. In the early 19th century, however, when Kings Maximilian I Joseph and Ludwig I decided to expand Munich northwards and westwards, their chief architect, Leo von Klenze, ordered the gate to be pulled down, as it stood in the way of the prestigious thoroughfare (Ludwigstrasse) that he intended to build.

Built in 1841–44, the Feldherrnhalle was designed by Friedrich von Gärtner, who modelled it on the Loggia dei Lanzi in Florence. Intended as a monument to the heroes of Bavaria, the interior contains statues of two great military leaders, Johann Tilly and Karl Philipp von Wrede by Ludwig Schwanthaler.

The central carved composition devoted to the heroes of the 1870–71 Franco-Prussian War is much newer, dating from 1882. It was designed by Ferdinand von Miller.

The Feldherrnhalle was the scene of Hitler's unsuccessful "Beer-hall Putsch". This resulted in the building acquiring a certain cult status in Nazi propaganda, and is no longer open to the public.

HITLER AND THE FELDHERRNHALLE

On the evening of 8 November 1923, Adolf Hitler announced the start of the "people's revolution" in the Bürgerbräukeller and ordered the takeover of the central districts of Munich. On 9 November a march of some 2,000 people acting on his orders was stopped by a police cordon outside the Feldherrnhalle in Residenzstraße. Four policemen and 16 of Hitler's supporters were shot. The marchers were dispersed, and Hitler fled to Uffing am Starnberger See, but was arrested and imprisoned. When Hitler finally came to power in 1933, he turned what became known as the Beer-hall Putsch into a central element of the Nazi cult.

The accused in the trial against the participants in the Beer-hall Putsch of 1923

Theatinerkirche (St Cajetan) ⑮

ST CAJETAN'S CHURCH

Theatinerstraße 22. **Map** 2 B3. **U** or **S** *Marienplatz.* 🚋 *19.* ⬤ *7am–6pm daily.*

IN ODEONSPLATZ, next to Feldherrnhalle, stands one of the most magnificent churches in Munich, St Cajetan's Church. When Henrietta Adelaide of Savoy presented the Elector Ferdinand with his long-awaited heir, Maximilian, the happy parents vowed to build an abbey in commemoration. The project was given to an Italian architect, Agostino Baralli,

who based his design on St Andrea della Valle, in Rome.

Although construction work on the church ended in 1690, the façade – designed by François de Cuvilliés – was not completed until 1765–68. The interior of the church is adorned with stuccos by Giovanni Antonio Viscardi and furnished in rich Baroque style. Its twin towers and copper dome are dominant features on the Munich skyline.

Haus der Kunst ⑯

ARTS HOUSE

Prinzregentenstraße 1. **Map** 3 D2.
C *(089) 21 12 70.* 🚌 *53, 55.*
⬤ *10am–10pm daily.* 🎟 *(free on Sundays and national holidays).*

BUILT BETWEEN 1933 and 1937, the Neo-Classical building is the work of a Nazi architect, Paul Ludwig Trost. It opened its doors in 1937 with a display of propaganda art, which was proclaimed by the Nazis as "truly German". This was followed by "The Exhibition of Degenerate Art", in which several masterpieces of modern art were ridiculed.

Since 1945 the building has become a dynamic centre of modern art that is famous far beyond Munich for its temporary exhibitions.

Its central hall, the Ehrenhalle (Hall of Honour), which was subdivided into smaller spaces, is currently being reopened in

Pediment on the gable of Theatinerkirche, with copper dome behind

stages, each stage accompanied by a special exhibition. This process will continue into 2005, when the hall will once again become the centre of the building. It will house new visitor facilities, as well as a permanent exhibition documenting the history of the Haus der Kunst.

Bayerisches Nationalmuseum ⓱

BAVARIAN NATIONAL MUSEUM

Prinzregentenstraße 3. **Map** 3 E3.
📞 (089) 211 24 01. 🚊 20. 🚌 53, 55. ◻ 10am–5pm Tue–Wed, Fri–Sun, 10am–8pm Thu. ⬤ Mon.

THE BAVARIAN National Museum was founded in 1855 by King Maximilian II. Between 1894 and 1900 it acquired a new building in Prinzregentenstrasse, which was designed by Gabriel von Seidel; this building alone is worth a closer look. The complex structure consists of wings representing various architectural styles, while the ground floor features halls that are built in styles that are appropriate to their exhibits. Romanesque and Gothic art can thus be seen in Neo-Romanesque and Neo-Gothic rooms, Renaissance art in Neo-Renaissance rooms and Baroque in Neo-Baroque rooms. The individual rooms have been arranged in subject groups, with paintings and sculptures supplemented by superb collections of decorative art and everyday objects. The exhibits include a beautiful sculpture of the Madonna by Tilman Riemenschneider.

Conrad Meit's *Judith* **(1515), Bavarian National Museum**

The first-floor collections are arranged thematically and include German porcelain, clocks, glass paintings, ivory carvings, textiles and gold

items. Particularly interesting is a collection of small oil sketches, painted by artists when designing some large-scale compositions, such as an altar or a ceiling painting.

In the basement rooms is a collection of folk art. This includes the popular Christmas cribs. These multi-figure compositions are the works of Bavarian and Italian artists.

Poster advertising an exhibition at the Schack-Galerie

Schack-Galerie ⓲

Prinzregentenstraße 9. **Map** 3 E3.
📞 (089) 23 80 52 24. ◻ 10am–5pm Wed–Mon. 🚌 53. 🚊 20.

THE MAGNIFICENT collection of German paintings on display in this gallery come from the private collection of Adolf Friedrich von Schack. They are housed in this elegant building built in 1907 by Max Littmann for use by the Prussian Legation.

As Schack's main interest was in 19th-century painting, the gallery features works that represent the Romantic period, including Leo von Klenze and Carl Spitz-weg, as well as witty, fairy-tale works by Moritz von Schwind. Particularly notable are his *Morning*, *In the Woods* and *Rübezahl* – in which the mythical Guardian of the Riesengebirge Mountains wanders through an enchanted

forest. Late 19th-century painters are represented by Franz von Lenbach, Anselm Feuerbach and, above all, by Arnold Bocklin. Bocklin's Romantic works, which are full of symbolism, include *Villa on the Coast* and *Man Scaring a Deer*. The gallery has a large collection of land-scapes, including interesting sun-soaked Italian scenes by German masters, as well as a valuable collection of paintings devoted to historic themes.

Archäologische Staatssammlung ⓳

PREHISTORY MUSEUM

Lerchenfeldstraße 2. **Map** 3 E2.
📞 (089) 211 24 02. 🚊 17. 🚌 53. ◻ 9am–4:30pm Tue–Sun. 🎟 admission free Sun and national holidays. ♿

IMMEDIATELY adjacent to the Bavarian National Museum is the Prehistory Museum, which was founded in 1885 by King Ludwig II. Since 1976, this spacious building has housed a rich collection of artifacts excavated in various parts of Bavaria. The oldest items in the collection date from the Palaeolithic era while later exhibits illustrate the region's early history. The collection includes Bronze Age, Roman and early Medieval treasures.

A 3rd-century mosaic floor from a Roman villa, on display in the Prehistory Museum

Bayerische Staatsbibliothek ⑳

BAVARIAN NATIONAL LIBRARY

Ludwigstraße 16. **Map** 2 C1, C2.
📞 *(089) 28 63 80.* 🚇 *Odeon, Universität.* ⏰ *9am–9pm Mon–Fri, 10am–5pm Sat–Sun.* ♿ *(telephone bookings required).*

THE MONUMENTAL Bavarian national library was designed by Friedrich von Gärtner, who took over, in 1827, from Leo von Klenze as the main architect on the prestigious Ludwigstrasse project – commissioned by King Ludwig I. Gärtner was also responsible for the Feldherrnhalle, Siegestor, St Ludwig's Church, and the University building.

This massive structure, in a style reminiscent of the Italian Renaissance, was erected between 1832 and 1843. Its external staircase is adorned with the seated figures of Thucydides, Hippocrates, Homer and Aristotle, by Ludwig von Schwanthaler.

Equally impressive are the stairs leading to the main rooms, which are modelled on the Scala dei Gianti of the Doge Palace in Venice. With its collection of 5 million volumes, the library is on a par with the Berlin Staatsbibliothek *(see p64)* as the biggest in Germany.

A statue of Hippocrates at the Bavarian National Library

The imposing twin-tower façade of Munich's Ludwigskirche

Ludwigskirche ㉑

ST LUDWIG'S CHURCH

Ludwigstraße 20. **Map** 2 C1.
🚇 *Universität.* ⏰ *7am–8pm daily.*

INSPIRED BY the Romanesque churches of Lombardy, Friedrich von Gärtner built this monumental triple-nave basilica with transept and twin-tower façade between 1829 and 1844.

The building's vast interior features magnificent original frescos that were designed by the main exponent of the Nazarene style, Peter von Cornelius, and painted by his associates. Von Cornelius himself painted the massive choir fresco, *The Last Judgement*. One of the biggest frescos in the world, it rivals in size Michelangelo's *Last Judgement*, which hangs in the Sistine Chapel, Rome.

Neue Pinakothek ㉒

THE NEW PINAKOTHEK

Barerstrasse 29. **Map** 2 A1. 📞 *(089) 23 80 51 95.* 🚇 *Theresienstraße.* 🚋 *18.* 🚌 *53.* ⏰ *10am–5pm Fri–Mon, 10am–8pm Wed–Thu.* ▦

THE BAVARIAN collection of modern European paintings and sculptures is housed in a building built by Alexander von Brancas between 1975 and 1981. It holds a representative collection of German works, from Neo-Classicism through Romanticism, the "Nazarenes", German and Austrian Biedermeier, Realism, Historicism, Impressionism, Pointillism and Secession paintings.

The collection also includes works by renowned French Realists, Impressionists, Post-Impressionists and Symbolists, purchased in 1909–11, when the gallery's director was the art historian Hugo von Tschudi.

The collection includes Ferdinand Georg Waldmüller's *Young Peasant Woman with Three Children Standing at the Window* (1840), Friedrich Overbeck's *Italia and Germania* (1828), Edouard Manet's *Breakfast in the Studio* (1868), Honoré Daumier's *Don Quijote* (1868), Edgar Degas' *Ironing Woman* (1869), Paul Gauguin's *Birth of Christ* (1869), Walter Crane's *Neptune's Horses* (1892), Gustav Klimt's *Music* (1895) and Lovis Corinth's *Portrait of Count Eduard von Keyserling* (1900). The gallery ends with a small selection of Symbolist and Art Nouveau paintings.

The space between the Old and New Pinakothek has been turned into a sculpture park that features, among others, a work by Henry Moore.

Goya's *Die Marquesa de Caballero* in the Neue Pinakothek

Alte Pinakothek ㉓

THE OLD PINAKOTHEK

See pp212–13.

Façade of the Glyptothek, with its central column portico

Pinakothek der Moderne ㉔

Barer Straße 40. **Map** 2 A2.
📞 (089) 23 80 53 60. Ⓤ Königsplatz. 🚌 53. 🚋 27. ⬤ 10am–5pm
Tue–Wed Sat–Sun, 10am–8pm
Thu–Fri. 🎫 except Sun. ♿ 📧
🌐 www.pinakothek-der-moderne.de

DESIGNED BY the German
architect Stephan
Braunfels, this gallery was
built to complement the
collections in the Alte and
Neue Pinakotheks nearby.
The modern building brings
together the worlds of art,
design, graphics, jewellery and
architecture under one roof.
   Highlights of the collection
include Cubist works by
Picasso and Georges Braque,
and paintings by Matisse,
Giorgio De Chirico and Max
Beckmann. Pop Art, Minimal
Art and Photorealism are also
represented. The design
exhibition is outstanding.

Glyptothek ㉕
GLYPTOTHECA

Königsplatz 3. **Map** 1 F2.
📞 (089) 28 61 00. Ⓤ Königsplatz.
⬤ 10am–5pm Wed, Fri, Sat, Sun,
10am–8pm Tue & Thu.

THE KÖNIGSPLATZ complex,
including Glyptothek and
Propylaeum, was the work of
Leo von Klenze. It was built in
1816–34 to house Ludwig I's
collection of Greek and Roman
sculptures and was the first
public museum to be devoted
to a single art discipline.
   The most famous pieces in
the museum's collection are
the ancient statue of a young
man, *Apollo of Terentia* (560
BC), the tomb stele of
Mnesareta (380 BC) and
sculptures from the front of
the Aphaia temple of Aegina.

Staatliche Antiken-sammlungen ㉖
THE NATIONAL COLLECTION OF ANTIQUITIES

Königsplatz 1. **Map** 1 F2. 📞 (089)
59 83 59. Ⓤ Königsplatz. ⬤ 10am–
5pm Tue–Sun. 🎫 Tue–Sat.

BUILT IN 1838–48 by Georg
Friedrich Ziebland, this
building is on the south side
of the Königsplatz. Since
1967, it has housed one of the
world's finest collections of
antique vases from the 5th
and 6th centuries BC. There
are also many other masterpieces of Greek, Roman and
Etruscan ornamental art,
jewellery and small statues.
Among the famous exhibits is
a golden Greek necklace from
the 4th century BC.

Propyläen ㉗

Königsplatz. **Map** 1 F2.
Ⓤ Königsplatz.

DERIVED FROM the Propylaea
to the Athenian Acropolis,
this magnificent Neo-
Classical structure
stands at the end of
Brienner Strasse and is
visible from as far as
Karolinenplatz. Built by
Leo von Klenze in
1846–62, its austere
form, featuring Doric
porticos, provides an
excellent final touch to
the composition of
Königsplatz by linking
together the National
Collection of Antiquities
and the Glyptotheca.
   The Propyläen is also
a symbolic gateway to
the new parts of the city.
It was funded by the
private foundation of
King Ludwig I, although
built after his abdication.

The carved decorations depict
scenes from the Greek War of
Liberation against Turkey
(1821–29), led by King Otto I,
son of Ludwig I.

Lenbachhaus ㉘

Luisenstraße 33. **Map** 1 F2. 📞 (089)
23 33 20 00. Ⓤ Königsplatz.
⬤ 10am–6pm Tue–Sun. 🎫

THIS ITALIAN-STYLE villa was
built between 1887 and
1891 by Gabriel von Seidl for
Franz von Lenbach, a painter
who was very popular with
the establishment.
   Since 1929, the villa has
housed the Municipal Art
Gallery. Apart from masterpieces such as *Portrait of a
Man*, by Jan Polak (c.1500)
and *Friends from the Young
Days* by Carl Spitzweg (1855),
it also has the world's biggest
collection of works by a group
known as *Der Blaue Reiter*
(The Blue Rider) artists. The
Russian painter Wassily
Kandinsky was a leading
proponent of this movement.

Fountain in the beautiful front garden of
the Lenbachhaus

Alte Pinakothek ㉓

ONSTRUCTION WORK on the Alte Pinakothek,
one of the world's most famous art galleries,
began in 1826 and was completed 10 years later.
Leo von Klenze designed the Italian-Renaissance-
style building. The history of its collections goes
back to the Renaissance period, when Wilhelm IV
the Steadfast (ruled 1508–50) decided to adorn his
residence with historic paintings. His successors
were equally keen art collectors and, by the 18th
century, an outstanding collection of 14th- to 18th-
century paintings had been amassed.

**St Luke Painting the
Madonna** (c.1440)
*This is one of the most frequently
copied masterpieces by
the Dutch painter Roger
van der Weyden.*

★ Four Apostles (1526)
*These two panels were
painted by Albrecht
Dürer, a founding
figure of the German
school of art. They were
purchased in 1627 by
Maximilian I from the
town of Nuremberg.*

**Seated Portrait of
Charles V** (1548)
*This portrait was
painted by the
Venetian artist
Titian during the
Emperor's visit to
the Reich's Parlia-
ment in Augsburg.*

**Main
entrance**

**Homage of the
Three Kings** (1504)
*The depiction of the
homage is just one
small part of the most
important work by Hans
Holbein the Elder.*

KEY

- ☐ Flemish and Dutch
  paintings
- ☐ German paintings
- ☐ Italian paintings
- ☐ French paintings
- ☐ Spanish paintings
- ☐ 16th–17th century paintings

STAR EXHIBITS

- ★ **Deposition from
  the Cross**
- ★ **Four Apostles**
- ★ **Land of Cockaigne**

Abduction of the Daughters of Leukippos (1618)
A highlight of the museum is the Rubens collection, which includes his depiction of the abduction of Hilaeria and Phoibe by Castor and Pollux.

VISITORS' CHECKLIST

Barer Straße 27. **Road map** 2
A1. (089) 23 80 52 16.
Königsplatz. 53. 27.
10am–5pm Wed & Fri–Sun,
10am–8pm Tue, Thu.
(admission free to children
up to age 14.)

GALLERY GUIDE
The ground-floor rooms of the gallery are devoted to the works of German old masters dating from the 16th and 17th centuries. On the first floor are works by Dutch, Flemish, French, German, Italian and Spanish artists.

First floor

★ Deposition from the Cross (1633)
Rembrandt's dramatic vision of the Saviour's sacrifice was originally intended to be part of a triptych.

Disrobing of Christ (c.1577–79)
The gallery's small but interesting collection of Spanish paintings includes this work by El Greco, one of his three most important compositions.

Ground floor

★ Land of Cockaigne (1566)
In this vividly detailed painting by Pieter Brueghel the Elder, the Flemish artist depicts the mythical land of plenty. The work is an ironic condemnation of gluttony and laziness, themes that are depicted in its many humorous scenes.

Schloss Nymphenburg ㉙

ONE OF EUROPE'S most beautiful palaces, Schloss Nymphenburg grew up around an Italianate villa built in 1663–64 for the Electress Henrietta-Adelaide to a design by Agostino Barelli. The palace was dedicated to the pastoral pleasures of the goddess Flora and her nymphs, hence the name. Several additions were made over the years, including four pavilions. These were designed by Joseph Effner who directed works from 1715. Built to the side of the original villa, these were connected by arcaded passageways.

Porcelain parrot in front of the factory

Gallery of Beauties
Portraits of royal favourites include this one of Helene Sedlmayr, a 17-year-old girl from Munich.

Entrance to Schloss Nymphenburg
Seen in this view are the original Italianate villa and two of the side pavilions that were added later.

Marstallmuseum
The former stables house a collection of carriages that once belonged to Bavarian rulers. They include the magnificent carriages of Ludwig II.

Porcelain Factory
Established in 1747 by Franz Anton Bustelli and transferred to Nymphenburg in 1761, this is one of the oldest porcelain factories in Europe.

KEY

– – – Suggested route

STAR SIGHTS

★ **Amalienburg**

★ **Festsaal**

★ **Lackkabinett**

★ Amalienburg
The interior of this hunting lodge in the Schlosspark is a superb example of Rococo style by François de Cuvilliés.

VISITORS' CHECKLIST

📞 (089) 17 90 80.
Ⓤ Rotkreuzplatz.
🕐 Apr–15 Oct: 9am–6pm daily; 16 Oct–Mar: 10am–4pm daily. 🏛

Magdalenenklause
After a lifetime of revels, Maximilian Emmanuel commissioned a hermitage where he could pray and meditate. It was completed in 1725.

Badenburg

Pagodenburg

Museum Mensch und Natur
This museum is devoted to geology and human biology.

★ Lackkabinett
This small 17th-century cabinet owes its name to its panels of black and red Chinese lacquer. It is on display in the Pagodenburg.

Botanical Garden
A collection of botanical specimens, including many rare plants, is featured in this fascinating garden.

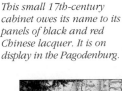

★ Festsaal
Featuring decorations devoted to the goddess Flora, this vast Rococo ballroom is the work of father and son – Johann Baptiste and Franz Zimmermann.

View from the platform of the television tower in Olympiapark

Olympiapark ⓴

[] *(089) 30 67 24 14.* [U] *Olympia-zentrum.* 📇 *20, 25, 27.* **Television tower** ◯ *9am midnight daily.* 🖼

BUILT FOR the 1972 Olympic Games, this vast sports stadium can be spotted from almost anywhere in Munich, as it is the site of a 290-m (950-ft) high television tower, the Olympiaturm. The entire complex was designed by Germany's leading architects, Behnisch and Partners.

The stadium has three main facilities: the Olympic Stadium, which seats 62,000 spectators, the Olympic Hall and the Swimming Hall. In what is one of the most original constructions of 20th-century German architecture, all three are covered by a vast transparent canopy, stretched between a series of tall masts to form an irregular tent.

The stadium includes many other facilities, such as an indoor skating rink, a cycle racing track and tennis courts.

The sports complex is located beside the park's artificial lake. Opposite it is a hill that was constructed from rubble removed from the city after war destruction.

Apart from sporting events, the Olympiapark hosts many popular events, including fireworks displays and regular open-air rock and pop concerts in the summer months.

Englischer Garten ㉛

[U] *Giselastraße.* 📇 *54.*

THE IDEA OF creating this garden, which would be open to all the inhabitants of Munich and not only to its aristocracy, came from Count von Rumford, an American-born chemist and physicist who lived in Bavaria from 1784. As the region's Minister of War, he was responsible for reorganizing the Bavarian army. His idea of creating a garden of this size – the garden covers an area of 5 sq km (1,235 acres) – right in the centre of a large city, was quite unique in Germany. In 1789, taking advantage of his influential position, he persuaded Karl Theodor to put his plans into action.

The project leader was Friedrich Ludwig von Sckell. He was brought to Munich from Schwetzingen by the Elector to create the garden on an area of former marshland.

Chinese Tower in the Englischer Garten

Opened in 1808, the Karl-Theodor-Park is today known simply as the Englischer Garten (English Garden). It is a popular place for long walks, jogging or just lying on the grass in the cool shade of a spreading old tree.

There are some interesting old buildings in the park, such as the Monopteros, a Neo-Classical temple by Leo von Klenze (1837), and the Chinese Tower (1789–90), which is similar to the pagoda in London's Kew Gardens. The Tower stands in one of the park's beer gardens.

It is also worth dropping in to the Japanese Teahouse, where the gentle art of tea brewing is demonstrated.

Deutsches Museum ㉜

See pp218–19.

Franz von Stuck's *Die Sünde*, on display in the Villa Stuck

Villa Stuck ㉝

Prinzregentenstraße 60. [] *(089) 45 55 51 25.* 📇 *18.* 📇 *51, 55.* ◯ *10am–6pm Tue–Sun.* 🖼

THIS VILLA was the home of the famous painter Franz von Stuck, the co-founder of the Munich Secession school of painting. As well as numerous portraits, nudes and sculptures, Von Stuck was the creator of many mythological and allegorical scenes, all painted in dark

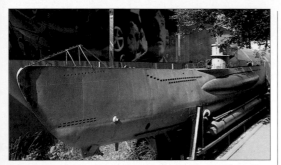
Submarine used in the film *Das Boot*, displayed in Bavaria-Filmstadt

colours and full of eroticism. These include eight variations (1893) on the theme of sin. His *Amazon* (1897) stands in front of the villa.

Franz von Stuck built the villa in 1897–98, to his own design, decorating it with his own paintings and sculptures. Since 1968, it has housed a museum. A permanent exhibition of Stuck's work is displayed in the magnificent music room on the ground floor, while the second-floor rooms are used for temporary exhibitions devoted mainly to early 20th-century art.

Bavaria-Filmstadt ❸

Bavariafilmplatz 7. *(089) 64 99 23 04.* 🚋 25. ◻ Mar–Oct: 9am–4pm daily; Nov–Feb: 10am–3pm daily. ♿ 🅿

COMMONLY known as Hollywood on Isar, this vast site in the southern suburb of Geiselgasteig covers an area of over 3.5 sq km (865 acres).

Since 1919 the world's greatest cinema stars have worked here, including Orson Welles and Billy Wilder. The British film director Alfred Hitchcock made his first films here (*The Pleasure Garden*, 1925 and *The Mountain Eagle*, 1926). Elizabeth Taylor, Gina Lollobrigida and Romy Schneider have all stood in front of the cameras here.

Strolling visitors to the site will often come across some well-known characters who have appeared in films such as *E.T.* or *The Neverending Story*, which were filmed here. The sets of other films made here, including *Enemy Mine* and *Cabaret*, can also

be seen. You can also peep into the submarine that was reconstructed for Wolfgang Petersen's classic film *Das Boot* (1981) – the film follows the voyage of one such boat during World War II.

VIP tours of the Filmstadt include stuntmen shows and fascinating demonstrations of many technical film-making tricks and techniques. A special attraction is the cinema called Showscan, whose seats move according to the story on the screen, giving visitors the sensation of a trip through the universe or of flying through the tunnels of an old silver mine.

While taking a look behind film sets you may even catch a glimpse of a movie star or a celebrity, as the studio is also used for recording TV shows.

Theresienwiese ❸

Theresienhöhe. Ⓤ *Theresienwiese.* ⛺ *Oktoberfest (Sep–Oct).*

FOR MOST OF THE YEAR this is simply a vast oval meadow encircled by the Bavariaring. Theresienwiese comes into its own once a year, however, during the Oktoberfest. Then it turns into a gigantic, boisterous beer-drinking venue, with stalls, marquees, funfair and loud music.

Towering above the meadow is a monumental 18-m (59-ft) high statue, symbol of the state of Bavaria. Made in 1844–50, the statue is the work of Ludwig Schwanthaler. It incorporates an internal staircase leading to the figure's head, where there is a viewing platform.

Just behind the statue is the Ruhmeshalle, a Neo-Classical building surrounded by a colonnade. Designed by Leo von Klenze and built in 1843–53, the building contains numerous busts of eminent Bavarians.

Bavaria statue in Theresienwiese

OKTOBERFEST

Munich's Oktoberfest is one of the biggest folk fairs in Europe. In 1810 the site on which it is held was the venue for a horse race, held to celebrate the marriage of Ludwig (later King of Bavaria) and Thérèse von Saxe-Hildburghausen. A few years later it became the venue for an autumn fair that has grown into an enormous event over the years. Chief amongst the attractions is beer, drunk in vast quantities, in marquees erected by the breweries. The festival starts in late September with a huge procession through the town and the ceremonial opening of the first barrel of beer. It finishes, 16 days later, on the first Sunday of October.

Revellers at the annual Oktoberfest in Theresienwiese

Deutsches Museum ㉜

THE DEUTSCHES MUSEUM, one of the oldest and largest museum of technology and engineering in the world, draws over 1.3 million visitors each year. It was founded in 1903 by Oskar von Miller, an engineer. The building in which it is housed, located on the island in the Isar, was designed by Gabriel von Seidl in 1925. The collections cover most aspects of technology, from its history to its greatest achievements. The museum also houses the world's largest library of technology.

Exterior of the Museum
The building combines Neo-Baroque, Neo-Classical and modern elements.

Decorative Arts
This plate with the portrait of a lady from Ludwig I's "gallery of beauty" is an example of reproduction techniques applied to porcelain. The ceramics section illustrates the development of faience, stoneware and porcelain.

★ Physics
Galileo's workshop features a large collection of the scientific equipment used by the famous astronomer and physicist to establish the basic laws of mechanics.

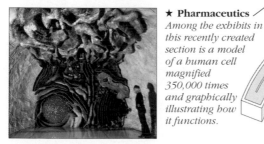

★ Pharmaceutics
Among the exhibits in this recently created section is a model of a human cell magnified 350,000 times and graphically illustrating how it functions.

Second floor

First floor

Main entrance

Ground floor

MUSEUM GUIDE
The museum's 18,000 exhibits are displayed over seven floors. While those on the lower floors include heavy vehicles and sections on chemistry, physics, scientific instruments and aeronautics, those on the middle floors relate to the decorative arts. The upper floors are devoted to astronomy, computers and microelectronics.

Sixth floor

Fifth floor

Fourth floor

Third floor

VISITORS' CHECKLIST

Museumsinsel 1. ☎ 21 791.
Ⓤ Frauenhoferstr. Ⓢ Isartor.
🚋 17, 18. 🚌 52, 56.
◯ 9am–5pm daily. 🅿️ (children under 6 free). 🚻 ◻ ♿ 🛗 by arrangement (21 79 252).
Ⓦ www.Deutsches-Museum.de

Telecommunications
The Philips camera of 1967 was one of the first colour television cameras in the world.

★ **Musical Instruments**
The keyboard instruments room contains the earliest southern German organ and a 17th-century inlaid harpsichord.

KEY

◻ Design and Technology

◻ Transport

◻ Kids' Kingdom

◻ Physics and Chemistry

◻ Musical Instruments

◻ Decorative Arts

◻ Time, Weights and Measures

◻ Automation, Microelectronics and Telecommunications

◻ Astronomy

◻ Agriculture and Geodesy

◻ Miscellaneous

Kids' Kingdom is a hands-on exhibition with computers and interactive games that teaches children about science and technology.

Basement

TRANSPORT

Land transport is the aspect of technology that is best and most fully presented in the Deutsches Museum. The numerous unique exhibits in the collection are soon to be moved to existing rooms on Theresienhöhe, which will be converted into a specialist museum of transport. This major project will result in the largest exhibition of transport the world over, from ancient times to the present day, laid out in an accessible way. The first section of this museum opened in 2003, with the final section due to be completed in May 2005.

Early locomotives in the museum collection

STAR EXHIBITS

★ **Musical Instruments**

★ **Pharmaceutics**

★ **Physics**

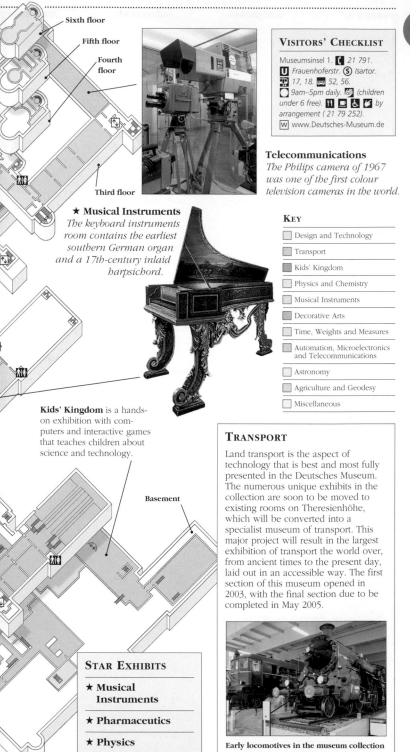

MUNICH STREET FINDER

MAP REFERENCES given in this chapter for sights (and in the Munich hotel and restaurant listings at the back of the book) refer to the maps here. The key map below shows the area of Munich covered by the *Street Finder*. The maps include the major sightseeing areas, historic attractions, railway stations, bus stations, U-Bahn and S-Bahn stations and train stations. The word Straße (Str.) indicates a street, Platz a square, Brücke a bridge and Bahnhof a railway station.

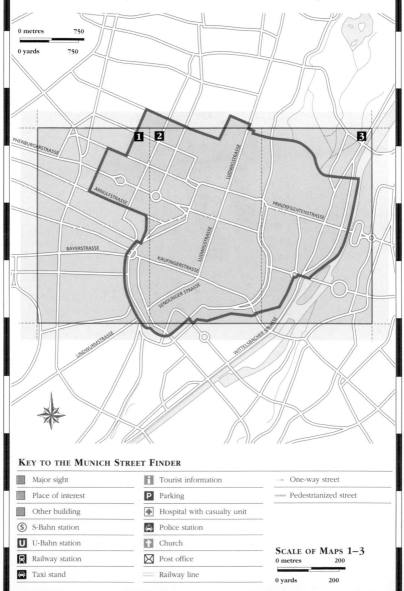

| 0 metres | 750 |
| 0 yards | 750 |

PHENBURGERSTRASSE

ARNULFSTRASSE

BAYERSTRASSE

LUDWIGSTRASSE

PRINZREGENTENSTRASSE

KAUFINGERSTRASSE

LUDWIGSTRASSE

SENDLINGER STRASSE

LINDWURMSTRASSE

WITTELSBACHER STRASSE

KEY TO THE MUNICH STREET FINDER

■ Major sight	ℹ Tourist information	→ One-way street
■ Place of interest	🅿 Parking	▬ Pedestrianized street
■ Other building	✚ Hospital with casualty unit	
Ⓢ S-Bahn station	Police station	
🅄 U-Bahn station	✝ Church	
Railway station	⊠ Post office	**SCALE OF MAPS 1–3**
Taxi stand	Railway line	

| 0 metres | 200 |
| 0 yards | 200 |

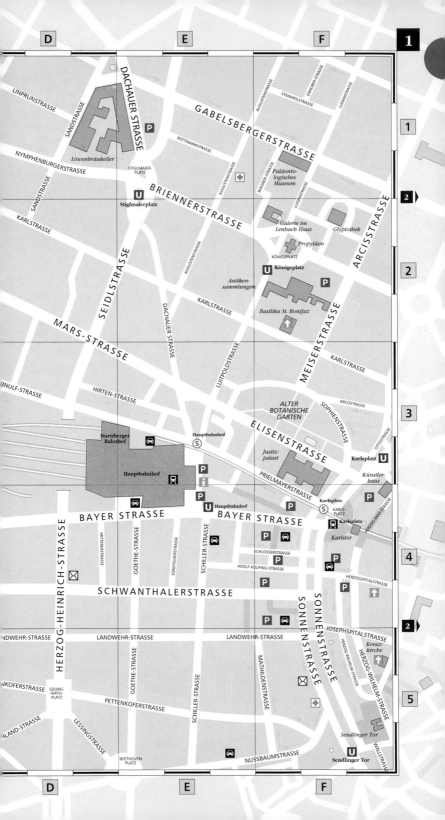

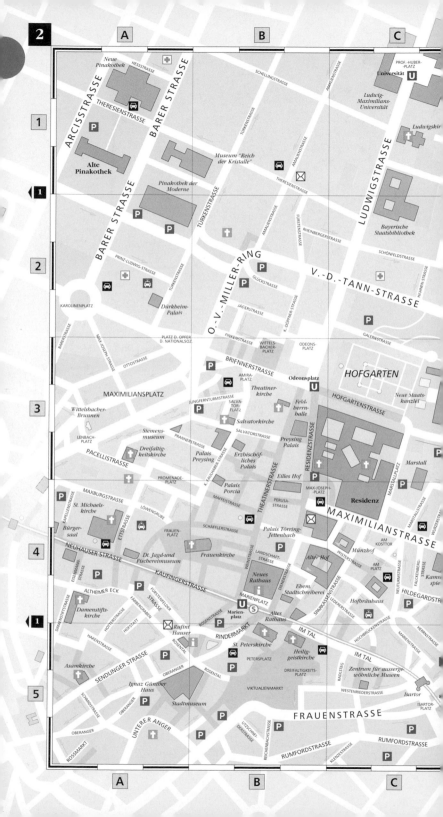

BAVARIA

B AVARIA *is the biggest federal state in the Federal Republic of Germany. It is made up of regions that, in the past, were either independent secular territories or bishoprics. It includes former free towns of the Holy Roman Empire, such as Nördlingen, Rothenburg ob der Tauber, Dinkelsbühl, Nuremberg and Augsburg, which lost their independence to Bavaria only in the early 19th century.*

The area that is now known as Bavaria was inhabited in early times by Celts and Romans. The German Baiovarii, which gave the territory its name, arrived here during the 5th and 6th centuries. In the second half of the 6th century, the area was conquered by the Franks then, from 1180 until 1918, Bavaria was ruled by the Wittelsbach dynasty. During Medieval times, this split into the Upper Bavarian line (Straubing, Ingolstadt and Munich) and the Lower Bavarian line (Landshut). In 1505, separate provinces were once again combined into a single country. During the 16th and 17th centuries the duchy of Bavaria was the bulwark of Roman Catholicism within the Holy Roman Empire and during the reign of Maximilian I, Bavaria fought against the Protestant Union in the Thirty Years' War. For his loyalty to Rome, Maximilian I was rewarded in 1623 with the title of Elector, which meant that he could vote in elections for the Emperor. Following the fall of the Holy Roman Empire, Bavaria became a kingdom and remained as such until 1918.

Bavaria's turbulent history has left behind a rich architectural and cultural heritage. In addition to Roman antiquities, Baroque fortresses and fairy-tale castles, the region also has more than its share of glorious Alpine scenery, beer halls and colourful festivals, all of which make this one of the most popular parts of Germany for tourists. The capital, Munich, is a lively cosmopolitan city of wide boulevards and leafy squares with a wide choice of shops, restaurants, cinemas and theatres.

Girls dressed in national costume celebrating St Leonard's Festival

◁ **Interior of the Abbey library, in Metten**

Exploring Bavaria

BAVARIA IS A PARADISE for tourists. Its beautiful lakes attract lovers of water sports, while the mountainous regions of the Bavarian Forest offer the unspoiled charms of nature. The Alps, with their charming mountain hostels and numerous ski-lifts, provide endless possibilities for enjoyment. Towns and villages feature magnificent historic sights and the capital, Munich, combines the advantages of a lively metropolis with a peaceful atmosphere that is not often found in large cities.

The façade and central rotunda of Bayreuth's Eremitage

SIGHTS AT A GLANCE

(map)

Fulda

RHÖN

EAST

Frankfurt

ASCHAFFENBURG **1**

SPESS

Men

MILTENBERG

WÜRZBURG **6**

BAMBER

POMMERSFEL

ROTHENBURG **17**

Heilbronn

ANSBACH **13**

Altmühl

DINKELSBÜHL **11**

NÖRDLINGEN **12**

AUGSBUR

LANDSBE
AM LEC

OTTOBEUREN **45**

KEMPTEN **41**

LINDAU **42**

LINDENBERG

LINDERHOF

Bodensee

FÜSSEN

NEUSCHWANSTEIN

Feldkirch

OBERSTDORF

| 0 km | 30 |
| 0 miles | 30 |

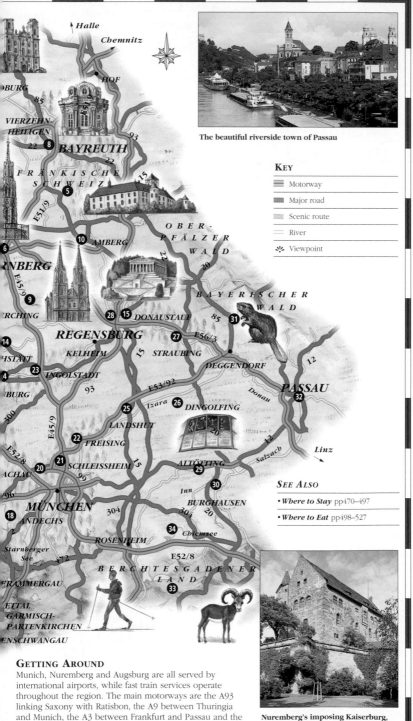

↑ *Halle*

Chemnitz

HOF

BURG

85

VIERZEHN-
HEILIGEN

22 **8** **BAYREUTH**

22

5

F R A N K I S C H E
S C H W E I Z

15

E51/9

O B E R -
P F Ä L Z E R
W A L D

10 AMBERG

22

20

6

NBERG

E45/9

9

B A Y E R I S C H E R
W A L D

RCHING

28 **15** DONAUSTAUF

85

31

14

REGENSBURG

27 E56/3

KELHEIM

15 STRAUBING

12

HSTÄTT

23

DEGGENDORF

4

INGOLSTADT

E53/92

PASSAU

BURG

93

25 Izara **26** DINGOLFING

Donau

32

300

E45/9

LANDSHUT

20

Linz

E52/8

22 FREISING

Salzach

ACHAU

20 **21** SCHLEISSHEIM

15

ALTÖTTING
29

96

99

30

Inn

18 **MÜNCHEN**

304

BURGHAUSEN

ANDECHS

304 20

*Starnberger
See*

472

34 Chiemsee

RAMMERGAU

B E R C H T E S G A D E N E R
L A N D

ETTAL

E52/8

ROSENHEIM

33

GARMISCH-
PARTENKIRCHEN

NSCHWANGAU

The beautiful riverside town of Passau

Key

▬ Motorway

▬ Major road

▬ Scenic route

▬ River

☼ Viewpoint

See Also

• *Where to Stay* pp470–497

• *Where to Eat* pp498–527

Getting Around

Munich, Nuremberg and Augsburg are all served by
international airports, while fast train services operate
throughout the region. The main motorways are the A93
linking Saxony with Ratisbon, the A9 between Thuringia
and Munich, the A3 between Frankfurt and Passau and the
A8, which runs between Stuttgart and Salzburg.

**Nuremberg's imposing Kaiserburg,
overlooking the city**

Red sandstone exterior of Schloss Johannisburg, Aschaffenburg

Aschaffenburg ❶

Road map C5. 👥 67 000. 🚃
ℹ️ *Schlossplatz (06021-39 58 00).*

SITUATED IN Lower Franconia, Aschaffenburg enjoys a scenic position on the hilly right bank of the river Main. The town became the second seat of the Mainz bishops in the 13th century, the first being Mainz.

The northwest part of the old town features a majestic, red sandstone riverside castle, **Schloss Johannisburg**, which was once occupied by the Mainz bishops-electors.

The castle gallery holds a fine collection of European paintings, dating from the 15th to the 18th century. It includes canvases by Lucas Cranach and Hans Baldung Grien. In the castle library are valuable medieval codices, such as the 10th-century *Book of Gospel Readings* (*Evangelarium*) from Fulda. Elegant interiors in the west wing are also noteworthy.

Occupying a scenic position above a vineyard a short distance to the northwest of the castle is Pompejanum. The Bavarian king Ludwig I was so fascinated with the discovery of Pompeii that he ordered a replica of the Castor and Pollux villa (*Casa di Castore e Polluce*) to be built. This he filled with his rich collection of antiquities.

After undergoing restoration work to repair war damage, the museum opened its doors to the public again in 1994.

♣ **Schloss Johannisburg**
Schlossplatz 4. 📞 *(06021) 38 65 70.*
🕐 *Apr–Sep: 9am–6pm Tue–Sun; Oct–Mar: 10am–4pm Tue–Sun.* 🦽

Pommersfelden ❷

Road map D5. ℹ️ *Hauptstraße 11 (09548-922 00).*

ON THE EDGE of the Steigerwald – a popular hiking area – is the small village of Pommersfelden, which is dominated by its magnificent Baroque palace, **Schloss Weissenstein**. The palace was commissioned by the Mainz Archbishop and Elector and the Prince-Bishop of Bamberg, Lothar Franz von Schönborn. It was built, in only five years (1711–16), to a design by the famous architect, Johann Dientzenhofer.

This masterpiece of secular Baroque architecture is worth visiting for several reasons. Particularly interesting is the three-storey-high ornamental ceiling by Johann Rudolf Byss. The most spectacular room is the Marble Hall, which features paintings by Michael Rottmayr. The well-preserved interior of the palace houses a gallery, a library, and a valuable collection of furniture. After visiting the palace, you can take a stroll around its gardens, which were

created by Maximilian von Welsch in 1715, in what was the then fashionable, geometric French style. It is now laid out in English-garden style.

♣ **Schloss Weissenstein**
📞 *(09548) 98180.* 🕐 *Apr–Oct: 10am–5pm daily.* 📷 *every hour. (Short tour: 11:30am and 4:30pm.)* 🦽

Coburg ❸

Road map D5. 👥 44,000. 🚃
ℹ️ *Herrngasse 4 (09561-741 80).*

FORMER RESIDENCE of the Wettin family, Coburg is situated on the bank of the river Itz. It is dominated by a massive fortress, the **Veste Coburg**, which is one of the largest in Germany. Coburg's origins go back to the 11th century, but its present-day appearance is mainly the result of remodelling that was carried out in the 16th and the 17th centuries.

The fortress consists of a number of buildings clustered around several courtyards and surrounded by a triple line of walls. The complex is now a museum, housing various collections, including prints and drawings, arms and armour.

In 1530, the fortress provided refuge to Martin Luther who, as an outlaw, hid here from April until October. The room in which he hid is

Ornate entrance to Coburg's Stadthaus

furnished with antique
furniture and features
a portrait of Luther,
painted by Lucas
Cranach the Younger.

Among the most
important buildings in
the old town are the
late-Gothic church of
St Maurice and a
beautiful Renaissance
college building that
was founded by Prince
Johann Casimir in
1605. On the opposite
side of the market
square is the town
hall, originally built in
1577–79 and remodelled in
the 18th century.

Further along is the town
castle, **Schloss Ehrenburg**,
which was built in the 16th
century on the site of a dissolved Franciscan monastery.
The castle burned down in
1693 and was subsequently
rebuilt. The façade facing the
square was remodelled by
Karl Friedrich Schinkel in
Neo-Gothic style.

The castle has some fine
interiors, including the
Baroque Riesensaal and
Weisser Saal and a chapel
with rich stucco decorations.

⚜ **Veste Coburg**
【 *(09561) 87 90.* ◯ *Apr–Oct:*
10am–5pm Tue–Sun; Nov–Mar:
1–4pm Tue–Sun. 🖼

⚜ **Schloss Ehrenburg**
Schlossplatz 1. 【 *(09561) 808 80.*
◯ *Apr–Sep: 9am–5pm Tue–Sun;*
Oct–Mar: 10am–3pm Tue–Sun. 🎫
every hour. 🖼

Vierzehnheiligen ❹

Staffelstein. **Road map** D5.
【 *(09571) 950 80.* ◯ *Apr–Oct:*
7am–7pm; Nov–Mar: 8am–5pm.

HIGH ABOVE the river Main
is Banz Abbey, a
Benedictine monastery built
in 1695 by Johann Leonhard
and Leonhard Dientzenhofer.
Directly opposite stands the
pilgrimage church of the
Fourteen Saints of Intercession.
The first chapel, erected on
this site in the 16th century,
proved to be too small to
accommodate the growing
numbers of pilgrims so, in
1741, the foundation stone

**Interior of the monumental, Baroque
Vierzehnheiligen church**

was laid for the monumental
new church, designed by
Balthasar Neumann. Built in
1741–72, this is one of the
most famous masterpieces of
South German Baroque, with
magnificent Rococo
furnishings. The building is
a cross-shaped basilica,
with a monumental twin-
tower façade.

The interior has
an exceptionally
dynamic style,
achieved by
combining the
longitudinal and
central planes: the
three ovals laid along
the main axis join with
the two circles of the
transept. The centrepiece
of the nave is the "Altar
of Mercy", which stands
at the spot where,
according to a 1519
legend, a shepherd
had visions of Christ
with the fourteen
Saints of Intercession. The
altar features statues of the
fourteen saints, the work of
J J M Küchel (1763). The rich
stucco decorations and wall
paintings are the work of
J M and F X Feuchtmayr,
J G Üblher and Giuseppe
Appiani.

**Madonna from
Marienkapelle in
Ebermannstadt**

Fränkische Schweiz ❺

Road map D5.

THE AREA POPULARLY known
as Franconian Switzerland
(*Fränkische Schweiz*) covers
the area between Nuremberg,
Bamberg and Bayreuth. One
of Germany's most beautiful
tourist regions, it offers its
visitors picturesque green
meadows, magnificent high-
lands covered with cornfields,
imposing castles perched on
top of high rocks, fabulous
dolomite rocks and deep
caves with stalactites. Its
towns and villages, with their
charming inns and timber-
frame houses, look like a
setting for *Snow White and
Seven Dwarfs*. The main
routes across the area
run alongside its
rivers – the Wiesent,
Leinleiter, Püttlach
and Trubach. The
Wiesent, which is
ideal for canoeing,
cuts across the
region from east to
west, joining the river
Regnitz near the town
of Forchheim. The
town features many
timber-frame houses,
including the old town
hall dating from the
14th to the 16th
century. Near
Forchheim, in
Ebermannstadt,
is a Marian church
with a fine Madonna.
The federal route
B470 leads to the picturesque
village of Tüchersfeld, which
is built into the rocks. A good
base for exploring this area is
the village of Pottenstein. St
Elizabeth of Thuringia is said
to have stayed here
in 1227. To the
east of the castle
is a cave with
impressive
stalactites.

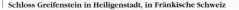

Schloss Greifenstein in Heiligenstadt, in Fränkische Schweiz

Würzburg 6

THE BOMBING RAID on Würzburg on 16 March 1945 lasted for about 20 minutes and destroyed over 80 percent of the town's buildings. It seemed that Würzburg, which occupies a picturesque position on the banks of the river Main, had been erased from the face of the earth. Like Dresden, however, the town rose from the ashes and once again it enchants visitors with its rich heritage of historic sights. As well as being a popular tourist destination, Würzburg is also an important commercial and cultural centre for Lower Franconia and home of the excellent Franconian wine.

View over Würzburg, with Dom St Kilian in the foreground

✦ Residenz
See pp232–3.

✦ Dom St Kilian
Domplatz. ✆ (0931) 321 18 30.
◯ Easter–1 Nov: 10am–5pm Mon–Sat, 1–6pm Sun and holidays; 2 Nov–Easter: 10am–noon, 2–5pm Mon–Sat, 12:30–1pm, 2–6pm Sun and holidays.

Next to the cathedral churches of Mainz, Speyer and Worms, this is Germany's fourth largest Romanesque church. It was built in 1045–1188, its patron saint an Irish monk who came to Würzburg in AD 686 and died a martyr's death.

The church is a three-nave basilica with a transept and a twin-tower façade. Inside, the Romanesque main nave with its flat roof contrasts sharply with the Baroque stucco embellishments of the choir.

In the north nave is an interesting group of bishops' tombs, including two that are the work of Tilman Riemenschneider. At the end of the north transept is a chapel, which was built by Balthasar Neumann for the bishops of the House of Schönborn.

✦ Neumünster-Kirche
St-Kilians-Platz.

Just north of the cathedral, the Neumünster-Kirche was built in the 11th century at the burial site of St Kilian and his fellow Irish martyrs, St Kolonat and St Totnan.

The church's imposing Baroque dome and its red sandstone façade date from the 18th century. Featured in

The beautiful red sandstone façade of Neumünster-Kirche

the interior are numerous works of art, including a late 15th-century Madonna and the *Man of Sorrow* by the 15th-century German sculptor Tilman Riemenschneider. The north door leads to a lovely small courtyard; the remains of the cloister date from the Hohenstauf period. Under a lime tree is the resting place of a famous medieval minstrel Walther von der Vogelweide.

A procession is held each year on St Kilian's day (8 July) when theological students carry the skulls of the martyrs, contained in a transparent box, from the west crypt to the cathedral where they are put on public display.

✦ Bürgerspital
Theaterstraße.

The Bürgerspital was founded in 1319 by Johann von Steren. Hospitals like this originally provided charitable care for the old as well as the infirm, and today this institution provides care for over one hundred elderly residents of Würzburg. It operates as a self-financing foundation, its main source of income being from vine-growing. Residents are given a quarter of a litre (½ pint) of an excellent home-produced wine each day, with double the ration on Sundays. Visitors can also sample various vintages.

✦ Juliusspital
Juliuspromenade.

Just a short distance away from Bürgerspital is another hospital. Founded in 1576 by Julius Echter, Juliusspital was remodelled in the 17th and the 18th centuries. The Rococo pharmacy (1760–65) in the hospital arcades has survived intact and is well worth a visit.

✦ Rathaus
Rueckermainstraße.

Würzburg's picturesque town hall was built in several stages. Begun in the 13th century, it was subsequently extended in the 15th and 16th centuries. Particularly noteworthy are the beautiful 16th-century paintings on the façade and the late-Renaissance tower, Roter Turm, which dates from around 1660.

An old crane near Alte Mainbrücke over the river Main

⊞ Alte Mainbrücke

Connecting the old town and Festung Marienberg, this beautiful bridge was built in 1473–1543. It is the oldest bridge over the Main.

♔ Festung Marienberg

Fürstenbau-Museum
📞 (0931) 438 38. ⏰ Apr–Oct: 9am–6pm Tue–Sun; Nov–Mar: 10am–4pm Tue–Sun. 🎟️
Mainfränkisches Museum
📞 (0931) 205 940. ⏰ Apr–Oct: 10am–5pm Tue–Sun; Nov–Mar: 10am–4pm Tue–Sun. 🎟️
Burgführungen 🎟️ Apr–Oct: 11am, 2pm Tue–Fri; 10am, 11am, 1pm, 2pm, 3pm, 4pm Sat–Sun.

Built on the site of an old Celtic stronghold, the Marienberg Fortress towers above the town. In AD 707 a church was built here and, in 1201, work commenced on a fortress that served as the residence of the prince-bishops until 1719. Within its fortifications stands the first original donjon church dating from the 13th century, and the Renaissance-Baroque palace. The museum exhibits illustrate the 1,200-year history of the town. The former arsenal now houses the Franconian Museum with its valuable collection of sculptures by Tilman Riemenschneider.

⛪ Käppele

Mergentheimer Strasse.
Standing at the top of a hill at the southwestern end of the city, this twin-towered Baroque chapel is the work of Balthasar Neumann (1747–50). Its interior is lavishly decorated with beautiful wall paintings by Matthias Günther.

Festung Marienberg, built on a hill overlooking the river Main

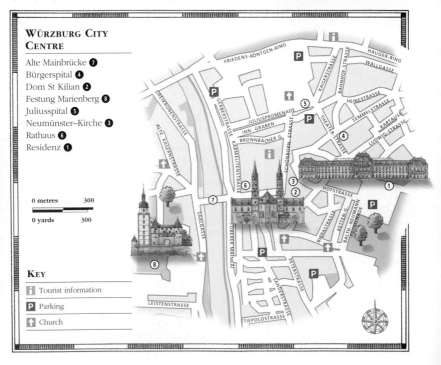

WÜRZBURG CITY CENTRE

Alte Mainbrücke ❼
Bürgerspital ❹
Dom St Kilian ❷
Festung Marienberg ❽
Juliusspital ❺
Neumünster–Kirche ❸
Rathaus ❻
Residenz ❶

0 metres 300
0 yards 300

KEY

🛈 Tourist information
🅿 Parking
✝ Church

Residenz in Würzburg

Sculpture from Residenz garden

THIS VAST COMPLEX on the eastern edge of the town was commissioned by two prince-bishops, the brothers Johann Philipp Franz and Friedrich Karl von Schönborn. Its construction between 1720 and 1744 was supervised by several architects, including Johann Lukas von Hilde-brandt and Maximilian von Welsch. However, the Residenz is mainly associated with the name of Balthasar Neumann, the creator of its famous Baroque staircase.

Napoleon's bedroom

Main entrance

Martin-von-Wagner-Museum entrance

★ Treppenhaus
The work of the Venetian artist Giovanni Battista Tiepolo, the largest fresco in the world adorns the vault of the staircase.

Frankonia-brunnen
A fountain, designed by Gabriel von Seidel, was constructed in the parade square in front of the Residenz in 1896. It was funded by donations from the inhabitants of Würzburg.

The Arms of the Patron
The richly decorated façade by Johann Wolfgang von der Auwery bears the personal arms of Friedrich Karl von Schönborn, Prince-Bishop of Bamberg and Würzburg.

★ Kaisersaal
The centrepiece of the palace, the sumptuous emperor's chamber, testifies to the close relationship between Würzburg and the Holy Roman Empire.

VISITORS' CHECKLIST

Residenzplatz 2. 📞 *(0931) 35 51 70.* ◯ *Apr–Oct: 9am–6pm daily; Nov–Mar: 10am–4pm daily.* ● *1 Jan, 24, 25, 31 Dec.* ◙

Garden Chamber
This vast, low hall has Rococo stucco works by Antonio Bossi, dating from 1749. There is also a painting on the vaulting by Johan Zick dating from 1750, depicting The Feast of the Gods *and* Diana Resting.

Venetian Room
This room is named after a tapestry depicting the Venetian carnival. Further ornaments include decorative panels with paintings by Johann Thalhofer, a pupil of Rudolph Byss.

★ Hofkirche
The church interior is richly decorated with paintings, sculptures and stucco ornaments. The side altars were designed by Johann Lukas von Hildebrandt and feature paintings by Giovanni Battista Tiepolo.

STAR SIGHTS

★ Hofkirche

★ Kaisersaal

★ Treppenhaus

Bamberg ⑦

Situated on seven hills like ancient Rome, Bamberg features a splendidly preserved old town, encircled by the branches of the river Regnitz. The town is famous not only for its exceptional artistic heritage but also for its excellent beer, produced by one of the nine breweries that operate here. Its long history goes back to AD 902, when the Babenberg family established their residence here. The town grew and prospered in the wake of the Thirty Years' War. In 1993, Bamberg became a UNESCO World Heritage Site.

Beautiful rose garden at the rear of the Neue Residenz

Exploring Bamberg
A good place to start sight-seeing is the Domplatz, one of Germany's loveliest squares, with its magnificent cathedral church and the old bishop's palace. After visiting the Neue Residenz you can go down to the river, where you will find the water palace, Concordia. The old town is reached by crossing one of two bridges – Untere or Obere Brücke.

🛆 Dom
See pp236–7.

🏛 Alte Hofhaltung
Historisches Museum
Domplatz 7. 📞 *(0951) 87 11 42.*
🕐 *9am–5pm Tue–Sun.* 🖼
On the west side of Domplatz stands a magnificent portal, featuring statues of the imperial couple Heinrich II and Kunigunde. This is the gate to the former bishop's residence, built at the turn of the 15th and 16th centuries in place of an old fortress of Heinrich II. Within the wings of the building is a pleasant courtyard. The museum that is housed here focuses on the history of the region.

🏛 Neue Residenz und Staatsgalerie
Domplatz 8. 📞 *(0951) 519 390.*
🕐 *Apr–Sep: 9am–6pm Mon–Wed, Fri–Sun, 9am–8pm Thu; Oct–Mar: 10am–4pm daily.* 🖼
The Neue Residenz, with its richly decorated apartments and the Emperor's Room, was built in 1695–1704 and is the work of Johann Leonhard Dietzenhofer. Its walls are adorned with magnificent frescos painted by the Tyrolean artist Melchior Steidl. The walls and pillars feature the Habsburg family tree, while 16 statues represent Emperors of the Holy Roman Empire. The Neue Residenz houses a collection of old German masters, including *The Flood* by Hans Baldung Grien and three canvases by Lucas Cranach the Elder.

🏛 Bishop's Palace
Behind the cathedral, along the quiet, picturesque Dom-strasse, are a number of ecclesiastical buildings, the oldest of which date from the 16th century. Domstrasse leads to the Baroque Bishop's Palace, built in 1763 by Johann Michael von Küchel.

🛆 Karmeliterkloster
Kreuzgang 🕐 *8:30–11.30 am, 2:30–5:30pm daily.*
The hospital-abbey complex of St Theodore was founded in the late 12th century by Bishop Eberhard. Since 1589 the church and abbey have belonged to the Carmelite order. The south tower and Romanesque portal are the remains of the massive 12th-century basilica. The interior of the church was redesigned in the late 17th and early 18th centuries so the altar is now situated at its western end, while the entrance is on the site of the previous presbytery. The layout of the cloisters on the south side of the church is typical of Cistercian designs.

⚓ Wasserschloss Concordia
Concordiastrasse. ⬤ *to the public.*
This magnificent Baroque palace, which enjoys a scenic position on the water's edge,

Façade of Schloss Seehof in Memmelsberg, flanked by two towers

Picturesque fishermen's cottages in Klein-Venedig

VISITORS' CHECKLIST

Road map D5. 🏘 71,000. ✈
8 km (5 miles) to the southeast.
ℹ Geyerswörthstraße 3 (0951-
297 62 00). 🎭 Calderon-
Festspiele (June), Sandkirchweih
(August). Ⓦ www.bamberg.info

was built for Counsellor Böttinger between 1716 and 1722, to a design by Johann Dientzenhofer. The building now houses a science institute.

🏛 Altes Rathaus

The Baroque lower bridge, Untere Brücke, provides a magnificent view over the upper bridge, Obere Brücke, with its fabulous town hall. This originally Gothic seat of the municipal authorities was remodelled in 1744–56 by Jakob Michael Küchel. The half-timbered structure of the Rottmeisterhaus, which seems to be gliding over the waves of the river Regnitz, was added in 1688.

🏛 Klein-Venedig

"Little Venice" is a district of fishermen's cottages, their picturesque façades adorned with pots of geraniums.

Visitors come here for a glass of Rauchbier – a local beer with a smoky flavour – while they enjoy the view.

🏛 Grünermarkt

With its historic houses and adjacent Maximilianplatz, Grünermarkt lies at the heart of the old town. Here you will find the magnificent Baroque St Martin's Church, built in 1686–91 by the Dientzenhofer brothers. Also notable are the late-Baroque buildings of the St Catherine Hospital and Seminary, built by Balthasar Neumann, which now serves as the town hall.

🏛 Kirche St Michael

Michaelsberg.
Fränkisches Brauereimuseum
🕐 Apr–Oct: 1–5pm Wed–Sun. 🎫
The Benedictine abbey that stood on this site was founded in 1015. The surviving church was built after 1121 and later remodelled in the 16th and 17th centuries. On the ceiling of the church, nicknamed the "Botanical Gardens", are paintings depicting almost 600 species of medicinal plants. The abbey's Baroque buildings date from the 17th and 18th centuries and are the work of Johann Dientzenhofer and Balthasar Neumann. The domestic quarters include the abbey's brewery, which now houses a museum.

The Baroque palace Concordia on the bank of the river Regnitz

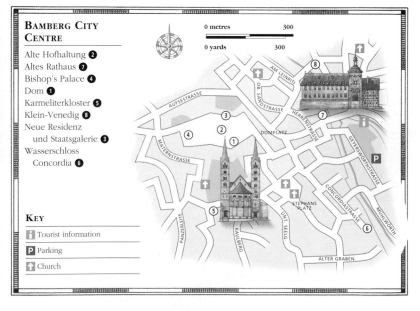

BAMBERG CITY CENTRE

Alte Hofhaltung ❷
Altes Rathaus ❼
Bishop's Palace ❹
Dom ❶
Karmeliterkloster ❺
Klein-Venedig ❽
Neue Residenz
    und Staatsgalerie ❸
Wasserschloss
    Concordia ❻

0 metres   300
0 yards   300

KEY

ℹ Tourist information
P Parking
✝ Church

Bamberg Cathedral

BAMBERG'S SKYLINE is dominated by the cathedral of St Peter and St George, which combines the late Romanesque and early French-Gothic styles. Its construction started about 1211 and the church was consecrated in 1237. This is a triple-nave basilica with two choirs, whose apses are flanked by two pairs of towers. The cloisters were built between 1399 and 1457, while the monumental sculptures adorning the portals date from the 13th century. The western choir of the cathedral holds the only papal grave in Germany, that of Pope Clement II, who had been the local bishop.

Sculpted figure of Ecclesia

Interior
The illuminated main nave features a graceful, early Gothic, cross-ribbed vault.

★ **Bamberger Reiter**
By the northwestern pillar of the eastern choir stands the famous equestrian statue of the "Bamberg Rider", dating from 1225–30. Many scholars have puzzled over the identity of the rider, but the riddle remains unsolved.

St George's Choir

★ **Tomb of Heinrich II and Kunigunde**
This beautiful sarcophagus of the imperial couple is the work of Tilman Riemenschneider, completed in 1513.

Main entrance

St Peter's Choir

Emperor's Cloak
The Diocesan Museum houses an exhibition of sacral art. It also features a collection of imperial vestments, including Heinrich II's blue cloak of stars.

VISITORS' CHECKLIST

Domplatz 5. █ (0951) 50 23 30.
◯ Apr–Oct: 10am–6pm daily;
Nov–Mar: 10am–5pm daily.
Diözesanmuseum █ (0951) 50
23 16. ◯ 10am–5pm Tue–Sun.
● Good Friday, 25, 31 Dec. ◿

Hochaltar des Peterschores
The main altar of the west choir is adorned with sculptures depicting the Crucifixion (1648–49) by Justus Glesker.

★ Marian Altar by Veit Stoss
Veit Stoss was commissioned to create this altar by his son, Andrew Stoss, who was a Carmelite prior in Nürnberg at the time. After the victory of the Reformation in Nürnberg, however, he moved to Bamberg.

Fürstenportal

Gnadenpforte
This magnificent stonework adorns the main entrance. The tympanum features reliefs depicting scenes from the Last Judgement.

STAR SIGHTS

★ **Bamberger Reiter**

★ **Marian Altar by Veit Stoss**

★ **Tomb of Heinrich II and Kunigunde**

Bayreuth ❽

LOVERS OF GERMAN music associate this town with the composer Richard Wagner (1813–83), who took up residence here in 1872. Established in 1231, Bayreuth originally belonged to the family of Count von Andechs-Meran; in 1248 it passed to the Margraves of Nuremberg (von Zollern) and, since 1806, Franconian Bayreuth has belonged to Bavaria. The town flourished during the 17th and 18th centuries when it was the residence of the Margraves, particularly during the time of Margravine Wilhelmine, sister of the Prussian King Frederick the Great and wife of Margrave Frederick.

Extraordinary Baroque interior of the Markgräfliches Opernhaus

🎭 Markgräfliches Opernhaus
Opernstraße 14. 📞 (0921) 759 69 22. ⏰ Apr–Sep: 9am–6pm daily; Oct–Mar: 10am–4pm daily. 🎫
One of the finest theatres in Europe, the Markgräfliches Opera House was built in the 1740s by Joseph Saint-Pierre. Its ornate Baroque interior was designed by Giuseppe Galli Bibiena and his son Carlo, who came from a famous Bolognese family of theatre architects.

♣ Neues Schloss
Ludwigstraße 21. 📞 (0921) 759 69 21. ⏰ Apr–Sep: 9am–6pm daily; Oct–Mar: 10am–4pm daily. 🎫
The Neues Schloss (New Castle) was commissioned by Margravine Wilhelmine and built by Joseph Saint-Pierre. The elongated, three-storey structure combines classical lines with a rustic ground floor. The Italian wing was added in 1759. To this day nearly all the rooms have retained their original Baroque and Rococo decor. The park is arranged in a typically English style.

🏛 Villa Wahnfried
Richard-Wagner-Museum. Richard-Wagner-Straße 48. 📞 (0921) 75 72 816. ⏰ Apr–Sep: 9am–5pm daily, 9am–8pm Tue; Oct–Mar: 10am–5pm daily. 🎫 ● Easter Sunday.
On the northeast side of the castle garden is Villa Wahnfried. Built for Wagner by Carl Wölfel, the villa was destroyed during World War II but was restored in the 1970s. In the garden is Wagner's tomb and that of his wife Cosima, the daughter of Franz Liszt.

🏛 Franz-Liszt-Museum
Wahnfriedstraße 9. 📞 (0921) 516 64 88. ⏰ Sep–Jun: 10am–noon, 2–5pm daily; Jul–Aug: 10am–5pm daily. 🎫
A short distance from Villa Wahnfried, at the junction of Wahnfriedstrasse and Lisztstrasse, stands the house in which Hungarian composer Franz Liszt died in 1886. It now houses a museum dedicated to the composer.

🏛 Eremitage
4 km (2.5 miles) northeast of town 📞 (0921) 759 60 37. ⏰ 16 Apr–14 Oct: 9am–6pm daily.
In 1715–18, following the example of the French king Louis XIV and the fashion among the nobility for playing at ascetism, Margrave Georg Wilhelm ordered the building of the Eremitage complex as a retreat. With its horseshoe-shaped orangery, the hermitage (or Altes Schloss) was given to Margravine Wilhelmine as a birthday present. She then set about transforming it into a glamorous, self-indulgent, pleasure palace.

RICHARD WAGNER (1813–1883)

The German composer is inseparably linked with Bayreuth, where he enjoyed his greatest artistic triumphs. His career, which did not run smoothly in early days, began in Magdeburg, Königsberg and Riga. From there he had to flee, via London to Paris, from his pursuing creditors. His reputation was firmly established by successful performances of his romantic operas *The Flying Dutchman* (1843) and *Tannhäuser* (1845) in Dresden. Wagner's long-time sponsor was the eccentric Bavarian king, Ludwig II. From 1872 Wagner lived in Bayreuth, where Festspielhaus was built specifically for the operas.

Bust of Wagner by Arno Breker (1939)

Tomb of Wagner and his wife in the garden of Villa Wahnfried

Festspielhaus, specially designed venue for the annual Wagner Festival

⊞ Festspielhaus

Festspielhügel. **[** (0921) 787 80.
[10am, 10:45am, 2:15pm, 3pm,
Tue–Sun (mornings only during the
Festival). **○** Nov.

Each July and August, Wagner
festivals are held in this theatre,
which was built in 1872–75 to
a design by Gottfried Semper.
The world premiere of *The
Ring of the Nibelung* was
performed here in 1876.

ENVIRONS: Approximately 20
km (12 miles) to the northwest
of Bayreuth is the town of
Kulmbach. Famous for its
countless breweries, the town
hosts a big beer festival each
year, in July and August.

Its town hall has a beautiful,
Rococo façade dating from
1752. From here you can walk
to the castle hill to visit the
Plassenburg Fortress, which
has belonged to the
Hohenzollern family
since 1340. Until 1604,
this was the seat of the
von Brandenburg-
Kulmbach Margraves.
This vast structure was
built in 1560-70. The
gem in its crown is the
Renaissance courtyard
with arcades (Schöner
Hof). The castle houses
a vast collection of tin
figurines, with some
30,000 items.

VISITORS' CHECKLIST

Road map D5. 🏘 75,000. ✈
10 km (6 miles) to northeast. 🚆
Hauptbahnhof. 🛈 Luitpoldplatz
9 (0921-885 88). 🎭 Musica Bayreuth (May), Fränkische Festwoche
(May), Richard-Wagner-Festspiele
(Jul–Aug), Bayreuther Barock (Sep).

In **Ködnitz**, just to the southeast of Kulmbach, can be seen
the Upper Franconian Village
School Museum. Based on the
original school furnishings and
various old photographs, the
exhibition illustrates the teaching methods that were used
in this region more than a
hundred years ago.

Some 25 km (16 miles) from
Bayreuth, in Sanspareil Park
near Hollfeld, is the **Felsentheater** – an unusual 80-seat
theatre set in a natural grotto.

Felsentheater, in a natural grotto in
Sanspareil Park near Bayreuth

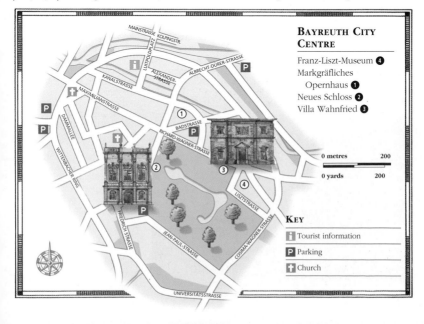

BAYREUTH CITY CENTRE

Franz-Liszt-Museum ❹
Markgräfliches
 Opernhaus ❶
Neues Schloss ❷
Villa Wahnfried ❸

0 metres   200

0 yards   200

KEY

🛈 Tourist information

🅿 Parking

✝ Church

Berching **9**

Map D6. 🏛 *7,500.* 🏨 *Petten-koferplatz 12 (08462-205 13).*

THIS CHARMING little town, situated in the valley of the river Sulz, boasts a history that stretches back to the 9th century. To this day it retains the complete enclosure of its medieval city walls, including towers and gates with old oak doors. The most beautiful of the towers is the *Chinesische Turm* (the Chinese Tower).

The regional museum is well worth visiting, as are some of the local churches. These include an early Gothic church, Mariae Himmelfahrt, remodelled after 1756 by M Seybold and featuring some beautiful Rococo stucco ornaments. The Baroque St Lorenz, with its 13th century tower and original late-Gothic altar, is also noteworthy.

Amberg **10**

Map D5. 🏛 *43,000.* 🏨 *Zeug-hausstraße 1A (09621-102 39).*

SITUATED AT THE EDGE of the Franconian Jura, on the banks of the river Vils, Amberg owes its development to local iron ore deposits and the steel industry. The well-preserved, oval-shaped old town is still encircled by medieval walls. At the centre is an enchanting market square with the vast 15th-century late-Gothic hall-church, Pfarrkirche St Martin, and Gothic town hall (1356), both still with their original interiors.

Amberg was once the residential town of the Rhine palatines, whose Renaissance palace and chancellery have survived to the present day.

The symbol of Amberg is the Stadtbrille, the bridge spanning the river Vils, whose arches reflected in the river resemble a pair of spectacles – hence its nickname "the town's spectacles".

The late-Gothic main altar in St George's Church, Dinkelsbühl

Dinkelsbühl **11**

Map D6. 🏛 *11,000.* 🚉 🏨 *Marketplatz (09851-902 40).* 🎭 *Kinderzeche (mid-Jul).*

THIS OLD Franconian town is one of the best-preserved medieval urban complexes in Germany. The walls surrounding the city include four towers – Wörnitzer, Nördlinger, Seringer and Rothenburger Tor – which are all almost intact. The residential district of the town consists

mainly of timber-framed houses. The finest example of these is the Deutsches Haus, which stands opposite St George's Church. Dating from the late 15th to the early 16th century, the house once belonged to the Drechsel-Deufstetten family and is now a hotel-restaurant.

The late-Gothic Church of St George is a triple-nave hall-church with no transept. Together with the presbytery, it forms one large interior crowned with magnificent network vaults. The most valuable items of the interior furnishings include the pulpit, the font – which dates from around 1500 – and the Crucifixion in the main altar, which is attributed to Michael Wolgemut. A fine view of the town can be obtained from the church tower.

In Turmgasse stands the Baroque palace of the Teutonic Order, built in 1760–64 by Mathias Binder.

Nördlingen **12**

Map D6. 🏛 *20,000.* 🚉 🏨 *Marktplatz 2 (09081-43 80 or 841 16.* 🎭 *Stabenfest (May), Nördlinger Pfingstmesse Schar-lachrennen (Jun–Jul), Sommerfestspiele (Jul), Historisches Stadtmauernfest (every third year in Sep; next in 2004).*

THE TOWN IS situated in the Ries Basin, which is an immense and well-preserved crater formed millions of years ago by a meteor.

During the Middle Ages Nördlingen was a free town of the Holy Roman Empire and an important trade centre. The fortification walls which surround the city, including fifteen towers (dating from the 14th to the 15th centuries) have survived almost intact to this day.

The late-Gothic church of St George was built by Nikolaus Eseler, who also built the St George Church in Dinkelsbühl. The church is a triple-nave hall-church with round pillars and network vaults. Its imposing west tower, known as the Daniel Tower, offers a magnificent panoramic view of the town

The symbol of Amberg is the bridge named "the town spectacles"

and its environs.

The St Salvator's Church features original Gothic altars and a portal that has the scene of the *Last Judgement* in the tympanum.

The former hospital of the Holy Spirit is now home to an interesting **Municipal Museum**. The 14th century town hall features a striking external stone stairway (1618).

🏛 **Municipal Museum**

Vordere Gerbergasse 1.
📞 *(09081-273 82 30).*
⏰ *Mar–Nov: 1:30–4:30pm Tue–Sun.*
📷 *Dec–Feb: open only to guided tours (reserve a place in advance by telephone).* ♿

Ansbach ⑬

Map D6. 👥 *40,000.* 🚉 ℹ️ *Johann-Sebastian-Bach-Platz 1 (0981-512 43 or 194 33.* 🎭 *Ansbacher Frülingsfest (May), Bach-Woche (every two years in Jul), Ansbacher Rokokospiele (Jul), Heimatfest (Jul).*

THE TOWN, situated west of Nuremberg, began its history in 748 AD with the foundation of a Benedictine Abbey by a man named Gumbert. A settlement called Onoldsbach, which sprang up nearby, is now called Ansbach. From 1460 until 1791 Ansbach was the home of the von Brandenburg-Ansbach Margraves and in 1791 it was incorporated into Prussia; after 1806 it passed into Bavaria. The Markgräfliche residence is situated in the north-eastern part of the Old Town. Remodelled several times it is now a Baroque neo-Classical structure. Its 27 original state apartments include the Mirror Room, Mirror Gallery, Dining Room and Audience Room. It now houses the Museum of Faience and Porcelain. The nearby Hofgarten has a 102-metre (335-ft) long Orangery. It also houses a Kaspar Hauser Collection. Hauser was killed in the town in 1833.

🏛 **Markgrafenmuseum**
Kaspar-Hauser-Platz 1.
📞 *(0981) 977 50 56.*
⏰ *10am–noon, 2–5pm Tue–Sun.* ♿
🏛 **Markgräfliche Residenz "Ansbacher Fayence und Porzellan"**
Promenade 27. 📞 *(0981) 953 83 90.*
⏰ *Apr–Sep: 9am–5pm Tue–Sun; Oct–Mar: 10am–4pm Tue–Sun.*
📷 *hourly.* ♿

Eichstätt ⑭

Map D6. 👥 *15,000.* 🚉
ℹ️ *Domplatz 8 (08421-988 00).*

WILLIBALD, a close companion and compatriot of the Anglo-Saxon missionary Boniface, established a missionary-abbey (Eihstat) here. Soon afterwards Eichstätt became an episcopal town. In 1634 a fire ripped through the town, destroying four-fifths of its houses and four churches; after this the town was rebuilt in Baroque style.

Eichstätt is home to the country's only Catholic university, established in 1980. On the outskirts of town, on a hill overlooking the River Altmühl, stands the picturesque Willibald Castle, which until the 18th century was the residence of prince-bishops. Now it houses an interesting museum of artifacts from the Jurassic era, where visitors can see a very well preserved skeleton of *archaeopteryx*.

A new bishop's residence was built nearby from 1702 until 1768. Its west wing features a magnificent staircase and the Mirror Room, in which the works of Mauritio Pedetti, Johann Jakob Berg and Michael Franz are displayed.

Donaustauf ⑮

Walhalla. 📞 *(09403) 96 16 80.*
⏰ *Apr–Sep: 9am–5:45pm; Oct: 9am–4:45pm; Nov–Mar: 10am–noon & 1–3:45pm.* ♿

IN 1830-1841 Leo von Klenze built the Walhalla *(see above)*. This monument to the national glory occupies a scenic location on the River Danube. The building stands on a raised terrace and has the form of a neo-Classical columned temple (similar to the Parthenon in Athens). It is adorned with 121 marble busts of artists and scientists.

Majestic Walhalla near Donaustauf

Orangery of the Markgräfliche residence, in Ansbach

Nürnberg (Nuremberg) ⓖ

SITUATED ON THE RIVER PEGNITZ, Nuremberg is not only a paradise for lovers of its famous gingerbread and sausages but is also the symbol of Germany's history. The earliest records of the town, the second largest in Bavaria, date from 1050 when it was a trading settlement. From 1219 Nuremberg, a free town of the Holy Roman Empire, was an important centre of craft and commerce. Its most rapid development took place in the 15th and 16th centuries, when many prominent artists, craftsmen and intellectuals worked here, making Nuremberg one of the cultural centres of Europe.

Picturesque alley near Frauentor

Exploring Lorenzer Seite
The southern part of the old town, known as Lorenzer Seite, is separated from the northern part by the river Pegnitz and encircled to the south by the city walls. Many of the area's historic treasures were carefully reconstructed following severe bomb damage during World War II.

🚪 Frauentor
Frauentorgraben.
Frauentor is one of the most attractive gates into the old town. It is installed in the massive city walls that were constructed during the 15th and 16th centuries. The vast tower, Dicker Turm, was erected nearby in the 15th century. Königstor, a magnificent gate that once stood to the right of Dicker Turm, was dismantled in the 19th century. Beyond Frauentor are a number of alleys with half-timbered houses, shops and cafés, built after the war.

🔒 Marthakirche
Königstraße 74–78.
Dating from the 14th century, the small hospital church of St Martha is tucked between the surrounding houses. Though its interior is virtually devoid of furnishing, it features some magnificent Gothic stained-glass windows, which date from around 1390.

🚪 Mauthalle
Hallplatz 2.
The massive structure that dominates Königstrasse is a Gothic granary built in 1498–1502 by Hans Beheim the Elder. It originally housed the town's municipal scales and the customs office. In the 19th century, the building was converted into a department store and continues in that role today, following postwar reconstruction.

🏛 Germanisches Nationalmuseum
See pp246–7.

🔒 St Lorenz-Kirche
Lorenzer Platz.
The most important building in Nuremberg is the Gothic church of St Lorenz, whose basilica-style main body was built around 1270–1350. The vast hall presbytery was added much later, in 1439–77. On entering the church it is worth taking a look at the magnificent main portal, which is adorned with

SIGHTS AT A GLANCE

Panoramic view over the rooftops of Nuremberg

One of four imposing gateways in the encircling city walls

sculptures. In the main nave of the church, suspended from the ceiling above the altar, is a superb group sculpture, *Annunciation*, the work of Veit Stoss (1519). He was also the creator of the crucifix within the main altar and the magnificent statue of the Archangel Michael standing by the second pillar of the main nave. There are

VISITORS' CHECKLIST

Road map D6. ⛨ 490,000. ✈ on the northeast outskirts of town. 🚉 ℹ️ *Königstrasse 93, Kopfbau (0911-233 60).* 🎵 *Internationale Nürnberger Orgelwoche (June–July); Christkindlesmarkt (late Nov–23 Dec).*

is the Nassauer Haus, a Gothic mansion whose lower storeys were built in the 14th century. The upper floors were added in the 15th century.

A short distance from the square, in Karolinenstrasse, is a fine sculpture by Henry Moore, which stands in the middle of this shopping street.

✚ Heilig-Geist-Spital

In the centre of town, on the banks of the river Pegnitz, stands the Hospital of the Holy Spirit. Founded in 1332, this is one of the largest hospitals built in the Middle Ages and features a lovely inner courtyard with wooden galleries. The wing that spans the river was built during extension works in 1488–1527. Lepers were kept at some distance from the other patients, in a separate half-timbered building that was specially erected for the purpose. From 1424 until 1796, the insignia of the Holy Roman Empire were kept here rather than in the castle.

The Heilig-Geist-Spital now houses an old-folks' home and a restaurant. The entrance to the building is on the northern side of the river.

also several Gothic altars and some magnificent 15th-century stained-glass windows (1493–95) by Adam Kraft. The pillars of the nave are adorned with a number of fascinating statues of the Apostles, dating from the late 14th century.

⛪ Lorenzer Platz

Overlooked by the church of St Lorenz, Lorenzer Platz is a popular meeting place for the citizens of Nuremberg and visitors alike. Outside the church is the Fountain of the Virtues, *Tugendbrunnen* (1589), with water cascading from the breasts of its seven Virtues. Nearby is a statue of St Lorenz, which is a copy of the 1350 Gothic original. Diagonally across the square

[Map of Nuremberg city centre with streets labelled including MAXTORGRABEN, VESTNERTORGRABEN, VESTNERTORMAUER, LANGEGASSE, SCHILDGASSE, LETZELGASSE, THERESIENSTRASSE, INN.-LAUFER GASSE, AUSSERE LAUFER GASSE, INN.-CRAMER-KLETT-STRASSE, JUDEN-GASSE, ROSENTAL, OBSTMARKT, STINER-WAAG-GASSE, LAUFERTOR-GRABEN, KATHARINENGASSE, MARIENTORGRABEN, BLUMENSTRASSE, LORENZER STRASSE, KÖNIGSTOR-GRABEN, GLEISSBÜHLSTRASSE, NENNSTRASSE, BREITE GASSE, GRASERG., NORD-ST-RING, KÖNIGSTRASSE, FRAUENTOR GRABEN]

0 metres 300
0 yards 300

KEY

ℹ️	Tourist information
🅿️	Parking
⛪	Church

Heilig-Geist-Spital reflected in the waters of the river Pegnitz

Exploring Nürnberg (Nuremberg)

NUREMBERG WAS ONCE an important publishing centre. Schedel's *Liber Cronicarum* was published here in 1493 and, in 1543 – following the town's official adoption of the Reformation in 1525 – *The Revolutions of the Celestial Spheres* by Copernicus was published. The Thirty Years' War ended the town's development but, during the 19th century, it became the focus for the Pan-German movement. In 1945–49 the town was the scene of the trials for war crimes of Nazi leaders.

Detail of *Schöner Brunnen*, in Hauptmarkt

🏛 Hauptmarkt

Each year the Hauptmarkt provides a picturesque setting for the town's famous Christkindlesmarkt, which goes on throughout Advent. At this famous market you can buy gingerbread, enjoy the taste of German sausages, warm yourself with a glass of red wine spiced with cloves and buy locally made souvenirs.

Nuremberg's star attraction is the Gothic *Schöner Brunnen* (Beautiful Fountain), which was probably erected around 1385 but replaced in the early 20th century with a replica. It consists of a 19-metre (62-ft) high, finely carved spire standing at the centre of an octagonal pool. The pool is surrounded by a Renaissance grille that includes the famous golden ring: the local tradition is that if you turn the ring three times, your wishes will come true. The pool is adorned with the statues of philosophers, evangelists and church fathers, while the spire is decorated with the statues of Electors and of Jewish and Christian heroes. Features and details of the original fountain are kept in the **Germanisches National-museum** (*see pp246–7*).

🏛 Frauenkirche

Hauptmarkt. ⬜ 9am–6pm Mon–Sat, 9am–12:30pm Sun.

Commissioned by Emperor Charles IV, this Gothic hall-church dates from 1352–58. Over its richly decorated vestibule is the oriel of the west choir. Its gable contains a clock from Männleinlaufen, installed in 1509. Each day at noon the clock displays a procession of Electors paying homage to the Emperor. Also noteworthy is the Gothic altar (*Tucher Altar*), which dates from 1445.

Heraldic arms adorning the tympanum of the town hall portal

🏛 Rathaus

Rathausplatz.

The present town hall consists of several sections. Facing the Hauptmarkt is the oldest, Gothic part, built in 1332–40 and remodelled in the early 15th century. Behind, facing Rathausplatz, is the Renaissance part, built in 1616–22 by Jakob Wolff. Its magnificent portals are decorated with heraldic motifs. The courtyard features a fountain dating from 1557.

🏛 Spielzeugmuseum

Karlstraße 13. ⬛ *(0911) 231 31 64.* ⬜ 10am–5pm Tue–Sun, 10am–9pm Wed. ⬤ Good Friday, 24, 25, 26, 31 Dec. 🖼

This enchanting toy museum, established in 1971, houses a magnificent collection of tin soldiers and a huge collection of dolls and puppets. Its greatest attraction, however, is a collection of antique dolls' houses, filled with miniature furniture and equipment.

🏛 Kirche St Sebaldus

Winklerstraße 26. ⬜ *year-round:* 11am–6pm Sun; Jan–Feb: 9:30am–4pm Mon–Sat; Mar–Whitsun & Oct–Dec: 9:30am–6pm Mon–Sat; Whitsun–Sep: 9:30am–8pm Mon–Sat.

The oldest of Nuremberg's churches, Kirche St Sebaldus was built in 1230–73 as a Romanesque, two-choir basilica. During remodelling in the 14th century, it was given two side naves and a soaring western hall-choir. The Gothic towers were completed in the late 15th century. At the centre of the presbytery is the magnificent tomb of St Sebald. This cast bronze structure was made by Peter Vischer the Elder. It houses a silver coffin (1397) containing relics of the saint. The church features some splendid carvings by Veit Stoss, including a statue of St Andrew (1505), standing in the ambulatory around the presbytery, the Volckamersche Passion (1499) and the Crucifixion scene in the main altar (1520). Also noteworthy is the magnificent Gothic font and the Tucher family epitaph by Hans von Kulmbach (1513).

The timber-frame building of the Dürerhaus

ALBRECHT DÜRER (1471–1528)

One of the most outstanding painters of the Renaissance era, Dürer was born in Nuremberg. He began his career as a goldsmith in his father's workshop, and learned painting at Michael Wolgemut's studio. He achieved fame not only as a painter, but also as a brilliant engraver and respected theoretician. He was a shrewd observer of the surrounding world and a sensitive artist, whose works are highly valued.

Dürer's self-portrait

🏠 Egidienkirche

Egidienplatz.
Egidienkirche is the only surviving Baroque church in Nuremberg. Its façade, built after the fire of 1696, hides a building containing elements of the previous Romanesque-Gothic Benedictine church. The older chapels, including the Euchariuskapelle, Tetzel-kapellethe and Wolfgang-kapelle, survive to this day.

⛪ Kaiserburg

Kaiserburg-Museum. Innerer Burghof. 📞 *(0911) 200 95 40.* ⏰ *Apr–Sep: 9am–6pm daily; Oct–Mar: 10am–4pm daily.* 🎟️
The three castles that tower over Nuremberg include the central burgraves' castle, with the Free Reich's buildings to the east, and the Imperial castle (whose origins go back to the 12th century) to the west. When climbing up the Burgstrasse you will first reach the Fünfeckturm (Pentagonal Tower), which dates from 1040. The oldest building in town, it is an architectural relic of the von Zollern burgraves' castle. At its foot are the Kaiserstallung (Emperor's stables), which now

houses a youth hostel. A continued climb will bring you, on the left, to the court-yard of the imperial palace, which features a round tower (*Sinwellturm*) dating from the 12th century, and a deep well – the *Tiefe Brunnen*. Passing through the inner gate of the castle you will finally reach its heart, the residential building.

🏛️ Albrecht-Dürer-Haus

Albrecht-Dürer-Straße 39.
📞 *(0911) 231 25 68.* ⏰ *10am–5pm Tue, Wed, Fri–Sun, 10am–8pm Thu.* 🎟️ 📷
Born in 1471 in a house on the corner of Burgerstrasse and Obere Schmiedgasse, the renowned artist and engraver Albrecht Dürer lived in this house from 1509 until his death in 1528. On the three-hundredth anniversary of his death, the building was bought by the town and many rooms have since been reconstructed. The ground-floor room now contains a printing press dating from Dürer's time. Copies of his pictures provide a useful insight into the work of this famous Nuremberg citizen.

🏛️ St-Johannis-Friedhof

Am Johannisfriedhof.
The St John's Cemetery is one of the best preserved and most important in Europe. Since it was established in 1518, it has provided a resting place for many famous people, including Albrecht Dürer (No. 649), the sculptor Veit Stoss (No. 268), the goldsmith Wenzel Jamnitzer (No. 664) and the painter Anselm Feuerbach (No. 715).

The cemetery also contains a rich array of tombs from the 16th, 17th and 18th centuries.

🏛️ Dokumentationszentrum Reichsparteitagsgelände

Bayernstr. 110. 📞 *(0911) 231 56 66.* ⏰ *9am–6pm Mon–Fri, 10am–6pm Sat–Sun.*
The vast, unfinished building complex in the southern part of town dates from the Nazi era. Its construction began in 1933 and it was intended to be a venue for National Party gatherings. The building now houses a historical exhibition and archive.

The buildings of the Kaiserburg, towering over the town

Nuremberg: Germanisches Nationalmuseum

THIS MUSEUM, WHICH WAS officially opened in 1852, was founded by a Franconian aristocrat named Hans von Aufsess. It houses a unique collection of antiquities from the German-speaking world. In 1945, towards the end of World War II, the buildings that had originally housed the museum were bombed. The modern architecture of the new building, which was completed in 1993, cleverly incorporates the remaining fragments of a former Carthusian abbey. Among the most valuable items in the museum's collection are works by Tilman Riemenschneider, Konrad Witz, Lucas Cranach the Elder, Adolf Altdorfer, Albrecht Dürer and Hans Baldung Grien.

Madonna with Child Crowned by Angels
This picture was painted by Hans Holbein the Elder (c.1465–1524) who created many festive altar-pieces using warm colours.

Archangel (1516)
This enchanting wood-carving of the archangel Raphaël is one of many works produced by Veit Stoss after his return from Cracow.

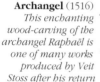

Cloisters

Former Carthusian church

Ground floor

Brooch from Domagnano
This Ostrogothic buckle from the 5th century AD, shaped like an eagle, was discovered in the late 19th century in Domagnano, in San Marino. It probably belonged to a rich Ostrogothic aristocrat.

★ **Cover of the Codex Aureus**
The richly ornamented cover of the Codex Aureus, *also known as the Golden Gospel Book of Echternach, was produced in Trier in the 11th century.*

GALLERY GUIDE

The exhibits have been arranged in sections, ranging from prehistory to the Middle Ages, and are located on the ground and first floors. Twentieth-century art is on the second floor and the toy collection is housed separately.

VISITORS' CHECKLIST

Kartäusergasse 1. ☎ (0911) 133 10. ◯ 10am–6pm Tue–Sun, until 9pm Wed. ● Shrove Tue, 24, 25, 31 Dec. ♿ ☒ www.gnm.de

First floor

Library

Library

★ Torquetum

Johannes Praetorius from Nuremberg produced this engraved copper device in 1568, designed to measure the positions of the stars.

KEY

- ▨ Prehistory and early history
- ▢ Middle Ages
- ▢ Renaissance and Baroque
- ▢ Baroque arts and crafts
- ▢ Arms and armour, garden sculpture
- ▢ Musical instruments and applied arts
- ▢ Crafts and guilds
- ▨ Scientific instruments and pharmaceutical history
- ▢ Textiles and folk art
- ▢ Archive, prints and drawings, coins and medals

★ Portrait of Michael Wolgemut (1516)

Albrecht Dürer painted this portrait of his predecessor and master, Wolgemut, 30 years after commencing work at his studio.

★ Schlüsselfeld Vessel

This beautiful silver-gold sailing ship, supported by a two-tailed mermaid, is an ornamental table vessel made in 1503 by an unidentified goldsmith from Nuremberg.

STAR SIGHTS

- ★ **Cover of Codex Aureus**
- ★ **Portrait of Michael Wolgemut**
- ★ **Schlüsselfeld Vessel**
- ★ **Torquetum**

Street-by-Street: Rothenburg ob der Tauber ⓱

Eagle crest from the town hall

IF YOU WANT TO SAMPLE the atmosphere of the Middle Ages, visit Rothenburg on the river Tauber, whose origins go back to the 12th century. Rothenburg was granted the status of a free town within the Holy Roman Empire in 1274 but its major growth took place in the 15th century. During the Thirty Years' War (1618–48) the town, which fought on the Protestant side, was captured by the Emperor's army. Little has changed since that time and the city walls still surround Gothic cathedrals and an array of gabled houses.

Reichsstadtmuseum
The former Dominican abbey now houses a museum devoted to the town's history. The abbey kitchen – the oldest surviving kitchen in Germany – is also open to visitors.

Franziskanerkirche
In this Gothic church is a retable depicting The Stigmatization of St Francis, *believed to be an early work by Tilman Riemenschneider.*

★ **St Jakobs Kirche**
In the Gothic church of St Jakob, which was built between 1373 and 1464, is this magnificent high altar by Friedrich Herlin.

★ **Mittelalterliches Kriminalmuseum**
Many blood-curdling exhibits are on display at this museum, which houses a collection of instruments of torture and punishment.

View from Burggarten

The castle garden (Burggarten) is reached through Burgtor, the tallest of the town's gates. The garden, which during the Middle Ages was the site of the Hohenstaufen family castle, provides a magnificent view over the town and the river valley.

VISITORS' CHECKLIST

Road map C5. 🏘 *12,000.* 🚉
🛈 *Marktplatz 2 (09861-404 92).* 🎪 *Reichsstadt-Festtage (second weekend in Sep), Meistertrunk (first weekend in Sep), Weihnachtsmarkt (Dec).*
Topplerschlösschen
📞 *(09861) 73 58.* ⬜ *1–4pm Fri–Sun.* ⬛ *in November.* 🅿

Galgentor

Galgentor, an old execution place, is also known as Würzburger Tor, since it is the gate leading to Würzburg.

Spitaltor

The best preserved segments of the old city walls are around Spitaltor. From here you can walk through Rödertor to Klingentor.

★ Rathaus

The town hall consists of the surviving Gothic section with a tower, and the later Renaissance structure with Baroque arcades.

KEY

— — — Suggested route

STAR SIGHTS

★ **Mittelalterliches Museum**

★ **Rathaus**

★ **St Jakobs Kirche**

Andechs ⑱

Road map D7. 🚌 *Andechserstrasse 16 (08152-932 50).*

THE VILLAGE OF Andechs, at the summit of the 700-m (2,300-ft) high Holy Mountain of the same name, is not only the destination of pilgrimages to the local church, but also of many less spiritual trips to the *Braüstüberl*, where visitors can refresh themselves with a glass or two of the excellent beer brewed by local monks.

The present triple-nave Gothic hall-church was built in 1420–25. Its Rococo interior dates from 1755. The lower tier of the main altar contains the famous *Miraculous Statue of the Mother of God* (1468), while the upper tier features the *Immaculata* by Hans Degler (1609). On selected feast days, holy relics are displayed on the altar gallery.

Lake at the foot of the Holy Mountain of Andechs

Landsberg am Lech ⑲

Road map D7. 🏘 *24,000.* 🚉
🛈 *Hauptplatz 152 (08191-12 82 46).*

THE HISTORY of Landsberg goes back to 1160 when Henry the Lion built his castle here, on the right bank of the river Lech. During the 13th century, the surrounding settlement grew into a town, which soon became a major trading centre. Religious conflicts, culminating in the Thirty Years' War, put an end to the town's development but, in the late 17th century, the town once again became

an important commercial and cultural centre. Adolf Hitler wrote *Mein Kampf* here, while serving a prison term for his unsuccessful coup attempt in Munich.

At the heart of Landsberg is the Hauptplatz with its Baroque town hall and the intricately carved 14th-century tower, Schmalztor.

In Ludwigstrasse is the late-Gothic parish church, Stadtpfarrkirche Mariä Himmelfahrt, whose Baroque-style interior features a statue of the *Madonna and Child* by Hans Multscher. Bayertor, the original town gate, is in the eastern part of the old town.

The town's **Neues Stadt-museum** is a useful source of information on local history.

🏛 Neues Stadtmuseum
Von-Helfenstein-Gasse 426. 📞 *(08191) 94 23 26.* ◯ *Apr–Jan: 2–5pm Tue–Sun.* 📷

Dachau ⑳

Road map D6. 🏘 *35,000.* 🚉
🛈 *Konrad-Adenauer-Straße 1 (08131-75286 or 75287).*

FOR MOST PEOPLE the name Dachau is inextricably linked with the concentration camp that was built here by the Nazis in 1933. Since 1965, the whole site has been designated as a memorial, **KZ-Gedenkstätte Dachau**, to the 32,000 prisoners who died there, with a permanent exhibition in the former domestic quarters of the camp.

Dachau is a beautiful town with many historic buildings. On the southwestern edge of the old town stands **Schloss Dachau**, summer residence of the Wittelsbachs. The palace that stands here today was created in the 18th century from the western wing of an earlier castle, the work of Joseph Effner. In the early 19th century the castle housed a colony

Relief from the church façade in Landsberg

of artists who had tired of city life. They were known as *Gruppe Neu Dachau*. Even earlier, however, the beauty of the surrounding countryside had been discovered by the impressionist painter Max Lieber-mann (1847–1935). The **Dachauer Gemäldegalerie** contains works of art inspired by local scenery, including one by Liebermann.

🏛 Dachauer Gemäldegalerie
Konrad-Adenauer-Straße 3.
📞 *(08131) 56 75 16.* ◯ *11am–5pm Tue–Fri, 1–5pm Sat–Sun.* 📷
♠ Schloss Dachau
Schlossstraße 7. 📞 *(08131) 879 23.*
◯ *Oct–Mar: 10am–4pm Tue–Sun; Apr Sep: 9am–6pm Tue–Sun.* 📷
⚰ KZ-Gedenkstätte Dachau
Alte Römerstrasse 75. 📞 *(08131) 66 99 70.* ◯ *9am–5pm Tue–Sun.* 📷

Schleissheim ㉑

Road map D6. Oberschleissheim.

SCHLEISSHEIM IS SITUATED barely 14 km (9 miles) from Munich, making it within easy reach for an afternoon visit to its Baroque palace and park.

Surrounded by canals and now somewhat neglected, the park was established in the 17th and 18th centuries and includes three palaces. The

Baroque façade of the Wittelsbach palace, Schloss Dachau

modest **Altes Schloss** was built in 1623 for Prince Wilhelm V. Now it houses an exhibition of religious folk art.

Schloss Lustheim is a small, Baroque, hermitage-type palace, built in 1684–87 by Enrico Zucalli for the Elector Max Emanuel. As well as its beautiful interiors and stunning frescoes, it boasts a magnificent collection of Meissen porcelain, which is displayed in the **Museum Meissener Porzellan**.

The newest building is the **Neues Schloss**, designed by Enrico Zucalli. Work began in 1701 but was not completed until the second half of the 18th century. Despite wartime damage, it retains many original features. It now houses exhibits belonging to the Bavarian State Museum.

The imposing bulk of the Neues Schloss in Ingolstadt

brothers, in 1724–25. The four-nave Romanesque crypt features a famous column, which is decorated with carvings of fantastic animals *(Bestiensäule)*. Nearby is the **Diözesanmuseum**, whose vast ecclesiastical collection includes two paintings by Rubens.

At the southwestern end of the old town stands a former monastery, Weihenstephan, which is home to the world's longest-established brewery.

Detail from Neues Schloss in Schleissheim

♣ **Altes Schloss**
◻ 10am–5pm Tue–Sun. 🎫
♣ **Neues Schloss**
☎ (089) 315 87 20. ◻ Apr–Sep: 9am–6pm Tue–Sun; Oct–Mar: 10am–4pm Tue–Sun. ● Mon. 🎫
♣ **Schloss Lustheim**
◻ Apr–Sep: 9am–6pm Tue–Sun; Oct–Mar: 10am–4pm Tue–Sun. 🎫
Museum Meissener Porzellan
☎ (089) 315 87 20. ◻ Apr–Sep: 9am–6pm Tue–Sun; Oct–Mar: 10am–4pm Tue–Sun. ● Mon.

Freising ㉒

Road map D6. 🚹 40,000. 🚉
ℹ Marienplatz 7 (08161-541 22).

SITUATED ON THE banks of the river Isar is the old town of Freising. Its history is closely connected with St Korbinian, who founded the bishopric here in the early 8th century. Korbinian died around AD 725 and his remains still lie in the crypt of the Dom – the Cathedral Church of the Birth of the Virgin Mary and St Korbinian (1159–1205). This is a five-nave basilica, without transept, with an elongated choir and a massive twin-tower western façade. Its interior was remodelled in Baroque style by the Asam

🏛 **Diözesanmuseum**
Domberg 21. ☎ (08161) 487 90. ◻ 10am–5pm Tue–Sun. 🎫

Ingolstadt ㉓

Road map D6. 🚹 115, 000. 🚉
ℹ Rathausplatz 2 (0841-305 30 30).

LYING ON THE river Danube, this former seat of the Wittelsbach family features many important historic buildings dating from the

Middle Ages and the Renaissance and Baroque periods. Among the most outstanding is the Church of the Virgin Mary, a triple-nave hall structure with circular pillars, chapels and choir with an ambulatory. Inside is the original Gothic-Renaissance main altar dating from 1572.

Another notable building is the Neues Schloss, built between the 15th and 18th centuries, with its stately rooms and Gothic chapel. It now houses the **Bayerisches Armeemuseum**.

A true gem of Bavarian architecture is the **Church of St Maria Victoria**, the work of Cosmas Damian Asam.

The **Deutsches Medizinhistorisches Museum** has a comprehensive collection of medical instruments.

🏛 **Bayerisches Armeemuseum**
Neues Schloss, Paradeplatz 4.
☎ (0841) 937 70. ◻ 8:45am–4:30pm Tue–Sun. 🎫
🏛 **Deutsches Medizinhistorisches Museum**
Anatomiestraße 18–20.
☎ (0841) 305 18 60. ◻ 10am–noon, 2–5pm Tue–Sun. 🎫

Striking Baroque interior of the Church of St Maria Victoria, Ingolstadt

Arcaded courtyard of Neuburg Castle

Neuburg an der Donau ㉔

Road map D6. 🏛 *25,000.* 🚉
🛈 *Ottheinrichplatz A118 (08431-552 40).*

PERCHED ON A promontory overlooking the river Danube, Neuburg is one of Bavaria's loveliest towns. During the Middle Ages, it changed hands frequently but was eventually ruled by Ottheinrich the Magnanimous, under whom the town grew and prospered on an unprecedented scale. He was the founder of the castle, built between 1534 and 1665, whose massive round towers still dominate the town. Its earliest part is the east wing. The courtyard, which is surrounded by arcades, features beautiful frescos by Hans Schroer. In the tower is a staircase adorned with paintings. The castle chapel, completed in 1543, is one of the oldest, purpose-built Protestant churches in Germany.

In Amalienstrasse, leading down towards the town, stands the former Jesuits' College and the Court Church (Hofkirche). Work on the church began in the late 16th century and was completed in 1627. It was intended to be a Protestant church, but the ruling family converted back to Catholicism during its construction and it was taken over by the Jesuits who turned it into a counter-reformation

Heraldic crest on Neuberg Castle

Marian church. The triple-nave hall-structure has an exquisite interior decorated in gold, white and grey.

Among many old buildings that survive in the town centre are the Graf-Veri-Haus and the Baron-von-Hartman-Haus in Herrenstrasse. To the east of town stands the Grünau Castle (Jagdschloss), built for Ottheinrich in 1530–55.

ENVIRONS: 18 km (11 miles) to the south, Schrobenhausen is the birthplace of the painter Franz von Lenbach, who was born in 1836. A museum in Ulrich-Peisser-Gasse is devoted to his life and work. While there, it is worth visiting St Jacob's Church, to see the fine 15th-century wall painting there.

🏛 Schlossmuseum Neuburg
Residenzstraße 2.
📞 *(08431) 88 97.* 🕐
Apr–Sep: 9am–6pm Tue–Sun; Oct–Mar: 10am–4pm Tue–Sun. 📷

Landshut ㉕

Road map E6. 🏛 *57,000.* 🚉
🛈 *Altstadt 315 (0871-92 20 50).*
🎭 *Fürstenhochzeit (every 4 years, next in 2005), Hofmusiktage (every 2 years, next in 2004), Frühjahrsdult (Apr–May), Bartlmädult (end Aug), Haferlmarkt (Sep).*

THE EARLIEST records of Landshut date from 1150. One hundred years later this was already a town and the main centre of power of the

Dukes of Lower Bavaria. In 1475 the town was the scene of a lavish medieval wedding, when Duke Georg of the House of Wittelsbach married the Polish Princess Jadwiga. Since 1903 the town has held regular re-enactments of the wedding feast (Landshuter Fürstenhochzeit).

Landshut has preserved its medieval urban layout, with two wide parallel streets, Altstadt and Neustadt, with clusters of historic 15th–16th century buildings. Opposite the town hall in Alstadt is the **Stadtresidenz**, a town house modelled on the Palazzo del Tè in Mantua. Sometimes known as the "Italian House", this was the first Renaissance palace to be built in Germany.

The vast brick church of St Martin (1385–1500) is a triple-nave, narrow hall-church featuring a presbytery, network vaults (1459) and the tallest church tower in Bavaria.

Landshut is dominated by the fortified 13th–16th century **Burg Trausnitz**, which features a medieval tower and a Renaissance palace dating from 1568–78. The palace features arcades around the courtyard and a series of frescos by Alessandro Scalzi, which date from 1578.

ENVIRONS: From Landshut, it is worth taking a trip to Moosburg, situated 14 km (9 miles) to the west. Its early

Stained-glass window in Landshut depicting Duke Georg and Jadwiga

13th-century Church of St Castulus features a 14-m (46-ft) high Marian altar by Hans Leinberger (1514). Leinberger was probably also the creator of the epitaph of Theoderich Mair and of the crucifix on the west wall.

♣ **Burg Trausnitz**
[(0871) 92 41 10. ○ Apr–Sep: 9am–6pm; Oct–Mar: 10am–4pm. 🖾
♣ **Stadtresidenz**
Altstadt 79. [(0871) 92 41 10.
○ Apr–Sep: 9am–6pm; Oct–Mar: 10am–4pm. 🖾 ● Mon.

Interior of St George's Chapel in Landshut

Dingolfing ㉖

Road map E6. 🏚 15,400.
ℹ Dr-Josef-Hastreiter-Straße 2 (08731-50 11 28).

THE MAIN TOURIST attraction in this small town on the banks of the river Isar is its Gothic castle. Built in the 15th century by the Bavarian dukes, this vast edifice now houses the Regional Museum. It is also worth taking a stroll to see Pfarrkirche St Johannes, a late-Gothic brick building dating from the late 15th century. Although what remains of its furnishings are merely the poor remnants of its former glory, nevertheless the church is still considered one of the most beautiful Gothic buildings in Bavaria.

ENVIRONS: In Landau an der Isar, situated 13 km (8 miles) to the east of Dingolfing, stands the picturesque Baroque church of Mariä Himmelfahrt, dating from the first half of the 18th century. There is also an interesting

small church, the Steinfelskirche (c.1700) inside a natural rock cave. In Arnstorf, 30 km (19 miles) to the east, is one of the few remaining Bavarian castles on water. Known as the Oberes Schloß, the castle was probably built in the 15th century and remodelled during the 17th and 18th centuries.

Straubing ㉗

Road map E6. 🏚 44,500. 🚇
ℹ Theresienplatz 20 (09421-94 43 07). 🎪 Gäubodenvolksfest (August), Agnes-Bernauer-Festspiel (July, every four years, next in 2007).

THIS MARKET TOWN enjoys a picturesque setting on the river Danube. The 60-m (200-ft) long Strassenmarkt, which consists of two squares, Theresienplatz and Ludwig-platz, is a part of the former trade route that led to Prague. The area is lined with historic buildings in Baroque, Neo-Classical and Secession styles.

At the centre of Strassen-markt stands the 14th-century municipal tower, which offers a splendid view over the towns of the Bavarian Forest. At Ludwigplatz 11 is the "Lion's Pharmacy", where the famous Biedermeier painter, Karl Spitzweg, worked as an apprentice in 1828–30.

Turning from Theresienplatz into Seminargasse or Jakobs-gasse, you will reach the monumental brick structure of the parish church of St Jakob (1400–1590). This triple-nave hall-church, crowned with a network vault, retains many original features, including stained-glass windows in the chapels of Maria-Hilf-Kapelle (1420) and St Bartholomew. The so-called Moses' Window in the Chapel of St Joseph was made in 1490 in Nuremberg, based on a sketch provided by Wilhelm Playdenwurff. In the Cobbler's Chapel (Schusterkapelle) hangs a painting of *Madonna and Child*, by Hans Holbein

(c.1500). Overlooking the Danube is a 14th–15th century castle, part of which is now used as a museum, **Museum im Herzogschloss**. The **Gäubodenmuseum** has a magnificent collection of Roman artifacts.

ENVIRONS: In the tiny village of Aufhausen, 21 km (12 miles) to the west, is the beautiful late-Baroque pilgrimage church of Maria Schnee. Built by Johann Michael Fischer in 1736–51, it includes magnificent wall paintings by the Asam brothers and a statue of the Madonna. Commissioned by Duke Wilhelm V of Bavaria, the Gnadenmadonna is believed to pardon sins.

In Oberaltteich, some 10 km (6 miles) to the east, is the beautiful church of St Peter and St Paul built in the early 17th century for the Benedictine order. Inside, an unusual hanging staircase leads to the galleries, while the vestibule is decorated with stucco ornaments, depicting bird motifs.

In Windberg, 22 km (14 miles) east of Oberaltteich, is a Romanesque Marian church whose main portal (c.1220) features an image of the Madonna in the tympanum.

🏛 **Gäubodenmuseum**
Frauenhoferstraße. [(09421) 818 11.
○ 10am–4pm Tue–Sun. 🖾
🏛 **Museum im Herzogschloss**
[(09421) 211 14. ○ mid-Mar–Jan: 10am–4pm Tue–Sun. 🖾

Main altar in Ursulinenkirche, Straubing

Regensburg (Ratisbon) 🄯

T HE AREA OF Regensburg was once a Celtic settlement and later a campsite of the Roman legions. The outline of the Roman camp is still visible around St Peter's Cathedral. In the early 6th century, Regensburg was the seat of the Agilolfa ruling family and, in AD 739, a monk named Boniface established a bishopric here. From AD 843, Regensburg was the seat of the Eastern Frankish ruler, Ludwig the German. From 1245 it was a free town of the Holy Roman Empire and throughout the Middle Ages remained South Germany's fastest growing commercial and cultural centre.

Picturesque Steinere Brücke leading to the old town of Regensburg

🎏 Steinerne Brücke

An outstanding example of medieval engineering, this 310-m (1,000-ft) long bridge over the Danube was built in 1135–46. It provides the best panoramic view of Regensburg. Near the bridge gate, Brückentor, stands an enormous salt warehouse topped with a vast five-storey roof.

🎏 Wurstküche (Wurstkuchel)

Thundorferstraße. ☐ May–Oct 8am–7pm daily; Nov–Apr: 10am–3pm daily.
Immediately behind the salt warehouse is the famous *Wurstküche* (sausage kitchen), which has probably occupied this site since as early as the 12th century and may have served as a canteen for the builders of the bridge. Its Regensburger sausages are regarded by local residents as the best in the world.

🎏 Altes Rathaus

Rathausplatz. 🎫 May–Sep: 3:15pm Mon–Sat. **Reichstagsmuseum**.
🛈 (0941) 507 44 10. 🎫 (every 30 mins) 9:30am–noon 2–4pm Mon–Sat, 10am–noon 2–4pm Sun. 📷
In Rathausplatz stands an old 15th-century town hall with a 13th-century tower. It contains a splendid, richly decorated

hall – *Reichssaal* – where the Perpetual Imperial Diet (the first parliament of the Holy Roman Empire) sat between 1663 and 1806. Benches in the chamber were coloured to indicate who could sit where: for example, red benches were set aside for Electors. The adjoining new town hall dates from the late 17th–early 18th century.

Late-Gothic oriel on the side elevation of the Altes Rathaus

🛈 Dom St Peter
Domschatzmuseum

Krauterermarkt 3. 🛈 (0941) 576 45.
☐ Apr–Oct: 6:30am–6pm; Nov–Mar: 6:30am–5pm. 🎫 May–Oct: 10am, 11am, 2pm Mon–Sat, noon & 2pm Sun; Nov–Mar: 11am Mon–Sat, noon Sun. 📷
Towering above the city, on the site of the former Roman military camp, is the massive brick structure of St Peter's Cathedral. Built between 1250 and 1525, its imposing western towers were added only in 1859–69. The master architect, Ludwig, modelled his design for the building on French examples (the

Sights at a Glance

19th-century towers on the Gothic St Peter's Cathedral

Rayonnant style). The stained-glass windows of the choir date from the early 14th century. The **Domschatz-museum** has a collection of ecclesiastical vestments.

⛪ Alte Kapelle

Alter Kornmarkt.
The Old Chapel is really a Marian collegiate church. It stands on the foundations of an older, early Romanesque chapel dating from the Carolingian period. The building has been remodelled several times and contains some beautiful Rococo stuccoes by Anton Landes.

♣ Schloss Thurn und Taxis

Emmeramsplatz 5. ☎ (0941) 504 81 33. ◯ daily. ◢ Apr–Oct: 11am, 2pm, 3pm, 4pm (also 10am Sat–Sun); Nov–Mar: 10am, 11am, 2pm, 3pm Sat–Sun. ◩
In the south end of the town you will find the buildings and churches of the former St Emmeram Abbey, which have been tastefully

VISITORS' CHECKLIST

Road map D6. 🏘 142,000.
🛈 Altes Rathaus (0941 507 44 10). 🎭 Frühjahrsdult (Whitsun), Bach-Woche (Jun), Bayerisches Jazz-Weekend (Jul), Herbstdult (Aug–Sep), Christkindlmarkt & Domspatzen concerts (Dec).
🖥 www.regensburg.de

Enchanting Rococo interior of Alte Kapelle

the burial chapel. In 1998, the Bavarian State Museum opened a branch here, which includes valuable collections of decorative art.

⛪ Baumburger Turm

Watmarkt.
Regensburg has many unique ancestral palaces dating from the 14th–15th centuries, with high towers modelled on Northern Italian architecture. Some 20 of the original 60 towers have survived. One of the most beautiful is the residential tower, Baumburger Turm. Nearby, at Watmarkt 5, stands the equally beautiful Goliathhaus, where Oskar Schindler lived for a time in 1945. A commemorative plaque has been placed at the rear of the building.

incorporated into the palace complex of the ducal family von Thurn und Taxis. These include a Gothic cloister dating from the 12th–14th centuries, a library with magnificent frescos by Cosmas Damian Asam and

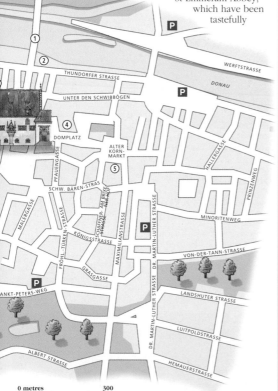

0 metres 300
0 yards 300

KEY

🛈 Tourist information

🅿 Parking

✝ Church

Gothic portals of St Emmeram Abbey in Schloss Thurn und Taxis

Winter view of Gnadenkapelle complex, from Altötting

Altötting ㉙

Road map E6. 🏛 *11,000.* 🚉
Kapellplatz 2a (08671-80 68). 🚌
🚉 *pilgrimages to Altötting (Whitsun).*

Altötting is renowned as the earliest destination of pilgrimages to the "Miraculous Statue" of the Virgin Mary (1330). The statue stands in the Wallfahrtskapelle St Maria, which consists of two parts. The central, octagonal chapel, **Gnadenkapelle** (c.AD 750) was once the baptistery. The external chapel was built in 1494 and the ambulatory in 1517. As well as the Miraculous Statue, it houses the so-called "Silver Prince", representing the miraculously cured son of the Prince-Elector, Karl Albrecht. Many Bavarian kings and princes wished to be buried here, including King Ludwig II, who requested that his heart be placed here after his death.

Nearby is the interesting Romanesque-Gothic church of St Philip and St Jacob (1228–30 and 1499–1520). Its Neo-Classical interior contains many tombstones, while a separate chapel, Tillykapelle, is the burial place of Johann Tserclaes von Tilly, a hero of the Thirty Years' War and the Emperor's general.

The **Schatzkammer** (Treasury) is housed in the former sacristy. Its collection includes an exquisite example of French enamel and gold artwork, the *Goldenes Rössl* (Golden Steed), which dates from around 1400. Despite its name, the theme of this work, by a celebrated Parisian goldsmith, is the Adoration of the Magi. It was commissioned by Isobel of Bavaria as a New Year gift for her husband, Charles VI of France.

Schatzkammer

Kapellplatz 21. 📞 *(08671) 51 66.*
⭕ *Apr–Oct:10am–noon, 2–4pm Tue–Sun.* 📷

Walkway around Gnadenkapelle, in Altötting, filled with offerings

Burghausen ㉚

Road map E6. 🏛 *17,000.* 🚉 *Stadtplatz 112 (08677-88 71 40).* 🚌

The very picturesque town of Burghausen is situated on the river Salzach. Towering over the town, the river and the lake is Wöhrsee Castle, a large castle complex built on a high ridge stretching for 1,100 m (1,200 yds). Work on the castle started in 1253, but most of the buildings were erected during the reign of King George the Rich and therefore have magnificent, late-Gothic forms. The king's wife, Jadwiga Jagiellon, whom he married in grand style in Landshut *(see p252)*, was later rejected by him and she spent her final days in the fortress of Burghausen.

The **Burg** consists of two main parts: the main castle, with tower, the residential quarters, the courtyard and domestic buildings; and the castle approach (Vorburg). The residential building has some fine 15th- and 16th-century paintings. A special door links the Prince's quarters with the "internal" Chapel of St Elizabeth. Next to the chapel is the mid-13th-century Dürnitz, which served originally served as a ballroom and banqueting hall .

The castle approach consists of five courtyards (Vorhof). In the fourth courtyard is the "external" Chapel of St Jadwiga (Aussere Burgkapelle St Hedwig) – the work of Wolfgang Wiesinger, a native of Salzburg (1489). This has numerous original buildings, including the town hall, which was created by combining three burgher houses dating from the 14th–15th centuries The parish church of St Jakob (1353-1513) in Burghausen is a three-nave basilica.

Burg

📞 *(08677) 4659.*
Staatliche Sammlung ⭕ *Apr–Sep: 9am–6pm daily; Oct–Mar: 10am–4pm daily.*

Panoramic view of Burghausen, with its vast castle complex on the hill

Bayerischer Wald ㉛

THE BAVARIAN FOREST STRETCHES north to the river Danube, between Regensburg and Passau. It is part of Central Europe's largest woodland and provides idyllic grounds for a variety of outdoor pursuits. The local rocks contain large quantities of quartz, which contributed to the early development of the glass industry here. To this day, the region produces some fine, blown-glass artifacts. The region also hosts a number of popular festivals throughout the year.

Spiegelau ❸
Spiegelau is one of the most popular starting points for tourists planning hiking trips into the mountains.

Zwiesel ❶
In the old glassworks, which survive to this day, you can watch workers using blow irons to produce vases, jugs and other objects made of glass.

Grafenau ❹
The main attractions of this small town are its snuff and furniture museums and the Baroque church.

Frauenau ❷
Along with Zwiesel, this is the oldest centre of glass production in the area. The local museum illustrates the town's history.

Finsterau ❻
Situated close to a vast artificial lake, Finsterau has an interesting open-air museum that displays examples of the local building trade.

Freyung ❺
The main attraction of the town is the Schloss (Castle) Wolfstein, which now houses a museum of hunting and fishing.

KEY

▬	Suggested route
═	Other road
▬	Scenic route
☼	Viewpoint

TIPS FOR WALKERS

Starting point: *Zwiesel.*
Distance: *82 km (51 miles)*
Getting there: *train to Frauenau, on the Zwiesel-Granau line; or Bodenmais, terminus of another branch line from Zwiesel.*

Street-by-Street: Passau ㉜

Passau, whose long history goes back to Roman times, lies on a peninsula between the rivers Danube and Inn, near the Austrian border. During the second half of the 5th century, St Severinus established a monastery in Passau as well as several more nearby. In 739, an Irish monk called Boniface, known as "Germany's Apostle", founded a bishopric here and for many years this was the largest diocese of the Holy Roman Empire. Large parts of the town were destroyed by fires in 1662 and 1680. Reconstruction was carried out by Italian artists, who gave the town its Baroque, Rococo and Neo-Classical façades. However Passau retains a medieval feel in its narrow alleys and archways.

Passauer Glasmuseum
Opposite the old town hall is the beautiful patrician Hotel Wilder Mann, which now houses the Glasmuseum. The museum's vast collection includes valuable examples of Bohemian, Austrian and Bavarian glasswork.

Deggendorf

ANGER STRA

★ Dom St Stephan
St Stephan's Cathedral is a true masterpiece of Italian Baroque, built by Italian architect Carlo Lurago to replace the original Gothic structure, which was largely destroyed by fire in the 17th century.

Passau-Hauptbahnhof

DOMPLATZ

GROSSE MESSE

University

★ Altes Rathaus
Dating from the 14th–15th century, the old town hall was created by combining eight patrician houses. The structure features a Neo-Gothic tower.

INNKAI

MARIEN-BRÜCKE

Neue Bischofsresidenz
Built by Domenico d'Angeli and Antonio Beduzzi in 1713–30, the Neue Residenz has a pilaster façade with protruding balconies and roof balustrade.

★ Veste Oberhaus
This former castle of the prince-bishops now houses the Kultur-historischesmuseum, with displays on local and regional history and the work of local artists.

VISITORS' CHECKLIST

🚶 50,000. 🚉 ℹ️ *Rathaus-platz 3, 94032 Passau (0851 95 59 80).* 🎭 *Festival Europäische Wochen (Jun-Jul) music and theatre events, plus exhibitions by European artists (mainly from Austria, Hungary, the Czech Republic, Slovakia and Poland).* 🌐 www.passau.de

Schaiblingsturm
On the bank of the river Inn are the remains of Passau's Gothic town walls. They include this tower, built in 1481.

PRINZREGENT LUITPOLD BRÜCKE

ORT

★ Wallfahrtskirche Mariahilf
High above the banks of the river Inn stands this early-Baroque abbey complex dating from 1627–30. It includes a pretty twin-towered pilgrimage church.

STAR SIGHTS

★ Altes Rathaus

★ Dom St Stephan

★ Veste Oberhaus

★ Wallfahrtskirche Mariahilf

0 metres 100
0 yards 100

KEY

– – – Suggested route

Berchtesgadener Land ⊛

Berchtesgadener land is one of the most beautiful regions, not just in Germany, but in the whole of Europe. It occupies the area of the Berchtesgadener Alps whose boundaries are defined by the river Saalach to the west, the river Salzach to the east, the "Stony Sea" *(Steinernes Meer)* to the south and, to the north, Untersberg, which is 1,972 m (7,500 ft) above sea level. To the south of Berchtesgaden village lies the National Park (Nationalpark Berchtesgaden).

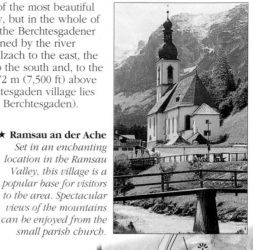

★ Ramsau an der Ache
Set in an enchanting location in the Ramsau Valley, this village is a popular base for visitors to the area. Spectacular views of the mountains can be enjoyed from the small parish church.

Hintersee
This scenic lake has given its name to a picturesque hamlet nearby. A walk around the lake takes about one hour.

LATTEN GEBIRG

REITER ALPE

HINTERSEE

Ramsau

Wimbachklar

NATIONAL- PARK BERCHTESGADEN

KEHLSTEINHAUS

Standing on the summit of Kehlstein, this stone building resembling a mountain shelter is known as the Adlerhorst (Eagle's Nest). It was given to Hitler as a birthday present in 1939 by one of his closest allies, Martin Bormann, and it became the Führer's favourite residence. The approach to the building is a true engineering masterpiece: the initial section, the Kehlsteinstrasse, is a scenic mountain road,

which passes through five tunnels and offers some breathtaking views. The final ascent is via a lift. The whole project took 13 months to complete. After the war, the Eagle's Nest fell into the hands of the Americans, then, in 1960, it passed into private hands. The building now houses a restaurant that is very popular with tourists, not only because of its history but also for the spectacular views that it provides over part of the Alps.

Nationalpark Berchtesgaden
This magnificent national park, which is home to many rare species of plants and animals, can be visited by joining organized tours between May and October.

Berchtesgaden

The capital of the region features many historic buildings. The Schloss, originally an Augustinian priory, now houses the art treasures collected by Crown Prince Ruprecht. The local salt mine has been a source of wealth since the 16th century.

VISITORS' CHECKLIST

Road map E7. *8,500.* Berchtesgaden. Kurdirektion, Königsseerstrasse 2, Berchtesgaden (08652-96 70).

Wallfahrtskirche Maria Gern

One of the loveliest Baroque buildings in the region, the pilgrimage church of Maria Gern was built in 1709 in this idyllic location.

UNTERS-
BERG

Vinkl

Maria
Gern

Bischofs-
wiesen

Hallein

Berchtes-
gaden

Mitterbach

Schönau
am Königssee

Königssee

KÖNIGSSEE

OBERSEE

KEY

■ Major road

═ Minor road

═ River

⚜ Viewpoint

STAR SIGHTS

★ **Königssee**

★ **Ramsau an der Ache**

★ Königssee

Germany's highest lake, Königssee is the focal point of Berchtesgadener Land. Lying 600 m (2,000 ft) above sea level, it covers an area of 5.5 sq km (1,360 acres) and reaches a depth of 188 m (616 ft).

Touring Chiemsee 🖲

BAVARIA'S LARGEST LAKE, Chiemsee is a real paradise for watersports enthusiasts, with sailors, water-skiers, swimmers and divers all enjoying the opportunities it offers. The lake is set amidst magnificent Alpine scenery in the region known as the Chiemgau, which stretches eastwards from Rosenheim to the border with Austria along the river Salzach. Chiemsee is surrounded by numerous small towns and villages and dotted with islands, some of which feature fascinating historic buildings. Excellent land, water and rail transport facilities ensure trouble-free travel to all destinations in the area.

Fraueninsel
Like its neighbour Herreninsel, this island is rich in art treasures. Its abbey (Klosterkirche) was founded in 766 and taken over by Benedictine nuns in the mid-9th century.

Stock
The harbour town of Stock is connected by narrow-gauge steam railway to the Chiemsee's main resort of Prien. The railway, the Chiemsee-bahn, is over one hundred years old.

Obing

Hinzing

Halfing

HARTSEE · Eggstädt

Bad Endorf

LANGBURGNER SEE

SIMSSEE

Prien · Stock

Hartas

Urschalling

Bernau

Urschalling
The 12th-century church of St James features magnificent wall paintings dating from the 13th and 14th centuries.

KEY

▬	Motorway
═	Major road
═	River
�背	Viewpoint

Herrenchiemsee Palace
In 1873, King Ludwig II bought Herreninsel, with the intention of building a replica of the Palace of Versailles here. Funds ran out and the project was not completed, but the magnificent central section and park are well worth visiting.

Seeon Abbey

This post-Benedictine abbey, surrounded by the waters of Klostersee, was built in stages during the 11th and 12th centuries. It was remodelled in 1438–43 by Konrad Pürkel, a master-builder from Burghausen.

VISITORS' CHECKLIST

Road map E7.
🛈 *Tourismusverband Chiemsee, Alte Rathausstrasse 11, 83209 Prien am Chiemsee (08051-690 50).* W *www.mychiemsee.de*

Altenmarkt
Stein
eeon
Truchtlaching
Traunreut
bach
Sondermoning
Chieming
Nußdorf
EMSEE
Traunstein
Grabenstätt
Übersee
Bergen

Castle in the Rock

One of the most interesting curiosities of this region is the "Höhlenburg" – a castle carved into a rock on the bank of the river Traun, some 30 m (98 ft) above water level. Visits are allowed only with a guide.

```
0 km          4
0 miles       4
```

Chieming

Chieming lies on the eastern shore of the lake. Its 6-km (4-mile) long beach is an ideal place for sunbathing and swimming in the waters of the lake.

Chiemsee

Lying at an altitude of 518 m (1,700 ft), the lake covers an area of 80 sq km (20,000 acres) with a depth of 70 m (230 ft). Its size makes it popular with sailing enthusiasts.

Colourful Alpine inn, dating from 1612, in Oberammergau

Garmisch-Partenkirchen ㉟

Road map D7. 👥 *27,000.* 🚉
ℹ️ *Richard-Strauss-Platz 2 (08821-18 07 00).* 🎭 *Neujahrs-Springen (1 Jan); Hornschlitten-Rennen (6 Jan); Ski World Cup Races; Richard Strauss Tage (Jun).*

LYING IN THE valley of the river Loisach, Garmisch-Partenkirchen is the best-known resort in the Bavarian Alps. To say that it offers ideal skiing conditions would be to state the obvious. In 1936, it hosted the Winter Olympic Games and, in 1978, the World Skiing Championships. From Garmisch-Partenkirchen, Germany's highest peak, Zugspitze (2964 m/9,720 ft), can be reached by taking the narrow-gauge railway to Zugspitzblatt and from there a cable car, which reaches the summit in a few minutes. Garmisch Partenkirchen's parish church of St Martin (Alte Pfarrkirche St Martin) is worth a visit. It was built in the 13th century and extended in the 15th century and features some well-preserved Gothic wall paintings and net vaulting. The **Werdenfelser Museum** shows how people in this region lived in the past, with a collection of furniture, clothing and room reconstructions.

Oriel window in Garmisch-Partenkirchen

🏛 **Werdenfelser Museum**
Ludwigstraße 47. 📞 *(08821) 21 34.* ⏰ *Dec–Oct: 10am–1pm, 3–6pm, Tue–Fri, 10am–1pm Sat–Sun.* 📷

Oberammergau ㊱

Road map D7. 👥 *4,700.* 🚉 *Eugen-Papst-Straße 9A (08822-923 10).* 🎭 *Oberammergauer Passionsspiele May–Oct, every ten years: next 2010); König-Ludwig-Lauf (Feb); König-Ludwig-Feiern (24 Aug).*

SITUATED SOME 20 km (12 miles) north of Garmisch-Partenkirchen, and standing on the site of a 9th-century Welfs' fort, Oberammergau is world famous for its folk art and passion plays. The Thirty Years' War (1618–48) and the plague of 1632 came close to wiping out the entire population of the village. Its surviving inhabitants pledged that if they were saved from extinction they would stage for ever more a play about Christ's Passion. No further deaths occurred and, to this day, the villagers have kept their pledge. Every ten years, some 2,000 people take part in the six-hour-long spectacle, in which they transform themselves from Bavarians into Jews and Romans from the time of Christ. About one hundred performances are staged between mid-May and mid-October. The venue for these magnificent plays is the huge Passionsspielhaus.

Buildings worth seeing in Oberammergau include the Rococo church of Saint Peter and Saint Paul (1735–40) and the famous *Pilatushaus*, with its illusionist painting of Christ before Pilate on the façade. The **Heimatmuseum** has a notable collection of carved wooden cribs.

🏛 **Heimatmuseum**
Dorfstraße 8. 📞 *(08822) 941 36.* ⏰ *15 May–15 Oct: 2–6pm Tue–Sun, Oct–May: 2–6pm Sat.* 📷

Ettal ㊲

Road map D7. 👥 *974.*

ABOUT 4 km (2.5 miles) from Oberammergau is the tiny resort of Ettal, which is best known for its Benedictine abbey, founded by Emperor Ludwig IV of Bavaria. The abbey's foundation stone was laid in 1330, while the Church of the Virgin Mary and the convent were consecrated in 1370. The church building is a Gothic structure but, in 1710–52, Josef Enrico Zuccalli and Franz Schmuzer carried out major remodelling work in the Baroque style. The church interior is decorated with rich Rococo stuccowork by Johann Baptist and Johann Georg Ubelhör, and wall paintings by Martin Knoller.

The monastery produces some fine fruit liqueurs, flavoured brandies and beer.

The Baroque Benedictine abbey in Ettal

Linderhof ③⑧

I N THE EARLY 1850s, Linderhof was bought by the
Bavarian King Maximilian II. This remote mountain
district had great appeal to the young heir to the throne,
Ludwig, later to become the eccentric King Ludwig II.
In 1874, work started on remodelling the existing
Königshäuschen (royal cottage) in the Neo-Rococo
style. The palace is surrounded by a delightful garden,
which is dotted with romantic little buildings, including
Schwanenweiher (Swan Lake), *Venusgrotte* (Venus grotto)
and the *Marokkanisches Haus* (Moroccan house).

VISITORS' CHECKLIST

Road map D7. **Schloss
Linderhof.** (08822) 920 30.
Apr–Sep: 9am–6pm daily;
Oct–Mar: 10am–4pm daily.

Tapestry Room
The walls of this room are
painted in a style that is reminiscent of tapestry work, with
depictions of pastoral scenes.

Reception Room
Although the palace was
intended as a private
residence, King Ludwig II
insisted on the provision
of a suitably ornate and
regal reception room.

Dining Room
Designed by Christian Jank,
the dining room was
completed in 1872. It features
gilded panelling by Phillip
Perron and stuccowork by
Theobald Behler.

Mirror Hall
The design of Linderhof's Mirror
Hall was based on the Mirror
Room of the royal residence in
Munich *(pp206–7)*.

Terraces
Terraces in front of the palace
are adorned with sculptures and
include a pool with a fountain.

Schloss Neuschwanstein ③⑨

SET AMIDST MAGNIFICENT mountain scenery on the shores of the Schwansee (Swan Lake), this fairy-tale castle was built in 1869–86 for the eccentric Bavarian King Ludwig II, to a design by the theatre designer Christian Jank. When deciding to build this imposing residence, the king was undoubtedly inspired by Wartburg Castle in Thuringia *(see pp176–7)*, which he visited in 1867. The pale grey limestone castle, which draws on a variety of historical styles, is a steep 30-minute walk from the nearby village of Hohenschwangau and offers spectacular views of the surrounding scenery.

★ Singers' Hall
The Sängersaal was modelled on the singing room of the Wartburg castle in Eisenach.

Study

Vestibule
The walls of the vestibule and of other rooms in the castle are lavishly covered with paintings depicting scenes from old German myths and legends.

★ Throne Room
The gilded interior of the throne room reminds one of Byzantine temples and the palace church of All Saints in the Residenz (see pp206–7) in Munich.

Dining Room
Like other rooms in the palace, the dining room includes fabulous pictures, intricately carved panels and beautifully decorated furniture, all bearing witness to the skill and artistry of the 19th-century craftsmen.

VISITORS' CHECKLIST

Road map D7. Neuschwanstein-
strasse 20. **(** (08362) 93 98
86. **◻** Oct–Mar: 10am–4pm
daily; Apr–Sep: 9am–6pm daily.
♨ ✔ ♿ (limited access).
🍴 🖼 🅿 ℹ

★ **Castle Building**
*Schloss Neuschwanstein is
the archetypal fairy-tale
castle and has provided the
inspiration for countless toy
models, book illustrations
and film sets.*

Courtyard
*The heart of the castle was
supposed to have been a
mighty 90-m (295-ft)
high tower with a
Gothic castle church.
It was never built,
but in 1988 its
planned position
was marked in
white stone.*

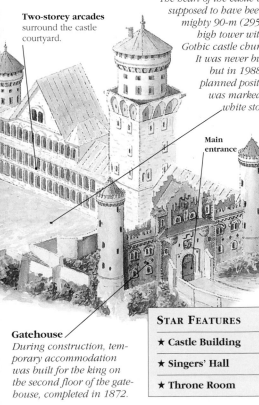

Two-storey arcades
surround the castle
courtyard.

**Main
entrance**

Gatehouse
*During construction, tem-
porary accommodation
was built for the king on
the second floor of the gate-
house, completed in 1872.*

STAR FEATURES

★ **Castle Building**

★ **Singers' Hall**

★ **Throne Room**

Hohen-
schwangau ④⓪

Road map D7. 🕌 Schwangau
3,818. ℹ (and tickets for both
castles) Kurverwaltung Schwangau,
Münchener Straße 2 (08362-8 19 80).

THE SKYLINE OF Schwangau is
dominated by two castles,
Schloss Neuschwanstein (left)
and the majestic **Schloss
Hohenschwangau**. The fortified castle that occupied this
site in the Middle Ages was
remodelled in 1538–47 and,
in 1567, it passed into the
hands of the Wittelsbach
family. The property was
destroyed during the course
of the Tyrolean War but in
1832 the heir to the throne
(later Maximilian II) ordered
the ruins to be rebuilt in Neo-
Gothic style. The plans were
prepared by the painter
Domenico Quaglio; after his
death, work on the castle was
continued by the architects
Georg Friedrich Ziebland and
Joseph Daniel Ohlmüller.
   This four-storey building,
standing on medieval foundations, is flanked by angular
towers. The wall paintings
that decorate the rooms of the
castle date from 1835–36.
Their iconographic content,
which is based on old Germanic sagas, is the work of
Moritz von Schwind. A walk
around the castle provides an
excellent opportunity to study
the Wittelsbach family history
and to see the mid-19th century furnishings. There are
magnificent views of the
surroundings from the castle's
lovely terraced gardens.

🏰 **Schloss Hohenschwangau**
((08362) 811 27. **◻** Apr–Sep:
9am–6pm Mon–Wed & Fri–Sun,
9am–8pm Thu; Oct–Mar: 10am–
4pm. **●** 24 Dec. **♨**

**Neo-Gothic castle of Maximilian II
in Hohenschwangau**

The Rococo Throne Room in the Kempten Residenz.

Kempten 🕙

Road map C7. 🏘 *68,000.* 🚉
🚉 *Rathausplatz 24 (0831-252 52 37 or 194 33).*

Kempten LIES at the centre of one of Germany's most attractive tourist regions, the Allgäu, which stretches from Bodensee lake to the west and the river Lech to the east. The town, which boasts a history of over 2,000 years, was first mentioned by the Greek geographer and historian Strabon as a Celtic settlement, Kambodounon. Later, the Romans established Cambodunum on the right bank of the river Iller. Along with Augusta Vindelicorum (Augsburg) and Castra Regina (Regensburg), this was one of the most important towns in the Roman province of Raetia.

Medieval Kempten grew around a Benedictine Abbey, founded in 752. In the north-western part of town, near the former abbots' residence,

is the church of St Lorenz. A triple-nave, galleried basilica with an octagonal cupola and a twin-tower façade, this is the work of Michael Beer and Johann Serro. The town's parish church of St Mang dates from the 15th century. In the Rathausplatz is an attractive town hall dating from 1474 and other historic buildings, including the Londoner Hof with its Rococo façade (1764). The **Römisches Museum** has a collection illustrating the town's Roman history and, on the right bank of the river Iller, is the **Archäologischer Park**, with impressive excavated remains of Roman Cambodunum.

🏛 Römisches Museum
Residenzplatz 31. 📞 *(0831) 123 67.*
🕙 *10am–4pm Tue–Sun.* 🎫
⛪ Archäologischer Park Cambodunum
Cambodunumweg 3. 📞 *(0831) 57 42 50.* 🕙 *May–Oct: 10am–5pm Tue–Sun; Nov–Apr:10am–4:30pm Tue–Sun.* ⚫ *Jan–Feb.*

Epitaph of the family of Andreas Bertsch, in the Stadtmuseum Lindau

Lindau 🕙

Road map C7. 🏘 *24,000.* 🚉 🚉
Ludwigstraße 68 (08382-26 00 30 or 19 433).

IN ROMAN TIMES Lindau was a fishing settlement, which used to lie over three islands. The first historic records of the town date from 882. On the south side of the old-town island lies the harbour with its 13th-century lighthouse (Mangturm). The new lighthouse (Neuer Leuchtturm), built in 1856, stands on the neighbouring pier and offers a splendid view over the lake and the Alps. The marble Lion of Bavaria opposite is the symbol of Lindau.

The old town features many historic buildings, such as the Gothic-Renaissance town hall in Reichsplatz, which was built in 1422–36 and later remodelled in 1578. The picturesque Maximilianstrasse is lined with the houses of rich patricians; their shady arcades *(Brodlauben)* are typical of Lindau architecture.

In Schrannenplatz, in the northwest area of the town, stands the church of St Peter. Since 1928 this has been the war memorial chapel for World War I victims. Its eastern section dates from the mid-12th century while the bigger, western section was built between 1425 and 1480. The interior contains many wall paintings, including some by Hans Holbein the Elder dating from 1485–90. Nearby stands the *Diebsturm* (Thief's Tower) of 1380. The **Stadtmuseum** (town museum) is housed in Haus zum Cavazzen (1729) in Markt-platz, which also features a lovely Neptune fountain.

On the south side of the Market Square stands the Protestant Church of St Stephen, which dates from the 12th century and was remodelled in Baroque style in 1782. The Catholic Church of St Mary, built in 1748–52, has a lovely Rococo interior.

🏛 Stadtmuseum Lindau
Marktplatz 6. 📞 *(08382) 94 40 73.*
🕙 *Apr–Oct: 11am–5pm Tue–Fri, Sun, 2pm–5pm Sat.* ⚫ *Nov–Mar.*

Oberstdorf ㊸

Road map C7. 🏔 *11,000.* 🚉 ℹ️
Verkehrsamt, Marktplatz 7 (08322-70 00).

OBERSTDORF LIES in the valley of the River Iller. The ideal skiing conditions and the mild all-year-round climate make this one of the most popular health resorts and winter sports centres in Germany. Nearby is the skiing stadium (Schattenberg-Skistadion) with its famous ski-jump, where the annual "four ski-jump" tournament starts each year.

Although the fire of 1865 destroyed large sections of the settlement here, some of the most important historic buildings escaped. These include Seelenkapelle, whose façade is decorated with a 16th-century wall painting typical of the region, and two chapels, Loretto-kapelle and Josephskapelle, which were joined together in 1707. Just to the east of Oberstdorf is the 2,224-m (7,300-ft) Mount Nebelhorn, whose summit can be reached in a few minutes by cable car. This offers a spectacular view over the majestic Allgäuer Alps as well as providing an excellent starting point for mountain hiking.

Füssen ㊹

Road map D7. 🏔 *16,000.* 🚉 ℹ️
Kurverwaltung, Kaiser-Maximilian-Platz 1 (08362-938 50).

SITUATED CONVENIENTLY on an important trade route, Füssen experienced its most rapid growth in the late Middle Ages, as witnessed by many of the buildings in Reichenstrasse and the remains of the town fortifications, which include Sebastiantor and sections of the walls with five turrets. Perched on a rock, high above the town, stands the palace of the Augsburg prince-bishops. Started in 1291 by the Bavarian Prince Ludwig II the Severe, construction was continued in 1490-1503 by the Augsburg bishops. The residential buildings of the palace range around a courtyard whose walls are decorated with trompe l'oeil door and window frames.

Madonna in the Church of St Mang, in Füssen

At the foot of the castle stands the former Benedictine Abbey (Kloster St Mang), which was erected in the 9th century at the burial site of St Magnus, the "Apostle of the Allgäu". The only surviving part of the abbey is the late 10th-century crypt with the remains of wall paintings.

Late-Baroque interior of the Abbey Library, in Ottobeuren

Ottobeuren ㊺

Road map D7. 🏔 *7,500.* ℹ️
Marktplatz 14 (08332-92 19 50).

SITUATED 8 km (5 miles) from Memmingen, the small health resort of Ottobeuren is the site of one of Germany's most famous Benedictine abbeys. Founded in 764, the abbey is still a place of prayer and work for the monks who live here, having withstood even the radical secularization of 1803. In the 18th century the abbey was remodelled by the Abbot Rupert II. The foundation stone for the building complex was laid in 1717 and work began under the direction of Simpert Kraemer. The new buildings were completed in 1731. The richly decorated interiors, with stuccoes by Andrea Maini, still survive. A new abbey church was built between 1737 and 1766 with construction super-vised initially by Simpert Kramer. In 1748, this was taken over by Johann Michael Fischer, who was responsible for its final appearance.

The interior of the church has a magnificent unity of style: Rococo stuccoes by Johann Michael Feuchtmayr are in perfect harmony with the vault frescos by Johann Jakob Zeiller as well as the splendid altars and stalls by Martin Hörmann and Johann Zeiller's brother Franz Anton Zeiller. The abbey's three organs, which are particularly beautiful, can be heard at regularly held recitals.

Ski-jump complex in Oberstdorf

Augsburg

Sᴵᵀᵁᴬᵀᴱᴰ ᴬᵀ ᵀᴴᴱ confluence of the Lech and Wertach rivers, Augsburg is the third largest town in Bavaria and one of the oldest in Germany. As early as 15 BC this was the site of a Roman camp, which later became a town known as Augusta Vindelicorum. Until the end of the 13th century, the town was ruled by powerful bishops. From 1316, as a Free Imperial City of the Holy Roman Empire, Augsburg grew to become one of the richest and most powerful cities in Germany. The Thirty Years' War (1618–48), however, put an end to the town's prosperity.

Augustusbrunnen
Incorporating a statue of the Emperor Augustus, the fountain was created in the workshop of Dutchman Hubert Gerhard in 1588.

Dom

RATHAUS PLATZ

PHIL. – WEISER – STRASSE

KAROL

Church of St Anna
The star attraction of this unassuming ex-Carmelite church is the Renaissance memorial chapel endowed by the brothers Ulrich and Jacob Fugger in 1509.

St Moritz Kirche

ANNASTRASSE

BGM. – FISCHER – STRASSE

Maximilian-museum
Set in a Renaissance patrician mansion, the museum has a splendid collection of work by local gold- and silversmiths.

KÖNIGS-PLATZ

ZEUGGASSE

Zeughaus
A bronze group by Hans Reichle, St Michael Overcoming Satan *(1607), adorns the façade of the former arsenal building.*

VISITORS' CHECKLIST

Road map D6. 👥 265,000.
✈ 5 km (3 miles) to the
north. 🚉 ℹ Bahnhofstraße 7
(0821-50 20 70). 🎭 Frühjahrs-
plärrer (week following Easter),
Herbstplärrer (Aug/Sep), Frieden-
fest (8 Aug), Mozartsommer
(Aug/Sep). W www.augsburg.de

★ Rathaus

The magnificent town hall,
built by Elias Holl in 1615–20,
is generally regarded as
Germany's finest example
of Mannerist architecture.

★ Maximilianstraße

Augsburg's main thoroughfare is the most
beautiful street in southern Germany, with
notable fountains by Adrian de Vries.

★ Fuggerhäuser

Commissioned by Jacob II
Fugger (1459–1525) for
himself and his family,
this Italian-style
building, with
two arcaded
courtyards,
was built in
1512–15.

St Ulrich-
und-Afra

STAR SIGHTS

★ Fuggerhäuser

★ Maximilianstraße

★ Rathaus

KEY

– – – Suggested route

View of the monumental Gothic
Dom of the Holy Virgin

🔒 Dom of the Holy Virgin
(Mariä Heimsuchung)

Frauenstraße 1. ⏱ 9am–5:30pm.
Originally a Romanesque
twin-choir, pillared basilica
with crypt, western transept
and two towers, dating from
994–1065, the structure was
remodelled between 1331 and
1431 along Gothic lines. The
church was given two further
side aisles, a choir with an
ambulatory and a French-style
ring of chapels. Original
features include the richly
carved portals and the famous
Romanesque bronze door
with 35 panels depicting
allegorical figures. There are
some unique stained-glass
windows, dating from 1140.

🏛 Fuggerei

Fuggerei-Museum, Mittlere Gasse 13.
☎ (0821) 319 88 10. ⏱ 1 Mar–23
Dec: 10am–6pm daily. ⬤ 24 Dec–28
Feb. 🎟
The Fuggerei, in Augsburg's
Jakobervorstadt (Jacob's
Suburb), is Europe's oldest
social housing estate. It was
founded in 1516 by Jacob
Fugger, a member of what
was then the richest family in
Europe. The intention was to
provide homes for the town's
poorest citizens, particularly
families with children. Today,
however, it has evolved into a
home for retired citizens.

The 52 houses in Fuggerei
were built in 1516–25 and line
six streets. They are surrounded by gardens. One of the
buildings houses the **Fuggerei-
Museum**, which is devoted to
the history of the estate and
has a fascinating shop, the
Himmlisches Fuggereilädle.

BADEN-WURTTEMBERG

T HIS GERMAN STATE, *which includes territories of the former Grand Duchy of Baden, is one of the country's most popular tourist destinations. Its charming old university towns, such as Tübingen and Heidelberg, historic castles, luxurious resorts and the magnificent recreation areas of the Schwarzwald (Black Forest) and Bodensee (Lake Constance) guarantee enjoyable and memorable holidays.*

This region's turbulent history, which has been ruled over the years by Palatinate electors, counts and finally kings of Wurttemberg, as well as by margraves and Grand Dukes of Baden, has given the province its cultural and religious diversity.

This southwestern area of Germany was the cradle of two great dynasties that played a significant part in German and European history and culture. The Hohenstaufen family – which originated from Swabia – produced kings and emperors who ruled during the most magnificent period of the German Middle Ages (1138–1254). These included Frederick I Barbarossa and Frederick II. The Hohenzollern family, also from Swabia, produced Brandenburg dukes, Prussian kings including Frederick the Great and German emperors from 1871–1918.

In Heidelberg the enlightened elector Ruprecht I founded the first university in Germany in 1386 and shortly after this epoch-making event, further universities were established in Tübingen and Freiburg im Breisgau. Many towns and villages in the region can boast a history going back to Roman times. The Romans used to grow vines in the area of Baden-Wurttemberg and now wines from the region are renowned worldwide for their high quality.

Baden-Wurttemberg, however, does not only represent an illustrious past, but also an impressive present. Unemployment figures for the region are the lowest in Germany, and many companies that are known and respected throughout the world – such as Bosch, DaimlerChrysler, Porsche and the software company SAP – have their production plants here.

Magnificent French-style garden in front of the palace in Ludwigsburg

◁ **Bodensee (Lake Constance), in the foothills of the Alps**

Baden-Wurttemberg

WITH ITS MAGNIFICENT castles, luxurious resorts and the beautiful recreation areas of the Black Forest, Baden-Wurttemberg is one of Germany's most popular tourist destinations. In addition, the region's long and turbulent history has given it a rich cultural and religious diversity. The southwest region of Germany was the cradle of two dynasties that played important roles in German and European history and culture – the Hohenstaufen and Hohenzollern families. The great number of urban centres in the state is due to the influence of these two families. Baden-Wurttemberg also has more universities than any other state in Germany, the oldest being located at Heidelberg, Tübingen and Freiburg im Breisgau.

The picturesque castle in Sigmaringen, in the region of Schwäbische Alb

KEY

▬	Motorway
▬	Main road
▬	Scenic route
‑‑‑	River
☀	Viewpoint

The Gothic town hall in Ulm

Kaiserslautern 6

MANNHEIM

SCHWETZINGEN 7   9

HEIDELBER

BRUCHSAL 8

MAULBRONN

KARLSRUHE 10

RASTATT

GAGGENAU

BADEN-BADEN 11

Strasbourg

OFFENBURG

FREUDENSTAD

28

8 EA

23 ROT

SCHWARZWALD (BLACK FOREST) 30

29   31

VILLINGEN-SCHWENNIGEN

FREIBURG IM BREISGAU

TUTIM

34

Zurich

SEE ALSO

• **Where to Stay** pp470–97

• **Where to Eat** pp498–527

WERTHEIM 1

TAUBER-BISCHOFSHEIM 2

BAD MERGENTHEIM 3

WEIKERSHEIM 4 5

CREGLINGEN

O D E N W A L D

AD WIMPFEN 16

6/E50

13 HEILBRONN

14 SCHWÄBISCH HALL

CRAILSHEIM

Ingolstadt

MARBACH

17

19 LUDWIGSBURG

STUTTGART

20 18 ESSLINGEN

15 AALEN

SCHWÄBISCH GMÜND

GÖPPINGEN

ELFINGEN

8/E52

TÜBINGEN

21 SCHWÄBISCHE ALB

UTLINGEN

24 ULM

Augsburg

CHINGEN

312 311

312

München

BIBERACH

Kempten

311

SALEM

27

26 WEINGARTEN

25 RAVENSBURG

ONSTANZ

FRIEDRICHSHAFEN

28 31

Bodensee

GETTING AROUND

The main communication centres of the area are Stuttgart, which has an international airport, and Mannheim. Main motorways include the A5 from Frankfurt to Basle, via Heidelberg, Karlsruhe, Baden-Baden and Freiburg; the A81 from Würzburg to Constance, via Tauberbischofsheim, Heilbronn, Stuttgart and Schwäbische Alb; the A6 from Mannheim to Ansbach, via Heilbronn and Crailsheim; and the A8 from Karlsruhe to Ulm, via Stuttgart.

SIGHTS AT A GLANCE

0 km   20

0 miles   20

Palace façade in Bruchsal

Wertheim ❶

Road map C5. 🏛 *24,500.* 🚉
ℹ️ *Wenzelplatz (09342-1066).* 🎭
Altstadtfest (Jul), Burgweinfest (Aug).

Sᴛᴀɴᴅɪɴɢ ᴀᴛ ᴛʜᴇ point where the rivers Tauber and Main meet is the town of Wertheim, whose earliest historic records date from 1183. A gunpowder explosion in 1619 plus the destruction caused by the Thirty Years' War turned the **Wertheimer Burg**, the von Wertheim family castle, into a romantic ruin. Its tall watchtower offers panoramic views.

Wertheim's market square is lined with half-timbered houses, while the Baroque Protestant church nearby, dating from the 15th–18th centuries, contains tomb tombs of members of the von Wertheim family. The most spectacular of these is the tomb of Count Ludwig II von Löwenstein-Wertheim and his wife, Anna von Stolberg. This is the work of Michael Kern (1618). Also worth visiting are the **Glasmuseum** and the **Grafschaftsmuseum Wertheim**, with collections of Frankish costumes, paintings and coins and displays on wine-making.

🏛 Glasmuseum
Mühlenstraße 24. 📞 *(09342) 68 66.* 🕐 *Apr–Oct & 1st Advent Sun–6 Jan: 10am–noon & 2–5pm Tue–Fri, 10am–5pm Sat & Sun.* **Glassmaking demonstrations** *daily.* 📷
🏛 Grafschaftsmuseum Wertheim
Rathausgasse 10. 📞 *(09342) 30 15 10.* 🕐 *10am–1pm, 2pm–5pm Tue–Fri, 10am–5pm Sat & Sun.* 📷

Half-timbered houses and tower by Schloss Tauberbischofsheim

Tauberbischofsheim ❷

Road map C5. 🏛 *13,000.* 🚉
ℹ️ *Marktplatz 8 (09341-803 13).*

Bᴏɴɪꜰᴀᴄᴇ, the Anglo-Saxon missionary to the German tribes, established Germany's first nunnery in AD 735. Its first prioress, Lioba, who was related to Boniface, gave her name to the Baroque church that stands in Tauberbischofsheim's market square.

The town, which enjoys a picturesque location in the valley of the river Tauber, still has a group of original half-timbered houses. On the market square is the Baroque Rehhof (1702) and the old "Star Pharmacy" in a

Heraldic crest from the castle in Bad Mergentheim

house once occupied by Georg Michael Franck, grandfather of the Romantic poets Clemens and Bettina Brentano.

In the eastern section of Hauptstraße stands Haus Mackert – a Baroque mansion built in 1744 for a wealthy wine merchant. In Schlossplatz is the Kurmainzisches Schloss, an imposing edifice built in the 15th–16th centuries, that now houses the **Landschaftsmuseum**.

🏛 Landschaftsmuseum Kurmainzisches Schloss
📞 *(09341) 37 60.* 🕐 *Easter–Oct: 2:30–4:30pm Tue–Sat, 10am–noon & 2–4:30pm Sun.* 📷

Bad Mergentheim ❸

Road map C5. 🏛 *25,000.* 🚉
ℹ️ *Marktplatz 3 (07931-5 71 35).* 🎭
Markelsheimer Weinfest (after Whitsun).

Lʏɪɴɢ ɪɴ ᴀ ᴄʜᴀʀᴍɪɴɢ spot on the river Tauber, Bad Mergentheim was, from 1525 until 1809, the seat of the Grand Masters of the religious order of the "House of the Hospitallers of Saint Mary of the Teutons in Jerusalem", more commonly known as the Teutonic Knights. When three Hohenlohe brothers entered the Order in 1220, they contributed to it their share of their father's estate. This laid the foundations for one of the most powerful Teutonic commands at the heart of the Holy Roman Empire. From 1244 until 1250 Heinrich von Hohenlohe held the office of Grand Master.

The former Hohenlohe's castle, built in the 12th–13th centuries, was remodelled in Renaissance style in 1565–74 by Michael Bronner and Blasius Berwart. They gave the castle its winding stairs and the opulent ornamental decor of the staircase. The Baroque-Rococo Schlosskirche dominates the complex. Its interior was designed by François Cuvilliés, while the

Scenic castle ruins in Wertheim

ceiling fresco *(The Victorious Cross)* is the work of Nicolaus Stuber. The castle is now the home of a very interesting museum of the Order, the **Deutschordensmuseum**.

Many of the town's historic buildings survive to this day, including the 13th-century Church of the Knights of St John of Jerusalem and the Dominican church containing the epitaph of the Grand Master Walther von Cronberg. The **Pfarrkirche** (Parish church) in the Stuppach district contains a masterpiece by Grünewald (1519), known as the *Madonna of Stuppach*.

Pfarrkirche in Stuppach
Kapellenpflege. ((7931) 26 05.
Mar–Apr: 10am–5pm daily; May–Oct: 9:30am–5:30pm daily; Nov: 11am–4pm daily. Dec–Feb.
Deutschordensmuseum
Schloss. ((07931) 522 12.
10am–5pm Tue–Sun.

Weikersheim ❹

Road map C5. 8,000. Am Marktplatz 12 (07934-99 25 75).

ELEVEN KILOMETRES (7 miles) east of Bad Mergentheim is the picturesque little town of Weikersheim. A Rococo fountain from 1768 stands at the centre of its market square while, on the north side, stands the late-Gothic parish church. The latter is a triple-nave hall-church with a single-tower western façade and two towers by the choir. Inside are many tombs of the von Hohenlohe family. Also on the market square stands the **Tauberländer Dorfmuseum**, which charts the history of rural life in Franconia.

In the western part of town stands the very well preserved **Schloss Weikersheim**, the palace complex of the Counts von Hohenlohe, which dates

gure of drummer Weikersheim's Hofgarten

from the 16th–18th centuries. Its highlight is undoubtedly the vast Rittersaal, a sumptuous banqueting hall that measures 35 m (115 ft) long × 12 m (39 ft) wide × 9 m (29 ft) high. The counts and their aristocratic guests used to enter this room on horseback. Its very rare, original furnishings include paintings and reliefs depicting hunting scenes.

A true rarity is the original Baroque Hofgarten (palace garden), designed by Daniel Matthieu and built in 1709.

Schloss Weikersheim
Apr–Oct: 9am–6pm daily; Nov–Mar: 10am–noon & 1:30–4:30pm daily.
Tauberländer Dorfmuseum
Marktplatz. ((07934) 12 09.
Easter–Nov: 2–5pm Wed, Fri–Sun, holidays.

Creglingen ❺

Road map C5. 5,000.
Rathaus (07933-6 31).

UPSTREAM FROM Weikersheim, on the Bavarian border, is the small town of Creglingen. Here, sometime in the distant past, a ploughman found a luminous holy wafer in a clod of earth and within a few years, the **Herrgottskirche** was built, where the host was put on display for visiting pilgrims. Between 1502 and

Altar by Tilman Riemenschneider, in Creglingen's Herrgottskirche

1506 Tilman Riemenschneider carved an altar for the church. The main theme of the polyptych is the *Assumption of the Virgin Mary*, considered to be the artist's masterpiece.

The town is also home to the esoteric collection of the famous **Fingerhutmuseum** (Thimble Museum).

Herrgottskirche
Kohlersmühle. ((07933) 631.
Apr–Oct: 9:15am–5:30pm daily; Nov–Mar: 10am–noon & 2–4pm Tue–Sun. 24, 25, 31 Dec.
Fingerhutmuseum
Kohlersmühle. ((07933) 370.
Apr–Oct: 10am–12:30pm 2–5pm Tue–Sun; Nov–Dec, Mar: 1–4pm Tue–Sun.

TEUTONIC ORDER

The Order of the Hospital of St Mary of the German House in Jerusalem was officially founded in Acre (Akkon) in 1190. Its aim was to care for sick pilgrims or Crusaders wounded in fights with the Saracens. In 1231–83, the Teutonic Knights took over all of Prussia and, in 1308–09 all Eastern Pomerania around Danzig, and they moved their headquarters from Venice to Marienburg on the river Nogat. In 1525 the Grand Master, Albrecht von Hohenzollern-Ansbach, converted to Lutheranism and secularized Teutonic Prussia. However, the Order remained in existence in the Holy Roman Empire: its German Master, Walter von Cronberg, who had his residence in Mergentheim, became *de facto* Grand Master. Napoleon abolished the Order in 1809, but it still exists today, with its headquarters based in Vienna since 1809.

The Wasserturm (Water Tower) in Friedrichsplatz, Mannheim

Mannheim ●

Road map B5. ● *326,000.* ● ●
Willy-Brandt-Platz 3 (0621-10 10 12).
● *Mannheim-Heidelberger
Filmfestival (mid-October).*

Mannheim existed as a small
fishing hamlet as far
back as 766. In 1606, Elector
Frederick IV the Righteous
ordered a fortress to be built
on the site, at the junction of
the rivers Rhine and Neckar.
A trading settlement sprang
up nearby, which was soon
granted town status. Having
been repeatedly destroyed
through the years, the town
was finally rebuilt in
Baroque style during the
reign of the Elector
Johann Wilhelm.

The town-centre
layout follows the
regular Baroque
pattern of the
early 18th
century, when the
town was divided
into 136 regular
squares. In 1720,
when Elector
Charles III Philip
decided to move
his residence from
Heidelberg to
Mannheim, the
foundation stone
for a Baroque
palace was laid in
the grounds of a
former citadel.

**Statue of Elector Karl
Theodor in Mannheim's
Jesuitenkirche**

With over 400 rooms, this
became one of the largest and
most opulent of all German
palaces. Like many other
residences built by European
rulers at that time, the palace
was modelled on Versailles.
The main palace is built to a
horseshoe layout, and its
symmetry is emphasized by a
central projecting entrance.
Building work was carried out
by Johann Clemens Froimont,
Alessandro Galli da Bibiena,
Guillaume d'Hauberat and
Nicolas de Pigage.

The second largest town of
the region, Mannheim boasts
many other historic buildings,
including the post-Jesuit
Church of St Ignatius and St
Francis Xavier, designed by
Alessandro Galli da Bibiena
and built in 1733–60. Original
wall-paintings by Egid Quirin
Asam no longer exist, but the
altars have survived to this
day. These include J I
Saler's *Silver Madonna
in Radiant Glory* (1747).
Also worth visiting are
the Baroque Altes
Rathaus (1701–23) and
Secessionist buildings
in Friedrichsplatz such
as the Kunsthalle and
Wasserturm – the
symbol of Mannheim.

The town has several
interesting museums: the
Städtische Kunsthalle
has a large collection of
19th- and 20th-century
art, including Francis
Bacon's *Study After
Velasquez's Portrait
of Pope Innocent X.*
The museum is
renowned for its
major temporary
exhibitions. The
**Reiss-Engelhorn-
Museen** has a fine
collection of 18th-
century Dutch
paintings and sections
devoted to early
history and ethno-
graphy. Another big
attraction is the
**Landesmuseum für
Technik und Arbeit**
(Museum of Techno-
logy and Labour).
Opened in 1990,
this houses a
collection of historic
machinery. Mann-

heim saw the first official
demonstration of many inventions that have now become
part of everyday life. In 1817,
Baron Karl Friedrich von
Sauerbronn demonstrated his
first bicycle here and, in 1886,
Carl Friedrich Benz unveiled
his first automobile, produced
at the nearby factory.

🏛 **Städtische Kunsthalle**
Moltkestraße 9. ● *(0621) 293 64
13.* ● *11am–6pm Tue–Sun.*
● *during Carnival, 1 May, 24, 31
Dec.* ●
🏛 **Landesmuseum für
Technik und Arbeit**
Museumsstraße 1. ● *(0621) 429 89.*
● *9am–5pm Tue, Thu & Fri, 9am–8pm
Wed, 10am–5pm Sat, 10am–6pm Sun.*
● *Good Friday, 24, 25, 31 Dec.* ●
🏛 **Reiss-Engelhorn-Museen**
Quadrat D5 and C5. ● www.
mannheim.de/reiss_museum.de
● *(0621) 293 31 50.* ● *11am–6pm
Tue–Sun.* ●

**Paul Cézanne's *Pipe Smoker* (c.1890), in
the Städtische Kunsthalle, Mannheim**

Schwetzingen ●

Road map B5. ● *21,500.* ●
Dreikönigstr. 3 (06202-94 58 75).
● *Schwetzinger Festspiele (May),
Mozartkonzerte (Sept).*

Schwetzingen's Baroque-
Renaissance palace was
built during the reign of the
Electors Johann Wilhelm,
Charles II Philip and Karl
Theodor as their summer
residence. Erected on the site
of a medieval castle that was
later converted into a hunting
lodge, it is one of the best
known palace complexes of

Baroque Schwetzingen Palace, set amid beautiful gardens

18th-century Europe. The conversion of the 16th-century hunting lodge was carried out by J A Breuning and the side wings were built by Alessandro Galli da Bibiena. The magnificent Rococo theatre, designed by Nicolas de Pigage, was built in 1752, while the palace garden is the work of Johann Ludwig Petri, who designed it in the French style. The garden includes a mosque with two minarets and a bathhouse. In 1776 Friedrich Ludwig von Sckell converted it into an English-style garden.

Heraldic insignia from Bruchsal Palace

Speyer to Bruchsal. He not only initiated the town's development but, most importantly, ordered a palace to be built for himself and his court. The foundation stone of **Schloss Bruchsal** was laid in 1720 and the building works were carried out by Maximilian von Welsch, who was responsible for the right wing, and Michael Rohrer, who built the left wing between 1723 and 1728. The main body, preceded by a ceremonial court-yard, was designed by Baron Anselm von Grünstein. The central part of the palace is

occupied by a magnificent staircase built by the great Balthasar Neumann, with stuccowork by Johann Michael Feuchtmayer and paintings by Johann and Januarius Zick. The palace suffered severe bomb damage in 1945, but its major part was reconstructed between 1952 and 1977.

St Peter's church was built in 1740–49 by Michael Rohrer to Balthasar Neumann's 1736 design. The church features magnificent Baroque tombs of Schönborn and his successor Cardinal Franz Christoph von Hutten. The palace garden was designed in the French style by Johann Scheer.

This former residence of prince-bishops now houses a section of the Karlsruhe Museum, which features the largest collection of Flemish and French tapestries in Germany. It is also home to the **Museum Mechanische Musikinstrumente**, which includes 200 mechanical musical instruments. Short demonstrations are given on these throughout the day.

♣ **Schloss Bruchsal**
[(07251) 74 26 61.] 9:30am –5pm Tue–Sun. ● 25, 31 Dec.
Museum Mechanischer Musik-instrumente [] Tue–Sun.
10am, 11am, 1pm, 2pm, 3pm, 4pm (obligatory). ● Shrove Tuesday, 24, 25, 31 Dec.

♣ **Schloss Schwetzingen**
[(06202) 12 88 28. **Schloss**
[] Apr–Oct: 11am–4pm Tue–Fri, 11am–5pm Sat–Sun; Nov–Mar: 2pm Fri, 11am, 2pm, 3pm Sat–Sun.
obligatory, every hour.
Garden [] Apr–Sep: 9am–7pm Tue–Sun; Oct & Mar: 9am–6pm Tue–Sun; Nov–Feb: 9am–5pm Tue–Sun.

Bruchsal **❽**

Road map B6. 🏘 40,000. 🚉 🛈
Am Alten Schloss 2 (07251-727 71).

BRUCHSAL BELONGED to the Bishops of Speyer from 1056 until 1806, since when it has been part of Baden. The town rose to prominence in the 17th century, when the Prince-Bishop of Speyer, Damian Hugo von Schönborn, moved his residence from

Central façade of the Baroque Schloss Bruchsal

Street-by-Street: Heidelberg ❾

Sɪᴛᴜᴀᴛᴇᴅ ᴏɴ ᴛʜᴇ ʙᴀɴᴋꜱ of the river Neckar, Heidelberg is one of Germany's most beautiful towns. For centuries it was a centre of political power, with a lively and influential cultural life. In 1386, Germany's first university was established here by the Elector Ruprecht I. Building of the palace began during his reign, continuing until the mid-17th century. However, in the late-17th century, French incursions totally destroyed medieval Heidelberg, including the castle. The town was subsequently rebuilt in the early 18th-century in Baroque style.

Marktplatz
Now adorned with the Neptune Fountain, the market square was, in the past, the site of executions and the burning of witches and heretics.

★ Heiliggeistkirche
Built in 1400–41 on the site of a late-Romanesque basilica, the Church of the Holy Spirit is the town's oldest sanctuary.

HAUPTSTRASSE

HEILIGGEISTSTRASSE

FISCHM

OBERE NECKARSTRASSE

STEINGASSE

LAUERSTRASSE

NECKARSTADEN

0 metres	60
0 yards	60

Philosophenweg
Built in 1817 on the slopes of Heiligenberg, at an altitude of 200 m (650 ft), the "Philosophers' Walk" offers magnificent views of Heidelberg and its castle.

★ Alte Brücke
This imposing, nine-span bridge over the river Neckar was built in 1786–88 by Mathias Maier. It was rebuilt after its destruction during World War II.

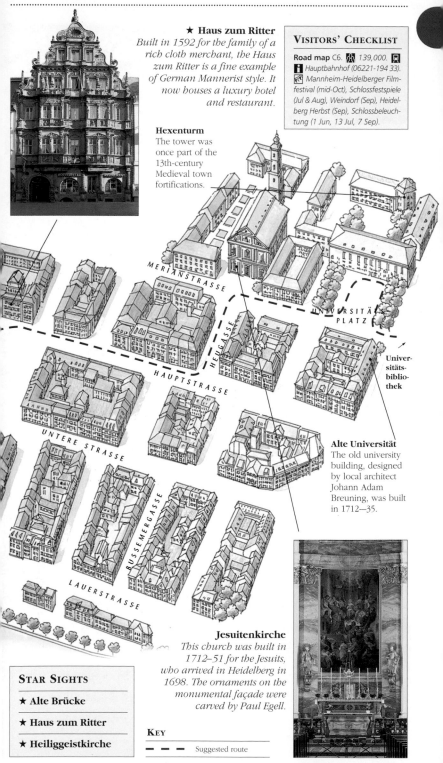

★ **Haus zum Ritter**
*Built in 1592 for the family of a
rich cloth merchant, the Haus
zum Ritter is a fine example
of German Mannerist style. It
now houses a luxury hotel
and restaurant.*

VISITORS' CHECKLIST

Road map C6. 🚶 *139,000.* 🚇
Hauptbahnhof (06221-194 33).
ℹ *Mannheim-Heidelberger Film-
festival (mid-Oct), Schlossfestspiele
(Jul & Aug), Weindorf (Sep), Heidelberg Herbst (Sep), Schlossbeleuch-
tung (1 Jun, 13 Jul, 7 Sep).*

Hexenturm
The tower was
once part of the
13th-century
Medieval town
fortifications.

MERIANSTRASSE

UNIVERSITÄTS
PLATZ

HEUGASSE

HAUPTSTRASSE

**Univer-
sitäts-
biblio-
thek**

UNTERE STRASSE

BUSSEMERGASSE

Alte Universität
The old university
building, designed
by local architect
Johann Adam
Breuning, was built
in 1712–35.

LAUERSTRASSE

Jesuitenkirche
*This church was built in
1712–51 for the Jesuits,
who arrived in Heidelberg in
1698. The ornaments on the
monumental façade were
carved by Paul Egell.*

STAR SIGHTS

★ **Alte Brücke**

★ **Haus zum Ritter**

★ **Heiliggeistkirche**

KEY

– – – Suggested route

Heidelberg Castle

Detail from Ruprechtsbau

Towering over the town, the majestic castle is really a vast residential complex that was built and repeatedly extended between the 13th and 17th centuries. Originally a supremely well-fortified Gothic castle, but now mostly in ruins, this was the seat of the House of Wittelsbach palatines. After remodelling in the 16th century, the castle became one of Germany's most beautiful Renaissance residences. However, its splendour was extinguished by the Thirty Years' War and the 1689 war with France, during which most of the structure was destroyed.

★ Ottheinrichsbau
The Deutsches Apotheken-museum is housed within the shell of this Renaissance building. It features Baroque and Rococo workshops and a travelling pharmacy.

The bell tower, which was erected in the early 15th century, was remodelled frequently in subsequent years.

★ Friedrichsbau
One of the latest parts of the castle is Friedrich's Palace, which dates from 1601–07. Inside are statues of members of the Wittelsbach dynasty, including Charles the Great.

Castle moat

Englischer Bau
These imposing ruins in the castle complex are the remains of a 17th-century building that Friedrich V built for his wife Elizabeth Stuart.

STAR SIGHTS

★ Friedrichsbau

★ Ottheinrichsbau

★ Ruprechtsbau

VISITORS' CHECKLIST

Schlossberg. ☎ (06221) 53 84
31. ◯ 8am–6pm daily.
Grosses Fass ◯ 8am–6pm
daily. 🖼 **Deutsches
Apothekenmuseum**
☎ (06221) 258 80.
◯ 10am–5:30pm. ⬛ 31 Dec,
1 Jan. 🖼

Pulverturm
*Built during the reign of the
Elector Ruprecht, this 14th-
century tower once formed
part of the castle defences.*

Brunnenhalle
This Gothic loggia features early-
Romanesque columns taken from the
palace of Charles the Great in Ingelheim.

Torturm

Main
entrance

★ **Ruprechtsbau**
*Built around 1400 by a
master builder from
Frankfurt, this is the oldest
surviving part of the castle.*

🏛 **Alte Universität**
Grabengasse 1. ☎ (06221) 54 21 52.
Universitätsmuseum ◯ Apr–Oct:
10am–4pm Tue–Sun; Nov–Mar:
10am–4pm Tue–Fri. 🖼
Designed by Mainz architect
Johann Adam Breuning, the
university was built in
1712–35. On the north wall
and ceiling are allegorical
paintings by Ferdinand Keller.
In front of the building is a
fountain crowned by a
sculpture in the form of the
heraldic Palatinate lion.

🏛 **Universitätsbibliothek**
Plöck 107–109. ☎ (06221) 54 23 80.
Ausstellungsraum ◯ 10am–6pm
Mon–Sat.
The monumental building of
the university library, designed
by Joseph Durm of Karlsruhe,
was erected in 1901–05 near
the church of St Peter. The
Heidelberg library, with over
2 million volumes, is one of the
largest in Germany. The
exhibition rooms hold many
precious manuscripts and old
prints, including the famous
Codex Manesse, illustrated
with 137 beautiful miniatures.

🏛 **Kurpfälzisches Museum**
Hauptstraße 97. ☎ (06221) 58 34
02. ◯ 10am–5pm Tue, Thu–Sun,
10am–9pm Wed. 🖼
The French Count Charles de
Graimberg spent the bulk of
his considerable fortune on
building up an extensive
collection of fine drawings,
paintings, arms and various
curios associated with the
history of the Palatinate and
the castle of Heidelberg. In
1879, his collection became
the property of the town and
forms the core of this very
interesting museum, which
also includes a fascinating
archaeology section.

⛪ **Heiliggeistkirche**
Hauptstraße.
This collegiate church, whose
Baroque dome is one of the
city's landmarks, was built in
1400–41. The canons of the
college were also university
scholars and therefore the
church aisle features special
galleries for the extensive
collections of library books –
Bibliotheca Palatina. The
choir features a tombstone of
Ruprecht III and his wife,
Elisabeth von Hohenzollern.

Karlsruhe ⑩

Road map B6. 🏛 *269,000.* 🚇
🚉 *Bahnhofsplatz 6 (0721-355 30 &
194 33; www.karlsruhe.de).*
🎭 *Internationales Trachten-und-
Folklorefest (Jun).*

KARLSRUHE, which is one of
the "youngest" towns in
Germany, flourished during
the 19th century as a centre
for science and art. In 1945,
it lost its status as a regional
capital, but is now the seat of
the Bundesverfassungsgericht
– the highest courts of the
Federal Republic.

The town originated in 1715
when the margrave of Baden,
Karl Wilhelm von Baden-
Durlach, ordered a lodge to
be built in the middle of his
favourite hunting grounds.
Karl liked the area and the
lodge so much that he decided to move his residence
here and live the remainder
of his days in peace – hence
the town's name, meaning
"Karl's rest". The original
Baroque-style design was
expanded during the reign of
his successor, Karl Friedrich.

The palace, which forms
the hub of 32 streets, was
designed by Leopoldo Retti,
Mauritio Pedetti, Balthasar
Neumann, Philippe de la
Gaupière and others, and
built in 1749–81. The town is
based on a fan-like plan,
spreading from a base formed
by the open-sided wings of
the palace. The rest of the
circle, whose centre is
marked by the octagonal
palace tower (1715), is filled
with green areas, including
the palace garden.

**A pyramid containing the tomb of Karl
Wilhelm von Baden Durlach in Karlsruhe**

In the early 19th century, the
town was remodelled along
Neo-Classical lines. The main
architect of this large-scale
project was Friedrich Weinbrenner, who created this
masterpiece of urban design.
The equilateral market square
is positioned along the palace
axis. It is filled with similar
but not identical buildings
and features a central pyramid
containing Karl Wilhelm's
tomb. South of Marktplatz is
the circular Rondellplatz.
Weinbrenner's other works
include the monumental town
hall (1811–25), the Protestant
town church and the Catholic
parish church of St Stephen.

Karlsruhe has some very
interesting museums. The
Badisches Landesmuseum in
the castle features a large
collection of antiquities,
decorative arts, sculpture,
porcelain and furniture, from
the Middle Ages to the

present day. In a
Neo-Renaissance
building (1843–46)
is the **Staatliche
Kunsthalle**, with
its large collection
of mainly German
and Dutch paintings
from the 16th–19th
centuries. These
include the famous
Crucifixion by
Grünewald (1523).

Entirely different
in character are the
collections of the
Zentrum für Kunst
und Medientech-
nologie (ZKM) – an
establishment that
has combined the
role of art college
and museum since 1997. It
occupies a former ammuni-
tions factory in the western
part of the town. Its core is
the **Museum für Neue Kunst**,
featuring installations, computer art and videos and
other work by contemporary
artists. The **Stadtmuseum im
Prinz-Max-Palais**, based in a
mansion named after the last
chancellor of the Second
Reich, contains the local
history museum.

🏛 **Staatliche Kunsthalle**
Hans-Thoma-Straße 2–6. 📞 *(0721)
9 26 33 55.* ⏰ *10am–5pm Tue–Fri,
10am–6pm Sat–Sun.* 🖼
🏛 **Museum für Neue Kunst**
Lorenzstraße 9. 📞 *(0721) 81 00 13
25.* ⏰ *10am–6pm Thu–Sun,
10am–8pm Wed.* 🖼
🏛 **Stadtmuseum im Prinz-
Max-Palais**
Karlstraße 10. 📞 *(0721) 1 33 42 30.*
⏰ *10am-6pm Tue, Wed, Fri & Sun,
10am–7pm Thu, 2–6pm Sat.*

The Baroque residence of the Dukes of Baden in Karlsruhe

Baden-Baden ⓫

Road map B6. 🚗 50,000.
✈ Baden Airport (5 km/3 miles
northwest of town). 🚉 ℹ️
Schwarzwaldstraße 52 & i-Punkt in
der Trinkhalle (07221-27 52 00).

K NOWN AS THE "summer
capital of Europe", this
elegant spa resort is one of
the oldest towns in Germany
and was once the favourite
destination of European
aristocracy from Russia to
Portugal. Even before the
Romans built their camp here
around AD 80, the site was
occupied by a Celtic settlement of the Latenian period.

In the early years of the
modern era, *Civitas Aurelia
Aquensis* – known simply as
Aquae – was already known
in Italy for the therapeutic
properties of its waters. In the
3rd century AD, Aquae was
conquered by the Germanic
tribe of Alamains and in the
6th century AD by the Francs,
who built a fortress in the
town. The Margrave Hermann
II, known as "Marchio de
Baduon", was the first
important ruler of Baden.

During the horrific Black
Death, the qualities of the
local waters were once again
recognized as being beneficial
to health. During the
Palatinate War of Succession,
Baden-Baden was almost
totally destroyed but, by the
end of the 18th century, it
had became one of Europe's
most fashionable
resorts.

The old town of
Baden-Baden lies at
the foot of the Schloss-
berg (castle hill). The
oldest surviving
building in the town is
the Gothic collegiate
church, built during
the 13th–15th centuries
and then remodelled
in the 18th century.
It contains several
valuable epitaphs. To
the south of the
church is the bathing
hall – Friedrichsbad –
which was built in
Neo-Renaissance style
in 1877. Nearby stands
the magnificent New
Palace, which was the

Baden-Baden's casino, set in the elegant Kurhaus

residence of margraves from
the 15th century onwards. It
was remodelled along
German Renaissance lines in
the 16th century by Kaspar
Weinhart. The interiors are
decorated with paintings by
Tobias Stimmer.

Most of the spa buildings
are the work of Friedrich
Weinbrenner. His elegant
Kurhaus in Werderstraße has
been used as a casino since
1838. The most famous
gamester at the casino was
Fyodor Dostoevsky, who was
not always lucky at roulette.
His novel *The Gambler* (1866)
is supposedly set in Baden-
Baden. Nearby is the Trinkhalle (pump room), with its
mineral water fountains. Built
in 1839–42, it is decorated
with wall paintings illustrating
Black Forest legends.

Rising behind the spa area
is the last project completed
by Leo von Klenze before his
death – the Orthodox burial

The Neo-Renaissance Trinkhalle (pump room) in Baden-Baden

chapel of a Romanian aristocratic family, the Stourdza
Mausoleum. In Schillerstraße
is the villa built in 1867 for the
Russian writer, Ivan Turgenev,
who lived here until 1872.

🎵 Brahmshaus
Maximilianstraße 85. 📞 (07221) 7 11
72. ⬤ 3–5pm Mon, Wed, Fri,
10am–1pm Sun. 🏷️
The exhibition displayed in
this house is devoted to the
life and works of the German
composer Johannes Brahms
who lived here from 1865
until 1874.

🔒 Kloster Lichtental
Hauptstraße 40. 📞 (07221) 50 49
10. ⬤ 3pm Tue–Sun. 🏷️ Group
tours (minimum 7 persons), advance
telephone booking required. 🏷️
This Cistercian nuns' abbey,
situated on the outskirts of
town, has a church dating
from the 14th–15th centuries.
Its ducal chapel contains
many epitaphs of the Baden
margraves. The abbey has
has an interesting museum.

🏛 Stadtgeschichtliche
Sammlungen
Schlossstraße 2. 📞 (07221) 2 21 80.
⬤ 11am–5pm Tue–Sun. 🏷️
This exhibition includes many
Roman archaeological finds
from the Baden-Baden region,
including a selection of
cooking utensils, an
interesting collection of toys,
dolls, medals and spectacles.

🏛 Stadtmuseum
Küferstraße 3. 📞 (07221) 93 22 72.
⬤ 10am–12:30pm & 2–5pm
Tue–Sun. 🏷️
The Stadtmuseum includes
sections on glass, porcelain
and paintings, as well as some
old gambling equipment.

Maulbronn ⓬

SITUATED AT THE HEART OF the Stromberg region, Maulbronn grew up around a Cistercian Kloster (monastery) which was founded in 1147 in the valley of the river Salzach by monks who came here from Alsace. The Klosterkirche, built in 1147–78, is an elongated, triple-nave basilica with a transept and a choir. The Gothic atrium on the western side was added in 1210–15. Outside the enclosure are domestic buildings, an inn and the guest chapel, which date from the 15th–17th centuries. Defence walls with turrets and a gate tower encircle the entire complex, which was designated a UNESCO World Heritage Site in 1993.

★ Chapter House
The monks assembled in this Gothic hall to discuss their private and public affairs. The hall has two naves, supported by three pillars.

★ Brunnenkapelle
Built opposite the entrance to the refectory, the Well Chapel, with its intricate Gothic forms, is where the monks used to wash their hands before meals.

Inner Courtyard
Once a garden, the monastery's inner courtyard is surrounded by cloisters. It is a place that inspires contemplation.

Cloisters

STAR FEATURES

- ★ Brunnenkapelle
- ★ Chapter House
- ★ Mourning
- ★ Stalls

The Porch
The porch, also known as "Paradise", was built onto the church façade in the early 13th century.

Cloisters
In the Middle Ages, monks meditated as they walked around the cloisters, which gave them protection from the vagaries of the weather. Talking was strictly forbidden.

Church Interior
Originally the church had a wooden ceiling. In 1424 it was replaced with a network vault, which stands in stark contrast to the plain walls.

VISITORS' CHECKLIST

Road map C6. 🏠 6,400.
ℹ️ Stadtverwaltung Maulbronn, Klosterhof 31 (07043-10 30).
Ⓦ www.maulbronn.de
Info-Zentrum Klosterhof.
📞 (07043) 92 66 10.
⌚ Mar–Oct: 9am–5:30pm daily; Nov–Feb: 9:30am–5pm Tue–Sun.
🕙 11:15am, 3pm. 📷

★ Mourning
This Gothic relief, made in around 1390 in the Parler family workshop, was part of an altar, which no longer exists. Today, it can be seen on the altar in the monastery's choir.

★ Stalls
Richly decorated with carved ornaments, the late-Gothic stalls date from around 1450.

Heilbronn ⑬

Road map C6. 👥 *119,000.* 🚆
ℹ️ *Kaiserstraße 17 (07131-56 22 70).*
🎭 *Pferdemarkt (Feb), Neckarfest
(Jun), Stadtfest (Jun), Heilbronner
Herbst (Sep).*

HEILBRONN'S EARLIEST records
date from the 8th century,
when the town was known as
"Helibrunna". By the late 19th
century, Heilbronn had
become Wurttemberg's main
industrial centre, with a large
port on the river Neckar.

Having suffered major destruction during World War II,
the town's surviving buildings
include the church of St Kilian,
a Gothic basilica from the
second half of the 13th century, with a triple-nave hall-
choir flanked by two towers.
The western tower was built
in 1508–29. The magnificent
altarpiece is an original late-
Gothic polyptych, the work of
Hans Seyffer (1498).

Near the 15th–16th-century
Rathaus (town hall) is a house
reputed to have been the
home of Käthchen, a char-
acter in Heinrich von Kleist's
play *Das Käthchen von Heilbronn.* Near the rebuilt
church of St Peter and St Paul
(originally the church of the
Teutonic Order) stands the
former Teutonic convent –
the Deutschhof.

**Isaak Habrecht's astronomical
clock on Heilbronn town hall**

**Half-timbered houses on the bank of the river
Kocher, in Schwäbisch Hall**

Schwäbisch Hall ⑭

Road map C6. 👥 *35,000.* 🚆
ℹ️ *Am Markt 9 (0791-75 12 46).*
🎭 *Kuchen-und Brunnenfest der
Haller Salzsieder (Whitsun).*

ARCHAEOLOGICAL exca-
vations in 1939
proved the existence
of a Celtic settlement
on this site as early as
500 BC. The town
features a great
number of historic
buildings from various
periods, including
many half-timbered
15th–16th-century
houses, Baroque town
houses, and a Rococo
town hall and town
palace (Keckenburg).
The most interesting
building is the hall-
church of St Michael,
whose Gothic main
body was built in
1427–56. The Romanesque
tower on the western façade,
however, dates from the 12th
century. The late-Gothic hall-
choir (1495–1527) is famous
for its decorative network
vaults. Original furnishings
include the main altar, the
stalls and the Holy Sepulchre.

Schwäbisch Gmünd ⑮

Road map C6. 👥 *63,400.* 🚆 ℹ️
*Kornhausstraße 14 (07171-60 34
250).* 🎭 *Internationales Schatten-
theater Festival (Jun), European
Church Music (Jul).*

THIS TOWN – the birthplace
of the architect Peter
Parler and painters Hans

**Madonna with Child,
in Marktplatz,
Schwäbisch Gmünd**

Baldung Grien and
Jörg Ratgeb – was
once renowned
throughout Europe
for the magnificent
goods produced by
its goldsmiths. It
has many great
historic buildings,
mainly churches,
such as the late-
Romanesque church
of St John, which
dates from around
1220, but was
subsequently
remodelled. The
church of St Cross is famous
not only for being the first
Gothic hall-church in
southern Germany, but also
the first major work of the
famous family of architects –
the Parlers. This triple-
nave hall with a hall-
choir, featuring an
ambulatory and a ring
of side chapels, was
built in several stages,
between 1320 and
1521. Its western
façade has a high
triangular top with
blind windows.

Inside the church
are many valuable
historic relics, such as
the Holy Sepulchre
(1400), the stalls,
which date from
around 1550, and
the organ gallery
(1688). Other
interesting structures
in the town include
the town fortifications and
several half-timbered houses.

Bad Wimpfen ⑯

Road map C6. 👥 *6,676.* 🚆 ℹ️
Carl-Ulrich-Straße 1 (07063-9 72 00).
🎭 *Talmarkt (Jun/Jul), Zunftmarkt
(Aug), Weihnachtsmarkt (Dec).*

THE TOWN of Bad Wimpfen
was created out of two
settlements, Bad Wimpfen am
Berg and Bad Wimpfen im
Tal, which remain distinct to
this day. The settlement on
top of the hill grew around
the Hohenstauf family palace,
whose chapel and well-
preserved arcade windows,
resting on pairs of decorated
columns, can still be seen.

Built at the order of Frederick I Barbarossa in 1165–75, this was the main and the biggest imperial palace (Kaiserpfalz) of the Holy Roman Empire. One of the surviving towers offers a spectacular view over the Neckar valley.

Set in a picturesque location, Bad Wimpfen features many half-timbered houses dating from the 16th–18th centuries.

Bad Wimpfen im Tal is built around the former collegiate church of St Peter and St Paul. This is a triple-nave basilica with transept, two eastern towers and cloister, dating from the 13th–15th centuries. The south façade of the transept and the portal are richly decorated with carvings, which are probably the work of Erwin von Steinbach, one of the builders of Strasbourg Cathedral. The church interior features many original carved statues and stalls.

Marbach ⓱

Road map C6. 🚶 1,450. 🚉
ℹ️ Marktstraße 23 (07144-10 20).

THIS SMALL TOWN would probably never merit an entry in any guidebook were it not for the fact that the great writer Friedrich Schiller was born here in 1759. The modest, half-timbered house, in which the famous poet spent his childhood, has survived to this day and is now a small museum – the **Schiller-Geburtshaus**. The town also possesses a vast museum of literature (**Schiller-Nationalmuseum**), which is housed in a Neo-Baroque palace. Its collection is not limited to the life and work of Schiller, but also includes many documents relating to German literature.

Other attractions in Marbach include some of the original half-timbered houses and the remains of the town walls and town gates in the old town. The late-Gothic Alexanderkirche is also worth a visit. Built in the second half of the 12th century by Aberlin Jörg, it features interesting network vaulting covered with ornamental paintings.

Friedrich Schiller statue in Marbach

🏚️ **Schiller-Geburtshaus**
Nicklastorstraße 31. 📞 (07144) 175 67. 🕐 9am–5pm daily. ⬤ 24–31 Dec. 📷

🏛️ **Schiller-Nationalmuseum**
Schillerhöhe 8–10. 📞 (07144) 84 86 10. 🕐 10am–5pm Thu–Tue, 10am–8pm Wed. ⬤ 24–31 Dec. 📷

Esslingen ⓲

Road map C6. 🚶 92,000.
ℹ️ Marktplatz 2 (0711-39 69 39 69).

SET AMONG vineyards on the banks of the river Neckar, the beautiful town of Esslingen is famous for its sparkling wines. The town's historic buildings were fortunate in surviving intact the ravages of World War II. A walk through the winding streets and narrow alleys of the old centre will yield many interesting sights, while a climb to the top of the hill affords a splendid view of the town and the Neckar valley, as well as the amazing **Innere Brücke**, a 14th-century bridge. From there visitors can descend towards the market square, stopping on the way to visit Frauenkirche, a Gothic hall-church dating from the 14th century. Its front tower, the work of Ulrich and Matthäus von Ensingen, was added later. In the market square is the Stadtkirche St Dionysius, the oldest church in town, built in the 13th century on the site of an earlier, 8th-century building. Inside are magnificent early-Gothic stained-glass windows and late-15th-century Gothic furnishings, including the choir partition, the sacrarium and the font. The nearby church of St Paul, built in the mid-13th century for the Dominicans, is the oldest surviving Dominican church in Germany. In neighbouring Rathausplatz stands the half-timbered old town hall, Altes Rathaus, with its beautiful Renaissance façade, and the Baroque new town hall. Designed as a palace for Gottlieb von Palm by Gottlieb David Kandlers, the Neues Rathaus was built between 1748 and 1751.

The picturesque houses and chapel of Esslingen's 14th-century Innere Brücke

Ludwigsburg ⑲

Palace crest

SITUATED NEAR Stuttgart and known as the "Versailles of Swabia", Ludwigsburg was founded in 1704 on the initiative of Eberhard Ludwig, Duke of Wurttemberg. At the heart of the town is the vast palace complex, which the Duke ordered to be built for his mistress, Countess Wilhelmina von Graevenitz. The construction of the palace, which was carried out between 1704 and 1733, involved many outstanding architects and interior decorators, including Philipp Jenisch, Johann Nette, Donato Frisoni and Diego Carlone.

Northern Garden
This magnificent Baroque park is the venue for a flower show ("Blooming Baroque") that is held here during the summer.

★ Western Gallery
The gallery features opulent stucco ornaments by Ricardo Retti and Diego Carlone (1712–15).

★ Marble Hall
This vast hall in the new wing of the palace was remodelled in 1816, but still retains some of its Baroque interior decor.

★ Queen's Library
The library is housed in the east wing of the palace, in the apartments arranged for Queen Charlotte Mathilde.

The new wing of the palace houses a museum devoted to court art of the Neo-Classical period.

VISITORS' CHECKLIST

Road map C6. 🏠 80,000. 🚆 🛈
Wilhelmstr. 10 (07141-910 22 52).
Residenzschloss Schlossstraße 30.
📞 (07141) 18 64 40. ⬜ 21
Mar–Oct: 10am–noon, 1–5pm
daily (tours every 20 mins); Nov–
20 Mar: 5 tours daily, 1st at
10:30am. 🎫 obligatory. **Theater-
museum** ⬜ 9am–5pm daily. 🌐

★ Schloss Favorite
The "Favorite" hunting lodge was
built between 1716 and 1723, but its
interior has been remodelled in
Neo-Classical style.

The old wing
contains the palace's
oldest apartments.

Märchengarten
The landscaped section
of the park includes the
"Fairy-tale Garden",
which contains figures
and models from
German fairy-tales.

**The upper fruit
garden** attracts
visitors with
its picturesque
paths, which are
lined with apple
trees and grapevines.

**Restaurant
and café**

Emichsburg
This romantic castle, built
in 1798–1802, was named
after the founder of the
Wurttemberg dynasty.

STAR SIGHTS

★ Marble Hall

★ Queen's Library

★ Schloss Favorite

★ Western Gallery

Stuttgart ⑳

THE CAPITAL of Baden-Wurttemberg, Stuttgart is one of the largest and most important towns of the Federal Republic. It grew from a 10th-century stud farm, known as Stutengarten, to become the ducal (1321) and later the royal (1806) capital of Wurttemberg. Beautifully situated among picturesque hills, the town is a major industrial centre with many important manufacturing plants. It is also a well-known publishing and cultural centre, with a world-famous ballet company, chamber orchestra and splendid art collections.

Exploring Stuttgart

Start your tour of Stuttgart at Schlossplatz, continuing along Königstrasse towards the Palace Gardens, with their many interesting buildings, and stopping to pay a visit to the Staatsgalerie, whose extension was designed by the British architect James Stirling. From there you can return via Konrad-Adenauer-Strasse, heading towards Karlsplatz, then to Schillerplatz and Marktplatz with its magnificent town hall, finally ending the walk at Hegelhaus museum.

⊞ Schlossplatz

At the centre of the square stands the **Jubiläumssäule** – a column erected in 1842–46 to celebrate the 25-year reign of Wilhelm I. The square also features sculptures by many famous artists, including Alexander Calder and Alfred Hrdlicka. The east side of the square features a huge palace complex, **Neues Schloss**, built in 1746–1807, while on the opposite side stands **Königs-bau**, a Neo-Classical structure erected in 1856–60.

Neo-classical façade of Stuttgart's Staatstheater

🏛 Kunstgebäude

Schlossplatz 2. **Galerie der Stadt Stuttgart** 🕿 (0711) 216 21 88. **Württembergischer Kunstverein** 🕿 (0711) 22 33 70. ◯ 11am–6pm Tue, Thu, Sun, 11am–8pm Wed. ⬚
Erected between 1912 and 1913, this building houses the regional association of the arts. The municipal art gallery, which has recently moved to Kliener Schlossplatz, features 19th- and 20th-century art, with an emphasis on artists from southern Germany, including Joseph Kosuth and Otto Dix.

❧ Schlossgarten

The magnificent gardens stretching north of the Neues Schloss were established in the early 19th century. They have maintained, to this day, much of their original charm, with neat avenues and interesting sculptures. The attractions include the **Carl-Zeiss-Planetarium**, which runs an excellent science programme, using equipment made by the famous optics company.

On the edge of the park stands a vast Neo-Classical theatre building, the **Württembergisches Staatstheater**, built in 1909–12 by Max Littmann. In 1982–3 it was given a new, dome-covered wing, the Theaterpavilion, designed by Gottfried Böhm.

🏛 Staatsgalerie

See pp298–9.

♣ Altes Schloss

Württembergisches Landes-museum Schillerplatz 6. 🕿 (0711) 27 90. ◯ 10am–1pm Tue, 10am–5pm Wed–Sun. ⬚
When Wurttemberg castle burned down in 1311, it was decided to move the family seat to Stuttgart. In 1325, the existing small castle was extended, creating Dütnitzbau. This wing has survived and can be seen from Karlsplatz. A large-scale Renaissance remodelling project, designed by Aberlin Tresch and carried out in 1553–78, gave the castle its square layout, with three-storey arcaded cloisters encircling the inner courtyard. The southwestern wing contains the Schlosskapelle (chapel), the first sacral building in Stuttgart built especially for the Protestants. The castle now houses the **Württem-bergisches Landesmuseum**,

The façade of Stuttgart's Neues Schloss, combining Baroque and Neo-Classical elements

Cloistered courtyard of the Renaissance Altes Schloss

which includes vast collections of decorative art, including those displaying the ducal and royal insignia of Wurttemberg. The prehistory section includes jewellery from the Frankish period and the preserved tomb of a Celtic nobleman from Hochdorf.

Schillerplatz

This is undoubtedly one of Stuttgart's most beautiful areas. It is here that the stud farm that gave Stuttgart its name is said to have stood. Today, a pensive statue of Friedrich Schiller, the work of the Danish sculptor Bertel Thorwaldsen (1839), occupies the centre of the square.

Schillerplatz is surrounded by historic buildings: the **Old Chancellery**, built in 1542–44 and extended upwards in 1566,

now houses a restaurant, the Prinzenbau (1605–78), and the Stiftsfruchtkasten, an attractive gabled granary (1578), now home to a museum of musical instruments.

Stiftskirche (Hl. Kreuz)
Stiftstraße 12.
From the south side of Schillerplatz there is a view of the presbytery of the collegiate church of the Holy Cross. This Gothic church, the work of Hänslin and Aberlin Jörg, was built in the 15th century and incorporated the walls of the previous, early-Gothic church. Despite World War II damage, this newly renovated church still has the original stone gallery of the dukes of Wurttemberg, built in 1576–84 by Simon Schlör to a design by Johann Steiner, as well as Gothic furnishings.

VISITORS' CHECKLIST

Road map C6. 586,000. south of town. Königstraße 1A (0711-22 28 20). Frühlingsfest (Apr/May), Stuttgarter Weindorf (Aug/Sep, Oct/Nov), Fellbacher Herbst (Oct), Weihnachtsmarkt (Dec). W www.stuttgart-tourist.de

Hegelhaus
Eberhardstraße 53. (0711) 216 67 33. 10am–5:30pm Mon–Fri, 10am–6:30pm Thu, 10am–4pm Sat.
Georg Wilhelm Friedrich Hegel – the creator of one of the most important modern philosophical systems – was born in this house on 27 August 1770. The house is now a museum, which houses an exhibition devoted to the life and work of the famous philosopher.

Figures of saints adorning the façade of the Stiftskirche

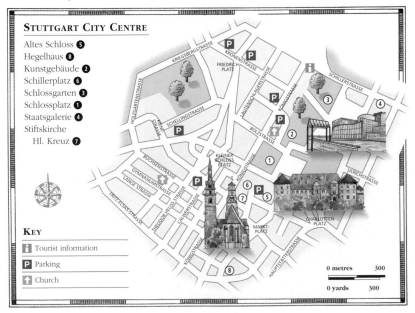

STUTTGART CITY CENTRE

Altes Schloss ❺
Hegelhaus ❽
Kunstgebäude ❷
Schillerplatz ❻
Schlossgarten ❸
Schlossplatz ❶
Staatsgalerie ❹
Stiftskirche
   Hl. Kreuz ❼

KEY

🛈 Tourist information

P Parking

🕇 Church

0 metres 300
0 yards 300

⛫ Linden-Museum/ Staatl. Museum für Völkerkunde

Hegelplatz 1. **⟦** *(0711) 2 02 24 56.* **◯** *10am–5pm Tue, Thu–Sun, 10am–8pm Wed.*

The Linden Museum is one of Germany's finest ethnology museums. It was founded by Count Karl von Linden, who was also its director from 1889 until 1910. The museum contains many fascinating exhibits from all over the world, including figures from the Indonesian theatre of shadows, a Tibetan sand mandala, a 6th–8th-century mask from Peru in South America and a full-size reproduction of an Islamic bazaar.

Peruvian mask in the Linden-Museum

🏛 Weißenhofsiedlung

Weißenhof 10. **Exhibition rooms** **⟦** *(0711) 2 57 91 87.* **◯** *10am–2pm Tue–Sat, 10–3pm Sun.* **◪** *from Am Weißenhof 15, 11am Sat.* **Architektur-Galerie ⟦** *(0711) 257 14 34.* **◯** *2–6pm Tue–Sat, 11am–4pm Sun.*

A building exhibition held in 1927 in Stuttgart had housing as its main theme. It left behind a complete housing estate that still exists today, although it was badly bombed during World War II. Most of the houses represent functionalism, which was being promoted at the time by the Bauhaus. The estate, which was to serve as an example to other towns and estates, has some interesting houses,

including works by Mies van der Rohe (Am Weißenhof 14–29), Le Corbusier (Rathenaustraße 1–3), Peter Behrens (Hölzelweg 3–5) and Hans Scharoun (Hölzelweg 1).

🏛 Liederhalle

Berliner Platz 1.

A must for all lovers of modern architecture, Liederhalle, in the centre of Stuttgart, is a successful synthesis of tradition and modernism. Built in 1955–56 by Adolf Abel and Rolf Gutbrod, this fine cultural and congress centre, with three concert halls clustered around an irregular hall, is still impressive today.

⛫ Mercedes-Benz-Museum

Mercedesstraße 137. **⟦** *(0711) 172 25 78.* **◯** *9am–5pm Tue–Sun.* **●** *public holidays.*

To the east of the town centre, in the Obertürkheim district, is the famous Mercedes-Benz-Museum. Its splendid collection illustrates the development of motorcar production, from the earliest models to today's state-of-the-art, computerized products. Set up to celebrate the centenary of their inventions, the museum features over 70 historic vehicles, all in immaculate condition. The collection includes the world's two oldest automobiles, Gottlieb Daimler's horseless carriage and Carl Benz's three-

Some of the models on display in the Mercedes-Benz-Museum

wheeled automobile from 1886. Also on display is a hand-made limousine that was built in the 1930s for the Emperor of Japan and the first "Popemobile", which was built for Pope Paul VI.

Another interesting exhibit is the famous 1950s racing car, *Silberpfeil* (Silver Arrow), as well as models that were built for attempts on world speed records. Also on display are scores of the latest models that have been produced by the company.

The visitor can also learn the history of Daimler-Benz AG, which was created by the merger in 1926 of Daimler-Motoren-Gesellschaft and Benz & Cie., Rhein. The company's subsequent 1999 merger with Chrysler created one of the world's largest car manufacturing concerns, DaimlerChrysler.

🏛 Fernsehturm

◯ *9am–10:30pm daily.*

Built between 1954 and 1956 this television tower was the world's first to be built entirely from ferro-concrete. It is 217 m (712 ft) high and stands on top of a wooded hill, Hoher Bopser. Its observation platform provides splendid views over Schwäbische Alb, Schwarzwald and, on a clear day, even the Alps.

⛫ Porsche-Museum

Porschestraße 42. **⟦** *(0711) 9 11 56 85.* **◯** *9am–4pm Mon–Fri, 9am–5pm Sat, Sun, public holidays.*

Stuttgart's other famous car manufacturer also has its own museum, which includes

House designed by Le Corbusier in Weißenhofsiedlung

around 50 examples of these fast and expensive vehicles, some of which are built to order. The history of the company is documented in a film shown in the museum's cinema. Free guided tours of the factory production lines are available. These are very popular and it is advisable to book well in advance.

♛ Markthalle

Dorotheenstraße 4. ◯ *7am–6pm Mon–Fri, 7am–4pm Sat.*

Stuttgart's market hall, built in 1912–14 in Art Nouveau style on the site of an earlier vegetable market, is one of the finest in Europe. Built as a food exchange, it has magnificent frescos. Today it still sells fresh fruit and vegetables to the general public, and it now also houses a small restaurant and café.

♦ Schloss Solitude

Solitudestraße. █ *(0711) 69 66 99.* ◯ *Apr–Oct: 9am–noon, 1:30–5pm Tue–Sun; Nov–Mar: 10am–noon, 1:30–4pm Tue–Sun.*

This exquisite small palace, standing on the slopes of a hill, was built for Prince Karl Eugene between 1763 and 1767. The Prince not only commissioned the project, but also took an active part in the design of the residence, which is the work of Pierre Louis Philippe de la Guêpière, who was responsible for introducing the Louis XVI-style to Germany. Many consider this palace to be his masterpiece.

Following its full restoration in 1990, and the provision of 45 residential studio apartments, the palace now serves art students on scholarships from all over the world. A 15-km (9-mile) long, straight road connects Schloss Solitude with Ludwigsburg.

JOHANNES KEPLER (1571–1630)

This outstanding astronomer and mathematician was born in Weil der Stadt. He studied theology in Tübingen, where he encountered the work of Nicolaus Copernicus, becoming a fervent advocate of his theory. Forced to flee in 1600, Kepler went to Prague where he worked with Tycho Brahe. Many years of research led him to formulate three laws of planetary motion. Kepler is also the inventor of the twin-lens telescope.

♛ Bad Cannstatt

Once an independent health resort, Bad Cannstatt is now a district of Stuttgart. Set in a beautiful park, it has a late-Gothic parish hall-church, a Neo-Classical town hall and a Kursaal (spa-house), built in 1825–42. One of its attractions is the Neo-Classical Schloss Rosenstein, built in 1824–29 at the request of King Wilhelm I, based on amended designs by John Papworth. The King was also the initiator of the beautiful "Wilhelm's complex". This includes a Moorish-style villa located in a symmetrically laid-out park, with many Oriental-style pavilions and other decorative elements. Completed in the 1840s, its main designer was Karl Ludwig Wilhelm von Zanth. The park has now been transformed into a botanical-zoological garden.

ENVIRONS: Stuttgart provides a convenient base for exploring the surroundings. In **Sindelfingen**, 15 km (9 miles) southwest, it is worth visiting the Romanesque Church of St Martin Canons, which was founded in 1083. While you are there, take a stroll along Lange Straße to the old town hall, which dates from 1478 and is joined with the Salt House (1592). The two buildings, both half-timbered in their upper sections, now house the town museum.

A little further to the west, **Weil der Stadt** is the birthplace of the astronomer Johannes Kepler and the reformer Johannes Brenz. The town's late-Gothic church of St Peter and St Paul was completed in 1492 by Aberlin Jörg. Inside is a beautiful Renaissance sacrarium, dating from 1611. The Marktplatz, with a statue of Kepler at its centre, has a Renaissance town hall (1582). Nearby, at Keplergasse 2, stands the house in which the famous astronomer was born and which now houses a small museum, the Kepler-Museum.

Another place worthy of a visit is **Waiblingen**, 10 km (6 miles) to the northeast of Stuttgart. It features a Romanesque church, the vaults of which are decorated with some splendid wall paintings dating from 1515.

The façade of the Schloss Solitude, in the hills to the west of Stuttgart's centre

Staatsgalerie

THE STAATSGALERIE grew from the museum of fine arts founded in 1843 by King Wilhelm I and containing the king's private collection. Now it ranks among the finest of German galleries. As well as its own magnificent collection of old masters and modern artists, the gallery has an extensive collection of graphics. In 1984 the art gallery acquired an extension designed by James Stirling.

★ The Mourning of Christ
This subtle depiction of Christ is the work of the Venetian artist Giovanni Bellini.

Bathsheba at her Toilet (c.1485)
In this painting, which is a fragment of a lost triptych illustrating Justice, Hans Memling uses the Old Testament story of Bathsheba to exemplify the abuse of power, intervention by God and the reformation of a sinner.

★ St Paul in Prison (1627)
In this, one of his earliest works, Rembrandt depicted the Apostle Paul awaiting death in a humble cell.

Entrance to Alte Staatsgalerie

Entrance to Neue Staatsgalerie

Crossing of the Rhine near Rhenen (1642)
The Dutch painter Jan von Goyen became famous for his evocative landscapes, which were often executed in uniform tones of lead-grey or brown-green.

STAR EXHIBITS

★ **Iphigenie**

★ **St Paul in Prison**

★ **The Mourning of Christ**

KEY

- Italian painting
- German painting
- Dutch painting
- 19th-century painting
- 20th-century painting
- Sculpture Garden
- Graphic arts
- Non-exhibition rooms

★ **Iphigenie** (1871)
Anselm Feuerbach's painting was inspired by a play by Goethe, Iphigenie on Tauris.

GALLERY GUIDE
Permanent exhibitions are located over the first floor of the two buildings. In the Alte Staatsgalerie are works by the old masters and from the 19th-century. The Neue Staatsgalerie holds 20th-century art. The extensive collection of graphic art is displayed in temporary exhibitions on both ground floors.

Spring Fields (1887)
One of the leading members of the French Impressionist movement, Claude Monet was unsurpassed in his rendition of iridescent light.

Mother and Child (1905)
This painting by Pablo Picasso represents his "pink period", which preceded the famous Cubist experiments of this great Spanish artist.

First floor

Female Nude Reclining on a White Pillow (1917)
Amedeo Modigliani became famous for his idiosyncratic portraits and female nudes.

Ground floor

Schwäbische Alb ㉑

THE MOUNTAIN RANGE of Schwäbische Alb (the Swabian Jura) extends like an arc, 220 km (137 miles) long and 40 km (25 miles) wide, from the Upper Rhine around Schaffhausen, in Switzerland, to Ries, at the border between the federal counties of Baden-Wurttemberg and Bavaria. The highest peak in the range is Lemberg (1,015 m/3,330 ft). Beech woods and scented juniper shrubs dominate the mellow landscape, whose whole system of inter-connected stalagmitic caves was carved from the underlying sedimentary limestone rocks.

Hechingen
On the outskirts of Hechingen, the remains of a 1st–3rd-century AD Roman villa are open to the public.

Haigerloch
In the vaults of this castle is a vast bunker that was used as an atomic research laboratory towards the end of World War II.

★ **Burg Hohenzollern**
The ancestral seat of the Hohenzollern family was remodelled in 1850-67. Only the 15th-century St Michaelkapelle survives from the original fortress.

★ **Beuron**
Beuron's magnificent Benedictine Abbey was founded in the 11th century. Its subsequent remodelling resulted in a Baroque structure, which survives to this day.

Böblinge

Herrenberg

Tübingen

Neckar

Rottenburg

Mössingen

Haigerloch

Hechingen

Burg Hohenzollern

Burladingen

Balingen

Albstadt

Dona

Messkirc

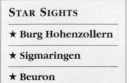

STAR SIGHTS

★ **Burg Hohenzollern**

★ **Sigmaringen**

★ **Beuron**

Swabian Jura Landscape
The gentle hills and enchanting villages attract hikers and tourists from all over the world.

VISITORS' CHECKLIST

ℹ️ *Schwäbische Alb Tourismusverband, Marktplatz 1, Bad Urach (07125-94 81 06).*
Ⓦ www.schwaebischealb.de

Hohenneuffen
A massive castle dominates the tiny town of Neuffen. It is the most impressive ruin in the Swabian Jura.

KEY

▭▭	Motorway
▬▬	Main road
▭▭	Secondary road
⋯⋯	River
☀	Viewpoint

Wendlingen•

Kirchheim•

•Nürtingen

Beuren

Hohenneuffen•

•Reutlingen ☀

Bad Urach

Lichtenstein

Burg Lichtenstein ☀

•Münsingen

S C H W Ä B I S C H E   A L B

Riedlingen•

Sigmaringen•

Lichtenstein
This romantic castle was immortalized in a novel by Wilhelm Hauff.

★ Sigmaringen
The town's skyline is dominated by the castle, which was reconstructed following a fire in 1893. Only the towers of the medieval fortress remain.

0 km   5

0 miles   5

Tübingen ②

Road map C6. 🦌 *85,000.* 🚃 ℹ️
*An der Neckarbrücke 1 (07071-913
60).* 🅰️ *Mon, Wed, Fri.*

Along with Heidelberg and Freiburg im Breisgau, Tübingen is the home of one of southern Germany's three most famous universities. It was founded in 1477 by Count Eberhard the Bearded.

The first records of the fortress that later gave rise to a settlement on this site date from 1078. By around 1231, the settlement had become a town. In 1342, Tübingen passed into the hands of the counts of Wurttemberg, having previously belonged to the counts Palatinate.

Schloss Hohentübingen, which towers over the town, has a magnificent gateway (Unteres Tor). Built in 1606, it is richly adorned with the coat of arms of the House of Wurttemberg. The walled castle complex, with its central courtyard and long approach, was built in stages during 1507–15, 1534–42 and 1606.

A walk along the Burgsteige will bring you to the picturesque old town. Here, at the centre of Marktplatz, is the Neptune Fountain, the work of Heinrich Schickhard, dating from 1617. In the western corner of the square is a lovely Renaissance town hall, built in 1435 and extended in the

Tübingen's Gothic-Renaissance town hall

16th century. It features an astronomical clock, which dates from 1511. *Sgraffiti* on the western façade dates from 1876; those on the elevations facing Haaggasse date from the 16th century.

The collegiate church of St George (**Stiftskirche St Georg**), built in 1440–1529, is a triple-nave hall with rows of side chapels, galleries and a single tower. Of particular note are the ducal tombs, the late-Gothic reading-room and the stained-glass windows of the choir, dating from 1475. Magnificent stalls, adorned with carved figures of the Prophets, date from the late 15th century.

The bookstore in Holzmarkt (*Buchhandlung Heckenhauer*) is where Hermann Hesse

once served as an apprentice bookseller. On the banks of the Neckar stands the **Hölderlinturm**, in which the German poet Hölderlin lived from 1807 until his death. Not far from here stands the large building of the Alte Burse, which was built in 1478–80 and later remodelled in 1803-1805. The building was once used to accommodate students and as a lecture hall. Martin Luther's close associate, Philipp Melanchthon, lectured here between 1514 and 1518.

The Protestant seminary in Neckarhalde was founded by Prince Ulrich in 1536. Its graduates include the poets Hölderlin, Mörike and Schiller and the philosophers Hegel and Schelling.

The **Kunsthalle** is famous throughout Germany not only for its temporary exhibitions, but also for its fine collection of modern art. Other popular attractions in Tübingen include the **Stadtmuseum**, which is devoted to the town's history, and the **Auto-und Spielzeugmuseum**.

🏛 **Museum Schloss Hohentübingen**
Burgsteige 11. 📞 *(07071) 297 73 84.*
⭕ *May–Sep: 10am–6pm Wed–Sun, Oct–Apr: 10am–5pm Wed–Sun.* 🖼

🛐 **Stiftskirche St Georg**
📞 *(07071) 275 50.* ⭕ *Apr–Sep: 9am–5pm daily, Oct–Mar: 9am–4pm daily.* 🖼

🎠 **Hölderlinturm**
Bursagasse 6. 📞 *(07071) 220 40.*
⭕ *10am–noon, 3–5pm Tue–Fri, 2–5pm Sat, Sun, public holidays.* 🖼

🏛 **Kunsthalle**
Philosophenweg 76. 📞 *(07071) 969 10.* ⭕ *10am–6pm Tue–Sun (during exhibitions).*

🏛 **Stadtmuseum**
Kornhausstraße 10. 📞 *(07071) 204 17 11 or 94 54 60.* ⭕ *3–6pm Tue–Fri, 11am–6pm Sat–Sun.* 🖼

🏛 **Auto- und Spielzeugmuseum**
Brunnenstraße 18. 📞 *(07071) 55 11 22.* ⭕ *Apr–Oct: 10am–noon, 2–5pm Wed–Sun; Nov–Mar: 10am–noon, 2–5pm Sun and public holidays only.* 🖼

Unteres Tor leading to Schloss Hohentübingen

Rottweil  ㉓

Road map C7. 🏘 *24,000.* 🚊 ℹ️
Hauptstraße 21–23 (0741-49 42 80).
🎭 *Fasnet (last Mon of Carnival),*
Jazzfest (May), Klassikfestival (Jun),
Ferienzauber (Aug).

Situated on the banks of the river Neckar, Rottweil is one of the oldest towns in Baden-Wurttemberg. It grew from a Roman settlement that was established on a hilltop here in AD 73. In 1234 Rottweil was granted town status and, by 1401, it had become a free town of the Holy Roman Empire. Between 1463 and 1802 it belonged to the Swiss Confederation, which was founded in 1291 by the cantons of Uri, Schwyz and Unterwalden. In 1802, the town passed into the rule of the dukes of Wurttemberg.

Rottweil has many historic remains, including sections of the fortified city walls, with several well-preserved turrets.

The parish church of St Cross (Heilig-Kreuz-Münster), built in 1230–1534, has a triple-nave basilica with stellar and network vaults. Late-Gothic altars, including St Bartholomew's, by Michael Wolgemut and a crucifix attributed to Veit Stoss, are among its features.

To the south of the church stands the late-Gothic town hall (1521). On the opposite side of the street, at Hauptstraße 20, the **Stadtmuseum** has an outstanding collection

Crucifixion **attributed to Veit Stoss in Heilig-Kreuz-Münster, Rottweil**

Fountain and "Black Gate" in Rottweil's main street, Hauptstraße

of prehistoric remains. The **Dominikanermuseum** has an interesting exhibition of Roman relics. These include the famous Orpheus mosaic, dating from the 2nd century AD, and an outstanding collection of late-Gothic sculpture, including the statue of St Barbara by Multscher (c.1450).

The Hauptstraße is lined with burghers' houses, displaying characteristic oriel windows. One of the most beautiful historic buildings in Rottweil is the Kapellenkirche, built in 1330–1478. Its 70-metre (230-ft) tower and three portals are adorned with carved ornaments reminiscent of the French Gothic style. The Baroque interior features frescos by Josef Fiertmayer, who was a pupil of renowned painter and architect Cosmas Damian Asam. The Gothic Dominican church, built in 1266–82 and remodelled in the 18th

Kapellenturm, Rottweil

century, has some frescos by Joseph Wannenmacher (1755). Roman baths dating from the 2nd century AD have been excavated at the corner of what is now the cemetery.

Rottweil is famous for its carnival processions *(Fasnet)*, a tradition that goes back to the Middle Ages. A collection of carnival costumes can be seen in the Stadtmuseum.

The **Puppen- und Spielzeugmuseum** has a fine collection of historic dolls and toys.

🏛 **Stadtmuseum**
Hauptstraße 20. ((0741)
942 96 34. ☐ 10am–noon,
2–5pm Tue–Sat, 10am–noon
Sun. ● Mon & Sun
afternoons. 🎫

🏛 **Dominikaner-museum**
Am Kriegsdamm. (
(0741) 78 62. ☐ 10am–1pm, 2–5pm
Tue–Sun. ● public holidays. 🎫

🏛 **Puppen- und Spielzeugmuseum**
Hochbrücktorstraße 9.
((0741) 942 21 77. ☐ 2–5pm
Mon–Sat, 11am–5pm Sun. 🎫

Ulm ㉔

Road map B6. 🎯 115,000. 🚉
ℹ️ *Münsterplatz 50 (0731-161 28 30.*
📷 *Fischerstechen (every fourth year in Jul: 2005, 2009 etc.), Schwörmontag (3rd Mon in Jul), Stadtfest (Jun).*

LYING ON the river Danube, Ulm dates back to 854. It became a town in 1165 then, in 1274, a free town of the Holy Roman Empire. During the 15th century Ulm was one of the richest towns in Europe but the Thirty Years' War put an end to its rapid development. In 1810 Ulm came under the rule of the Wurttemberg kings. The town is renowned as the birthplace of Albert Einstein. During World War II, most of the old town was destroyed during bombing raids.

The Münster is a true masterpiece of European Gothic architecture. A vast, five-nave basilica, its 161-m (530-ft) high west tower is the highest church tower in the world. The cathedral's construction, from 1377 until 1545, was overseen by the greatest builders of the German Gothic – Heinrich and Michael Parler, Urlich von Ensingen, Hans Kun and Matthäus Böblinger. The unfinished cathedral was extended in 1844–90, based on the original medieval design. The interior contains many outstanding features,

Gothic font in Ulm Cathedral

including the altar by Hans Multscher (1443), the famous stalls with figures of philosophers, poets, prophets and apostles carved by Jörg Syrlin the Elder, 15th-century stained-glass windows, and the font, by Jörg Syrlin the Younger.

The town has many fine historic buildings, including the Gothic-Renaissance town hall, which is decorated with brightly coloured frescos and features an astronomical clock. Other features of Marktplatz include the Gothic fountain *Fischkasten* (Fish Crate), dating from 1482, and the Reichenauer Hof, which dates from 1370–1535.

The **Ulmer Museum**, which is housed in a number of historic 16th- and 17th-century buildings, has a collection of art spanning a period from the Middle Ages to the present day. The collection includes the work of local artists, such as Hans Multscher.

The **Deutsches Brotmuseum** specializes in artifacts related to bread and bread-making, including items depicting bread in art and graphic designs.

🏛 **Ulmer Museum**
Marktplatz 9. 📞 *(0731) 161 43 30.*
🕐 *11am–5pm Tue–Sun, 11am–8pm Thu (during exhibitions).* 📷
🏛 **Deutsches Brotmuseum**
Salzstadelgasse 10. 📞 *(0731) 699 55.* 🕐 *10am–5pm Tue, Thu–Mon, 10am–8:30pm Wed.* 📷

Ravensburg ㉕

Road map C7. 🎯 45,000. 🚉
ℹ️ *Kirchstraße 16 (0751-823 24).*
📷 *Fasnet (Feb), Rutenfest (Jul).*

THE FIRST HISTORIC records of the "Ravespurc" fortress date from 1088, when it was one of the seats of the Welf family. It is believed to be the

Main altar by Hans Multscher in Ravensburg's Liebfrauenkirche

birthplace of Henry the Lion, the powerful Duke of Saxony and Bavaria, born in 1129. The settlement that sprang up at the foot of the castle was granted town status in 1251. From 1395, paper was produced here and, during the 15th century, the town became one of the richest in Germany from its involvement in the linen trade.

Standing in Kirchstraße is the 14th-century parish church of Liebfrauenkirche, which retains original 15th-century features, including the main altar and some fine stained-glass windows.

In Marienplatz stands the late-Gothic town hall (14th–15th century), with its lovely Renaissance bay window. Also in Marienplatz is the Waaghaus (1498), which housed the weigh-house and mint on the ground floor, with a trading hall upstairs, when Ravensburg was engaged in coin production. The watchtower *(Blaserturm)* is crowned by a Renaissance octagon that has become the symbol of the town. Another attractive building here is the Lederhaus, which dates from 1513–14. Near the town hall is the old 14th–15th century granary *(Kornhaus)*.

Marktstraße features many old burgher houses. No. 59, the oldest house in town, dates from 1179. The neighbouring house was built in 1446. The tall white cylindrical tower that can be seen from here is known as the "sack of flour" *(Mehlsack)*. It was erected in the 16th century. A magnificent view of the town can be obtained from Veitsburg, which occupies the site of the original Welf castle.

Astronomical clock on Ulm's Gothic-Renaissance town hall

Former Cistercian abbey complex in Salem, now a secular building

Weingarten ㉖

Road map C7. 🏃 22,500. 🚉
ℹ️ Münsterplatz 1 (0751-40 51 25).
🎠 Blutritt (day after Ascension).

COUNT HENRY OF THE House of Welf founded a Benedictine abbey in Weingarten in 1056. During the Romanesque period, around 1190, the monks of the abbey produced a chronicle of the House of Welfs, known as the *Welfenchronik*.

Ambitious plans, drawn up in the 18th century at the initiative of Abbot Sebastian Hyller, provided for an extension of the abbey and the construction of another vast complex of buildings. Two side courtyards and four external courtyards, encircled with curved galleries with smaller pavilions, were planned to be grouped around the church. These were designed by Casper Moosbrugger, Franz Beer, Enrico Zucalli and others, and built in 1715–24.

The church is reminiscent of the Basilica of St Peter's in Rome. Although it is half the size of the latter, it is nevertheless an immense structure. Inside are some magnificent ceiling frescos by Cosmas Damian Asam, while the carved and inlaid choir stalls are the work of Joseph Anton Feuchtmayer. Also of note is the organ by Josef Gabler. In an ingenious design, the organ pipes are concealed within a series of towers to avoid obscuring the windows of the façade.

The **Alamannenmuseum** has a fascinating exhibition of relicts that have been found in graves dating from the Merovingian period.

🏛 **Alamannenmuseum**
Karlstr. 28. 📞 (0751) 405 125. 🕐
3–5pm Tue–Sun, 3–6pm Thu. 🤚

Salem ㉗

Road map C7. 🏃 8,500.

THE FIRST CISTERCIAN monks arrived in Salmansweiler (now known as Salem) in 1134. Between 1299 and 1414 they built a church according to the rules of their order, which espoused poverty and banned any decoration of the monastic buildings.

The abbey is a triple-nave basilica with transept and straight-end choir. Its austere façade is relieved by blind windows, some of which have attractive traceries. In later years the restraints of poverty were relaxed to the extent that the abbey now has an interesting tabernacle (1500), stalls (1594) and early-Renaissance altars (dating from the 18th century).

The new abbey buildings were built between 1700 and 1710 and constitute **Schloss Salem**. The buildings include some richly decorated abbot's apartments and the extremely impressive Emperor's room *(Kaisersaal)*, which was built between 1708 and 1710.

Since its secularization in 1802, the abbey has been the private property of the Baden margraves who keep some of their art collection here. The west wing houses a private boarding school founded by Kurt Hahn, who also founded Gordonstoun in Scotland.

⚓ **Schloss Salem**
📞 (07553) 814 37. 🕐 Apr–Oct:
9:30am–6pm Mon–Sat, 10:30am–
6pm Sun. 🤚

Ceiling fresco in Weingarten's abbey

The Bodensee ㉘

SOMETIMES KNOWN as Lake Constance, the Bodensee lies on the border of Germany, Switzerland and Austria. The area surrounding the lake is one of the most attractive in Germany, in terms of both natural beauty and cultural heritage. Towns and villages around the shores feature countless reminders of past times and cultures. The best time for a visit is summer, when local fishermen stage colourful fairs and water sports are possible.

The Bodensee
The lake is 15 km (9 miles) across at its widest point and 74 km (46 miles) long. It lies at an altitude of 395 m (1,295 ft) and reaches 252 m (826 ft) in depth.

Reichenau
The greatest attraction of this island is the Bene-dictine abbey, which was famed during the era of Otto the Great (10th century) for its illumi-nated manuscripts. It has a beautiful Romanesque-Gothic church and an intoxicating herb garden.

Stockach

Ludwigshafen

ÜBERLINGER SEE

Überlin

Singen

Radolfzell

Gottmadingen

ZELLERSEE

Mair

Reichenau

Konstanz

UNTERSEE

Kreuzlingen

★ **Mainau**
Mainau is known as the "Island of Flowers". The most beautiful displays are in the park surrounding the Baroque palace, which was built in 1739–46. It is currently owned by the Lennart Bernadotte family.

STAR SIGHTS
★ **Konstanz**
★ **Mainau**
★ **Wasserburg**

★ **Konstanz (Constance)**
The largest town in the region, its main attraction is the magnificent 11th-century Romanesque cathedral. The vaults over the central aisle were built between 1679 and 1683.

Meersburg
The exquisite Baroque town of Meersburg has two residences – the Baroque Neues Schloss and the Altes Schloss. The latter is a 16th-century structure built on top of a hill. It contains within its walls an old Carolingian palace.

VISITORS' CHECKLIST

Map 7 C. ⓘ *Bahnhofsplatz 13, Konstanz (07531-13 30 30).* Ⓦ www.konstanz.de ⓘ *Seenachtfest (mid-August); Büllefest (1st Sun in October).* **Bodensee-Naturmuseum** *Hafenstr. 9, Konstanz (07531-12 87 39 00).* ⓘ *10am–6pm.* ⓘ **Heimat-museum Reichenau** *Ergat 1.* ⓘ *(07534) 920 70.* ⓘ *May–Oct: 3–5pm Tue–Sun.* ⓘ

★ Wasserburg
This charming church, with a tower crowned with an onion-shaped dome, is one of the most frequently photographed sights in this region.

Lindau
This island town has so many historic buildings that the whole area has been listed as a historic monument.
(see p270).

Friedrichshafen is best known for its Zeppelin-Museum. The first Zeppelin airships were tested here in 1900.

Meersburg
Friedrichshafen
Langenargen
BODENSEE
Wasserburg
Lindau
Arbon
Bregenz
Rorschach

KEY
▅	Motorway
▅	Major road
▅	Minor road
▅	River
⚓	Ferry route

Langenargen has an enchanting, small Moorish-style palace named Montfort.

0 km   5
0 miles   5

Freiburg im Breisgau ㉙

THE COUNTS von Zähringen first established Freiburg in 1120. The town, which later belonged to the counts von Urach, became so rich over the years that, in 1368, it bought its freedom and voluntarily placed itself under the protection of the Habsburgs. Marshal Vauban fortified the town in the 17th century, when Freiburg briefly belonged to France. Since 1805 it has been part of Baden. Situated between Kaiserstuhl and Feldberg, it is a natural gateway to the southern Black Forest.

Freiburg University
Freiburg University occupies a Baroque post-Jesuit complex. In the main entrance stands this statue of the pensive Aristotle.

This former Jesuit church belongs to the university complex.

Tourist information

RATHAUS–PLATZ

RATHAUSGASSE

Railway station

BERTHOLDSTRASSE

Fischerau
Fischerau and, parallel to it, Gerberau are picturesque streets in the old town, running along the Gewerbebach stream.

Bertholdsbrunnen (Berthold's fountain) stands at the intersection of Bertholdstraße and Kaiser-Joseph-Straße, known as "Kajo".

| 0 metres | 50 |
| 0 yards | 50 |

Martinstor
St Martin's Gate was part of the 13th-century town fortifications. Its present appearance is the result of work carried out in 1900.

KEY

--- Suggested route

STAR SIGHTS

★ **Bächle**

★ **Münster – the Main Altar**

★ **Kaufhaus**

◁ **Picturesque scene with fruit trees in blossom in the Schwarzwald (Black Forest)**

Haus zum Walfisch
The façade of the Whale House in Franziskanergasse, with its lovely bay window, is a magnificent example of late-Gothic style.

VISITORS' CHECKLIST

Road map B7. 197,000. Rotteckring 14 (0761-388 18 80). Fasnet (end of carnival), Frühlingsmesse (May), Internationales Zeltmusikfest (Jun), Weintage (Jun), Weinkost (Jun), Herbstmesse (Oct), Umwelt-Film-Festival (Oct). www.freiburg.de

Münsterplatz
The picturesque square at the foot of the cathedral, lined by houses of various periods, from Gothic to Rococo, is still used for markets.

★ Bächle
From the Middle Ages, fast-flowing canals have been running along the streets, draining excess surface waters, and providing the water needed to extinguish the frequent fires.

★ Münster – the Main Altar
The cathedral, which started in c.1200 as a Romanesque basilica, was completed by 1513 in the French Gothic style. Inside is the original main altar by Hans Baldung Grien.

★ Kaufhaus
Completed in 1520, with ground-floor arcades and richly adorned gables, the Kaufhaus (literally buying house) was used by local merchants for meetings, conferences and lively festivities.

KAISER–JOSEPH–STRASSE

SCHUSTERSTRASSE

SALZSTRASSE

MUNSTER-PLATZ

Schwarzwald (Black Forest) ③⓪

COVERED WITH TALL FIR TREES and spruces, the Schwarz-
wald is one of Germany's most picturesque regions.
The area is famous not just for its cuckoo clocks,
Kirschwasser (schnaps) and *Schwarzwälder Kirschtorte*
(Black Forest Gâteau); in the past, Celts and later the
Romans came to appreciate the therapeutic qualities
of the local spring waters. (The sources of the rivers
Donau and Neckar are here.) The area is also
a paradise for skiers, climbers, ramblers,
hang-glider pilots and sailors.

★ **Staufen
im Breisgau**
*The town is also
known as Faust-
stadt: Dr Faustus,
who had resided
here, died in 1539
– he is variously
reputed to have
blown himself up,
to have been stran-
gled or to have had
his neck broken.*

Todtnau
*Todtnau is not only a sports centre and a
base for hikers: it is also a major centre of
toothbrush production and the birthplace
of Karl Ludwig Nessler (1872–1951), who
invented the process of hair-perming.*

Todtmoos
*The heart of this resort is the Baroque
pilgrimage church, which dates from the
17th–18th centuries. Popular dog-sleigh
races are held annually in the town.*

Friesenheim
Lahr
Herbolzheim
Teningen
Emmendi
Denzlingen
Freiburg
im Breisg
Bad Krozingen
Staufen im Breisgau
Müllheim
Tod
Todtmo
SCHWARZWALD
Kandern
Wiese
Wehr
Lörrach
Rheinfelden
Rhein
Dreisam

Gutach
In the open-air museum near the small town of Gutach visitors can see the Schwarzwald's oldest house – the Vogtsbauernhof – which dates from the 16th century.

★ Furtwangen
The main attraction of Furtwangen is its clock museum (Uhrenmuseum), which houses a collection of more than 4,000 varied chronometers.

```
0 km          10
0 miles       10
```

Hangloch-Wasserfall
This magnificent mountain waterfall near Todtnau is one of the most beautiful in the Black Forest.

KEY

▬ Motorway

▬ Main road

▬ Secondary road

▬ River

❉ Viewpoint

★ St Blasien
In the beautiful health resort of St Blasien is a Benedictine Abbey, founded in the 9th century. Crowned with a vast dome, its church (1783) is an excellent example of early Neo-Classical style.

STAR SIGHTS

★ **Furtwangen**

★ **St Blasien**

★ **Staufen im Breisgau**

WESTERN GERMANY

Western Germany at a Glance

FAMED FOR ITS excellent wines and the festivities of Cologne's annual carnival, Western Germany is the country's wealthiest and most heavily industrialized region. The Ruhr district still harbours enormous industrial potential, while Frankfurt am Main is Germany's largest financial centre. The region is also rich in tourist attractions – visitors are drawn to the romantic castles which line the Rhein and Mosel valleys, to Cologne with its majestic twin-towered cathedral, the spa town of Aachen, the museums of Frankfurt and Kassel and the imposing Romanesque cathedrals of Speyer, Worms and Mainz.

NORTH RHINE-WESTPHALIA
See pp368–401

Cologne Cathedral (see pp388–9), *which was not completed until the 19th century, is generally considered one of the most outstanding Gothic buildings in Germany.*

0 kilometres   100

0 miles   100

RHINELAND-PALATINATE & SAARLAND
See pp322–45

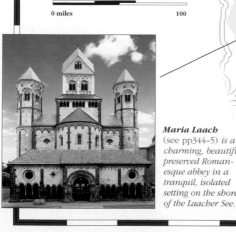

Maria Laach (see pp344–5) *is a charming, beautifully preserved Roman-esque abbey in a tranquil, isolated setting on the shores of the Laacher See.*

Detmold is best known for its magnificent castle (see p401) – one of the most beautiful examples of the "Weser Renaissance" style of architecture.

The Museum Fridericianum in Kassel (see pp350–51), *originally built to house Friederich II's art collection, has hosted the* documenta *since 1955, a four-yearly exhibition of contemporary art that has achieved international acclaim.*

HESSE
See pp346–67

Fulda Cathedral (see p354) *is one of the finest Baroque churches in Hesse. It was built on the site of the previous Romanesque church and follows the original layout.*

The old town in Frankfurt am Main (see p361) *is centred around the Römerberg – a square surrounded by attractive half-timbered houses, with the Fountain of Justice as a focal point.*

Wine in Western Germany

O F THE GREAT EUROPEAN vineyards, Germany's are the farthest north. There are 13 wine-growing regions in Germany, but the most famous German vineyards are those in the western part of the country, especially the Rheingau, Pfalz, Rheinhessen and Mosel-Saar-Ruwer regions. The most widely drunk alcoholic beverage in Germany is beer – unlike in France, Italy or Spain – and therefore the wines produced here are mainly high-quality wines of named vineyards, with a relatively low production of table wine.

Vineyards in Edenkoben, in the southern part of the Weinstraße (*see p333*), in the Palatinate

The Mosel-Saar-Ruwer *region produces superb white wines from the Riesling grape. The highest quality wines are those marked with the letters QmP.*

IMPORTANT FACTS ABOUT GERMAN WINE

Region and climate

Gentle, rocky hills stretching along the river bends – perfect for Rieslings – are typical of the Mosel-Saar-Ruwer and Rheingau regions. Clay and limestone soil, appropriate for the Müller-Thurgau variety, are found in Hesse on the Rhine. The German climate is considerably more severe than that of southern countries, which gives the wines a slightly sharp, refreshing taste.

Typical grape varieties

The red grape is not cultivated in great quantities. The most popular red variety is the Spätburgunder, known in France as Pinot Noir, which produces a heavy wine with a strong flavour. White grapes are much more popular, especially the famous Rieslings, from which the best white wines are produced, the Müller-Thurgau, which gives a light wine with a fruity bouquet, the Grauburgunder (Pinot Grigio) and the Weißburgunder (Pinot Blanc). Less well-known are: Silvaner, Gewürztraminer, Grüner Veltliner and Gutedel. Rosé wines are produced from the Portugieser variety, cultivated in the Rhineland–Palatinate (Pfalz) and Rheinhessen.

Famous wine producers

Mosel-Saar-Ruwer: Fritz Haag, Heymann-Löwenstein, Karthäuserhof, Dr. Loosen, Egon Müller, J.J. Prüm, C. von Schubert, Willi Schaefer; **Rheingau:** Georg Breuer, Robert Weil; **Rheinhessen:** Gunderloch, Keller; **Pfalz:** Müller-Catoir, Georg Mosbacher, Dr. Bürklin-Wolf, von Buhl.

The Nabe *is famous for its white wines, produced from Silvaner as well as Riesling and Müller-Thurgau grapes.*

The Rheingau, where the "Rhine" wines are made, is well known for its Rieslings, particularly the Johannisberg Riesling. A famous vineyard is Prinz von Hessen.

The fountain of the "Wine Witch" in the small town of Winningen, in the Mosel-Saar-Ruwer region

Wine cellars in the former Cistercian monastery at Eberbach in the Rheingau region

WINE REGIONS

The two best-known wine regions are Mosel-Saar-Ruwer and Rheingau. Mosel, Saar and Ruwer are the three rivers whose names have been combined to give the region its name. Exceptional Rieslings are produced here as well as smaller amounts of other wines. The Rheingau produces a full-bodied red wine in addition to the dominant Rieslings. Rheinhessen produces not only several types of white and red wines, but also a rosé, as does the Palatinate.

Liebfraumilch has been produced in the Rheinhessen region for over 40 years. Mainly designed for export, it is a sweetish, medium-class of wine, a blend of several grape varieties.

0 km   70

0 miles   70

KEY

- Mosel–Saar–Ruwer
- Rheinhessen
- Mittelrhein
- Pfalz
- Nahe
- Rheingau
- Ahr
- Hessische Bergstraße

Romanesque Architecture

WESTERN GERMANY boasts some of the most interesting examples of Romanesque architecture in the whole of Europe. Charlemagne's famous chapel in Aachen was erected as early as the Carolingian period. The cathedral in Trier and the church of St Maria im Kapitol in Cologne are among the most outstanding creations of early-Romanesque architecture of the Frankish dynasty. In the 12th century, the most important German centres of art were Cologne and the towns of the central Rhineland, with three magnificent cathedrals in Speyer, Mainz and Worms, and the monastery in Maria Laach, preserved to this day.

The choir of St Martin in the Dom in Mainz is an example of the spaciousness that is typical of the late-Romanesque style.

The front elevation of the St Gotthard-Kapelle in Mainz has upper galleries with arcades decorated with friezes – a common feature of Romanesque architecture.

Twin western towers

Gallery above the vestibule

The northern portal of the Dom in Worms is framed by an offset architrave and flanked by pairs of columns, as are the portals of many other Romanesque cathedrals.

Lavishly decorated main portal

The monastery in Maria Laach has many capitals with intricate decorations, such as these carvings with human faces.

Cross-vaulting
(or cross-
ribbed
vaulting)

Tower at the
intersection of
the nave and
transept

The portal of the Dom in Trier
*has a magnificent tympanum,
depicting Christ with the Virgin
Mary and St Peter.*

ROMANESQUE CATHEDRALS

Cathedrals of the type
shown here were built with
a basilica-type internal
arrangement, including a
transept and presbytery,
and a double choir usually
ending in a semicircular
apse. The Dom in Speyer
has a massive twin-towered
west front, as shown here.
The other pair of towers
rises above the presbytery,
and the intersection of the
nave and transept has a
lower, broad fifth tower.

The system of vaults
also acts as support.

Twin
eastern
towers

ROMANESQUE CAPITALS

Romanesque churches in the Rhine
Valley feature exquisite stone
sculptures. The capitals, with their
extraordinary variety of form, ranging
from simple blocks to fine figurative
or animal-decorated compositions, are
of particular interest.

Water-leaf capital of a bonded column	**Simplified Corinthian capital**
Cushion (or block or cube) capital	**Zoömorphic (animal-decorated) capital**

The St Gotthard-Kapelle in Mainz, *next to the
Dom, was the archbishop's personal chapel for
private prayer. It is comparable to similar private
buildings in secular palaces.*

RHINELAND–PALATINATE AND SAARLAND

T*HE RHINELAND-PALATINATE is one of Germany's most romantic regions, attracting visitors with its vineyards, gentle hills and fairy-tale castles along the Rhine and Mosel valleys. Several towns, such as Trier, have kept reminders of their Roman heritage.*

These two states, which border France in the west, did not emerge in their present form until after World War II. The Rhineland-Palatinate was created from the previously independent Bavarian Palatinate and the southern part of the Central Rhineland, making it a true jigsaw-puzzle of territories without a coherent history. The Saarland was under French rule until 1956. Today, it forms a bridge between France and Germany, the two driving forces of European unity.

The turbulent history of the region has left many traces. The picturesque Mosel Valley is lined with grand Medieval fortresses, such as Burg Eltz, while Worms on the Rhine is the setting for most of the Nibelungen legend as well as the residence of the mythical king of Burgundy, Gunther.

The Nibelung treasure is still said to lie at the bottom of the Rhine. The impressive cathedral in Worms, along with the Romanesque cathedrals of Speyer and Mainz, is a fascinating example of Medieval sacral architecture.

The "Deutsches Eck" in Koblenz is the strategic spot where the Mosel flows into the Rhine, and Koblenz also marks the beginning of the romantic Rhine Valley. A boat trip upriver, justifiably popular with visitors, will pass some spectacular rocky scenery, including the famous Lorelei Rock and countless castles set among vineyards on either side of the gorge.

The famous ironworks complex in Völklingen is a reminder of a bygone era, when most of the Saarland's inhabitants were active in mining, steelworks and other heavy industries.

Panorama of Saarbrücken, with the Saar river in the foreground

◁ **The snow-covered Medieval fortress of Burg Eltz, in the Mosel Valley**

Exploring Rhineland-Palatinate and Saarland

WHITE WINE enthusiasts come here, attracted by the beautiful, picturesque valleys of the Rhine and Mosel rivers, with their Medieval castles and small towns. Travelling along the Deutsche Weinstraße (German wine route), Germany's oldest tourist route, visitors can see fascinating historic buildings and taste the different types of wine made by the numerous small vineyards scattered throughout the entire region. Speyer and Mainz have monumental Romanesque cathedrals, while Trier boasts many interesting Roman relics. The huge ironworks in Völklingen is a surprising sight, transporting visitors back to a time when heavy industry ruled much of the region.

SEE ALSO

- *Where to Stay* pp487–8
- *Where to Eat* pp516–17

The imposing red-sandstone building of the Dom in Mainz

The proud complex of Schloss Stolzenfels near Koblenz, designed by Karl Friedrich Schinkel

Bonn

Cologne (Köln)

BAD NEUENAHR- -AHRWEILER

61

MARIA LAACH

H O H E - E I F E L

SCHNEE - EIFEL

PRÜM

Kyll

257

E42/60

Our

BITBURG

50

MOSELTAL 3

E422/1

TRIER 1

Luxembourg

Mosel

268

327

Saar

268

E422/1

41

ST. WENDEL

SAARLAND 2

NEUKIRCHEN

E29

SAARBRÜCKEN

E50/6

Metz

0 km   20

0 miles   20

The interior of the Dom in Trier

SIGHTS AT A GLANCE

Koblenz pp342–3 **9**
Mainz pp334–7 **7**
Maria Laach pp344–5 **10**
Saarland p330 **2**
Speyer **4**
Trier pp326–9 **1**
Worms **5**

Suggested routes

Deutsche Weinstraße **6**
Moseltal **3**
Rheintal **8**

GETTING AROUND

The A65 motorway links Karlsruhe with Ludwigshafen, and
continues from there towards
Luxembourg or Lorraine, via
Homburg and Saarbrücken.
The A32, and later the A4,
leads from Saarbrücken to
Metz or Strasbourg. The A1
runs northwards from
Friedrichsthal to Trier and
the Mosel Valley. Inter-City
trains offer a frequent and
convenient service; Frankfurt
am Main and Köln/Bonn
(Konrad-Adenauer-Flughafen)
have international airports.

KEY

▭	Motorway
▭	Main road
▭	Scenic route
═	River
☼	Viewpoint

Map labels:
Siegen
256
ALTENKIRCHEN
WESTERWALD
54
E35/3
Labn
NDERNACH
WIED
9
KOBLENZ
54
Frankfurt am Main
E31/61
8 RHINE VALLEY (RHEINTAL)
NSRÜCK
Rhein
WIESBADEN
50
7
MAINZ
BAD KREUZNACH
41
OBERSTEIN
RHEINLAND PFALZ
63
E31/61
E31/61
5 WORMS
E50/6
FRANKENTHAL
E50/6
KAISERSLAUTERN
LUDWIGSHAFEN
270
NEUSTADT
SPEYER
DEUTSCHE WEINSTRASSE 6
4
10
PIRMASENS
LANDAU
65
Karlsruhe

Trier ❶

ONE OF GERMANY'S OLDEST towns, Trier was founded in 16 BC as *Augusta Treverorum*, supposedly by the Emperor Augustus himself. In the 3rd and 4th centuries it was an imperial seat and the capital of the *Belgica prima* province. In the 5th century the town, which now numbered 70,000 inhabitants, was conquered and destroyed by Germanic tribes. Trier never returned to its former importance – in the 17th century it had a mere 3,600 inhabitants, and 100 years later they still numbered fewer than 4,000. The town, which is also the birthplace of Karl Marx, has a rich architectural heritage.

🚩 Porta Nigra

🔳 *(0651) 754 24.*
⏱ *Apr–Sep: 9am–6pm daily; Oct–Mar: 9am–5pm daily.* 🖼

This town gate, named *Porta Nigra* (black gate) in the Middle Ages because of the colour of its weathered stone, was erected in the 3rd century. The oldest German defensive structure, it still impresses with its colossal size: 36 m (118 ft) long, 21.5 m (70.5 ft) wide and 30 m (27 ft) high. Two gateways lead onto a small inner courtyard, and there are two tiers of defence galleries with large open windows. It is flanked by two towers – the four-storey western tower and the three-storey unfinished eastern tower. The entire structure was made of huge blocks of sandstone, connected by iron rods, without mortar.

In the 12th century, the building was transformed into the two-storey church of St Simeon and served as such until the early 19th century.

The magnificent *Porta Nigra*, gigantic Roman gateway into Trier

Petrusbrunnen (fountain of St Peter) in Hauptmarkt

🚩 Hauptmarkt

Trier's main market square, undoubtedly one of the most attractive in Germany, dates back to the 10th century. The Marktkreuz (market cross) erected around the same time symbolized the town's right to hold markets. Today there is a copy of the original cross mounted on a granite Roman column, with a relief of the Lamb of God. On the southeastern side of the square is the Petrusbrunnen (St Peter's fountain), from 1595, with sculptures of St Peter and the Four Virtues. On the south-western side stands the 15th-century Steipe, with a steep gabled roof. Originally it was used by the town councillors as guesthouse and banqueting hall. The Baroque Rotes Haus (red house) next door dates from 1683. Löwenapotheke, in a 17th-century building on the southeastern side of the square, is Germany's oldest pharmacy, its records dating back to the 13th century.

🏛 Bischöfliches Dom- und Diözesanmuseum

Windstraße 6–8. 🔳 *(0651) 710 52 55.* ⏱ *9am–5pm Mon–Sat, 1–5pm Sun.* ⬛ *1 Jan, 24 & 25 Dec.* 🖼

A 19th-century building near the cathedral, once a Prussian prison, now houses the art collection of the Diocese, including early Christian works of art. Its pride of possession is a 3rd-century ceiling painting from the imperial palace which once stood on the site of the cathedral. The fresco was rediscovered in 1945, and some 70,000 pieces were painstakingly reassembled over the following decades. Another important historic exhibit is the reconstructed crypt of the Benedictine church of St Maximin, which has important 9th-century Carolingian wall paintings.

🔐 Dom St Peter

🔳 *(0651) 979 07 90.*
⏱ *Apr–Oct: 6:30am–6pm daily; Nov–Mar: 6:30am–5:30pm daily.* 🖼

The present cathedral incorporates the remains of an older 4th-century church. The oldest cathedral in Germany, it was constructed in stages – in the early 11th century, late 12th century, mid-13th century and 14th century. It is a triple-nave, two-choir basilica with transept and six towers, and its furnishings include several outstanding objects, such as the tomb of the papl envoy Ivo (1144).

🔐 Liebfrauenkirche

An der Meerkatz 4. 🔳 *(0651) 425 54.* ⏱ *Apr–Oct: 7:30am–6pm daily; Nov–Mar: 7:30am–5:30pm daily.* 🖼

Adjoining the cathedral is the Liebfrauenkirche (Church of Our Dear Lady), built in 1235–60. Along with the

The Liebfrauenkirche – one of the country's earliest Gothic churches

cathedral in Magdeburg, this is one of the earliest examples of German Gothic architecture. Its ground plan is based on the Greek cross, and the tower above the dome accentuates the intersection of the naves. Its western portal is richly decorated with carved ornaments and iconographic symbols. The interior features many outstanding relics, including 15th-century wall paintings on twelve columns, which symbolize the 12 apostles. There are also some impotant tombs, including that of a local nobleman, Karl von Metternich (1636), which is found in the northeast chapel.

�ï Aula Palatina

Konstantinplatz. ☎ (0651) 42 570.
◐ Apr–Oct: 10am–6pm Mon–Sat, noon–6pm Sun; Nov–Mar: 11am–noon & 3–4pm Tue–Sat, noon–1pm Sun.

The *Aula Palatina* (Palatinate hall) dates from AD 310. An elongated, rectangular brick building 67 m (220 ft) long, 27.5 m (90 ft) wide and 30 m (98 ft) high with a vast semicircular apse, it served as the throne hall of the Roman emperor or his representative. Following the town's sacking by Germanic tribes, the building was reduced to rubble. In the 12th century the apse was converted into a tower, to

VISITORS' CHECKLIST

Road map A5. 🏠 99,000.
🚉 An der Porta Nigra.
🛈 Simeonstraße 60 (0651-97 80 80). Ⓦ www.trier.de

accommodate the archbishop. In the 17th century, the *Aula Palatina* was integrated into the newly-built palace and its eastern wall partly demolished. During Napoleonic and Prussian times, the hall served as army barracks. The Prussian king Friedrich Wilhelm IV eventually ordered its reconstruction. From 1856 it has served as the Protestant church of St Saviour. Restored after bombing in 1944, its giant size still seems remarkable.

The monumental, austere exterior of the Aula Palatina

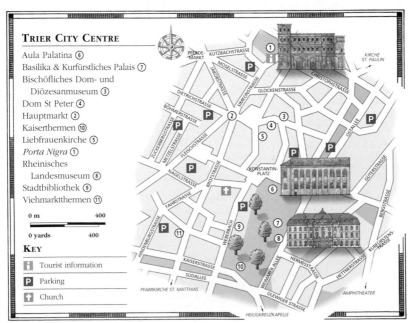

TRIER CITY CENTRE

Aula Palatina ⑥
Basilika & Kurfürstliches Palais ⑦
Bischöfliches Dom- und
 Diözesanmuseum ③
Dom St Peter ④
Hauptmarkt ②
Kaiserthermen ⑩
Liebfrauenkirche ⑤
Porta Nigra ①
Rheinisches
 Landesmuseum ⑧
Stadtbibliothek ⑨
Viehmarktthermen ⑪

0 m   400

0 yards   400

KEY

🛈 Tourist information

🅿 Parking

✝ Church

Portal of the Kurfürstliches Palais

♣ Kurfürstliches Palais

Konstantinplatz. ☎ (0651) 949 42 02.
⬤ *the Palais is an administrative building and so visits that are not part of a public function are possible only by appointment.*
The Kurfürstliches Palais is considered to be one of the most beautiful Rococo palaces in the world. It has undergone several transformations over the centuries and remains of the earlier buildings can still be seen. The present building was designed by Johannes Seiz and built in 1756–62 for Archbishop Johann Philipp von Walderdorff. The sculptures were created by Ferdinand Tietz. The central tympanum shows Pomona, Venus, Apollo and a group of angels. The stairs, which lead from the garden to the inner staircase, were designed in the 18th century, but not built until 1981. They have beautiful handrails with typical Rococo motifs. The gardens are equally beautiful and include a miniature garden, a landscape garden and a mother-and-child area.

🏛 Rheinisches Landesmuseum

Weimarer Allee 1. ☎ (065) 977 40.
⬤ 9:30am–5pm Tue–Fri, 10:30am–5pm Sat & Sun; May–Oct: 9:30am–5pm Mon. ⬤ 1 Jan, 24, 25 & 26 Dec. 🎟 (free 1st Mon of the month).
Only a few steps separate the electoral palace from the Rhine regional museum foun-

ded in 1877. Its collections are grouped into four sections: prehistoric, Roman, Franconian-Merovingian, and medieval to contemporary. The largest space is devoted to Roman relics. Star exhibits include a magnificent mosaic depicting Bacchus, from the dining room of a Roman villa, and the lovely statuette of a nymph, undoubtedly the work of a major artist. Equally impressive is a stone carving showing a ship loaded with four giant barrels, sailing on the Mosel River. Dating from AD 220, it decorated the tomb of a local wine-merchant.

📖 Stadtbibliothek

Weberbach 25.
The municipal library contains a number of important collections that were assembled here in the early 19th century, when many monastic libraries closed down. Among its treasures the library holds 74 full-page miniatures of the famous Trier Apocalypse (c.800), as well as one of the few surviving copies of the first Bible printed by Gutenberg.

♣ Kaiserthermen

Weimarer Allee/Kaiserstr.
☎ (0651) 442 62. ⬤ Apr–Sep: 9am–6pm daily; Oct–Jan: 9am–5pm (4pm Dec) daily. 🎟
Not far from the Rheinisches Landesmuseum are the remains of the vast imperial

baths. Built in the early 4th century, during the reign of Constantine, they were the third largest bathing complex in the Roman world. The remaining sections of the walls and foundations indicate the former layout. Best preserved are the walls of the *caldarium*, the room with the hot water pool. Next to it is the round *tepidarium*, the warm baths. The spacious *frigidarium* was used for cold baths. Considerable room was given to the *palaestra*, an outdoor exercise area.

♣ Viehmarktthermen

Viehmarktplatz.
☎ (0651) 994 10 57. ⬤ Apr–Sep: 9am–6pm Tue–Sun; Oct–Mar: 9am–5pm Tue–Sun.
Following excavations completed in 1994, the remains of these Roman baths, along with those of medieval refuse pits and the cellars of a Capucin monastery, are now on display to the pubic under a large glass canopy.

Nymph in Rheinisches Landesmuseum

📖 Jesuitenkolleg

Jesuitenstr. 13. ⬤ 8:30am–5:30pm daily.
The Gothic Church of the Holy Trinity was built for Franciscan monks, who settled in Trier before 1238. The surviving church, from the late 13th century, went to the Jesuits in 1570. The college (1610–14) was transferred to the university following the dissolution of the Jesuit Order. It now houses a theological seminary. In the church, the tomb of Friedrich von Spee (1591–1635) is worth a visit.

Vast complex of the Kaiserthermen (imperial baths)

⋔ Amphitheater

Petrisberg. 🅲 *(0651) 730 10.*
⬭ *Apr–Sep: 9am–6pm; Oct–Mar:*
9am–5pm. 📷

Near the imperial baths are the ruins of the Roman amphitheatre, dating from the 1st century AD. This was the scene of gladiatorial fights and animal contests. The entire structure, consisting of an elliptical arena and a stepped auditorium, was surrounded by a high wall, divided into individual storeys by colonnaded arcades. The complex was designed to seat up to 20,000 people. In the 5th century the inhabitants of Trier used the amphitheatre as a place of refuge from the increasingly frequent raids by Germanic tribes.

⌂ Heiligkreuzkapelle

Arnulfstraße/Rotbachstraße.
The Chapel of the Holy Cross, in a secluded spot, is one of Trier's more interesting historic buildings. Built in the Romanesque style in the second half of the 11th century, at the initiative of the parson of Arnulfa Cathedral, it is a small building with a ground plan in the shape of the Greek cross and an octagonal tower set within the cross. Although it suffered serious damage during World War II, it was meticulously restored to its original state in the years 1957–8.

⌂ Pfarrkirche St Matthias

Matthiasstraße. 85. 🅲 *(0651) 310 79.* ⬭ *6:30am–8pm daily.*
This church's history dates back to the 5th century, when it became the burial place of St Eucharius, the first bishop of Trier. From the 8th century, the church was run by Benedictine monks. In the 10th–11th centuries a new church was erected as burial site of the relics of the apostle, St Matthew. It was twice remodelled at the turn of the 15th to 16th centuries, when it acquired its rich Gothic vaults. The present abbey dates from the 16th century. The shrine holding the apostle's relics ensured that the church became one of the most important destinations for pilgrims in the region.

The ruins of Barbaratherme, ancient Roman baths

⋔ Barbaratherme

Südallee. 🅲 *(0651) 994 10 57.*
⬭ *Apr–Sep: 9am–6pm; Oct–Mar:*
9am–5pm. 📷

Not far from the Roman bridge across the Mosel River are the ruins of the Barbara baths, dating from the 2nd century AD. Although above ground not much has been preserved, the extensive system of underground heating channels, the *hypocaustum*, clearly demonstrates the original size of this public bath complex. In the Middle Ages, Patrician and aristocratic families transformed the baths into their residences. In the 17th century Jesuit monks dismantled the remaining structures, and used the recovered building materials to construct their own college.

⋔ Kirche St Maximin

Maximinstraße. 🅲 *(0651) 710 52 55.*
📷 *obligatory.*

In the Middle Ages there were as many as four abbeys in Trier. St. Maximin Abbey was founded on the burial site of its patron saint, who died in AD 325. The surviving church was built in the 13th century, on the foundations of the previous buildings. Its Romanesque–Gothic forms were partly obscured by the remodelling work carried out in 1580–1698. The church's most valuable historic remains were the Carolingian wall paintings, which originally adorned the crypt. These are now displayed in the Rheinisches Landesmuseum.

⌂ Kirche St Paulinus

Thebäerstraße. 🅲 *(0651) 27 08 50.*
⬭ *Mar–Sep: 9am–6pm daily;*
Oct–Feb: 9am–5pm daily.

This church was built in the 12th century, on the foundations of an older Christian chapel. In 1674 it was blown up by the French army. St Paulin, its patron saint and bishop in Trier, was one of the few to voice his opposition to the Aryan credo of Emperor Constantine II, in which he rejected the divinity of Christ and proclaimed himself alone to be made in God's image. Paulin did not meet with a martyr's death, but was exiled to Phrygia (now Turkey), where he died in 358. The present church, which is a true gem of Rococo architecture, was designed by Balthasar Neumann, who also created the main altar. The wall paintings are by Thomas Scheffler.

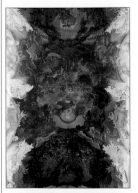
Baroque ceiling paintings in the Rococo Kirche St Paulinus

Saarland ❷

THIS GERMAN state, bordered by Luxembourg and France, was long disputed between France and Germany, but has now been firmly integrated into the Federal Republic. Almost forgotten are its coal and steel industries, which declined in the 1960s and 70s. The region has seen a turbulent history – it was ruled in turn by Celts, Romans and Franks. In the 17th century, on the order of Louis XIV, Vauban built the town-fortress of Saarlouis. Saarbrücken, an 18th-century town, is famous for its Baroque architecture, mostly created by Friedrich Joachim Stengel.

Von Nassau-Saarbrücken family tombs in Saarbrücken

Saarbrücken

Road map B6. 🏛 *190,000.* 🚊 🏢
Saargalerie, Reichsstr. 1 (0681-194 33 or 93 80 90). 🎭 *Max Ophüls-Preis (Jan), Perspectives du Théâtre (May), Saar Spektakel (Aug).*

The capital of Saarland, Saarbrücken was first built as the Franconian fortress of *Sarabrucca*. The town, situated on the banks of the Saar River, flourished in the 17th and 18th century, under the rule of Duke Wilhelm Heinrich von Nassau-Saarbrücken.

The churches and other prestigious buildings are largely the work of Friedrich Joachim Stengel, court architect to the von Nassau-Saarbrücken family. He designed the Catholic **Basilika St Johann** (1754–8) in the market square, as well as the monumental **Schloss**, the palace on the opposite bank of the Saar (1739–48). Its original, modern façade, created in 1989 after damage in World War II, is the work of the architect Gottfried Böhm.

Opposite the Schloss stands the **Altes Rathaus** (old town hall), dating from 1748–50, which today houses an interesting museum of ethnography. The Protestant **Ludwigskirche** (1762–75) is

one of the last works completed by Stengel. A truc architectural gem, it is laid out in the shape of a Greek cross. The **Stiftskirche St Arnual**, in the southwestern part of the town, contains the splendid Gothic and Renaissance tombs of the von Nassau-Saarbrücken family. Since 1960 it has also featured a "German–French Garden". One of the garden's entrances leads to Gulliver-Miniwelt (miniature world of Gulliver), where small versions of the world's most famous buildings are exhibited.

Völklinger Hütte, the historic steelworks in Völklingen

Völklingen

Road map B6. 🏛 *43,500.*
🏢 *Rathausstr. 57 (06898-211 00).*
About 10 km (6 miles) west of Saarbrücken lies the small industrial town of Völklingen, which was granted town status in 1937. In 1881, Carl Röchling, a native of Saarbrücken, bought a small steel mill, the **Völklinger Hütte**, which he soon developed as the heart of his family's industrial empire. The steel mill still exists, and in 1994 it became a UNESCO World Heritage Site, listed as a historical object of international importance. Another attraction is an original, early 20th-century housing estate.

Homburg

Road map B6. 🏛 *42,000.* 🏢 *Rathaus, Am Forum 5 (06 841-10 11 66).*
This town grew up around the Hohenburg castle, which now is just a picturesque ruin. In the Schlossberg nearby were unearthed the remains of a fortress, which was built in 1680 92 by Sébastien Le Preste Vauban on the orders of the French King Louis XIV. The greatest attraction of Homburg, however, is its Schlossberg caves, the largest man-made caves in Europe, cut into the red sandstone.

Ottweiler

Road map B5. 🏛 *16,000.*
🏢 *Schlosshof 5 (06 824-35 11).*
The small picturesque town of Ottweiler has a beautifully preserved old town. The Alter Turm (old tower), which in the 15th century formed part of the town's fortifications, now serves as a belfry for the parish church, whose origins go back to the 15th century. Its present Baroque form was the work of Friedrich Joachim Stengel from 1756–7.

Rathausplatz is a beautifully proportioned complex of historic houses, mostly the homes of wealthy citizens, dating from the 17th and 18th centuries. Many have half-timbered upper halves. The Altes Rathaus (old town hall, 1714) combines two different building methods – the base is stone, the top half-timbered. In Schlossplatz is the Renaissance Hesse Haus (c.1590).

Moseltal ❸

THE MOSEL RIVER, 545 km (338 miles) long, is
one of the longest tributaries of the Rhine.
The Mosel valley between Trier and Koblenz,
where the Mosel flows into the Rhine, is one of
the most beautiful parts of Germany. On both
sides of the river, romantic castles tower over
endless vineyards, where excellent white grapes
are grown – both are typical features of the
charming landscape.

Burg Thurant ②
Near the town of Alken
stands Thurant castle, which
was built in the 13th century.
It is the only twin-towered
castle along the Mosel.

Kobern-Gondorf ①
An ancient cemetery, dating from
Roman and Franconian times, was
discovered here in 1874. It yielded
many interesting artifacts, including
necklaces, rings and weapons.

Burg Pyrmont ⑤
Pyrmont's grim 13th-century
medieval castle was remodelled
and extended several times
during the Baroque era.

Cochem ⑥
The castle in Cochem,
originally built in the
11th century, was
completely destroyed
by French soldiers in
1689. The present castle
was rebuilt in the
19th century.

416

49

Mosel

Baybach

Dünnbach

Bremm

Ehrenburg ③
The first fortress, rising to
235 m (771 ft) above sea
level, was built in 1120. It
was frequently remodelled
in later years.

Burg Eltz ④
The von Eltz family
castle, whose history
goes back to the 16th
century, remains in
private hands to this day,
but it is open to visitors.

Burg Arras ⑦
This fortress built around
900–950 as part of the fortifications against frequent
pillaging raids by Normans.

KEY

▬	Suggested route
▬	Scenic route
═	Other road
┄	River, lake
☼	Viewpoint

0 km   5

0 miles   5

TIPS FOR DRIVERS

Length of the route: about
75 km (46 miles).
Stopping-off points: *there are
numerous restaurants and cafes
in Cochem; small pubs can be
found along the entire route.*
Additional attractions: *a boat
trip on the Mosel River, from
Koblenz to Cochem or Trier.*

Altar in the Dreifaltigkeitskirche, in Speyer

Speyer ❹

Road map B6. 👥 *46,000.* 🚉 ⓘ
Maximilianstraße 13 (06232-14 23 92).
🎪 *Brezelfest (Jul), Kaisertafel (Aug), Altstadtfest (Sep), Bauernmarkt (Sep).*

In the 7th century, Speyer was the seat of a diocese. As a free city of the Holy Roman Empire from 1294 until 1779, 50 sessions of the imperial parliament took place here. The most famous session was in 1529, when the Protestant states of the Holy Roman Empire lodged a protest (hence "Protestant") against the decisions of the Catholic majority.

The most important historic building in Speyer is the Romanesque **Dom St Maria und St Stephan**, a World Heritage Site. For a time, before being superseded by the gigantic abbey of Cluny in Burgundy, this was the largest monumental Romanesque building in Europe. The Dom, built in 1025–61 on the initiative of Conrad II, is a triple-nave, cross-vaulted basilica with transept, vestibule, choir, apse and several towers. Its magnificent triple-nave crypt, the burial place of Salian emperors, has stunning stone carvings, some worked by Lombard stonemasons. **St Afra's**, dating from around 1100, has some interesting sculptures, including *Christ Bearing His Cross* and *Annunciation* (c.1470). The Domnapf, a vast stone bowl seen at the forecourt of the cathedral, dates from 1490. It was used during enthroning

ceremonies, when the newly anointed bishop would order it to be filled with wine right to the brim in order to win the hearts of his flock.

Another 11th-century interesting building is the **Mikwe** in Judenbadgasse, a ritual Jewish bath for women, and the remains of a synagogue nearby. To the west of the Dom stand the remains of the medieval fortifications including the **Altpörtel**, a 14th- to 16th-century town gate. The late-Baroque **Dreifaltigkeitskirche** (church of the Holy Trinity), built in 1701–17, is an architectural masterpiece with marvellous interiors.

Worms ❺

Road map B5. 👥 *82,000.* 🚉
ⓘ *Neumarkt 14 (06241-250 45).*

Worms is one of the oldest towns in Germany. In the Middle Ages it was the home of the Reich's Parliament, hosting more than 100 sessions. The **Dom St Peter** is one of the largest late-Romanesque cathedrals in Germany, along with the cathedrals in Mainz and Speyer. It was built in 1171–1230 as a two-choir basilica, with eastern transept, four towers and two domes. Its northern nave includes five beautiful sandstone reliefs from a Gothic cloister, which no longer exists. The interior furnishings date mainly from modern times. Particularly noteworthy is the high altar designed in the 18th century by Balthasar Neumann, and the stalls dating from 1760.

A relief from 1488, in the Dom in Worms

Tombstones in the Heiliger Sand Jewish cemetery in Worms

A short distance from the cathedral is the Marktplatz (market square), with the interesting **Dreifaltigkeitskirche** church of the Holy Trinity (1709–25). Northeast of the square stands the **Stiftskirche St Paul** (church of St Paul), built in the 11th–12th centuries and completed in the 18th century, with original 13th century wall paintings. Nearby is the only surviving Renaissance residential building in Worms, the **Rotes Haus** (red house).

In the western part of the old town is the **Heiliger Sand** (holy sands), the oldest Jewish cemetery in Europe, where the earliest tombstones date from the 11th and 12th centuries. Also worth a visit is the 14th-century **Liebfrauenkirche** (Church of Our Dear Lady). The most noteworthy feature of the **Magnuskirche** (11th–12th centuries) is its crypt, from around AD 800, while the **Stiftskirche St Martin** (late 11th century) has some interesting portals.

The vast Romanesque Dom St. Peter in Worms

Deutsche Weinstraße ❻

THE "German Wine Route" starts in Bockenheim and ends in Schweigen, near the Alsatian town of Weißenburg. The tour suggested here includes the most interesting sections of this route. This is one of the most beautiful parts of Germany, where visitors will encounter aspects of German and European historical and cultural heritage at every step, set among the picturesque scenery of the endless vineyards covering the sun-drenched slopes of the Pfälzer Wald.

St Martin ⑥
Not much remains of the Romanesque church of St Martin, but the 16–18th-century buildings surviving in the town continue to enchant visitors.

Hambacher Schloss ⑦
Only a romantic ruin remains of this vast hill-top fortress, whose fame is based on the Hambacher Fest when, on 27 May 1832, students protested against the fragmentation of Germany.

Trifels ④
This grim, ruined castle once served as a prison for many important people, including the King of England, Richard the Lionheart.

Bad Dürkheim ⑧
This famous resort is best known for its annual Wurstmarkt, held in September. Despite its name, it celebrates the wine harvest, and sausages take second place.

Landau ⑤
This little town has the remains of the fortress built by Vauban, and an extraordinarily beautiful post-Augustinian church.

NATURPARK
PFÄLZER
WALD

0 km   5

0 miles   5

Bad Bergzabern ②
This town has some interesting Renaissance remains, including the Gasthaus zum Engel (Angel's Inn) and a royal castle.

Leinsweiler ③
Hilltop Hof Neukastel was once the home of the German impressionist artist Max Slevogt, and to this day, wall paintings by the artist can be seen here.

Klingbach

Dörrenbach ①
The star attractions in this small town are the half-timbered town hall and the Gothic church surrounded by fortifications.

KEY

▬ Suggested route

▭ Scenic route

= Other road

░ River, lake

🌿 Viewpoint

TIPS FOR DRIVERS

Length: 83 km (51 miles).
Stopping-off points: *Landau has many cafés and restaurants. The spa town of Bad Dürkheim, with its cafés and wine bars, is also a good place to stop.*
Signs: *Look for signposts showing a bunch of grapes or a wine jug.*

Mainz ❼

THE TOWN, which grew out of the Roman military camp *Moguntiacum* established in 39 BC, is today the capital of the Rhineland-Palatinate. Mainz is the home of two important German television stations (ZDF and SAT 1). It is also the main centre of trade for the popular Rhine wines. Its late-Romanesque cathedral symbolizes the power of the Kurfürsten, the prince-electors, who used to crown German kings. Indisputably the town's most famous son is Johannes Gutenberg – the inventor of printing.

🏛 Kurfürstliches Schloss

Dieter-von-Isenburg-Straße. **Römisch-Germanisches Museum** 📞 *(06131)* 912 40. ⏱ *10am–6pm Tue–Sun.*

Construction of the Baroque electoral palace, which began in 1627 during the rule of Archbishop Georg von Greifenclau, was completed more than a century later, in 1775–6, under Johann Friedrich Carl Joseph von Erthal. Today the palace houses the fascinating museum of Roman and Germanic history.

🏛 Gutenberg-Museum

Liebfrauenplatz 5. 📞 *(06131) 12 26 40.* ⏱ *9am–5pm Tue–Sat, 11am–3pm Sun.* ● *public holidays.*

Johannes Gensfleisch zum Gutenberg became famous as the inventor of the printing process using movable metal type. The letters were cast in a special apparatus and set in

Statue of Gutenberg in Gutenbergplatz

columns. Gutenberg himself prepared the Bible for printing and publication in 1454–5. From the original 200 copies, only 46 have survived to this day.

The museum, which opened in 1900, shows a reconstruction of the master's workshop from 1450. The collection comprises priceless early books, including the Gutenberg Bible and the Psalter published in 1457 by Fust & Schöffer, Gutenberg's erstwhile partners and latterday creditors. The Psalter was the first work to be printed using three different colours of inks.

🏛 Kaiserdom

See pp336–7.

🏛 Gutenbergplatz

A short distance from the Protestant parish church of St John is Gutenbergplatz, a pleasant square with a statue of the inventor. Set in its

paving stones is a line marking the 50th parallel. The Staatstheater (state theatre) in the square is an interesting late Neo-Classical building from 1829–33.

Historic half-timbered houses in Kirschgarten

🏛 Kirschgarten

Near the Baroque hospital of St Roch, built in 1721 and now an old people's home, runs a street called Kirschgarten (cherry orchard). This is one of the loveliest parts of old Mainz, which suffered serious damage in World War II. The well-preserved complex of historic half-timbered houses, dating from the 16th–18th centuries, makes this district worth visiting and a pleasant place for a stroll.

⛪ Kirche St Stephan

Kleine Weißgasse 12. 📞 *(06131) 23 16 40.* ⏱ *10am–noon 2–5pm Mon–Sat, 2–5pm Sun.* ● *4:30pm Dec–Jan.*

A short distance from Kirschgarten stands the Gothic parish church of St Stephen. It was built in stages, on the site of an older building dating from the 10th century. Construction began in the mid-13th century and continued until the end of the 15th century. The resulting church is a triple-nave hall with eastern transept and a single-nave choir. The adjacent late-15th century cloisters are a true gem of late-Gothic design. The original stained-glass windows in the presbytery, destroyed during World War II, were replaced by six new ones in 1978–81, designed and partly made by

The Baroque Kurfürstliches Schloss and museum

Landing stage for boats on the Rhine

VISITORS' CHECKLIST

Road map B5. 🏙 190,000. 🚂
🛈 Im Brückenturm am Rathaus
(06131-28 62 10). 🎭 Mainzer
Fastnacht (Jan/Feb), Johannis-
nacht (Jun), OpenOhr Festival
(Whitsun), Mainzer Zeltfestival
(end of Jun/early Jul) Weinforum
Rheinhessen (last weekend in
Oct). 🖥 www.mainz.de

Marc Chagall. Set against a beautiful blue background, they depict biblical scenes, including Abraham with the three travellers, the Patriarch pleading to God to spare the righteous in Sodom and Gomorrah, Jacob's dream, and Moses with the Tablets of the Ten Commandments.

The church interior contains many other interesting original features. The four large brass candelabra were cast in Mainz in 1509. The small polyptych depicting the Crucifixion dates from around 1400,

while its movable wings were made some 100 years later. The niche below the tower contains the Holy Tomb (c.1450).

⋔ Römersteine
Southeast of the University campus are the impressive remains of the Roman aqueduct, dating from the 1st century AD. The Zahlbach valley was a vantage point for the southwestern flank of the Roman camp, *Castrum Moguntiacum*, but it presented a major technical problem of supplying the camp with

drinking water. The aqueduct was built by Roman engineers. Although some of its pillars were 23 m (75 ft) high, the present remains only reach up to 10 m (32 ft).

ENVIRONS: It is also worth making an excursion to **Oppenheim**, a centre of the wine trade 20 km (12 miles) to the south. The pride of this town is its Gothic Katharinenkirche, a church built of red sandstone in the 13th–14th centuries. The neighbouring hill and the ruins of Landskron castle provide the most spectacular view over the Rhine valley. The Weinbaumuseum, museum of viticulture, is also worth visiting.

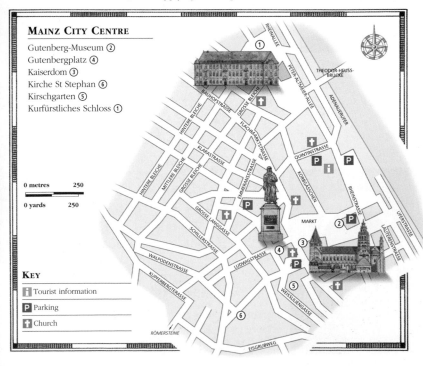

MAINZ CITY CENTRE

Gutenberg-Museum ②
Gutenbergplatz ④
Kaiserdom ③
Kirche St Stephan ⑥
Kirschgarten ⑤
Kurfürstliches Schloss ①

0 metres 250
0 yards 250

KEY
🛈 Tourist information
P Parking
⛪ Church

Mainzer Dom

Crucifix in the St Gotthard-Kapelle

T**HE GREATEST** attraction of Mainz is its superb cathedral, gleaming red in the sunshine. Together with those of Speyer and Worms it is one of the only three Romanesque imperial cathedrals to have survived almost intact to this day. Its basic framework was laid out in 1081–1137 and 1183–1239, but its oldest parts date from the early 11th century, with the rows of Gothic side chapels added during the 13th and 14th centuries. Although neither the Gothic altars nor the magnificent choir screen have survived to this day, it is still possible to see the large group of bishops' monuments from the 13th to the 19th century.

Portal of the "Memorie" Burial Chapel
The late-Gothic portal, leading to the Romanesque burial chapel of the cathedral canons, was made by Madern Gerthener, after 1425.

Pulpit
This Neo-Gothic pulpit was made in 1834 by Joseph Scholl.

Two large and two small towers are symmetrically positioned on the ends of the cathedral.

St Stephen's Choir
The Romanesque eastern choir, one of the first parts to be built, is simpler in style than other parts of the cathedral.

Round staircase towers are from the previous building, built in the early 11th century.

★ **Monument of Heinrich Ferdinand von der Leyen**
This Baroque monument of the Dom rector, the work of Johann Mauritz Gröninger, was erected during his lifetime, in 1706.

VISITORS' CHECKLIST

Bischöfliches Dom- und Diözesanmuseum Domstr. 3.
☎ (06131) 25 33 44.
◯ 10am–5pm Tue–Sun.

St Martin's Choir
The late-Romanesque western choir with its trefoil closing is an early 13th-century addition.

★ **Stalls**
These superb Rococo oak stalls encircle almost the entire presbytery. They were created by Franz Anton Hermann, who completed them in 1767.

Main entrance

Tomb of Jakob von Liebenstein
The late-Gothic tomb of the archbishop von Liebenstein, who died in 1508, is the work of Hans Backoffen. It depicts the deceased in draped robes, lying under an ornate canopy.

STAR FEATURES

★ **Monument of Heinrich Ferdinand von der Leyen**

★ **Stalls**

Rhine Valley (Rheintal) ❽

THE CELTS called it *Renos*, the Romans *Rhenus*, while to Germanic tribes it was the Rhein, or *Vater Rhein* ("Father Rhine"), as it is known today. The source of this mighty, 1320-km (825-mile) long river is in Switzerland, from where it flows through Liechtenstein, Germany, Luxembourg and Holland, yet the Germans regard it as "their" river. The Rhine is steeped in many legends – it was into this river that Hagen von Tronje, faithful follower of King Gunther and slayer of Siegfried, threw the treasure of the Nibelungs, and Lohengrin's swan is said to appear near the town of Kleve *(see p374)* to this day.

Bonn

Bendorf

Rhein

Siegen

Kob

Trier

Saarbrücken

Stolzenfels ①

The existing castle complex has little in common with the original 13th-century fortress, which burned down in 1688. In the early 19th century, the ruins were bought by the future king Friedrich Wilhelm IV. The castle, designed by the famous Prussian architect Karl Friedrich Schinkel, was built in 1833–45.

```
0 kilometres        5
0 miles             5
```

Saarbrücken

Boppard ②

Boppard's most famous sights are the remains of the Roman military camp of Bodobric, the church of St Severus (12th–13th centuries), famous for its wall paintings, and the Medieval market square, built on the site of Roman hot baths. Michael Thonet, the creator of famous chairs made from bent wood, was born here in 1796.

TIPS FOR DRIVERS

Length of the route: *About 125 km (78 miles).*
Stopping-off points: *The best places to stop are Boppard or Bacharach, offering the widest choice of bars and restaurants.*
Further attractions: *A boat trip on the Rhine river, from Koblenz to Mainz.*

St Goar ③

The town takes its name from Goar, an Aquitanian hermit who settled here in the mid-6th century. His burial place is in the magnificent 11th-century crypt of the Stiftskirche (the parish church, which today is a Protestant church).

Marksburg ⑧

From 1117 this castle, which towers over the Rhine and the small town of Braubach, has been owned at different times by the von Braubachs and the powerful Epstein family. The Marksburg is the only castle along this stretch of the Rhine which has never been damaged.

Loreley ⑦

The Loreley Rock, onto which many boats have been smashed by the strong currents, has been a source of inspiration for many poets. A 19th-century legend tells of a beautiful blonde combing her hair and luring unlucky sailors to their deaths with her song.

Pfalzgrafenstein ④

In the middle of the Rhine River stands the proud and mighty fortress of Pfalzgrafenstein – one of the most beautifully situated castles in the Rhineland. Its origins date back to 1326, but its present shape is the result of Baroque refurbishments in the 17th–18th centuries.

Bacharach ⑤

The town has a unique complex of historic buildings, with fortified town walls, the church of St Peter, the ruins of the Gothic chapel of St Werner, and Burg Stahleck – the castle towering over the town which today houses a youth hostel.

Burg Sooneck ⑥

In the 13th century, Sooneck castle was the home of various robber knights. The fortress fell into ruin in the late 17th century, due to frequent raids by the French. In the 19th century it was bought by the Hohenzollerns, who rebuilt the castle in its original form.

Limburg

ms

ms

rg

rwesel *Kaub*

⑦

④

⑤

Lorch

⑥

Rüdesheim

Bingen

Kaiserslautern *Mannheim*

KEY

Motorway
Main road
Scenic route
River
☀ Viewpoint

Koblenz ⑨

THE NAME which the Romans gave to their camp in 9 BC – *castrum ad confluentas,* meaning the "camp at the confluence" – reflects the town's strategic importance, for it is here that the Mosel flows into the Rhine. From the Middle Ages until the 19th century, Koblenz was the seat of the powerful archbishop–electors of Trier. It was also the birthplace of Prince von Metternich, the 19th-century Austrian statesman. Today it is a modern metropolis which attracts many visitors, and is the main centre of the region's cultural life.

Romanesque twin-tower façade of the Basilika St Castor

🏛 Deutsches Eck
Ludwig-Museum im Deutsch-herrenhaus. 📞 *(0261) 30 40 40.* ⏰ *10:30am–5pm Tue–Sat, 11am–6pm Sun & public holidays.*
The "German corner" is the place where the Mosel flows into the Rhine. Here stands the enormous equestrian statue of Emperor Wilhelm I. Designed by Bruno Schmitz, it was erected in 1897, destroyed in World War II and replaced with a copy in 1993. The name refers to the complex of buildings known as Deutschherrenhaus belonging to the Order of Teutonic Knights. Only part of the three-wing residence of the Order's Commander, built in the early 14th century, has survived to this day. Following its refurbishment in 1992 the building now houses the Ludwig-Museum, with a collection of modern art (mainly German and French post-1945 artists) donated by Peter and Irene Ludwig.

🏛 Basilika St Castor
Kastorstraße 7.
The collegial church of St Castor was built in 817–36 on the initiative of the archbishop of Trier, on a site previously occupied by an early Christian church. The treaty of Verdun, which divided the Carolingian Empire between the three sons of Ludwig I the Pious, was signed here in 843. The present appearance of the church is the result of extensions from the 11th–13th centuries. Inside are beautiful wall epitaphs of the Trier archbishops Kuno von Falkenstein (1388) and Werner von Königstein (1418). Also noteworthy is the pulpit dating from 1625.

🏛 Florinsmarkt
Mittelrheinisches Museum
Florinsmarkt 15. 📞 *(0261) 129 25 02.* ⏰ *10:30am–5pm Tue–Sat, 11am–6pm Sun.*
This square takes its name from the Romanesque-Gothic church of St Florin, dating from the 12th and 14th centuries. The Mittelrheinisches Museum with its collection of archaeology and medieval art of the Central Rhine region occupies three historic buildings. The Kaufhaus, in the centre, dates from 1419–25 and 1724. The image of a horse-rider shows the robber baron Johann von Kobem, beheaded in 1536, who now sticks his tongue out at passers-by every half hour. To its right stands the late-Gothic Schöffenhaus, and to its left is the Baroque Bürresheimer Hof, from 1659–60.

The Renaissance Alte Burg, now housing archives and a library

♣ Alte Burg
Burgstraße 1.
In the Middle Ages, the powerful von Arken family had a fortified residence built for themselves in the north-western section of the Roman fortifications. In 1277 it was taken over by Heinrich von Finstingen, the archbishop of Trier, who ordered its extension. The fortress was to protect him from the citizens of Koblenz who were striving for independence. Successive archbishops continued with the conversion of the building, which acquired its final shape in the 17th century. The eastern Renaissance façade of the complex is particularly attractive. Today it houses the municipal archives and parts of the library.

The spur between the Mosel and the Rhine, called Deutsches Eck

⛪ Liebfrauenkirche

Florinspfaffengasse 14.
📞 (0261) 315 50.
🕐 8am–6pm Mon–Sat,
9am–12:30pm Sun.

At the highest point
in the old town
stands the
Romanesque church
of Our Dear Lady. Its
history dates back to
early Christian times,
but its present form
is the result of
remodelling work
carried out in
1182–1250. A triple-
nave basilica with galleries,
it has a twin-tower western
façade. The beautiful, elongated Gothic choir was added
in 1404–30.

♜ Kurfürstliches Schloss

Clemensplatz.

Not far from the bridge across
the Rhine stands the electoral
palace, an example of the
Rhineland's early Neo-Classical architecture. It was built,
and for a short time occupied,
by Clemens Wenzeslaus von
Sachsen, the last of Trier's
electors. Construction of the
castle began in 1777, to a
design prepared by Michael
d'Ixnard, and continued until

**Statue of the
Madonna in
Liebfrauenkirche**

1786, overseen by
Antoine François
Peyère the Younger.

🏛 Festung Ehrenbreitstein

Landesmuseum Koblenz
📞 (0261) 970 30.
🕐 15 Mar–15 Nov:
9:30am–5pm daily.

On the opposite side
of the Rhine stands the
mighty fortress of
Ehrenbreitstein, one
of the largest in the
world. A smaller fort-
ress was erected on
this site in 1000, and extended in subsequent years by
the archbishops and electors
of Trier, who lived in this
indomitable fortress from 1648
to 1786. Trier's holiest relic,
the Rock Christi (vestments
of Christ) was kept here. The
appearance of the fortress has
not changed much since Prus-

VISITORS' CHECKLIST

Road map B5. 🏠 109,300. 🚉
🏨 Bahnhofplatz 17 (0261-313
04); Jesuitenplatz (0261-13 09 20).
🎭 Internationale Musiktage (Mar/
Apr), Altstadtfest mit dem Fest
der Stadtteile (Jun/Jul), Koblenzer
Gauklerfest (Jul), Rhein in Flammen
(Aug), Schängelmarkt (Sep),
Koblenzer Mendelssohn-Tage
(autumn). Ⓦ www.koblenz.de

sian days. It offers splendid
views over Koblenz, the
Rhine and the Mosel. Today,
it is home to the **Landesmuseum Koblenz** (regional
museum) with an interesting
collection on the development of technology, and
to the **Rhein-Museum** with
hydrological collections. At
Wambachstraße 204, in the
same district, is the house
of Beethoven's mother.

The Classical façade of the Kurfürstliches Schloss

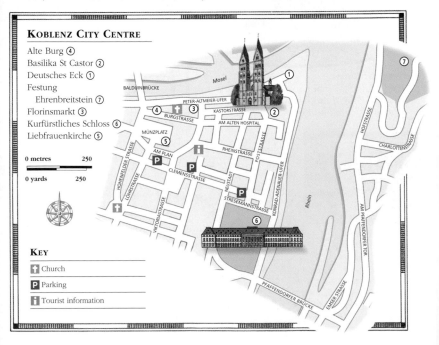

KOBLENZ CITY CENTRE

Alte Burg ④
Basilika St Castor ②
Deutsches Eck ①
Festung
   Ehrenbreitstein ⑦
Florinsmarkt ③
Kurfürstliches Schloss ⑥
Liebfrauenkirche ⑤

0 metres   250

0 yards   250

KEY

⛪ Church

🅿 Parking

ℹ Tourist information

Maria Laach ⑩

Capital of a vestibule column

A TRUE MASTERPIECE of German and European Romanesque architecture, the Maria Laach Abbey stands next to the Laacher See, a lake formed in the crater of an extinct volcano. Its construction started in 1093 at the behest of Heinrich II, who also lies buried here. Building continued from 1093 until 1220. Until secularization in 1802, the Abbey was the home of the Benedictines. Since 1892 the church has once again been resounding with Gregorian chants, which are sung here several times a day.

View from the West
The monumental western façade of the abbey consists of the semicircular apse, a massive, square 43-m (141-ft) tall central tower, and two slim 35-m (115-ft) tall flanking towers.

★ Tomb of Heinrich II
The tomb of the Palatine Heinrich II, who died in 1095, dates from about 1280. His effigy has been reproduced in a magnificent walnut wood block, which to this day has kept its original colours.

Löwenbrunnen
The lion fountain, which adorns the atrium, was made in 1928. It was modelled on the famous Alhambra fountain in Granada, Spain.

Main entrance

Detail from a Column Capital
The western door is surrounded by columns with interesting capitals. Carved figures can be seen, including that of a devil recording the sins of each entrant and others which are pulling each other's hair out.

The "Paradise", the courtyard, is meant to symbolize the Garden of Eden.

Church entrance

Mosaics
The interior is decorated with paintings and mosaics created over centuries by artists of the Beuron School. In the eastern apse is a mosaic of Christ the Ruler dating from 1911.

VISITORS' CHECKLIST

Road map B5. 🚌 6032 *from Niedermendig or Mayen, 6031 from Andernach.* ☎ *(02652) 590.* ⏰ *5:30am–8pm daily.* **Crypt** – *information by video show.* 🍴 🛍 🚻  W *www.maria-laach.de*

The church towers have arcaded galleries, typical of Romanesque style.

Stained-glass Windows
Three vast stained-glass windows in the eastern apse were made by a contemporary artist, W. Rupprecht, in 1956.

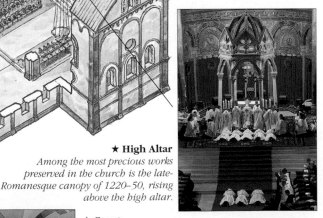

★ High Altar
Among the most precious works preserved in the church is the late-Romanesque canopy of 1220–50, rising above the high altar.

★ Crypt
The vaults of the exquisite early-Romanesque crypt are supported by austere square capitals. This is also the resting-place of Gilbert, the first abbot at Maria Laach.

STAR SIGHTS

★ Tomb of Heinrich II

★ High Altar

★ Crypt

HESSE

Hesse lies in *the very heart of present-day Germany. Scattered over the region are reminders of its former glory: Roman camps, Carolingian buildings, Romanesque churches and Gothic cathedrals with lofty spires. Territorial partitions, so typical of the former German Reich, brought about the blossoming of art and architecture during the Renaissance and the Baroque eras.*

A post-World War II creation, the borders of this federal state roughly approximate those of its 13th-century forerunner. For most of its history, Hesse was divided between Hesse-Darmstadt and Hesse-Kassel.

Today, when admiring the distinctive panorama of Frankfurt am Main – its towering banks and skyscrapers more reminiscent of New York's Manhattan than of a European metropolis – it is hard to believe that this was the birthplace of Goethe. The importance of this city extends far beyond Hesse: it is the financial centre of the European Union, and its annual Book Fair is the largest event of its kind in the world.

Darmstadt became famous as a centre for Jugendstil (Art Nouveau) early in the 20th century. Wiesbaden is the seat of Hesse's state government, and Marburg is one of the best-known university towns. In the 16th century, at the times of fierce religious feuds, the first Protestant university was built here. The Church of St Elizabeth is one of the earliest examples of Gothic architecture in the region. Lovers of modern art will know of Kassel – every five years it hosts the *documenta*, an exciting exhibition of artistic developments.

Hesse has much more to offer. The Waldecker Land, near Kassel, boasts the Eder lake and attractive health resorts. Eberbach in the picturesque Rheingau, the wine-growing area around Eltville, has a well-preserved former Cistercian abbey, which was used as a film setting.

Park and Baroque Orangery of the palace complex in Fulda

◁ **Frankfurt's skyscraper district, nicknamed "Mainhattan"**

Exploring Hesse

ELTVILLE, situated in the Rheingau, one of Germany's most important wine-producing regions, is famous for its Riesling wine. Frankfurt am Main, known around the world as a great financial and commercial centre, also has fantastic museums, drawing visitors with their outstanding art collections, while the International Book Fair is a true paradise for readers and bookworms. In the 19th century, wealthy socialites chose Bad Homburg as their favourite spa, while the romantic town of Marburg still has the lively atmosphere of a university town.

The Dom in Limburg, overlooking the Lahn river

The giant Niederwalddenkmal near Rüdesheim

SIGHTS AT A GLANCE

*Map labels: Paderborn, FRANKENBERG, Siegen, Siegen, MARBURG **6**, WESTERWALD, E41/45, 54, GIESSEN **7**, WETZLAR **8**, Cologne (Köln), 49, WEILBURG **9**, E451/5, E40, LIMBURG **10**, BAD NEUH..., BAD HOMBURG **11**, HANAU, KIEDRICH **14**, WIESBADEN **13**, **16**, FRANKFURT AM MAIN, **12** ELTVILLE, **15**, RÜDESHEIM, RÜSSELSHEIM, DARMSTADT **17**, LORSCH **18**, MICHELSTADT, E35/5, Heidelberg*

The Messeturm in the Frankfurt
fairgrounds, designed by Helmut Jahn

SEE ALSO

• *Where to Stay* pp488–90.

• *Where to Eat* pp517–19.

GETTING AROUND

The A7 motorway, cutting across Hesse
in a north–south direction, provides a
fast transport link. Starting from Hannover, it runs through Göttingen, Kassel
and Fulda to Würzburg in Bavaria. The
A4 runs from Dresden, via Weimar, to
Bad Hersfeld. From there visitors can
take the A7 or the A5, towards Gießen,
Bad Homburg, Frankfurt am Main and
onwards to Darmstadt and Heidelberg.
The fast ICE railway connects Kassel
and Frankfurt am Main with Basel (in
Switzerland), Stuttgart, Berlin and
Munich. Frankfurt am Main has one
of Europe's largest airports.

KEY

▬	Motorway
▬	Main road
▬	Scenic route
═	River
⚡	Viewpoint

Statue of the Brothers Grimm in Hanau

Kassel ❶

THE CULTURAL, scientific and commercial centre of northern Hesse, Kassel suffered severe damage during World War II due to the armaments industries based here, and much of the town has been rebuilt in functional 1950s style. Today, Kassel has become synonymous with one of the most important shows of contemporary art – *documenta* – held here every five years (the 12th documenta is scheduled for 2007). The town is equally famous for its outstanding collection of European art, housed in the splendid Schloss Wilhelmshöhe, as well as for its parks and gardens, especially the large forest-park adjoining the castle.

17th century cameo-decorated tureen in the Landesmuseum

🏛 Hessisches Landesmuseum
Brüder-Grimm-Platz 5. 【 (0561) 784 60. ◻ 10am–5pm Tue–Sun. ● 1 May, 24, 25, 31 Dec. 🖼 (free Fri.)

Outstanding items in the Neo-Baroque Hesse Regional Museum, built in 1910–13, are the astronomical instruments, originally installed in 1560 in a landgrave's castle, which no longer exists. The ethnographic section has displays of Hessian folk costumes and regional craft items.

The Landesmuseum also houses one of Europe's most unusual museums: the fascinating Tapetenmuseum (wallpaper museum). Established in 1923, the museum presents the history of wallpaper and the methods of its production around the world. The collection includes examples of leather wall coverings (cordovans) and wallpapers representing Secession and Art-Deco styles as well as the "world's literature on wallpaper". *Vues de Suisse* (views of Switzerland), dating from 1802, is one of the earliest examples of scenic wallpaper. It was printed using 95 different inks and 1,024 wooden blocks. Equally famous is the panoramic *Rénaud et Armide*, from the workshop of Joseph Dufours, printed in 1828 using 2,386 wooden blocks.

🏛 Neue Galerie
Schöne Aussicht 1. 【 (0561) 70 96 30. ◻ 10am–5pm Tue–Sun. ● 1 May, 24, 25 & 26 Dec. 🖼 (free Fri.)

The New Gallery, founded in 1976 and devoted to 19th- and 20th-century art, occupies a Neo-Classicist building from 1871–4. The main emphasis of the gallery's collection is on Romantic and Impressionist paintings. It includes canvases by artists such as Carl Schuch, Max Slevogt and Lovis Corinth.

The splendid collection of 20th-century paintings focuses on German Expressionism. An entire room is also devoted to the installations of the controversial sculptor and performance artist Joseph Beuys.

Wallpaper (1670–80), in the Tapetenmuseum

🏛 Brüder-Grimm-Museum
Schöne Aussicht 2. 【 (0561) 10 32 35. ◻ 10am–5pm daily. ● 1 Jan, Good Friday, 24, 25, 31 Dec. 🖼

Next to the New Gallery is the small Schloss Bellevue, built in 1714 by Paul du Ry. Although brothers Jacob and Wilhelm Grimm were born in Hanau, they lived in Kassel from 1798 until 1830, and in 1960 a museum devoted to the lives and work of the famous fairy-tale tellers and philologers was opened, containing the first editions of their most important works.

An illustration for Cinderella, one of the Grimm fairy-tales

🏛 Kunsthalle Fridericianum
Friedrichsplatz 18. 【 (0561) 707 27 20. ◻ 10am–6pm Wed & Fri–Sun, 10am–8pm Thu. 🖼

Königsplatz and Friedrichsplatz were designed by the court architect, Simon Louis du Ry. The northwestern side of the latter is occupied by the Neo-Classical Fridericianum, built by du Ry in 1769–76. Its founder, Landgrave Friedrich II, had always intended it to be a museum, and it became the second public museum (after the British Museum in London) to be built in Europe, and the first one on the European mainland. Since 1955, the Fridricianum has been the main venue for Kassel's multimedia contemporary art show – the *documenta*, which every five years takes over the entire city. An additional exhibition hall, the Documentahalle, was opened in 1992, in the nearby Staatstheater.

The Ottoneum, home of the first permanent theatre in Germany

Ottoneum

Steinweg 2. **Naturkundemuseum**
☎ (0561) 787 40 14. ⏱ 10am–
5pm Tue–Sun. 🎟
The Ottoneum (1604–5), built
for Landgrave Maurice the
Learned, was Germany's first
permanent theatre. Designed
by Wilhelm Vernukken and
remodelled in the late 17th
century by Paul du Ry, it was
converted into a natural history
museum in 1885.

Orangerie

An der Karlsaue 20c. ☎ (0561) 70 13
20. **Museum für Astronomie und
Technikgeschichte** ⏱ 10am–
5pm Tue–Sun. **Zeiss-Planetarium**
🎟 2pm Tue, Sat, 2 & 8pm Thu, 3pm
Wed, Fri, Sun. 🎟 (free Fri.)
The southern part of Kassel is
home to Karlsaue, a vast

palace and garden complex
named after its founder, Landgrave Karl. The site was
earlier occupied by a small
Renaissance Schloss (1568),
surrounded by a garden. In
1702–10 Pierre-Etienne Monnot built the large Orangery,
which now houses a museum
of astronomy and technology.
Monnot is also the creator of
Marmorbad, a bath pavilion
from 1722, while the kitchen
pavilion was designed by
Simon Louis du Ry in 1765.

Wilhelmshöhe

Gemäldegalerie Alter Meister.
Schloss Wilhelmshöhe. ☎ (0561)
937 77. ⏱ 10am–5pm Tue–Sun.
● 1 May, 24, 25, 31 Dec. 🎟
At the top of Wilhelmshöher
Allee, designed in 1781, stands
Wilhelmshöhe, a magnificent
palace and park. The palace
is situated along the axis of
the avenue that runs up the
hill, through a long forest
glade. The original intention
was to fill it with a series of
cascades, but only a few of
these were ever built. At the
top of the hill is the Octogon,
crowned with the statue of
Hercules, the symbol of the
town. The palace was
designed by Simon Louis du
Ry and Heinrich Christoph

Jussow and built in 1793–1801
for the Elector Wilhelm. Now
it houses the Gemäldegalerie
Alte Meister with its outstanding collection of European
masters including paintings
by Rubens, Titian, Rembrandt,
Dürer and Poussin. The large
and attractive park has many
pavilions and sculptures.

**Cascades, with Octogon and
Hercules statue, in Wilhelmshöhe**

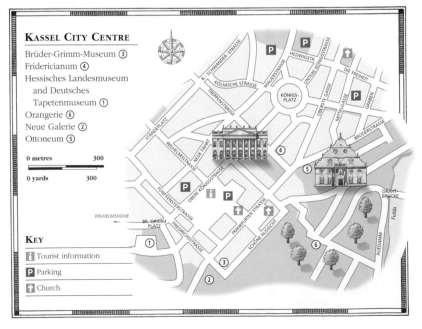

KASSEL CITY CENTRE

Brüder-Grimm-Museum ③
Fridericianum ④
Hessisches Landesmuseum
and Deutsches
Tapetenmuseum ①
Orangerie ⑥
Neue Galerie ②
Ottoneum ⑤

| 0 metres | 300 |
| 0 yards | 300 |

KEY

🛈 Tourist information

P Parking

✝ Church

Fritzlar ②

Road map C4. 🏛 *15,000.* 🚉 🚌
Kasseler Straße. 🛈 *Rathaus,
Zwischen den Krämen 5 (05622-98
86 43).* 🎭 *Pferdemarkt (Jul),
Stadtfest (Aug).*

THE BEAUTIFUL town of Fritzlar has preserved its original, nearly complete ring of
medieval walls with watch-
towers, bastions and over 450
half-timbered houses from
various periods. In the early
8th century, St Boniface, the
apostle of Germany, had the
holy oak of the Germanic god
Donar, which grew here, cut
down to build a Christian
chapel. In 724 he founded the
Benedictine **Dom** (abbey of
St Peter). In 1118 the original
church was replaced by a cruci-
form, vaulted basilica with a
triple-nave crypt, and this was
remodelled in the 13th and
14th centuries. Adjacent to the
church is a lovely 14th-cen-
tury ambulatory. The church
interior is rich in historic
treasures. The east wall of the
transept is decorated with
wall paintings from c.1320,
and the south nave includes a
Pietà (1300). The 14th-century
parish church of the Franciscan Order nearby has a lovely
painting of the Madonna, on
the northern wall of the choir.

In Fritzlar's picturesque old
town stands the **Rathaus**
(town hall), whose lower
floors date from the 12th
century, while the upper ones
were added in the 15th century. The exquisite **Hochzeitshaus** (wedding house),
in the street of the same
name, is a Renaissance half-
timbered house, built in
1580–90, which now houses a
museum. Another interesting
sight is the **Alte Brücke**, a
13th-century stone bridge
spanning the Eder River.

Relief of St Martin, on the walls of
the Rathaus in Fritzlar

Waldecker Land ③

THE WALDECKER LAND, situated west of Kassel, was
once an independent county and later, until
1929, a free state within the German Reich. Today
this region, with its Eder-Stausee (reservoir), is
one of the most attractive tourist regions in
Germany. The wooded hills provide a perfect
setting for long rambles, the roads and tracks
are ideally suited for cycling tours and the
rivers and lakes permit visitors to practise
a wide variety of watersports.

Korbach ②
Korbach is a beautiful
old town with many
half-timbered houses.
Worth seeing are the
Gothic church of St
Kilian with its inter-
esting 14th-century
pulpit, and the
church of St Nicho-
las, with the
Baroque tomb of
Georg Friedrich
von Waldeck
(1692).

Frankenberg ⑤
This small town is brimming
with half-timbered houses.
The town hall (1509), also
half-timbered, has humorous
polychrome wood-carvings.
The Gothic Marienkirche with
its 15th-century wall paintings
is also worth visiting.

0 km   10

0 miles   10

KEY

▦	Motorway
▬	Suggested route
▦	Scenic road
═	Other road
⌇	River, lake
☀	Viewpoint

Bad Arolsen ①

Both the sculptor Christian Daniel Rach and the painter Wilhelm von Kaulbach were born in this spa town, and they are commemorated in two museums. The star attraction, however, is the Baroque castle (1713–28) of the von Waldeck family, designed by Julius Ludwig Rothweil.

Waldeck ③

The old fortress of Waldeck is now a hotel. It offers superb views over the Eder-Stausee reservoir and the small town of Waldeck with its 18th-century half-timbered houses. The Gothic town church has a high altar (c.1500), devoted to the Virgin Mary.

TIPS FOR VISITORS

Length of route: *110 km (68 miles).*
Stopping-off points: *There are many good cafés and restaurants in every town along the route.*
Further attractions: *Cruises and ferries run on the Edersee. A viewing platform on top of the Peterskopf hill, near Hemfurth, can be reached by electric train.*

Bad Wildungen ④

This popular spa town has many charming half-timbered houses. The church has a priceless altar painted with scenes of the Passion by Konrad von Soest (1403).

Projecting gate of the Baroque Stadtschloss in Fulda

Fulda ❹

Road map C5. 🏛 60,000. 🚊 ℹ
Bonifatiusplatz 1 (0661-1 02 18 14).

FULDA'S HISTORY began in March 744, when Sturmius, a pupil of St Boniface, laid the foundation stone for the Benedictine abbey. Ten years later the body of St Boniface, who had been murdered by Frisian pagans, was laid to rest here. The town, which grew around the abbey, experienced its heyday during the Baroque period, and a new Baroque building, designed by Johann Dientzen-hofer, was built in 1704–12 on the foundations of the old abbey. The **Dom St Salvator und Bonifatius** is a triple-nave basilica with a dome above the nave intersection, a monumental eastern façade and a shrine with the saint's relics under the high altar, in the western section.

Opposite the cathedral stands the **Stadtschloss** (former episcopal palace), a shoe-shaped edifice, built by Johann Dientzenhofer and Andreas Gallasini, with richly decorated Baroque and Rococo interiors. Particularly noteworthy are the Kaisersaal (imperial hall) on the ground floor, the magnificent Mond-saal (moon chamber, formerly the ballroom) and the charming Rococo-style Spiegelsaal (chamber of mirrors) on the first floor. Today, some of the palace chambers hold an impressive collection of porcelain. The palace complex includes a large landscaped garden and an orangery, which houses a café.

THE BROTHERS GRIMM

The two brothers are known around the world as collectors of German folk-tales, which were first published in 1812 and sub-sequently translated into most languages. Fairy-tales such as *Hänsel and Gretel*, *Cinderella* and *Little Red Riding Hood* have been favourites for generations of children. Above all, however, the brothers were scholars. In his *German Grammar*, published in 1819, Jacob Grimm proved that all German dialects sprang from a common origin, and thus laid the foundations of German philology. The Grimm Brothers also initiated the publication of the *Dictionary of the German Language*.

To the north of the Dom stands the round **Michaels-kirche**, a Carolingian chapel dating from 822, one of the oldest church buildings in Germany. Inside the church has a ring of eight columns and a crypt supported by a single column. The circular gallery, the long side nave and the western tower are 11th-century additions.

Other interesting sights in Fulda are the Baroque **Heilig-Geist-Kirche** (church of the Holy Spirit), built in 1729–33 by Andreas Gallasini, and the late-18th century parish church of St Blasius. In the 8th century, five abbeys were established on the four hills surrounding the town. On Petersberg stands the former Benedictine **Peterskirche**, from the 9th–15th centuries, with a Carolingian crypt.

Inside the church is one of Germany's oldest wall paintings, dating from 836–47.

Alsfeld ❺

Road map C4. 🏛 18,000. 🚊 ℹ
Am Markt 13 (06631-9 11 02 43).
🎭 *Pfingstfest (Whitsun), Akademischer Marktfrühschoppen (May), Stadt- und Heimatfest (Aug), Historischer Markt (Sep).*

THE FIRST historic records of Alsfeld date from the late 9th century. Today the town attracts visitors with its pretty old town with numerous 16th–17th century half-tim-bered houses. On the eastern side of the town square stands a grand late-Gothic **Rathaus** (town hall), built in 1512–16, and one of the finest examples of half-timbered structures

Half-timbered houses in Alsfeld

anywhere in Germany. Other interesting features in the market square are the stone **Weinhaus**, with its distinctive stepped gable (1538), and the Renaissance **Hochzeitshaus** (wedding house), dating from 1565. Oposite the town hall stands the **Stumpfhaus** (1609), its façade beautifully decorated with wood carvings and paintings. From the town hall runs the picturesque Fulder Gasse, with the Gothic parish church **Walpurgiskirche** (13th–15th centuries), which has 15th-century wall paintings. In Rossmarkt stands the former Augustian **Dreifaltigkeitskirche** (church of the Holy Trinity), from the 13th–15th centuries. It was from here that in 1522 the monk Tilemann Schnabel began to spread the Reformation in Alsfeld. The 18th-century **castle** in Altenburg, 2km (1 mile) from Alsfeld, enjoys a hilltop position.

Detail on the Rathaus, in Marburg

Marburg ⑥

Road map C4. 🏠 80,000. 🚉
ℹ️ *Pilgrimstein 26 (06421-991 20).*
🎭 *Maieinsingen (30 Apr) Marktfrühschoppen (Jul), 3-Tage Marburg (Jul), Elisabethmarkt (Oct), Weihnachtsmarkt (Dec).*

WHEN IN 1248 the county of Hesse broke away from Thuringia, Marburg became one of the most important seats of the landgraves. The first landgrave, Heinrich II, lived in the castle that towers over the town. The town's history is inseparably linked with the 13th-century figure of Elisabeth of Thuringia, wife of Ludwig IV, who devoted her life to the poor and died here. In 1527, Philipp the Magnanimous founded the first Protestant university in the Reich at Marburg. He also instigated the first Marburg Colloquy in 1529, to unify the Protestant faith. The "articles" presented by Martin Luther to Melanchthon and Zwingli later formed the basis for the Augsburg

Creed. Today, Marburg is a picturesque university town. A tour of the town should start from the **Elisabethkirche**, at the bottom of the hill. Built in 1235–83, it is (after Trier) Germany's second purely Gothic church. There is a large set of Gothic altars from the early 16th century, including the altars of St Elisabeth (1513) and of the Holy Family (1511). Next to the north choir entrance stands the statue of St Elisabeth with a model of the church (1480). The choir contains the tomb of the Saint, positioned under the baldachin (c.1280). The vestry houses the greatest treasure, the reliquary of St Elisabeth (1235–49). In the south choir is an interesting group of monuments to the Hessian landgraves, from the 13th–16th centuries.

The **Universitätsmuseum für Bildende Kunst** holds a collection of paintings produced after 1500, with a predominance of 19th- and 20th-century German artists. Around the market square stands a group of historic, half-timbered houses from the 14th–17th centuries. Particularly pretty are the Sonne (sun, No. 14), the Stiefel (boot, No. 17) and the house at No. 19. The Steinhaus (stone house, No. 18), built in 1318, is the oldest in Marburg, along with that at No. 13 Hirschgasse. At No. 16 Markt is the Renaissance

The Gothic portal of the Elisabethkirche in Marburg

Künstlerhaus (artists' house). High above the town (287 m/942 ft above the sea) towers the **Landgrafenschloss**, the landgraves' castle dating from the 10th–16th centuries. The two-storey Fürstenbau (dukes' building) has a large ducal chamber, dating from 1330. The Wilhelmsbau was built in 1492–8. It houses a museum of sacral art with mementos of the debate between Luther, Zwingli and Melanchthon.

🏛 **Elisabethkirche**
Elisabethstraße. 📞 *(06421) 655 73.*
🕐 *Apr–Oct: 9am–6pm; Nov–Feb: 10am–4pm.*

🏛 **Universitätsmuseum für Bildende Kunst**
Biegenstraße 11. 📞 *(06421) 282 54 31.* 🕐 *11am–1pm & 2–5pm Tue–Sun.*

🏛 **Landgrafenschloss und Universitätsmuseum für Kulturgeschichte im Wilhelmsbau**
Schloss 1. 📞 *(06421) 282 58 71.* 🕐 *Apr–Oct: 10am–6pm Tue–Sun; Nov–Mar: 11am–5pm Tue–Sun.*

The Alte Universität (old university) in Marburg

Gießen ❼

Road map C4. 🏛 *72,000.* 🚉 🛈
Berliner Platz 2 (0641-194 33).

GIESSEN was granted town status in 1248, and in 1607 it acquired its university. In Brandplatz stands the partially reconstructed **Altes Schloss** (old palace), dating from the 14th–15th centuries. Now the home of the Oberhessisches Museum, it holds a large collection of art dating from the Gothic period to today.

The **Botanischer Garten** is one of Germany's oldest botanical gardens, established in 1609 for the purposes of scientific research. To the north of it stands the **Neues Schloss** (new palace), built in 1533–9 for Landgrave Philipp the Magnanimous. It miraculously escaped damage when the town was bombed in 1944. The Wallenfelssches Haus nearby houses interesting ethnological collections. The only remaining part of the Gothic **Pfarrkirche St Pankratius**, which was almost completely destroyed in 1944, is its tower, dating from 1500.

At No. 2 Georg-Schlosser-Straße is the **Burgmannenhaus**, an attractive half-timbered mansion dating from the 14th century.

Portal of the Altes Schloss in Gießen

Along with the old stable block in Dammstraße, it is the only half-timbered building that has survived to this day.

Wetzlar ❽

Road map C5. 🏛 *54,000.* 🚉
🛈 *Domplatz 8 (06441-993 38).*

OCCUPYING A picturesque spot on the banks of the Lahn river, Wetzlar is overlooked by the ruins of the 12th-century **Kalsmunt** fortress. It was built for the Emperor Friedrich I Barbarossa (1122–90). Only parts of the tower remain intact. The **Dom** (Collegiate Church of St Mary) was begun in 897 but by the late 15th century had only been partly completed. The splendid western double portal has remained unusable for the last 500 years – although the iconography of the tympanum was finished, the stairs leading to the entrance were never built. If they had been built, they would have led not to the church's nave, but to a courtyard. Wetzlar's Dom is a rare, perhaps even unique surviving example of the typical appearance of most European churches in the mid-15th century. Inside the church are several interesting historic artifacts, including the statue of the *Madonna on the Moon Crescent* (mid-15th century) and a late-Renaissance *Crucifixion.*

In 1772, the young Johann Wolfgang von Goethe spent three months in Wetzlar working as an apprentice at the court of appeal. During this time he fell in love with Charlotte Buff, called Lotte, who was engaged to one of Goethe's friends. The **Lottehaus**, her former home, has a collection of items relating to Goethe and Lotte. It was the suicide of a friend, Karl Wilhelm Jerusalem, who lived in the 18th-century **Jerusalemhaus** at No. 5 Schillerplatz, that inspired Goethe to write his tragic novel, *The Sorrows of Young Werther* (1774). Jerusalem had suffered unrequited love, just like Goethe. The novel, which was published two years later, made Goethe famous around Europe, but it also unwittingly led many young men to commit suicide.

The Gothic south tower of the Dom in Wetzlar

Weilburg ❾

Road map B5. 🏛 *13,500.* 🚉
🛈 *Mauerstraße 6 (06471-76 71).*

WEILBURG enjoys a particularly scenic location in a bend of the Lahn River. The town is dominated by the majestic Renaissance–Baroque **Schloss** of the Nassau-Weilburg family. The monumental castle complex was created in stages. Its main section dates from the Renaissance era; the east wing was built in 1533–9; the south and west wings in 1540–48 and the west tower in 1567. The northern part of the palace was completed in 1570–73. In the late-17th century, various Baroque additions were made, mainly to the interior of the castle. The 16th-century furnishings show the rich ornamentation typical of the German Renaissance. The **Obere Orangerie** (upper orangery), built in 1703–5 and today used for temporary exhibitions, and the **Hofkirche** (castle church), dating from 1707–13, are the work of Ludwig Rothweil. Terraces lead from the castle

to the Lahn river, which is crossed by an 18th-century stone bridge. In Frankfurtstraße stands the **Heiliggrabkapelle** (Chapel of the Holy Sepulchre), dating from 1505.

Limburg ⑩

Road map B5. 🏠 *31,000.* 🚉
🛈 *Hospitalstraße 2 (06431-61 66).*

LIMBURG'S history dates back to the 8th century. In 1821, the town became the see of a newly created diocese.

The **Dom** (collegiate cathedral church of St George) towers high above the Lahn river. This monumental building, whose style combines late-Romanesque and early French-Gothic, was erected in 1190–1250. Its well-proportioned interior contains a rich variety of historic artifacts, including some 13th-century wall paintings in the presbytery and the transept, a font dating from the same period and the tombstone of Konrad Kurzbold, who founded the first church on this site.

To the south of the Dom stands the **Burg** (castle), an irregular structure built in the 13th–16th centuries. It houses the interesting **Diözesanmuseum** (Diocese museum).

Limburg has many original examples of beautiful half-timbered buildings. The houses at No. 1 Römerstraße, No. 6 Kolpingstraße, No. 4 Kleine Rütsche and No. 11

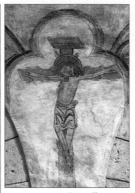

Romanesque–Gothic wall paintings in the Dom in Limburg

Kornmarkt date from the last decade of the 13th century. Near the 14th-century **Alte Lahnbrücke** (old Lahn bridge), with its defensive towers, stands a mansion belonging to the Cistercians of Eberbach. The post-Franciscan Sebastiankirche (church of St Sebastian) dates from the 14th and 18th centuries.

Bad Homburg ⑪

Road map C5. 🏠 *52,000.* 🚉
🛈 *Kurhaus, Louisenstraße 58 (06172-17 81 10).* 🎭 *Fugato (Sep every two years – the next is in 2005).*

BAD HOMBURG grew up around a fortress whose earliest records date back to 1180. Friedrich II von Hessen-Homburg initiated the conversion of the medieval castle into the **Schloss**, a Baroque palace built in 1678–86. It features a magnificent Festsaal (ballroom) and Spiegelkabinett (hall of mirrors). The only part of the former complex remaining today is the 14th-century Weißer Turm (white tower). Following the annexation of Hesse-Homburg by Prussia in 1866, the palace became the favourite summer residence of the royal (and, from 1871, of the imperial) family.

Along with Baden-Baden and Wiesbaden, Homburg was one of Germany's most fashionable spas, and today the town reflects its former splendour. The **Kurpark**, a landscaped park established in 1854–67, was designed by Peter Joseph Lenné.

The **Spielbank** (1838), in Brunnenallee claims to be the oldest casino in the world. Built in 1887–90, the **Kaiser-Wilhelm-Bad** is still used as the main bath complex for therapeutic treatments. An Orthodox chapel, designed by Leonti Nikolayevich Benois for the Russian Orthodox nobility, was finished in 1899.

ENVIRONS: Saalburg, 7 km (4 miles) to the northwest, has a Roman fortress, which was completely reconstructed in 1898–1901. The fortress formed part of the *limes*, the fortified border that separated the Roman Empire from its Germanic neighbours in the 1st to 3rd century AD.

The grand edifice of the Kaiser-Wilhelm-Bad in the Kurpark, Bad Homburg

Eltville ⑫

Road map B5. 🏃 *17,000.* 🚉 **ℹ**
Schmittstr. 2 (06123-90 98 0). 📷
Biedermeier- und Sektfest (Jul).

IN THE 2nd century, the area
that is now the old town
was a Roman *latifundium,* a
large agricultural estate. In
1332, Eltville was granted
town status. Part of the Mainz
diocese, it is today known for
its excellent sparkling wine.

In 1337–45 the **Burg**
(castle) was extended at the
request of Archbishop Heinrich von Virneburg. The east
wing of the castle was added
in 1682–3 by Giovanni Angelo
Barell. The only part of it
remaining today is the five-
storey residential tower; the
rest of the building is a picturesque ruin. In the tower
are original 14th-century wall
paintings and friezes.

The twin-naved **Pfarrkirche
St Peter und St Paul** (parish
church) was built in
1350–1430. The vestibule has
well-preserved wall
paintings (1405)
showing scenes
from the Last
Judgement. The
town boasts
several attractive
mansions,
including Hof
Langenwerth
von Simmern
(1773), Stock-
heimer Hof (1550) and
Gräflich-Eltzscher Hof
(16th–17th century).

**Crest of the Hessische Staats-
weingüter-Vinothek, in Eltville**

Wiesbaden ⑬

Road map C5. 🏃 *270,000.* 🚉
ℹ *Markstr. 6 (0611-172 97 80).*
📷 *Internationale Maifestspiele (May),
Theatrium (Jun).*

WIESBADEN is the modern
capital of Hesse. Highly
valued as a spa by the
Romans, who exploited the
healing properties of its
waters, the town grew from
a small settlement known as
aquae mattiacorum after the
Germanic tribe of the Mattiacs.
In 1774 the Nassau-Usingen
family chose Wiesbaden as
their residence. This, as well
as the subsequent rapid

**The Baroque Biebrich Palace,
south of Wiesbaden**

growth of the town as a spa
resort in the 19th century, laid
the foundations for its lasting
prosperity. Today, the town is
still dominated by large-scale
developments carried out in
the spirit and style of Classi-
cism and Historicism.

The **Stadtschloss** (municipal castle), today the seat of
the state parliament, was built
in 1835–41. In Schlossplatz
the Neo-Renaissance **Marktkirche,** built in 1853–62,
soars above the town's
other buildings.
In front of the
church stands a
statue of Wilhelm
I the Great von
Nassau-Oranien.
The oldest
building in the
town is the
Altes Rathaus
(old town hall),
dating from 1610. In Wilhelmstraße is the imposing Neo-
Renaissance and Neo-Baroque
Hessisches Staatstheater
(state theatre). It was built in
1892–4 for Kaiser Wilhelm II
to the designs of the theatre

architects Fellner and Helmer.
Adjacent to the Marktkirche is
the attractive Kurhauskolon-
nade (spa house colonnade).
It was erected in 1825 and is
the longest colonnade in
Europe. The early 20th-century
Kurhaus (spa house) itself,
with its grand façade and
portico, is the work of Friedrich Thiersch. Inside is the
original **Spielbank** (casino),
where Fyodor Dostoyevsky
and Richard Wagner tried
their luck at the tables.

To the south of the town
centre stands **Schloss Biebrich,** where the counts von
Nassau-Usingen resided until
the early 19th century, when
they moved to the newly built
palace in the town centre.
The Schloss was built in
stages during the 18th century. The north pavilion was
built first, in 1700, followed
nine years later by the south
pavilion. The wings, which
join the two pavilions, and
the central rotunda were
added during the first two
decades of the 18th century.
Finally, the two external
wings were added in 1734–44,
creating an overall horseshoe
layout. The interior is richly
furnished, predominantly in
Baroque-Rococo style.

On the northern outskirts of
the town is a large hill, the
Neroberg, whose summit can
be reached by funicular railway. At the top is the so-
called **Griechische Kapelle**
(Greek chapel). Built in 1847–
55 by Philipp Hoffmann, it
served as a mausoleum for
Princess Elisabeth von Nassau,
the niece of Alexander I Tsar of
Russia, who died young.

The attractive façade of Hessisches Staatstheater in Wiesbaden

The ornate Gothic portal of Pfarrkirche St Valentin, in Kiedrich

Kiedrich ⓮

Road map B5. 🏠 *3,400.* 🚉
🅷 *Markstr. 27 (06123-90 50 11).*

THE EARLIEST recorded mention of Kiedrich was in the mid-10th century, in a document produced by the Archbishop Friedrich of Mainz. One of the town's main attractions is the **Pfarrkirche St Valentin**, a gem of Gothic architecture. The church was built in stages, beginning with the main hall (1380–90). The west tower was added in the early 15th century and the light, lofty choir in 1451–81. Some time later the central nave was raised to the level of the choir, creating a row of galleries above the aisles, and at the same time the magnificent star vaults were created. The whole project was financed from donations made by countless pilgrims who came to pray to the relics of St Valentine, kept here since 1454. A statue of the saint adorns the western portal. The early 15th-century tympanum depicts the *Annunciation* (on the left) and the *Coronation of the Virgin Mary* (on the right);

above is an image of *God the Father giving His Blessing*, with two archangels playing musical instruments. Inside, the church harbours an incredible wealth of ancient art treasures. The high altar and St Catherine's altar in the south aisle date from the late-Renaissance period. The magnificent Gothic stalls were created in 1510, while the church organ is one of the oldest in Germany, with pipes made in 1310. Next to the parish church stands a late-Gothic, two-storey funeral chapel built in 1445.

Kiedrich has several interesting old mansion houses, such as the Schwalbacher Hof (1732). The **Rathaus** (town hall) is evocative of the late-Gothic style, although it was built much later (1585–6).

ENVIRONS: Five km (3 miles) west of Kiedrich, in Oestrich, is **Kloster Eberbach**, a former Cistercian abbey. This vast complex, built between the 12th and 14th centuries, was once home to nearly 300 monks and is one of the best-preserved medieval monasteries in Germany. The church interior provided the setting for some of the scenes in the film *The Name of the Rose*, based on the novel by Umberto Eco. The Cistercians used to have their own vineyards here, and today the abbey buildings are used by

the Hessian Wine Co-operative to press, ferment, store and sell Eberbacher Steinberg, a famous white Rheingau wine.

A short way to the west, in **Winkel**, stands the Baroque castle of Reichardshausen, which in the early 19th century was the home of Princess Luise von Nassau.

🏠 **Kloster Eberbach** ☎ *(06723) 91 78 0.* ◻ *Apr–Oct: 10am–6pm daily; Nov–Mar: 11am–5pm daily.* 🖼

Rüdesheim ⓯

Road map B5. 🏠 *10,000.* 🚉
🅷 *Geisenheimerstr. 22 (06722-194 33).* 🎆 *Fireworks (Jul), Weinfest (Aug).*

RÜDESHEIM, enjoying a picturesque location on the banks of the Rhine, has a long history going back to Roman times. The town is famous for its main street, the **Drosselgasse**, which is lined with countless wine bars and shops. There are also the remains of three castles: the **Boosenburg**, the **Vorderburg** and the 12th-century **Brömserburg**. The Brömserburg's keep today houses a wine museum.

Rüdesheim also has several historic mansions, including the half-timbered Brömserhof (1559) with a collection of musical instruments, and the early 16th-century Klunkhardshof. Above the town towers the **Niederwalddenkmal**, a statue of Germania, 10.5 m (34 ft) high, built to commemorate victory in the Franco-Prussian War of 1870–71, which resulted in German unification. The monument affords excellent views of Bingen and the Rhine valley.

Gabled and half-timbered houses in Drosselgasse, in Rüdesheim

Frankfurt am Main ⑯

FRANKFURT, nicknamed "Mainhattan" and "Chicago am Main" because of its skyscrapers, is one of the main economic and cultural centres of both Germany and Europe. The headquarters of many major banks and newspaper publishers are based here, including those of the *Frankfurter Allgemeine Zeitung*, one of Europe's most influential newspapers. The city's International Book Fair is the world's largest event of its kind. Goethe was born in Frankfurt, and the Johann-Wolfgang-Goethe-Universität is one of Germany's most famous universities. The city also boasts magnificent art collections.

The Neo-Renaissance façade of the Alte Oper

🎭 Alte Oper

Opernplatz 8. 📞 (069) 134 04 00.
The monumental old opera house stands near the Stock Exchange. Built in 1872–80, it was completely burned down during World War II. Subsequently rebuilt, it is today used as a conference centre. Its façade and decorations are a fine imitation of the Italian Renaissance style.

🏛 Eschenheimer Turm

Große Eschenheimer Straße
The Eschenheimer Turm, at the corner of Hochstraße, presents a silhouette typical of old Frankfurt. A relic of the medieval town's fortifications, it was designed by Klaus Mengoz; construction began in 1400 and was completed in 1428 by Madern Gerthener. The façade of the tower features

Putti with model ship, at the front of the Börse

many attractive bay windows; it also has two reliefs depicting eagles, the symbol of the German empire and the city of Frankfurt.

🏛 Börse

Börsenplatz.
According to historical records, local merchants founded the town's first Stock Exchange in 1558. The new building, designed by Heinrich Burnitz and Oskar Sommer, was erected in 1864–79. It has been used again by stockbrokers since 1957, and is open to the public. Like the old opera house, the stock exchange is designed in Neo-Renaissance style.

🏛 Hauptwache

An der Hauptwache.
Built in 1730, the Hauptwache was originally a guardhouse. Later it was turned into a prison. Dismantled stone by stone during the construction of the town's underground system, it was reassembled in its original form following the completion of the project. Since 1904 the Hauptwache has been a chic café and a popular meeting place.

🏛 Goethehaus

Großer Hirschgraben 23. 📞 (069) 13 88 00. ⏰ Apr–Sep: 9am–6pm Mon–Fri, 10am–4pm Sat & Sun; Oct–Mar: 9am–4pm Mon–Fri, 10am–4pm Sat & Sun. 📷
Southwest of the Hauptwache is Johann Wolfgang Goethe's family home. The great German poet, novelist and dramatist was born here on 28 August 1749. The house, along with many other buildings in Frankfurt, was totally destroyed in World War II, but later lovingly restored. Its interior was reconstructed to represent the style typical of the mid- to late- 18th century. Goethe lived in this house until 1775, when he moved to Weimar. The desk at which he wrote his early works, including the first versions of *Götz von Berlichingen* (1771) and *Egmont* (1774), has been preserved.

The adjacent building now houses the Goethemuseum. Opened in 1997, the museum recreates the atmosphere of the 1750–1830 period, and holds a collection of items related to the writer. There is an excellent library, which contains some of his writings.

The distinctive Neo-Classical rotunda of the Paulskirche

Portal of the Goethehaus, with the ancestral family crest

⛪ Paulskirche

Paulsplatz. ☎ (069) 21 23 85 89.
🕐 10am–5pm daily.

The distinctive Neo-Classical rotunda of the church was begun in 1786 but not completed until 1833, due to continuous hostilities with France. Today, however, this building is no longer thought of, or indeed used as, a church. After the first, albeit ill-fated, German National Assembly met here following the revolutionary upheavals of 1848–9, the church became a symbol of republican and liberal Germany. The Paulskirche now serves as a venue for many important events. Each year the awards ceremony for the prestigious German Publishers' Peace Prize takes place here.

🏛 Römerberg

Located in the centre of Frankfurt's old town, this square contains the Gerechtigkeitsbrunnen (fountain of justice). Its highlight, however, is the **Römer** (literally the Roman). So-called after the remains of ancient settlements, it is a complex of 15th- to 18th-century houses, including the Altes Rathaus (old town hall), which were rebuilt after World War II. Opposite is a group of half-timbered houses, commonly referred to as Ostzeile. The Steinernes Haus (stone house) was originally built in 1464 for a Cologne silk merchant. Recently reconstructed, it is now the home of the Frankfurter Kunstverein (artists' league).

VISITORS' CHECKLIST

Road map C5. 🏙 660,000. ℹ
Hauptbahnhof (069-21 23 88 00);
Am Römerberg (069-21 23 88 00).
🎭 Dippemesse (spring, autumn),
Wäldchestag (Whitsun), Kunsthandwerk Heute (May/Jun), Mainfest (Aug), Book Fair (Oct), Christkindlmarkt (Dec). 🅆 www.frankfurt.de

The Ostzeile on the Römerberg, one of the symbols of Frankfurt

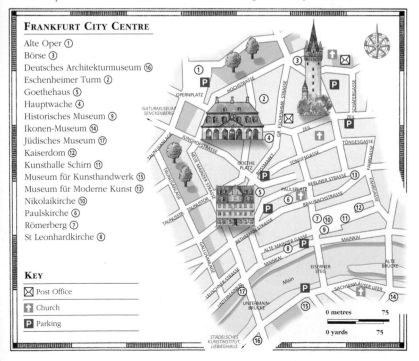

FRANKFURT CITY CENTRE

KEY

⊠ Post Office

✝ Church

🅿 Parking

0 metres 75
0 yards 75

🏛 Jüdisches Museum

Untermainkai 14–15. ☎ *(069) 21 23 50 00.* ○ *10am–5pm Tue & Thu–Sun, 10am–8pm Wed.* ✎

The Jewish community of Frankfurt was the second largest in Germany, after that of Berlin. This museum, in the former Rothschild Palace, documents the rich cultural heritage of Frankfurt's Jews.

⛪ St Leonhardkirche

Alte Mainzer Gasse.

Close to the banks of the Main stands the church of St Leonhard, a fine example of Gothic and Romanesque architecture. A five-naved hall-church with an elongated choir, it was built in stages in the 13th and 15th centuries. Inside are many treasures, including at the front of the main nave a copy of Leonardo da Vinci's *Last Supper* by Hans Holbein the Elder, from 1501. Next to it is St Mary's altar, created by master craftsmen from Antwerp in 1515–20. On the north wall of the choir visitors can see a fresco depicting the *Tree of Life and the Apostles* (1536) by Hans Dietz.

🏛 Historisches Museum

Saalgasse 19. ☎ *(069) 21 23 55 99.* ○ *10am–5pm Tue, Thu–Sat, 4–8pm Wed, 1–5pm Sun.* ✎

The new building housing the history museum was finished in 1972. The museum has an interesting display of items relating to Frankfurt's history, including a fascinating model of the medieval town, a collection of local prehistoric finds and several decorative

The early-Gothic Alte Nikolaikirche, in Frankfurt's Römerberg

architectural fragments from buildings that were destroyed during World War II.

The adjacent building is the Saalhof, which dates back to the time of the Emperor Friedrich I Barbarossa (1122–90). In 1333, the building passed into private hands and from then on it frequently changed its appearance.

⛪ Alte Nikolaikirche

Römerberg.

The twin-naved church of St Nicholas, also known as Alte Nikolaikirche, was consecrated in 1290. Used as a court church until the late 15th century, it now serves a Lutheran congregation. Popular attractions are its many statues of St Nicholas (Santa Claus) and the 40-bell carillon, which twice a day plays German folk songs.

🏛 Kunsthalle Schirn

Römerberg. ☎ *(069) 299 88 20.* ○ *10am–7pm Fri–Sun & Tue, 10am–10pm Wed & Thu.* ✎

One of Europe's most prestigious exhibition buildings, the Kunsthalle opened in 1986. It hosts temporary art exhibitions featuring archaeological themes and the work of old masters and contemporary artists.

⛪ Kaiserdom

Domplatz 14. ☎ *(069) 297 03 20.* ○ *9am–noon, 2:30–6pm daily; 2:30–6pm Fri.* ✎ *3pm daily.*
Dommuseum ☎ *(069) 13 37 61 86.* ○ *10am–5pm Tue–Fri, 11am–5pm Sat & Sun.*

Near the archaeological park, where the ruins of a Carolingian fortress have been unearthed, stands the imperial cathedral, used for the coronation of German kings from 1356, and of Holy Roman Emperors from 1562. The cathedral, dedicated to St Bartholomew and Charlemagne, was built during the 13th, 14th and 15th centuries, on the site of a Carolingian chapel. It has several priceless masterpieces of Gothic art, including the magnificent 15th-century Maria-Schlaf-Altar and a high altar dating from the second half of the 15th century. The choir has original 14th-century stalls; above these there is a fresco painted in 1427 depicts scenes from the life of the cathedral's patron saint, Bartholomew.

The Dom's huge tower affords magnificent views of the town. In the cloisters is the Dommuseum with an interesting collection of liturgical objects, sacred art and precious artifacts.

🏛 Museum für Moderne Kunst

Domstraße 10. ☎ *(069) 21 23 04 47.* ○ *10am–5pm Tue & Thu–Sun, 10am–8pm Wed.* ✎

The modern art museum occupies a building that looks like a slice of cake. It was designed by Hans Hollein in 1989–92. The museum's collection represents all the major artistic trends from the 1960s until the present day, and includes works by Roy Lichtenstein, Andy Warhol

The magnificent late-Gothic high altar in the Kaiserdom

Hollein's modern design, housing the Museum für Moderne Kunst

and Claes Oldenburg. Temporary exhibitions held here focus on multi-media shows, incorporating photography and video art.

♦ Ikonen-Museum
Brückenstraße 3–7. *(069) 21 23 62 62.* ○ *10am–1pm daily, 1:30–5pm Tue & Thu–Sun, 10am–8pm Wed.*
The museum of icons holds an extensive collection of Russian-Orthodox icons from the 16th–19th centuries. It is housed in the Deutschordens-haus, originally built in 1709–15 by Maximilian von Welsch for the Order of the Teutonic Knights. The present building is a faithful copy of the earlier Baroque three-wing structure destroyed in World War II. Inside is the 14th-century Teutonic Church of St Mary, with original altars and 14th- to 17th-century wall paintings.

🏛 Museum für Angewandte Kunst
Schaumainkai 17. *(069) 21 23 40 37.* ○ *10am–8pm Tue–Sun.*
The museum of applied arts was opened in 1983, in a building designed by Richard Meier. He used a Biedermeier house, the Villa Metzler, and added a modern wing. The museum has a striking collection of around 30,000 objects of applied art from Europe and Asia.

Nearby, in a villa with a large garden in Schaumainkai, is the small but fascinating Museum der Weltkulturen (ethnography museum), which is well worth a visit.

🏛 Deutsches Architekturmuseum
Schaumainkai 43. *(069) 21 23 88 44.* ○ *10am–5pm Tue & Thu–Sun, 10am–8pm Wed.*
One of the most interesting museums in the Schaumainkai complex is undoubtedly the museum of architecture, opened in 1984 in an avant-garde building designed by Oswald Mathias Ungers. The museum has a permanent collection as well as temporary exhibitions concentrating mainly on developments in 20th-century architecture.

Nearby, at No 41 Schau-mainkai, is the Deutsches Filmmuseum, which holds documents and objects relating to the art of film-making and the development of film technology. The museum has its own cinema, which shows old and often long-forgotten films.

♦ Liebieghaus
Schaumainkai 71. *(069) 21 23 86 17.* ○ *10am–5pm Tue & Thu–Sun, 10am–8pm Wed.*
The Liebieghaus was built in 1896 for the Czech industri-alist Baron Heinrich Liebieg. Today it houses a museum of sculpture, with works ranging from antiquity through to Man-nerism, Baroque and Rococo. The museum also has superb examples of ancient Egyptian and Far Eastern art, as well as works from the Middle Ages and the Renaissance. Its highlights are the works of Neo-Classical masters such as Antonio Canova, Bertel Thorwaldsen and Johann Heinrich Dannecker.

The Liebieghaus, home of the museum of sculpture

🏛 Naturmuseum Senckenberg
Senckenberganlage 25. *(069) 754 20.* ○ *9am–5pm Mon, Tue, Thu & Fri, 9am–8pm Wed, 9am–6pm Sat & Sun.*
This museum, near the uni-versity, is one of the best natural history museums in Germany. Besides a vast col-lection of plants and animals, including dinosaur skeletons, it contains human and animal mummies from Egypt.

Environs: **Hanau**, 30 km (19 miles) east of Frankfurt, is the birthplace of the brothers Wilhelm and Jakob Grimm. An exhibition devoted to their lives and work is held at the local history museum, in Phil-ippsruhe, a Baroque palace.

The Deutsches Architekturmuseum, in Schaumainkai

Frankfurt – Städelsches Kunstinstitut

THE FOUNDER of this excellent museum, the banker Johann Friedrich Städel, bequeathed his art collection to the town in 1815. He also founded an art college for the training of new artists and the upkeep of the collection. Since then, the museum has grown through acquisitions and donations. It moved to a Neo-Renaissance building in 1878, on the picturesque "museum embankment" by the Main. In the 1920s it acquired the Hohenzollern collection from Sigmaringen. The building gained a new wing in 1990 (designer Gustav Peichl), and was renovated in 1995–9.

Ideal Portrait of a Woman (c.1480)
Simonetta Vespucci, mistress of Giuliano Medici, is the subject of this painting by Sandro Botticelli. Her pendant belonged at the time to the Medici collection.

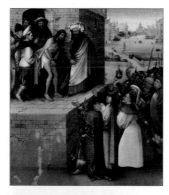

Ecce Homo
Members of the family who commissioned this painting from Hieronymus Bosch also originally figured in it, but they were later painted over and now only a few figures are partially visible.

First floor

★ Lucca Madonna
This small painting by Jan van Eyck, which evokes an intimate and intensely private atmosphere, takes its name from its former owner, Charles Ludwig de Bourbon, Duke of Lucca.

Around 100,000 prints and drawings, dating from the 14th century to the present day and making up one of Germany's most valuable collections, are exhibited in this exhibition hall.

Main entrance

Library

KEY

- ☐ 19th-century paintings
- ☐ 20th-century paintings
- ☐ German, Dutch and Flemish 17th- and 18th-century paintings
- ☐ Italian, French and Spanish 17th- and 18th-century paintings
- ☐ German and Dutch 14th–16th-century paintings
- ☐ Italian 14th–16th-century paintings

★ **The Geographer** (1669)
Although the signature on the painting is not genuine, there is no doubt that this picture, depicting a scholar at work, is the work of Jan Vermeer van Delft.

VISITORS' CHECKLIST

Schaumainkai 63.
☎ (069) 605 09 80.
Ⓦ www.staedelmuseum.de
🕐 10am–5pm Tue–Sun,
10am–8pm Wed & Thu. 🎫 (free
Tue.) 🅿 🖿 🏠 ✔

Second floor

★ **Blinding of Samson** (1636)
Rembrandt's dramatic painting depicts the violent blinding of Samson by the Philistines after Delilah cut off his hair.

GALLERY GUIDE
The ground floor of the building is used for changing exhibitions of prints and drawings, as well as a book store and a museum shop. The first floor is devoted to 19th- and 20th-century art and the second floor to the Old Masters.

Pilgrimage to the Isle of Cythera (c.1710)
Jean-Antoine Watteau painted three pictures on this theme, inspired by Dancourt's play The Three Sisters. *The museum holds the earliest of the three, which shows a Flemish influence.*

Ground floor

Orchestra Players (1870–74)
Edgar Degas, not completely satisfied with his painting, retrieved it from its owner. In 1874, he cropped it on three sides, added a bit at the top and repainted the entire painting.

STAR EXHIBITS

★ **Lucca Madonna**

★ **Blinding of Samson**

★ **The Geographer**

Darmstadt ⑰

Road map C5. 🏛 *138,000.* 🚊
ℹ️ *im Karree (06151-13 27 82);*
Luisenplatz 5, for tickets only (06151-
13 27 81). 🎭 *Frühlingfest (Mar/Apr),*
Schlossgrabenfest (May), Heinerfest
(early Jul), Herbstfest (Oct).

THE EARLIEST historical
records of Darmstadt,
which was probably named
after Darimund, a Frankonian
settler, date from the 12th
century. Until 1479, the castle
and the town belonged to the
Counts von Katzenelnbogen,
and later to Hessian landgraves. In 1567, the Landgraves von Hessen-Darmstadt
chose Darmstadt as their residence, and they continued to
live here until 1918.

To the north of the old
town stands the **Residenzschloss**, initially a ducal
palace, and from 1806 residence of the Landgraves von
Hessen-Darmstadt. The Re-
naissance-Baroque complex is
centred around three courtyards. The earlier medieval
castle, which stood on the
same site, burned down in
1546. The present palace was
created in stages, with its
earliest parts, the Renaissance
wings, dating from 1567–97.
The Glockenbau has a 35-bell
carillon which can be heard
every half hour; it was completed after the Thirty Years'
War, in 1663. Further modifications, planned in 1715–30,
were never completed. Two

Baroque wings, the so-called
Neubau or Neuschloss (new
castle), surround older buildings to the south and west.
The Schloss was bombed in
World War II and subsequently rebuilt. Today it houses the
provincial and university
library, while the Glockenbau
is home to the fascinating
Schlossmuseum (castle
museum). As well as a
splendid collection of
coaches and furniture,
it contains the famous
Darmstädter Madonna
(1526), by Holbein.

Also worth seeing,
the late-Renaissance
Rathaus (town hall),
built in 1588–90, sur-
vived World War II.
The 15th-century choir
of the **Stadtkirche** has
an enormous monu-
ment (1587) to Magda-
lena zur Lippe, first
wife of Landgrave
Georg I the Pious. To
the southwest of the
Stadtkirche stands the
Altes Pädagog, built
in 1629 as an educa-
tional establishment.

To the north of the Schloss
is the **Hessisches Landesmuseum** (regional museum
of Hesse), erected in 1892–
1905. Its collection includes
artifacts dating from the Roman era to the 20th century.
The museum also has an
excellent natural history section, whose exhibits include
the impressive skeleton of a

mammoth as well as birds of
every species native to
southern Hesse. Set in the park
behind the museum is the
Baroque Prinz-Georg-Palais
(1710), which houses the
**Großherzoglich-Hessische
Porzellansammlung**, an
extensive porcelain collection.

The last Grand Duke of
Hesse, Ernst Ludwig, was
an important patron of the
Jugendstil, the German
Art Nouveau movement.
He initiated the build-
ing of an exhibition
and residential com-
plex, the **Mathil-
denhöhe**, which
was established in
1901 in the grounds of
the former ducal park,
to serve the existing
artists' colony led by
Joseph Maria Olbrich.
Olbrich designed the
Ernst-Ludwig-Haus,
which now houses
the **Museum
Künstlerkolonie**,
an exhibition space
for the colony's
artists, as well as the
famous **Hochzeits-
turm** (wedding tower), erected in 1907–8 to celebrate the
Grand Duke's wedding. The
Behrens-Haus, designed by
the Hamburg architect Peter
Behrens, is sober in contrast.
The Orthodox church of **St
Mary Magdalene** was built in
1897–9 by the Russian architect Leonti Nikolayevich
Benois, in honour of Alice,
wife of the last tsar of Russia
and sister of Ernst Ludwig.

**Statue on the door
of the Behrens-
Haus in Darmstadt**

🏛 **Schlossmuseum**
Residenzschloss. 📞 *(06151) 240 35.*
🕐 *10am–1pm & 2–5pm Mon–Thu,*
10am–1pm Sat & Sun.
🏛 **Hessisches
Landesmuseum**
Friedensplatz 1. 📞 *(06151) 16 57*
03. 🕐 *10am–5pm Tue & Thu–Sat,*
10am–9pm Wed, 11am–5pm Sun. 🖼
🏛 **Museum
Künstlerkolonie**
Olbrichweg/Bauhausweg.
📞 *(06151) 13 33 85.* 🕐 *10am–5pm*
Tue–Sun. 🖼
🏛 **Großherzoglich-
Hessische Porzellan-
sammlung**
Schlossgartenstr. 10. 📞 *(06151) 71*
32 33. 🕐 *10am–1pm & 2–5pm*
Mon–Thu, 10am–1pm Sat & Sun.

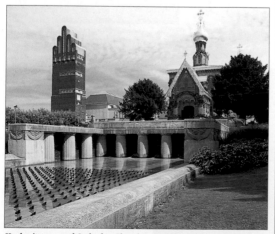

Hochzeitsturm and Orthodox Church in Mathildenhöhe, Darmstadt

The Carolingian Torhalle (gate-house) of the Kloster (abbey) in Lorsch

Lorsch ⑱

Road map B5. 🏛 *10,700.* 🛈 *Rathaus, Marktplatz 1 (06251-596 74 00).*

THIS SMALL town is mainly known for the **Kloster**, a Benedictine abbey first founded in 764 by Chrodegang of Metz and one of the most important cultural and intellectual centres in Europe in the Carolingian era. It reached the peak of its power in the 8th–13th centuries, before being sold to the Archbishop of Mainz in 1232. The Benedictines were forced to leave, and in their place the Cistercians arrived. The monastery was dissolved during the Reformation, and in 1621 the Spanish Army destroyed and plundered the greater part of the complex.

Fragments of the 13th-century nave, the towers and the gate-house, dating from c.790, are all that has survived. The original 8th-century church, a basilica without transept, burned down in 1090 and was rebuilt in the 12th century. The original crypt is the burial place of Ludwig II the German, the first ruler of the Eastern Franks. The **Torhalle** (gate-house) is one of the most important architectural remains of the Carolingian period, and it was listed as a UNESCO World Heritage Site in 1991. Its lower section is made up of three arcades, equal in height and width, modelled on Roman triumphal arches. The first-floor quarters above were probably used as a guest room or courtroom, and from the 14th century they served as a chapel. Remains of the original wall paintings are still visible here. The façade is decorated with red and white stone mosaics, which were inspired by Franco-Merovingian art. The vertical divides, created by pilasters and entablature, are copies of ancient designs – an architectural feature typical of the Carolingian Renaissance. The chapel's high roof and vaults date from the 14th century.

Michelstadt ⑲

Road map B5. 🏛 *16,000.* 🛈 *Marktplatz 1 (06061-194 33).* 🗓 *Bienenmarkt (Whitsun).*

MICHELSTADT, set among the hills of the Odenwald, is first mentioned in historical records in 741. From the 13th century the town belonged to the von Erbach family (the future Counts von Erbach).

The town has preserved many historic half-timbered houses and presents a typical image of medieval Germany. The 16th-century **Kellerei** is built around the remains of an earlier castle dating from 970. It now houses a regional museum. The sight most popular with photographers is the half-timbered **Rathaus** (town hall), dating from 1484, with its three towers and an open ground-floor gallery. Nearby stands the late-Gothic, 15th-century **Pfarrkirche St Michael** (parish church of St Michael). Inside are some interesting epitaphs including the double tombstone of Philipp I and Georg I, dating from the late 15th century. A true rarity is the 18th-century **synagogue**, which escaped being burned by the National Socialists in 1938.

In the Steinbach district of Michelstadt stands the **Einhardsbasilika**, a church dating from around 821. The first church built on this site, at the initiative of Einhard, a courtier of Charlemagne, was a small, pillared and vaulted basilica with a short choir ending with a rounded apse. Under the eastern section is a crypt. The parts which remain to this day include the main nave, the north aisle with an apse and the crypt which holds precious religious relics.

ENVIRONS: In **Fürstenau**, situated about 1 km (0.6 mile) northwest of Michelstadt, is a beautiful complex including the Altschloss (old palace), remodelled from a medieval castle, the Neuschloss (new palace), dating from 1810, the park and its garden pavilions.

Erbach, 5 km (3miles) south of Michelstadt, became famous as a centre for the art of ivory carving. In No. 1 Otto-Glenz-Straße is the Deutsches Elfenbeinmuseum (German ivory museum), which is devoted to this craft. Other attractions in this town include the overbearing Baroque Schloss (castle) and its interesting art collection.

The Carolingian Einhardsbasilika in Michelstadt-Steinbach

NORTH RHINE-WESTPHALIA

ORIGINALLY consisting of two distinct provinces with somewhat diverging histories, the region of North Rhine-Westphalia today has its own strong identity. It encompasses the vast valley of the Ruhr river, rich in mineral deposits, where over the past 200 years huge conurbations have developed, comprising dozens of industrial cities that are gradually merging into one another.

As a province, the North Rhineland, situated along the lower Rhine valley, goes back to Roman times. In the Middle Ages most of this area was ruled by the Bishops of Köln. The North Rhineland cities grew and prospered thanks to their trade links, and in the 19th century they became major centres of mining and heavy industry.

Westphalia forms the eastern part of the land. Once a Saxon territory, its history was often intertwined with that of the Rhineland. Only its western end has been heavily industrialized.

North Rhine-Westphalia is not the largest of the German regions, but with a population of nearly 18 million it is the most heavily populated one. It is often thought that the region, and in particular the heavily industrialized Ruhr valley, has little to offer to its visitors, but this is a mistaken belief. Its splendid past has left many priceless historic monuments and more recently, thanks to great investment, its industrial cities have transformed themselves into attractive cultural centres.

The history of towns such as Bonn, Aachen, Cologne (Köln) and Xanten goes back to Roman times, and they have preserved much of their ancient heritage to this day. Evidence of Romanesque art, which flourished in the Rhineland, is today apparent in numerous impressive abbeys dotted throughout the region and in the churches of Cologne, which also boasts the colossal Gothic Dom.

Much of North Rhine-Westphalia is rural, and the region offers thousands of kilometres of tracks for walking in the Teutoburg Forest and in the Northern Eifel mountains, as well as splendid conditions for watersports and fishing in the Sauerland. It also has surprisingly good ski slopes, such as in the Rothaar Mountains.

A typical lowland landscape near Xanten, in the Rhineland

◁ The imposing Gothic Kölner Dom (Cologne cathedral), lit up at night

Exploring North Rhine-Westphalia

DESPITE BEING heavily industrialized, the land of North Rhine-Westphalia has many attractions for visitors. At least two days should be set aside to admire the historic treasures in Cologne, while those who prefer museums – or shopping – might allocate more time for Düsseldorf. The towns of Bonn, Aachen and Münster should also feature on every visitor's schedule. The best areas for rest and relaxation are the mountain ranges of the Eifel and the Teutoburg Forest, ideally suited for walking and cycling holidays.

SEE ALSO

• *Where to Stay* pp490–92

• *Where to Eat* pp519–23

Burg Altena in the Sauerland

SIGHTS AT A GLANCE

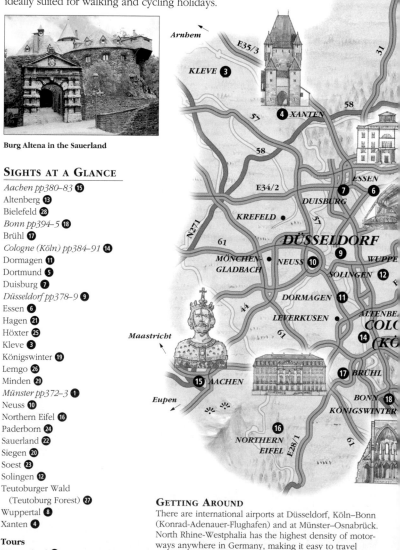

GETTING AROUND

There are international airports at Düsseldorf, Köln–Bonn (Konrad-Adenauer-Flughafen) and at Münster–Osnabrück. North Rhine-Westphalia has the highest density of motorways anywhere in Germany, making it easy to travel between cities, and providing links with other German regions, Belgium and the Netherlands.

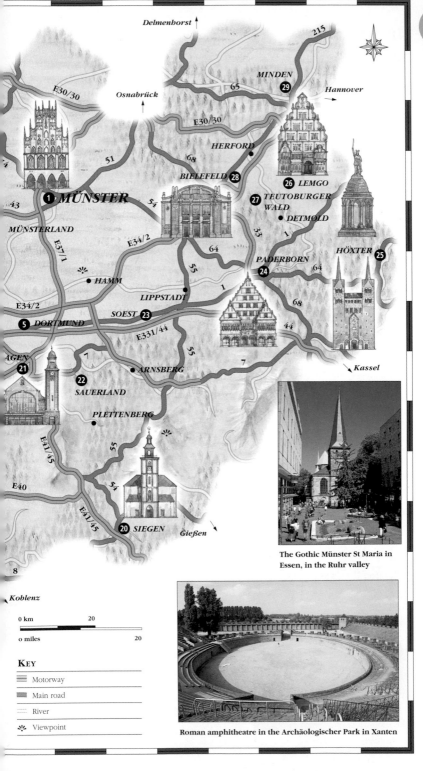

Delmenhorst

Osnabrück

Hannover

MINDEN 29

E30/30

215

65

E30/30

HERFORD

51

68

BIELEFELD 28

LEMGO 26

MÜNSTER 1

54

27 TEUTOBURGER WALD

DETMOLD

MÜNSTERLAND

33

E37/1

E34/2

64

1

HÖXTER 25

PADERBORN

24

64

HAMM

55

LIPPSTADT

68

E34/2

1

DORTMUND 5

SOEST 23

44

E331/44

Kassel

55

7

AGEN 21

7

22

ARNSBERG

SAUERLAND

PLETTENBERG

E41/45

55

E40

54

E41/45

SIEGEN 20

Gießen

Koblenz

The Gothic Münster St Maria in Essen, in the Ruhr valley

Roman amphitheatre in the Archäologischer Park in Xanten

0 km   20

0 miles   20

KEY

▬▬ Motorway

▬▬ Main road

═══ River

☼ Viewpoint

Münster ❶

MÜNSTER and its surroundings were already inhabited in Roman times, but its history proper started in the 9th century, with the establishment of a bishopric. Town status was granted in 1137, and in the 13th century Münster joined the Hanseatic League. In 1648 the Westphalian Peace Treaty was signed here, ending the Thirty Years' War. Münster's Westfälische Wilhelms-Universität (1773) is one of Germany's largest universities. World War II saw 90 percent of the old town laid to ruins, but most of it has now been rebuilt.

🏛 Erbdrostenhof
Salzstraße 38. ● *Closed to the public.*
This beautiful mansion was skilfully positioned diagonally across a corner site. Designed by Johann Conrad Schlaun, it was built in 1753–7, and despite destruction in World War II it still enchants with its "wavy", late-Baroque façade.

🏛 Rathaus
Prinzipalmarkt. **Friedensaal**
📞 *(0251) 492 27 24.* ○ *9am–5pm Mon–Fri, 9am–4pm Sat, 10am–1pm Sun.* ● *25 Dec.* 🎫
The imposing Gothic town hall, the pride of Münster, was almost completely destroyed during World War II. After its splendid reconstruction, it is again a major draw for visitors. The only parts that had escaped destruction were the furnishings of the main council chamber, which have been returned to their rightful place after the rebuilding work. It

The beautifully restored façade of the late-Gothic Rathaus

Houses on Prinzipalmarkt, reconstructed in the medieval style

was here that on 15 May 1648 part of the Westphalian Treaty was signed, ending the Thirty Years' War.

🏰 Lambertikirche
Prinzipalmarkt.
St Lamberti is an excellent example of the hall-churches characteristic of Westphalia. It was built in 1375–1450, but the openwork finial of the tower dates from 1887. The cages hanging on the tower held the bodies of the leading Anabaptists, following the crushing of their commune in 1536. It is also worth taking a look at the relief depicting the *Tree of Jesse*, above the southwest entrance, and the figures of the apostles (c.1600) by Johann Koess.

🏛 Dom St Paulus
Domplatz. **Domkammer**
○ *11am–4pm Tue–Sun.* 🎫
The most precious historic relic in Münster is undeniably

its massive St Paulus' cathedral, built in 1225–65 and representing a transitional style between late-Romanesque and early-Gothic. The vast basilica has two transepts, two choirs and a couple of massive towers at the western end. The northern cloister was added in the 14th century, and in the 16th–17th centuries the passage that runs around the presbytery acquired a ring of chapels. In the vestibule stands a group of 13th-century sculptures. Especially worth seeing are the two altars by Gerhard Gröninger (1st half of the 17th century), the early 16th-century stained-glass windows brought here from Marienfeld, the Gothic candelabra and monuments of many bishops. The cathedral's best-known treasure is the astronomical clock (1540), with paintings by Ludger tom Ring the Elder and sculptures by Johann Brabender. At noon, moving figures show the Magi paying tribute to the infant Jesus to the sounds of the carillon.

🏛 Westfälisches Landesmuseum für Kunst und Kulturgeschichte
Domplatz 10. 📞 *(0251) 590 701.* ○ *10am–6pm Tue–Sun.* 🎫 *(free Fri.)*
The Westphalian regional museum specializes mainly in Gothic art, with a large collection of sculptures and altars rescued in World War II. Its most noteworthy exhibits include the works by Heinrich and Johann Brabender. The upstairs galleries show works by Conrad von Soest and the tom Ring family. Contemporary art is represented by, among others, August Macke's work.

Figure of a saint in Dom St Paulus

🏰 Überwasserkirche
Überwasserkirchplatz.
The Liebfrauenkirche (Church of Our Lady) is popularly named Überwasserkirche (church above the water), after the district on the banks

The Baroque-Classical Schloss, residence of Münster's prince-bishops

of the tiny Aa river. This Gothic edifice was built in c.1340–46, on the site of a Romanesque Benedictine church. Inside are 16th-century votive paintings by Ludger and Hermann tom Ring.

♦ Residenzschloss
Schlossplatz 2.
This beautiful Baroque residence was built in 1767–87, by Prince-Bishop Maximilian Friedrich. It was designed by Johann Conrad Schlaun, a local master of Baroque architecture. Maximilian Friedrich started the redevelopment of Münster in the northern Baroque style. On his initiative the town acquired a large park, part of which was transformed into a botanical garden in 1803. After World War II, the castle was rebuilt and became the headquarters of Münster university.

🏛 Museum für Lackkunst
Windthorststraße 26. *(0251) 41 85 10.* 🕐 *noon–8pm Tue, noon–6pm Wed–Sun & public holidays.* 🗓
This unique museum, devoted to lacquer ware, has a good collection with items from around the world and from different periods, making a visit to the museum a treat for those interested in this craft.

Watermill in the open-air museum in Mühlenhof

♠ Mühlenhof
Theo-Breider-Weg 1. *(0251) 98 12 00.* 🕐 *16 Mar–Oct: 10am–5pm daily; Nov–15 Mar: 1–4:30pm Tue–Sat, 11am–4pm Sun.* 🗓
This small but interesting open-air museum is situated on the banks of the picturesque Aasee, Münster's lake and main recreation area. Displayed are a number of rural dwellings with authentic furnishings and two mills (17th and 18th centuries).

♦ Drostenhof
Wolbeck, Am Steintor 5.
Southeast of the town, in Wolbeck (now part of the city), is an original Renaissance mansion from the mid-16th century. Its exquisite gatehouse leads into the courtyard of the mansion, which has original fireplaces, doors and ceiling paintings.

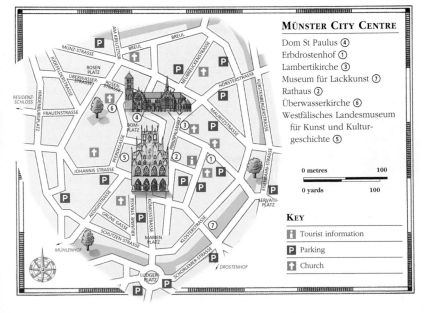

MÜNSTER CITY CENTRE

Dom St Paulus ④
Erbdrostenhof ①
Lambertikirche ③
Museum für Lackkunst ⑦
Rathaus ②
Überwasserkirche ⑥
Westfälisches Landesmuseum für Kunst und Kulturgeschichte ⑤

0 metres	100
0 yards	100

KEY

ℹ Tourist information
🅿 Parking
✝ Church

Münsterland ❷

THE REGION stretching in a narrow strip to the north of Münster is the land of horses and Wasserburgen (moated castles). The castles were surrounded by moats or built on islands to give their owners protection in the surrounding lowlands. Almost 50 Wasserburgen have survived, some converted into residences. Not all are open to visitors as most remain to this day in the hands of the family of the original owners. The best way to tour the flat Münsterland region is by car or bicycle.

Vischering ②
The magnificent Burg Vischering is one of the oldest and best-preserved castles in Westphalia. Founded in 1270, it was extended in the 16th and 17th centuries.

Schloss Raesfeld ⑤
The beautiful 17th-century castle has some original 14th-century elements. Particularly worth seeing is the castle chapel with its Baroque altar.

Havixbeck ①
Two interesting castles are near this small town: the Renaissance Haus Havixbeck and the Renaissance-Baroque Burg Hülshoff, birthplace of and museum to the 19th-century writer Annette von Droste-Hülshoff.

Schloss Nordkirchen ③
This vast moated castle, nicknamed the "Westphalian Versailles", was designed by Gottfried Laurenz Pictorius and built in 1703–34 for the Plettenberg family.

Schloss Lembeck ④
In its present shape, the Lembeck castle complex is the result of Baroque remodelling, under the direction of Johann Conrad Schlaun. Nearby is a nature reserve.

0 km   16
0 miles   16

KEY

■ Suggested route

■ Scenic route

═ Other road

⋯ River, lake

☼ Viewpoint

TIPS FOR DRIVERS

Length of route: 97 km (58 miles).
Stopping-off points: Every town has inns, and there is a hotel in Schloss Lembeck.
Suggestions: All castles are open to visitors Tuesday to Sunday, with the exception of Nordkirchen, which opens only at weekends.

Kleve (Cleves) ❸

Road map A3. 🏘 *50,000.* 🚉 🚌 🚗
Kavariner Str. 20–22 (02821-89 50 90).

THE TOWN OF Kleve is named after the high cliff, on which a castle was built in the 10th century. Around it a settlement developed, which became a town in 1242. It was ruled by the dukes of Kleve, whose ambitions were far greater than the size of their dominions and reached their peak in 1539, when Anne of Cleves married the English King Henry VIII.

During World War II Kleve lost most of its historic buildings. One that has survived to this day is the imposing Gothic church of the Assumption of the Virgin Mary, **St Mariä Himmelfahrt** (1341–1426). It has remains of the high altar, dating from 1510–13, with reliefs by Henrik Douvermann and Jakob Dericks, as well as beautiful monuments and epitaphs to the von Kleve dukes. Equally worth seeing is the former Franciscan **St Mariä Empfängnis**, a Gothic twin-nave hall-church from the first half of the 15th century. Its noteworthy features include the Gothic stalls (1474) and a magnificent Baroque pulpit (1698). The well-preserved ducal castle of **Schwanenburg** was remodelled twice: in Gothic style in the late 15th century, and in Baroque style in 1636–66. Testifying to former splendour are the parks established in the mid-17th century by Johann Moritz von Nassau. The most beautiful of these is the **Tiergarten** (animal garden). **Haus Koekkoek**, located nearby, once belonged to the Romantic painter, Barend Cornalis Koekkoek, after whom it was named.

⛪ Schwanenburg
Am Schlossberg. 📞 *(02821) 22 884.*
🕐 *May–Oct: 11am–5pm Mon–Fri, 10am–5pm Sat & Sun; Nov–Apr: 10am–5pm Sat & Sun.* 📷

ENVIRONS: The suspension bridge across the Rhine – at 1,228 m (4,028 ft) the longest such structure in Germany – connects Kleve with **Emmerich**. Here it is worth visiting the Martinskirche, which has the exquisite, late-10th-century shrine of St Willibrod.

Twelve km (7 miles) to the southeast of Kleve lies the charming town of **Kalkar** which, in around 1500, was home to the famous Kalkar School specializing in wood-carving. The church of St Nicolai has superb furnishings dating from the same period.

Six km (4 miles) southeast stands **Moyland**, a moated castle. It houses a modern art collection, which belongs to the brothers von der Grinten and includes over 4,000 works by the artist Joseph Beuys.

Xanten ❹

Road map B4. 🏘 *19,500.* 🚉 🚌
ℹ *Kurfürstenstr. 9 (02801-983 00).*

THE HISTORY of Xanten goes back to the Romans, who founded the settlement of *Colonia Ulpia Traiana* near the local garrison. The present town, however, did not rise out of the ruins of the Roman town. It was established nearby, around the memorial church built on top of the grave

The Hafentor in the Archäologischer Park in Xanten

of the martyr St Viktor. It was named *ad sanctos* (by the saints), soon to be shortened to Xanten. A powerful town in the Middle Ages, Xanten also features in the Nibelung myth, and was said to be the birthplace of Siegfried.

Undoubtedly the most important historic building in the town is the **Dom St Viktor**, built on the graves of St Viktor and members of the Thebian Legion. The surviving Gothic cathedral dates from 1263–1517. It is worth taking a look at the Gothic sculptures standing by the pillars of the main nave, the shrine of St Victor (1129), the early-Gothic stalls (c.1240) and, above all, the exquisite Marienaltar by Henrik Douvermann. Equally fascinating are the collegial buildings and the cloister holding the tombs and epitaphs of the canons.

Xanten also has many pretty old houses, mainly clustered around the central market square. Another sight worth visiting is the **Klever Tor**, a magnificent double town-gate, dating from the late 14th century, in the northwest of the town. The **Archäologischer Park,** established in 1974 on the site of the Roman town, displays many reconstructed Roman public buildings including the impressive Hafentor (harbour gate).

⛪ Archäologischer Park
Wardter Str. 📞 *(02801) 29 99.* 🕐 *Mar–Oct: 9am–6pm daily; Nov: 9am–5pm daily; Dec–Feb: 10am–4pm daily.* 📷

The Gothic Dom St Victor in Xanten

The Young Horses by Emil Nolde, in the Museum am Ostwall

Dortmund ❺

Road map B4. 🏛 600,000. 🚉 🚌
ℹ️ *Königswall 18A (0231-14 03 41).*
🎭 *Dortmund aller art (Aug), Dortmund à la carte (Jun), Hansetage (Nov).*

THE LARGE CITY of Dortmund is famous not only for its excellent beer and highly developed industry, but also for its more than 1,000 years of history. In the Middle Ages, the town grew rich through trade and joined the Hanseatic League; after a period of decline it flourished again in the 19th century.

A walk through the small old town will take visitors to the **Museum für Kunst-und Kulturgeschichte** (museum for art and cultural history) with displays of interiors from various periods, including Secessionist designs by Joseph Maria Olbrich. A short distance from here is the **Petrikirche**, a Gothic 14th-century hall-church, whose greatest attraction is its high altar (1521), the work of Gilles, a master from Antwerp. Also noteworthy is the former Dominican **Propsteikirche**, with its exquisite late-Gothic main altar. A shortcut across the market square and along Ostenhellweg takes the visitor to two more churches: the **Reinoldikirche** and the **Marienkirche**. The former,

Statue on Alter Markt, in Dortmund

dedicated to St Reinold, the patron saint of Dortmund, has an early-Gothic 13th-century main body and a late-Gothic, 15th-century presbytery. It includes many Gothic sculptures and furnishings. The second one, the church of St Mary, is a 12th-century Romanesque structure. It has a magnificent main altar, by Conrad von Soest (1415–20) and a statue of the Madonna (c.1230). The **Museum am Ostwall** has an excellent modern art collection.

🏛 **Museum für Kunst-und Kulturgeschichte**
Hansastr. 3. 📞 *(0231) 502 55 22.* 🕙 *10am–5pm Tue, Wed, Fri, Sun, 10am–8pm Thu, noon–5pm Sat.* 🖼

🏛 **Museum am Ostwall**
Ostwall 7. 📞 *(0231) 502 32 47.* 🕙 *as above.* 🖼

ENVIRONS: 10 km (6 miles) northwest, in **Waltrop**, on the Dortmund-Ems Canal, is the Schiffshebewerk Henrichenburg, a hoist built in 1899 to lift ships.

Essen ❻

Road map B4. 🏛 600,000. 🚉 🚌
ℹ️ *Im Handelshof (0201-194 33).*
🎭 *Essen Original (Aug).*

IT IS HARD TO believe that this vast industrial metropolis has grown from a monastery, established in 852. The town owes its growth and prominence to the Krupp family,

who, over several generations from the mid-19th century, created the powerful German steel and arms industry.

The most important historic building in the town is the **Münster**, the former collegiate church of the canonesses. This unusual edifice consists of the 15th-century Gothic church of St John, an 11th-century atrium and the main church, which in turn has a Romanesque 11th-century frontage and a Gothic 14th–century main body. Without doubt the most precious object held by the church is the *Goldene Madonna*, a statue of the Virgin Mary with the Infant, made from sheet gold, probably c.980. The treasury has an outstanding collection of gold items from the Ottonian period.

Another important sight in Essen is the **Synagogue** built by Edmund Körner in 1911–13. The largest synagogue in Germany, it managed to outlast the Third Reich and is now a place of commemoration.

Visitors who are interested in 20th-century architecture should see the church of **St Engelbert** in Fischerstraße, designed by Dominikus Metzendorf (1934–6), the towngarden in **Margarethenhöhe** built from 1909 to a design by Georg Metzendorf, and the opera house designed by the Finnish architect, Alvar Aalto.

Essen has much to offer to modern art enthusiasts. The **Museum Folkwang** boasts an excellent collection of 20th-century paintings, mainly German Expressionists. It also has a division devoted to the graphic arts and posters.

The **Grugapark** is a large green area with botanical gardens, zoo and the Grugahalle, where major concerts are held. To the south of the centre, on the banks of the Baldeneysee, stands **Villa Hügel**, which belonged to the Krupp family until 1945. Today interesting art exhibitions are frequently hosted here. Further south, in **Werden**, is the former Benedictine church of St Ludger, consisting of a 13th-century body preceded by a 10th-century imperial frontage. The

The grand Villa Hügel, former home of the Krupp family in Essen

treasury holds many precious objects including a bronze crucifix from around 1060.

🏛 Museum Folkwang
Goethestr. 41. **C** (0201) 884 53 14. ◯ 10am–6pm Tue–Thu, Sat & Sun, 10am–midnight Fri. ● 1 Jan, Easter, 1 May, 24 & 31 Dec. ☒

ENVIRONS: Visitors interested in technology should visit **Bochum**, which is also the seat of the excellent Ruhr-Universität. There are two excellent museums: the **Deutsches Bergbau-Museum** devoted to mining, and the **Eisenbahnmuseum** (railway museum) in Dahlhausen. Both have world-class exhibits.

Duisburg ❼

Road map B4. 🏚 540,000. 🚊 🚌 🖪 Königstr. 86 (0203-285 44 11).

DUISBURG, on the edge of the Ruhr region, underwent a period of rapid development in the 19th and 20th centuries. Once a small town, it became the world's largest inland harbour thanks to its location at the spot where the Ruhr flows into the Rhine.

The small old town was almost totally destroyed in World War II, but the 15th-century Gothic **Salvatorkirche** (church of St Saviour) has been rebuilt. Some of the town's greatest attractions are its museums. The **Wilhelm-Lehmbruck-Museum** focuses on the work of the sculptor Lehmbruck, who was born in Duisburg. The museum has an interesting collection of 20th-century sculptures, including works

by famous artists such as Salvador Dali, Henry Moore, Max Ernst, Emil Nolde and Joseph Beuys. Also worth visiting is the **Museum der Deutschen Binnenschifffahrt** with its collection of barges and inland waterway vessels. In the 16th century, Duisburg was the home of the famous geographer and cartographer Gerhard Mercator, whose collection of globes, maps and charts can now be seen in the **Kulture- und Stadthistorisches Museum**.

🏛 Wilhelm-Lehmbruck-Museum
Düsseldorfer Str. 51. **C** (0203) 283 26 30. ◯ 11am–5pm Tue–Sat, 10am–6pm Sun. ☒

ENVIRONS: CentrO in **Oberhausen**, 14 km (9 miles) north of Duisburg, is the largest shopping and leisure complex in Europe.

Krefeld, 6 km (4 miles) southwest of Duisburg, has been a centre of silk fabric production from the 17th century, and the Deutsches Textilmuseum has over 20,000 exhibits, ranging from antiquity to the present day.

Wuppertal ❽

Road map B4. 🏚 380,000. 🖪 🖪 Elberfeld, Informationszentrum am Döppersberg (0202-194 33); Rathaus (0202-563 21 80).

WUPPERTAL, capital of the Bergisches Land area, was created in 1929 by combining six towns strung along a 20-km (12-mile) stretch of the Wupper river. The towns are joined by the **Schwebebahn**, a monorail constructed in 1900. Carriages are suspended from a single rail, which rests on tall pillars.

The most interesting of the former towns is Elberfeld, with a museum of clocks, and the **Von-der-Heydt–Museum** of 19th- and 20th-century German art. The museum in the Friedrich-Engels-Haus in Barmen (Engelsstr. 10) is worth seeing, and Neviges has a Baroque pilgrimage church, with a much-visited miraculous picture of the Virgin Mary.

🏛 Von-der-Heydt-Museum
Elberfeld, Turmhof 8. **C** (0202) 563 62 31. ◯ 11am–6pm Tue, Wed, Fri–Sun, 11am–8pm Thu. ☒ 🖿 🖊

The unusual monorail, linking Wuppertal's six constituent towns

Düsseldorf **9**

DÜSSELDORF, the administrative capital of North Rhine-Westphalia, received its municipal rights in 1288. From the late 14th century it was the capital of the Duchy of Berg, and from 1614 that of the Palatine. The town owes much to Duke Johann Wilhelm (called Jan Wellem), who lived here in 1690–1716. One of the most important industrial and cultural centres in the Rhine Valley, this European metropolis has a renowned university, superb museums and theatres and, as the German capital of fashion, many excellent shops.

🏛 Museum Kunst Palast
Ehrenhof 5. **(** *(0211) 892 42 42.* 🔲 *11am–8pm Tue–Sun.* 🈲 🔳 🈲 🔳
This art museum is one of the most interesting in Germany, with a collection of paintings dating from the 16th to the 20th centuries, including works by Rubens, Cranach and Dutch masters of the 17th century. It also holds a large collection of paintings by the Düsseldorf Academy, active in the first half of the 19th century, whose best known artists were Peter von Cornelius and Friedrich Wilhelm Schadow.

🏯 Altstadt
The small old town area suffered severe damage during World War II. Among the surviving monuments it is worth seeing some of the beautiful town houses and the late-Gothic **Rathaus** (town hall), built in the years 1570–73. In

Interior of the Pfarrkirche St Andreas

front of it stands a famous equestrian statue of the Elector Jan Wellem, built in 1703–11 by Gabriel Grupello. The Düsseldorf castle, burned down in 1872, only has the **Schlossturm** (castle tower) remaining, which now houses a museum of navigation. Another building worth visiting is the Baroque, post-Jesuit **Pfarr-kirche St Andreas** (parish church of St Andrew), from the years 1622–9. It has a central ducal mausoleum complex situated behind the presbytery, where the remains of Jan Wellem and others are kept. The **Lambertuskirche**, the former collegiate church of St Lambertus, is a Gothic hall-church with a tall front tower, built in 1288–1394. Some valuable furnishings have survived, including the Gothic sacramentarium and important Gothic ducal tombs, such as that of Duke Wilhelm V, from 1595–9.

Detail from the façade of the Lambertuskirche

🏛 Kunstsammlung Nordrhein-Westfalen
Grabbeplatz 5. **(** *(0211) 838 10.* 🔲 *10am–6pm Tue–Fri, 11am–6pm Sat-Sun, 10am–10pm 1st Wed of the month.* ⬤ *24,25 & 31 Dec.* 🈲 🔳 🔳 🔳
The art collection of the state of North Rhine-Westphalia is enormous, featuring mainly the work of 20th-century artists. Particularly valuable are 88 paintings by

Paul Klee, which were acquired in 1960. There are also works by Wassily Kandinsky, Marcel Duchamp, Piet Mondrian and Pablo Picasso. The gallery at Grabbeplatz is known as K20, and a second building at Stäudehaüsstr. 1, where contemporary art is exhibited, is known as K21. Temporary exhibitions are held nearby, at No. 4 Grabbeplatz.

🏛 Hetjens-Museum
Schulstraße 4. **(** *(0211) 899 42 10.* 🔲 *11am–5pm Tue & Thu–Sun, 11am– 9pm Wed.* 🈲
This museum, in the Nesselrode Palace, is the oldest German museum devoted entirely to ceramics. Visitors can learn about techniques for producing faïence and porcelain, and admire global exhibits from prehistory to the present day.

🏛 Königsallee
The "kings' avenue", often just referred to as Kö, was laid out at the beginning of the 19th century, along the edge of the old city moat.
One of the most elegant shopping streets in Europe, the Kö is lined with expensive shops. Luxurious galleries, exclusive boutiques, department stores, fashion houses and modern shopping malls are interspersed with numerous bars and restaurants. Particularly noteworthy is the Art Nouveau Warenhaus Tietz (now housing the Kaufhof-Galleria department store), which was built in the years 1907–9, to a design by Joseph Maria Olbrich.

🌿 Hofgarten
Jägerhofstr. **Goethemuseum:** Jacobistraße 2. **(** *(0211) 899 62 62.* 🔲 *11am–5pm Tue & Fri, 1–5pm Sat.* 🈲
This charming park, originally laid out in 1769 for Elector Karl Theodor, was recreated in the English style at the beginning of the 19th century. The park is a marvellous setting for Schloss Jägerhof, a Baroque hunting lodge dating from the years 1752–63 and built according to a design by

The late-Baroque Schloss Benrath

VISITORS' CHECKLIST

Road map B4. 👥 *600,000.* 🚆 *Konrad-Adenauer-Platz.* ✈ *north of the centre (0211-42 10).* ℹ️ *Immermannstr. 65B, Berliner Allee (0211-17 20 20).* 🚢 🚣 *Bootsausstellung (Jan), Rosenmontagsumzug (Carnival Mon), Größte Kirmes am Rhein (end Jul), St Martinsfest (Nov).* 🌐 W *www.duesseldorf.de*

Johann Josef Couven and Nicolas de Pigage. The castle was rebuilt after World War II. It now houses the Goethe-Museum, holding memorabilia and documents related to the writer's life, and a collection of 18th-century art, funded by Ernst Schneider.

🏛 Heinrich-Heine-Institut

Bilker Str. 12–14. [(0211) 899 55 71. ◯ 11am–5pm Tue–Fri & Sun, 1–5pm Sat. 🖼

The celebrated German poet Heinrich Heine was born in Düsseldorf in 1797. This institute was established to preserve his legacy, to conduct research into his work and to organize exhibitions. Düsseldorf's university and a number of streets have also been named after Heine.

♔ Schloss Benrath

Benrather Schlossallee. [(0211) 899 72 71. ◯ Apr–Oct: 10am–5pm Tue–Sun; Nov–Mar: 11am–6pm Tue–Sun. Wed until 8pm. 🖼 🔲

Benrath, part of Düsseldorf since 1929, is home to this beautiful Neo-Classical hunting palace, built for the electors of the Palatine in 1755–73 by Nicolas de Pigage. Decor, beautiful furnishings and an extensive park have survived.

The former city moat which runs alongside Königsallee

Kaiserswerth

Today a part of Düsseldorf, this area prides itself on a history dating back to the 8th century. Its Pfarrkirche St Suitbertus, a Romanesque basilica from the 12th century, has the magnificent 13th-century golden relic of its patron saint. There are also the ruins of a palace, built in the 12th century for Friedrich I Barbarossa.

ENVIRONS: The "Neanderthal" part of the Düssel valley was originally named after the poet Joachim Neander. It became famous in 1856, when the remains of ape-like creatures were uncovered in a cave. A museum dedicated to these "Neanderthal Men" is located in Mettman, 17 km (11 miles) east of Düsseldorf.

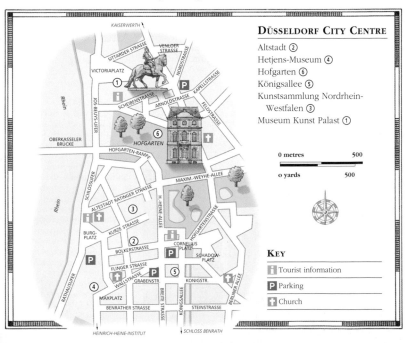

DÜSSELDORF CITY CENTRE

Altstadt ②
Hetjens-Museum ④
Hofgarten ⑥
Königsallee ⑤
Kunstsammlung Nordrhein-
  Westfalen ③
Museum Kunst Palast ①

0 metres   500
0 yards   500

KEY

ℹ️ Tourist information

🅿 Parking

✝ Church

Neuss 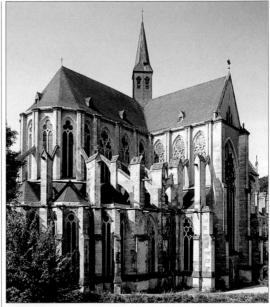 ❿

Road map B4. 👥 *150,000.* 🚆 🚌
ℹ️ *Büchel 6 (02131-403 77 95).*

THE HISTORY of Neuss goes
back to Roman days. The
town developed around a
Bernhardine monastery, which
became a girls' boarding
school in the 12th century.
The most famous building is
the magnificent 13th-century
Romanesque **Münster St
Quirinus**. After a fire in 1741,
a Baroque dome with a statue
of St Quirin, the patron saint,
was added to the eastern
tower of the church. Also
worth seeing is the Obertor
(upper gate), built in 1200,
one of the mightiest gates in
the Rhineland.

Dormagen ⓫

Road map B4. 👥 *62,000.* 🚆 🚌
ℹ️ *Zons, Schlossstraße 2–4 (02133
97 497 70).* 🎭 *Freilichtspiele in Zons
(Jun–Sep).*

THIS MEDIUM-SIZED town,
which principally relies on
its chemical industry, would
not be found in a guide book
were it not for two remarkable historic monuments
within the city limits. On the
banks of the Rhine lies the
fortified customs town of
Zons, established around
1373–1400 at the instigation
of archbishop Friedrich von
Saarwerden. This small regular, four-sided fortress has
survived in excellent condition. The buildings in the
settlement are mainly from a
later time, but the walls and
gates, as well as the ruined
castle **Schloss Friedestrom**
are among the most fascinating examples of Medieval fortifications in the Rhine Valley.
Equally interesting is an excursion to **Knechtsteden,**
west of Dormagen, where an
amazing monastery was built
for the Norbertines in the
12th century. Set amid woods
and orchards, the vast twin-
choired basilica has mighty
towers in the eastern section.
There are impressive murals,
including a 12th-century mural
of Christ in the western apsis,
as well as attractive cloisters.

The Gothic post-Cistercian Bergischer Dom in Altenberg

Solingen ⓬

Road map B4 👥 *165,000.* 🚆 🚌
ℹ️ *Clemens-Galerien Mummstr. 10
(0212-290 32 05).* 🎭 *Frühjahrskirmes
(Mar).*

SOLINGEN IS ALMOST synonymous with its famous fac-
tory, where quality scissors
and knives are produced. The
main attraction in town is the
Klingenmuseum, which
shows cutting tools from the
Stone Age to the present day.

ENVIRONS: Remscheid, 7 km
(4 miles) east of Solingen has
the Röntgenmuseum, dedi-
cated to the German Nobel
Prize winner Alfred Röntgen,
who was born here and dis-

**Baroque façade of the local
Heimatmuseum in Remscheid**

covered the X-ray. One of the
most beautiful buildings is the
Heimatmuseum with displays
of typical regional interiors.
    Schloss Burg, on the Wup-
per river, is the 12th-century
fortress of the von Berg family. Many times rebuilt, it now
houses a museum.

Altenberg ⓭

Road map B4. 👥 *5,745.* 🚆 🚌
ℹ️ *Altenberger-dom-str. 29–31,
51519 Odenthal (02202-71 01 31).*

ALTENBERG NEAR Odenthal has
preserved its **Bergischer
Dom**, a former Cistercian
cathedral and one of the most
important destinations for pilgrims. Built in 1259–1379, it is
also one of the most beautiful
Gothic buildings in Germany.
In accordance with their
rules, the Cistercians built the
church without a tower. The
interior is furnished with
Gothic works of art and has
stunningly beautiful stained-
glass windows, the altar of
the *Coronation of the Blessed
Virgin Mary* from the late
15th century, a beautiful 14th-
century *Annunciation* and a
sacrarium (1490). After the
dissolution of the Order in
1803, the cathedral suffered a

turbulent history. It now serves as a church for both Catholics and Protestants.

Children also enjoy a visit to Altenberg because of its **Märchenwald** (fairy-tale wood), an enchanted forest, with interactive scenes and statues representing all the most popular fairy tales.

Köln (Cologne) ⑭

See pp384–91.

Aachen ⑮

Road map A4. 🏛 *254,000.* 🚉 🚌
🛈 *Elisenbrunnen (0241-194 33).*
🎭 *Frühjahrsbend (Apr), horse-riding competitions CHIO (Jun), Europamarkt des Kunsthandwerks (Sep).*

AACHEN OWES ITS fame to its hot springs, whose healing powers were already highly rated by the Romans when they established baths here in the 1st–2nd centuries AD. The name of the town, *aquae grani* or Aquisgrani, also relates to the source.

The settlement grew mainly in the 8th century, when Charlemagne chose it as his principal residence in 768. He built a huge palace complex with chapel, cloistered courtyard and hall for himself.

When Charlemagne was crowned emperor in 800, Aachen became the capital of the Holy Roman Empire. Although the town soon lost this title, it remained an important destination for pilgrims because of the valuable relics brought here by Charlemagne. From the 10th to the 14th centuries, all German kings were crowned in the palace chapel.

Subsequently, in the 18th and 19th centuries, Aachen gained great importance as a spa. Many magnificent buildings dating from this splendid era have long since vanished. A further wave of destruction was inflicted by World War II, yet some particularly magnificent historic

monuments have survived. The most important of these, in the centre of the old town, is the **Pfalz** *(see pp382–3)*, a complex of buildings belonging to Charlemagne's former palace. They include a cathedral with a palace chapel and a hall which was rebuilt as the **Rathaus**.

In the old town, not far from the cathedral complex, it is worth visiting the church of St Folian, where a Gothic Madonna dating from 1411 has survived. A short distance south from here stands the Elisenbrunnen (fountain of St Elizabeth), an exceptionally beautiful building where mineral water can be taken. It was built in 1822–7 according to designs by Johann Peter Cremer and Karl Friedrich Schinkel.

After admiring the attractive houses around the central market square visitors can enjoy the **Couven-Museum**. Based in an historic middle-class town house, it has an interesting collection dedicated to the life of the bourgeoisie in the 18th and 19th centuries. There is also a collection of ceramic tiles from the 17th–19th centuries.

The house where Israel Berr Josaphat Reuter established the first-ever news agency in 1850 (transferred to London

Statue of David Hansemann

a year later) now houses the **Internationales Zeitungsmuseum**, devoted to the history of the press, with over 100,000 newspapers from the 17th century to today.

It is also worth visiting the **Suermondt-Ludwig-Museum**, a short distance beyond the compact town centre, which has a great collection of art from the Middle Ages until the present day, including some beautiful sculptures and paintings from the 17th century.

To the northeast of the old town extends the spa district of Aachen. Here, visitors can stroll through the spa park at their leisure or spend an evening at the casino. Aachen also has much to offer lovers of modern art: the Ludwig-Forum für Internationale Kunst hosts interesting exhibitions, performances and concerts.

🏛 **Internationales Zeitungsmuseum**
Pontstr. 13. 🔒 *(0241) 432 45 08.*
⏰ *9:30am–1pm & 2:30–5pm Tue–Fri, 9:30am–1pm Sat.*
🏛 **Suermondt-Ludwig-Museum**
Wilhelmstr. 18. 🔒 *(0241) 47 98 00.*
⏰ *11am–7pm Tue & Thu–Fri, 11am–9pm Wed, 11am–5pm Sat & Sun.* 🏷
🚻 🖻 📷
🏛 **Couven-Museum**
Hühnermarkt 17. 🔒 *(0241) 432 44 21.* ⏰ *10am–5pm Tue–Sun.* ⬤ *public holidays.* 🏷

ENVIRONS: **Kornelimünster**, 6 km (4 miles) southeast of the centre, is a beautiful place with a well-preserved old town and churches. The most important of these is the Pfarrkirche St Kornelius, a former Benedictine monastery which dates from the early 9th century. The surviving building is a 14th-century Gothic basilica, extended by the early 16th century to an imposing five-nave structure. In the 18th century the octagonal chapel of St Kornelius was added to this at the axis of the presbytery.

The Neo-Classical building which houses the casino in Aachen's spa park

The Pfalz in Aachen

THE ORIGINAL palace of Charlemagne in Aachen did not survive; of his vast construction only the Pfalzkapelle (palatine chapel) remains. Modelled on the church of San Vitale in Ravenna, Italy, it was built by Odo von Metz in 786–800. In the mid-14th century a front tower was added, and in the years 1355–1414 a new presbytery was built. Side chapels were added later, and in the 17th century the central section was covered by a dome.

Charlemagne, effigy on his shrine

Antique Columns
The arcaded ambulatory is divided by beautiful columns, made from red marble and porphyry which had been brought from Ravenna and Rome.

Hubertus- and Karls- kapelle

Charlemagne's Throne
This modest throne, fashioned from marbled tiles, served as the coronation throne for successive German leaders.

Candelabra
This copper candelabra, a masterpiece of Romanesque craftsmanship, was a gift from Emperor Friedrich I Barbarossa.

Main entrance

Ungarn- kapelle

STAR SIGHTS

★ **The Shrine of Charlemagne**

★ **Lotharkreuz**

★ **Pala d'Oro**

Bronze doors
The doors, dating from the time of Charlemagne, are the oldest historic monument of their kind in Germany.

★ Lotharkreuz
This magnificent cross (c.1000), decorated with a cameo showing a portrait of Emperor Augustus, is one of the most valuable exhibits in the Schatzkammer.

The Gothic presbytery was modelled on Sainte-Chapelle in Paris.

VISITORS' CHECKLIST

Cathedral Münsterplatz. (0241) 47 70 90. ☐ 7am–7pm daily. ☐ from 10:45am Mon–Fri, from 12:30pm Sat & Sun.
Treasury Klosterplatz 2. (0241) 47 70 91 27. ☐ 10am–1pm Mon, 10am–6pm Tue, Wed, Fri–Sun, 10am–9pm Thu. ☐ W www.aachen-dom.de

★ The Shrine of Charlemagne
The Emperor Charlemagne was canonized as a saint in 1165 and shortly after, probably at the beginning of the 13th century, a golden shrine was made to keep his bones in. It is now on display in the presbytery.

★ Pala d'Oro
The front of the main altar is adorned with valuable gold sheets from c.1020, which were funded by Heinrich II.

Matthiaskapelle

Annakapelle

Proserpina's Sarcophagus
This sarcophagus, in the Schatzkammer (treasury), is an exceptionally beautiful example of Roman sculpture. It is thought that the body of Charlemagne rested in this coffin until he was canonized.

Ambo
The ambo, a pulpit fashioned from gold-plated copper and inlaid with precious stones and ivories, was donated by Heinrich II in 1014.

Köln (Cologne) ⑭

Detail on the Rathaus

ORIGINALLY FOUNDED by the Romans as *Colonia Agrippina*, Köln is one of the oldest towns in Germany. The Franks ruled the town from the end of the 5th century, and Charlemagne raised its status to that of an archbishopric. Köln has remained a powerful ecclesiastical centre – it boasts 12 Romanesque churches as well as the famous Gothic cathedral. In the Middle Ages the city also played a significant role in the Hanseatic League, and from 1388 it had a university.

⛪ St Andreas

Komödienstraße 4–8.
This late-Romanesque basilica was founded c.1200, with a presbytery added in 1414–20. The saint Albertus Magnus lies buried in the crypt. Particularly noteworthy are the beautiful capitals, which link the pillars between the naves, and the stalls (c.1420–30).

⛪ Pfarrkirche St Mariä Himmelfahrt

Marzellenstraße 32–40.
The parish church of the Assumption of Mary is one of the few Baroque buildings in Köln. It was built for the Jesuit Order in 1618–89, under the direction of Christoph Wamser. It is easy to discover numerous Romanesque and Gothic elements, although these are not surviving parts of an earlier building, but the result of a consciously created link with earlier styles.

Picturesque houses on Fischmarkt

⛪ Dom St Peter und Santa Maria

See pp388–9.

🏛 Römisch-Germanisches Museum

Roncalliplatz 4. ☎ (0221) 22 12 45 90. ⏰ 10am–5pm Tue–Sun.
This modern, glazed building houses archaeological finds dating from the Roman and pre-Roman eras that have been uncovered in Köln and

the Rhine Valley. On display are weapons, many items of everyday use, ornamental and artistic objects as well as the superb Dionysus mosaic and the monument to Poblicius.

🏛 Museum Ludwig

Bischofsgartenstraße 1. ☎ (0221) 22 12 23 82. ⏰ 10am–8pm Tue, 10am–6pm Wed–Fri; 11am–6pm Sat & Sun. 📷
This museum, combining the private collection of the Ludwig family with the 20th-century works originally held by the Wallraf-Richartz-Museum, has one of Europe's best collections of modern art. There are paintings by Picasso, German Expressionists, Surrealists, American Pop Artists and the Russian Avantgarde as well as many sculptures.

⛪ Groß St Martin

An Groß St Martin 9. ☎ (0221) 16 42 56 50. ⏰ 10am–6pm Mon–Fri, 10am–12:30pm & 1:30 6pm Sat, 2–4pm Sun.
This church, with its attractive triangular presbytery and vast tower dominating Fischmarkt, was founded by the Benedictine Order in the late 12th century. The Romans built a sports arena on this site with a swimming pool, remains of which have been uncovered under the crypt. The houses in the surrounding Martinsviertel are post-World War II, however they were built to historic designs and with a medieval street lay-out, making this an intimate and romantic area to explore.

Panorama with the Rathaus, Groß St Martin and the Dom, with the Rhine in the foreground

A detail of the Gothic section of the Rathaus façade

🏛 Wallraf-Richartz-Museum – Fondation Corboud
See pp390–91.

🏯 Rathaus
Alter Markt. ℹ (0221) 22 10. ⬤ 10am–5pm Mon–Fri, 10am–noon Sat. **Jewish Baths** ⬤ 8am–4:45pm Mon–Thu, 8am–noon Fri, 10am–4pm Sat, 11am–1pm Sun. **Praetorium** Kleine Budengasse. ⬤ for renovation.
The town hall is an irregular shape created by successive modifications. In the first phase, around 1330, a wing with a Hanseatic Hall was built, decorated with Gothic sculptures of heroes and prophets. In 1407–14 a vast Gothic tower was added, and in the 16th century the arcaded Renaissance Lions Courtyard and a magnificent front lodge were built. In front of the town hall, under a glass pyramid, are the remains of 12th-century ritual Jewish baths, that were destroyed after the expulsion of the Jews in 1424. From Kleine Budengasse an entrance leads to the *Praetorium*, the remains of a Roman town hall.

🏛 Gürzenich
Gürzenichstraße
This Gothic building has a huge celebration hall (1437–44), which occupies the entire first floor. Next to it are the ruins of the Romanesque church Alt St Alban. It has a copy of the sculpture *Parents* by Käthe Kollwitz.

⛪ Minoritenkirche Mariä Empfängnis
Minoritenstraße
This modest Gothic Franciscan church was established in the 13th–14th centuries. It is an elegant three-naved basilica without a tower, modelled on the Elisabethkirche in Marburg. There are historic furnishings and a 14th-century shrine with the remains of Johannes Duns Scotus, a Scottish Minorite.

VISITORS' CHECKLIST

Road map B4. 🏙 1,005,000. 🚉 Hauptbahnhof. 🚌 ZOB Breslauer Platz. ✈ Konrad-Adenauer Flughafen (02203-400). ℹ Unter Fettenhennen 19 (0221-22 13 04 00). 🛒 Markt bei der Apostelkirche 7am–noon Tue & Fri. 🎭 Rosenmontagsumzug (Carnival Rose Mon, Jan/Feb), Bierbörse (Aug/Sep). 🅦 www.koelntourismus.de

Place of remembrance, in Alt St Alban, near the Gürzenich

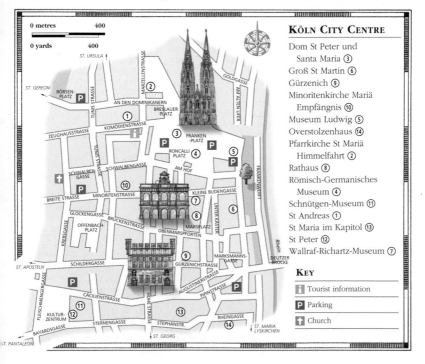

KÖLN CITY CENTRE

KEY

ℹ Tourist information

🅿 Parking

✝ Church

Exploring Köln (Cologne)

PRESENT-DAY Köln is a metropolis, known primarily for its trade fairs. It is also an important centre of art and culture, its reputation forged by several excellent museums, numerous historic buildings and superb art galleries. Book and newspaper publishers have their head offices here, as do radio and television stations. The highest number of visitors, however, come to Köln for the five days preceding Ash Wednesday, to join in the fun and watch the grand carnival processions.

🏛 Schnütgen-Museum
Cäcilienstraße 29. ☎ (0221) 22 12 36 20. ☐ 10am–5pm Tue–Fri, 11am–5pm Sat & Sun. 🖼
The Romanesque church of St Cecilia, built in 1130–60 as a nunnery, was taken over in 1479 by the Augustinian Sisters, today it houses the Schnütgen-Museum. Destroyed during World War II and subsequently rebuilt, this museum specializes in religious art, mainly from the Middle Ages. Its collection includes magnificent sculptures, gold and ivory items and sacral objects.

The Romanesque church of St Gereon, with its vast dome

🏰 St Peter
Leonhard-Tietz-Straße 6.
The late-Gothic church of St Peter is a galleried basilica, built in 1515–39. Following its destruction in World War II, the former vaulting was replaced by a ceiling. The church's greatest attractions include its Renaissance stained-glass windows (1528–30) and the magnificent *Crucifixion of St Peter*, painted after 1637 by Peter Paul Rubens, who spent his childhood here and whose father lies buried in the church.

Detail from Stadtmuseum

🏰 St Maria im Kapitol
Marienplatz 19.
Originally built in the early part of the 11th century, as a convent, the church's extension and remodelling took until the early 13th century. Noteworthy among the furnishings are its extensive crypt and the mid-11th-century wooden door in the west closure, richly carved with reliefs depicting scenes from the life of Christ. It also has a superb Renaissance rood screen, and is the only church in Köln with cloisters.

🏵 Overstolzenhaus
Rheingasse 8.
World War II deprived Köln of many of its historic residential buildings, but this one has been lovingly restored. Built for a prosperous patrician family in the second quarter of the 13th century, it is regarded as one of the town's finest Gothic houses.

🏰 St Maria Lyskirchen
An Lyskirchen 12.
This, the smallest Romanesque church in Köln, was built around 1220 and slightly remodelled in the 17th century. Its greatest attractions are magnificent frescos depicting scenes from the Bible and the lives of the saints, which adorn the vaults (c.1250), as well as the *Schöne Madonna*, a huge statue of the Virgin with the Infant Christ (c.1420).

🏛 Imhoff-Stollwerck-Museum
Rheinauhafen 1a. ☎ (0221) 931 88 80. ☐ 10am–6pm Tue–Fri, 11am–7pm Sat & Sun. 🖼
This fantastic museum of chocolate explains the history of cocoa bean cultivation as well as the cultural significance, use and marketing of chocolate. It also shows the production process, and lets visitors sample the product.

🏰 St Georg
Georgsplatz 17.
This church was built around the middle of the 11th century, originally as a transept basilica with two choirs. In

---

ROMANESQUE CHURCHES
Köln has 12 surviving Romanesque churches, bearing testimony to the importance of the Church in the town's development. Built on the graves of martyrs and early bishops of Köln, the forms of the churches influenced the development of Romanesque architecture well beyond the Rhineland. Almost all the churches were damaged in World War II. Some, such as the church of St Kolumba, have not been restored, but most were returned to their former glory.

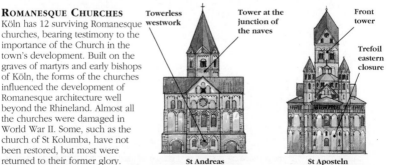

Towerless westwork

Tower at the junction of the naves

Front tower

Trefoil eastern closure

St Andreas

St Aposteln

The attractive Romanesque church of St Kunibert, seen from the Rhine

the mid-12th century the west choir was replaced by a massive frontage (westwork), but the towers were never added.

🔒 St Pantaleon
Am Pantaleonsberg 2.

A little way from the centre is this exquisite church, a former Benedictine monastery founded c.950 by Archbishop Bruno, brother of Emperor Otto I. The archbishop and the Empress Theophanu, who completed the building, are both buried here. The church has a superb late-Gothic choir screen with richly carved ornamentation. From the crypt, the remains of a Roman villa are accessible.

🏛 Severinsviertel

The Severin Quarter, a district on the southern edge of the old town, owes its name to the 13th-century Romanesque church of St Severinus. The church, largely remodelled in the Gothic style in the 15th and 16th centuries, features rich original furnishings and has a mid-10th-century crypt.

🔒 St Aposteln
Neumarkt 30.

This enormous 12th-century church of the Apostles, which towers over Neumarkt, a central square in Köln, is one of the most interesting Romanesque churches in the Rhineland. The original basilica has a trefoil eastern closure, a low tower at the junction of the naves and a tall front tower. It was given two further slim turrets flanking the apse of the presbytery.

From Neumarkt, Hahnenstrasse leads to Rudolfplatz and the Hahnentor, perhaps the most beautiful of all surviving medieval gates.

🔒 St Gereon
Gereonsdriesch 2–4.

This church must be the most unusual edifice not only in the Rhineland, but in all of Germany. Its oldest part, an oval building surrounded by small conchas, was built in the late 4th century on the graves of martyrs and – according to legend – founded by St Helen. The Romanesque

presbytery is an 11th-century addition and, in 1219–27, the oval was encircled with a ten-sided, four-storey structure in early-Gothic style. This is topped with a massive dome, 48 m (157 ft) in diameter, with ribbed vault.

🔒 St Ursula
Ursulaplatz 24.

This church was built in the 12th century, on the site of an earlier church probably dating from c.400. In the late 13th century the presbytery was rebuilt in Gothic style. The Baroque golden chamber at the southern end, added in the 17th century, is lined with many shrines. According to legend, these hold the remains of St Ursula and 11,000 virgins, all of whom were reputedly killed at the hands of the Huns. The town insignia of Köln also testify to the veneration of the virgins.

🔒 St Kunibert
Kunibertskloster 2.

Bishop Kunibert was buried in a church on this site in 663. The present Romanesque church (1215–47) has precious Romanesque stained-glass windows (c.1220–30).

The medieval Hahnentor, exit from Köln towards Aachen

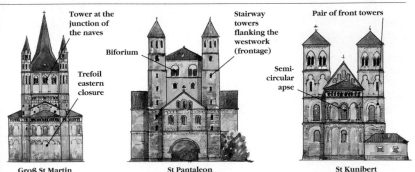

| Groß St Martin | St Pantaleon | St Kunibert |

Tower at the junction of the naves
Trefoil eastern closure
Biforium
Stairway towers flanking the westwork (frontage)
Pair of front towers
Semi-circular apse

Cologne Cathedral (Kölner Dom)

10th-century Gero Cross

THE MOST FAMOUS Gothic structure in Germany, the Kölner Dom is also unusually complex, whether in terms of its splendour, its size or even simply the date of its construction. The foundation stone was laid on 15th August 1248, the presbytery consecrated in 1322. The cathedral was built gradually until c.1520. It then remained unfinished until the 19th century, when Romanticists revived interest in it. The building was finally completed in 1842–80, according to the rediscovered, original Gothic designs.

Pinnacles
Elaborately decorated pinnacles top the supporting pillars.

Cathedral Interior
The presbytery, the ambulatory and the chapels retain a large number of Gothic, mainly early-14th-century, stained-glass windows.

Engelbert Reliquary (c.1630)
The cathedral treasury is famous for its large collection of golden objects, vestments and the fine ornamentation of its liturgical books.

Main entrance

Petrusportal, or the portal of St Peter, the only one built in the second half of the 14th century, has five Gothic figures.

STAR SIGHTS

★ **Gothic Stalls**

★ **Shrine of the Three Kings**

★ **Altar of the Magi**

★ **Gothic Stalls**
The massive oak stalls, built in 1308–11, were the largest that have ever been made in Germany.

Semicircular arches transfer the thrust of the vaults onto the buttresses.

Buttresses support the entire bulk of the cathedral.

High Altar
The Gothic altar slab, which dates back to the consecration of the presbytery, depicts the Coronation of the Virgin Mary, flanked by the twelve apostles.

★ **Shrine of the Three Kings**
This huge Romanesque reliquary was made by Nikolaus von Verdun in 1181–1220, to hold the relics of the Three Kings. These relics were brought to Köln in 1164 for Emperor Friedrich I Barbarossa.

★ **Altar of the Magi**
This splendid altar (c.1445), the work of Stephan Lochner, is dedicated to the Three Kings, the patrons of Köln.

Mailänder Madonna
This fine early-Gothic carving of the Milan Madonna and Child dates from around 1290. It is currently displayed in the Marienkapelle.

Wallraf-Richartz-Museum – Fondation Corboud

THIS MUSEUM WAS named after Ferdinand Franz Wallraf, who bequeathed his art collection to the city in 1824, and Johann Heinrich Richartz, who funded the first building. In 1977, all 20th-century works of art were combined with the private collection of the Ludwig family and exhibited in the Museum Ludwig, initially located on the upper floors of the museum. In 2001 the Wallraf-Richartz-Museum moved to a brand-new building, incorporating many new works from the collection of Gerard Corboud.

Bleaching the Linen (1882)
Max Liebermann created this painting in the early stages of his career, when his work was largely concerned with Realism.

★ Stigmatization of St Francis (c.1616)
This dark and mysterious painting, originally created by Peter Paul Rubens for the Capuchin church in Köln, is untypical of the artist's work

Third floor

Reclining Girl (1751)
This young nude, arranged on her bed in a provocative pose, is an example of the light-hearted works of so-called "boudoir art" that François Boucher specialized in.

Ground floor

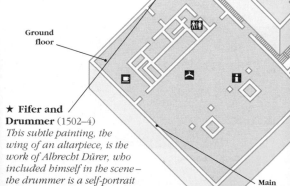

★ Fifer and Drummer (1502–4)
This subtle painting, the wing of an altarpiece, is the work of Albrecht Dürer, who included himself in the scene – the drummer is a self-portrait of Dürer himself.

Main entrance

Girls on a Bridge
(1905)
Edvard Munch covered the same subject several times (see p423). The version held in Köln is one of the earliest, and features an urbanized landscape.

Fifth floor

GALLERY GUIDE
Each floor in the museum displays paintings belonging to one era. On the second floor, the exhibition begins with the collection of 14th-century art; the third floor holds 16th–18th century art, and on the fifth floor works of art from the 19th century are displayed, organized by the schools of art they represent.

Jacob accuses Laban of giving him Lei instead of Rachel as a wife
(1628)
This biblical scene was painted by one of the most outstanding Dutch masters, Hendrick ter Brugghen.

Second floor

Old Woman and Boy
(c.1650–60)
This scene was painted by Bartolome Esteban Murillo. The artist excelled not only as the master of charmingly senti-mental depictions of the Madonna, but was also an excellent observer of everyday life in 17th-century Spain.

Madonna and Child
(1325–30)
This central panel of a trip-tych by Simone Martini is thought to have originated from the San Agostino church in San Giminiano.

KEY

☐ Medieval paintings
☐ 17th- and 18th-century paintings
☐ 19th-century paintings
☐ Non-exhibition space

STAR EXHIBITS

★ **Fifer and Drummer**

★ **Stigmatization of St Francis**

One of the artificial reservoirs in the northern Eifel

Northern Eifel

Road map A4. ⓘ *Bad Münstereifel, Kölner Strasse 13 (0180) 500 22 83.* 🎭 *Bad Münstereifel: Burg in Flammen (Jul).*

BARELY 20 percent of the Eifel mountain range is in North Rhine-Westphalia. Low, forested mountains line the valley of the Rur river, which has been dammed in several places. The resulting artificial lakes provide a perfect opportunity for relaxation and sporting activities. There are also many attractive towns and fascinating monuments.

Blankenheim is famed for its picturesque half-timbered houses, the late-Gothic church and the frequently modified 12th-century castle of the counts von Manderscheid-Blankenheim, which today is a youth hostel. The source of the Ahr river can also be seen here – a house was built over the top of it in 1726.

In **Schleiden**, the castle, built in the 12th century and frequently rebuilt up until the 18th century, is worth visiting. There is also a late-Gothic church with valuable stained-glass windows and an impressive organ dating from 1770.

Probably the most beautiful town in this region is **Monschau**, which until 1919 was called Montjoie. It is known also for the Montjoier Düttchen (croissants) and an excellent mustard. The ruin of a 13th-century castle towers on a hill. At its foot, the Rur river runs through a narrow valley, with attractive small towns, narrow, steep streets and timber-frame houses from various eras. In Hasenfeld

visitors can see a dam dating from 1904, and an amazing hydro-electric building, decorated in a way that reflects its purpose. One of the most interesting monuments of this region is the Steinfeld monastery, with a history dating from the 10th century. In 1121 the Augustinians settled here, and in 1126 they accepted the rule of St Norbert of Xanten, and this became the first monastery on German territory. A beautiful Romanesque basilica was built in the second half of the 12th century. It has retained wall paintings from the 12th and 14th centuries, and vaulted ceilings from the 16th century. The **Rheinisches Freilichtmuseum Kommern** is an open-air museum with examples of the building styles typical of the Northern Eifel. It is also worth visiting the town of **Euskirchen**, which has an attractive Gothic church with superb furnishings, and the moated castle of Veynau (14–15th centuries).

Picturesque half-timbered houses in Monschau

The spa town of **Bad Münstereifel** dates back to 830, when a Benedictine monastery was established here. The present church is a 12th-century Romanesque basilica with impressive 11th-century frontage. Also worth seeing are the Gothic town hall and a Romanesque house, now housing a museum.

🏛 **Rheinisches Freilichtmuseum Kommern**
Auf dem Kahlenbusch. Mechernich-Kommern. ⓘ *(02443) 998 00.* ⏱ *Apr–Oct: 9am–6pm; Nov–Mar: 10am–4pm.* ♿

Brühl ⑰

Road map B4. 🚶 *42,000.* 🚉 🚌 ⓘ *Uhlstr. 1 (02232-79 34 50).* 🎭 *Hubertusmarkt (Oct).*

THE SMALL TOWN of Brühl has one of the most beautiful residential complexes, since 1984 a UNESCO World Heritage Site. As early as the 13th century, a palace was established here for the archbishops of nearby Köln, but this was destroyed in 1689. A Baroque palace, **Augustusburg**, was built on its foundations in 1725–8, according to a design by Johann Conrad Schlaun. It was named after the instigator of the building, Elector Klemens August. The building was almost immediately refurbished, with a new façade and furnishings, the work of François Cuvilliés, and in the 1940s a new staircase was completed to a design by Balthasar Neumann. After devastation in World War II, the palace was carefully restored, and the magnificently furnished late-Baroque and Rococo interior, especially a stunning dining room designed by Cuvilliés, can now be seen again. A path leads from the orangery to a Gothic church built for the Franciscans in the 15th century. The *Annunciation* on the high altar is the work of Johann Wolfgang van der Auwer, while the magnificent

Merry-go-round at the Phantasialand in Brühl

Phantasialand, the largest theme park in Germany, near Brühl

canopy above was designed by Balthasar Neumann. The castle is surrounded by a Baroque park, designed by Dominique Girard.

About 2 km (1 mile) east of the main residence is another castle, **Falkenlust**, built in 1729–40, to a design by Cuvilliés. Its captivating interior includes a lacquered and a mirror cabinet. Nearby stands an octagonal chapel, its interior decoration modelled on a secluded grotto.

It is also worth visiting the small villa near Augustusburg where the great Surrealist artist Max Ernst was born. It now houses a small display commemorating his work.

Another attraction, which draws a large number of visitors is **Phantasialand**, Germany's largest theme park. Visitors will need several days to see all the attractions of this vast fairground with its roller-coaster, water-rides and numerous merry-go-rounds.

♟ Augustusburg
((02232) 440 00. ☐ Feb–Nov: 9am–noon & 1:30–5pm Tue–Fri, 10am–6pm Sat & Sun.

☐ Falkenlust
((02232) 440 00. ☐ Feb–Nov: 9am–12:30pm & 1:30–5pm Tue–Fri, 10am–6pm Sat & Sun.

☐ Phantasialand
Berggeiststr. 31–41. **(** (02232) 362 00. ☐ Apr–Oct: 9am–6pm daily, later in summer. 📷

ENVIRONS: Two moated houses await the visitor at **Kerpen**, 27 km (17 miles) to the north: the small 16th-century castle of Lörsfeld, and the Baroque palace of Türnich, built in 1756–66.

In **Pulheim-Brauweiler**, 30 km (19 miles) to the north, is an extremely beautiful Benedictine monastery, founded in 1024. Building began in 1048, funded by Rycheza, the wife of the Polish King Boleslav Chrobry.

From here it is worth travelling another 23 km (14 miles)

west to **Bedburg**, where the moated castle is worth seeing. This is a vast brick structure with four wings, which was established in stages over 300 years, starting in around 1300.

Bonn ⑱

See p394.

Königswinter ⑲

Road map B4. 🏛 35,000. 🚍 📠
ℹ Drachenfelsstr. 11 (02223-91 77 11).

KÖNIGSWINTER lies in the centre of the Siebengebirge, an attractive range of small, wooded mountains (the "seven mountains"), excellently suited for walking. The most popular mountain is the Drachenfels (dragon's rock). The oldest mountain railway in Germany, built in 1883, takes visitors to the top (321 m/1,053 ft). During the ascent visitors can see the Neo-Gothic Drachenburg, a palace dating from 1879–84, and on the top are the ruins of the Gothic Drachenburg, dating from the 12th century. The "dragon" in the name relates to the myth of the Nibelungs – the dragon slain by Siegfried was supposed to have lived here.

The little town of Königswinter, at the foot of the mountains, has picturesque 17th-century half-timbered houses, town houses and late 19th-century hotels.

ENVIRONS: Bad Honnef, 6 km (4 miles) to the south, is a charming spa town known as "Nice on the Rhine", where the former chancellor Konrad Adenauer lived until his death. A museum commemorates this great politician.

Situated 15 km (9 miles) to the north is **Siegburg**, where a Benedictine monastery (1064) is worth visiting. The walls of the crypt are from the 11th century, but the present church is a 17th-century building, rebuilt after World War II. The Anno-Schrein is a magnificent Romanesque reliquary box dating from 1183.

The Baroque Schloss Augustusburg in Brühl

Bonn ⑱

BONN was founded by the Romans in 11 BC, and flourished thanks to the archbishops of Cologne. It gained fame because of Ludwig van Beethoven, who was born here in 1770, and Robert Schumann, who spent the final years of his life here. The world heard of Bonn when, on 10 May 1949, it was elevated to the status of capital of the Federal Republic of Germany. When parliament decided in 1991 to make Berlin the capital of the newly unified country, Bonn was deprived of its role, although seven ministries stayed on.

The Baroque portal of the Beethovenhaus in Bonn

🏠 Beethovenhaus
Bonngasse 20. 📞 (0228) 981 75 25. 🕐 Apr–Sep: 10am–6pm Mon–Sat, 11am–4pm Sun; Oct–Mar: 10am–5pm Mon–Sat, 11am–4pm Sun. 📷
The museum is housed in the Baroque 18th-century house where the composer Ludwig van Beethoven was born and lived until the age of 22. He never returned to his home town, but there is a large and impressive collection of memorabilia from his entire life.

🏠 Markt
The central market square in Bonn, shaped like a triangle, owes its present appearance to a mixture of modern and Baroque architecture. Its most outstanding feature is the late-Baroque **Rathaus** (town hall), built in 1737–8, to a design by Michel Leveilly. The centre of the market square is decorated with the Marktbrunnen, a fountain in the shape of an obelisk, erected in 1777 in honour of the Elector Maximilian Friedrich.

Not far from the Markt are some churches worth seeing. The first is the Gothic **Remigius-kirche**, built for the Franciscans in the years 1274–1317, and the second is the Baroque **Namen-Jesu-Kirche** built for the Jesuits according to a design by Jacob de Candreal in the years 1686–1717.

🏠 Rheinufer
The Rhine embankment, which changes its name several times along its course, runs along the western bank of the Rhine. Many of Bonn's attractions are grouped along this street. To the north of Kennedybrücke (Kennedy bridge) lies the Beethovenhalle, a vast concert and congress hall, and to the south of the bridge is the Bonn opera house.

Gold clasps in the Rheinisches Landesmuseum

Next to the opera is the Alter Zoll, the former customs house, based in one of the bastions that was part of the 17th-century city defences.

🏠 Universität
Am Hofgarten.
Founded in 1818, Bonn University is based in what is probably the most beautiful home for an educational institution anywhere in Germany. The stunningly attractive Baroque castle was built for the Elector Joseph Klemens in 1607–1705, to a design by Enrico Zuccalle, and extended after 1715 by Robert de Cotte.

🔒 Münster St Martin
Münsterplatz.
Bonn's cathedral is a magnificent example of Romanesque architecture in the Rhine Valley. The church was built in around 1150–1230, on the site of an earlier 11th-century cathedral, of which a three-naved crypt has survived. South of it, the romantic 12th-century Romanesque cloister is also worth seeing.

🏛 Rheinisches Landesmuseum
Colmantstraße 14–16. 📞 (0228) 988 10. ⏺ Reopening after renovation end 2003; until then the collection is displayed at "Alte Rotation", Justus-von-Liebig-Str. 115. 🕐 11am–5pm Tue–Sun, 11am–8pm Wed.
This interesting regional museum has a vast collection of excavated items dating back to Roman times, as well as medieval and modern art. The skull of a Neanderthal Man is also exhibited here.

The Baroque Elector's palace, housing Bonn University

♨ Regierungsviertel

Until recently this was the central authority of one of the most powerful countries in Europe, and teeming with life. Now it creates a somewhat desolate impression. Some ministries and offices have remained in Bonn, and the transfer to Berlin is taking time, but the town is definitely changing.

The former Bundestag building, in the Regierungsviertel

♨ Haus der Geschichte der BR Deutschland

Willy-Brandt-Allee 14. ((0228) 916 50. ○ 9am–7pm Tue–Sun.
This excellent new history museum details the history of Germany after World War II, with fascinating multi-media displays and vast amounts of illustrative material.

ฏ Kunstmuseum Bonn

Friedrich-Ebert-Allee 2. ((0228) 77 62 60. ○ 10am–6pm Tue & Thu–Sun, 10am–9pm Wed. ● 24, 25 & 31 Dec; Sat, Sun & Mon in carnival.
This superb museum of 20th-century art, in an interesting building designed by Axel Schultes, has a great collection of Expressionist paintings, including many works by August Macke. Next to the museum is the Kunst- und Ausstellungshalle, which opened in 1992 as a venue for temporary exhibitions.

🎎 Bad Godesberg

The small spa town of Bad Godesberg was incorporated into Bonn as recently as 1969. An elegant neighbourhood, its villas line the spa park. On top of the hill is the Godes-burg, a castle dating from the 13th century, which has been a ruin since the 16th century.

♠ Poppelsdorf

In this leafy southwestern suburb, the Baroque Schloss Clemensruhe (1715–18) is well worth visiting. Both the castle and its extensive park with an attractive botanical garden belong to the university. It is also worth making a detour to the Baroque pilgrimage church on the Kreuzberg, a low hill. The church houses the chapel of the Holy Steps, attributed to Balthasar Neumann.

The Baroque Schloss Clemensruhe, in Poppelsdorf

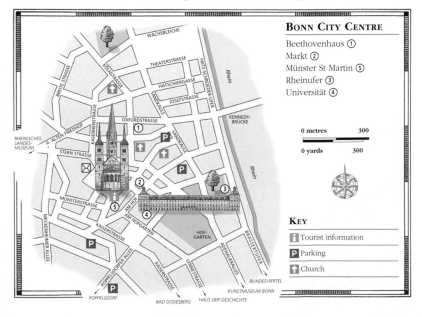

BONN CITY CENTRE

Beethovenhaus ①
Markt ②
Münster St Martin ⑤
Rheinufer ③
Universität ④

0 metres 300
0 yards 300

KEY

🛈 Tourist information
P Parking
✝ Church

The medieval Oberes Schloss in Siegen

Siegen ❷⓿

Road map B4. 🏛 *100,000.* 🚆 🚌
🛈 *Markt 2 (0271-404 13 16).*
🎭 *Kultur Pur (May/Jun), Rubensfest (Jun/Jul), Weihnachtsmarkt (Dec).*

BEAUTIFULLY located amidst the hills on the high banks of the Sieg river, Siegen is the largest town in the Siegerland region. For centuries the city was the residence of the dukes of Nassau. Religious divisions in the family resulted in two castles being built in Siegen. The **Oberes Schloss** (upper castle) is a medieval building, frequently refurbished in the 16th, 17th and 18th centuries. The museum, which has been opened inside the castle, has some paintings by Peter Paul Rubens, who was born in Siegen. The lower **Unteres Schloss** is a Baroque palace, which replaced an earlier building. In the centre of Siegen it is also worth visiting

the **Nicolaikirche**, a 13th-century hexagonal church with a presbytery and tower, which served as the ducal family mausoleum.

ENVIRONS: In **Freudenberg**, 10 km (6 miles) northwest of Siegen, is the small settlement of Alter Flecken, which is reproduced in virtually all German guidebooks. Founded in 1666 at the instigation of Duke Johann Moritz von Nassau, the village consists of identical half-timbered houses.

Hagen ❷❶

Road map B4. 🏛 *210,950.* 🚆 🚌
🛈 *Pavilion im Volkspark (02331-207 58 88).* 🎭 *Marktschreiertage (Jan).*

HAGEN would probably not feature in the guidebooks, were it not for Karl Ernst Osthaus, who created an artists' colony here at the beginning of the 20th century, inviting Art Nouveau designers such as Peter Behrens and Henry van de Velde. The magnificent **Hohenhof**, Osthaus' home, was created by van de Velde. It houses the **Karl-Ernst-Osthaus-Museum**, with a collection of modern art. Behrens designed the crematorium in the suburb of Delstern and the beautiful villas **Haus Como** (Hafleyer Str. 35) and **Haus Goedeke** (Amselgasse). In the south of the town is the Westfälisches

Freilichtmuseum, a popular open-air museum, which displays many historic workshops and factories with reconstructed equipment.

Sauerland ❷❷

Road map B4. 🛈 *Sauerland-Touristik, Brilon, Heinrich-Jansen-Weg 14 (02961-94 32 29).*

THE SAUERLAND is the region to the south and east of the Ruhr coalfields, making an obvious holiday destination for the inhabitants of this large, industrialized conurbation. Embracing the northern part of the Rhenish slate massif, its densely wooded mountains are not high – the highest peak is Hegekopf at 843 m (2,766 ft). Crossed by rivers teeming with fish and full of artificial lakes, the area is perfect for walking, cycling and fishing.

Enjoyable days can be had on an excursion to one of the caves such as **Attahöhle**, **Dechenhöhle** and **Heinrichshöhle** near Iserlohn. There are charming towns, too, and in **Breckerfeld**, the Gothic parish church has preserved a superb altar, from around 1520. The main attraction in **Altena** is the superb, gigantic Burg (castle), built in the 12th century and restored in the early 20th century. In 1910 the world's first youth hostel for tourists

One of the charming villages, nestling in the hilly landscape of the Sauerland

Timber-frame house, typical of the Sauerland landscape

was created here. The 14th-century Schloss Wocklum in **Balve** was rebuilt in the 18th century. One of the greatest tourist draws in the Sauerland is the **Möhnesee**, a lake with a huge dam, built in 1908–12 and bombed by Allied "dambusters" in 1943 with catastrophic consequences. **Arnsberg** has a regional museum and the lovely Neo-Gothic moated castle Herdringen with assorted furnishings from other castles.

In the south extend the Rothaargebirge (red-haired mountains). Their most beautiful town is the spa resort of Bad Berleburg, while the Kahler Asten mountain and the town of Winterberg are popular winter sports areas.

Soest ㉓

Road map B4. 🚶 50,000. 🚌 🚃
🛈 Am Seel 5 (02921-103 14 14).
🎭 Bördetag (May), Gauklertag (Sep), Jahrmarkt Allerheiligenkirmes (Nov).

THE WESTPHALIAN town of Soest made its mark in history when, in about 1100, the town's civic rights were formulated and subsequently adopted by 65 other towns. Today the town captivates visitors with its well-preserved old town, its historic churches, and the almost completely intact walls which surround the town. The focus of the old town is the Romanesque **Propsteikirche St Patrokli**, founded in 965 by Bruno, archbishop of Cologne, and built in stages until the 13th century. Further historic buildings are grouped around the church: the 18th-century, Baroque **Rathaus** (town hall),

the 12th-century Romanesque **Petrikirche** with its Gothic presbytery, and the 12th-century **Nicolaikapelle**, a chapel with 13th-century wall paintings and an altar painted by Konrad von Soest.

In the northern part of the old town, two churches are worth seeing: the **Hohnekirche** with beautiful Gothic and early Baroque furnishings, and the **Wiesenkirche** with equally valuable furnishings and a magnificent group of stained-glass windows from the 14th and 15th centuries. The window above the northern portal shows the so-called Westphalian Last Supper, depicting a table laden with plentiful Westphalian smoked ham and local pumpernickel bread.

An ornate window in the Dom in Paderborn

ENVIRONS: In **Lippstadt**, 23 km (14 miles) east of Soest, it is worth visiting the Gothic Marienkirche. In the suburb of Bökenförde is the 18th-century Baroque moated palace Schwarzenraben, and there is an early-Baroque castle in Overhagen.

Paderborn ㉔

Road map C3. 🚶 140,000. 🚌 🚃
🛈 Marienplatz 2 (05251-88 29 80).
🎭 Puppenfestspiele (Feb), Schützenfest (Jul), Liborifest (Jul–Aug), Liborikirmes (Oct).

PADERBORN has featured on the historical map for over 1,000 years. In the 8th century Charlemagne built a palace here, and in about AD 800, a bishopric was established. The town's most important monument is the beautiful **Dom St Maria, St Kilian und St Liborius**, a Romanesque-Gothic cathedral. This enormous hall-church with two transepts and tall front tower suffered greatly during World War II, but it continues to captivate visitors with its magnificent decor on the richly carved portal, the great

Romanesque crypt, interesting plaques and richly decorated bishops' tombs and epitaphs. The diocesan museum holds the Imad-Madonna, funded by Bishop Imad, an outstanding figure of the Madonna and Child dating from 1051–8. On the northern side of the cathedral a section of the foundations of the emperor's palace can be seen, together with the **Bartholomäuskapelle** (chapel of St Bartholomew), the oldest hall-church in Germany, completed in 1017. To the south of the cathedral complex, on Rathausplatz, is the exceptionally beautiful **Rathaus** (town hall) dating from 1613–20. An example of the Weser-Renaissance style, it is crowned with richly ornamented gables. The **Heinz-Nixdorf-Museumsforum** provides a pleasant break from the past – this museum is dedicated to the history of computers.

ENVIRONS: Near **Stukenbrock**, 15 km (9 miles) north of Paderborn, is the theme park Hollywood-Park and the fascinating Safariland, where more than 500 African animals roam freely.

Tower of the Romanesque-Gothic Dom in Paderborn

the centre of Höxter is a Gothic church built for the Franciscans in 1248–1320.

The city's greatest attraction, however, is the magnificent **Abtei Corvey**, a monastery founded in 822. It was originally built as the church of St Stephen and St Vitus, but only the grandiose two-storey frontage completed in 885 survived. It became the model for several other churches built in Westphalia, while the main body of the church was rebuilt in the 17th century.

Front of the early-Romanesque Abtei Corvey in Höxter

Höxter ㉕

Road map C3. 🏘 *35,000.* 🚪 🚌
🛈 *Weserstraße 11 (05271-194 33).*
🎭 *Corveyer Musikwochen (May–Jun), Huxorimarkt (Sep), Kirchenmusiktage (Nov–Dec).*

IN A PICTURESQUE situation on the Weser river, Höxter can pride itself on its beautiful old town with many timber-frame houses, fragments of the city walls, a Renaissance **Rathaus** (town hall) from 1610, and important churches. The history of **Kilianikirche**, in the centre of the old town, goes back to the late 8th century, although in its present form it is a Romanesque building from the 11th–12th centuries. Also in

Lemgo ㉖

Road map C3. 🏘 *42,000.* 🚪 🚌
🛈 *Am Historischen Marktplatz (05261-988 20).*

THIS EXCEPTIONALLY pretty town was founded in 1190 by Bernhard II von Lippe. It was a member of the Hanseatic League, and had its heyday during the witch hunts of the 17th century. Today, Lemgo has numerous Renaissance monuments – it was spared during World War II, and the Gothic Nicolaikirche and Marienkirche, with Gothic wall paintings and a Renaissance organ by Georg Slegel, have survived. The pearl of the city is the beautiful **Rathaus** (town hall), built in the 15th–17th centuries. It contains an original pharmacy that is still in use. Many timber-frame houses have also survived, the best ones in Papen-, Mittel- and Echternstraße.

Façade of a Renaissance pharmacy inside the Rathaus in Lemgo

The most beautiful house in Lemgo is the **Hexenbürger-meisterhaus**. This "witches' mayor's house" (1571), an excellent example of Weser Renaissance, belonged to the mayor, Hermann Cothmann, who started the witch hunt. It now houses a town museum. Also worth visiting are the **Junkerhaus** (1891), the architect's home, and **Schloss Brake** (13th-16th centuries), a castle which now houses the **Weserrenaissance-Museum**.

🏛 **Weserrenaissance-Museum**
Schloss Brake. 📞 *(05261) 945 00.*
🕐 *10am–6pm Tue–Sun.*

Teutoburger Wald (Teutoburg Forest) ㉗

Road map C3. 🛈 *Detmold, Rathaus Am Markt 5 (05231-97 73 28).*
🎭 *Andreas-Messe in Detmold (Nov).*

A RANGE OF LOW mountains extending from Osnabrück through Bielefeld right up to Paderborn, the Teutoburg Forest is one of the most attractive tourist regions in Westphalia. The best base for walking and cycling holidays is **Detmold**, which has a very attractive old town with well-preserved timber-frame buildings from various periods, and the elegant Residenz-schloss, the castle of the zur Lippe family. Originally medieval, the palace was rebuilt in the 16th century in the Weser-

The picturesque Renaissance Rathaus in Höxter

Renaissance style. The interior is composed of 17th and 19th century furnishings. The star feature is a set of eight gobelins crafted in a Brussels workshop around 1670, showing scenes of Alexander the Great's triumphs. Furnishings from the 19th century include designs by Charles Le Brun.

Three km (2 miles) south of Detmold is the spot where in the year AD 9 Cherusko Arminius, known as Hermann, leader of the Germanic tribes, triumphed against the Roman army led by Varus. At the top of the mountain, the **Hermannsdenkmal**, a huge monument designed by Ernst von Bandel, was erected in 1838–75. It was supposed to symbolize the German struggle for unification.

Two fascinating attractions near Detmold are the **Adlerwarte Berlebeck**, an ornithological research station, where eagles and many other birds of prey can be observed, and the **Vogelpark Heiligenkirchen**, a bird park with over 2,000 varieties of birds in all shapes and sizes from around the world.

Hermannsdenkmal, near Detmold

Bielefeld ㉘

Road map C3. 🏛 *325,000.* 🚉 🚌
🛈 *Niederwall 23 (0521-51 69 98) or Bahnhof 6 (0521-51 69 99).* 🎭 *Hermannslauf (Apr), Leinenweber-Markt (May), Bielefelder Kultur-Sommer (May–Sep), Sparrenburgfest (Jul), Weinmarkt (Sep), Weihnachtsmarkt (Dec).*

ON THE EDGE of the Teutoburg Forest, Bielefeld owes its evolution to the production of and trading in linen. The old town is dominated by the **Sparrenburg** castle, built in the 13th century for the von Ravensberg family. In the 16th century the castle was surrounded by new fortifications including new bastions, and in the 19th century the residential part of the city was greatly extended.

The central feature of the old town is Alter Markt (old

market), on which stands the **Nicolaikirche**. This Gothic church suffered heavily in World War II, although the marvellous Antwerp altar (c.1520) was preserved. Nearby, on Obernstraße, stands the **Crüwell-Haus**, an interesting late-Gothic town house from the early 16th century. The street leads to **St Jodokus-Kirche**, a late-Gothic church, whose greatest treasure is the amazing figure of the Black Madonna (c.1220). Further south is the **Kunsthalle**, a modern building with a significant collection of 20th-century art. It is also worth visiting the **Marienkirche** in the new town. Built in 1280–1330, this Gothic church holds the tomb of one of the von Ravensberg dukes (c.1320) and a high altar (c.1400) with a central Gothic section.

ENVIRONS: Picturesque **Herford**, 17 km (11 miles) north of Bielefeld, has a lovely old town with timber-frame houses and beautiful Gothic churches. In **Enger**, 21 km (13 miles) to the north, in the former church of the canons, a tomb dating from 1100 holds the remains of the Saxon Duke Widukind, buried in 807.

The spa town of **Bad Salzuflen** with its pretty old town and spa park is the ideal place for those seeking relaxation.

An observation tower in the Sparrenburg complex in Bielefeld

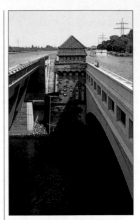

The Wasserstraßenkreuzung (waterway junction) in Minden

Minden ㉙

Road map C3. 🏛 *85,000.* 🚉 🚌
🛈 *Domstraße (0571-829 06 59).* 🎭 *Klassik-Open-Air (Jul/Aug).*

CHARLEMAGNE created a bishopric here as early as 798. The town evolved thanks to its strategic location on the Weser river. The city's most important monument is the cathedral, **Dompfarrkirche St Petrus und St Gorgonius**. It has a Romanesque presbytery, transept and monumental frontage built in the 11th–12th centuries, although the body of the church is an example of early-Gothic style from the 13th century. It is worth visiting the church treasury with its 11th-century crucifix.

The **Rathaus** (town hall), with 13th-century lower sections, is worth seeing, as are Minden's many charming houses around the market square. A great attraction is the **Wasserstraßenkreuz** (waterway junction), where a 375-m (1,230-ft) long bridge takes the Mittellandkanal across the Weser river.

ENVIRONS: On top of a hill in **Porta Westfalica**, 6 km (4 miles) south of Minden, is a giant monument to Kaiser Wilhelm (1892–6), designed by Bruno Schmitz.

The **Westfälische Mühlenstraße**, (Westphalian mill route), signposted around Minden, takes visitors past 42 different mills and windmills.

NORTHERN
GERMANY

Northern Germany at a Glance

NORTHERN GERMANY has very varied landscapes, ranging from the sandy beaches on the Baltic and North Sea coasts to the moraine hills of Schleswig-Holstein and the moorlands of the Lüneburger Heide. Nature-lovers are enchanted by the countless lakes in Mecklenburg and the Harz mountains, while those interested in history or architecture enjoy the Renaissance castles along the Weser River and the Gothic brick architecture in former Hanseatic towns. Historic buildings in Goslar and Hildesheim testify to the importance of these two towns.

Helgoland *is a popular tourist destination. Red cliffs as high as skyscrapers, a picturesque town and the sea aquarium are the star attractions of this island.*

SCHLESWIG-HOLSTEIN
(see pp440–51)

LOWER SAXONY, HAMBURG AND BREMEN
(see pp410–39)

Oldenburg, *symbolized by its heraldic shield, is famous for its large collection of paintings and interiors in its Kunstmuseum (art museum).*

Bremen, *a historic harbour town, draws visitors with its many historic buildings and monuments, including a Renaissance-Gothic town hall.*

Fehmarn, one of the largest of the German islands, is linked with the German mainland by a railway bridge constructed in 1963.

Rügen enchants visitors with its chalky white cliffs, which contrast starkly with the deep blues and greens of the surrounding Baltic Sea.

MECKLENBURG
LOWER POMERANIA
(see pp452–67)

Lübeck suffered massive damage in World War II, but its Gothic town hall survived the attacks and the city's beautiful old town has been rebuilt.

0 km   50

0 miles   50

Hamburg not only has attractive museums and valuable monuments, but also such lively and bustling places as the Fischmarkt, a huge market held every Sunday morning where it is possible to purchase virtually anything.

Gothic Brick Architecture

Terracotta decoration

BRICK WAS used as a building material in many parts of medieval Europe, but in Northern Germany it gave rise to the distinctive style of *Backsteingotik* (brick Gothic). Brick technology was introduced in the mid-12th century by Norbertine monks arriving from Lombardy. The style is characterized by a rich variety of vaults, the use of buttresses instead of supporting arches, and colourful designs achieved by using glazed bricks. Through trade and the activities of religious orders these forms spread throughout the Baltic region.

The storeys are divided by friezes.

MARIENKIRCHE IN LÜBECK
Considered the crowning achieve-ment of *Backstein-gotik*, this church, built from around 1260, became the model for countless others, including the cathedral in Schwerin. It is a triple-naved basilica, with a twin-towered façade, braced with buttresses.

The eastern façade of many churches, such as the Marienkirche in Prenzlau (above) was often crowned by an elaborate, orna-mental gable.

A pointed arched portal, decorated with ceramic borders, was a typical feature of many village churches.

Main portal

Gables with tiled decorations and intricate openwork, such as this gable of the south chapel of the Nikolai-kirche in Wismar, are a feature of many Lower Pomeranian churches.

The vast twin-towered façade symbolizes the power of its founders – wealthy Lübeck patricians.

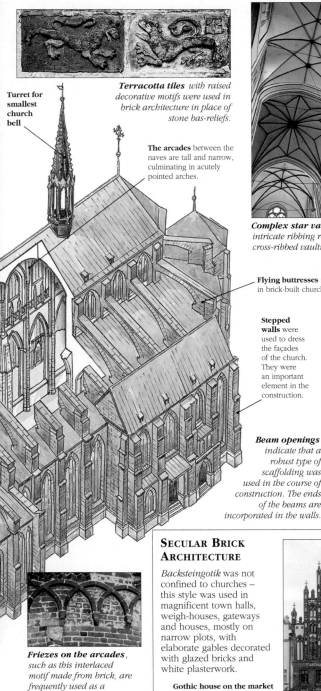

Terracotta tiles with raised decorative motifs were used in brick architecture in place of stone bas-reliefs.

Turret for smallest church bell

The arcades between the naves are tall and narrow, culminating in acutely pointed arches.

Complex star vaulting with intricate ribbing replaced the earlier cross-ribbed vaulting.

Flying buttresses are rare in brick-built churches.

Stepped walls were used to dress the façades of the church. They were an important element in the construction.

Beam openings indicate that a robust type of scaffolding was used in the course of construction. The ends of the beams are incorporated in the walls.

Friezes on the arcades, such as this interlaced motif made from brick, are frequently used as a decorative element, even in village churches.

SECULAR BRICK ARCHITECTURE

Backsteingotik was not confined to churches – this style was used in magnificent town halls, weigh-houses, gateways and houses, mostly on narrow plots, with elaborate gables decorated with glazed bricks and white plasterwork.

Gothic house on the market square in Greifswald

The German Coastline

T HE WATERS of two seas – the North Sea and the Baltic Sea – lap on northern Germany's shores, linked by the Kiel Canal, which cuts across the base of the Jutland peninsula. The cool climate on the coast makes for short summers yet, on a sunny day, the beaches are packed with holidaymakers, and a holiday here can have a lot to offer. Heiligendamm was the first seaside resort to be established in Germany, in 1783 by a duke of Mecklenburg. By the end of the 19th century, spas with elegant villas, promenades and piers were springing up everywhere. A popular attraction are the *Strandkörbe* – huge wickerwork beach chairs.

The sand dunes form part of a nature reserve in the northern part of Sylt, the largest of the North Frisian islands.

The Cliffs of Helgoland have a characteristic reddish hue indicating the red sandstone from which they are composed.

NORDSEE (NORTH SEA)

NORDFRIESISCHE INSELN

Sylt

NORDFRIESLAND

Flensburg

Schleswig

Rendsburg

Kiel

Helgoland

Neumünst

OSTFRIESLAND

Itzehoe

Elmshorn

Pinneberg

Hambur

Wilhelmshaven

Bremerhaven

Reinbek

Emden

Oldenburg

Borkum, one of the East Frisian islands, was once inhabited by whalers. Garden fences were often constructed from whale bones, and some have survived to the present day.

The Kiel Canal, known in Germany as the Nord-Ostsee-Kanal, was constructed in 1887–95. Around 40,000 vessels pass through the canal every year.

Bremerhaven is a vast port at the mouth of the Weser river. It was constructed from 1837 to support the port of Bremen, which is located farther inland, away from the sea.

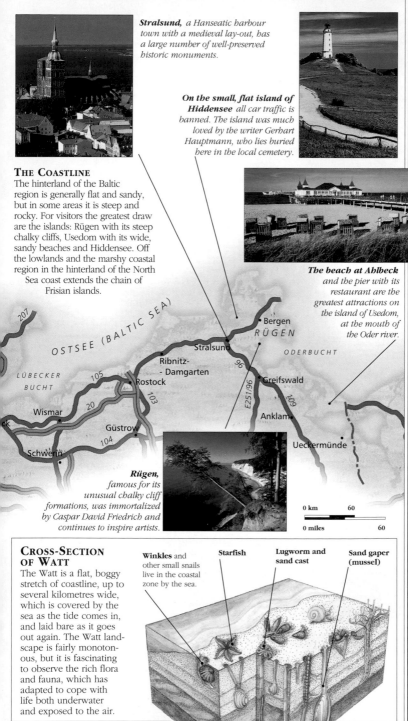

Stralsund, *a Hanseatic harbour town with a medieval lay-out, has a large number of well-preserved historic monuments.*

On the small, flat island of Hiddensee *all car traffic is banned. The island was much loved by the writer Gerhart Hauptmann, who lies buried here in the local cemetery.*

THE COASTLINE

The hinterland of the Baltic region is generally flat and sandy, but in some areas it is steep and rocky. For visitors the greatest draw are the islands: Rügen with its steep chalky cliffs, Usedom with its wide, sandy beaches and Hiddensee. Off the lowlands and the marshy coastal region in the hinterland of the North Sea coast extends the chain of Frisian islands.

The beach at Ahlbeck *and the pier with its restaurant are the greatest attractions on the island of Usedom, at the mouth of the Oder river.*

207

OSTSEE (BALTIC SEA)

LÜBECKER BUCHT

Bergen
RÜGEN

Stralsund

ODERBUCHT

Ribnitz-
- Damgarten

105

Rostock

103

Greifswald

Wismar

20

409

Anklam

104

Güstrow

Schwerin

Ueckermünde

Rügen, *famous for its unusual chalky cliff formations, was immortalized by Caspar David Friedrich and continues to inspire artists.*

0 km   60

0 miles   60

CROSS-SECTION OF WATT

The Watt is a flat, boggy stretch of coastline, up to several kilometres wide, which is covered by the sea as the tide comes in, and laid bare as it goes out again. The Watt landscape is fairly monotonous, but it is fascinating to observe the rich flora and fauna, which has adapted to cope with life both underwater and exposed to the air.

Winkles and other small snails live in the coastal zone by the sea.

Starfish

Lugworm and sand cast

Sand gaper (mussel)

LOWER SAXONY, HAMBURG AND BREMEN

THREE *federal states – Lower Saxony and the independent city states of Hamburg and Bremen – cover an enormous terrain, embracing the whole of northwestern Germany. For the visitor they provide a series of memorable snapshots: the mighty cosmopolitan port of Hamburg, enchanting towns and villages with half-timbered houses and the blooming heather of the Lüneburger Heide.*

Lower Saxony was formed in the 19th century through the merging of the kingdom of Hannover with the duchy of Brunswick, Oldenburg and Schaumburg-Lippe and other parts of northern Germany. The second-largest German state after Bavaria, it only ranks fourth in terms of the number of its inhabitants, being less densely populated than other states.

Lower Saxony is characterized by lowlands that become hillier in the south, culminating in the Harz Mountains. The only large cities are Hannover, a modern centre renowned for its trade fairs and for hosting Expo 2000, and Braunschweig, a venerable town that cherishes its link with the Saxon king Heinrich der Löwe, its first important ruler. The Romanesque splendour of Hildesheim is a magnet for visitors, as are the Renaissance centres along the Weser River including Hameln, the charming towns of Celle, Lüneburg and Einbeck, and Wolfenbüttel, Stadthagen and Bückeburg which contain some remarkable Mannerist works of art.

Nature lovers will enjoy excursions to the Lüneburger Heide or paddling in the endless expanses of mud-flats in the North Sea. Tourists are also attracted by the sandy beaches of the East Frisian islands, as well as the solitary rock of the island of Helgoland.

The "free and Hanseatic" towns of Hamburg and Bremen rejoice in a different atmosphere, urban and urbane, tolerant and multicultural, based on centuries of trade with the world.

The glorious moorlands of the Lüneburger Heide, with tall juniper bushes and flowering heathers

◁ The charming Gänselieselbrunnen (goose girl fountain) in the market square in Göttingen

Exploring Lower Saxony, Hamburg and Bremen

Hamburg and Bremen, the region's largest cities, are also the most convenient bases for tourists, offering accommodation in every price category. The most attractive area in this region is the south-eastern section, extending to the foothills of the Harz Mountains with picturesque towns, such as the university town of Göttingen, Romanesque Hildesheim or the stunningly beautiful mer-chant town of Goslar. A visit to the seaside and an excursion to the islands are also enjoyable.

SEE ALSO

• *Where to Stay* pp492–5

• *Where to Eat* pp523–5

OSTFRIESISCHE INSELN

OSTFRIESLAND

WILHELMSHAVEN

EMDEN

OLDENBURG

BREMEN

CLEMENSWERTH

CLOPPENBURG

NORDHORN

WIEHENGEBIRGE

OSNABRÜCK

BÜCKEB

The crowning feature of the bay window of the Dempter-haus in Hameln

The massive edifice of the Neues Rathaus in Hannover

| 0 km | 40 |
| 0 miles | 40 |

KEY

▬ Motorway

▬ Main road

▬ Scenic route

═ River

☆ Viewpoint

GETTING AROUND

There are international airports in Hamburg, Bremen and Hannover. A network of motorways links Lower Saxony with Scandinavia (via Schleswig-Holstein), and with the rest of western Europe (via the Netherlands or southern Germany). There are good ferry connections between Hamburg and Harwich (England). An extensive rail network makes the entire state accessible, although bus connections are limited.

The Grosse Wallanlagen Park in Hamburg, laid out along the city's former fortifications

SIGHTS AT A GLANCE

Altes Land **9**
Braunschweig (Brunswick) **18**
Bremen pp416–19 **7**
Bückeburg **17**
Celle **14**
Clemenswerth **3**
Cloppenburg **5**
Duderstadt **25**
Einbeck **23**
Goslar pp436–7 **22**
Göttingen **24**
Hamburg pp420–25 **8**
Hannover (Hanover) pp430–31 **20**
Hildesheim pp434–5 **21**
Lüneburg **11**
Lüneburger Heide **12**
Oldenburg **4**
Osnabrück **6**
Ostfriesische Inseln (East Frisian Islands) **1**
Ostfriesland (Eastern Frisia) **2**
Soltau **13**
Stade **10**
Stadthagen **16**
Wolfenbüttel **19**
Wolfsburg **15**

Tours
The Weser Renaissance Trail **26**

Ostfriesische Inseln (East Frisian Islands) ❶

Road map B2. 🚢 *Emden-Borkum, Norden-Norddeich to Juist and Norderney, Nessmersiel-Baltrum, Bensersiel-Langeoog, Neuharlingersiel-Spiekeroog, Harlesiel-Wangerooge.*
ℹ️ *(0180) 522 96.*
🌐 *www.die-nordsee.de*

Moormuseum in Elisabethfehn, Ostfriesland

ALONG THE North Sea Coast extends the belt of East Frisian Islands consisting of, from west to east: Borkum, Juist, Norderney, Baltrum, Langeoog, Spiekeroog and Wangerooge. All around them is the **Nationalpark Niedersächsisches Wattenmeer**, a large national park established to protect the unique ecosystem of the shallow seas. At low tide it turns into vast mud-flats, extending to the horizon. This is the time to tour the Watt, as it is known locally, either by horse-drawn carriage or barefoot – always making sure to return before the tide comes in!

The islands themselves, with their beautiful sandy beaches, sand dunes and healthy climate, are among the most popular holiday destinations in Germany.

The car-free island Juist, a 17-km (11-mile) strip of land less than 500 m (1,640 ft) wide, and Norderney with its main town of the same name are the most interesting islands. Neo-Classical villas recall the days when such figures as Heinrich Heine and Otto von Bismarck spent their holidays here. It is also worth

Nationalpark Niedersächsisches Wattenmeer in the Greefsiel area

visiting Wangerooge, another island where cars are banned. Three lighthouses – Westturm, Alter Leuchtturm and Neuer Leuchtturm – indicate the island's role in the navigation of the Weser River estuary.

Ostfriesland (East Frisia) ❷

Road map B2. 🚉 *Emden, Leer, Norden.* ℹ️ *(01805) 20 20 96 or (04931) 93 83 200.* 🌐 *www.die-nordsee.de* 🎪 *Kiewittmarkt (end Mar); Altstadtfest (Aug).*

EAST FRISIA is a peninsula near the border with the Netherlands and the Jadebusen bay, at Wilhelmshaven. This is a land of flat meadows, grazing cows and windmills.

Emden, the region's capital, has an attractive town hall resembling that in Antwerp, and a town centre crossed by many canals. The **Nannen-Kunsthalle Emden**, founded in the early 1990s by Henri Nannen, publisher of the magazine *Stern*, holds a remarkable collection of 19th-century paintings, including the works of many German Expressionists such as Emil Nolde, Max Beckmann and Oskar Kokoschka.

Another attraction is the **Moor- und Fehnmuseum** (moor and fen museum) in Elisabethfehn, which is dedicated to the extraction of peat. Its exhibits include the world's largest plough, as well as the story of Jever, the local beer. Also worth visiting are the Renaissance palace whose reception hall has a ceiling with sunken panels, and next

to the parish church the wood and stone tomb of the Frisian leader Edo Wiemken, made in 1561–4 by master craftsmen from Antwerp.

🏛️ **Nannen-Kunsthalle Emden**
Hinter dem Rahmen 13. 📞 *(04921) 975 00.* 🕐 *10am–8pm Tue, 10am–5pm Wed–Fri, 11am–5pm Sat & Sun.* ● *1 May, 25 & 31 Dec.* 📷
🏛️ **Moor- und Fehnmuseum**
Elisabethfehn. 📞 *(04499) 22 22.*
🕐 *end Mar–end Oct: 10am–6pm Tue–Sun & bank holidays.*

Clemenswerth ❸

Road map B3. 🚉 *Sögel or Lathen.* ℹ️ *Papenburg, Rathausstr. 2 (04961-839 60).* **Schloss** 📞 *(05952-93 23 25.* 🕐 *Apr–Oct: 10am–1pm, 2–6pm Tue–Sun.* ● *winter.*

EMSLAND, to the south of East Frisia, extends along the Dutch border, a poor area since time immemorial, with moors and boglands. Only the discovery of oil in the 20th century engineered its progress. Sögel, 33 km (21 miles) south of Greater Papenburg, has the region's greatest attraction, the palatial hunting lodge or schloss Clemenswerth, built from 1737–49. In search of solitude, the elector and archbishop of Cologne Clemens August commissioned the lodge from Johan Conrad Schlaun. The design was modelled on the pavilion-pagoda of Nymphenburg in Munich. Altogether it comprises seven pavilions with mansard roofs and a chapel. All the brick buildings were laid out on a green lawn, creating a star shape around the palace. Inside there is a museum of the region.

Oldenburg ➍

Road map B2. 👥 *155,000.* 🚉
ℹ️ *Wallstr. 14 (0441-361 61 30).*
📅 *Hafenfest (7 days after Whitsun); Altstadtfest (end Aug); Kramermarkt (Sep/Oct).*

A THOUSAND YEARS old, and once part of Denmark, this town remained the seat of a duchy until 1918.

The **Lambertikirche**, in the central market square, is a late-Gothic hall-church with a Neo-Classical rotunda added in 1797. The **Schloss**, the ducal residence, displays a similar marriage of styles, particularly Baroque and Neo-Classical. The **Landesmuseum für Kunst und Kulturgeschichte** (state museum of art and culture), based in the castle, is known mainly for its collection of paintings assembled by Wilhelm Tischbein, who lived here for 25 years. The affiliated **Augusteum**, a Neo-Renaissance building in a picturesque spot, holds the museum's modern collection.

🏛 **Landesmuseum für Kunst und Kulturgeschichte**
Damm 1. 📞 *(0441) 220 73 00.*
🕐 *9am–5pm Tue, Wed & Fri, 8pm Thu, 10am–5pm Sat & Sun.*
⬤ *1 Jan, Good Friday, Easter, 1 May, 24, 25 & 31 Dec.* 🎟️

ENVIRONS: The small spa town of **Bad Zwischenahn** is worth a visit. Its star attraction is the Gothic St Johanniskirche with frescoes from 1512.

A windmill in the open-air museum in Cloppenburg

Cloppenburg ➎

Road map B2. 👥 *29,000.*
ℹ️ *Eschstr. 9 (04471-152 56).*
📅 *Mariä Geburtsmarkt (Sep).*

T HE SMALL market town of Cloppenburg boasts the **Museumsdorf**, the oldest open-air museum in Germany, established in 1934. On a vast site, 50 architectural monuments from all over Lower Saxony have been assembled. There are houses, including charming examples of the half-timbered style of Wehlburg, windmills and a small 17th-century church from Klein-Escherde near Hildesheim.

To the east of Cloppenburg lies Visbek. Here the visitor is

Epitaph for Albert von Bevessen in the Dom in Osnabrück

taken back to the Stone Age, with megalithic graves from 3,500 to 1,800 BC, including the 80-m (262-ft) long grave known as "Visbeker Bräutigam" (bridegroom) and the even larger, 100-m (321-ft) long "Visbeker Braut" (bride).

🏛 **Museumsdorf Cloppenburg**
Bether Straße 6. 📞 *(04471) 948 40.*
🕐 *Mar–Oct: 9am–6pm daily, Nov–Feb: 9am–4:30pm daily.* 🎟️

Osnabrück ➏

Road map B3. 👥 *157,000.* 🚉
ℹ️ *Kranstr. 58 (0541-32 32 202).*

T HIS WESTPHALIAN town has been a bishop's see since the time of Charlemagne. In 1648, negotiations took place here between representatives of Sweden and the Protestant duchies of the Reich. The signing of the Peace of Westphalia in 1648, which ended the Thirty Years' War, was announced from the town hall steps. It was also the birthplace of the writer Erich Maria Remarque in 1899.

Despite damage in World War II, the **Dom St Peter**, Osnabrück's 13th-century cathedral, is worth visiting. It has a bronze baptismal font and enormous triumphal cross, and the late-Gothic Snetlage-Altar of the Crucifixion. From here a short walk takes the visitor to the market square, Marienkirche and the Gothic **Rathaus** (town hall), with a sculpture of Charlemagne.

ENVIRONS: South of Osnabrück is the western part of the Teutoburger Wald (Teutoburg Forest). The spa town of **Bad Iburg**, 12 km (8 miles) to the south of Osnabrück, has a monumental Benedictine monastery and bishop's palace. The Rittersaal (knights' hall) is worth seeing, with its giant ceiling fresco depicting an architectural fantasy of foreshortened perspectives.

The Schloss in Oldenburg, featuring Baroque and Neo-Classical styles

Bremen ⑦

BREMEN, together with its deep-water port Bremerhaven, constitutes a separate town state. Not so much a bustling modern metropolis as a peaceful country town, it is conscious of its historical origins dating back to Charlemagne. The townscape is not dominated by the port as in Hamburg, but by the old town with its magnificent cathedral and town hall. Bremen enjoyed prosperity from 1358 when it joined the Hanseatic League, its wealth based on the coffee and wool trade. Today, Bremen still benefits from its port, which ships around 700,000 cars a year.

Statue of the Bremen Town Musicians, by Gerhard Marcks

Gabled houses and the statue of Roland in the Marktplatz

Exploring Bremen

Most of Bremen's tourist attractions are in the old town, on the east bank of the Weser River. The area is easy to pick out on a map as it is surrounded by a green belt, established when the town's fortifications were demolished. The Übersee-museum (ethnography museum) is close to the old town, and trams run to Schwachhausen, where the Focke-Museum is based.

🏛 Marktplatz

On the main square of Medieval Bremen stand the town hall and the cathedral and, on the west side, several gabled houses. This lovely view is slightly marred by the unattractive 1960s Haus der Bürgerschaft, the state parliament building.

In front of the town hall stands a 10-m (32-ft) statue of Roland, dating from 1404. It is the largest of many similar statues in German towns, and the prototype for others. A nephew of Charlemagne, Roland symbolizes a town's

independence. His gaze is directed toward the cathedral, the residence of the bishop, who frequently sought to restrict Bremen's autonomy. Roland's sword of justice symbolizes the judiciary's independence, and the engraved motto confirms the emperor's edict, conferring town rights onto Bremen.

The second, more recent (1953) monument in the square is dedicated to the Bremen Town Musicians – a donkey, dog, cat and cockerel, who according to the Grimm fairy tale trekked to Bremen.

🏛 Rathaus

Marktplatz. ☎ (0421) 30 80 00. ◔ 11am, noon, 3pm, 4pm daily. 🖼
The original Gothic building dating from the years 1405–10 was clad with a magnificent Renaissance façade, one of the finest examples of Weser Renaissance architecture in northern Germany, designed by Lüder von Bentheim. He masterfully incorporated the Gothic figures of Charlemagne and seven Electors, as well as four prophets and four wise men. In the 40-m (131-ft) Große Halle (great hall) new laws were passed, as symbolized by the fresco (1932) of Solomon's court. Among its many other treasures, the meticulously crafted Renaissance spiral staircase is worth mentioning. On the western side of the town hall is the entrance to the "Ratskeller" where you can sample 600 different wines, and delight in the murals from 1927, by the Impressionist Max Slevogt.

The late-Renaissance façade of Bremen's Rathaus

♖ Schütting

Marktplatz.

On the southwestern side of Marktplatz stands this mansion used by the Merchants' Guild for their conventions. It was built in 1537–9 by the Antwerp architect Johann der Buschener in Dutch Mannerist style. The eastern gable, more classically Renaissance in style, is the work of the local builder Carsten Husmann.

⚲ Dom

Tower and "Bleikeller":
◻ *Easter–1 Nov: 10am–5pm Mon–Fri, 10am–2pm Sat, 2–5pm Sun.*

This magnificent Romanesque cathedral with its vast twin-towered façade dates from the 11th century. Over the years it was extensively refurbished. At the end of the 19th

The Mannerist Schütting, a meeting place for merchants

century, while the southern tower was rebuilt, the façade was also reconstructed and a tower was added at the junction of the naves. Inside, it is worth looking at the sandstone bas-reliefs which divide the western choir stalls as well as fragments of Gothic stalls that were destroyed in the 19th century, with scenes of the Passion and the battle

VISITORS' CHECKLIST

Road map C2. 👥 556,000. 🚉
ℹ️ *Am Bahnhofplatz (0421-30 80 00).* ⚓ *Tours of the port (0421-33 89 89).* **Cruises:** *Apr–Oct: 10:15 & 11:45am, 1:30, 3:15 & 4:45pm daily.* 🎭 🛒 *Sat & Sun.* 🎉 *6 Tage Rennen (Jan); Osterwiese (Apr); Breminale (May/Jun); Vegesack Harbour Festival (Jun); Bremer Freimarkt (second half Oct/ early Nov).* 🌐 *www.bremen.de*

of Judas Machabeus. There is also a Baroque pulpit paid for by Christina the Queen of Sweden in 1638, and numerous multi-coloured memorials, including one to Segebad Clüver by the entrance to the north tower (1457). The larger eastern crypt has interesting Romanesque capitals, while in the second eastern crypt visitors can admire the oldest Bremen sculpture of Christ the Omnipotent (1050) as well as the baptismal font. The latter has 38 bas-reliefs, and a bowl supported by four lions with riders. In the so-called "Bleikeller" (lead cellar) underneath the former church cloisters, eight perfectly preserved mummies are on show.

Bas-reliefs on the western choir stalls in the Dom

BREMEN TOWN CENTRE

0 metres	500
0 yards	500

KEY

ℹ️ Tourist information

☒ Parking

✚ Church

♨ Böttcherstraße

Paula-Modersohn-Becker-Museum and **Roseliushaus**
Böttcherstr. 6–10. ☎ *(0421) 336 50 77.* ○ *11am–6pm Tue–Sun.*

This once insignificant lane where coopers lived was transformed into Art Deco style in 1926–30 by Ludwig Roselius, a wealthy coffee merchant. The National Socialists preserved the street as an example of degenerate art. At the entrance to the street is a bas-relief by Bernhard Hoetger from 1920, of the Archangel Michael fighting a dragon.

The **Paula-Modersohn-Becker-Museum**, built in the Expressionist style, contains an art museum, while in the neighbouring 16th-century **Roseliushaus** the original period interiors can be admired. The street's other attraction is a carillon which chimes tuneful melodies every day at noon, 3pm and 6pm.

♨ Schnoorviertel

Spielzeugmuseum im Schnoor
Schnoor 24. ☎ *(0421) 32 03 82.* ○ *11am–6:30pm Mon–Fri, 11am–7pm Sat; 1 Apr–31 Dec: 11am–6pm Sun.*

The Schnoorviertel is a historic district of small houses dating from the 15th–18th centuries. One of Bremen's poorest areas before World War II, it miraculously escaped destruction. It has been restored gradually since

Archangel Michael fighting a dragon, on a bas-relief in Böttcherstrasse

1958 and now teems with restaurants, cafés, souvenir shops and tourists. In the centre of the district is the Gothic **Johanniskirche**, which once belonged to the Franciscans. In accordance with the order's rules it has no tower, although this is compensated for by a decorative gable on the western façade, and three levels of arched alcoves and herringbone brickwork. The **Spielzeugmuseum** (toy museum) nearby is also worth visiting.

⋔ Kunsthalle

Am Wall 207. ☎ *(0421) 32 90 80.* ○ *10am–9pm Tue, 10am–5pm Wed–Sun.* ✍

On the edge of the old town is this art gallery, which actually lost most of its collection to Russia during World War II. The pieces that remained, as well as works subsequently acquired, make the collection of great importance. There

are works by Dürer, Altdorfer, Rubens, Jan Breughel, van Dyck and Rembrandt. There is also an excellent French section, with works by Delacroix, Denis, Monet and Manet, as well as 19th- and 20th-century German painters such as Beckmann and Kirchner. At the heart of the collection are about 40 paintings by Paula Modersohn-Becker.

⋔ Übersee-Museum

Bahnhofplatz 13. ☎ *(0421) 160 38 190.* ○ *9am–6pm Tue–Fri, 10am–6pm Sat & Sun.* ✍

This museum of overseas countries transports the visitor to faraway destinations. Founded in 1891, it was originally a museum of German colonialism and is now dedicated to the culture of non-European nations. Of special interest are exhibits on Pacific cultures, with life-sized models of houses and boats from the Solomon Islands.

⋔ Focke-Museum

Schwachhauser-Heerstr. 240. ☎ *(0421) 361 35 75.* ○ *10am–9pm Tue, 10am–5pm Wed–Sun.* ✍

The excellent collections of this museum compensate for its distant location. Founded in 1918, when the history museum was amalgamated with the decorative arts museum, it presents Bremen's art and culture from the Middle Ages to the present day. Exhibits from patrician houses and original sculptures from the façade of the town hall testify to the wealth of the Hanseatic town. Other sections are devoted to the archaeology of the region as well as to whaling and emigration to the US in the 19th and 20th centuries.

The nearby Rhododendronpark offers a pleasant respite from the museums. It includes 1,600 varieties of rhododendron which become a sea of flowers from late April to June.

ENVIRONS: Three places in the Bremen area are particularly worth a detour. About 50 km (31 miles) to the north lies Bremen's deep-sea harbour **Bremerhaven,** with the **Deutsches Schifffahrtsmuseum**. This wonderful,

Camille Pissarro, *Girl lying on a grassy slope,* **Kunsthalle**

PAULA MODERSOHN-BECKER (1876–1907)

A pupil of Fritz Mackensen and wife of Otto Modersohn, Paula Modersohn-Becker was the most significant artistic figure in Worpswede. She learned about the Impressionist use of colour during visits to Paris, and her own unique sensibility made her a

precursor of Expressionism. She became famous for her naturalistic paintings of poor, starving and even dying country folk. She died in childbirth, aged only 31, and this is how she was commemorated on her tombstone, in the peaceful village cemetery in Worpswede, by the sculptor Bernhard Hoetger.

Girl playing a flute in birch woods (1905)

Exhibits in the Große Kunstschau in Worpswede near Bremen

marine museum, designed by the renowned architect Hans Scharoun, displays both originals and models of a wide range of ships, dating from the Roman Empire to the present day. A special hall displays the *Hanse Kogge*, a merchant ship dredged from the bottom of the Weser River in 1962. This type of ship was capable of holding 120 tons of cargo, and handled the entire merchandise of northern Europe during the late Middle Ages. Displayed outside, in the open-air part of the museum, are the last great German sailing boat *Seute Deern*, the polar ship *Grönland* and *Wilhelm Bauer*, a U-boat from World War II.

The small village of **Worpswede**, northeast of Bremen, takes the visitor into the world of art. From 1889 until the end of World War II it was a famous artists' colony, situated in the middle of peat bogs. Apart from poets, such as Rainer Maria Rilke, and such architects as Bernhard Hoetger, the fame of this village rested principally on the painters: Fritz Mackensen, Otto Modersohn, Hans am Ende, Fritz Overbeck and Heinrich Vogeler. Unquestionably the greatest artist in Worpswede was Paula Modersohn-Becker, whose sad fairytale world of rustic subjects cannot be defined within one style. Work by the founding members is on display in the **Große Kunstschau** and the **Worpsweder Kunsthalle**.

Verden an der Aller, the picturesque bishops' residence and once a free town of the Reich, is known to sports enthusiasts thanks to its horseracing tracks, training centres and stadiums, and the **Deutsches Pferdemuseum** (horse museum), with a large collection of equestrian artifacts. Seven horse auctions are held in the town each year, and the most important are in April and October.

Apart from horses, Verden an der Aller has a picturesque town centre with small houses, the Andreaskirche, a church with the famous brass tomb of bishop Yso, as well as the Johanniskirche with a rainbow-arched wall dating from the 18th century.

Above the town rises the Dom with a large, steep roof. The hall of this cathedral, a modification of earlier basilicas, is architecturally interesting, with a multi-sided presbytery, a passageway dating from 1268–1311 and Romanesque cloisters and a tower. North of the cathedral is the Domherrenhaus, housing the Historisches Museum, with exhibits on regional history and archaeological and ethnographic departments.

🏛 **Deutsches Schifffahrtsmuseum**
Bremerhaven, Hans-Scharoun-Platz 1.
📞 *(0471) 482 070.* ⬜ *Apr–Oct: 10am– 6pm daily; Nov–Mar: 10–6pm Tue–Sun.* ⬛ *24, 25 & 31 Dec.* 🖼
Wilhelm Bauer ⬜ *Apr–Oct.* 🖼
🏛 **Große Kunstschau**
Worpswede. Lindenallee 3 & 5.
📞 *(04792) 13 02.* ⬜ *10am–6pm (5pm Nov–mid-Mar) daily.* 🖼
🏛 **Worpsweder Kunsthalle**
Bergstr. 17. 📞 *(04792) 12 77.*
⬜ *10am–6pm daily.* 🖼
🏛 **Deutsches Pferdemuseum**
Holzmarkt 9. 📞 *(04231) 80 71 40.*
⬜ *10am–5pm Tue–Sun.*

The Dom in Verden an der Aller, with its unusually large roof

Hamburg ⑧

Crest on the town hall

Gᴇʀᴍᴀɴʏ's second largest city, Hamburg has an openness to the world and a variety of architectural styles in its districts, making it a fascinating place to visit. For many years, Hamburg was a leading member of the Hanseatic League and an independent trading town, and in 1945 it became a city-state of the Federal Republic. Visitors are attracted by Hamburg's enormous port, situated right in the centre of the city, colourful entertainments in the red-light district St Pauli, many attractive parks and lakes as well as the warm welcome extended by the locals who, on first encounter, may seem a little cool.

A fountain in the Neo-Renaissance Rathausmarkt

Exploring Hamburg

The best way to get around Hamburg is by metro (U-Bahn and S-Bahn), using an all-day ticket (Tageskarte) since parking space is scarce. The city centre can be explored on foot, including the area between the main railway station and the lake, along with the rest of the old town, the port and Hamburg's two largest museums.

🏛 Rathausmarkt

The symbol of Hamburg is the enormous Neo-Renaissance town hall, the fifth in the city's history. Previous town halls were destroyed by wars as well as a catastrophic fire in 1842. Little remains of the old town. The city's current appearance is characterized by 19th-century style as well as Modernism. The town hall itself, with its ornamental halls representing the pride of Hamburg's middle class, is worth visiting.

The town hall square is enclosed on one side by Alsterfleet. Originally a small river, it is today one of numerous canals which have given Hamburg the name "Venice of the North". A monument in memory of the victims of World War I is the work of the artist Ernst Barlach. Between Rathausmarkt and Gänsemarkt runs a network of elegantly roofed shopping arcades. These were built in the 19th century, and have since been continually extended.

🏛 Alster

Elegant arcades lead from the Rathausmarkt to Binnenalster, a large lake in the middle of the city. Like the much larger Außenalster lake further north, it was created by damming the Alster River. On a sunny day, the Jungfernstieg, an elegant boulevard running the length of the Alster, is a pleasant place for a walk.

Great views of the city can be had from the café in the Alsterpavilion. There is a small quay from which boats depart for the "Alsterrundfahrt", an excursion which takes the visitor all the way to the Außenalster and to smaller canals with views of the villas in the north of Hamburg and the cityscape of the centre with its five main towers.

Door knocker on St Petrikirche

🔒 St Petrikirche

Mönckebergstr. 📞 *(040) 325 74 00.* ⏲ *8am–6pm Sun–Fri, 9am–5pm Sat.* The church of St Petri, originally Gothic, was extensively rebuilt in the Neo-Gothic style after the Great Fire of 1842. The Grabower Altar that once belonged to the church has been transferred to the Kunsthalle *(see pp422–3).* Tourists can still admire the Gothic sculpture of the Madonna, dating from 1470.

🏛 Jakobikirche

Jakobikirchhof 22. 📞 *(040) 303 73 70.* ⏲ *10am–4pm Mon–Fri, 10am–1pm Sat.* The church of St Jacobi, from 1340, was bombed during World War II, and subsequently rebuilt in its original style. Its captivating interior includes the largest Baroque

The main altar in Jakobikirche

organ in northern Germany, the work of Arp Schnitger. The triptych of St Luke in the presbytery of the southern nave, a magnificent example of late-Gothic art, was originally created in 1499 for Hamburg's cathedral, which was pulled down in 1804.

⊞ Kontorhausviertel

Deichtorhallen Deichtorstr. 1–2 *(040) 32 10 30.* ◯ *10am–6pm (during exhibitions).*

After World War I a district of commercial offices known as Kontorhausviertel was built between Steinstraße and Messberg. The **Chilehaus**, built by Fritz Höger in 1922–4, was an experiment in creating a traditional brick building with a Modernist design. This ten-storey building, with its pointed eastern façade resembling a ship's bow, became internationally famous as a symbol of Expressionist architecture.

Nearby are the enormous **Deichtorhallen**, market halls of the port built in 1911–12. Turned into dramatic exhibition halls in 1997, they are now used for major art exhibitions.

The Expressionist Chilehaus in Kontorhausviertel

⊞ Speicherstadt

Deutsches Zollmuseum
Alter Wandrahm 16a. *(040) 30 08 76 11.* ◯ *10am–5pm Tue–Sun.*
The atmosphere of the giant warehouse district by the port will seem depressing to some, charming to others. Located within the toll-free area of the port, this district is reached after crossing the customs post. It is the largest complex of warehouses in the world. The Neo-Gothic buildings, dating from the end of the 19th century, are separated by canals. They still serve as

storerooms for coffee, tea and carpets, waiting here in customs-free limbo until the owners are ready to sell them. Recently listed as one of the city's historic monuments, Speicherstadt is waiting for a new owner and a new purpose. The **Deutsches Zollmuseum** (German customs museum), temporarily located here by Kornhausbrücke, (corn house bridge), tells the story of customs and excise over the past hundred years.

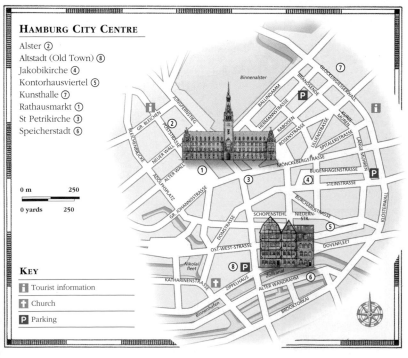

HAMBURG CITY CENTRE

Alster ②
Altstadt (Old Town) ⑧
Jakobikirche ④
Kontorhausviertel ⑤
Kunsthalle ⑦
Rathausmarkt ①
St Petrikirche ③
Speicherstadt ⑥

0 m   250
0 yards   250

KEY

ℹ Tourist information

✝ Church

P Parking

Kunsthalle

THE MOST interesting art gallery in northern Germany, the Kunsthalle in Hamburg has a tradition dating back to 1817, when the Kunstverein (friends of the fine arts), proud of its middle-class, non-aristocratic background, was established. The museum opened to the public in 1869. The collection has a standard chronological review of European art movements, with an emphasis on 19th-century German Romantics, with works by Caspar David Friedrich and Philipp Otto Runge. A four-storey extension, the Galerie der Gegenwart (contemporary gallery), was built in 1996 to a design by the architect Matthias Ungers. The building is reached by an underground link from the basement of the main gallery.

The Polar Sea (1823–4)
Caspar David Friedrich's dramatic seascape, with a sinking ship in the background behind the rising flow, is loaded with symbolism.

★ **Offering in the Temple**
(c.1627) *Thanks to his mastery of a sense of drama, Rembrandt succeeded in depicting the psychological make-up of his elderly subjects, who have recognized the Saviour in an unspoken message conveyed to the temple by Mary and Joseph.*

High Altar of St Peter in Hamburg (1383)
This panelled painting, displaying a stunning wealth of detail, was produced by Master Bertram of Minden, the first artist in Germany to be identified by his name.

★ **Morning** (1808)
This painting by Phillip Otto Runge centres around Aurora, goddess of dawn, and was intended to be part of a series called "Times of the Day". The other works were never completed due to the artist's untimely death aged 33.

115
114
113
112
111
110
109
108
107
106
105
104
103
102
101
120
119
125
124
123
118

Main entrance

Ground floor

Self-Portrait with Model (1910 and 1926) *Sixteen years after first painting this picture, Ernst Ludwig Kirchner repainted areas, in order to emphasize the distance between model and artist.*

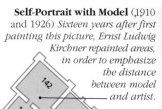

VISITORS' CHECKLIST

Glockengießerwall. (040) 4 28 13 12 00. 10am–6pm Tue–Sun, 10am–9pm Thu.
Library 11am–5pm Tue–Sat.
Café Liebermann 10am–6pm Tue–Sun, 10am–9pm Thu.

GALLERY GUIDE

On the ground floor, Rooms 2–10 and 16–19 contain works of art from the first half of the 20th century. On the first floor, Rooms 101–116 display the works of old masters. In Rooms 117–136 paintings from the 19th century are exhibited, and more works from the first half of the 20th century are shown in Rooms 137–148.

142
141
143
139
138
140
144
136A
136
145
147
135
148
134
133
132
131
130

First floor

★ **Girls on the Pier** (c.1900) *This painting is one of six variations on the same theme painted by Edvard Munch. The painter omitted the landscape, concentrating on the relationship and tensions between the girls.*

18
19

Stairs down to underground link to Galerie der Gegenwart

KEY

- Gallery of old masters
- 19th-century paintings
- 20th-century paintings (first half)
- Gallery of drawings
- Non-exhibition space

10
9
8
7
6
5

Stairs to basement and Hubertus-Wald-Forum with temporary exhibitions

STAR EXHIBITS

★ **Girls on the Pier**

★ **Morning**

★ **Offering in the Temple**

Nana (1877) *The subject of Édouard Manet's painting was the heroine of a Zola novel. Manet was not allowed to exhibit the painting in the Paris Salon because Nana was known as a Parisian courtesan.*

⚜ Altstadt (Old Town)

Hamburg's old town extends to the south of the Rathaus (town hall) but, following the Great Fire of 1842 and bombing during World War II, only a few original buildings remain. **Katharinenkirche** (St Catherine's), with its characteristic tower, was begun in the 13th century and completed in the 17th century. It has been restored after damage in World War II. Of the neighbouring Neo-Gothic **Nikolaikirche** only a single tower remained after 1945, the Nikolaiturm, which is the third tallest in Germany. It serves as a monument to the tragic consequences of war.

Deichstrasse is one of a few surviving streets in the old town, with the original façades visible from both the road and the canal (the best view is from Hohe Brücke, a bridge). One of the many famous restaurants is at No. 25, "Zum Brandanfang", where The Great Fire of 1842 was said to have broken out, which eventually destroyed most of the city.

Ornate Baroque pulpit in Hamburg's Michaeliskirche

⛪ Michaeliskirche

Observation tower 📞 (040) 37 67 81 00. ◯ Apr–Sep: 9am–6pm Mon–Sat, 11am–5:30pm Sun; Oct–Mar: 10am–5pm Mon–Sat, 11:30am–5:30pm Sun.
The massive Baroque church of St Michaelis, visible from afar with its 132-m (433-ft) tower (the "Michel"), is the main symbol of Hamburg. The interior is preserved in a white, grey and gold colour

The neon-lit Reeperbahn in St Pauli

scheme, and some of the fittings are made from tropical wood. The observation platform affords splendid views of the city and its harbour.

⚜ Krameramtswohnungen

Krayenkamp 10. 📞 (040) 37 50 19 88. ◯ 10am–5pm Tue–Sun.
Near the Michaeliskirche a section of the old town, the Krameramtswohnungen, has miraculously survived. These half-timbered houses, linked by a courtyard, were funded by the merchants' guild and built to house the widows of shopkeepers. Today they are occupied by tourist shops, cafés and restaurants.

🚢 The Port

Cap San Diego 📞 (040) 36 42 09. ◯ 10am–6pm daily. **Rickmer Rickmers** 📞 (040) 319 59 59. ◯ 10am–6pm daily.
Situated 104 km (62 miles) inland along the Elbe River, Hamburg is Europe's second largest port after Rotterdam,

and the port dominates the panorama. Every year 12,000 ships dock here from 90 countries. From the U3 Baumwall metro station it is best to walk to **Landungsbrücken**, past the museum ships moored here: the freighter *Cap San Diego* and the sailing boat *Rickmer Rickmers* (1896). Landungsbrücken is a 200-m (656-ft) long building from where the passenger ferries depart. A tour of the harbour is highly recommended. Near Landungsbrücken, in a copper-domed building, is the entrance to Alter Elbtunnel (the old tunnel under the Elbe) where people and cars are lowered in a giant lift.

⚜ St Pauli

Infamous around the world, this area is also known as **Reeperbahn**, after the main street. It is a world of nightclubs and bars, pubs and theatres, sex clubs and brothels. It is here, in Hamburg's red-light district, that some teenage seasonal workers from Liverpool, the Beatles, started their careers. On Herbertstrasse, scantily clad women offer their services behind a metal barrier – women and those under 18 are forbidden entrance. St

---

FISCHMARKT – A MARKET FOR EVERYTHING

This is an attraction for early risers or for those who never get to bed at all. From 5am (7am in winter) on Sundays the Auktionshalle (auction hall) and the nearby waterside turn into a colourful market place. Fishermen returning from the sea with their freshly caught fish compete with noisy greengrocers offering their wares and bric-à-brac merchants setting out stalls. Thousands of tourists mingle with sailors and ladies of the night relaxing with a cup of steaming mulled wine after a hard night's work in St Pauli. Here and there you can hear Plattdeutsch being spoken, the northern patois. Morning mass at 10am used to mark the end of this colourful spectacle, but today's public lingers on and then hurries off to bed instead of church.

Bric-à-brac on sale at a market stall in Fischmarkt

Pauli even has an Erotic-Museum, where next to the exhibits are reproductions of works by artists from Rembrandt to Picasso, which are said to "prove" that everything revolves around the female posterior.

ENVIRONS: The magnificent palace in **Ahrensburg** (1595), 23 km (14 miles) to the northeast, has Baroque and Rococo interiors open to visitors.

Façade of Schloss Ahrensburg, flanked by towers

Altes Land ●

Road map C2.

O N THE FLOOD plains stretching for more than 30 km (19 miles) between Hamburg and Stade, along the Lower Elbe River, is the Altes Land (old land). This area is fertile and has the largest number

of orchards in Germany. Many visitors come here in May, when cherry and apple tree blossom turns everything into a sea of white and pink. In this riot of colour stand sturdy red-brick houses with white half-timbered panels, thatched roofs and carved gates. The most beautiful villages are **Neuenfelde**, **Jork**, **Borstel**, **Steinkirchen** and **Hollern**, with their richly furnished Baroque churches.

Stade ●

Road map C2. 47,000.
U3 to Neugraben, then by train or catamaran from Landungsbrücken.
Hansestrasse 16 (04141-40 91 70 & 40 91 75).

T HIS MEDIEVAL Hanseatic town has retained most of its half-timbered buildings, with the most attractive in the **Alter Hafen** (old harbour). There is a also a quaint crane and the **Schwedenspeicher** (Swedish granary) dating from the Swedish occupation during the Thirty Years' War (1692–1705). It is now home to the **Schwedenspeicher-Museum**, Stade's regional museum with exhibits on the town's history and defence system, including wheels from 700 BC, which were part of a Bronze-Age cart. Nearby, an interesting building at Am Wasser West 7 houses the **Kaufmann Collection**, with works by Worpswede artists. The entire old

The Baroque portal of the Dutch-influenced Rathaus in Stade

town is surrounded by preserved modern fortifications. Other attractions are the **Bürgermeister-Hintze-Haus** at Am Wasser West 23, a house built for the mayor, Hintze, in 1617–46, and the exquisite Baroque **Rathaus** (town hall) from 1667, its design revealing Dutch influence.

It is also worth visiting two Gothic churches: **St Wilhadi** from the 14th century which boasts an interesting Gothic hall and a leaning tower, and **St Cosmas and Damiani**, founded after the Great Fire of 1659, with marvellous Baroque furnishings.

Ⓜ Schwedenspeicher-Museum
Am Wasser West 39. (04141) 32 22. 10am–5pm Tue–Fri, 10am–6pm Sat & Sun.

The half-timbered houses along the waterside of Alter Hafen in Stade

Lüneburg ⑪

Road map D2. 🏔 *70,000.*
🅿 ℹ *Rathaus, Am Markt (04131-207 66 20).*

I T IS HARD TO believe that this small, former Hanseatic town was once one of the wealthiest in Germany. Its prosperity was founded on salt mines. Opened in 956, they provided work for more than 2,000 people by the late Middle Ages and were the largest industry in Europe.

Lüneburg's most important monument is the **Rathaus** (town hall). The interior is even more intriguing than the frequently re-built façade, in particular the Großer Ratssaal (the main hall) with its Gothic stained-glass windows and 16th-century frescoes of the Last Judgement, as well as the Große Ratsstube (council chamber) with Renaissance woodwork by Albert von Soest. The **Museum im Rathaus** (town hall museum) holds a remarkable collection of municipal silverware.

Johnniskirche, one of Lüneburg's three Gothic churches, stands on Am Sande. It has a 108-m (354-ft) west tower, which leans more than 2 m (6 ft) from the perpendicular. In one of its five naves there is a panelled painting dating from 1482–5, the masterful work of the German painter Hinrik Funhof. Also interesting is the soaring basilica of **Michaeliskirche**, consecrated in 1409.

Not far from here is the old port on the Ilmenau River. On Lüner Straße stands the **Altes Kaufhaus**, a former herring warehouse with a Baroque façade. The 14th-century wooden crane was rebuilt in the 18th century. It was used to load salt onto ships. The decorative wavy brick lines *(Taustäbe)* on many of the old buildings are charac-teristic of the town.

🏛 Museum im Rathaus
Am Markt. 📞 *(04131) 30 92 30.* 🕐 *10am–5pm daily.* ⬤ *1 Jan, 24–26 & 31 Dec.* 🎫

A typical farmstead in Lüneburger Heide

Lüneburger Heide ⑫

Road map D2. ℹ *Lüneburg, Barg-hausenstr. 35 (04131-737 30).*

S OUTH OF Hamburg, between the rivers Elbe and Aller, is a large sprawling area of heathland, grazed by heifers and sheep and buzzing with bees in the heathers and pine forests. Until the Middle Ages, this area was covered by dense mixed forests, but these were felled in order to satisfy demand for wood in

the saltworks of Lüneburg. The half-stepped terrain provides grazing land for Heidschnucken, the local breed of sheep. The heather moors are best seen at the **Naturschutzpark Lüneburger Heide**, a large area of nature reserve founded in 1921. From the village of Undeloh it is best to continue by foot, bike or carriage to the traditional village of Wilsede. From Wilsede it is not far to Wilseder Berg, the highest peak of this moraine region. The view of the sur-rounding countryside is parti-cularly beautiful at the end of August, when the purple heather is blooming.

Soltau ⑬

Road map C3. 🏔 *23,000.* ℹ
Bornemannstr. 7 (05191-82 82 82).

T HE MAIN attraction of the town of Soltau is **Heide-park Soltau**, a vast funfair with trains, water rides and a genuine Mississippi steam-boat. For nature lovers, the **Vogelpark Walsrode**, 20 km (12 miles) southwest of Soltau, may be a more attractive al-ternative. It holds about 1,000 species of birds from every continent, from penguins to birds of paradise. Aviaries, some 12-m (40-ft) tall, seek to simulate an impression of the birds' natural environment.

🌿 Heidepark Soltau
📞 *(05191) 91 91.* 🕐 *Apr–Oct: 9am–6pm daily (admission till 4pm).*
🌿 Vogelpark Walsrode
📞 *(05161) 604 40.* 🕐 *Mar–Oct: 9am–7pm daily.*

ENVIRONS: In grim contrast to both parks stands **Bergen-Belsen**, a concentration camp built by the National Socialists in the moorland of Osterheide, about 30 km (19 miles) south of Soltau. A monument and small museum commemorate the place where 50,000 people were murdered, among them Anne Frank.

🏛 Gedenkstelle Bergen-Belsen
Lohheide. 📞 *(05051) 60 11.*
🕐 *9am–6pm daily.*

Eighteenth-century wooden crane in Lüneburg

Vogelpark Walsrode – a paradise with 1,000 different bird species

Celle

Road map C3. 🚗 *74,000.*
🚉 *Bahnhofplatz.* ℹ *Markt 14–16
(05141-12 12).*
ⓦ *www.region-celle.de*

BETWEEN THE years 1378 and
1705, Celle was the seat of
distant relations of the Welf
family, the reigning dynasty in
the Duchy of Brunswick-Lüne-
burg. The **Schloss** (castle), rebuilt in Renaissance style after
1533, has a preserved eastern
façade with octagonal towers
at the corners, gables and bay
windows. It is one of the
most important early-Renaissance buildings in Germany.
The Gothic chapel is worth
visiting. It was rebuilt in a
Mannerist style to a design by
Martin de Vos, who painted
76 of its paintings, including
the famous *Crucifixion* (end
of the 16th century).
  Celle prides itself on 500
half-timbered houses, with
the most interesting ones in
picturesque Kalandgasse and
Zöllnerstrasse. **Hoppner
Haus**, at Poststrasse 8, is
richly decorated

with reliefs of mythological
beasts. Equally interesting is
the painted decoration of the
Rathaus (town hall), a great
example of Weser Renais-
sance *(see p439)* from 1579.
From the **Stadtkirche** church
tower great views unfold. The
Baroque **Synagoge**, beyond
the old town, is the only one
surviving in northern Germany.

♣ Schloss
[*(05141) 12 373.* ⏱ *Apr–Oct:
11am, noon, 1, 2 & 3pm Tue–Sun;
Nov–Mar: 11am & 3pm Tue–Sun.* 🎟

♠ Stadtkirche
[*(05141) 7735.* ⏱ *10am–6pm
Tue–Sat.* **Tower:** *Apr–Oct:
10–11:45am 2–4:45pm Tue–Sat.*

✡ Synagoge
Im Kreise 24. ⏱ *3–5pm Tue–Thu,
9–11am Fri, 11am–1pm Sun.*

ENVIRONS: The town of
Wietze, 11 km (7 miles) west
of Celle, has been a centre of
petroleum since 1858. The
**Deutsches Erdölmuseum
Wietze** provides a very
interesting overview on the
history of oil extraction.
The neighbouring village of
Wienhausen has a Cistercian

Kloster (monastery) with a
beautiful 13th–14th century
church. Worth seeing are its
Gothic frescoes, the presbytery vaults and the 14th- and
15th-century tapestries.

🏛 Deutsches Erdölmuseum
Schwarzer Weg 7–9. [*(05146) 92
340.* ⏱ *Mar–Oct: 10am–5pm
Tue–Sun; Jun–Aug: 10am–6pm
Tue–Sun.* 🎟
♠ Wienhausen Kloster
[*(05149) 357.* 🎟 *Apr–Oct: 10 &
11am, 2–5pm Tue–Sat, noon–5pm
Sun.* 🎟

Wolfsburg

Road map D3. 🚗 *123,000.* 🚉
ℹ *Willy-Brandt-Platz 5 (05361-14
333).*

DURING THE 1930s, this small
village began to develop
into a sizeable town, based
around the Volkswagen car
works. Production of the
"people's car" was conceived
by Hitler – every German was
to be able to afford this inexpensive car, designed by Ferdinand Porsche. The model
reached its peak during the
post-war economic boom
years. The **Volkswagenwerk**
factory is open to visitors.
  Wolfsburg also has some
outstanding examples of
modern architecture: a
cultural centre designed by
Alvara Aalto, a city theatre
designed by Hans Scharoun
and a planetarium.

**🚗 Volkswagenwerk
Autostadt**
Stadtbrücke. [*(0800) 28 86 78 23.*
⏱ *9am–8pm daily.*
🎟 *guided tours every 15 mins.*

The façade of the Schloss with octagonal towers at the corners, in Celle

The Renaissance Schloss in Stadthagen

Stadthagen ⑯

Road map C3. 🏛 *23,800.* 🚉
ℹ *Am Markt 1 (05721-92 60 70).*

THE COUNTS OF Schaumburg-Lippe used the Renaissance **Schloss** (castle) as their private residence. Apart from this and the town hall, the main attraction is the church of **St Martini** which has an early Baroque mausoleum of Ernst zu Holstein-Schaumburg built onto its eastern wall. Adrian de Vries, court artist to Rudolf II in Prague, created a masterful monument of bronze figures.

🏛 St Martini
Schulstr.18. ⬜ *3–5pm Wed & Fri.*

ENVIRONS: A gem of Romanesque architecture can be found at **Idensen** near Wunsdorf, 22 km (14 miles) from Stadthagen. The church interior (1120) is entirely painted with scenes from the Old and New Testaments, and there is a vast, Byzantine-style image of Christ's Enthronement (*maiestas domini*) on the vaulted ceiling of the apsis.

Bückeburg ⑰

Road map C3. 🏛 *21,000.* 🚉
ℹ *Marktplatz 4 (05722-20 61 81).*

IN THE 16TH century this town became the capital of the principality of Schaumburg-Lippe. The philosopher Johann Gottfried von Herder was the preacher here. The **Stadtkirche** (town church), one of the first Protestant churches in Germany, is a pinnacle of Mannerism with

its fantasy façade. Another attraction is the **Schloss** with its enchanting chapel. The Goldener Saal (golden hall), from 1605, has a Götterpforte (portal of the divinities) and a beautiful panelled ceiling.

🏛 Stadtkirche
Lange Str. 📞 *(05722) 957 70.*
⬜ *15 Apr–15 Oct: 3–5pm Mon; 10:30am–noon, 3–5pm Tue–Fri, 3–5pm Sun; 16 Oct–14 Apr 2:30–4:30pm Wed & Sun.*

⬥ Schloss
📞 *(05722) 50 39.* ⬜ *Apr–Sep: 9:30am–6pm; Oct–Mar: 9:30am–5pm.*

The opulent Goldener Saal in Schloss Bückeburg

Braunschweig (Brunswick) ⑱

Road map E3. 🏛 *240,000.* 🚉
ℹ *Vor der Burg 1 (0531-27 35 50).*
🎭 *Festival of Chamber Music (May); Medieval Fair (May/Jun).*

AN IMPORTANT commercial and political centre from the early Middle Ages, Braunschweig was chosen as town of residence by Heinrich der Löwe (Henry the Lion), ruler of Saxony

and Bavaria. A member of the Welf family, he eventually lost in his struggle against the German emperor.

Very different in character but equally famous was Till Eulenspiegel, an ordinary man who poked fun at dim-witted citizens, the aristocracy and the clergy. His exploits were fictionalized in the 16th century, and he was immortalized with a fountain on Bäckerklint Square.

Braunschweig's continued decline culminated in the almost total destruction of the town in 1944. During reconstruction, the concept of the "Traditionsinsel" was developed: small islands of reconstructed historic monuments adrift in a sea of modernism.

A tour of the town is best started from Burgplatz (castle square). Here is the **Burglöwe**, the monument of a lion funded by Heinrich in 1166 (the original is in a museum). Symbolizing Heinrich's rule, it was the first such sculpture to be erected since Roman days. The **Dom** (cathedral), Romanesque in style but modified, is well worth seeing. In the north nave, an extension, are unusual turned pillars, and in the transept and presbytery are 13th-century frescoes. Its marvellous treasures include a gigantic seven-armed bronze candlestick, the tomb of Heinrich and his wife Mathilde, the Crucifix of Imerward and a wooden cross with the figure of Christ modelled on the sculpture of *Voltosanto* in Lucca. Visitors can also see the column of the Passion with the figure of Christ, the work of Hans Witten.

To the west of the cathedral lies the **Altstadtmarkt** (old town market). Here are the L-shaped **Rathaus** (town hall), with a two-storey open cloister, and the Gothic church

The Burglöwe, Heinrich der Löwe's monument in Braunschweig

of **St Martini**. The beautiful **Gewandhaus** (cloth hall), rebuilt in the Renaissance, is also worth seeing.

East of the cathedral is the **Herzog-Anton-Ulrich-Museum**, the oldest in Germany. It was opened to the public as a gallery by Duke Anton Ulrich and holds such gems as Rembrandt's *Family Portrait*, a Giorgioni self-portrait and Vermeer van Delft's *Girl with a Glass of Wine*.

⌂ Dom
Burgplatz. ☐ 10am–5pm daily.
⌂ St Martini
Altstadtmarkt. ☐ May–Dec: 10am–1pm, 3–5pm Tue–Fri, 10am–5pm Sat, 10am–noon, 3–5pm Sun; Jan–Apr: 10am–1pm Tue–Sat.
🏛 Herzog-Anton-Ulrich-Museum
Museumsstr. 1. 📞 (0531) 122 50. ☐ 10am–5pm Tue & Thu–Sun, 10am–8pm Wed. ✎

The richly decorated portal of the Gewandhaus in Braunschweig

ENVIRONS: In **Königslutter**, 35 km (22 miles) east of Braunschweig, Emperor Lothar initiated the building of the Benedictine **Abteikirche**, a monastery church and later his burial place. The portal with figures of lions, a frieze with figures of fishermen on the exterior of the apse and the cloisters reflect the taste of the times and the northern Italian origin of architects and sculptors; only the frescoes are late 19th-century additions.

Helmstedt, 45 km (28 miles) to the east, is unjustifiably only associated with the former border crossing between East and West Germany. In 1576,

The Marienbrunnen fountain on Altstadtmarkt in Braunschweig

Duke Julius of Brunswick founded the Julius Academy, one of Germany's most popular Protestant universities, where the Italian philosopher Giordano Bruno taught. Juleum (1592–7), the main building, has a central tower and two decorative gables. Repainted in the original bold red, it is now home to the **Kreisheimatmuseum**, a regional museum and library.

⌂ Abteikirche
Königslutter. ☐ 9am–6pm daily, in winter until 5pm.
🏛 Kreisheimatmuseum
Helmstedt. ☐ 9–11am, 3–5pm Mon–Fri, 3–5pm Sat, 11am–12:30pm Sun. **Library** ☐ 3–5pm Tue, Thu.

Wolfenbüttel ⓳

Road map E3. 🚶 53,000. 🚉
🛈 Stadtmarkt 7 (05331-86 280). 🎭 Theaterfest (Jun/Jul); Altstadtfest (Aug).

THIS SMALL town has had a remarkably turbulent past. From 1432 until 1753 the Welf dukes moved their seat here from Braunschweig. In the 16th century, innovative town design introduced wide avenues and spacious squares. Largely unscathed by World War II attacks, the town has 500 historic half-timbered houses, and a magnificent library. The **Herzog-August-Bibliothek** contains 130,000 volumes, including the most

valuable book in the world, Heinrich der Löwe's Gospel book. Associated with the town are the philosopher Gottfried Wilhelm Leibniz and writer Gotthold Ephraim Lessing. The **Lessinghaus** houses a literature museum.

The centre of the town is dominated by the **Schloss**, the largest castle in Lower Saxony, refurbished in the Baroque style in 1714–16. It houses the **Schlossmuseum** with regional items such as furniture and tapestries. The Venussaal (hall of Venus) has beautiful Baroque ceiling frescoes. Opposite the castle is the **Zeughaus** (armoury), with its interesting Mannerist façade, built in 1613–19 to a design by Paul Francke.

Continuing eastwards the visitor will get to the **Hauptkirche**, the 16th-century church dedicated to *Beatae Mariae Virginis*, the ducal pantheon and the leading example of Protestant Mannerist architecture. Begun in 1608, the church's façade has delicate reliefs, while the interior reveals an unusual combination of styles, including the very late-Gothic.

♠ Schloss and Schlossmuseum
Schlossplatz. 📞 (05331) 924 60.
Lessinghaus, Museum & Zeughaus
📞 (05331) 80 80. ☐ 10am–5pm Tue–Sun. **Herzog-August-Bibliothek** ☐ 8am–8pm Mon–Fri, 9am–1pm Sat. ● 24 & 31 Dec. ✎
⌂ Hauptkirche
Michael-Praetorius-Platz 9.
📞 (05331) 28 92.

Baroque façade of Schloss Wolfenbüttel

Hannover (Hanover) ❷⓿

THE CAPITAL OF Lower Saxony, Hannover does not at first glance seem particularly exciting, but appearances can be deceptive: the town boasts interesting architecture in the historic centre, magnificent Baroque gardens and one of Europe's most important museums of modern art. Hannover's past was marked by its dynastic links with England, sharing the same ruler during the years 1714–1837. Annual industrial trade fairs have earned the town an international reputation, and in 2000 Hannover hosted the international exhibition Expo 2000 which attracted 18 million visitors.

Exploring Hannover

After the near-total destruction of the old town in 1944, many historic monuments have been rebuilt, and large green spaces encourage the visitor to explore the town on foot. It is best to follow an extensive circuit, starting from and returning to the railway station. The Baroque gardens at Herrenhausen in the northwest of the town are reached by metro (U-Bahn 4, 5).

🏛 Opernhaus

Opernplatz 1. 📞 *(0511)* 99 99 11 11.
The opera house was built in 1845–57 by George Ludwig Friedrich Laves, Hannover's most important architect, to a fine Neo-Classical design. Particularly charming is the façade with portico columns.

🏛 Niedersächsisches Landesmuseum

Willy-Brandt-Allee 5. 📞 *(0511)* 980 77 25. ⏰ *10am–5pm Tue–Wed, Fri–Sun, 10am–7pm Thu.* 🖼
The most interesting part of the state museum of Lower Saxony is the picture gallery, which holds excellent German medieval and Renaissance paintings (Dürer, Spranger, Cranach), a good section with Dutch and Flemish paintings (Rubens, Rembrandt, van Dyck) as well as German paintings of the 19th and 20th centuries, with fine examples of Romanticism and Impressionism (Friedrich, Corinth, Liebermann).

🏛 Sprengel-Museum

Kurt-Schwitters-Platz. 📞 *(0511) 16 84 62 10.* ⏰ *10am–8pm Tue, 10am–6pm Wed–Sun.* 🖼
One of Europe's finest museums of modern art, the Sprengel-Museum reflects the city's role as an artists' mecca in the 1920s, before the National Socialists destroyed works of art that they designated as "degenerate". Hannover's controversial artist Kurt Schwitters worked here, as did El Lissitzky, whose *Kabinett der Abstrakten* (school of abstraction, 1928, reconstructed) is worth seeing. Funded by Bernhard Sprengel, a chocolate magnate, the museum was built in 1979, and holds works by Munch, Chagall and Picasso, as well as many more recent artists, including Christo.

The museum is located by Maschsee, a large artifical lake created in the centre of the city in 1936. During the summer it teems with motor and sailing boats, while Hanoverians stroll around its banks.

Mueller's *The Lovers* (1920), in the Sprengel-Museum

🏛 Neues Rathaus

Trammplatz 2. 📞 *(0511) 168 45 333.*
Dome ⏰ *Apr–Oct: 9:30am–6:30pm Mon–Sat, 10am–6:30pm Sun.*
The gigantic town hall symbolizes the lofty ambitions of the wealthier citizens at the beginning of the 20th century. It was built from 1901–13, on more than 6,000 beech pillars, modelled on a Baroque palace with a central dome, and decorated with Neo-Gothic and Secessionist detail. The Swiss artist Ferdinand Hodler created a vast painting entitled *Einigkeit* (unity) for the Debating Hall, which depicts the arrival of Protestantism in the town in 1533. A unique oblique lift takes you up to the dome from where there are wonderful views.

⚜ Leineschloß

Hinrich-Wilhelm-Kopf-Platz.
In the historic city centre by the Leine River stands the Leineschloß, a 17th-century palace completely rebuilt by the local architect Laves between 1817 and 1842. It had to be rebuilt again after destruction in World War II, and now serves as headquarters for the Niedersächsischer

Façade of the vast Neues Rathaus, with its central dome

Interior of the church of St Georg und St Jacobus, in Marktplatz

Landtag (Lower Saxony state parliament). The porticos on the façade were modelled on ancient Greek temples.

Marktplatz

Although the houses on this square had to be almost completely rebuilt after World War II, this is one of the best examples of 15th-century red-brick architecture, with amazing gables with projections as well as figurative friezes of glazed terracotta. Nearby, the Marktkirche St Georg und St

Jacobus (church of St George and St Jacob) features a 14th-century nave with a characteristic four-pinnacled tower. The most valuable object among its furnishings is the Gothic altar, with scenes of the Passion and copper engravings by the renowned artist Martin Schongauer.

Herrenhäuser Gärten

Despite having been razed to the ground during World War II, the gardens in Hannover's Herrenhausen district are among the most beautiful Baroque gardens in Germany. They were established by Duchess Sophie von der Pfalz, daughter of Elizabeth Stuart and mother of England's

VISITORS' CHECKLIST

Road map C3. 522,000. Ernst-August-Platz. Ernst-August-Platz 2 (0511-16 84 97 00). Sat. Schützenfest (Jun/Jul). www.hannover.de

George I. The Großer Garten, the most important of the four gardens, has a formal layout modelled on 17th- and 18th-century Dutch parks. It is a botanical garden with fountains, including the Große Fontäne, the tallest in Europe with a 82-m (269-ft) water spout. There are grottoes, mazes, sculptures and decorative urns, and the hedges are some 21 km (13 miles) long.

The stunningly beautiful Baroque gardens in Herrenhausen

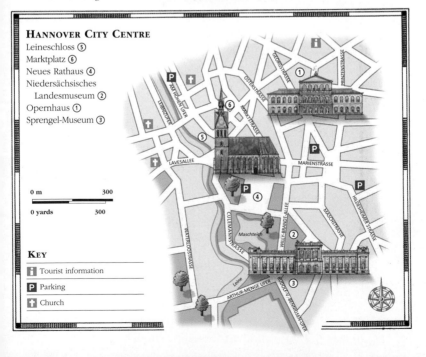

HANNOVER CITY CENTRE

Leineschloss ⑤
Marktplatz ⑥
Neues Rathaus ④
Niedersächsisches
    Landesmuseum ②
Opernhaus ①
Sprengel-Museum ③

0 m   300
0 yards   300

KEY

🛈 Tourist information

🅿 Parking

✝ Church

Hildesheim ㉑

THE UNDISPUTED CAPITAL of Romanesque culture, the old town of Hildesheim was transformed into a heap of rubble by heavy bombing on 22 March 1945. The most important monuments have now been re-created, with mixed results, surrounded by modern developments. Two churches, the Michaeliskirche and the Dom St. Mariä, are UNESCO World Heritage sites, and the Roemer-Pelizaeusmuseum of Egyptian Culture also makes a visit to Hildesheim worthwhile.

Wedekindhaus, a beautiful half-timbered house on Marktplatz

Exploring Hildesheim

Contrary to received wisdom, the city is best visited on foot. Visitors can park in the centre, for example near the church of St Michael, and then explore the main sights from here. A round tour, including the museums, should not take longer than around 4–5 hours. It is also possible to follow the Rosenroute (rose trail) around town which is marked on the pavements by white roses.

🏛 Marktplatz

Since gaining civic rights in the 11th century, the heart of the bishopric town has been its market square. Every detail has now been faithfully reconstructed, and it is easy to forget that the square looked totally different only a few years ago. In 1987, the Knochenhaueramtshaus (butchers' guild hall) was rebuilt, the largest and most famous half-timbered house in Germany, dating from 1529. Opposite are the Gothic town hall and the Tempelhaus, an original 15th-century building with round turrets and a half-timbered annexe, added in 1591. Reliefs depict the story of the Prodigal Son.

🏛 Andreaskirche

Andreasplatz. ◯ Apr–Sep: 9am–6pm Mon–Fri, 9am–4pm Sat, 11:30am–4pm Sun; Oct–Mar: 10am–4pm Mon–Sat, 11:30–4pm Sun. **Tower** Apr–Oct: 11–4pm Mon–Sat, noon–4pm Sun.

The reconstructed Gothic church of St Andrew is notable for the brightness and the quality of the light that passes through its vast windows, as well as its soaring proportions. The 115-m (377-ft) tower was added in the 19th century.

Presbytery of Michaeliskirche

🏛 Michaeliskirche

Michaelisplatz. ◯ Apr–Oct: 8am–6pm Mon–Sat, noon–6pm Sun; Nov–Mar: 9am–4pm Mon–Sat, noon–4pm Sun.

Built on the instructions of Bishop Bernward, the church is a textbook example of what became known as the Ottonian style, the early Romanesque culture of the Otto dynasty. Its characteristic feature is the streamlined simplicity of interior and exterior, with square pillars intersecting with the naves. The sarcophagus of the founder, St Bernward, is in the crypt in the western part of the church.

Luckily, a rare painted 12th-century ceiling was removed during World War II and thus largely survived. It depicts the story of Redemption, from Adam and Eve with the Tree of Life, through to Mary and the Saviour.

🏛 Roemer-Pelizaeus-museum

Am Steine 1. 🔲 (05121) 93 690. ◯ 10am–6pm daily.

Bas-relief on the façade of Andreaskirche

The pride of this museum is the Ancient Egyptian collection, one of the best in Europe, which includes the burial figures of Hem Om and the writer Heti from the Old Kingdom (c.2600 BC). It also has fine collections of Chinese porcelain and Inca artefacts, and it is famed for its temporary exhibitions on ancient cultures, from Tutankhamun to the Mayans.

🏛 Dom St Mariä

Domhof. 🔲 (05121) 179 17 60. ◯ 15 Mar–15 Oct: 9:30am–5pm Mon–Sat, noon–5pm Sun; 16 Oct–14 Mar: 10am–4:30pm Mon–Sat, noon–5pm Sun.

During a hunting expedition in 815, Ludwig der Fromme (the devout), son of Charlemagne, allegedly hung relics of the Virgin Mary on a tree. When he tried to remove them they would not budge – which he took to be a heavenly sign that a church should be founded on this site and a town alongside it. The Tausendjähriger Rosenstock (1,000-year-old rose) of

The Bernwardsäule in the Dom St. Mariä – a huge bronze column

this legend grows to this day in the cathedral's apse, and even survived bombing. The cathedral was reconstructed after World War II, using a model of the church's 11th-century appearance.

Original works of art bear witness to the cathedral's foundry which flourished under bishop Bernward. Bronze double doors depict the Old Testament version of the Creation on one side, and the life of Christ according to the New Testament on the other. The Bernwardsäule, a huge bronze column from 1022, was once topped by a crucifix. The column, with scenes from the life of Christ arranged as a spiralling picture story, recalls the column of Emperor Trajan in Rome. Two further important works of art are a chandelier from 1060, with a diameter of 3 m (10 ft), and a baptismal font (c.1225) based on the personifications of the four rivers of the Garden of Eden.

⛪ Godehardkirche

Godehardsplatz. ☐ *Apr–Sep: 9am–6pm Mon–Fri, 9am–5pm Sat, noon–6pm Sun; Oct–Mar: 9am–4:30pm Mon–Sat, noon–4:30pm Sun.*
This church is dedicated to Bernward's successor, bishop Godehard, who like him has been included in the canon of saints. Built in 1133–72, it is typical of local architecture, and also recalls the earlier church of St Michaelis. It has interesting carved capitals as well as a northern doorway with the Blessed Jesus Christ accompanied by St Godehard and St Epiphany.

⛪ Mauritiuskirche

Moritzberg.
Another Romanesque church worth visiting in Hildesheim

VISITORS' CHECKLIST

Road map C3. 👥 *106,000.* 🚉 *Bahnhofsplatz.* 🛈 *Rathausstr. 18–20 (05121-179 80).* 🎷 *Jazz-Time (before Whitsun); Frühlingsfest (Mar); Weinfest (May); Bauernmarkt (Sep); Drachenflugtag (Oct).* 🖵 *www.hildesheim.de*

is the church of St Maurice, west of the centre. Founded by bishop Hezilo and built in the years 1058–68, the church has enchanting cloisters, dating from the 12th century, and the sarcophagus of the founder of the church.

Presbytery of the massive Godehardkirche, flanked by towers

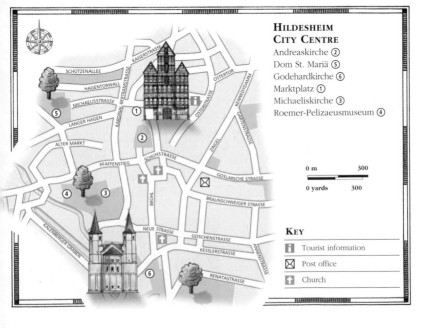

HILDESHEIM CITY CENTRE

Andreaskirche ②
Dom St. Mariä ⑤
Godehardkirche ⑥
Marktplatz ①
Michaeliskirche ③
Roemer-Pelizaeusmuseum ④

0 m   300
0 yards   300

KEY

🛈 Tourist information

☒ Post office

✝ Church

Street-by-Street: Goslar ㉔

GOSLAR, at the foot of the Harz mountains, is a captivating town with 1,800 charming, half-timbered houses, the largest number in Germany. For 300 years the Holy Roman Emperors of Germany resided in Goslar, a member of the Hanseatic League also known as "the treasure chest of the North". Goslar's main source of wealth was the nearby mine in Rammelsberg, where zinc, copper and especially silver were mined. The townscape has remained largely unchanged, making it a great tourist attraction as well as a UNESCO world heritage site.

Guildhouse (Hotel Kaiserworth)

Jakobikirche

MARKT

HOHER WEG

KAISERBLEEK

DOM PLATZ

★ **Rathaus**
On the western side of the market square stands the 15th-century town hall. Its beautiful Huldigungssaal (hall of homage) has a ceiling and walls with Gothic frescos.

Siemens-haus

★ **Pfarrkirche**
The Gothic Church of Saints Cosmas and Damian has Romanesque stained-glass windows and a bronze Renaissance baptismal font.

Statue of the Emperor Barbarossa

KEY

– – – Suggested route

The Kaiserpfalz
The Emperors' palace is a stone building (1005–15), largely rebuilt in the 19th century. The chapel and the Emperors' hall with its superb paintings are worth seeing.

★ **Historic Half-
Timbered Houses**
*Many charming
half-timbered
buildings from
various periods
have survived in
Goslar, creating
compact rows of
houses in the streets
of the city centre.*

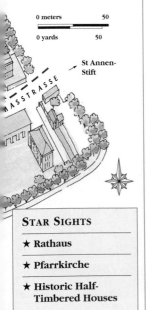

```
0 meters      50
0 yards        50
```

→ **St Annen-
Stift**

STAR SIGHTS

★ **Rathaus**

★ **Pfarrkirche**

★ **Historic Half-
Timbered Houses**

🏠 Siemenshaus
Schreiberstraße 12. 📞 *(05321) 238
37*. 🕐 *9am–noon Tue & Thu*.
This half-timbered house, one
of the most attractive, was
once owned by the Siemens
family who have their roots in
Goslar. The former brewery
on this site is open to visitors.

⛪ St Peter and St Paul
Frankenberger Platz.
Located in the Frankenberg
neighbourhood, this was one
of 47 churches which once
stood in the town. It was built
in the 12th century, and the
tympanum of the south portal
dates from this period. Extensively refurbished, the church
prides itself on its magnificent
Baroque furnishings.

⛪ St Jakobi
Jakobi-Kirchhof. 📞 *(05321) 235 33*.
🕐 *Apr–Sep: 8:30am–5pm daily*.
The present appearance of
this church, the only Catholic
one in Goslar, is the result of
Gothic additions, although the
structure of the walls remains
Romanesque. The famous
work of art in the church is
the *Pietà* by Hans von Witten,
but it is also worth looking at
the wall paintings, the organ
and the baptismal font.

⛪ Neuwerkkirche
Rosentorstraße. 📞 *(05321) 228 39*.
🕐 *Apr–Oct: 10am–noon & 2:30–
4:30pm Mon–Fri, 10am–noon Sat*.
This impressive late-Romanesque church was built in the
12th–13th centuries for the
Cistercian Order, although the
surviving monastic buildings
date from the early 18th century. Inside, the wall paintings
and the choir partition are
of interest. The church is surrounded by a peaceful garden.

**The train in the Bergbaumuseum
in Rammelsberg**

🏠 Breites Tor
Breite Straße.
Some parts of the defensive
system, dating mainly from
c.1500, are well preserved.
This "wide gate", which can
be seen on the eastern
approach of the town, is the
most imposing part.

🏠 St Annen-Stift
Glockengießerstraße 65. 📞 *(05321)
247 62*. 🕐 *11am–1pm & 2–4pm
Mon–Thu, 11am–1pm Fri & Sat*.
The hospice of St Anna for
orphans, the elderly and infirm still fulfills the same function. Behind its picturesque
façade is a beautiful small
chapel with superb paintings
on a wooden ceiling.

🏛 Bergbaumuseum
Rammelsberg
Bergtal 19. 📞 *(05321) 75 00*.
🕐 *9am–6pm daily*
Goslar's mining museum is
based in the 10th-century
silver mine. One of the oldest
surviving industrial structures
in the world, it was entered in
UNESCO's list of world heritage sites. On display are the
mining tools and utensils that
were used in various periods.
Visitors can take a train ride
through the mine and learn
about the history of mining.

The above-ground buildings of the silver mine in Rammelsberg

Einbeck ❷❸

Road map C3. 🏘 *29,400.* 🚉
ℹ *Rathaus, Marktplatz 6 (05561-91 61 21).*

IN THE MIDDLE AGES, this town had 600 breweries – more than houses – and today it is still known for its beers; Bockbier, the famous German strong beer, was invented here. Burned down in 1540 and 1549, the town was subsequently rebuilt in a uniformly Renaissance style. The historic town centre is enclosed by the city walls. More than 100 half-timbered houses have survived to this day. **Eickesches Haus** (Marktstraße 13) is particularly eye-catching, with a sculpted façade based on biblical and Classical stories. Other picturesque houses can be found in Tiedexer Straße and in **Marktplatz**. The latter boasts the **Rathaus** (town hall), Einbeck's main attraction, as well as the **Ratswaage** (municipal weigh house) and **Ratsapotheke** (chemist). The tower of the neighbouring **Pfarrkirche St Jakobi** (parish church) leans 1.5 m (5 ft) from the perpendicular. In 1741, a Baroque façade was added to hide this.

ENVIRONS: 15 km (9 miles) from Einbeck is the spa town of **Bad Gandersheim**. It grew up around a Benedictine monastery established here in 852, which in the 10th century was the home of Roswitha von Gandersheim, the first known German poet.

Göttingen ❷❹

Road map C4. 🏘 *129,000.* 🚉
ℹ *Altes Rathaus, Markt 9 (0551-499 800 or 194 33).* 🎭 *Händelfest (Jun); Literaturherbst (Oct); Jazzfestival (Nov); student festivals, such as Stiftungsfest.*

ALONG WITH Tübingen, Marburg and Heidelberg, Göttingen is one of the most renowned German university towns. Established in 1737 by the English King George II, who was also the ruler of Hannover, the university taught the sons of wealthy German, English and Russian aristocrats. Important cultural figures worked here, including the writer Heinrich Heine, the brothers Grimm and the explorer Alexander von Humboldt. Göttingen's reputation as an educational centre continues today, partly due to the establishment of the Max Planck Institute, named after the scientist who was born in the city and developed the quantum theory.

Göttingen is a lively town thanks to its student population, with dozens of cafés, cosmopolitan restaurants and bars. University buildings are scattered all over town, and the **Aula**, a Neo-Classical Assembly Hall, is worth a visit. On the Marktplatz in the town centre stands the **Rathaus** (town hall) with a Gothic stone façade. The **Gänselieselbrunnen**, the goose girl fountain, in front dates from 1901. It is kissed by students who have passed their exams, and much loved by tourists.

From the southeastern end of the market square, Göttingen's four main churches can be seen: St Michael to the south, St Johannis to the west, St Albani to the east and St Jakobi to the north. The latter two boast late-Gothic altars worth visiting. Together, they testify to Göttingen's early importance in the Middle Ages.

Stone crest on Göttingen's Rathaus

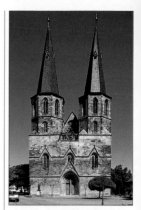

The twin-towered Gothic façade of St Cyriakus in Duderstadt

Duderstadt ❷❺

Road map C4. 🏘 *24,500.* 🚉
ℹ *Marktstr. 66 (05527-84 12 00).*

TO THE SOUTH of the Harz mountains, not far from the former border with East Germany, lies this often overlooked gem. A walk around the medieval town is best started on **Obermarkt** (upper market). Here stands the half-timbered **Rathaus** (town hall), with an interesting façade and spiky towers. Inside it has exhibition halls and a cultural centre. East of the town hall rises the Catholic **Probsteikirche St Cyriakus** with its rich interior of altars and 15 Baroque statues. **St Servatius**, its Protestant counterpart, combines Gothic architecture with a Secessionist interior. Nearby is the **Westchurchtorturm**, the only surviving town gate. Its strangely spiralling finial is not a decorative feature, but the consequence of a weakness in its design.

The Gothic Rathaus on Marktplatz in Göttingen

The Weser Renaissance Trail 26

THE WESER Renaissance is an architectural and decorative style of northern Germany, dating from the mid-16th to the mid-17th century. Its tall roofs and gables were inspired by Dutch architecture, although it has many original features: the *Zwerchhäuser* (bay windows, one or more storeys high), the *Utlucht* (protruding sections of the façade), lavish decorations and multi-wing castles, some with spiral staircases in their towers.

Hameln ①
Rattenfängerhaus (rat catcher's house), Hochzeitshaus (wedding house) and Dempstersches Haus (Dempsters' house) are good examples of the Weser Renaissance style. The Romanesque-Gothic Münster (collegiate church) is also worth seeing.

Bevern ③
Another gem of the Weser Renaissance style, the castle in Bevern, near Holzminden, was built from Prussian stone in the years 1602–12. It has four wings as well as two towers in the corners of its courtyard.

Hämelschenburg ②
The castle, built in 1588–1612, is a three-winged building, surrounded by a moat. It has an impressive exterior with towers and decorative gables; its original interiors are also preserved.

Münden ④
The principal buildings that exemplify the Weser Renaissance style are the town hall and the castle, now a regional museum with a collection of ceramics. Fragments of a Renaissance fresco of Duke Eryk II of Calenberg can also be admired here.

0 km   20

0 miles   20

TIPS FOR DRIVERS

Starting point: *Hameln.*
Length: *112 km (70 miles).*
Stopping-off places: *good restaurants and bistros can be found in all the towns and villages along the route.*

WESERGEBIRGE

Emmer   *Weser*

SOLLING

Weser

Diemel

SCHLESWIG-HOLSTEIN

*S*CHLESWIG-HOLSTEIN *is the northernmost German state, situated between the Baltic and the North Sea and bordered by the Elbe River and Denmark. Weather-beaten by the unstable marine climate, the Gothic brick buildings of Lübeck, queen of the Baltic coast, testify equally to the turbulent history of this region. Today, tourists visit Schleswig-Holstein for its wide sandy beaches and impressive lakes.*

Originally, this state comprised two territories: Schleswig in the north, which was inhabited by Germanic tribes (Angles, Saxons, Vikings and Danes) in the Middle Ages, and Holstein in the south, mainly populated by Slavs, who converted to Christianity as late as the 12th century. Its more recent history was characterized by struggles between the Hanseatic towns and the rulers of Denmark. In the 18th century, the entire region, from Altona in the south (now part of Hamburg) to Kolding in the north, belonged to Denmark, but in 1866 it was annexed to Bismarck's Prussia. In 1920, the political borders that exist today were established when Denmark regained the northern part of Schleswig after a plebiscite, leaving a significant Danish minority on the German side.

Schleswig-Holstein is principally an agricultural region, and less densely populated than any other state in Germany. Art lovers are mainly drawn to Lübeck, the most powerful Hanseatic town in the Baltic during the Middle Ages. Lübeck's old town, an architectural gem, has now been listed as a world heritage site by UNESCO. Other places offer surprises aplenty – the visitor will be captivated by the Romanesque churches around Flensburg, while the magnificent countryside more than compensates for the lack of major cultural monuments. A walk through the national park of Schleswig-Holsteinisches Wattenmeer, the moving sand dunes of the elegant island of Sylt, or a romantic sunset on the lake shores in Plön will leave lasting impressions.

The moated Renaissance Wasserschloss in Glücksburg

◁ Idyllic landscape with a lighthouse on Sylt island

Exploring Schleswig-Holstein

U NDOUBTEDLY the greatest attraction in this two-part state is Lübeck, and at least one day should be set aside to visit this town. Kiel is a popular destination during the annual Kieler Woche, the world's largest sailing festival. The sun-kissed island of Sylt invites the visitor to linger for a few days, while the stunning scenery of Helgoland is best explored in a one-day trip from Cuxhaven or Husum. Hotels in the larger towns, such as Schleswig, Kiel or Flensburg, and many provincial boarding houses, provide a good base for excursions.

0 km   25

o miles   25

Buildings in Plön, in the Holstein Switzerland Nature Reserve

GETTING AROUND

The nearest international airport is Hamburg. Two motorways bisect Schleswig-Holstein: leaving Hamburg and the long queues for the Elbe Tunnel behind, the E47 (No 7) takes the visitor to Kiel and via Flensburg on to the Danish peninsula of Jutland, while the E22 (turning off the E47) leads via Lübeck to the Danish capital, Copenhagen.

Esbjerg (Denmark

NORDFRIESL

NORDFRIESISCHE INSELN

199

HALLIGEN

5

Nordsee (North Sea)

EIDERSTEDT

5

203

HUSUM

HELGOLAND

MELDORF

DITHMARSCHEN

CUXHAVEN

73

495

The lake at Westensee Nature Reserve, where visitors can experience the captivating nature and wildlife close up

KEY

▬ Motorway

▬ Main road

～ River

🔆 Viewpoint

Ferries departing for excursions from the harbour in Kiel

NSBURG 41

199

201

6 SCHLESWIG

*Kieler Bucht
(Bay of Kiel)*

76

7 KIEL

210

202

207

WAGRIEN

RENDSBURG

E45/7

404

*HOLSTEINISCHE
SCHWEIZ* **8**

205

4

21

*Lübecker
Bucht*

NEUMÜNSTER

PLÖN 76

77

206

21

LÜBECK
10

ÜCKSTADT

E45/7

4

F22/1

LMSHORN 23

RATZEBURG 9

PINNEBERG

Hamburg

Hamburg

E26/24

REINBEK

Berlin

GEESTHACHT *Berlin*

BOIZENBURG

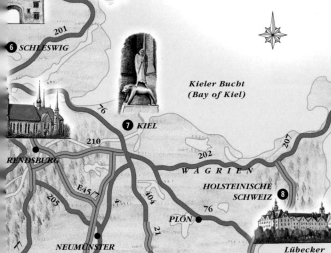

Helgoland ●

FOR LOVERS OF SPICES in Germany, it may have seemed a bad deal when in 1890 Germany received Helgoland from Britain in return for Zanzibar, but the island is nevertheless worth a visit. Farthest out in the open sea (50 km/31 miles from the mainland), the island always had great strategic importance, and after 1945, Britain used it as a bombing target before it was returned to Germany in 1952. Today its fresh air and spectacular red cliffs attract thousands of tourists.

VISITORS' CHECKLIST

Road map B1. 👥 *1,900.* ⛴
Bremerhaven, Cuxhaven and Wilhelmshaven. 🚩 *Lung Wai 28 (04725-81 37 11 & 14).*
Ⓦ www.helgoland.de

Port ①
On the flat part of the island is Unterland, a small post-war town with 1,900 inhabitants and a port. Fishermen store their nets in the colourful little houses, referred to as Hummerbuden (lobster huts).

Lange Anna ③
Tall Anna, measuring about 40 m (131ft) high, is the best known red sandstone cliff. Nearby is the Lummenfelsen, which is the smallest nature reserve in Germany.

0 metres 100
0 yards 100

Oberland ②
In the upper part of the island stands the Nikolai-kirche, dating from 1959. Close by, and worth a visit, are 16th-century tombs.

KEY

– – – Suggested route

TIPS FOR TOURISTS

Starting point: *the port of Helgoland*
Length: *1.7 km (1.1 miles).*
Stopping places: *there are numerous restaurants, bars and cafés all over the island .*

Glückstadt ❷

Road map C2. 🕍 *12,000*. 🚪 🛈
Grosse Nübelstraße 31 (04124-93 75 85).

THE DANISH king, Christian IV, founded this little town in 1617 and although less impressive than Hamburg, the town is worth a visit for its layout – roads radiate out from the hexagonal market square, once surrounded by fortifications. On the square stands the reconstructed 17th-century town hall as well as the Baroque Stadtkirche (town church). In 1648, parts of the duchy of Holstein were transferred to Glückstadt. Most of the palaces built to house the Dukes survived, for example the Palais Werner with its amazing ballroom. The regional **museum** is now in Brockdorf-Palais, another palace from 1632.

🏛 **Detlefsen-Museum**
Am Fleth 43. 📞 *(04124) 93 76 30.*
🕐 *2–5pm Tue; 2–6pm Fri; 10am–noon, 2–5pm Sun.*

Meldorf ❸

Road map C1. 🕍 *7,500*. 🚪
🛈 *Nordermarkt 10 (04832-97 800).*

MELDORF HAS preserved the **Dithmarscher Dom**, its cathedral, a 13th-century basilica with an exterior extensively rebuilt in the 19th century. The vaulting in the transept, resembling a cupola, is decorated with Gothic frescos, depicting the legends of saints Catherine, Christopher and Nicholas. There is a richly decorated dividing wall (1603) and a grand triptych of the Crucifixion (c.1520).

The port and waterfront of Flensburg

Sylt ❹

Road map B1. 🕍 *50,000*. 🚪 *in Westerland.* 🛈 *Westerland, Stephanstrasse 6 (04651-820 20).*

THE ISLAND OF Sylt, the largest of the North Frisian islands, has long attracted wealthy German visitors. The 50-km (31-mile) long island offers a rich variety of landscapes: white, sandy beaches, shifting sand dunes near List, towering up to 25 m (82ft) high, steep shorelines, the Rotes Kliff (red cliff) near Kampen and the Watt, the endless expanse of mudflats in the national park, Schleswig-Holsteinisches Wattenmeer. **Westerland** is Sylt's main town, and its promenade, Friedrichstrasse, is "the" place to be seen. There is also an interesting casino in a former Secessionist spa building.

Flensburg ❺

Road map C1. 🕍 *84,500*. 🚪
🛈 *Rathausstrasse 1 (0461-909 09 20).* 🎏 *Rum-Regatta in Flensburger Förde (Jun).*

THE MOST NORTHERLY town in Germany, Flensburg was an important trading centre in the 16th century with 200 ships, although at times it belonged to Denmark. The **Nordertor** (northern gate), dating from 1595, is an emblem of the city. The shipping museum is fascinating while the Marienkirche has a Renaissance altar, sculptures and the painting *The Last Supper* (1598). Nearby is the **Heilig-Geist-Kirche** (church of the Holy Ghost), which has belonged to the town's Danish community since 1588. Other interesting churches are **Nikolaikirche** which boasts a magnificent Renaissance organ, and Johanniskirche with a vaulted ceiling dating from around 1500. Its painted scenes show people disguised as animals, which was a covert way of criticizing the church and the system of indulgences.

ENVIRONS: Schloss Glücksburg, 9 km (6 miles) northeast of Flensburg, a square castle with massive corner towers on a granite base, was built from 1582–7. Visit its captivating castle chapel, the Roter Saal (red hall) with its low vaulting, and the valuable collection of 18th-century tapestries from Brussels. The artist Emil Nolde lived and worked in **Seebüll**, west of Flensburg, from the age of 20 until his death in 1956.

The sandy beaches of the North Frisian island of Sylt, extending far to the horizon

The inner courtyard of Schloss Gottorf in Schleswig

Schleswig ❻

Road map C1. 🏘 *27,000.* 🚉
ℹ️ *Plessenstr. 7 (04621-98 16 16).*
🎭 *Schleswig-Holstein Musik Festival throughout the region (Jul/Aug); Wikinger-Tage (Aug every other year).*

THE MAIN SEAT of the Vikings, Schleswig became a bishop's see as early as 947, and from 1544 to 1713 it was the residence of the dukes of Schleswig-Holstein-Gottorf, once related to the rulers of Denmark and Russia. They resided in **Schloss Gottorf**, a castle with four wings which now houses the **Schleswig-Holsteinisches Landesmuseum** (regional museum) as well as northern Germany's most famous archaeological museum, the **Archäologisches Landesmuseum**, exhibiting the *Moorleichen*, prehistoric corpses preserved in peat. It is also worth seeing the two-storey chapel (1590).

The **Dom** (cathedral) was built in stages between the 12th and 15th centuries. Its largest treasure is the Bordesholmer Altar, a triptych altar carved by Hans Brüggemann in 1514–21. A masterpiece of Gothic carving, it is 12 m (39 ft) high and comprises 392 figures; the only one to look straight at the visitor is the sculptor himself, bearded and hat askew (in the house of Abraham and Melchisede).

Visitors can also walk around the historic fishermen's district of **Holm**, and visit the **Wikinger-Museum Haithabu**, about 4 km (2 miles) from the town centre. The fortifications have survived in the grounds of this historic Viking settlement. The museum is housed in a modern building, which looks like an upturned boat. Exhibits include the depiction of Viking life, models of boats, jewellery and everyday items.

🏛 **Schloss Gottorf/ Schleswig-Holsteinisches Landesmuseum/Archäologisches Landesmuseum**
📞 *(04621) 81 30.* 🕐 *Mar–Oct: 10am–6pm daily; Nov–Feb: 10am–4pm Tue–Sun.*
🏛 **Wikinger-Museum Haithabu**
📞 *(04621) 81 32 22.* 🕐 *Apr–Oct: 9am–5pm daily; Nov–Feb: 10am–4pm Tue–Sun.*

Kiel ❼

Road map C1. 🏘 *245,000.* 🚉
ℹ️ *Andreas-Gayk-Straße 31 (0431-67 91 00).* **Town hall** 🕐 *May–Sep: 12:20 Wed & Sun.* 🎭 *Kieler Woche (end Jun).*

LOCATED AT THE end of the Kieler Förde inlet, Kiel marks the beginning of the Nord-Ostsee-Kanal (Kiel Canal), in service since 1895, with two giant locks. Ferries depart from Kiel for Scandinavia, and in the summer the "Kieler Woche" turns the town into a mecca for yachtsmen from around the world.

A walk along the Schweden-Kai (embankment) and surroundings will take visitors to the vast **Rathaus** (town hall), dating from the beginning of the 20th century, and the **Nikolaikirche** (church of St Nicholas) which was rebuilt after the devastation of World War II, with its baptismal font and Gothic altar. Ernst Barlach created *Geistkämpfer*, the sculpture outside the church, which symbolizes the triumph

ROMANESQUE BAPTISMAL FONTS
There are few places in the world where visitors can see as many Romanesque baptismal fonts as in Angeln. Generally fashioned from granite, they have been preserved in enchanting 12th-century churches, which can be visited by following a 63-km (39-mile) route along the roads linking Flensburg and Schleswig, Munkbrarup, Sörup, Norderbrarup, Süderbrarup and finally Ulsnis.

Font in the church in Borbry

Font in the church in Munkbrarup

Font in the church in Sörup

A house in Kiel's Schleswig-Holsteinisches Freilichtmuseum

of mind over matter. Pieces of the sculpture, which had been cut up by the National Socialists, were found and reassembled after the war.

The most interesting of Kiel's many museums is the **Schleswig-Holsteinisches Freilichtmuseum**, an open-air museum in Molfsee, 6 km (4 miles) from the centre of Kiel, where German rural architecture from the 16th–19th centuries is on show. Pottery, basket-making and baking are demonstrated, and the products are sold here.

🏛 **Schleswig-Holsteinisches Freilichtmuseum**
Hamburger Landstraße 97. 📞 *(0431) 65 96 60.* ⭕ *Apr–Oct: 9am–6pm daily; Nov–Mar: 11am–4pm Sun & public holidays.* 📷

Holsteinische Schweiz (Holstein's Switzerland) ❽

Road map D1. 🚉 🏨 *Bad Malente, Kurverwaltung, Bahnhofstraße 4a (04523-20 01 00).* 🎷 *Jazz-Festival in Plön; open-air opera during Sommerspiele in Eutin.*

THE MORAIN hills, which reach a height of 164 m (538 ft), and 140 lakes are the reasons why this area is known as Holstein's Switzerland. The best means of transport here is the bicycle, allowing visitors to appreciate the beauty of nature and the wealth of the fauna – ornithologists have counted 200 species of birds. The main centre of this holiday area is **Plön** on the

Born Emil Hansen, this great artist later adopted the name of the town in which he was born. After studying art in Copenhagen, Munich and Paris, Nolde devoted himself to painting, and was also successful in the graphic arts. From 1906–7 he belonged to the Expressionist group *Die Brücke*. He is known particularly for his use of vivid colours and highly expressive features, embuing his subjects with great emotion. Rejected and forbidden to paint by the National Socialists as an exponent of "degenerate art", Nolde settled and continued to paint in Seebüll, where a house was built for him to his own designs.

Großer Plöner See (large Plön lake). Nearby is **Preetz**, an old shoemakers' town, which has a towerless Gothic church that belonged to a former Benedictine monastery. Older still is the Romanesque church in **Bosau**, a small town in a picturesque location on the Großer Plöner See. It was the first bishopric in this area, and home to Vizelin – the apostle of the Slavs.

It is also worth visiting **Eutin**, a small town full of picturesque buildings, which is sometimes referred to as the "Weimar of the north". The original Schloss, a brick structure with four wings, was built in the Middle Ages as the residence of the Lübeck bishops, but it was substantially altered in the years 1716–27. Worth seeing inside are the palace chapel, the Blauer Salon (blue salon) with Rococo stucco work, as well as paintings by Johann Heinrich Wilhelm Tischbein, which were inspired by the *Iliad* and the *Odyssey*, epic poems written by Homer.

The Dom in Ratzeburg

Ratzeburg ❾

Road map D2. 🏘 *12,500.* 🚉
🏨 *Schlosswiese 7 (04541-85 85 65 or 800 080).*

RATZEBURG, situated on an island in the Großer Ratzeburger See, is linked with the mainland by three causeways. The town was named after Ratibor, the duke of the Elbe River area. Henry the Lion established a missionary bishopric here in 1154, and later it became the residence of the Lauenburg dukes.

The **Dom** (cathedral) is one of the earliest examples of brick architecture, a style that was imported from Lombardy. The southern vestibule of the Romanesque basilica is particularly impressive – with herringbone-pattern brickwork and lines of black tiles as interior decoration. The Romanesque stalls, a 13th-century crucifix in a rainbow arch, the ducal gallery above the nave and the Baroque altar in the southern transept are some of its treasures.

The 17th-century Schloss in Plön, in Holstein's Switzerland

Street-by-Street: Lübeck ⑩

This "specific nest", as Lübeck was described by its
most famous resident, Thomas Mann, is well worth
a visit. The most important town in the Baltic basin by
the end of the Middle Ages, it is now a magnet for fans
of Backsteingotik, Gothic brick architecture which has
been elevated to a national style. In Lübeck it is easy to
see why: church interiors, the façades of buildings, the
city gates, the unique town hall and even the Medieval
hospital resemble pictures from an illustrated history of
architecture brought to life. Despite a few blunders, the
city has been beautifully rebuilt after World
War II and enjoys a positive revival.

Mengstraße
*This street is full of
picturesque Gothic
buildings fronted
by typical brick
façades and
crowned by
stepped gables.*

Rathaus
*Germany's most famous
brick town hall, dating
from 1226, has unusual
walls and turrets.*

**Heiligen-Geist-
Hospital**

★ Marienkirche
*St Mary's Church, larger than the
cathedral and situated behind the
town hall, holds great art treasures.*

Holstentor
*This gate, once the only entrance
into Lübeck, was built by Hinrich
Helmstede in the years 1466–78,
based on Flemish designs. It has
become the emblem of the town.*

Petrikirche
The church of St
Peter, from the
first half of the
14th century, is
Lübeck's only
five-naved church.

KEY

– – – Suggested route

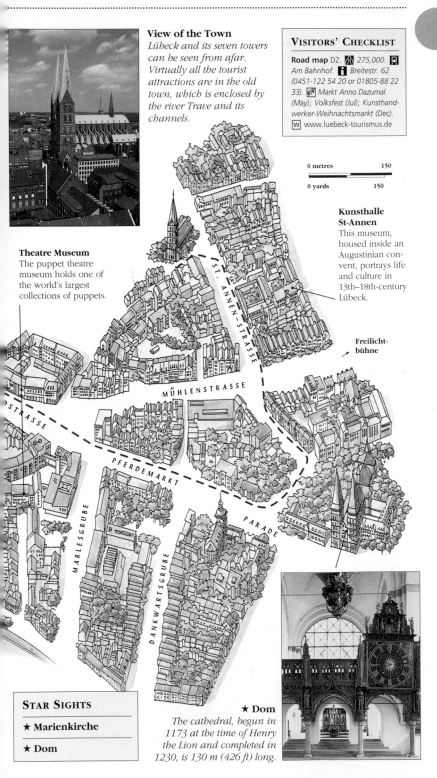

View of the Town
Lübeck and its seven towers can be seen from afar. Virtually all the tourist attractions are in the old town, which is enclosed by the river Trave and its channels.

VISITORS' CHECKLIST

Road map D2. 275,000. *Am Bahnhof.* Breitestr. 62 (0451-122 54 20 or 01805-88 22 33). Markt Anno Dazumal (May); Volksfest (Jul); Kunsthandwerker-Weihnachtsmarkt (Dec). www.luebeck-tourismus.de

0 metres 150

0 yards 150

Kunsthalle St-Annen
This museum, housed inside an Augustinian convent, portrays life and culture in 13th–18th-century Lübeck.

Theatre Museum
The puppet theatre museum holds one of the world's largest collections of puppets.

Freilicht-bühne

ST. ANNEN-STRASSE

MÜHLENSTRASSE

...STRASSE

PFERDEMARKT

MARLESGRUBE

DANKWARTSGRUBE

PARADE

STAR SIGHTS

★ **Marienkirche**

★ **Dom**

★ **Dom**
The cathedral, begun in 1173 at the time of Henry the Lion and completed in 1230, is 130 m (426 ft) long.

MARZIPAN FROM LÜBECK

A favourite present from Lübeck is marzipan, which has been popular throughout Europe since the 19th century. The sweets are made from two-thirds sweet almonds imported from Venice and one-third sugar and aromatic oils. The Persians referred to it as *marsaban*, and in 1530 its name was recorded for the first time in Lübeck as *Martzapaen*. From 1806, the Niederegger patisserie perfected the recipe; they established a patisserie on Breite Strasse which operates to this day.

Exploring Lübeck

All the most important monuments, with the exception of the Holstentor, are situated within the old town, which is best explored on foot.

🏠 Marienkirche

🕐 *9am–5pm daily, in winter to 3pm.*
St Mary's church was constructed by the Lübeckers as a monument to themselves. The twin-towered basilica with transept and a passageway around the polygonshaped presbytery is the brick modification of a NeoClassical French cathedral.

Its vast interior boasts the highest vaulted brick ceiling in the world (40 m/131 ft) which dominates the other interior features. These include a 10 m (32 ft) bronze Holy Sacrament (1476–9); a baptismal font in the main nave dating from 1337; the altar dedicated to the Virgin Mary in the Sängerkapelle (singers' chapel) made in Antwerp in 1518; and the main, late-Gothic Swarte-Altar with the Madonna. The Briefkapelle, the south-

western side chapel built around 1310, is one of the earliest examples of star vaulting in Europe.

In one of the towers, the shattered fragments of the church bells have been left embedded in the floor where they fell during the bombing in 1942; the present bells are from St Catherine's in Gdansk.

🏛 Buddenbrook-Haus

Heinrich-und Thomas-Mann-Zentrum, Mengstr. 4. 📞 *(0451) 122 41 92.*
🕐 *Apr–Oct: 10am–6pm daily; Nov–Mar: 10am–5pm daily.* ● *24, 25, 31 Dec.* 📷
Literature lovers will wish to visit the Buddenbrook house Behind its Rococo façade from 1758 is a museum devoted to the Mann family, the great writers who lived here in 1841–91. It is here that Thomas Mann wrote the family saga of the Buddenbrooks, after whom the house is named, and for which he was awarded the Nobel Prize in 1929. The centre exhibits

documents relating to this famous family, in particular to Thomas and Heinrich Mann, concentrating on their time in Lübeck and their emigration and exile after 1933.

🏛 Schabbelhaus

Mengstraße 48 & 50.
Originally the western, wealthier half of Lübeck had many patrician houses, facing the streets with their ornate brick gables. Many of these were damaged in the bombing raids of March 1942, but after World War II they were carefully restored. The most interesting buildings survived in Mengstrasse, in particular the famous Schabbelhaus at No. 48. Built in 1558, this house gained a magnificent Baroque hall in the 18th century. Today it is an attraction in its own right as well as a restaurant.

Stepped gables of the Haus der Schiffergesellschaft

🏛 Haus der Schiffergesellschaft

Breite Straße 2.
The house of the Marine Guild, which dates from 1535, has a splendid interior and now houses one of the city's most elegant restaurants. The façade has stepped gables and terraces/forecourts, typical of Lübeck.

🏛 Füchtingshof

Glockengießerstr. 23.
The eastern part of the town is of an entirely different character: narrow streets link charming Höfe (courtyards) and small, modest houses. The most interesting Höfe can be

The multi-storey Burgtor, crowned by a Baroque cupola

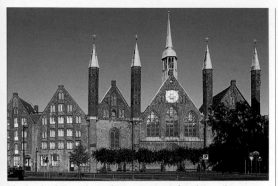

The façade of the Gothic Heiliger-Geist-Hospital, with its spiky towers

found at numbers 23 and 39. The Baroque portal of the Füchtingshof, at No. 23, leads to houses which, from 1639, were built for the widows of merchants and captains.

🏰 Burgtor

On the northern limits of the old town stands the castle gate, a second surviving gate of the historic fortifications. A Baroque finial was added to the gate in 1685. The five storeys of the tower are decorated with uniform rows of windows and windbreaks.

✠ Heiliger-Geist-Hospital

Große Burgstr. ☐ Apr–Sep: 10am–5pm Tue–Sun; Oct–Mar: 10am–4pm Tue–Sun.
The Holy Ghost hospital is the best preserved Medieval building of its type in central Europe. Built in the shape of the letter T, it has a shorter western section with a twin-aisled hall-church (c. 1286), containing frescos of *Christ and the Madonna on Solomon's Throne* and *Majestas Domini*. The second section contains the actual hospice. In 1820, small cubicles were created for the elderly, who lived here until 1970.

⛪ Jakobikirche

This 15th-century church, which suffered only insignificant damage during World War II, has preserved its original, mainly Baroque features. Of particular note are the main altar as well as the side altar in the south chapel. The latter was established around 1500 by the mayor, Heinrich Brömbse,

and depicts a scene of the Crucifixion carved in sandstone. Both the small and the large organ originate from the 15th century.

⛪ Katharinenkirche

Königstraße. **Museumskirche St. Katharinen** ☐ Apr–Sep: 10am–1pm, 2–5pm Tue–Sun.
St Catherine's, the only surviving monastic church, was built by the Franciscans, as is apparent from the absence of a tower and its monastic gallery in the presbytery of the main nave. The western façade, with its glazed brickwork, is of a high artistic quality. In the 20th century, sculptures carved by Ernst Barlach were added (*Woman in the Wind, Beggar on Crutches* and *The Singing Novitiate*). On the western side hangs the painting of *The*

The bright interior of the Gothic Dom

Resurrection of Lazarus by Jacopo Tintoretto, bought by a wealthy patrician; the sculpture of St George and the dragon is a copy of the famous original by the Lübeck artist Bernt Notke, which is now in Stockholm.

🏛 Kunsthalle St-Annen

St-Annen-str. 15. ☎ (0451) 122 41 37. ☐ Apr–Sep: 10am–5pm Tue–Sun; Oct–Mar: 10am–4pm Tue–Sun. ● Easter, 24, 25, 31 Dec. 🈂
The Augustinian convent houses unusual Lübeck art treasures. There is an impressive number of wooden Gothic altars, commissioned by wealthy families for their private chapels in one of the five churches. The altars were supposed to bring them eternal salvation after death, and to symbolize the wealth and prestige of the family during their lifetime. Gems of the collection are the Hans Memling altar with Christ's Passion, and the external side wings of the Schonenfahrer Altar by Bernt Notke.

⛪ Dom

☐ Apr–Sep: 10am–5pm daily; Oct–Mar: 10am–3pm daily.
The cathedral, completed in 1341, takes the form of a Gothic hall-church. Its most precious possession is the Triumphal Cross sculpted from a 17-m (55-ft) oak tree by Bernt Notke, a celebrated local artist. The giant figures, resplendent with emotion, include Adam and Eve, as well as the founder, bishop Albert Krummedick. Among numerous memorials, that dedicated to bishop Heinrich Bocholt, made from bronze, stands out. Additionally, two valuable sculptures can be seen; *Holy Mary Mother of God* with a crown composed of stars, as well as the *Beautiful Madonna* in the southern nave (1509). Note the bronze baptismal font by Lorenz Grove from 1455, with three kneeling angels supporting the bowl.

MECKLENBURG-LOWER POMERANIA

THE MEDIEVAL *towns of Schwerin, Wismar, Rostock and Stralsund, as well as several magnificent architectural monuments, provide reason enough to visit this part of Germany, yet it also offers a largely untouched landscape of forests and lakes. Along the Baltic coastline, tourists delight in the beautiful sandy beaches of Darß or Usedom, but above all they head for the island of Rügen, with its famous white cliffs.*

Mecklenburg-Vorpommern (Lower Pomerania), a mosaic of regions, can look back on an eventful history. In the 12th century, indigenous Slav tribes were colonized and converted to Christianity. The region became part of the Holy Roman Empire and German colonialism resulted in the Slavs' rapid assimilation. In the Middle Ages, several towns became rich trading centres and joined the Hanseatic League. From the 18th century, the Swedish Empire was the most powerful political force in this part of Europe. It ruled Wismar, Rügen and Stralsund until 1803 and 1815 respectively, when the territories became part of Prussia, and later the German Reich. During World War II the Baltic towns suffered terrible destruction and then from neglect under the German Democratic Republic: in 1953 all the hotels were nationalized and the unique buildings in the Hanseatic towns were left to decay or were destroyed.

After reunification, although still one of the poorest states in Germany, Mecklenburg-Lower Pomerania today has become an idyllic holiday destination. Improvements in the infrastructure, new hotels and restaurants have brought positive change, and it has much to offer. Nature lovers, walkers and cyclists, for example, can enjoy the Mecklenburg lake district and the island of Rügen. Fans of architecture will find a wealth of interest in the palace in Ludwigslust and the castle of Güstrow, as well as the Gothic brick architecture in town halls, churches and smaller buildings.

The beautiful white chalk cliffs on the island of Rügen sweep down to the blue Baltic Sea

◁ The superb Schloss of Schwerin, on an island in the middle of Schwerin lake

Exploring Mecklenburg-Lower Pomerania

THIS IS A large region with only minor roads so visitors are well advised to allow extra time to explore it. The area can be divided into three: the west, stopping off in pretty Wismar or charming Schwerin with its fairy-tale castle; the centre, with the major port of Rostock as a base, and the east, which can be explored from Stralsund or Greifswald. In the central Mecklenburger Seenplatte is Müritz National Park, a vast area of lakes and forests that is ideal for camping, walking and sailing. It is also a good plan to set aside a few days for relaxation on the sandy beaches of Darß, Zingst, Usedom or Rügen.

Mecklenburg's glorious beaches

Sights at a Glance

See Also

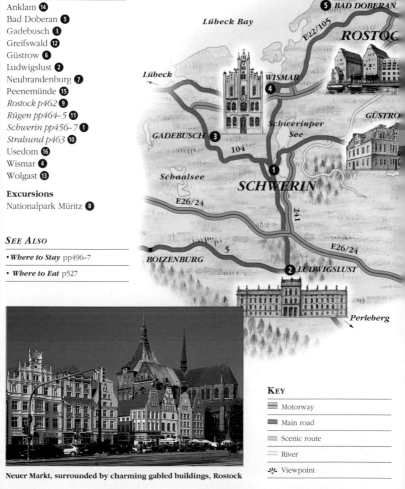

Mecklenburg Bay

Lübeck Bay

Lübeck

GADEBUSCH ③

Schaalsee

E26/24

BOIZENBURG

⑤ **BAD DOBERAN**

E22/105

ROSTOC

WISMAR ④

GÜSTRO

Schweriner See

104

① **SCHWERIN**

241

E26/24

② **LUDWIGSLUST**

Perleberg

Neuer Markt, surrounded by charming gabled buildings, Rostock

Key

▬	Motorway
▬	Main road
▬	Scenic route
—	River
☆	Viewpoint

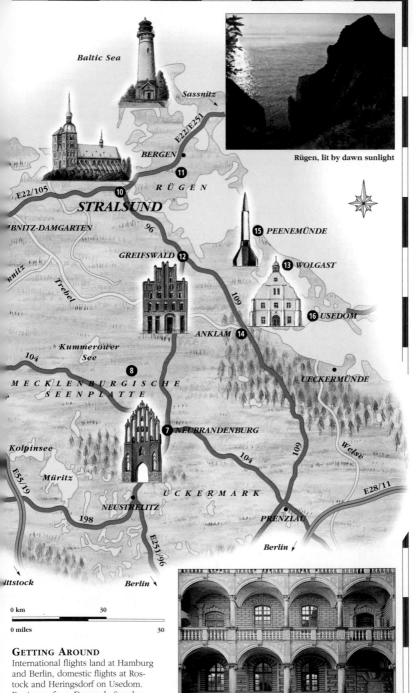

Baltic Sea

Sassnitz

E22/E251

BERGEN

11

R Ü G E N

10

E22/105

STRALSUND

BNITZ-DAMGARTEN

96

GREIFSWALD 12

Rügen, lit by dawn sunlight

15 **PEENEMÜNDE**

13 **WOLGAST**

rnitz

Trebel

109

16 **USEDOM**

ANKLAM 14

Kummerower See

104

8

MECKLENBURGISCHE SEENPLATTE

UECKERMÜNDE

7 *NEUBRANDENBURG*

104

109

Welse

Kolpinsee

E55/19

Müritz

U C K E R M A R K

E28/11

NEUSTRELITZ

198

PRENZLAU

E251/96

Berlin

ittstock

Berlin

0 km	30
0 miles	30

GETTING AROUND

International flights land at Hamburg and Berlin, domestic flights at Rostock and Heringsdorf on Usedom. Ferries go from Denmark, Sweden and Lithuania to Saßnitz and Rostock, and the E55 motorway runs from the south to Schwerin and Rostock.

The attractive cloisters of Schloss Güstrow

Schwerin ❶

DESPITE protests from Rostock, the smaller town of Schwerin was chosen as the capital of the newly united state of Mecklenburg-Lower Pomerania. This was an inspired choice as the town is picturesquely situated amid several lakes, with a fairy-tale castle on an island, and an enchanting old town with many Neo-Classical and historic buildings that survived World War II largely unscathed. Apart from a brief spell, the Mecklenburg dukes resided in Schwerin from 1318–1918. Intellectual life flourished here in the 16th century and so the city is known as "Florence of the North".

The Neo-Renaissance Schloss on an island in Schweriner See

Exploring Schwerin

The old town of Schwerin is situated between Pfaffenteich railway station and Schweriner See, a vast 65-sq km (25-sq mile) lake. All the town's most important tourist attractions can easily be visited on foot. Close by to the north is Schelf, which was once a separate town.

♠ Schloss

Schlossinsel. **((0385) 56 57 38.**
☐ 15 Apr–14 Oct: 10am–6pm Tue–Sun; 15 Oct–14 Apr: 10am–5pm Tue–Sun.

Situated on Burg Island, this castle is often referred to as the "Neuschwanstein of Mecklenburg", after the famous Bavarian castle. The Schweriner Schloss was in fact largely built in 1843–57 to an eclectic design by Georg Adolph Demmler and Friedrich August Stüler, who were inspired by the turrets of Château Chambord in France. Major refurbishment tried to recreate some of the castle's original Renaissance features,

of which only the ceramic decorations have remained. Inside, the castle chapel built by Johan Batista Parra in 1560–63 has survived. The elegant rooms in the castle – Thronsaal (throne chamber), Ahnengalerie (ancestral gallery), Rote Audienz (red auditorium), Speisesaal (dining chamber) – are decorated with gilded stucco work. Despite the proliferation of their styles these rooms delight visitors, transporting them back to the 19th century.

♣ Burg- und Schlossgarten

The remaining part of the island is occupied by the Burggarten (fortress garden), which has an orangery and an artificial grotto, built from granite around 1850. A bridge leads to the larger Schlossgarten (castle garden) which is a favourite place for the town's inhabitants to relax. The Kreuzkanal, a canal built in 1748–56, one of the garden's axes, is lined with copies of Baroque statues

including the *Four Seasons*, created by the renowned sculptor of the Dresden Zwinger, Balthasar Permoser.

▥ Staatliches Museum

Am Alten Garten 3. **(** (0385) 595 80. ☐ 10am–8pm Tue, 10am–6pm Wed–Sun. ● 24 & 31 Dec.

The state museum stands in Alter Garten, one of the most attractive squares in Germany, where the waters beautifully reflect the castle and the Neo-Renaissance theatre. The museum, which features lions on its façade and a portico with Ionic columns, houses an art collection based on that of Duke Christian Ludwig II, a lasting testimony to his taste and erudition. Apart from works by German artists such as Cranach, Liebermann and Corinth, and the Dutch painters Hals and Fabritius, it holds works by many French artists. This includes 34 paintings by Jean-Baptiste Oudry, who was court painter to Ludwig XIV, as well as a good selection of paintings by the much more recent Dadaist artist Marcel Duchamp.

▦ Rathausplatz

The town hall square is surrounded by the homes of wealthy citizens, often with 19th-century façades concealing older walls. This is true of the Gothic town hall, which is hidden under an English mock-Tudor-style façade. Demmler was the architect who is responsible for numerous Neo-Renaissance

***Venus and Amor* (1527) by Lucas Cranach in the Staatliches Museum**

The Dom and houses in Schwerin

and Neo-Gothic buildings, the showpieces of Schwerin. One of the outstanding buildings in the market square is Neues Gebäude on the north side. This "new building" is a covered market from 1783–5, with a showpiece façade comprising 12 Doric columns.

🏛 Dom St Maria und St Johannes

Markt. **(** (0385) 56 50 14.
Tower ○ telephone for opening times.

This cathedral is regarded as the most important work of Gothic brick architecture in the Baltic region, in spite of its Neo-Gothic tower, which affords a marvellous view of the entire town. The basilica, dating from 1240–1416, with its wide transept and passageway around the presbytery

and its wreath of chapels, is reminiscent of the design of French cathedrals. A small number of outstanding original features remain in the cathedral, which compare well with the finest works from Antwerp during this time. They include the wooden late-Gothic multi-panelled Crucifixion worked in sandstone, the 14th-century baptismal font, a memorial to Duchess Helen of Mecklenburg created by the Vischer workshop in Nuremberg, as well as the tombstones of Duke Christopher and his wife (1595).

VISITORS' CHECKLIST

Road map D2. 🏘 110,000. 🚉
Am Bahnhof. 🛈 *Markt 10 (0385-592 52 22).* 🎭 *Schlossfestspiele (Jun–Jul), Drachenbootfestival (Aug).* 🏘 W *www.schwerin.de*

🏛 Freilichtmuseum Schwerin-Mueß

Alte Crivitzer Landstraße 13.
((0351) 20 84 10. ○ 15 Apr–15 Oct: 10am–6pm Tue–Sun.

The museum contains a collection of Mecklenburg folk architecture, including 17 houses of the 17th–19th centuries, which strive to recreate the look of an original village. Combine a visit to this open-air museum with a leisurely day on the beach in nearby Zippendorf.

Houses of an earlier era in open-air Freilichtmuseum in Schwerin-Mueß

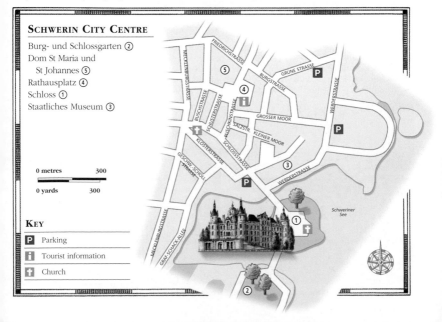

SCHWERIN CITY CENTRE

Burg- und Schlossgarten ②
Dom St Maria und
 St Johannes ⑤
Rathausplatz ④
Schloss ①
Staatliches Museum ③

0 metres   300
0 yards   300

KEY

P	Parking
🛈	Tourist information
✝	Church

One of 24 waterfalls in Ludwigslust Park

Ludwigslust ❷

Road map D2. 🏘 *12,600.*
🚉 *north of centre, 15 min. walk.*
ℹ *Schlossstr. 36 (03874-52 62 51).*

A T THE BEGINNING of the 18th century, the small village of Klenow was founded here, which from 1765 grew into a town. The town was laid out around the **Schloss**, residence of the dukes of Mecklenburg-Schwerin until 1837. The "Versailles of Mecklenburg" is in fact quite different from its French namesake. The Baroque palace was built entirely in brick, concealed beneath sandstone from the Ruda hills. The ornate interior, particularly the elegant Goldener Saal (gold hall), was decorated in Ludwigsluster Carton, a type of papier-mâché, in order to cut costs.

In the mid-19th century, the vast **Schlosspark** was redesigned by Peter Joseph Lenné as an English-style landscaped garden. On a scenic walk round the garden, the visitor can discover some 24 waterfalls, a canal, artificial ruins, a stone bridge and the mausoleum of Helena Pavlovna, daughter of Tsar Peter I,

who died tragically young. In the town you will find the Protestant **Stadtkirche**, built in 1765–70 to look like an antique temple. In the presbytery is a giant mural, *The Adoration of the Shepherds*.

⚜ **Schloss**
🎟 *(03874) 57 19 12.*
🕐 *15 Apr–15 Oct: 10am–6pm Tue–Sun; 16 Oct–14 Apr: 10am–5pm Tue–Sun.* ⬤ *24, 31 Dec.* 🎫
🏛 **Stadtkirche**
🎟 *(03874) 284 57.* 🕐 *Mar–Oct: 11am–6pm Tue–Sat, 3–4pm Sun.*

Gadebusch ❸

Road map D2. 🏘 *6,600.* 🚉
ℹ *Lübsche Str. 5 (03886-29 76).*

T HIS SMALL TOWN, situated right next to the former East–West border, has two interesting historic monuments. The **Stadtkirche**, which dates from 1220, is the oldest brick church in Mecklenburg. Its cross vaulting, chunky pillars and goblet-shaped capitals are Romanesque in style. One of its most precious pieces is the bronze baptismal font (1450). Angels hold the bowl, on which 22 scenes of the Passion were sculpted by an unknown artist.

Baptismal font in the Stadtkirche in Gadebusch

In the 16th and 17th centuries, the **Schloss** was the

residence of distant relations of the dukes of Mecklenburg. Resembling the castle in Wismar, it is decorated with glazed reliefs and pilasters. It is not open to visitors.

Wismar ❹

Road map D2. 🏘 *55,000.* 🚉
🚊 *Am Markt 11 (03841-194 33).*

W ISMAR is undoubtedly one of the most attractive towns in Mecklenburg. During the Middle Ages, it was an important Hanseatic centre, as evidenced by the monumental brick church, which is completely out of proportion with the provincial town of today. After the Thirty Years' War, in 1648, the Swedes were established in the town, and rebuilt it as the strongest fortress in Europe. In 1803 they leased Wismar to Mecklenburg, but never claimed it back.

The town centre has a grand market square measuring 100 x 100 m (328 x 328 ft), with **Wasserspiele** (water feature), a Dutch-Renaissance pavilion from 1602 in the centre. Water was piped here from a source 4 km (2 miles) away, until 1897, to supply 220 private and 16 public buildings. The most beautiful house on the square is the **Alter Schwede** (old Swede), built about 1380, with a protruding Gothic

The Baroque residence of the dukes of Mecklenburg-Schwerin in Ludwigslust

Alter Schwede and Wasserspiele in the market square in Wismar

brick gable. To the west of the market there are two churches, which act as sad examples of the GDR's neglect of its historical legacy. The reconstruction of the **Georgenkirche**, badly damaged in World War II, was begun in 1989, and it will soon be returned to its former glory. The **Marienkirche** has only one surviving tower – the ruined nave was blown up in 1960. Nearby lies the **Fürstenhof**, residence of the dukes of Wismar. The north wing is the most interesting – its Mannerist style was inspired by the Italian town of Ferrari and northern European ceramic traditions (such as Lübeck workshop). The magnificent sandstone portal is flanked by pairs of intertwined fauns.

A pair of fauns from the portal Fürstenhof in Wismar

Nikolaikirche is a gem of Wismar architecture. Spared in World War II, the façade of this late-Gothic basilica from the 14th and 15th centuries is decorated with glazed friezes of mythological creatures, saints and, at the peak of the transept, a huge rose window. The proportions of the interior and the height of the vaulted main nave measuring 37 m (121 ft) are captivating. Some of the interior fixtures and fittings came from other churches in the city, which were either ruined or no longer exist, including the so-called Krämeraltar with a sculpture of the *Beautiful Madonna and Child* (c.1420). The room by the tower has the most complete cycle of frescos in the region (c.1450).

Bad Doberan ❺

Road map D1. 🏘 *11,900.* 🚉
🛈 *Alexandrinenplatz 2 (038203-621 54).*

WHEN Duke Henry Borwin was hunting deer, a passing swan reportedly shouted "*Dobr Dobr*" (a good location) as the deer fell. Borwin duly founded the most important Cistercian monastery of the Baltic region here. The **Münster** was built in 1295–1368, with a severe interior and a small bell, in accordance with the order's rules which stipulate that no tower should be built. The interior is fascinating, its walls surfaced in red, with white plasterwork and colourful ribbing. Most of the original fixtures and fittings have survived almost intact. Among the treasures are a vast, gilded panelled painting, produced in Lübeck in 1310, a 12-m (39-ft) Holy Sacrament made from oak, a small cupboard holding the chalice and relics

from an earlier Romanesque building, as well as a statue of the Virgin Mary. Beautiful tombs mark the resting places of the rulers of Mecklenburg, of the Danish Queen Margaret, and Albrecht, King of Sweden, who died in 1412. Visitors can walk around the outside of the church which has a pleasant lawn. Beyond you can find a small octagonal building, beautifully decorated with glazed brickwork – this lovely piece of 13th-century architecture is the morgue.

A stroll around the health spa is also recommended. Right in its centre it has two early 19th-century pavilions with Chinese features – an ideal place for a coffee break.

ENVIRONS: Another adventure the visitor could try is a trip on the "Molli", a narrow-gauge railway that links Bad Doberan with Heiligendamm and Kühlungsborn, where there is a 4-km (2-mile) long beach. On the way, a little gem of 13th-century country architecture, the church in **Stefenshagen,** calls for a visit. On its south portal, see the terracotta figures of the Apostles. Across the presbytery runs a brickwork relief with mythological creatures.

🏠 Doberaner Münster

Klosterstrasse. 📞 *(038203) 627 16.*
🕐 *May–Sep: 9am–6pm Mon–Sat, noon–6pm Sun; Mar, Apr, Oct: 10am–5pm Mon–Sat, noon–5pm Sun; Nov–Feb: 10am–4pm Tue–Sat; noon–4pm Sun.* 📷 *daily.*

The monumental Cistercian Münster in Bad Doberan

The imposing Schloss, dominating the skyline of Güstrow

Güstrow **❻**

Road map D2. ⚄ *32,500.* ⊟
ℹ *Domstr. 9 (03843-68 10 23).*

Güstrow is one of the most
harmonious towns of the
former German Democratic
Republic, with an attractive
old town, unmarred by pre-
fabricated tower blocks. All
the most important monu-
ments are within easy reach.
The town is dominated by the
Schloss, built from 1558 by
Franz Parr, a member of a
renowned family of sculptors
and architects from northern
Italy. German, Italian and
Dutch elements come
together here, including fanta-
stical chimneys and two-
storey arcades in the courtyards. The architect's brother
decorated the Festsaal
(ballroom) with a hunting
frieze – the stucco heads of
the deer have real antlers.

In the nearby **Dom**, a brick
cathedral of the 13th and 14th
centuries, there is a
fascinating Gothic altar
(c.1500). Look for the vast
figures of the Apostles on the
pillars of the nave and the
16th century tomb of Duke
Ulrich and his two wives,
with a large genealogical
family tree of all three of
them. In the north nave hangs
the burly *Schwebende*
(Hovering Angel), a
remarkable work by Ernst
Barlach, who lived here from
1910 until his death in 1938.
He described his works to
Bertolt Brecht as: "beautiful
without beautifying, sizeable

without enlarging, harmonious without smoothness, and
full of vitality without brutal-
ity". Barlach's work bore the
brunt of National Socialist
condemnation – the original
Schwebende was melted
down and made into cannons
but the copy that replaced it
was made from the original
plaster cast. Other works by
Barlach can be seen in the
museum dedicated to him.

It is worth concluding a
visit to this town in the
market, near which rises the
Pfarrkirche St Marien. This
church has a magnificent high
altar, a panelled work of art
with painted wings by
Belgian artists (c.1522).

Environs: The open-air
museum in **Groß-Raden**,
near Sternberg, is popular
with tourists as well as
archaeology students. A
village has been re-created
with houses, workshops and
a system of fortifications.

**🏛 Archäologisches
Freilichtmuseum**
Groß-Raden. **☎** *(03847) 22 52.*
⬜ *Apr–Oct: 10am–5:30pm
daily; Nov–Mar: 10am–5pm
Tue–Sun.*

Neubrandenburg **❼**

Road map E2. ⚄ *75 000.* ⊟
ℹ *Marktplatz 1 (0395-194 33).*

Founded in 1248 as a sister
town to Brandenburg on
the Havel, the town was laid
out in the form of a regular
oval. It prospered as a trading
centre until the Thirty Years'
War, after which it fell into
disrepair. As a result it now
has what is probably the only
example of post-World War II
concrete tower blocks
surrounded by medieval town
walls, which have survived
virtually intact. The walls
extend for 2.3 km (2515 yds),
originally with a keep open to
the interior, and subsequently
interspersed with half-
timbered houses, known as
Wickhäuser (there were
once 58, of which 24 survive).
Of the four city gates the
most interesting are **Fried-
länder Tor** (begun in 1300),
with inner and outer gateways and a tower, as well as
Neues and Stargarder Tor,
decorated on the town side
with mysterious terracotta
figures of women with raised
hands (c.1350).

In the town centre stands
the Medieval **Marienkirche**,
which was damaged during
World War II and is now
restored as a concert hall.

Environs: The castle in **Star-
gard**, some 10 km (6 miles) to
the south, is the oldest secular
building in Mecklenburg. Its
4 m (13 ft) walls were begun
in 1200; the residence in 1236.
Today it houses a youth hostel.

A typical half-timbered Wiekhaus in the town wall in Neubrandenburg

Nationalpark Müritz ⑧

THERE ARE ABOUT a thousand lakes between Schwerin and Neubrandenburg; the largest of these is Müritzsee, to the east of which a national park was established in 1990. A particularly attractive part of the lake district is the so-called Mecklenburgische Schweiz (Swiss Mecklenburg), with its hilly moraines, such as Ostberg, 115 m (377 ft) above sea level. Tourists are attracted by the breathtaking scenery, perfect conditions for water sports and fascinating castles and palaces.

VISITORS' CHECKLIST

Road map E2. 🛈 *Waren, Neuer Markt 19. (03991-66 61 83); Neustrelitz, Markt 1 (03981-25 31 19).*

Basedow ①
For 600 years Basedow was in the hands of the von Hahn family, who built this irregular three-winged palace.

Schlitz ②
This palace is the most important Neo-Classical monument in Mecklenburg (1800–1823). In its beautiful landscaped park stands the Nymphenbrunnen, the famous fountain of nymphs. Cast in 1903 in Secessionist style for the Berlin department store Wertheim, it was transferred to this site in 1930.

Müritzsee ④
Müritzsee (meaning "small sea") is, at 115 sq km (44 sq miles), the second largest lake in Germany after Lake Constance.

KEY

▬	Tour route
▬	Scenic route
=	Minor road
≈	River, lake
☀	Viewpoint

Neustrelitz ⑤
The palace (1712) was the seat of distant relations of the Mecklenburg-Strelitz dukes who established the town and its church, and after 1733 resided here.

0 km   15

0 miles   15

Waren ③
Waren, an ideal base for tourists, is close to Binnen-müritz with its beaches and shops with watersports equipment for sale or hire.

Rostock **⑨**

THE HISTORY OF THE most important German port in the Baltic has been turbulent. This prosperous Hanseatic town had established trade links with distant ports such as Bergen (Norway), Riga (Latvia) and Bruges (Belgium) as early as the 15th century. In 1419 the first university in northern Europe was founded here, and it flourished again in the 19th century. After it suffered heavy damage in the Allied air raids of 1942, Rostock was rebuilt on a grand scale as the GDR's showpiece, since Szczecin had been lost to Poland.

VISITORS' CHECKLIST

Road map D1. 🚗 *200,000.*
🚉 🛈 *Neuer Markt 3. (0381-194 33).*
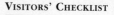 www.rostock.de
🎭 *Warnemünder Woche (Jul), Weihnachtsmarkt (Nov–Dec).*

Kröpelinerstraße – a promenade with 17th century houses

Exploring Rostock

A visit to the town is best started from the Neuer Markt (new market), from where the most important monuments can easily be reached on foot.

🏛 Rathaus

The town hall, on Neuer Markt, has a Baroque façade (added in 1727–9), from which seven Gothic towers of the original building emerge. At the rear of the building, in Große Wasserstraße, it is worth seeking out Kerhofhaus, the best preserved Gothic house in Rostock with a splendidly ornate façade featuring glazed brickwork, dating from 1470.

🏛 Steintor

A few minutes south of Neuer Markt is the Steintor, the best known of the gates in the old city wall. One of only three surviving gates of the original fortifications (at one time with 22 gates), it received its characteristic crowning feature during the Renaissance.

🏛 Marienkirche

Am Ziegenmarkt. ○ *10am–5pm Mon–Sat, 11:15am–noon Sun.* 📷
This church, meant to exceed the height of its Lübeck counterpart, was completed in the mid-15th century, after almost 250 years of construction. The nave, built after the original roof had collapsed, has an untypical, short body, while the massive western tower is as wide as three naves. Interconnected swathes of glazing decorate the exterior of the church, while much of the whitewashed interior features star vaulting. The main attraction is the astronomical clock, constructed in 1472 by maestro Düringer of

Baptismal font in the Marienkirche

Nuremberg. Its mechanism will show the correct time and date until 2047. Every afternoon its clockwork apostles parade before the tourists.

🏛 Kröpelinerstraße

The most popular street in the city is lined by houses from the 17th to the 19th centuries. In summer students congregate around the "Brunnen der Lebensfreude" (fountain of happiness) on the Universitätsplatz (university square). The main university building was built in the years 1867-70 in Neo-Renaissance style. The southern part of the square is occupied by a palace with a beautiful Baroque hall where concerts are performed. A Neo-Classical annexe with a Doric colonnade (1823) stands nearby. A statue on the square commemorates the town's most famous resident, Field Marshal Blücher, who helped defeat Napoleon at Waterloo.

ENVIRONS: Between Rostock and Stralsund lies a delightful coastal area. The peninsula, with the three former islands of **Fischland**, **Darß** and **Zingst**, attracts visitors to its quiet, beautiful beaches and splendid natural scenery. Particularly attractive are the villages of **Ahrenshoop**, which was originally an artists' colony, **Prerow**, which has traditional fishermen's houses and churches, and **Wieck**, with its charming thatched houses. A national park has been established here, and includes Darß and its magnificent forest, Zingst, the west coast of Rügen and the island of Hidensee.

The richly decorated pulpit in the Marienkirche

Stralsund

VISITORS' CHECKLIST

Road map E1. 🚗 62,000. 🚉
ℹ️ *Alter Markt 9 (03831-246
90).* 🌐 *www.stralsund.de*
🎭 *Sundschwimmen (Jun);
Wallenstein-Tage (Jul);
Stralsunder Segelwoche (Jul).*

AFTER LÜBECK, STRALSUND IS the most interesting Hanseatic town in northern Germany. During its history, it has had to defend its independence against Lübeck, Denmark, Holland and Sweden. In the Thirty Years' War, General Wallenstein vowed that he would take the town even if it were chained to heaven – but he failed. Subsequently, Lower Pomerania stayed under Swedish rule for 200 years until 1815, when it became Prussian. Despite its turbulent history, 811 protected buildings survived in the old town, among them some truly remarkable examples of architecture.

The Rathaus with its small turrets

Exploring Stralsund
The town centre of Stralsund is surrounded by water on all sides – in the north by the Strelasund bay, and on the other sides by lakes formed in the moats of the former bastions, Knieperteich and Frankenteich. All the most interesting historic monuments are easily accessible on foot from here.

🏛 Alter Markt
The old market square affords the best view of the filigree façade of the town hall,

Portal of the Nikolaikirche

beyond which stands the vast edifice of St Michael's church. It is surrounded by houses from various eras, of which the two most important are the Gothic Wulflamhaus, and the Commandantenhaus, Baroque headquarters of the town's former Swedish commandant. The Rathaus dates from the 13th century with a 14th-century façade and ground-floor arcades, and resembles the one in Lübeck. In 1370 the Hanseatic League

and the defeated Danish king signed a peace treaty here.

The Nikolaikirche, built from 1270–1360, was inspired by French Gothic cathedrals as well as the Marienkirche in Lübeck. It has rare free-standing flying buttresses in brick, which are much more unusual than in stone. Inside there are several intriguing furnishings, for example, the statue of St Anna (c. 1290), an astronomical clock (1394), as well as fragments of the Novgorod stall with various fascinating scenes including one of hunting for sables. The Baroque main altar was designed in 1798 by renowned Berlin architect and sculptor Andreas Schlüter.

🏛 Kulturhisto-risches Museum
Mönchstr. 25/27
📞 *(03831) 287 90.*
🕐 *10am–5pm Tue–Sun.*
🎫

The Katharinenklos-ter, a former 15th-century Dominican abbey, now houses two museums. Its abbey rooms provide an appropriate setting for historic exhibitions – the refectory has vaults supported by stylish columns – including copies of the famous Viking treasure from Hiddensee and a collection of 18th- and 19th-century toys and dolls' houses. A branch of the Museum, in Böttcherstraße, has a collection devoted to village life, folklore and costumes of the Baltic region.

🏛 Deutsches Museum für Meereskunde und Fischerei
⭕ *10am–5pm daily; Jul, Aug:
9am–6pm; 25, 26 Dec: 10am–5pm;
1 Jan: noon–5pm.* ⚫ *24, 31 Dec.* 🎫

Highlights of this museum of the sea and fishing, based in a former convent, include colourful aquariums and a 16-m (52-ft) long skeleton of a whale. It is also a scientific establishment researching the life of sea organisms.

🏛 Marienkirche
Tower ⭕ *May–Oct: 9am–5pm
Mon–Sat, 11:30am–5pm Sun;
Nov–Mar: 10am–noon, 2–4pm Mon–Fri, 10am–noon Sat, 2:30–4pm Sun;
Apr: 10am–4pm Mon–Sat, 2:30–4pm
Sun.* **Organ concerts:** *summer: 11am
Mon–Wed, Fri–Sun.* 🎫

Dominating the Neuer Mark is the town's largest church, St Mary's, built in 1383–1473, with an octagonal tower (with good views of Stralsund). Star vaulting lightens the impact of the monumental 99-m (325-ft) high interior. Main attractions are Gothic frescos, carved wooden figures of saints and a late-Gothic baptismal font. The huge Baroque organ is used for concerts in summer.

Marienkirche with its dominant, octagonal tower

Rügen ⑪

THE LARGEST of Germany's islands at 926 sq km (357 sq miles), Rügen is also the most beautiful and diverse, boasting steep cliffs next to sandy beaches and a hilly hinterland with forests and peat bogs. The island is only 50 km (31 miles) across, yet its rugged coastline extends for hundreds of miles. The Huns once ruled here, and their tombs can still be seen. It was fortified by the Slavs, then ruled by Danes and Swedes. In 1815 Rügen came under Prussian rule, and in 1936 it was linked to the mainland by the 1 km- (0.6 mile-) long Rügendamm.

Kap Arkona
An attractive walk around the rugged cape, 46 m (150 ft) high, passes the ruins of the Jaromar ancestral home and a temple to the Slav god Svantevit.

Hiddensee
This small island is accessible from Stralsund or Schaprode on Rügen. Horse-drawn carts and bikes replace cars in this oasis of tranquillity.

KEY

▬	Motorway
═	Main road
☀	Viewpoint

★ Waase
At this typical fishing village on the island of Ummanz, an unusual work of art has survived: an altarpiece from Antwerp, from around 1520.

STAR SIGHTS

★ **Nationalpark Jasmund**

★ **Putbus**

★ **Waase**

Map labels: Nobbi · Altenkirchen · Dranske · Wiek · Breege · WITTOW · Grieben · BUG · Hiddensee · Lebbi Bodd · Schaprode · Trent · HIDDENSEE · UMMANZ · Gingst · Kubitzer Bodden · Samtens · Stralsund · Poseritz · G. · Brandshagen · Reinberg

Jasmund Peninsula

The northeast of the peninsula is occupied by the Stubnitz forest of oak and beech trees, which continues down to the sea, interrupted by dazzling white chalk cliffs. The symbol of Rügen, they inspired artists like Caspar David Friedrich.

★ Nationalpark Jasmund

An attractive walk starts at the viewpoint of Königsstuhl (king's seat; 119 m/390 ft), continues along the Hochuferweg (cliff-top walk), past Victoriasicht and Wissower Klinken viewpoints, to end at Sassnitz.

Ostseebad Binz

Rügen's largest and most popular seaside resort, Binz has a beautiful white beach, grand early 20th-century villas and a pier.

★ Putbus

This elegant late Neo-Classical town was planned after 1807 on the model of Bad Doberan. Its centrepiece is the theatre, which was built in 1819 to a design by Wilhelm Steinbach.

0 km 5

0 miles 5

Greifswald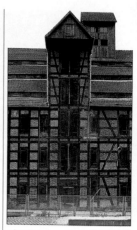

Road map E1. 🏙 *54,000.* 🚉 🚌 ℹ️
Rathaus Am Markt (03834-52 13 80).
🎵 *Musical concerts "Greifswalder Bachwochen" (Jun); Jazz Evenings in Eldena (Jul); Fischerfest (Jul).*

This former Hanseatic town is situated 5 km (3 miles) from the Bay of Greifswald. From afar the picturesque silhouette of the town with its three church towers, nicknamed Fat Mary, Little Jakob and Long Michael, appears like a painting by Caspar David Friedrich – the town's most famous resident – come to life. Charm pervades the old town, its architectural mix resulting from 40 years of East German rule. Greifswald, an important academic centre and market town, has geared up for more for tourism since 1989. It is certainly worth a visit – a short walk from east to west will enable the visitor to see all the most important monuments in town.

The 14th-century **Marienkirche** has a vast square tower, giving it a rather squat appearance and its nickname, Fat Mary. Inside, the church contains the remains of frescos and an amazing Renaissance pulpit depicting the Reformation figures of Luther, Bugenhagen and Melanchthon. The city museum has a collection of paintings by Caspar David Friedrich, including his famous landscapes of the ruined monastery of Eldena, *Ruined Eldena in the Riesengebirge*, which he transposed to the mountains of present-day Poland and Czech Republic.

The market square with its Baroque town hall is surrounded by patrician houses, with exemplary rich brickwork façades (particularly numbers 11 and 13). Nearby rises the vast **Dom St Nikolai.** The cathedral's octagonal tower, topped with a Baroque helm, affords extensive views of the town. The Rubenow-Bild (1460), one of the paintings inside, depicts the founding professor of Greifswald's university in front of Mary, Mother of God.

ENVIRONS: Wieck, an attractive working fishing village, is now incorporated into Greifswald. It has a drawbridge dating from 1887, reminiscent of typical Dutch bridges. The Cistercian monastery of **Eldena**, just 1 km (0.6 mile) south of Wieck district, was made famous by the Romantic paintings of Caspar David Friedrich. The monastery was founded in 1199 and plundered by the Swedes in 1637. Its ruined red walls amid the green grass and trees look wildly romantic.

Alter Speicher – the half-timbered granary in Wolgast

Wolgast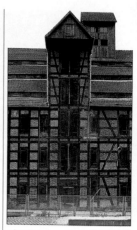

Road map E1. 🏙 *15,000.* 🚉
ℹ️ *Rathausplatz 10 (03836-60 01 18).*

From 1295 the seat of the Pomeranian-Wolgast dukes, Wolgast castle was destroyed in 1713, when Peter the Great ordered the town to be burned down. An interesting building still remaining is the 12-sided cemetery chapel with star vaulting, which is supported by a single column. The most valuable work of art can now be seen in **Pfarrkirche St Petri**, a 14th-century parish church.

Renovated houses around the Fischmarkt in Greifswald

Dating from the turn of the 17th to the 18th century, the *Totentanz* frieze is an imitation of the famous *Dance of Death* by Hans Holbein in Basle. Another notable artifact is the epitaph of Duke Philip I, crafted in 1560 by the Saxon artist Wolf Hilinger.

Other attractions in the town are the **Alter Speicher**, an 80 m- (262 ft-) long half-timbered granary (Burgstraße, 1836), and the family home of Philipp Otto Runge, famous romantic painter and adopted son of Hamburg.

Fishing boat on the beach at Usedom

🖼 Philipp-Otto-Runge-Gedenkstätte
Kronwieckstraße 45. **📞** *(03836) 20 20 00.* **◻** *Jun–Aug: 10am–6pm Tue–Fri, 10am–2pm Sat, Sun; Sep–May: 10am–5pm Tue–Fri, 10am–2pm Sat.*

One of the models in the Otto Lilienthal-Museum in Anklam

Anklam ⓮

Road map E2. **👥** *16,400.* **🚉**
ℹ *Markt 3, Rathaus (03971-21 05 41).*

A FORMER HANSEATIC town, Anklam's erstwhile importance is revealed by its vast defensive walls, in which is set the city gate, **Steintor**, dating from the mid-15th century. It is worth visiting the Gothic **Marienkirche**. Inside, the church's octagonal pillars and the arches of its arcades are painted with graceful figures, which reveal a Lübeck influence.

A museum recalls the life and inventions of Otto Lilienthal who was born here in 1848. After observing storks, he constructed a flying machine and completed his first flight in 1891. In total he created some 2000 machines,

none of which flew further than 350 m (1148 ft). His last flight ended in his death.

🏛 Otto-Lilienthal-Museum
Ellbogenstraße 1. **📞** *(03971) 24 55 00.* **◻** *May–Sep: 10am–5pm Tue–Fri, 2–5pm Sat, Sun; Oct–Apr: 10am–4pm Tue–Fri, 2–5pm Sun.*

Usedom ⓰

Road map E1. **🚉 ℹ** *Heringsdorf, Kurverwaltung, Kulmstr. 33 (038378-24 51); Ahlbeck, Kurverwaltung, Dünenstr. 45 (038378-244 97).*

T HE ISLAND, named after the village of Usedom and separated from the mainland by the Peenestrom, is the second largest in Germany at 445 sq km (172 sq miles). A small corner in the east was incorporated into Poland after 1945. Usedom is almost as attractive as Rügen, possessing white beaches, forests, peat bogs and bays overgrown with rushes in the south. It is linked with the mainland by two drawbridges (near Anklam and Wolgast). The resorts follow one another like pearls on a string: Bansin, Heringsdorf and Bad Ahlbeck, known as the "three sisters", are connected by a wide beach. At the beginning of the 20th century they evolved into elegant holiday resorts, with white villas, hotels and boarding houses, as typical of seaside resorts. Worth a visit is the industrialist

Oechler's house in Heringsdorf (Delbrückstr. 5), which has an antique appearance with mosaics on its façade. During the past few years, the early 20th-century piers in all three spas have been rebuilt and restored. The longest, in Heringsdorf, is also the second largest in Europe, after one in Poland. The Marienkirche, one of the island's main attractions, was erected in the 19th century.

Peenemünde ⓯

Road map E1. **👥** *650.*

H ISTORICALLY THE most interesting spot on the island of Usedom is the **museum** at Peenemünde, based on military territory. It demonstrates the evolution of space travel, pioneered at this research station since 1936.

During World War II, long-distance rockets, powered by liquid fuel and known as V-2 *(Vergeltungswaffe; retaliatory weapon)*, were produced here, which inflicted heavy damage on London and Antwerp in 1944. After the war, the chief engineer, Wernher von Braun, worked for NASA and helped develop the Apollo rockets.

🏛 Historisch-technisches Informationszentrum
Am Kraftwerk. **📞** *(038371) 205 73.* **◻** *Apr–Oct: 9am–6pm Tue–Sun (Jun–Sep: also Mon); Nov–Mar: 10am–4pm Tue–Sun.*

V-2 rocket in Peenemünde

TRAVELLERS' NEEDS

WHERE TO STAY

I T IS RELATIVELY EASY to find a room in a hotel or pension in Germany, even in small towns or large villages. The range of prices for a night's accommodation is wide, depending on the standard of services offered and the location of the establishment. In smaller towns located in attractive tourist areas, you can also find rooms to rent at a reasonable rate in private homes. In large towns and cities it is harder to find inexpensive accommodation.

If cost is a consideration, it may be necessary to take a room in a hotel that is some distance from the city centre. Within the list of hotels provided on pages 474–497 there is a choice of around 250 hotels and pensions, which represent various price categories and a high standard of services. Tourist offices supply lists of accommodation and may be able to find a room for you. Information about other accommodation options can be found on pages 472–3.

The atmospheric lobby of the Kempinski Hotel, Berlin *(see p475)*

THE RANGE OF HOTELS

G ERMAN HOTELS ARE awarded stars following the same system that is used in other countries, with the number of stars awarded depending on the facilities offered by the hotel rather than the standard of service. This means that it may be possible to enjoy a more pleasant stay in a small hotel that has only a single star than in a three-star hotel that offers lifts, a swimming pool, restaurant and business centre, but where refurbishment is long overdue.

If the general name of the hotel includes the appellation *"Garni"*, this indicates that there is not a restaurant on the premises, but only a dining room where breakfast is served. *"Hotel Apart"* means that the establishment is comprised of suites that include equipped kitchens or a kitchen annexe. The price of suites is such that it is not worth booking them for just one night, although a booking

of several days for a family or group of friends can turn out to be very economical.

Standards vary enormously between hotels. In large cities there will be no difficulty in finding a deluxe (and, of course, expensive) hotel, which typically will be part of an international chain. The choice of less expensive accommodation usually, though not necessarily always, entails accepting a lower standard of service or a less convenient location.

Away from cities, high prices generally apply to rooms in comfortable hotels in particularly peaceful and beautiful locations, or to those provided within historic palaces or villas. Smaller hotels in such areas usually offer good accommodation at very affordable prices, where visitors can enjoy their stay in small, but cosy and comfortable rooms.

HOW TO BOOK

A S IN OTHER countries, hotel accommodation can be booked directly by telephone, letter or fax, as well as by e-mail or through the Internet. Reservations can be made directly with the hotel or through a local tourist office. They may request written confirmation of the booking, and will almost certainly ask for a credit card number. Tell the owners what time you will be turning up, and let them know if you are delayed, in order not to lose the room.

For those who have not pre-booked, the local tourist office can usually find a hotel room or provide information about rooms in private homes. They are also a good source of advice about the availability of other accommodation options in the area.

Entrance of Opera Hotel, Munich

◁ The Hotel Alte Post in Oberammergau

The deluxe Hotel Vier Jahreszeiten in Hamburg *(see p494)*

INTERNATIONAL AND GERMAN CHAIN HOTELS

THROUGHOUT GERMANY there are hotels belonging to virtually all the well-known international chains, as well as to German national chains. Many places in Germany have an IBIS, which can be relied on to provide inexpensive, usually two-star accommodation. In season, they offer a double room for little more than €51.

Somewhat more expensive, and of a higher standard, are hotels belonging to the Best Western chain. Their excellent standard of service, combined with an affordable price, ensures their popularity with tourists. Hotels belonging to the Sorat group are also recommended. Their standard is similar to that of Best Western establishments and can be two-, three- or even four-star, but their premises always have interesting interiors, designed by renowned architects. Many hotels belonging to chains are, in fact, four- or deluxe five-star. Among the finest are the Kempinski and Vier Jahreszeiten hotels. In addition to these, there is no shortage of hotels belonging to chains such as Hilton, Holiday Inn, Inter-Continental, Mercure, Ramada and Hyatt Regency.

HOTELS IN HISTORIC BUILDINGS

GERMANY, LIKE many other countries, has numerous palaces, castles and other historic buildings that have been converted into hotels. Often the name *Schlosshotel* is used to indicate that an establishment is a hotel

within a palace. Many of these hotels are members of international organizations, such as **European Castle Hotels and Restaurants** or **Romantik Hotels und Restaurants**, who can provide further information.

Sign for the four-star Parkhotel in Dortmund

HOTEL PRICES

IN GERMANY, a complicated hotel categorization system operates, with a diverse range of prices depending on the season, as well as on various events that are taking place. In summer resort areas, it is obviously most expensive during the summer, while in large cities visited frequently by businessmen the most expensive seasons are spring and autumn. In cities where commercial fairs are held, prices may double during the

most popular fairs – for example, in Berlin during the tourist fair ITB, in Hanover during the information-computer fair CEBIT and in Frankfurt during the car and publishing fairs. It is the same, of course, in Munich during the October beer festival.

Many hotels offer significant reductions at weekends, and often there is the opportunity of a discount for those who turn up without a reservation. Prices can also sometimes be negotiated for longer bookings, especially during periods when business is slack.

ADDITIONAL COSTS

TAX IS INCLUDED in the basic price of a hotel room, but tips should be given for additional services such as having your baggage taken to your room or having theatre tickets reserved for you. Additional costs can come as a surprise when you settle your bill. In the most expensive hotels, for example, breakfast is not included in the cost of the room. Most hotels have their own parking facilities, but the cost may be unacceptably high. Check in advance the cost of making direct-dialled telephone calls from the hotel room, as well as the commission charged by the hotel for cashing traveller's cheques and the rate offered when exchanging currency. Using the mini-bar and pay-to-view TV channels in your room can also prove to be expensive.

Swimming pool in the Grand Hotel Esplanade in Berlin

The picturesque Alte Wirt Hotel in Bernau

PENSIONS AND GASTHÖFE

A GASTHOF IS A traditional inn with a restaurant on the ground floor and rooms to rent on the upper floor. A wide range of establishments is covered by this simple description, however, from small, inexpensive, family-run hotels, with modestly equipped rooms, to the most luxurious and elegant accommodation in an exquisitely restored country inn.

Pensions are less formal establishments than hotels and are typically run by a family. They usually provide modest accommodation, breakfast and a pleasant family atmosphere. They are always comfortable and very clean, at affordable prices.

INEXPENSIVE ACCOMMODATION

G ERMANY has a very widely developed chain of youth hostels *(Jugendherberge)* and these provide the cheapest option for an overnight stay. A youth hostel can be found in every large town, as well as in small holiday centres. The most attractive are those that are located in old castles, beautiful villas or other historic buildings. Most hostels are of a high standard. Accommodation may be provided in double and triple rooms, as well as in dormitories. In order to be eligible to use youth hostels, you must carry a valid membership card of the Youth Hostels Association. Membership is available from the YHA of your own country. The fee for overnight accommodation with breakfast is around DM 20–25 (€10–13). Unless you are carrying a sheet sleeping bag with you, you must hire one at the hostel, for which an additional charge will be made. The hostels are usually closed during the day, so you must ensure that all arrangements connected with your stay are arranged before 9am or after 4–4:30pm. In large cities during the high season, when demand for beds is particularly heavy, your stay may be limited to 2–3 days. Apart from in Bavaria, overnight accommodation is open to everyone who is in possession of a valid membership card. In Bavaria, only members aged 26 and under may use the hostels. Older members may stay, however, when they are in charge of a group of youngsters.

The Alpenrose Pension in Neuschwanstein

Private accommodation offers another inexpensive option. In attractive tourist areas, it is common for owners of larger villas and private houses to rent rooms to tourists, often offering breakfast as well. Houses with rooms available to rent are indicated by the sign *Fremdenzimmer* or *Zimmer frei*. Details of such accommodation can be obtained and booked in tourist information offices.

During the summer months, students may also benefit from acommodation in student hotels that otherwise house university students during term times in German university towns. Again, information about such accommodation may be obtained from tourist offices.

Mountain hut at Feldberg, Black Forest

AGROTOURISM

A GROTOURISM is very popular in Germany, and has become an attractive and low-cost alternative holiday, particularly for families with children. The rooms that are available are of a perfectly acceptable standard and meals can often also be provided by the farmers.

For younger children, and especially those from towns and cities, it is a great thrill to observe the daily work on a farm and to have contact with farm animals. Often, farmers who take holidaymakers keep a number of different animals on the farm. They may also offer the possibility of horse-riding, or hiring bicycles, a boat or fishing tackle, so that a full programme of outdoor activities can be enjoyed. Agrotourist holidays can be booked through **Zentrale für den Landurlaub Landschriften** and by **Agratour GmbH**.

MOUNTAIN HOSTELS

MOUNTAINOUS REGIONS of Germany are generally well prepared to accommodate walkers. Shelters, hostels and mountain hotels can be found not only along Alpine trails, but also in the Thuringian Forest, the Black Forest and the Harz Mountains. Details about such accommodation can be obtained from local tourist information bureaus.

CAMPING

TRAVELLING WITH a camping trailer, camper van or just a tent continues to be very popular in Germany, with a highly developed network of more than 2,000 camping sites throughout the country. Of a generally high standard, sites are equipped with washrooms and kitchens. There is usually a shop and café and some have swimming pools.

DISABLED TRAVELLERS

VIRTUALLY ALL HOTELS of a higher standard are equipped to accommodate disabled guests. At least one entrance will have ramp access, and a few rooms will have bathrooms adapted to the needs of those who are confined to a wheelchair. Facilities for the disabled are worse in lower-category hotels, where specially adapted fixtures and fittings are rarer. In such hotels, you may have to negotiate steep stairs, as many rooms are located on the upper floors of buildings.

In order to receive additional help during a journey, a disabled person can contact the **Bundesarbeitsgemeinschaft Hilfe für Behinderte e.V.**, or the **Bundesverband Selbsthilfe Körperbehinderter e.V**.

A mountain shelter in Oybin, Saxony

TRAVELLING WITH CHILDREN

TRAVELLING WITH children through Germany should not present any problems. In most hotels, facilities such as cots and high chairs can be obtained and there is often no additional accommodation charge for a young child. In better hotels, a few hours of babysitting for the children can usually be booked. Few hotels, however, provide children's playrooms. The standard equipment in every hotel includes a high chair for toddlers, while menus always include the option of children's portions.

DIRECTORY

INFORMATION ON ACCOMMODATION & RESERVATIONS

Deutsche Zentrale für Tourismus (DZT)
Beethovenstr. 69,
60325 Frankfurt.
☎ (069) 974640.
ⓦ www.deutschlandtourismus.de

Hotel Reservation Service (HRS)
Drususgasse 7–11,
50667 Cologne.
☎ (0221) 207 76 00.
ⓦ www.hrs.com

YOUTH HOSTELS

Deutsches Jugendherbergswerk DJH Service GmbH
Bismarckstr. 8,
32756 Detmold.
☎ (05231) 740 10.
ⓦ www.jugendherberge.de

AGROTOURISM

Agrartour GmbH (DLG)
Eschborner Landstr. 122,
60489 Frankfurt am Main.
☎ (069) 24 78 80.
ⓦ www.agrartour.de

Zentrale für den Landurlaub Landschriften––Verlag GmbH
Heerstraße 73, 53111 Bonn.
☎ (0228) 96 30 20.
ⓦ www.bauernhofurlaub.com

MOUNTAIN SHELTERS

Dav Summit Club
Am Perlacher Forst 186,
81545 Munich.
☎ (089) 64 24 00.
ⓦ www.dav-summit-club.de

Verband Deutscher Gebirgs- und Wandervereine e.V.
Wilhelmshöher Allee 157–159,
34121 Kassel.
☎ (0561) 93 87 30.
ⓦ www.wanderverband.de

CAMPING & CARAVANNING

Deutscher Camping-Club e.V.
Mandlstr. 28,
80802 Munich.
☎ (089) 380 14 20.
ⓦ www.camping-club.de

DISABLED TRAVELLERS

Bundesarbeitsgemeinschaft Hilfe für Behinderte e.V.
Kirchfeldstr. 149,
40215 Düsseldorf.
☎ (0211) 31 00 60.
ⓦ www.bagh.de

Bundesverband 'Selbshilfe' Körperbehinderter e.V. (BSK)
Altkrautheimerstr. 20,
74238 Krautheim.
☎ (06 294) 428 10.
ⓦ www.bsk-ev.de

Touristik Union International (TUI)
Karl-Wiechert-Allee 23,
30625 Hanover.
☎ (0511) 56 70.
ⓦ www.tui.de

Choosing a Hotel

THE HOTELS IN THIS GUIDE have been chosen on the basis of good value, attractive location and range of amenities offered. Entries are listed by price category within each town or region, with colour-coded thumb tabs in the margins to indicate the areas covered on each page. A map of Berlin can be found on pages 104–109; a road map is featured inside the back cover.

	NUMBER OF ROOMS	RESTAURANT	GARDEN OR TERRACE	SWIMMING POOL	AIR CONDITIONING

BERLIN

BERLIN – EASTERN CENTRE: *DeragHotel Grosser Kurfürst* €€€
Neue Rosstr. 11–12, 10179. **Map** 5 E3. ☎ (030) 24 60 00. ☏ (030) 24 60 03 00.
Ⓦ www.deraghotels.de
A good medium-class hotel, furnished in a modern style and located near a U-Bahn station. It belongs to the DeragHotel chain of hotels that specialize in providing additional services. Here, for example, hire of a bicycle is included in the room price.
① 🛏 🗲 🍴 🛁 🔁 🍸 — **144** ●

BERLIN – EASTERN CENTRE: *Hackescher Markt* €€€
Grosse Präsidentenstr. 8, 10178. **Map** 5 D1. ☎ (030) 28 00 30.
☏ (030) 28 00 31 11. Ⓦ www.hackescher-markt.com
Charming small hotel opposite Hackeschen Höfen, with excellent restaurant, terrace and elegantly furnished rooms.
① 🛏 🗲 🛁 🔁 🅿 🍸 — **31** ▪

BERLIN – EASTERN CENTRE: *Hilton Berlin* €€€€
Mohrenstr. 30, 10117. **Map** 5 C3. ☎ (030) 202 30. ☏ (030) 20 23 42 69.
Ⓦ www.hilton.com
Excellent location with views from front rooms of Deutscher Dom and Französischer Dom. Rooms are comfortably furnished and spacious. Three excellent restaurants. ① 🛏 🗲 🖥 🍴 🛁 🔁 🅿 🍸 — **589** ● ▪ ● ▪

BERLIN – EASTERN CENTRE: *Maritim proArte Hotel Berlin* €€€€
Friedrichstr. 151, 10117. **Map** 1 C4, 5 C2. ☎ (030) 203 35.
☏ (030) 20 33 42 09. Ⓦ www.maritim.de
One of the city's most attractive hotels, furnished with modern furniture and contemporary works of art. Some luxury rooms have bathrooms finished with marble and granite. ① 🛏 🗲 🍴 🛁 🔁 🅿 🍽 🍸 — **402** ● ● ▪

BERLIN – EASTERN CENTRE: *Four Seasons Hotel* €€€€€
Charlottenstr. 49, 10117. **Map** 5 C2. ☎ (030) 203 38. ☏ (030) 20 33 61 19.
Ⓦ www.fourseasons.com
Located near the Gendarmenmarkt, this is regarded as one of Berlin's top-three hotels. The façade of the modern building is inlaid with travertine and marble, while the interiors are furnished in a lavish Neo-Baroque style. ① 🛏 🗲 🍴 🛁 🔁 🅿 🍸 — **204** ● ▪

BERLIN – EASTERN CENTRE: *Hotel Adlon* €€€€€
Unter den Linden 77, 10117. **Map** 1 B4, 4 B2. ☎ (030) 22 610.
☏ (030) 22 61 22 22. Ⓦ www.hotel-adlon.de
Deluxe hotel near the Brandenburg Gate. Its acclaimed designers used the most expensive materials, including marble, leather and cherry and myrtle wood. Special rooms cater for those with allergies.
① 🛏 🗲 🍴 🛁 🔁 🅿 🍸 — **337** ● ● ▪

BERLIN – WESTERN CENTRE: *Hotel Palace Berlin* €€€€
Budapester Str. 45, 10787. **Map** 2 C4. ☎ (030) 250 20. ☏ (030) 25 02 11 19.
Ⓦ www.palace.de
Luxury hotel located in the Europa-Center. Elegant interiors are concealed within a rather uninteresting exterior. Guests, including major politicians and film stars, value its intimate atmosphere, excellent service and renowned gourmet restaurant, First Floor *(see p504)*.
① 🛏 🗲 🍴 🛁 🔁 🅿 🍸 — **282** ● ▪

BERLIN – WESTERN CENTRE: *Savoy Hotel* €€€€
Fasanenstr. 9–10, 10623. **Map** 2 A4. ☎ (030) 31 10 30. ☏ (030) 31 10 33 33.
Ⓦ www.hotel-savoy.com
Perfectly located, with well-furnished rooms and a charming atmosphere. In addition to excellent restaurants and bars, its Casa del Habano is Berlin's first cigar lounge. ① 🛏 🗲 🍴 🛁 🔁 🅿 🍸 — **125** ● ▪

	Price categories / Key	NUMBER OF ROOMS	RESTAURANT	GARDEN OR TERRACE	SWIMMING POOL	AIR CONDITIONING

Price categories for a twin room with bathroom or shower, and including breakfast, service and tax:
€ up to €77
€€ €78–€128
€€€ €129–€179
€€€€ €180–€230
€€€€€ over €230

RESTAURANT
The hotel has a restaurant that is open to non-residents as well as to hotel guests.

GARDEN OR TERRACE
The hotel is set in a garden or has an outside terrace or courtyard, often with tables for eating outside.

SWIMMING POOL
The hotel has a swimming pool.

AIR CONDITIONING
All rooms are air-conditioned.

Hotel	No. of Rooms	Restaurant	Garden or Terrace	Swimming Pool	Air Conditioning
BERLIN – WESTERN CENTRE: *Grand Hyatt Berlin* €€€€€	342	●		●	■
BERLIN – WESTERN CENTRE: *Hotel Brandenburger Hof* €€€€€	82	●			
BERLIN – WESTERN CENTRE: *Kempinski Hotel Bristol Berlin* €€€€€	301	●		●	■
FURTHER AFIELD: *Artemisia* €€	12		■		
FURTHER AFIELD: *Best Western Hotel City-Consul, Berlin* €€	99	●			■
FURTHER AFIELD: *Märkischer Hof* €€	20				
FURTHER AFIELD: *Villa Kastania* €€€	45	●		●	■
FURTHER AFIELD: *Hecker's Hotel* €€€	69	●			■
FURTHER AFIELD: *Hotel Berlin* €€€€	701	●	■		■

BERLIN – WESTERN CENTRE: *Grand Hyatt Berlin* €€€€€
Marlene Dietrich Platz 2, 10785. **Map** 4 A3. ((030) 25 53 12 34. FAX (030) 25 53 12 35.
Reservations ((0180) 523 12 34. W www.hyatt.com
This is one of the most luxurious hotels in Berlin, with a superb restaurant (Vox), a sushi bar, bistro and the discreet Café Tizian. Nearby is a vast commercial centre, with music theatre, casino and giant multi-screen cinema in which the Berlin Film Festival is held.

BERLIN – WESTERN CENTRE: *Hotel Brandenburger Hof* €€€€€
Eislebener Str. 14, 10789. **Map** 2 B5. ((030) 21 40 50. FAX (030) 21 40 51 00.
W www.brandenburger-hof.com
An elegant atmosphere, perfect service, tranquil location and luxury rooms ensure this hotel's reputation as one of the best in Berlin. Dating from the Wilhelm era, the captivating building has been restored, furnished with furniture in the Bauhaus style and decorated with works of art.

BERLIN – WESTERN CENTRE: €€€€€
Kempinski Hotel Bristol Berlin
Kurfürstendamm 27, 10719. **Map** 2 B4. ((030) 88 43 40. FAX (030) 883 60 75.
W www.kempinskiberlin.de
One of the most famous hotels in Berlin, the Kempinski occupies a distinctive semi-circular building. It has a classic interior with luxurious rooms, an excellent restaurant and bistro-café.

FURTHER AFIELD: *Artemisia* €€
Brandenburgische Str. 18, 10707 Berlin-Wilmersdorf. ((030) 873 89 05.
FAX (030) 861 86 53.
The Artemisia is the only women-only hotel in Berlin. The rooms, on the fourth and fifth floors of an old building, are comfortable.

FURTHER AFIELD: *Best Western Hotel City-Consul, Berlin* €€
Rathausstr. 2–3, 10367. ((030) 55 75 70. FAX (030) 55 75 72 72.
W www.consul-hotels.com
This modern hotel is just a 10-minute walk from Alexanderplatz. It is furnished to a high standard, and equipped with video, fax and modem facilities for guests' use. An excellent breakfast buffet is served.

FURTHER AFIELD: *Märkischer Hof* €€
Linienstr. 133, 10115. **Map** 1 C2. ((030) 282 71 55. FAX (030) 282 43 31.
Housed within a historic 19th-century building, not far from Oranienburger Strasse, this small hotel has a family atmosphere. The standard is astonishingly high in relation to the prices.

FURTHER AFIELD: *Villa Kastania* €€€
Kastanienallee 20, 14052 Berlin-Charlottenburg. ((030) 300 00 20.
FAX (030) 30 00 02 10. W www.villakastania.com
Situated in a tranquil street, with good connections by U-Bahn to the city centre, this intimate hotel maintains high standards. Standard rooms are fitted with small kitchens.

FURTHER AFIELD: *Hecker's Hotel* €€€
Grolmannstr. 35, 10623. **Map** 2 A4. ((030) 889 00. FAX (030) 889 02 60.
W www.heckers-hotel.com
Located right by the Kurfürstendamm, this hotel has tastefully furnished interiors with unpretentious furniture, lighting by famous designers and contemporary works of art.

FURTHER AFIELD: *Hotel Berlin* €€€€
Lützowplatz 17, 10785. **Map** 2 D4. ((030) 26 050. FAX (030) 26 05 27 16.
W www.blueband.de
The large, light rooms are comfortably furnished. In summer it is pleasant to eat lunch in the patio restaurant.

For key to symbols *see back flap*

Price categories for a twin room with bathroom or shower, and including breakfast, service and tax:
€ up to €77
€€ €78–€128
€€€ €129–€179
€€€€ €180–€230
€€€€€ over €230

RESTAURANT
The hotel has a restaurant that is open to non-residents as well as to hotel guests.
GARDEN OR TERRACE
The hotel is set in a garden or has an outside terrace or courtyard, often with tables for eating outside.
SWIMMING POOL
The hotel has a swimming pool.
AIR CONDITIONING
All rooms are air-conditioned.

		NUMBER OF ROOMS	RESTAURANT	GARDEN OR TERRACE	SWIMMING POOL	AIR CONDITIONING
FURTHER AFIELD: *Regent Schlosshotel Berlin* €€€€€ Brahmsstr. 10, 14193 Berlin-Wilmersdorf. ((030) 89 58 40. FAX (030) 89 58 48 00. W www.regenthotels.com The most exclusive hotel in Berlin, with furnishings and interior decor by Karl Lagerfeld. The restaurant is renowned. 1 🛏 ⚡ 🍴 🕗 🔖 P 🐾		54	●		●	■
BRANDENBURG						
BRANDENBURG: *Hotel Lindenhof* € Chaussestr. 21, 14774. **Map** E3. ((03381) 40 430. FAX (03381) 40 43 33. The hotel is housed within an attractive Art Nouveau building, with comfortable modern rooms. The restaurant serves regional and classic food. Hotel bar and beer garden. 1 🛏 🔖 P 🐾		15	●	■		
CHORIN: *Haus Chorin* € Neue Klosterallee 10, 16230. **Map** E2. ((033366) 500. FAX (033366) 326. W www.haus-chorin.de Housed in a beautiful 100-year-old villa located by a lake, the hotel has a pleasant garden and comfortably furnished rooms. 1 🛏 🔖 P 🐾		63	●	■		
COTTBUS: *Radisson SAS Hotel Cottbus* €€ Vetschauer Str. 12, 03048. **Map** F3. ((0355) 476 10. FAX (0355) 476 19 00. W www.radissonsas.com Located in the centre of town in the Pücklerpassage complex. Comfortable rooms, restaurant and piano bar. 1 ⚡ 🛏 🔖 P 🍴 🐾		241	●	■	●	
JÜTERBOG: *Zum Goldenen Stern* € Markt 14, 14913. **Map** E3. ((03372) 40 14 76. FAX (03372) 40 16 14. W www.hotel-goldener-stern.de Comfortable, modern rooms within a traditional old house. Bicycles can be hired and function rooms are available. 1 🛏 P 🐾		25	●	■		
LEHNIN: *Markgraf* € Friedensstr. 13, 14797. **Map** E3. ((03382) 76 50. FAX (03382) 76 54 30. Recently restored hotel with pleasantly furnished rooms. The restaurant offers tasty regional and Austrian dishes. 1 🔖 ⚡ 🛏 🔖 P 🐾		40	●	■		
NEURUPPIN: *Altes Kasino am See* € Seeufer 11, 16816. **Map** E2. ((03391) 30 59. FAX (03391) 35 86 84. W www.hotel-altescasino.de Located at the edge of a lake, this hotel has pleasant and modern rooms, a good restaurant and a café on the terrace. 1 🔖 🛏 P 🐾		20	●	■		
POTSDAM: *art'otel Potsdam* €€ Zeppelinstr. 136, 14471. **Map** E3. ((0331) 981 50. FAX (0331) 981 55 55. W www.artotel.de This luxury hotel for art lovers displays an interesting architectural approach in linking the new section with the old part, which is housed in a 19th-century granary. The leading English designer Jasper Morrison was responsible for the innovative design. 🛏 🔖 P 🔖 ⚡ 🐾		123	●	■		
POTSDAM: *Mercure Potsdam* €€ Lange Brücke, 14467. **Map** E3. ((0331) 27 22. FAX (0331) 272 02 33. W www.mercure.com Modern hotel situated in the centre of the town, directly by the river Havel. Hotel bar and restaurant with terrace. 1 🛏 🔖 P ⚡ 🔖 🐾		210	●	■		
POTSDAM: *Relexa Schlosshotel Cecilienhof* €€€€ Neuer Garten, 14469. **Map** E3. ((0331) 370 50. FAX (0331) 29 24 98. W www.relaxa-hotel.de Formerly owned by the Hohenzollern family, this is the castle in which the Potsdam treaty was signed in 1945. Stylishly decorated rooms, elegant restaurant and salon with an open fire. 1 🔖 🛏 🔖 🐾		41	●	■		

WITTSTOCK: *Stadt Hamburg*   €   44
Röbelerstr. 25, 16909. **Map** E2. █ and ⨎ (03394) 44 45 66.
Recently renovated hotel located fairly close to the old town. Cosy rooms
and a good restaurant. 1 🚪 🔃 P ⌘

SAXONY-ANHALT

BERNBURG: *Parkhotel Bernburg*   €€   103
Aderstedter Str. 1, 06406. **Map** E3. █ (03471) 36 20. ⨎ (03471) 36 21 11.
W www.parkhotel-bernburg.de
This hotel was built in 1994 and has good service, comfortable rooms
and an excellent restaurant. 1 🚪 🔃 🎴 P ⌖ 🔒 ⌘

DESSAU: *NH Hotel*   €€   153
Zerbster Str. 29, 06844. **Map** E3. █ (0340) 251 40. ⨎ (0340) 251 41 00.
W www.astronhotel.com
This hotel in the Bauhaus style is near Dessau's historic town hall. Rooms
are comfortable and there is a good restaurant. 1 🚪 🔃 P ⌖ 🔒 ⌘

HALBERSTADT: *Parkhotel Unter den Linden*   €€   42
Klamrothstr. 2, 38820. **Map** D3. █ (03941) 600 077. ⨎ (03941) 6254 444.
W www.pudl.de
This hotel is housed in an attractive 100-year-old villa in the centre of
town. It features stylish, comfortable rooms and a high standard of
cuisine in the elegant restaurant. 1 🚪 🔃 P 🔒 ⌘

MAGDEBURG: *Herrenkrug Parkhotel*   €€€   147
Herrenkrugstr. 3, 39114 Magdeburg-Ausserhalb. **Map** D3. █ (0391) 850 80.
⨎ (0391) 850 85 01. W www.herrenkrug.de
Located in a vast park between the river Elbe and the racecourse, with
spacious and luxuriously furnished rooms, many in Art Nouveau style.
Several restaurants, pleasant café and hotel bar. 1 🚪 🎴 🔃 P 🎴 ⌖ 🔒 ⌘

MERSEBURG: *Radisson SAS*   €€   134
Oberaltenburg 4, 06217. **Map** D4. █ (03461) 452 00. ⨎ (03461) 45 21 00.
W www.radissonsas.com
The hotel is housed within a small, refurbished, Baroque palace. It has
superbly furnished rooms, several restaurants, café with a terrace and
hotel bar. 1 🚪 🔃 P ⌖ 🔒 ⌘

NAUMBURG: *Zur alten Schmiede*   €   41
Lindenring 36–37, 06618. **Map** D4. █ (03445) 243 60. ⨎ (03445) 24 36 66.
This hotel with tastefully furnished rooms is housed in a former forge.
1 🚪 🔃 P ⌘

QUEDLINBURG: *Romantik Hotel Am Brühl*   €€   47
Billungstr. 11, 06484. **Map** D4. █ (03946) 961 80. ⨎ (03946) 961 82 46.
W www.hotelambruehl.de
A small, romantic, family-run hotel with tastefully furnished rooms.
A good dinner is served in the intimate wine bar. 1 🚪 🔃 P ⌖ ⌘

STENDAL: *Altstadt-Hotel*   €€   27
Breite Str. 60, 39576. **Map** D3. █ (03931) 698 90. ⨎ (03931) 69 89 39.
W www.altstadt-hotel-stendal.de
Nice rooms in city-centre hotel with fax facility available. 1 🚪 ⌖ ⌘

TANGERMÜNDE: *Ringhotel Schwarzer Adler*   €   56
Lange Str. 52, 39590. **Map** D3. █ (039322) 23 91. ⨎ (039322) 36 42.
W www.schwarzer-adler-tangermuende.de
A hotel that has been family-run for generations. The rooms are furnished
in a modern style and the restaurant offers home cooking. Sauna,
solarium and swimming pool are available. 1 🎴 🚪 P 🔒 ⌘

WERNIGERODE: *Ringhotel Weisser Hirsch*   €€   54
Marktplatz 5, 38855. **Map** D3. █ (03943) 60 20 20. ⨎ (03943) 63 31 39.
W www.hotel-weisser-hirsch.de
Recently restored and modernized, this family-run, 18th-century hotel is
the oldest hotel in town. Regional and international cuisine are available
in the restaurant. 1 🚪 🔃 P ⌖ 🔒 ⌘

WITTENBERG: *Best Western Stadtpalais Wittenberg*   €€   78
Collegienstrasse 56–57, 06886. **Map** E3. █ (03491) 42 50. ⨎ (03491) 42 51 00.
W www.stadtpalais.bestwestern.de
Large and comfortable rooms, bar, rustic restaurant serving regional
cuisine combined with Best Western service. 🍽 ⚿ ⌖ P 🔒 ⌘

Price categories for a twin room with
bathroom or shower, and including breakfast,
service and tax:
€ up to €77
€€ €78–€128
€€€ €129–€179
€€€€ €180–€230
€€€€€ over €230

RESTAURANT
The hotel has a restaurant that is open to
non-residents as well as to hotel guests.
GARDEN OR TERRACE
The hotel is set in a garden or has an
outside terrace or courtyard, often with
tables for eating outside.
SWIMMING POOL
The hotel has a swimming pool.
AIR CONDITIONING
All rooms are air-conditioned.

		NUMBER OF ROOMS	RESTAURANT	GARDEN OR TERRACE	SWIMMING POOL	AIR CONDITIONING
WÖRLITZ: *Wörlitzer Hof*	€€	50	●			
Markt 96, 06786. **Map** E3. ☏ *(034905) 41 10.* **FAX** *(034905) 411 22.* 🆆 www.woerlitzer-hof.de Newly built hotel near the main entrance to the park. Sunny and pleasant rooms. The restaurant serves home cooking. 🔟 📶 🔃 **P** 🏊 🚲 🍴 🌳						
SAXONY						
BAUTZEN: *Goldener Adler*	€€	30	●			
Hauptmarkt 4, 02625. **Map** F4. ☏ *(03591) 48 660.* **FAX** *(03591) 48 66 20.* Recently opened hotel within a 16th-century building. Each room is individually decorated. The restaurant serves regional and international cuisine. Bar and winebar. 🔟 📶 🔃 **P** 🌳						
CHEMNITZ: *Ringhotel Schlosshotel Klaffenbach*	€€	49	●			
Wasserschlossweg 6, 09123 Chemnitz-Klaffenbach. **Map** E4. ☏ *(0371) 261 10.* **FAX** *(0371) 26 11 10.* 🆆 www.schlosshotel-klaffenbach.de The hotel is located next to a 17th-century moated castle, which is classified as a protected monument. The hotel restaurant has Gothic vaulting. 🔟 📶 🔃 **P** 🏊 🍴 🌳						
DRESDEN: *Am Blauen Wunder*	€€	38	●	■		
Loschwitzer Str. 48, 01309 Dresden-Blasewitz. **Map** E4. ☏ *(0351) 336 60.* **FAX** *(0351) 33 66 299.* 🆆 www.hotel-am-blauen-wunder.de Comfortably furnished hotel near the renowned "Blue Miracle" bridge. The restaurant serves Italian cuisine. 🔟 📶 🔃 **P** 🏊 🍴 🌳						
DRESDEN: *art'otel Dresden Design Hotel*	€€€	174	●		●	
Ostra-Allee 33, 01067. **Map** E4. ☏ *(0351) 492 20.* **FAX** *(0351) 492 27 77.* 🆆 www.artotel.de Newly built, interestingly designed hotel, which is located near the renowned Zwinger gallery. Its comfortable rooms feature paintings by well-known artists, while exhibitions are held in the art gallery. The restaurant serves Californian cuisine. Excellent recreational facilities include a sauna. 🔟 📺 📶 🔃 **P** 🏊 🍴 🌳						
DRESDEN: *Romantik Hotel Pattis*	€€€	47	●			■
Merbitzer Str. 53, 01157 Dresden-Briesnitz. **Map** E4. ☏ *(0351) 425 50.* **FAX** *(0351) 425 52 55.* 🆆 www.pattis.net The hotel is located within a former 16th-century mill, set in a beautiful park. The restaurant's renowned chef prepares dishes according to recipes from the royal Saxon court. A particularly attractive offer is a two- night stay in the hotel, including a magnificent dinner served on Meissen porcelain and a visit to the nearby Meissen porcelain factory. 🔟 📶 🔃 **P** 🍴 🌳						
DRESDEN: *Kempinski Hotel* *Taschenbergpalais Dresden*	€€€€€	215	●	■	●	■
Taschenberg 3, 01067. **Map** E4. ☏ *(0351) 491 20.* **FAX** *(0351) 491 28 12.* 🆆 www.kempinski-dresden.de Now one of the world's leading hotels, this recently restored building has been used to accommodate guests from the time of Augustus the Strong. The hotel's restaurants serve dishes from many countries. First-class facilities include a large ballroom and a business centre. 🔟 🍴 📺 📶 🔃 **P** 🏊 🌳						
FREIBERG: *Silberhof*	€€	32	●			
Silberhofstr. 1, 09599. **Map** E4. ☏ *(03731) 268 80.* **FAX** *(03731) 26 88 78.* 🆆 www.silberhof.de Comfortable hotel in the centre of Freiberg. Rooms are comfortably equipped with top-quality furniture and furnishings. Buffet breakfast. 🔟 📶 🍴 🔃 **P** 🌳						

GÖRLITZ: *Sorat Hotel Görlitz* €€ 46
Struvestr. 1, 02826. **Map** F4. ▐ *(03581) 40 65 77.* ▐ *(03581) 40 65 79.*
Ⓦ www.sorat-hotels.com
Based in a former merchant's house, this hotel has modern rooms and
the excellent Am Goldenen Strauss restaurant. ① ⊟ ⓝ ⚡ ⓑ ⓔ

KAMENZ: *Goldner Hirsch* € 22
Markt 10, 01917. **Map** F4. ▐ *(03578) 30 12 21.*
▐ *(03578) 30 44 97.* Ⓦ www.hotel-goldner-hirsch.de
This city-centre hotel is located in a historic house dating from 1550. It
has recently been restored and rooms are elegantly furnished. Facilities
include free car parking and restaurants. ① ⊟ ⓝ ⓟ ⓑ ⓔ

LEIPZIG: *Balance Hotel Leipzig Alt Messe* €€ 126
Breslauerstr. 33, 04299 Leipzig-Stötteritz. **Map** E4. ▐ *(0341) 867 90.*
▐ *(0341) 867 94 44.* Ⓦ www.holiday-inn-hotel.de
This modern hotel was built in 1995. The restaurant serves international
cuisine. ① ⊟ ⓝ ⚡ ⓑ ⓣ ⓔ

LEIPZIG: *Leipzig Marriott Hotel* €€ 231
Am Hallischen Tor 1, 04109. **Map** E4. ▐ *(0341) 965 30.* ▐ *(0341) 965 39 99.*
Ⓦ www.marriott.com
city-centre hotel, opposite the railway station. Rooms are furnished in a
modern style, with exclusive suites for VIPs. The hotel also offers a
business centre with extensive facilities. ① ⊟ ⓝ ⓟ ⓣ ⚡ ⓑ ⓔ

LEIPZIG: *Kempinski Hotel Fürstenhof* €€€€ 92
Tröndlinring 8, 04105. **Map** E4. ▐ *(0341) 14 00.* ▐ *(0341) 140 37 07.*
Ⓦ www.arabellasheraton.com
This long-standing hotel features elegant rooms, marble floors and
interesting ceilings. ① ⚡ ⓑ ⊟ ⓝ ⓟ ⓣ ⓔ

MEISSEN: *Ross* €€ 41
Grossenhainer Str. 9, 01662. **Map** E4. ▐ *(03521) 75 10.* ▐ *(03521) 75 19 99.*
Ⓦ www.meiland.de/partnerhotels/ross
This hotel occupies a 100-year-old building. Facilities include a sauna,
solarium, restaurant and café with a terrace. ① ⊟ ⓝ ⓟ ⚡ ⓑ ⓔ

MORITZBURG: *Landhaus* €€ 17
Schlossallee 37, 01468. **Map** E4. ▐ *(035207) 816 02/03.* ▐ *(035207) 816 04.*
Hotel with spacious rooms, located near the castle. The elegant restaurant
serves both light and classic cuisine. Other features include an intimate
wine bar and a garden. ① ⊟ ⓝ ⚡ ⓔ

PIRNA: *Romantik Hotel Deutsches Haus* €€ 40
Niedere Burgstr. 1, 01796. **Map** F4. ▐ *(03501) 52 81 03.*
▐ *(03501) 46 88 20.* Ⓦ www.romantikhotels.com/pirna
Located in a beautiful Renaissance building, this hotel has a long tradition
of hospitality. Its rooms are furnished in a variety of styles, so that every
guest can feel at home. Bicycles are available for hire. The hotel offers an
attractive "gourmet weekend", which comprises three nights' accommodation with breakfast and dinner, plus a ticket for a musical event.
① ⚡ ⊟ ⓑ ⓟ ⓔ

ZITTAU: *Schwarzer Bär* € 16
Ottokar-Platz 12, 02763. **Map** F4. ▐ *(03583) 55 10.*
▐ *(03583) 55 11 11.*
Hotel with a tradition dating back over 300 years. Rooms furnished in
contemporary style. Good, unpretentious cooking. ① ⊟ ⓝ ⓟ ⓔ

ZWICKAU: *Achat* €€ 204
Leipziger Str. 180, 08058. **Map** E4. ▐ *(0375) 87 20.* ▐ *(0375) 87 29 99.*
Ⓦ www.achat-hotel.de
This recently opened hotel has comfortable rooms and apartments with
small kitchens. Its restaurant serves regional cuisine. ⓔ ① ⓑ ⚡ ⊟ ⓝ ⓟ

THURINGIA

ALTENBURG: *Parkhotel am Grossen Teich* €€ 65
August-Bebel-Str. 16/17, 04600. **Map** E4. ▐ *(03447) 58 30.*
▐ *(03447) 58 34 44.* Ⓦ www.parkhotel-altenburg.bestwestern.de
The hotel occupies a recently restored Neo-Classical building on the edge
of town and features newly equipped conference halls. The restaurant
serves classic and regional cuisine. ① ⊟ ⓝ ⓟ ⚡ ⓑ ⓔ

For key to symbols *see back flap*

Price categories for a twin room with bathroom or shower, and including breakfast, service and tax:
€   up to €77
€€   €78–€128
€€€   €129–€179
€€€€   €180–€230
€€€€€   over €230

RESTAURANT
The hotel has a restaurant that is open to non-residents as well as to hotel guests.
GARDEN OR TERRACE
The hotel is set in a garden or has an outside terrace or courtyard, often with tables for eating outside.
SWIMMING POOL
The hotel has a swimming pool.
AIR CONDITIONING
All rooms are air-conditioned.

	NUMBER OF ROOMS	RESTAURANT	GARDEN OR TERRACE	SWIMMING POOL	AIR CONDITIONING
EISENACH: *Best Western Hotel Kaiserhof* €€ Wartburgallee 2, 99817. **Map** D4. ☎ *(03691) 21 35 13.* FAX *(03691) 20 36 53.* W www.kaiserhofeisenach.de Housed in a beautiful Renaissance building, this hotel offers a Thuringian weekend package, which includes two nights with breakfast and dinner, a welcome cocktail, a city sightseeing tour and a visit to the Lutherhaus – a museum devoted to the Reformation.	64	●			
ERFURT-APFELSTADT: *Country Inn* € Riedweg 1, 99192. **Map** D4. ☎ *(036202) 850.* FAX *(036202) 854 10.* W www.countryinns.de This hotel is located beyond the city limits and offers a wonderful view of several medieval castles. Rooms are tastefully furnished, and the hotel has an elegant restaurant, café and hotel bar.	97	●			
ERFURT: *Zumnorde* €€ Anger 50/51, 99084. **Map** D4. ☎ *(0361) 568 00.* FAX *(0361) 568 04 00.* W www.hotel-zumnorde.de The ZumNorde has beautifully furnished rooms, an intimate hotel bar and a spacious roof terrace.	52	●	■		
GERA: *Comfort Inn* € Hoferstr. 12d, 07548 Gera-Dürrenebersdorf. **Map** D4. ☎ *(0365) 821 50.* FAX *(0365) 82 152 00.* W www.comfort-inn-gera.de Recently built hotel on the edge of a forest. Pleasant rooms and apartments with kitchens. A full breakfast is served in the morning, while light snacks are available in the evening.	69				
GOTHA: *Toscana* € Pfortenwallgasse 1, 99867. **Map** D4. ☎ *(03621) 295 93.* FAX *(03621) 295 96.* W www.toscana.de.tt Located in the city centre, the Toscana has elegantly furnished rooms and a restaurant serving mainly Italian cuisine.	20	●			
GREIZ: *Schlossberg Hotel* € Marienstr. 1–5, 07973. **Map** E4. ☎ *(03661) 62 21 23.* FAX *(03661) 62 21 66.* W www.schlossberghotel-greiz.de Situated at the foot of the castle hill, in the centre of the old town, this hotel is quiet and tranquil yet close to everything. Every room is brightly decorated. The hotel offers a large business centre and conference halls. The restaurant serves regional cuisine and an excellent breakfast buffet is available.	33				
JENA: *Jembo Park* € Rudolstädter Str. 93, 07745 Jena-Göschwitz. **Map** D4. ☎ *(03641) 68 50.* FAX *(03641) 68 52 99.* W www.jembo.de Recently built motel complex located within the grounds of a large park. As well as hotel rooms, 22 bungalows are available. Within the complex is a bowling alley and a variety of other sports facilities.	48	●			
MÜHLHAUSEN: *Mirage* € Karl-Marx-Str. 9, 99974. **Map** D4. ☎ *(03601) 43 90.* FAX *(03601) 43 91 00.* W www.mirage-hotel.de Situated in the centre of the city, the Mirage has attractively decorated rooms and a number of elegant suites.	75				
WEIMAR: *Hotel Elephant* €€€€€ Markt 19, 99423. **Map** D4. ☎ *(03643) 80 20.* FAX *(03643) 80 26 10.* W www.arabellasheraton.com Guests, including many celebrities, have been received here since the 16th century. Very comfortable rooms and two restaurants, which include Thuringian dishes in their repertoire.	99	●	■		

MUNICH

Cosmopolitan Hotel €€ 71
Hohenzollernstr. 5, 80801. **Map** D7. **(** (089) 38 38 10. **FAX** (089) 38 38 11 11.
[W] www.cosmopolitan-hotel.de
Located in the centre of the Schwabing district, the hotel has comfortable,
modern rooms. The hotel bar is a popular meeting place in the evenings.
[1] 🛏 🔄 **P** 🛎 ⚡ 🅿

Romantik Hotel Inselmühle €€€ 37
Von-Kahr-Str. 87, 80999 München-Untermenzing. **Map** D7. **(** (089) 810 10.
FAX (089) 812 05 71. [W] www.weber-gastronomie.de
One of the most beautiful hotels in Munich. Most of its stylish rooms
have balconies. The restaurant is highly recommended. [1] 🛏 **P** 🛎 🅿

Bayerischer Hof €€€€€ 399
Promenadeplatz 2–6, 80333. **Map** D7. **(** (089) 212 00.
FAX (089) 212 09 06. [W] www.bayerischerhof.de
Situated in the centre of the city, this is an internationally renowned
hotel. It offers elegantly furnished rooms, a choice of restaurants, a
winter garden, tropical bar, bar with live music, night club, roof-top
swimming pool, designer boutiques and a business centre.
[1] ⚡ 🛎 🛏 🔄 **P** 🅿

Kempinski Hotel Vier Jahreszeiten München €€€€€ 316
Maximilianstr. 17, 80539. **Map** D7. **(** (089) 212 50.
FAX (089) 21 25 20 00. [W] www.kempinski-vierjahreszeiten.de
Situated on one of the most architecturally beautiful streets in the world,
this hotel is renowned for excellent service and its elegant restaurant.
[1] 🛏 🔄 **P** 🅿

BAVARIA

ALTÖTTING: *Zur Post* €€€ 102
Kapellplatz 2, 84503. **Map** E7. **(** (08671) 50 40. **FAX** (08671) 62 14.
[W] www.zurpostaltoetting.de
Renowned hotel features stylishly furnished rooms. The elegant restaurant
serves both Bavarian and international cuisine. Bicycles can be hired at
the hotel, which also has a swimming pool. [1] 🛏 🔄 **P** 🛎 ⚡ 🅿

ANSBACH: *Bürger-Palais* €€ 12
Neustadt 48, 91522. **Map** D6. **(** (0981) 951 32. **FAX** (0981) 956 00.
The Bürger-Palais is located in a Baroque building in the centre of the
town. Elegant rooms include bathrooms finished with marble. There is a
café with a terrace, while the hotel's Bratwurststüble restaurant serves
both Franconian and international specialities. [1] 🛏 🛎 🅿

ASCHAFFENBURG: *Wilder Mann* €€ 70
Loeherstr. 51, 63739. **Map** C5. **(** (06021) 30 20. **FAX** (06021) 30 22 34.
[W] www.hotel-wilder-mann.de
This hotel is based in a 16th-century building in the heart of the old
town. The hotel's comfortably furnished rooms will please the most
demanding of guests. [1] 🛏 🔄 **P** 🛎 🅿

AUGSBURG: *Dom-Hotel* €€ 52
Frauentorstr. 8, 86152. **Map** D6. **(** (0821) 34 39 30. **FAX** (0821) 34 39 32 00.
[W] www.domhotel-augsburg.de
This hotel is located near the cathedral, in a recently restored historic
building. Facilities include a swimming pool, sauna and solarium.
[1] 🛏 🔄 **P** 🛎 ⚡ 🅿

AUGSBURG: *Romantik Hotel Augsburger Hof* €€ 36
Auf dem Kreuz 2, 86152. **Map** D6. **(** (0821) 34 30 50. **FAX** (0821) 34 30 555.
[W] www.augsburger-hof.de
One of a chain that specializes in hotels based in beautiful historic
buildings. Located near Mozart's house, the hotel has a stylish restaurant
offering exquisitely prepared dishes. [1] 🛏 🔄 **P** 🅿

AUGSBURG: *Steigenberger Drei Mohren* €€€ 106
Maximilianstr. 40, 86150. **Map** D6. **(** (0821) 503 60.
FAX (0821) 15 78 64. [W] www.augsburg.steigenberger.de
Although this comfortable hotel is situated near the city's main street, the
rooms are completely quiet. The hotel offers a choice of restaurants,
including a fish restaurant, and a dance hall. [1] 🛏 🔄 **P** 🛎 ⚡ 🅿

For key to symbols *see back flap*

Price categories for a twin room with bathroom or shower, and including breakfast, service and tax: € up to €77 €€ €78–€128 €€€ €129–€179 €€€€ €180–€230 €€€€€ over €230	**RESTAURANT** The hotel has a restaurant that is open to non-residents as well as to hotel guests. **GARDEN OR TERRACE** The hotel is set in a garden or has an outside terrace or courtyard, often with tables for eating outside. **SWIMMING POOL** The hotel has a swimming pool. **AIR CONDITIONING** All rooms are air-conditioned.	NUMBER OF ROOMS	RESTAURANT	GARDEN OR TERRACE	SWIMMING POOL	AIR CONDITIONING
BAMBERG: *Alt Ringlein*　　€€ Dominikanerstr. 9, 96049. **Map** D5. ((0951) 953 20. FAX (0951) 953 25 00. w www.alt-ringlein.com Based in a 14th-century building, this well-known establishment offers all the virtues of a modern hotel. 1 ▦ ▧ P ▨	52	●			
BAMBERG: *Romantik Hotel Weinhaus Messerschmitt*　　€€ Lange Str. 41, 96047. **Map** D5. ((0951) 29 78 00. FAX (0951) 297 80 29. w www.hotel-messerschmitt.de This hotel has been owned by the same family for many years. Cosy atmosphere and classic regional cuisine. 1 ▦ P ▤ ▥ ▨	19	●			
BAMBERG: *Residenzschloss*　　€€€ Untere Sandstr. 32, 96049. **Map** D5. ((0951) 609 10. FAX (0951) 609 17 01. w www.residenzschloss.com Beautifully located by a river, this hotel is a charming complex of skilfully combined new and historic buildings. Facilities include an elegant restaurant and café with a terrace. 1 ▦ ▧ ▦ P ▤ ▥ ▨	185	●	■		
BAYREUTH: *Bayerischer Hof*　　€€ Bahnhofstr. 14, 95444. **Map** D5. ((0921) 786 00. FAX (0921) 786 05 60. w www.bayerischer-hof.de A popular, comfortable hotel with interestingly furnished rooms. Facilities include a restaurant, bar and wine bar. 1 ▦ ▧ P ▤ ▥ ▨	55	●	■	●	
BAYREUTH: *Lohmühle*　　€€ Badstr. 37, 95444. **Map** D5. ((0921) 530 60. FAX (0921) 530 64 69. w www.hotel-lohmuehle.de Although the hotel is constructed in traditional Franconian style, the rooms are equipped with every modern convenience. The restaurant offers both Franconian and international cuisine. 1 ▦ ▧ P ▤ ▨	42	●	■		
BAYREUTH: *Treff Hotel Rheingold*　　€€ Austrasse 2/Unteres Tor, 95445. **Map** D5. ((0921) 756 50. FAX (0921) 756 58 01. w www.ramada-treff.de This new hotel is located in a supremely beautiful area. An English-style pub, café with a terrace, as well as a magnificent swimming pool, gym, sauna, solarium and golf course. 1 ▦ ▧ P ▦ ▦ ▤ ▥ ▨	146	●	■	●	
BURGHAUSEN: *Glöcklhofer*　　€€ Ludwigsberg 4, 84489. **Map** E7. ((08677) 961 70. FAX (08677) 655 00. w www.hotel-gloecklhofer.de In a beautiful location by the entrance to the castle, this hotel belongs to the EuroRing chain. Facilities include a large swimming pool, bicycle hire, tennis courts and pleasant gardens. 1 ▦ ▦ ▧ P ▤ ▨	56	●	■	●	
COBURG: *Festungshof*　　€€ Festungshof 1, 96450. **Map** D5. ((09561) 802 90. FAX (09561) 80 29 33. w www.festungshof.de Small hotel, beautifully located opposite the castle. It was built 100 years ago, but has been modernized. 1 ▦ P ▤ ▨	14	●	■		
COBURG: *Romantik Hotel Goldene Traube*　　€€ Am Viktoriabrunnen 2, 96450. **Map** D5. ((09561) 87 60. FAX (09561) 87 62 22. w www.romantikhotels.com/coburg Hotel with comfortably furnished rooms, offering an excellent breakfast buffet and restaurant serving sophisticated cuisine. 1 ▦ ▧ P ▤ ▥ ▨	74	●	■		
DACHAU: *Fischer*　　€€ Bahnhofstr. 4, 85221. **Map** D6. ((08131) 782 05. FAX (08131) 785 08. w www.hotel-fischer-dachau.de A comfortable hotel opposite the railway station. Rooms are contemporary and the restaurant serves regional and international food. 1 ▦ ▧ P ▥ ▨	26	●	■		

DINKELSBÜHL: *Deutsches Haus* €€ 10
Weinmarkt 3, 91550. **Map** D6. [(09851) 60 58. FAX (09851) 79 11.
W www.deutsches-haus-dkb.de
The comfortable rooms in this hotel are furnished with antique furniture.
The renowned restaurant is highly recommended. 1 🔧 🔼 **P** 🗐

EICHSTÄTT: *Adler garni* € 15
Marktplatz 22–24, 85072. **Map** D6. [(08421) 67 67. FAX (08421) 82 83.
Based in a recently restored building dating from the 16th century, this
hotel has stylishly decorated, intimate rooms. The extensive breakfast
buffet includes "healthy eating" options. 1 🔧 🔼 **P** 🗗 🗐

FREISING: *Isar-Hotel* €€ 55
Isarstr. 4, 85356. **Map** D6. [(08161) 86 50. FAX (08161) 86 55 55.
W www.isarhotel.de
This recently built hotel is located in the city centre. The rooms are
pleasantly furnished. Bicycles can be hired. 1 🔧 🔼 **P** 🗗 🗐

FÜSSEN: *Alpenblick* € 66
Uferstr. 10, 87629 Füssen-Hopfen am See. **Map** D7. [(08362) 505 70.
FAX (08362) 50 57 73.
Attractive rooms and luxurious suites offer fine views of the Alps and the
Hopfensee. Evenings can be spent by an open fire. 1 🔧 🔼 **P** 🗐

GARMISCH-PARTENKIRCHEN: *Garmischer Hof* €€ 49
Chamonixstr. 10, 82467. **Map** D7. [(08821) 91 10.
FAX (08821) 514 40. W www.garmischer-hof.de
Beautifully located hotel with rooms decorated in the Alpine style.
Convenient for rail access to the Zugspitze mountain. 1 🔧 🔼 **P** 🗐

GARMISCH-PARTENKIRCHEN: *Posthotel-Partenkirchen* €€ 59
Ludwigstr. 49, 82467. **Map** D7. [(08821) 936 30. FAX (08821) 93 63 22 22.
W www.post-hotel.de
This hotel is decorated in typical Bavarian style, with wooden features,
stylized furniture and comfortable rooms. 1 🔧 🔼 **P** 🗐

INGOLSTADT: *Ara Hotel* €€ 94
Schollstr. 10A, 85055. **Map** D6. [(0841) 954 30. FAX (0841) 954 34 44.
W www.hotel-ara.de
Newly built hotel with Italian-style furnishings. Italian specialities are
served in the restaurant. Pleasant café with terrace. 1 🔧 🔼 **P** 🗐

KEMPTEN: *Bayerischer Hof* €€ 52
Füssener Str. 96, 87437. **Map** C7. [(0831) 571 80.
FAX (0831) 571 81 00. W www.bayerischerhof-kempten.de
Conveniently located hotel in the centre of the city with rooms furnished
in a modern style, a pleasant bar and Chinese restaurant. 1 🔧 🔼 **P** 🗐

LANDSHUT: *Romantik Hotel Fürstenhof* €€ 24
Stethaimer Str. 3, 84034. **Map** E6. [(0871) 925 50. FAX (0871) 92 55 44.
W www.romantikhotels.com/landshut
This hotel is based in a beautiful villa near the town centre. Two
restaurants offer a wide selection of dishes, including regional cuisine.
Lovers of tennis and golf will also enjoy staying here. 1 🔧 🔼 **P** 🗐

LINDAU: *Reutemann Seegarten* €€€ 64
Seepromenade, 88131. **Map** C7. [(08382) 91 50. FAX (08382) 91 55 91.
W www.bayrischerhof-lindau.de
The hotel is situated by a lake, with a beautiful view of the Swiss and
Austrian Alps. Bicycles can be hired. 1 🔧 **P** 🗐

NEU-ULM: *Römer Villa* €€ 23
Parkstr. 1, 89231. **Map** C6. [(0731) 80 00 40. FAX (0731) 800 04 50.
W www.roemer-villa.de
Elegant rooms are a feature of this hotel, which occupies a beautiful Art
Nouveau building. Facilities include a restaurant, lounge with an open
fire, wine bar and winter garden. 1 🔧 🔼 **P** 🔒 🗐

NEUBURG AN DER DONAU: *Klosterbräu* € 27
Kirchplatz 1, 86633 Neuburg a.d. Donau-Bergen. **Map** D6. [(08431) 677 50.
FAX (08431) 411 20.
At this historic, modernized hotel, there are good facilities for taking part
in various sports, including tennis. The restaurant serves regional cuisine,
specializing in game dishes and local fish. 1 🔒 🔧 🔼 **P** 🗐

For key to symbols *see back flap*

Price categories for a twin room with bathroom or shower, and including breakfast, service and tax:

€ up to €77
€€ €78–€128
€€€ €129–€179
€€€€ €180–€230
€€€€€ over €230

RESTAURANT
The hotel has a restaurant that is open to non-residents as well as to hotel guests.

GARDEN OR TERRACE
The hotel is set in a garden or has an outside terrace or courtyard, often with tables for eating outside.

SWIMMING POOL
The hotel has a swimming pool.

AIR CONDITIONING
All rooms are air-conditioned.

	NUMBER OF ROOMS	RESTAURANT	GARDEN OR TERRACE	SWIMMING POOL	AIR CONDITIONING
NÜRNBERG (NUREMBERG): *Burghotel-Grosses Haus* €€ Lammsgasse 3, 90403. **Map** D6. 📞 *(0911) 23 88 90.* 📠 *(0911) 23 88 91 00.* 🆆 www.altstadthotels-nuernberg.de From this hotel you can enjoy a beautiful view of the old town. Facilities include a swimming pool, sauna and a rustic bar. 1 🛏 🔼 P 🖪	57			●	
NÜRNBERG (NUREMBERG): *Romantik Hotel Am Josephsplatz* €€ Josephsplatz 30/32, 90403. **Map** D6. 📞 *(0911) 21 44 70.* 📠 *(0911) 21 44 72 00.* 🆆 www.romantikhotels.com/Nuernberg This splendid hotel lies in the heart of Nürnberg's old town. Some of the elegant rooms open onto a flower-filled courtyard. 1 🖪 🛏 🔼 P 🖫 🖪	36		■		
NÜRNBERG (NUREMBERG): *Maritim* €€€€ Frauentorgraben 11, 90443. **Map** D6. 📞 *(0911) 236 30.* 📠 *(0911) 236 38 23.* 🆆 www.maritim.de A hotel of international standard, close to the railway station. Rooms are elegant and there are numerous dining options. 1 🖪 ≈ 🛏 🔼 🖫 P 🖪	316	●			
OBERAMMERGAU: *Turmwirt* €€ Ettalerstr. 2, 82487. **Map** D7. 📞 *(08822) 926 00.* 📠 *(08822) 14 37.* A typical Bavarian hotel, with carefully chosen furnishings. Facilities include a restaurant, café and patisserie. 1 🛏 🔼 P 🖪 ≈ 🖪	22	●			
OBERSTDORF: *Kappeler Haus* € Am Seeler 2, 87561. **Map** C7. 📞 *(08322) 968 60.* 📠 *(08322) 96 86 13.* This hotel has a family atmosphere and a swimming pool. 1 🛏 🔼 P 🖪	45		■	●	
PASSAU: *Passauer Wolf* €€ Rindermarkt 6, 94032. **Map** E6. 📞 *(0851) 931 51 10.* 📠 *(0851) 931 51 50.* 🆆 www.passauerwolf.de Beautifully located in a historic building between the old town and the Danube. Modern rooms and excellent cuisine. 1 🖪 🛏 🔼 🖪	39	●			
REGENSBURG: *Bischofshof* €€ Krauterer Markt 3, 93047. **Map** D6. 📞 *(0941) 584 60.* 📠 *(0941) 584 61 46.* 🆆 www.hotel-bischofshof.de Located opposite the cathedral, the Bischofshof's rooms have been refurbished in rustic style. Elegant restaurant. 1 🖪 ≈ 🛏 🔼 P 🖪	55	●	■		
ROTHENBURG OB DER TAUBER: *Markusturm Romantik Hotel* €€ Rödergasse 1, 91541. **Map** C6. 📞 *(09861) 942 80.* 📠 *(09861) 94 28 113.* 🆆 www.markusturm.de Housed in a building dating from 1264, this hotel has rooms furnished with valuable antique furniture. 1 ≈ 🛏 P 🖪	23	●			
ROTHENBURG OB DER TAUBER: *Prinzhotel* €€ Hofstatt 3, 91541. **Map** C6. 📞 *(09861) 97 50.* 📠 *(09861) 975 75.* 🆆 www.prinzhotel.rothenburg.de This hotel is located in the old city, near the Röderturm. All the rooms are attractively furnished in a modern style. 1 🛏 🔼 P 🖪	52	●	■		
WÜRZBURG: *Alter Kranen* €€ Kärrnergasse 11, 97070. **Map** C5. 📞 *(0931) 351 80.* 📠 *(0931) 500 10.* 🆆 www.hotel-alter-kranen.de This middle-range hotel has a beautiful location on the bank of the river Main. A buffet breakfast is served. 1 🛏 🔼 P 🖪	14				

BADEN-WÜRTTEMBERG

BADEN-BADEN: *Tannenhof* €€ Hans-Bredow-Str. 20, 76530. **Map** B6. 📞 *(07221) 30 09 90.* 📠 *(07221) 300 99 51.* 🆆 www.hotel-tannenhof-baden-baden.de Good hotel with attractively decorated, spacious rooms. North Italian cuisine is a speciality of the hotel restaurant. 1 🛏 P 🖪 🔼 🖪	27	●			

BADEN-BADEN: *Romantik Hotel Der Kleine Prinz*   €€€€   40
Lichtentaler Str. 36, 76530. **Map** B6. **(** *(07221) 346 60 04*.
FAX *(07221) 346 60 59*. **W** www.derkleineprinz.de
Based in a beautifully furnished and decorated villa, the hotel is named
after the children's novel *The Little Prince* by Antoine Saint-Exupéry.

BADEN-BADEN: *Steigenberger Badischer Hof*   €€€€   139
Lange Str. 47, 76530. **Map** B6. **(** *(07221) 93 40*.
FAX *(07221) 93 44 70*. **W** www.badischer-hof.steigenberger.de
This hotel is housed in a former monastery, which has been tastefully
refurbished to the highest international standards.

BAD MERGENTHEIM: *Hotel Gästehaus Alte Münze*   €   31
Münzgasse 12, 97980. **Map** C5. **(** *(07931) 56 60*. **FAX** *(07931) 56 62 22*.
Opened in 1993, this hotel is situated in a central yet tranquil location
near the Knight's Castle.

BAD MERGENTHEIM: *Romantik Hotel Victoria*   €€   78
Poststr. 2–4, 97980. **Map** C5. **(** *(07931) 59 30*. **FAX** *(07931) 59 35 00*.
W www.victoria-hotel.de
An intimate spa hotel with excellently equipped rooms, sauna and solarium.
Very highly regarded among connoisseurs.

BAD WIMPFEN: *Am Rosengarten*   €€€   60
Osterbergstr. 16, 74206. **Map** C6. **(** *(07063) 99 10*. **FAX** *(07063) 991 80 08*.
W www.hotel-rosengarten.net
Beautifully located on the edge of the old town. Pleasant hotel bar, café
with terrace and fitness studio.

BRUCHSAL: *Ritter*   €€   98
Au in den Buchen 72 & 83 & 92, 76646. **Map** C6. **(** *(07257) 880*. **FAX** *(07257) 881 11*.
W www.ritterbruchsal.de
A hotel with a long tradition, the Ritter has luxurious rooms, two
restaurants and a beer garden.

ESSLINGEN: *Am Schelztor garni*   €€   36
Schelztorstr. 5, 73728. **Map** C6. **(** *(0711) 396 96 40*. **FAX** *(0711) 35 98 87*.
The hotel is housed in a recently renovated period building within the
historic town centre. Breakfast only is served.

FREIBURG IM BREISGAU: *Zum Roten Bären*   €€€   25
Oberlinden 12, 79098. **Map** B7. **(** *(0761) 38 78 70*. **FAX** *(0761) 387 87 17*.
W www.roter-baeren.de
This is one of the oldest hotel buildings in Germany. Its traditions date
back to the 14th century and even to the 12th century in parts. It is
comfortably furnished in a modern manner.

FREIBURG IM BREISGAU: *Colombi-Hotel*   €€€€   120
Rotteckring 16, 79098. **Map** B7. **(** *(0761) 210 60*.
FAX *(0761) 31 410*. **W** www.colombi.de
Quiet, centrally situated hotel with impeccable service and luxurious rooms
furnished in the Schwarzwald style. Facilities include swimming pool,
sauna, gym and excellent restaurant.

HEIDELBERG: *Holländer Hof garni*   €€€   39
Neckarstaden 66, 69117. **Map** C6. **(** *(06221) 605 00*. **FAX** *(06221) 60 50 60*.
W www.hollaender-hof.de
Beautifully located within the environs of the old town and with a view
of the famous castle, this hotel has a long tradition of hospitality. It is
very conveniently situated for sightseeing.

HEIDELBERG: *Marriott Hotel*   €€€€   248
Vangerowstr. 16, 69115. **Map** C6. **(** *(06221) 90 80*.
FAX *(06221) 90 86 60*. **W** www.marriott.com
Located by the river Neckar, this modern hotel has a private jetty as well
as a well-equipped conference hall, bar and wine bar. From the café
there is a beautiful view along the river.

HEILBRONN: *Ringhotel Burkhardt*   €€   82
Lohtorstr. 7, 74072. **Map** C6. **(** *(07131) 622 40*.
FAX *(07131) 62 78 28*. **W** www.burkhardt-ringhotel.de
This old-established hotel is conveniently located in the centre of town,
near the river Neckar. It has a pleasant restaurant.

For key to symbols *see back flap*

Price categories for a twin room with bathroom or shower, and service and tax:
€ up to €77
€€ €78–€128
€€€ €129–€179
€€€€ €180–€230
€€€€€ over €230

RESTAURANT
The hotel has a restaurant that is open to non-residents as well as to hotel guests.

GARDEN OR TERRACE
The hotel is set in a garden or has an outside terrace or courtyard, often with tables for eating outside.

SWIMMING POOL
The hotel has a swimming pool.

AIR CONDITIONING
All rooms are air-conditioned.

		NUMBER OF ROOMS	RESTAURANT	GARDEN OR TERRACE	SWIMMING POOL	AIR CONDITIONING
KARLSRUHE: *Alfa garni*	€€	40				
Bürgerstr. 4, 76133. **Map** B6. ☎ (0721) 299 26. ℻ (0721) 299 29. W www.karlsruhe-hotel.de Situated in the centre of Karlsruhe, this hotel has attractively furnished rooms and a restaurant run by the Mövenpick chain. ① 🛏 📶 **P** 🖾						
KARLSRUHE: *Renaissance*	€€€	215	●			
Mendelssohnplatz, 76131. **Map** B6. ☎ (0721) 371 70. ℻ (0721) 37 71 56. W www.renaissancehotels.com This hotel, near the Congress Centre, has several conference halls. The restaurant serves regional and international dishes. ① 🛏 📶 **P** 🖾 🏊 🖾						
KONSTANZ: *Steigenberger Inselhotel*	€€€€	102	●	■		
Auf der Insel 1, 78462. **Map** C7. ☎ (07531) 12 50. ℻ (07531) 264 02. W www.steigenberger.com Based in a former monastery building, this comfortable hotel has a sauna and solarium as well as private access to the lake. 🛏 📶 **P** 🏊 🖾						
LUDWIGSBURG: *Nestor*	€€€	151	●	■		■
Stuttgarter Str. 35/2, 71638. **Map** C6. ☎ (07141) 96 70. ℻ (07141) 96 71 13. W www.nestor-hotels.de This elegant hotel occupies two 18th-century buildings. Regional and international dishes are served in the restaurant. ① 🛏 📶 **P** 🖾 🏊 🖾						
LUDWIGSBURG: *Schlosshotel Monrepos*	€€€	80	●	■	●
Domäne Monrepos 22, 71634. **Map** C6. ☎ (07141) 30 20. ℻ (07141) 30 22 00. W www.schlosshotel-monrepos.de Beautifully located by the lake near Prince Ludwig's palace Monrepos. There is an attractive café nearby. ① 🛏 📶 **P** 🖾 🖾						
MANNHEIM: *Maritim Parkhotel*	€€€€	173	●		●	■
Friedrichsplatz 2, 68165. **Map** B5. ☎ (0621) 158 80. ℻ (0621) 158 88 00. W www.maritim.de This elegant hotel offers beautiful interiors, excellent service and a restaurant serving regional cuisine. ① 🛏 📶 **P** 🖾 🏊 🖾						
MARBACH: *Parkhotel*	€€	56				
Schillerhöhe 14, 71672. **Map** C6. ☎ (07144) 90 50. ℻ (07144) 905 88. Located on Schillerhöhe, this hotel has pleasantly furnished, comfortable rooms. A buffet breakfast is served. ① 🛏 📶 **P** 🏊 🖾						
RAVENSBURG: *Waldhorn*	€€€	30	●	■		
Marienplatz 15, 88212. **Map** C7. ☎ (0751) 361 20. ℻ (0751) 361 21 00. W www.waldhorn.de Well known for its excellent food, the Waldhorn's restaurant serves French cuisine, specializing in game and fish. ① 🛏 📶 **P** 🖾 🏊 🖾						
ROTTWEIL: *Haus zum Sternen & Romantikhotel*	€€	11	●	■		
Hauptstr. 60, 78628. **Map** C7. ☎ (0741) 533 00. ℻ (0741) 53 30 30. W www.romantikhotels.com Based in a 13th-century building but with modern facilities, this hotel overlooks the Neckar valley. ① 🛏 **P** 🖾 🖾						
SALEM: *Reck*	€€	20	●	■		
Bahnhofstr. 111, 88682. **Map** C7. ☎ (07553) 201. ℻ (07553) 202. Hotel with a family atmosphere and rooms in various categories. The pleasant restaurant offers a large choice of wines. ① 🛏 📶 **P** 🖾						
SCHWÄBISCH GMÜND: *Einhorn*	€	18	●	■		
Rinderbachergasse 10, 73525. **Map** C6. ☎ (07171) 630 23. ℻ (07171) 616 80. W www.hoteleinhorn.com City-centre hotel with pleasant rooms. Located in a 12th-century cellar, the restaurant serves international cuisine. ① 🛏 📶 **P** 🖾 🖾						

SCHWÄBISCH HALL: *Der Adelshof* €€ 47
Am Markt 12–13, 74523. **Map** C6. 【 *(0791) 758 90.* ℻ *(0791) 60 36.*
ⓦ www.hotel-adelshof.de
In a beautiful location near the market. Excellent breakfast buffet,
exclusive restaurant and pleasant bar. 🔲 ⛵ 🔲 P 🔲 🔲

STUTTGART: *Kronen-Hotel* €€€ 84
Kronenstr. 48, 70174. **Map** C6. 【 *(0711) 225 10.* ℻ *(0711) 225 14 04.*
ⓦ www.vch.de
Situated in a tranquil part of the city centre, not far from the railway
station. Excellent breakfast. Garden with terrace. 🔲 ⛵ 🔲 P 🔲 🔲 🔲

STUTTGART: *Inter-Continental* €€€€ 276
Willy-Brandt-Str. 30, 70173. **Map** C6. 【 *(0711) 202 00.* ℻ *(0711) 20 20 20 20.*
ⓦ www.stuttgart.intercontinental.com
Located opposite the castle park, the hotel's facilities include a business
centre with internet access, gym and golf course. 🔲 ⛵ 🔲 P 🔲 🔲 🔲

TÜBINGEN: *Krone* €€€ 48
Uhlandstr. 1, 72072. **Map** C6. 【 *(07071) 133 10.* ℻ *(07071) 13 31 32.*
ⓦ www.krone-tuebingen.de
Regarded as one of the best hotels in the city, the Krone has elegantly
furnished rooms and a renowned restaurant. 🔲 ⛵ 🔲 🔲 P 🔲 🔲

ULM: *Engel* €€ 46
Loher Str. 35, 89081 Ulm-Lehr. **Map** C6. 【 *(0731) 14 04 00.* ℻ *(0731) 14 04 03 00.*
ⓦ www.hotel-engel-ulm.de
A well-known inn was converted into this modern, comfortable hotel.
Pleasant rooms are furnished with wooden furniture. 🔲 ⛵ 🔲 P 🔲 🔲

WEINGARTEN: *Walk'sches Haus* €€ 27
Marktplatz 7, 76356. **Map** B6. 【 *(07244) 70 37 0.* ℻ *(07244) 70 37 40.*
ⓦ www.walksches-haus.de
Beautifully located in a 16th century building near the market. A pleasant
restaurant in the garden offers French cuisine. 🔲 ⛵ P 🔲 🔲

RHINELAND-PALATINATE AND SAARLAND

KOBLENZ: *Top Hotel Krämer garni* €€ 22
Kardinal-Krementz-Str. 12, 56073. **Map** B5. 【 *(0261) 40 62 00.* ℻ *(0261) 413 40.*
ⓦ www.tophotel-k.de
A family-run hotel in a quiet area of the city centre, providing a warm,
comfortable atmosphere. 🔲 ⛵ 🔲 P 🔲 🔲 🔲

KOBLENZ: *Mercure* €€€ 169
Julius-Wegeler-Str. 6, 56068. **Map** B5. 【 *(0261) 13 60.* ℻ *(0261) 136 11 99.*
ⓦ www.mercure.com
The Mercure has a vast, mirrored façade and elegant restaurant. Rooms
are comfortable and well furnished. 🔲 ⛵ 🔲 P 🔲 🔲 🔲

MAINZ: *Dorint Hotel Mainz* €€€ 217
Augustusstr. 6, 55131. **Map** B5. 【 *(06131) 95 40.*
℻ *(06131) 95 41 00.* ⓦ www.dorint.de
Baroque cellars dating from the 17th century have been integrated into this
unique hotel building. The Bajazzo restaurant offers international and
regional dishes. 🔲 ⛵ 🔲 P 🔲 🔲 🔲

MAINZ: *Günnewig Bristol Hotel* €€€ 75
Friedrich-Ebert-Str. 20, 55130 Mainz-Weisenau. **Map** B5. 【 *(06131) 80 60.*
℻ *(06131) 80 61 00.* ⓦ www.guennewig.de
Popular with business travellers, this conveniently located hotel has air-
conditioned rooms and a good restaurant. 🔲 ⛵ 🔲 P 🔲 🔲 🔲

MARIA LAACH: *Seehotel Maria Laach* €€€ 69
Ortsteil Maria Laach, 56653 Maria Laach. **Map** B5. 【 *(02652) 58 40.*
℻ *(02652) 58 45 22.* ⓦ www.maria-laach.de
Tranquil hotel with comfortable rooms. Popular with tourists visiting the
nearby Benedictine monastery. Good restaurant and café with a terrace.
🔲 ⛵ 🔲 P 🔲 🔲 🔲

SAARBRÜCKEN: *Mercure Kongress* €€ 150
Hafenstr. 8, 66111. **Map** B6. 【 *(0681) 389 00.* ℻ *(0861) 389 09 89.*
ⓦ www.mercure.com
Situated by the Congress Centre and urban motorway, this hotel has
spacious, comfortably furnished rooms. 🔲 ⛵ 🔲 P 🔲 🔲 🔲

For key to symbols *see back flap*

Price categories for a twin room with bathroom or shower, and including breakfast, service and tax:
€ up to €77
€€ €78–€128
€€€ €129–€179
€€€€ €180–€230
€€€€€ over €230

RESTAURANT
The hotel has a restaurant that is open to non-residents as well as to hotel guests.
GARDEN OR TERRACE
The hotel is set in a garden or has an outside terrace or courtyard, often with tables for eating outside.
SWIMMING POOL
The hotel has a swimming pool.
AIR CONDITIONING
All rooms are air-conditioned.

	NUMBER OF ROOMS	RESTAURANT	GARDEN OR TERRACE	SWIMMING POOL	AIR CONDITIONING
SAARBRÜCKEN: *La Residence* €€€ Faktoreistr. 2, 66111. **Map** B6. ((0681) 388 20. FAX (0681) 388 21 85. W www.la-residence.net Well located in the city centre, this hotel has comfortable rooms. A buffet breakfast is served in the winter garden. 1 📶 🔼 P 🛏 ⚡ 🍴	142	●	■		
SPEYER: *Domhof* €€ Bauhof 3, 67346. **Map** B6. ((06232) 132 90. FAX (06232) 13 29 90. W www.domhof.de Newly opened stylish hotel in a historic building near the Dom. 1 📶 🔼 P ⚡ 🛏 🍴	49				
SPEYER: *Binshof* €€€€ Binshof 1, 67346 Speyer-Binshof. **Map** B6. ((06232) 64 70. FAX (06232) 64 71 99. W www.lindner.de Located in a landscaped park some distance from the city is this excellent hotel. Features include a huge swimming-pool complex. 1 📶 📶 🔼 P ⚡ 🛏 🍴	67	●	■	●	■
TRIER: *Römischer Kaiser* €€ Porta Nigra-Platz 6, 54292. **Map** A5. ((0651) 977 00. FAX (0651) 97 70 99. W www.hotels-trier.de A modern hotel, with an elegant restaurant, has been created within the walls of a historic building. 1 📶 🔼 P 🍴	43	●	■		
TRIER: *Dorint Hotel Porta Nigra* €€€ Porta-Nigra-Platz 1, 54292. **Map** A5. ((0651) 270 10. FAX (0651) 270 11 70. W www.dorint.de One of the finest hotels in Trier, with rooms providing a high degree of comfort and a restaurant to satisfy gourmets. 1 📶 🔼 P ⚡ 🛏 🍴	106	●			
HESSE					
ALSFELD: *Zum Schwalbennest* € Pfarrwiesenweg 12–14, 36304. **Map** C4. ((06631) 91 14 40. FAX (06631) 710 81. W www.hotel-schwalbennest.de A modern hotel with intimate rooms and a rustic restaurant. There is also a wine bar and a bar with a dance floor. 1 📶 🔼 P ⚡ 🍴	65	●	■		
BAD HOMBURG: *Parkhotel* €€€ Kaiser-Friedrich-Promenade 53–55, 61348. **Map** C5. ((06172) 80 10. FAX (06172) 80 14 00. W www.parkhotel-bad-homburg.de Located near the spa park, close to the Taunus baths and the casino. Large recreation room and several restaurants. 1 📶 🔼 P 🛏 ⚡ 📺 🍴	123	●	■		
DARMSTADT: *Jagdschloss Kranichstein* €€€ Kranichsteiner Str. 261, 64289 Darmstadt-Kranichstein. **Map** C5. ((06151) 977 90. FAX (06151) 97 79 20. W www.hotel-jagdschloss-kranichstein.de This hotel occupies one of Germany's most beautiful Renaissance castles. Comfortably furnished rooms and several restaurants. 1 📶 🔼 P 🛏 🍴	15	●	■		
ELTVILLE AM RHEIN: *Kronenschlösschen* €€€ Rheinallee, 65347 Eltville-Hattenheim. **Map** B5. ((06723) 640. FAX (06723) 76 63. W www.kronenschloesschen.de Housed in a beautiful villa, this recently restored and modernized hotel is located close to the Rhine. Features include an elegant restaurant, bistro, wine bar, hotel bar and a restaurant in the garden. 1 🛏 📶 P 🍴	18	●	■		
FRANKFURT AM MAIN: *Borger garni* €€ Triebstr. 51, 60388 Frankfurt-Bergen-Enkheim. **Map** C5. ((06109) 309 00. FAX (06109) 30 90 30. This hotel with a long family tradition is located in a historic area of Frankfurt. The rooms are comfortable and the area has good transport connections to the city centre. 1 📶 P 🍴	36	●	■		

FRANKFURT AM MAIN: *Best Western Alexander am Zoo garni* €€€ 59
Waldschmidtstr. 59–61, 60316. **Map** C5. **(** (069) 94 96 00. **FAX** (069) 94 96 07 20.
W www.alexanderamzoo.de
Italian-style hotel near the zoo, with modern, comfortably furnished
rooms. Pleasant hotel bar and varied breakfast buffet. Ideal venue for
businessmen. 🗍 🚗 🖳 P 🍴 🛅 🌫 🥂

FRANKFURT AM MAIN: *Frankfurt Hotel Savoy* €€€ 144
Wiesenhüttenstr. 42, 60329. **Map** C5. **(** (069) 27 39 60.
FAX (069) 27 39 67 95. W www.savoyhotel.de
High-class hotel with rooms decorated in a Swedish style and a roof-top
recreational centre. 🗍 🚗 🖳 🍴 🌫 🛅 🥂

FRANKFURT AM MAIN: *Steigenberger Frankfurter Hof* €€€€€ 332
Kaiserplatz, 60311. **Map** C5. **(** (069) 215 02. **FAX** (069) 21 59 00.
W www.frankfurter-hof.steigenberger.de
A flagship of the Steigenberger-Hotels chain. Rooms, including the vast
presidential suite, are luxurious. Several well-equipped function rooms
and a number of excellent restaurants. 🗍 🚗 🖳 P 🌫 🛅 🥂

FULDA: *Romantik Hotel Goldener Karpfen* €€€ 50
Simpliziusbrunnen 1, 36037. **Map** C5. **(** (0661) 868 00.
FAX (0661) 868 01 00. W www.hotel-goldener-karpfen.com
In perfect harmony with its Baroque surroundings, this hotel is located in
the city centre. Guests can relax in the hotel bar or intimate wine bar,
and enjoy the highly recommended cuisine. 🗍 🚗 🖳 P 🍴 🛅 🌫 🥂

KASSEL: *Hotel Residenz Domus* €€ 54
Erzbergerstrasse 1–5, 34117. **Map** C4. **(** (0561) 70 33 30. **FAX** (0561) 70 33 34 98.
W www.hotel-domus-kassel.de
Beyond the Art Nouveau façade lies a comfortable hotel with elegant
rooms and a winter garden with glass roof. 🗍 🚗 🖳 P 🌫 🛅 🥂

KASSEL: *Schlosshotel Wilhelmshöhe* €€€ 101
Schlosspark 8, 34131 Kassel-Wilhelmshöhe. **Map** C4. **(** (0561) 308 80.
FAX (0561) 308 84 28. W www.privathotel.net
Beautifully located in the most exclusive part of the city, with pleasant,
comfortably furnished rooms. 🗍 🚗 🖳 P 🍴 🛅 🥂

LIMBURG: *Romantik Hotel Zimmermann* €€ 20
Blumenröder Str. 1, 65549. **Map** B5. **(** (06431) 46 11. **FAX** (06431) 413 14.
W www.romantikhotel-zimmermann.de
Celebrities stay at this hotel whose motto is "Our guests are also our
friends." The hotel is elegantly furnished with various eye-catching and
interesting architectural features, including marble bathrooms.
🗍 🚗 P 🛅 🌫 🥂

MARBURG: *Sorat Hotel Marburg* €€ 146
Pilgrimstein 29, 35037. **Map** C4. **(** (06421) 91 80. **FAX** (06421) 91 84 44.
W www.sorat-hotels.com
New hotel in the heart of the city, with attractively furnished rooms.
Facilities include a sauna, solarium and gym. 🗍 🖳 P 🍴 🌫 🚗 🥂

MARBURG: *Waldecker Hof garni* €€ 40
Bahnhofstr. 23, 35037. **Map** C4. **(** (06421) 600 90.
FAX (06421) 60 09 59. W www.waldecker-hof-marburg.de
This family-run hotel with comfortable rooms is conveniently situated
close to the railway station. 🗍 🛅 🌫 🚗 🖳 P 🍴 🥂

RÜDESHEIM AM RHEIN: *Jagdschloss Niederwald* €€€ 52
Am Niederwald 1, 65385. **Map** B5. **(** (06722) 710 60. **FAX** (06722) 710 66 66.
W www.niederwald.de
Housed in a former hunting lodge/castle and beautifully located in the
midst of a forest above the Rhine. Stylized interiors create a unique
atmosphere. The panoramic restaurant serves fish and game dishes,
accompanied by a wide choice of wines. There is a small zoo near the
hotel. 🗍 🚗 🖳 P 🥂

WEILBURG: *Schlosshotel* €€€ 33
Langgasse 25, 35781. **Map** B5. **(** (06471) 50 900.
FAX (06471) 50 90 111. W www.schlosshotel-weilburg.de
This comfortable hotel is located within the administrative buildings of a
former Renaissance castle. Among its attractions are a good choice of
dishes in the restaurant and café with a terrace. 🗍 🚗 🖳 P 🌫 🛅 🥂

For key to symbols *see back flap*

Price categories for a twin room with bathroom or shower, and including breakfast, service and tax:
€ up to €77
€€ €78–€128
€€€ €129–€179
€€€€ €180–€230
€€€€€ over €230

RESTAURANT
The hotel has a restaurant that is open to non-residents as well as to hotel guests.
GARDEN OR TERRACE
The hotel is set in a garden or has an outside terrace or courtyard, often with tables for eating outside.
SWIMMING POOL
The hotel has a swimming pool.
AIR CONDITIONING
All rooms are air-conditioned.

	NUMBER OF ROOMS	RESTAURANT	GARDEN OR TERRACE	SWIMMING POOL	AIR CONDITIONING
WETZLAR: *Landhotel Naunheimer Mühle* €€ Mühle 2, 35584. **Map** C5. (*(06441) 935 30.* **FAX** *(06441) 93 53 93.* W www.naunheimer-muehle.de This modern hotel occupies a converted water mill on the bank of the river Lan. Facilities include tennis courts.	32	●	■		
WIESBADEN: *Klee am Park* €€€ Parkstr. 4, 65189. **Map** B5. (*(0611) 900 10.* **FAX** *(0611) 900 13 10.* W www.klee-am-park.de Excellent location close to theatres, park and spa buildings. Comfortable rooms.	54	●	■		
WIESBADEN: *Nassauer Hof* €€€€€ Kaiser-Friedrich-Platz 3, 65183. **Map** B5. (*(0611) 13 30.* **FAX** *(0611) 13 36 32.* W www.nassauer-hof.de This long-established hotel has a beautiful Baroque façade and distinguished interiors. A particular attraction is the pool, which features water from the hotel's own spring. Other facilities include a luxurious beauty salon and good restaurant.	186	●	■	●	■

NORTH RHINE-WESTPHALIA

	NUMBER OF ROOMS	RESTAURANT	GARDEN OR TERRACE	SWIMMING POOL	AIR CONDITIONING
AACHEN: *Best Western Hotel Royal garni* €€€ Jülicher Str. 1, 52070. **Map** A4. (*(0241) 18 22 80.* **FAX** *(0241) 18 22 86 99.* W www.royal.bestwestern.de Located in a recently refurbished historic building dating from the 18th century. Guests can relax in the wine bar.	35				■
AACHEN: *Dorint Aachen Quellenhof* €€€€ Monheimsallee 52, 52062. **Map** A4. (*(0241) 913 20.* **FAX** *(0241) 913 21 00.* W www.dorint.com/aachen This hotel recently re-opened following extensive refurbishment of the highest standard. Every technological facility is available, as well as a swimming pool and 12 tennis courts.	174	●		●	
BIELEFELD: *Brenner Hotel Diekmann* €€ Otto-Brenner-Str. 133, 33607. **Map** C3. (*(0521) 299 90.* **FAX** *(0521) 299 92 20.* W www.brenner-hotel.de Family-run hotel with attractive, spacious rooms. Facilities include a bowling alley, hotel bar and conference halls.	65	●	■		
BONN: *Schlosshotel Kommende Ramersdorf* €€ Oberkasslerstr. 10, 53227 Bonn-Beuel. **Map** B4. (*(0228) 44 07 34.* **FAX** *(0228) 44 44 00.* This establishment, which belongs to a chain of castle hotels, is housed within the imposing Teutonic Knights Castle. Former meeting halls have been converted into a restaurant and function rooms.	18	●	■		
BONN: *Kaiser Karl* €€€ Vorgebirgsstr. 56, 53119. **Map** B4. (*(0228) 985 570.* **FAX** *(0228) 985 5777.* W www.kaiser-karl-hotel-bonn.de Comfort and good service are guaranteed in this exclusive hotel. Rooms are elegantly furnished and decorated, and each one is equipped with a safe. Breakfast is served in the lounge or garden, and there is a pub-style bar.	42	●	■		
BONN: *Best Western Domicil* €€€€ Thomas-Mann-Str. 24–26, 53111. **Map** B4. (*(0228) 72 90 90.* **FAX** *(0228) 69 12 07.* W www.bestwestern.de A hotel complex consisting of a number of buildings that have been carefully integrated. Features include a pleasant bar, a winter garden and a restaurant serving international cuisine.	44	●	■		

DETMOLD: *Lippischer Hof* €€ 27
Willy-Brandt-Platz 1, 32756. **Map** C3. [(05231) 93 60. FAX (05231) 244 70.
Housed in a historic 18th-century building; facilities include a bar and
wine bar. 🛏 ↻ P 🄴

DÜSSELDORF: *Ibis Hauptbahnhof* €€ 166
Konrad-Adenauer-Platz 14, 40210. **Map** B4. [(0211) 167 20. FAX (0211) 167 21 01.
W www.ibishotel.com
Located behind the historic façade of the railway station, this hotel has
been built around an atrium, so that guests' windows open onto a
courtyard filled with greenery. 1 🛏 ↻ 🄴

DÜSSELDORF: *Madison I* €€€ 100
Graf-Adolf-Str. 94, 40210. **Map** B4. [(0211) 168 50. FAX (0211) 168 53 28.
W www.madison-hotels.de
Attractively furnished rooms with pine furniture. The hotel complex
includes a sports club. 1 🛏 ↻ 🍴 ≠ 🄴 🄴

DÜSSELDORF: *Nikko* €€€€€ 301
Immermannstr. 41, 40210. **Map** B4. [(0211) 83 40. FAX (0211) 16 12 16.
W www.nikko-hotel.de
This hotel complex is reminiscent of a small village with charming
architecture and modern technology. The Benkay restaurant specializes
in Japanese cuisine. 1 🛏 ↻ 🍴 ≠ 🄴 🄴

ESSEN: *Schlosshotel Hugenpoet* €€€€ 25
August-Thyssen-Str. 51, 45219 Essen-Kettwig. **Map** B4.
[(02054) 120 40. FAX (02054) 12 04 50. W www.hugenpoet.de
Housed within a former castle, this hotel is elegantly furnished with
stylish furniture and marble stairways. Some rooms feature original pieces
of furniture from the 16th century. Renowned restaurant in the park has a
large choice of wines and delicacies. 1 ↻ P 🄴 🛏 🄴

HÖXTER: *Ringhotel Niedersachsen* €€ 80
Grube 3–7, 37671. **Map** C3. [(05271) 68 80. FAX (05271) 68 84 44.
W www.hotelniedersachsen.de
This hotel is renowned for its hospitality, with comfortable rooms and an
intimate hotel bar for guests. The restaurant serves both regional and
international dishes. 1 🛏 ↻ P ≠ 🄴 🄴

KÖLN (COLOGNE): *Coellner Hof* €€ 79
Hansaring 100, 50670. **Map** B4. [(0221) 166 60.
FAX (0221) 166 61 66. W www.coellnerhof.de
A well-known, beautifully furnished hotel with excellent service. Facilities
include a good restaurant and hotel inn with an extensive choice of drinks.
1 🛏 ↻ P ≠ 🄴

KÖLN (COLOGNE): *Rheinblick garni* €€ 27
Uferstr. 20, 50996 Köln-Rodenkirchen. **Map** B4. [(0221) 340 91 40.
FAX (0221) 39 21 39.
The hotel is attractively located overlooking the Rhine. Rooms are
attractively furnished and breakfast is served in the winter garden, which
offers a beautiful view of the river. 1 🛏 P 🍴 🄴

KÖLN (COLOGNE): *Im Wasserturm* €€€€ 88
Kaygasse 2, 50676. **Map** B4. [(0221) 200 80.
FAX (0221) 200 88 88. W www.hotel-im-wasserturm.de
Housed in a 19th-century former water tower, this hotel has an excellent
location in a park, just a few minutes from the old town. The wonderful
interiors were designed by a well-known Parisian artist and architect.
Sophisticated service and a panoramic restaurant on the 11th floor add to
guests' enjoyment of their stay here. 1 🛏 ≠ 🄴 ↻ P 🄴

KÖLN (COLOGNE): *Hyatt Regency* €€€€€ 305
Kennedy-Ufer 2a, 50679. **Map** B4. [(0221) 828 12 34.
FAX (0221) 828 13 70. W www.cologne.regency.hyatt.com
With beautiful greenery and fountains gracing even the entrance hall, this
hotel has the feel of a botanical garden. 1 🛏 ≠ 🄴 P 🍴 🄴

LEMGO: *Im Borke* € 37
Salzufler Str. 132, 32657 Lemgo-Kirchheide. **Map** C3. [(05266) 16 91.
FAX (05266) 12 31. W www.hotel-im-borke.de
Pleasant family hotel set in a garden. Guests can spend their time pleasantly
in the stylish restaurant, bowling alley or sauna. 1 🛏 ↻ 🄴 P 🄴

For key to symbols *see back flap*

Price categories for a twin room with bathroom or shower, and including breakfast, service and tax:

€ up to €77
€€ €78–€128
€€€ €129–€179
€€€€ €180–€230
€€€€€ over €230

RESTAURANT
The hotel has a restaurant that is open to non-residents as well as to hotel guests.

GARDEN OR TERRACE
The hotel is set in a garden or has an outside terrace or courtyard, often with tables for eating outside.

SWIMMING POOL
The hotel has a swimming pool.

AIR CONDITIONING
All rooms are air-conditioned.

	NUMBER OF ROOMS	RESTAURANT	GARDEN OR TERRACE	SWIMMING POOL	AIR CONDITIONING
MÜNSTER: *Romantik Hotel Hof zur Linde* €€€ Handorfer Werseufer 1, 48157 Münster-Handorf. **Map** B3. ☎ *(0251) 327 50.* FAX *(0251) 32 82 09.* W www.hof-zur-linde.de This hotel was converted from a former 17th-century farm. The restaurant has an open fireplace and antique furniture. 1 ⟰ 🔓 ⟲ 🔄 P 🍴 ▣	48	●	▪		
MÜNSTER: *Schloss Wilkinghege* €€€€ Steinfurter Str. 374, 48159 Münster-Ausserhalb. **Map** B3. ☎ *(0251) 21 30 45.* FAX *(0251) 21 28 98.* W www.schloss-wilkinghege.de Modern, elegantly furnished rooms within the 16th-century walls. The highly recommended restaurant specializes in regional dishes. Other features include a knights' hall and golf course. 1 ⟲ P 🔓 ▣	35	●	▪		
SIEGEN: *Best Western Parkhotel Siegen* €€ Koblenzer Str. 135, 57072. **Map** B4. ☎ *(0271) 338 10.* FAX *(0271) 338 14 50.* W www.parkhotel-siegen.bestwestern.de This modern hotel has spacious rooms and elegantly furnished suites as well as several fully equipped conference halls. 1 ⟲ 🔄 P ⟰ 🔓 ▣	88	●	▪		
WINTERBERG: *Steymann* € Schneilstr. 4, 59955. **Map** C4. ☎ *(02981) 70 05.* FAX *(02981) 36 19.* W www.hotel-steymann.de A spa hotel, which also features a sauna and solarium. The restaurant offers various specialist dishes, at reasonable prices. 1 ⟲ 🔄 P ▣	60	●	▪	●	
WUPPERTAL: *Lindner Golfhotel Juliana* €€€ Mollenkotten 195, 42279. **Map** B4. ☎ *(0202) 647 50.* FAX *(0202) 647 57 71.* W www.lindner.de Comfortably furnished suites and rooms as well as conference halls and a swimming pool. 1 ⟲ 🔄 P ⟰ 🔓 ▣	132	●	▪	●	
LOWER SAXONY, HAMBURG AND BREMEN					
BRAUNSCHWEIG (BRUNSWICK): *Ritter St. Georg* €€€ Alte Knochenhauerstr. 13, 38100. **Map** D3. ☎ *(0531) 130 30.* FAX *(0531) 130 38.* W www.ritter-st-georg-bs.de This hotel occupies a recently restored 500-year-old building. Rooms are comfortable and there is an atmospheric, rustic restaurant. ⟲ 1 🔓 ▣	22	●			
BREMEN: *Lichtsinn* €€ Rembertistr. 11, 28203. **Map** C2. ☎ *(0421) 36 80 70.* FAX *(0421) 32 72 87.* W www.hotel-lichtsinn.de Ten suites with small kitchens as well as individual rooms are available in this family-run hotel in the city centre. 1 ⟲ 🔄 🔓 ⟰ P ▣	35				
BREMEN: *Tulip Inn Schaper-Siedenburg* €€ Bahnhofstr. 8, 28195. **Map** C2. ☎ *(0421) 308 70.* FAX *(0421) 30 87 88.* W www.schaper-siedenburg.de This well-known, long-established hotel is conveniently located near the main railway station. 1 ⟲ 🔄 ⟰ ▣	88				
BREMEN: *Best Western Zur Post* €€€ Bahnhofsplatz 11, 28195. **Map** C2. ☎ *(0421) 305 90.* FAX *(0421) 305 95 91.* W www.bestwestern.de On the sixth floor of this super deluxe establishment, the L'Orchidée restaurant offers panoramic views of the city. 1 ⟲ 🔄 P ⟰ 🔓 ▣	177	●	▪	●	
BREMEN: *Park Hotel* €€€€€ Im Bürgerpark, 28209. **Map** C2. ☎ *(0421) 340 80.* FAX *(0421) 340 86 02.* W www.park-hotel-bremen.de A luxurious hotel, renowned for its family atmosphere, excellent service, comfortable rooms and well-equipped conference halls. The restaurant specializes in fish, poultry and game dishes. 1 ⟲ 🔄 P 🍴 🔓 ▣	150	●	▪	●	▪

BÜCKEBURG: *Grosse Klus* €€ 25
Am Klusbrink 19, 31675. **Map** C3. ((05722) 951 20. FAX (05722) 95 12 50. "
W www.klus.de
This hotel occupies two buildings, one dating from the 18th century.
Rooms are furnished in a modern manner and the cuisine includes
regional and classical dishes. Bicycles can be hired.
1 �

CELLE: *Best Western Celler Hof* €€ 47
Stechbahn 11, 29221. **Map** C3. ((05141) 91 19 60. FAX (05141) 911 96 44.
W www.residenzhotels.de
Very high standard hotel with wonderful service. Facilities include a gym,
sauna and nearby golf course. 1 �

CLOPPENBURG: *Park Hotel* €€ 51
Burgstr. 8, 49661. **Map** B2. ((04471) 66 14. FAX (04471) 66 17.
W www.parkhotel.cloppenburg.de
Recently built hotel, with comfortably furnished rooms and a pleasant
location in a park, close to the civic hall. Facilities for playing golf and
skittles are available. 1 �

DUDERSTADT: *Zum Löwen* €€€ 42
Marktstr. 30, 37115. **Map** D4. ((05527) 30 72. FAX (05527) 726 30.
W www.hotelzumloewen.de
Housed in a 16th-century building with a Neo-Classical façade, this hotel
has been modernized to a very high standard. It features pleasant rooms
and a number of dining venues. 1 �

EINBECK: *Der Schwan* €€ 12
Tiedexerstr. 1, 37574. **Map** C3. ((05561) 46 09. FAX (05561) 723 66.
This hotel is based in an Art Nouveau building with intimate rooms.
The elegant restaurant serves both classical and light cuisine.
1 �

GOSLAR: *Der Achtermann* €€€ 152
Rosentorstr. 20, 38640. **Map** D3. ((05321) 700 00. FAX (05321) 700 09 99.
W www.der-achtermann.de
Rooms in this hotel are furnished in a modern manner, while the
Altdeutsche Stuben restaurant specializes in typical German cooking.
1 🚏

GOSLAR: *Treff Hotel Das Brusttuch* €€€ 13
Hoher Weg 1, 38640. **Map** D3. ((05321) 346 00. FAX (05321) 34 60 99.
A well-maintained late Gothic building has been converted into this
modern hotel. 1 🚏

GÖTTINGEN: *Romantik-Hotel Gebhard* €€€ 63
Goetheallee 22, 37073. **Map** C4. ((0551) 496 80. FAX (0551) 496 81 10.
W www.romantikhotels.com/goettingen
Conveniently located opposite the railway station, this long-established
hotel is housed in a historic building. Facilities include an elegant
restaurant, hotel bar and several function rooms.
1 🚏

HAMBURG: *Best Western Raphael Hotel Altona* €€ 39
Präsident-Krahn-Str. 13, 22765. **Map** C2. ((040) 38 02 40. FAX (040) 38 02 44 44.
W www.altona.bestwestern.de
This hotel is conveniently located between the port and the business
centre, near the Altona railway station. Facilities include modern rooms
with safes and double-glazed windows, breakfast buffet and bar.
1 🚏

HAMBURG: *Hafen Hamburg* €€ 230
Seewartenstr. 9, 20459. **Map** C2. ((040) 31 11 30. FAX (040) 31 11 37 55.
W www.hotel-hamburg.de
Formerly a mariner's house, this building has been extended and
refurbished as a hotel with large comfortable rooms. From the restaurant
a panoramic view of the port can be enjoyed. 1 🚏

HAMBURG: *Europäischer Hof* €€€ 320
Kirchenallee 45, 20099. **Map** C2. ((040) 24 82 48. FAX (040) 24 82 47 99.
W www.europaeischer-hof.de
Modern, luxurious interiors, excellent service, a good restaurant and a
hotel bar with music. The hotel also issues guests with a card entitling
them to three days' free travel by public transport. 1 🚏

For key to symbols *see back flap*

Price categories for a twin room with bathroom or shower, and including breakfast, service and tax:

€ up to €77
€€ €78–€128
€€€ €129–€179
€€€€ €180–€230
€€€€€ over €230

RESTAURANT
The hotel has a restaurant that is open to non-residents as well as to hotel guests.
GARDEN OR TERRACE
The hotel is set in a garden or has an outside terrace or courtyard, often with tables for eating outside.
SWIMMING POOL
The hotel has a swimming pool.
AIR CONDITIONING
All rooms are air-conditioned.

	NUMBER OF ROOMS	RESTAURANT	GARDEN OR TERRACE	SWIMMING POOL	AIR CONDITIONING
HAMBURG: *Kempinski Hotel Atlantic Hamburg* €€€€€ An der Alster 72, 20099. Map C2. 【 (040) 288 80. FAX (040) 24 71 29. W www.kempinski.atlantic.de This long-established hotel has beautifully furnished rooms and excellent service. The restaurant serves sophisticated dishes. 1 ⚟ ⬆ P ⚡ 🔒 ⬛	252	●	■	●	■
HAMBURG: *Vier Jahreszeiten* €€€€€€ Neuer Jungfernstieg 9–14, 20354. Map C2. 【 (040) 349 40. FAX (040) 34 94 26 01. W www.raffles-hvj.de A luxury-class hotel with stylized interiors, decorated with precious woods, valuable rugs and antiques. The restaurant, well-stocked wine bar and excellent patisserie are very popular. 1 ⚟ ⬆ P ⚡ 🔒 ⬛	156	●	■		■
HANNOVER: *Best Western Parkhotel Kronsberg* €€€ Gut Kronsberg 1. 18, 30539. Map C3. 【 (0511) 874 00. FAX (0511) 86 71 12. W www.kronsberg.bestwestern.de Situated opposite the Hannover trade fair area, this modern hotel is surrounded by beautiful greenery. 1 ⚟ ⬆ P ⬛ ⚡ 🔒 ⬛	200	●	■	●	
HANNOVER: *Hotel Georgenhof* €€€ Herrenhäuser Kirchweg 20, 30167. Map C3. 【 (0511) 70 22 44. FAX (0511) 70 85 59. W www.hotelgeorgenhof.de Set in a park, this hotel is near the city centre. The restaurant is one of the best in the country, and there is a wide choice of wines. 1 ⚟ P 🔒 ⬛	14	●	■		
HANNOVER: *Grand Hotel Mussmann garni* €€€€ Ernst-August-Platz 7, 30159. Map C3. 【 (0511) 365 60. FAX (0511) 365 61 45. W www.grandhotel.de Well-maintained hotel in the city centre, opposite the railway station. Comfortable rooms and excellent service. 1 ⚟ ⬆ P ⚡ 🔒 ⬛	140				
HILDESHEIM: *Parkhotel Berghölzchen* €€ Am Berghölzchen 1, 31139. Map C3. 【 (05121) 97 90. FAX (05121) 97 94 00. W www.berghoelzchen.de Beautifully located within a landscaped park, this hotel has traditions dating back to the 18th century. 1 ⚟ ⬆ P ⚡ 🔒 ⬛	80	●	■		
KÖNIGSLUTTER: *Avalon Hotelpark Königshof* €€ Braunschweigerstr. 21A, 38154. Map D3. 【 (05353) 50 30. FAX (05353) 50 32 44. W www.avalon-hotels.com Large hotel complex with comfortably furnished rooms and excellent sports facilities. Other features include several restaurants, café, beer garden and various banqueting halls. 1 ⚟ ⬆ ⚡ 🔒 P ⬛	174	●	■	●	
LÜNEBURG: *Bremer Hof* €€ Lüner Str. 12, 21335. Map D2. 【 (04131) 22 40. FAX (04131) 22 42 24. W www.bremer-hof.de This hotel has traditions going back to the 16th century. Features include intimate rooms and regional cuisine. 1 ⚟ ⬆ P ⬛	53	●			
OLDENBURG: *Heide* €€ Melkbrink 49–51, 26121. Map B2. 【 (0441) 80 40. FAX (0441) 88 40 60. Occupying a modern building with every comfort, this hotel has well-equipped conference rooms and recreational areas. Two restaurants serve local specialities. 1 ⚟ ⬆ ⚡ 🔒 P ⬛	93	●	■	●	
OSNABRÜCK: *Walhalla* €€ Bierstr. 24, 49074. Map B3. 【 (0541) 349 10. FAX (0541) 349 11 44. W www.hotel-walhalla.de This long-established hotel, with an elegant restaurant, has recently been modernized. Guests can enjoy the sauna and solarium, and there is a golf course available nearby. 1 ⚟ ⬆ P ⚡ 🔒 ⬛	66	●			

STADTHAGEN: *Gerber Hotel La Tannerie* €€ 29
Echternstr. 14, 31655. **Map** C3. **[** (05721) 98 60. **FAX** (05721) 986 66.
W www.gerber-hotel.de
Conveniently located in the city centre, this hotel has pleasant,
individually decorated rooms. An excellent breakfast buffet is served.
① ↻ P ⇆ 🛏 🖼

WOLFENBÜTTEL: *Parkhotel Altes Kaffeehaus* €€ 75
Harztorwall 18, 38300. **Map** D3. **[** (05331) 88 80. **FAX** (05331) 88 81 00.
W www.parkhotel-wolfenbuettel.de
A recently modernized hotel housed in a historic building. The restaurant
menu includes a variety of international dishes. ① 🛏 ↻ P ⇆ 🎿 🍽 🖼

WOLFSBURG: *Brackstedter Mühle* €€ 50
Zum Kühlen Grunde 2, 38448 Wolfsburg-Brackstedt. **Map** D3. **[** (05366) 900.
FAX (05366) 90 50. **W** www.brackstedter-muehle.de
This comfortable hotel is located in a converted 17th-century building
with a water mill. The restaurant serves regional cuisine as well as
exquisitely innovative dishes. ① 🛏 ⇆ 🖼

SCHLESWIG-HOLSTEIN

BAD MALENTE: *Gartenhotel Weisser Hof* €€ 18
Vossstr. 45, 23714. **Map** D1. **[** (04523) 992 50. **FAX** (04523) 68 99.
This hotel is beautifully sited amid greenery. The stylishly furnished
restaurant has been run by the same family for many years. Among its
specialities are fish and game dishes. ① 🛏 ⇆ 🎿 🖼

FLENSBURG: *Am Wasserturm* €€ 36
Blasberg 13, 24943 Flensburg-Mürwik. **Map** C1. **[** (0461) 315 06 00.
FAX (0461) 31 22 87. **W** www.hotel-restaurant-am-wasserturm.de
Located in a tranquil spot, this hotel has rooms furnished in a modern
style. There is a café with a terrace. ① 🛏 P ⇆ 🖼

HELGOLAND: *Atoll* €€€ 50
Lung Wai, 27498. **Map** B1. **[** (04725) 80 00. **FAX** (04725) 80 04 44.
W www.atoll.de
This super-modern hotel is constructed from glass and chrome, but some
of the rooms are furnished in a traditional manner. The restaurant serves
excellent cuisine, particularly fish and crab dishes. ① 🛏 🎿 ⇆ 🖼

KIEL: *Berliner Hof garni* €€ 103
Ringstr. 2–6, 24103. **Map** C1. **[** (0431) 663 40. **FAX** (0431) 663 43 45.
W www.berlinerhof-kiel.de
Convenient located in the city centre near the railway station. Rooms are
attractively decorated and a buffet breakfast is served. ① 🛏 ↻ P ⇆ 🖼

KIEL: *Kieler Yacht-Club* €€€ 58
Hindenburgufer 70, 24105. **Map** C1. **[** (0431) 881 30. **FAX** (0431) 881 34 44.
W www.yachtclub.bestwestern.de
A hotel with elegantly furnished, modernized rooms, offering beautiful
views of the Baltic and Kiel fjord. The restaurant serves various regional
and international specialities and the bar is popular with yachtsmen.
① 🛏 ↻ ⇆ 🎿 🖼

LÜBECK: *Alter Speicher garni* €€ 45
Beckergrube 91–93, 23552. **Map** D2. **[** (0451) 710 45.
FAX (0451) 70 48 04. **W** www.hotel-alter-speicher.de
Built in the style of a traditional granary, this hotel has comfortably furnished
rooms and a sauna and solarium for the benefit of guests. ① 🛏 ↻ ⇆ 🎿 🖼

LÜBECK: *Kaiserhof garni* €€ 60
Kronsforder Allee 11–13, 23560. **Map** D2. **[** (0451) 70 33 01.
FAX (0451) 79 50 83. **W** www.kaiserhof-luebeck.de
A modern hotel has been created within two beautiful bourgeois houses,
which have been restored and linked together. All the rooms are
exquisitely furnished and the hotel has a terrace. ① 🛏 ↻ P 🍽 🖼

LÜBECK: *Radisson SAS Senator Hotel Lübeck* €€€ 224
Willy-Brandt-Allee 6, 23554. **Map** D2. **[** (0451) 14 20. **FAX** (0451) 142 22 22.
W www.senator-hotel.de
Beautifully located on the river Trave, this hotel has been harmoniously
integrated with the surrounding architecture. The hotel houses a well-
known restaurant, rustic wine bar and bar. ① 🛏 ↻ P 🍽 ⇆ 🎿 🖼

For key to symbols *see back flap*

Price categories for a twin room with bathroom or shower, and including breakfast, service and tax: € up to €77 €€ €78–€128 €€€ €129–€179 €€€€ €180–€230 €€€€€ over €230	RESTAURANT The hotel has a restaurant that is open to non-residents as well as to hotel guests. GARDEN OR TERRACE The hotel is set in a garden or has an outside terrace or courtyard, often with tables for eating outside. SWIMMING POOL The hotel has a swimming pool. AIR CONDITIONING All rooms are air-conditioned.	NUMBER OF ROOMS	RESTAURANT	GARDEN OR TERRACE	SWIMMING POOL	AIR CONDITIONING

OEVERSEE: *Romantik Hotel Historischer Krug* € € — 50 — ● ■ ●
Grazer Platz 1, 24988. **Map** C1. (*(04630) 94 00.* FAX *(04630) 780.*
W www.romantikhotels.com
Located 9 km (5 miles) south of Flensburg, this hotel dates back to the 16th century; it has been run by the same family for almost 200 years. There is a good restaurant, a café with a terrace, hotel bar and garden.
1 🛏 P 🏊 🔒 🍴

RATZEBURG: *Der Seehof* € € — 45 — ● ■
Lüneburger Damm 1–3, 23909. **Map** D2. (*(04541) 86 01 00.*
FAX *(04541) 86 01 02.* W www.derseehof.de
A comfortable hotel perched on pillars above the lake. As well as tastefully furnished rooms and a number of cafés and restaurants, the hotel has its own jetty and a beach. 1 🛏 🔄 P 🍴

SCHLESWIG: *Waldschlösschen* € € — 117 — ● ■
Kolonnenweg 152, 24837. **Map** C1. (*(04621) 38 30.* FAX *(04621) 38 31 05.*
W www.hotel-waldschloesschen.de
Standing on the edge of the forest, this hotel has rooms furnished in a variety of styles. There are good facilities for taking part in sporting activities and bicycles can be hired. 1 🛏 🔄 P 🏊 🔒 🍴

SYLT: *Miramar* € € € — 93 — ● ■ ●
Friedrichstr. 43, 25980 Westerland. **Map** B1. (*(04651) 85 50.* FAX *(04651) 85 52 22.*
W www.miramar.de
Service is impeccable in this hotel by the sea. Fine views can be enjoyed from the terrace. 1 🛏 🔄 P 🔒 📺 🍴

SYLT: *Benen-Diken-Hof* € € € € — 40 — ● ■ ●
Süderstr. 3, 25980 Keitum. **Map** B1. (*(04651) 938 30.* FAX *(04651) 9383 183.*
W www.benen-diken-hof.de
A charming hotel in a quiet area. Rooms are comfortable, service is courteous and an abundant breakfast buffet is provided. There is a golf course nearby. 1 🛏 P 🍴

MECKLENBURG-LOWER POMERANIA

ANKLAM: *Hotel Friedrich-Franz Palais* € — 18
Demminer Str. 5, 17389. **Map** E2. (*(03971) 83 31 36.* FAX *(03971) 83 31 37.*
Recently built hotel with pleasant rooms and a hall, in which a hearty breakfast is served. 1 🛏 P 🍴

BAD DOBERAN: *Romantikhotel Bad Doberan* € € — 45 — ● ■
August-bebel-str. 2, 18209. **Map** D1. (*(038203) 630 36.* FAX *(038203) 621 26.*
W www.romantikhotels.com
One of the oldest hotels on the Baltic sea and one of the finest in Germany. An excellent restaurant serves Mecklenburg specialities.
1 🛏 🔄 P 🍴

DARGUN: *Kloster-Schänke* € € — 27 — ● ■
Am Klosterdamm, 17159. **Map** E2. (*(039959) 25 20.* FAX *(039959) 252 28.*
This hotel is situated in a quiet, tranquil spot, on the edge of the forest and near the lake. Some of the pleasant rooms have balconies with a view of the lake. Other features include a lounge with an open fireplace and a beer garden. The restaurant serves regional cuisine.
1 🛏 🍴

GREIFSWALD: *Parkhotel Greifswald* € € — 71 — ■
Pappelallee 1, 17489. **Map** E1. (*(03834) 87 40.* FAX *(03834) 87 45 55.*
W parkhotel.greifswald.de
Set amidst greenery, this city-centre hotel has well-furnished rooms. The breakfast room serves regional cuisine and a good breakfast buffet.
1 🛏 🔄 P 🏊 🔒 🍴

GÜSTROW: *Am Güstrower Schloss*   €€   47
Schlossberg 1, 18273. **Map** D2. 【 *(03843) 76 70.*
FAX *(03843) 76 71 00.* W www.schlosshotel-guestrow.de
This modern hotel is housed within a former prison building opposite the
castle. 1 🛏 🔁 P 🍴 🛗 ⚡ 🌐

NEUBRANDENBURG: *Landhotel Broda*   €   13
Oelmühlenstr. 29, 17033. **Map** E2. 【 *(0395) 56 91 70.*
FAX *(0395) 569 17 29.* W www.landhotel-broda.de
A new hotel situated in a tranquil spot on the edge of the Teulensee.
Rooms are furnished in a comfortable, attractive manner. Bicycles can be
hired. 1 🛏 🔁 P 🌐

ROSTOCK: *Courtyard by Marriott*   €€   150
Kröpeliner/Schwaansche Str. 6, 18055. **Map** D1. 【 *(0381) 497.00.*
FAX *(0381) 497 07 00.* W www.courtyard.com
Rooms are comfortable in this hotel close to the city centre and the old
harbour. There is a good restaurant and bar. 1 🛏 🔁 P ⚡ 🛗 🌐

ROSTOCK: *Godewind*   €€   59
Warnemünder Str. 5, 18146 Rostock-Markgrafenheide. **Map** D1. 【 *(0381) 60 95 70.*
FAX *(0381) 60 95 71 11.* W www.hotel-godewind.de
Recently opened hotel with comfortable rooms, close to the Baltic Sea.
1 🛏 🔁 P ⚡ 🛗 🍴 🌐

RÜGEN: *Kurhotel Sassnitz*   €€   83
Hauptstr. 1, 18546 Sassnitz. **Map** E1. 【 *(038392) 530.* FAX *(038392) 533 33.*
W www.ruegen-hotel.de
This elegant spa hotel is housed in a former mariner's house, which has
recently been restored. Rooms are spacious and regional cuisine is
served. 1 🛏 🔁 🍴 ⚡ 🌐

RÜGEN: *Landhotel Herrenhaus*   €€   20
Dorfstr. 6, 18556 Bohlendorf bei Wiek. **Map** E1. 【 *(038391) 770.* FAX *(038391) 702 80.*
This family-run hotel is housed in what was once an aristocratic
residence. Facilities include a pleasant restaurant and a lounge with an
open fireplace. 1 🛏 P ⚡ 🌐

SCHWERIN: *Ramada Hotel Schwerin*   €€   78
Am Grünen Tal, 19063 Schwerin-Grosser Dreesch. **Map** D2.
【 *(0385) 399 20.* FAX *(0385) 399 21 88.* W www.ramadahotels.com
This hotel, with sumptuously furnished rooms and a modern recreational
centre, belongs to the Best Western hotel group. The elegant Primavera
restaurant serves Italian delicacies. 1 🛏 🔁 P 🍴 ⚡ 🛗 🌐

SCHWERIN: *Ringhotel Arte*   €€   40
Dorfstr. 6, 19061 Schwerin. **Map** D2. 【 *(0385) 634 50.*
FAX *(0385) 634 51 00.* W www.ringhotel-arte.de
Housed within a former country inn dating from the 19th century, this
recently modernized hotel has retained many interesting features.
Seasonal cuisine and an abundant breakfast buffet are served.
1 🛏 🔁 P ⚡ 🛗 🌐

STRALSUND: *Royal Hotel am Bahnhof*   €€   60
Tribseer Damm 4, 18437. **Map** E1. 【 *(03831) 29 52 68.*
FAX *(03831) 296 50.* W www.royal-hotel.de
An excellent starting point for seeing Stralsund on foot, this hotel has a
beautiful Art Nouveau façade. The restaurant serves both international
and regional cuisine. 1 🛏 🔁 P ⚡ 🍴 🌐

USEDOM: *Residenz Waldoase*   €€   42
Dünenstr.1, 17419 Ahlbeck. **Map** E2. 【 *(038378) 500.*
FAX *(038378) 502 99.* W www.schoener-inseln.de
This charmingly located modern hotel is based in a refurbished former
holiday home. Also available are 26 self-catering bungalows that are
serviced by the hotel. Within the hotel grounds there are several dining
venues, offering interesting dishes throughout the day.
1 🛏 🔁 P ⚡ 🛗 🌐

WISMAR: *Altes Brauhaus*   €   14
Lübschestr. 37, 23966. **Map** D2. 【 *(03841) 28 32 23.*
FAX *(03841) 28 32 23.*
Housed within a 16th-century building, this recently restored hotel has
pleasantly furnished rooms. 1 🛏 🌐

For key to symbols *see back flap*

WHERE TO EAT

The crest of the Forsthaus Paulsborn restaurant in Berlin

ERMAN CUISINE does not enjoy the same reputation as that of, say, France, but nevertheless you can eat very well here. There are many establishments that specialize in regional cuisine, which, although somewhat heavy, is always very appetizing. It is also easy to find good restaurants serving ethnic cuisine, such as Italian, Greek, Indian, Chinese, Thai or Turkish. In the past few years, some fine restaurants have opened. Run by renowned master chefs, they serve excellent cuisine of the very highest European standards.

From the many thousands of restaurants throughout Germany, we have chosen the finest for inclusion in this guidebook, with a view to catering for a variety of budgets. Detailed information on the selected restaurants can be found on pp504–527.

TYPES OF RESTAURANTS

THE TERM *Restaurant* is used to define both restaurants offering exquisite cuisine and excellent service, at steep prices, and popular local establishments with affordable prices. The word *Gasthaus* usually indicates a traditional style of inn that specializes in straightforward regional cuisine. In many towns, there is a *Ratskeller* established in the cellar of the town hall. These are usually good, not overly expensive restaurants serving dishes that represent the regional cuisine. They usually have atmospheric, stylized interiors that are well adapted to the vaulted, dark spaces of the historic cellars. A *Weinstube* is a wine bar, where good, usually local, wine is served. Often decent

food is also available here. A *Bierstube* is similar in style, except that the beverage is beer. The term *Café* has a variety of connotations in Germany. This is a place that serves an excellent breakfast with various options in the mornings, while from noon they offer lunch dishes. The choice is usually somewhat heavy, though varied. In addition, at any time of the day and evening, customers can have a coffee here, eat some ice cream or a cake, drink beer or some other alcoholic beverage. In the evenings there is often music.

A typical venue in which you can spend an evening is a *Kneipe*. In terms of its atmosphere, this is somewhat reminiscent of an English pub. Patrons generally come here to have a drink, but there are usually a few hot dishes on offer to appease their hunger. Self-service venues offering snacks are known as *Imbiss*. These can have a very varied character, from a stall serving baked sausages and cans of drink, to elegant kiosks offering a large choice of salads and fast food. These kiosks are often run by immigrants. In fact in most large German towns there are numerous kiosks serving Arabic, Turkish, Chinese and American food. If shoppers feel the need for a snack, they might like to take advantage of the restaurant or cafeteria facilities in department stores. These are usually self-service establishments known as *Stehcafé*, which means "Stand Up Café".

Entrance to a *Gasthaus* near the cathedral in Cologne

WHAT AND WHEN TO EAT

BREAKFAST IS USUALLY a hearty affair with various types of bread accompanied by cheese, sausages and marmalade. On Sundays brunch is served in most places until 2pm: this is a combination of breakfast and lunch, in the form of a Swedish buffet. During the lunch period (between noon and 2pm) most establishments serve an excellent salad or a bowl of filling soup, while many restaurants offer a special fixed-price menu that is significantly cheaper than in the evenings. Restaurants start to fill up in the evenings between 6 and 7pm, although dinner is most usually eaten after 8pm.

Altdeutsche Weinstube in Dörrenbach

Wine festival in Alter Hof in Freiburg im Breisgau

OPENING HOURS

CAFÉS GENERALLY open from 9am, while restaurants are open from noon, sometimes with a break from 3 to 6pm. The most expensive places do not open until dinner time and are frequently closed for one day during the week.

A street stall serving snacks of freshly cooked sausages

MENU

IN MOST GOOD restaurants the menu is written in German and English, and sometimes also in French. In cafés and less expensive restaurants, the menu may be handwritten, in which case the staff may be able to help with a translation. In many of the less expensive places there is, in addition to the regular menu, a daily menu with attractive seasonal dishes. Sometimes the chef's special offers are written on a blackboard. In all restaurants and cafés, a menu showing prices will be displayed outside the establishment.

RESERVATIONS

MAKING A PRIOR reservation is essential in all the best restaurants while in most good and medium standard restaurants it is advisable to do so, particularly on a Friday or Saturday night. If you have not made a reservation, try one of the popular restaurant complexes where you can usually get a table.

PRICES AND TIPS

THE COST OF restaurant meals in Germany is unusually diverse depending on location. A three-course meal without alcohol can be found for around €10–13, but in the centre of larger cities a minimum of €18–22 would be more usual. In a luxury restaurant, the bill for a six-course meal, without drinks, can cost in excess of €76. The price of alcoholic drinks also varies, but beer is the cheapest drink.

Prices include service and tax, but it is usual to leave a tip – generally around 10 per cent of the total bill. When paying for a meal by credit card, the tip can be added to the total. Restaurants and cafés that accept credit cards usually display the logos of acceptable cards near the entrance. Before ordering, it is best to find out whether a minimum charge is applied to customers who wish to pay their bill by credit card.

DRESS CODE

GERMANS USUALLY prefer to dress comfortably, casually and practically, preferring a sporty style to more formal attire. When going out in the evenings, many women – regardless of their age – wear trousers and comfortable low-heeled shoes, though some prefer elegant dresses. Men generally wear jackets and ties only during office hours.

Going to a restaurant does not require any particular preparation unless you wish to go to a luxurious, gourmet restaurant, for which you will probably have to book up to two months in advance.

Interior of the Bamberger Reiter restaurant in Berlin

CHILDREN

RESTAURANTS USUALLY provide high chairs for toddlers and, particularly during the lunch period, there will be light dishes for children – or you can order small portions.

VEGETARIANS

INCREASINGLY, GERMANS are turning to vegetarianism, although the number of vegetarian restaurants is still limited. However, a few vegetarian dishes can usually be found on most menus. If necessary, choose a restaurant that serves a national cuisine in which there is no shortage of vegetarian dishes – for example Indian or Thai.

DISABLED VISITORS

IF A TABLE WITH wheelchair access is required, it is best to specify this when making the reservation. At the same time, check whether toilets are easily accessible.

Picnicking – a popular form of relaxation in Germany

What to Eat

Bavarian dessert

GERMAN CUISINE IS very varied, good value and of a generally high standard. In the north, delicious fish dishes can be found while, throughout the country, wonderful, hearty meat dishes in thick sauces are served. Germany is renowned not just for sausages *(Wurst)* but also for excellently prepared pork knuckle, roast beef and pork, poultry dishes, as well as various types of dumpling, delicious bread and cakes.

Matjestopf
Young, salted herrings with onion and cream are often served with jacket potatoes.

Reibekuchen
Otherwise known as Kartoffelpuffer, *these potato pancakes are served either savoury or sweet.*

Maultaschen
These square dumplings with a savoury (usually meat) filling are typical of Schwabian cuisine.

Sweet mustard

Tomato sauce

Weisswurst (white sausage)

A beer pretzel

Pieces of meat

Leek

Potatoes

String beans

Sliced carrots

Pichelsteiner
This is a typical Eintopf, *a one-pot dish that replaces soup and the main course. It comprises meat, potatoes and various vegetables stewed in an aromatic sauce.*

Kartoffelsalat
This delicious potato salad is flavoured with piquant marinated cucumbers, onion and mayonnaise.

Kartoffelsuppe
Flavoured with marjoram, this creamy potato soup is served with slices of sausage.

Linsensuppe
When served with sausages, this lentil soup provides a satisfying lunch.

Leberknödelsuppe
A speciality of Bavaria, this clear consommé is served with liver dumplings.

Oven-baked
goose with
crunchy skin

Stuffing of
chestnuts
and diced
apple

Martinsgans
Traditionally served on St Martin's Day (November 11, see p38), the goose is stuffed with chestnuts and apples before being roasted in the oven.

Eisbein mit Erbspüree
A dish of baked pork knuckle is served with puréed peas and cabbage cooked in champagne.

Sweet and sour
sauce

Potato
dumplings

Apple
puree

Sliced roast
meat

Kartoffelklösse
Often prepared from a mixture of raw and cooked potatoes, dumplings may accompany main courses.

Sauerbraten mit Kartoffelklössen und Apfelmus
Roast beef marinated in vinegar is served here with apple purée and dumplings prepared from cooked potatoes.

Karpfen
Carp, a popular freshwater fish, is prepared in different ways in different parts of the country. Here it is served with a smooth tomato sauce.

KAFFEE UND KUCHEN
A mouth-watering selection of cakes is generally offered with afternoon coffee. Germany is renowned for its light fruit tarts, apple charlottes, cheesecake and plum or cherry cakes.

Schwartenbraten
Roast pork is here served with sauerkraut and bread dumplings.

This almond-
flavoured
gingerbead
is known as
Weisse
Nürnberger
Lebkuchen

Yeast
doughnuts,
deep-fried
in fat, are
known as
Berliners

Rote Grütze
A thick, jellied dessert made from fruit juice and wine, with the addition of fruit.

Schwarzwälder Kirschtorte
Chocolate gateau filled with cherries and cream is a speciality of the Black Forest.

What to Drink

THROUGHOUT GERMANY, beer is undoubtedly the most popular drink, and each region has its own beer-brewing traditions. However, the country is also renowned for excellent wines, which are produced in the south. The most well known are Mosel and Rhine wines, although these are not necessarily better than Franconian wines. Stronger spirits and liqueurs are also available, as are some very pleasant non-alcoholic cold drinks.

Shop in Eberbach stocked with wine from the adjoining monastery

HOT DRINKS

Herbal infusions include mint and camomile tea

IN GERMAN ESTABLISHMENTS there is no difficulty in getting a cup of tea *(Tee)*, but don't be surprised if the waiter asks whether you mean mint tea *(Pfefferminztee)* or camomile *(Kamillentee)*, since herbal infusions are popular in Germany. To be sure of being served Indian tea, it is advisable to specify *Schwarztee* when placing the order.

Coffee is another popular drink. In general, filter coffee, which is fairly mild, is served. For customers who prefer a stronger coffee, it is best to order an espresso.

NON-ALCOHOLIC COLD DRINKS

VARIOUS TYPES OF carbonated drinks and fruit juices – ubiquitous throughout Europe and the US – are popular, and an extensive choice is available in every café and restaurant in Germany. A refreshing non-alcoholic drink is *Apfel-Schorle*, which is apple juice mixed with equal proportions of sparkling mineral water. (The alcoholic version is *Wein-Schorle*, which is wine mixed with mineral water.) Another popular non-alcoholic drink is *Spezi*, which is a mixture of cola and Fanta.

Although tap water is generally safe to drink, it is not usually served with restaurant meals. To order a bottle of mineral water, ask for *Mineralwasser*, adding the phrase "*ohne gas*" if still water is preferred.

Apfel-Schorle

Limonade (Lemonade)

Mineralwasser (Mineral water)

SPIRITS AND LIQUEURS

Bitter-sweet spirit, Jägermeister

Herbal/root-flavour spirit, Kümmerling

STRONG SPIRITS ARE often drunk after heavy meals, particularly pork dishes. It is best to order one of the popular drinks distilled from rye or wheat, such as *Doppel Korn*. Brandy (known as *Weinbrand*) is also produced in Germany. Liqueurs are also popular, as is a spirit flavoured with herbs and roots (known as bitters). Among the most popular are *Kümmerling* and *Jägermeister* while, in Berlin, *Kaulzdorfer Kräuter Likör* is served. In many restaurants various kinds of whisky can be ordered, including well-known Scottish and Irish brands and popular American bourbons, but connoisseurs may miss their personal favourites. Italian restaurants often serve grappa, a grape spirit, after a meal, while in Greek restaurants ouzo – an aniseed spirit – may be offered.

Weizen Doppel Korn (rye spirit)

WINES

G ERMANY IS RENOWNED for its excellent white wines, particularly those made from the Riesling grape. Among the most highly prized wines are those from the Rheingau region. Lovers of red wine might like to try Assmannshausen Spätburgunder wine, which is produced from the Pinot Noir grape.

Germany has a system of classifying wines into three groups according to their quality: the lowest quality is *Tafelwein*, then *Qualitätswein* and the highest quality *Qualitätswein mit Prädikat*. The latter includes wines produced from appropriately selected grapes, which is always confirmed on the bottle label. The term *Trocken* indicates a dry style, *Halbtrocken*, semi-dry and *Süss* means sweet. Very good sparkling wines, known as *Sekt*, are also produced in Germany

Mainstockheimer Hofstück Spätburgunder

Spätburgunder from the Rheingau region

Riesling Schloss Vollrads

BEERS

Beermat with brewery logo

E ACH REGION OF Germany has its own beer-brewing tradition: the most popular breweries in the north are Jever in Freesia and Beck's in Bremen, along with Bitburger, Warsteiner and Karlsberg. In the Rhine region, the biggest producers are DAB from Dortmund and König in Duisburg. In Berlin, Schultheiss, Berliner Kindl and Engelhardt compete for the primary position, while in Dresden the principal beers are produced by a brewery in Radeberg. However, Bavaria is by far the major brewing centre – the names of the breweries Löwenbräu, Hofbräu and Paulaner are known to every beer lover around the world. The most commonly drunk beer is Pils, a bottom-fermented lager of the pilsner type. Brown ales are also popular, particularly in the south. Schwarzbier, a top-fermented brown ale of over 4 per cent alcohol, is increasingly popular. Weizenbier, a bitter top-fermented beer, also has many fans, as has Bock, which is strong, at around 6 per cent alcohol.

Löwenbräu beer

König Ludwig Dunkel beer

Schultheiss beer

Wheat beer mixed with fruit juice, Berliner Weisse mit Schuss – speciality of Berlin

Franziskaner Hefe Weissbier beer

A tankard of beer with the essential head of foam

Choosing a Restaurant

THE RESTAURANTS IN THIS guide have been selected because of their good food and interesting location. Venues are listed state by state, beginning with Berlin. The colour-coded thumb tabs on the side of the page correspond to the relevant pages in the book. A map of Berlin can be found on pages 104–9, and the road map for Germany is at the back of the book.

	CREDIT CARDS	GARDEN OR TERRACE	GERMAN WINES	VEGETARIAN DISHES

BERLIN

BERLIN – EASTERN CENTRE: *Zum Nussbaum*   € | ● | ■ | ● |
Am Nussbaum 3, 10178. **Map** 5 E2. **[** *(030) 242 30 95.*
This inn, based in one of the lanes of Nikolaiviertel, is one of the most popular places in town. The cuisine is traditional Berlin style – both pork knuckle and herrings feature on the menu. **&** **†**

BERLIN – EASTERN CENTRE: *Art'otel Berlin Mitte*   €€€ | ● | ■ | ● | ■
Wallstrasse 70–73, 10179. **Map** 5 E3. **[** *(030) 24 06 20.* **FAX** *(030) 24 06 22 22.*
Good regional cuisine, with a light, modern touch. The hotel's function room is a unique room of an 18th-century palace with an ornamental Rococo ceiling.

BERLIN – EASTERN CENTRE: *Reinhard's*   €€€ | ● | ■ | ● | ■
Poststr. 28, 10178. **City map** 5 E2. **[** *(030) 242 52 95.*
A captivating restaurant with a stylish interior themed as the Roaring Twenties, serving an excellent selection of dishes from various countries. The speciality is *Das Geheimnis aus dem Kaiserhof* (the secret from the emperor's court) – a succulent steak served with a sauce, apparently created for Max Liebermann. **†**

BERLIN – EASTERN CENTRE: *Borchardt*   €€€€ | ● | ■ | ● | ■
Französische Str. 47, 10117. **Map** 1 C5, 4 C2. **[** *(030) 20 38 71 10.*
FAX *(030) 20 38 71 50.*
One of a small number of restaurants that have retained their original interior in early 20th-century style, with marble columns, mosaics and parquet floors. Prices are reasonable, and the Italian food is very good. A favourite venue with German politicians. **&**

BERLIN – EASTERN CENTRE: *Lorenz-Adlon-Gourmet*   €€€€ | ● | | ● | ■
Unter den Linden 77, 10117. **Map** 1 B4, 4 B2. **[** *(030) 226 10.*
FAX *(030) 22 61 22 22.*
The restaurant lives up to the name of the famous Adlon Hotel, in which it is based. Thanks to the culinary art of its current chef, Rainer Sigg, the Lorenze-Adlon-Gourmet continues to be one of the best restaurants in town. **&** **†**

BERLIN – EASTERN CENTRE: *Margaux*   €€€€€ | ● | | | ■
Unter den Linden 78, 10117. **Map** 1 B4, 4 B2. **[** *(030) 22 65 26 11.*
This Michelin-starred restaurant represents the new Berlin better than any other gourmet establishment. It is stylish and urban in character, offering a selection of classic yet creative French dishes with discrete service all in a sophisticated setting. Complementing the *à la carte* menu, there is a set menu and excellent wine list. **&**

BERLIN – WESTERN CENTRE: *Ottenthal*   €€€ | ● | | | ■
Kantstr. 153, 10623. **Map** 2 B4. **[** *(030) 313 31 62.*
Almost opposite the Theater des Westens, the modest interior of this restaurant is decorated with the mechanism of a church clock from the eponymous village of Ottenthal in Austria. Good Austrian food and an excellent selection of Austrian wines, accompanied by tunes from Mozart. Reservation is advisable. **†**

BERLIN – WESTERN CENTRE: *First Floor*   €€€€ | ● | | ● | ■
Budapester Str. 45, 10787. **Map** 2 C4. **[** *(030) 25 02 10 20.*
FAX *(030) 25 02 11 61.*
Elegant restaurant of the highest calibre. The menu includes traditional German fare, such as pork knuckle with cabbage, as well as more sophisticated creations with fish, crab and aromatic truffles. Besides the *à la carte* selection, there are also lunchtime set menus which are significantly lower in price. Reservation is necessary. **&** **†**

<table>
<tr><td colspan="2"></td><td>CREDIT CARDS</td><td>GARDEN OR TERRACE</td><td>GERMAN WINES</td><td>VEGETARIAN DISHES</td></tr>
</table>

Prices of a three course meal without drinks, including cover charge, tax and service:

€ up to €20
€€ €21–€29
€€€ €30–€39
€€€€ €40–€49
€€€€€ over €49

CREDIT CARDS
Credit cards are accepted.
GARDEN OR TERRACE
Weather permitting, it is possible to eat al fresco.
GERMAN WINES
A good selection of German wines.
VEGETARIAN DISHES
The restaurant offers a good selection of meat free and vegetarian dishes.

	CREDIT CARDS	GARDEN OR TERRACE	GERMAN WINES	VEGETARIAN DISHES
BERLIN – WESTERN CENTRE: *Die Quadriga* €€€€€ Eislebener Str. 14, 10789. **Map** 2 B5. 🅲 *(030) 21 40 50.* FAX *(030) 21 40 51 00.* This gourmet restaurant is based in the Brandenburger Hof Hotel, which has long been one of Berlin's finest. The relatively small dining room is well equipped with furniture designed by Frank Lloyd Wright. Impeccable service complements the sophisticated French cuisine. Reservation is required. 🅿 ♿ 👶	●		●	
FURTHER AFIELD: *Oren* € Oranienburger Str. 28, 10117. 🅲 *(030) 28 59 93 13.* FAX *(030) 28 59 93 13.* This restaurant, near the synagogue and the Centrum Judaicum, specializes in Jewish and Arabic vegetarian dishes for groups of 10 people or more. The menu includes such delicacies as falafels, tofu-stuffed peppers and excellent aubergine dishes. Wines from Israel. ♿	●	■	●	■
FURTHER AFIELD: *Globe Restaurant* €€ Lützowplatz 17, 10785. **Map** 2 D4. 🅲 *(030) 26 05 25 61.* FAX *(030) 26 05 27 16.* This is an exquisite restaurant which serves international cuisine of a very high quality. In summer it is pleasant to eat lunch in the patio restaurant.	●	■		■
FURTHER AFIELD: *Mare Bê* €€€ Rosenthaler Str. 46–48, 10178. **Map** 5 D1. 🅲 *(030) 283 65 45.* An excellent address for lovers of southern French, Italian and Spanish cooking, with a hint of the Middle East. It is worth eating here on a Tuesday, when the house speciality – oysters – are served. The courtyard has a peaceful garden. 👶	●	■		■
FURTHER AFIELD: *Ana e Bruno* €€€€€ Sophie-Charlotten Str. 101, 14059. 🅲 *(030) 325 71 10.* FAX *(030) 322 68 95.* Quite definitely the finest Italian restaurant in town. The elegant pastel interior and soft Italian melodies create an ideal setting for the delicious specialities created by the chef.				■
FURTHER AFIELD: *Harlekin* €€€€€ Lützowufer 15, 10785. **Map** 3 D4. 🅲 *(030) 25 47 88 630.* FAX *(030) 265 11 71.* The Grand Hotel Esplanade has one of the finest restaurants in the city. Guests can observe the chefs at work in the open kitchen. The exceptional menu lists European, including many Italian, and Asian dishes, which are served in an impeccable manner. A reservation is essential. 🅿 ♿ 👶	●	■	●	■
BRANDENBURG				
BRANDENBURG: *Sorat Hotel Brandenburg* € Altstädtischer Markt 1, 14770. **Road map** E3. 🅲 *(03381) 59 70.* FAX *(03381) 59 74 44.* This restaurant belongs to a hotel located in the old town market square. It is a very pleasant venue which serves tasty and varied food, including a selection of dishes which are typical for different German regions. ♿ 👶	●	■		■
CHORIN: *Haus Chorin* € Neue Klosterallee 10, 16230 Chorin. **Road map** E2. 🅲 *(033366) 500.* FAX *(033366) 326.* This hotel–restaurant is based in a stylish Art Nouveau villa situated on the shores of a lake. The regional fish and game dishes are particularly highly recommended. ♿ 👶	●	■	●	■
COTTBUS: *Branitz–Fürst Pückler* € Heinrich-Zille Str., 03042. **Road map** F3. 🅲 *(0355) 751 00.* FAX *(0355) 71 31 72.* This elegant restaurant with open fireplace is based in the Best Western Branitz Hotel. ♿ 👶	●	■	●	■

<table>
<tr><td colspan="2">

Prices of a three course meal without drinks, including cover charge, tax and service:

€ up to €20
€€ €21–€29
€€€ €30–€39
€€€€ €40–€49
€€€€€ over €49

</td><td>

CREDIT CARDS
Credit cards are accepted.
GARDEN OR TERRACE
Weather permitting, it is possible to eat *al fresco*.
GERMAN WINES
A good selection of German wines.
VEGETARIAN DISHES
The restaurant offers a good selection of meat free and vegetarian dishes.

</td></tr>
</table>

	Price	CREDIT CARDS	GARDEN OR TERRACE	GERMAN WINES	VEGETARIAN DISHES
LEHNIN: *Markgraf* Friedensstr. 13, 14797. **Road map** E3. 📞 *(03382) 76 50.* FAX *(03382) 76 54 30.* Elegant yet unpretentious restaurant in the Markgraf Hotel, serving regional cuisine. After the meal, coffee can be taken on the terrace. ♿ 🚶	€	●	■	●	■
NEURUPPIN: *Altes Kasino am See* Seeufer 11, 16816. **Road map** E2. 📞 *(03391) 30 59.* FAX *(03391) 35 86 84.* This hotel–restaurant serves delicious, no-nonsense food reminiscent of home cooking. Good selection of fish and game dishes. ♿ 🚶 🎵	€	●	■		
ORANIENBURG: *Galerie* Andre-Pican-Str. 23, 16515. **Road map** E3. 📞 *(03301) 69 00.* FAX *(03301) 69 09 99.* This new restaurant, part of the Stadthotel Oranienburg, is in the centre of town. The interior is presented like an art gallery, and there is also a bar. Excellent regional dishes and French cuisine. ♿	€	●	■		
POTSDAM: *Hofgarten* Friedrich-Ebert-Str. 88, 14467. **Road map** E3. 📞 *(0331) 231 70.* FAX *(0331) 231 71 00.* Modern restaurant in the Voltaire Hotel, serving mainly dishes of the day. Regional cuisine predominates. ♿ 🚶	€	●	■	●	■
POTSDAM: *Speckers Gaststätte zur Ratswaage* Am neuen Markt 10, 14467. **Road map** E3. 📞 *(0331) 280 43 11.* FAX *(0331) 280 43 19.* Unpretentious, modern, family run restaurant. Exquisite and original creations, mainly French-influenced, are prepared from locally grown produce. Excellent service. ♿ 🚶	€€€€	●	■	●	■
WITTSTOCK: *Stadt Hamburg* Röbelerstr. 25, 16909. **Road map** E2. 📞 and FAX *(03394) 44 45 66.* This restaurant, based in the Hotel Stadt Hamburg, is situated close to the old town of Wittstock. The interior is pleasant, and the menu is characterized by regional dishes. ♿ 🚶	€	●	■		

SAXONY–ANHALT

	Price	CREDIT CARDS	GARDEN OR TERRACE	GERMAN WINES	VEGETARIAN DISHES
BERNBURG: *Amadeus* Breite Str. 2–3, 06406. **Road map** D3. 📞 *(03471) 35 39 71.* FAX *(03471) 35 41 35.* This restaurant, based in the Askania Hotel, serves regional food and Mediterranean cuisine. ♿ 🚶	€	●		●	■
DESSAU: *Fürst Leopold* Friedensplatz, 06844. **Road map** E3. 📞 *(0340) 251 50.* FAX *(0340) 251 51 77.* This restaurant, part of the Steigenberger Seminar & Konferenzhotel, was built to cater especially for the needs of business people attending conferences and seminars, but other guests are equally welcome. The restaurant serves a large number of interesting and delicious German dishes. There is also a small bistro and a bar. ♿ 🚶 🎵	€	●	■	●	■
HALLE: *Dorint Hotel Charlottenhof* Dorotheenstr. 12, 06108. **Road map** D4. 📞 *(0345) 292 30.* FAX *(0345) 292 31 00.* The restaurant belongs to the Dorint Hotel Charlottenhof, which is located in the city centre. Guests can watch their food being prepared while in the restaurant. The food is generally very tasty, the service friendly. Pleasant hotel bar. ♿ 🚶	€€	●	■	●	■
MAGDEBURG: *Alt Prester* Alt Prester 102, 39114 Magdeburg-Prester. **Road map** D3. 📞 *(0391) 819 30.* FAX *(0391) 819 31 18.* This restaurant, in the Alt Prester Hotel, is in a beautiful location on the banks of the Elbe river. It specializes mainly in traditional German cooking. Beer garden.	€		■	●	■

MERSEBURG: *Belle Epoque* €
Oberaltenburg 4, 06217. **Road map** D4. **☎** *(03461) 452 00.*
FAX *(03461) 45 21 00.*
Exquisite restaurant, based in the Radisson SAS Hotel, specializing in
Scandinavian and German cuisine. Interesting decor and very good
service. There is also a café with terrace and a bar. **&** **⚑**

NAUMBURG: *Zur alten Schmiede* €
Lindenring 36–37, 06618. **Road map** D4. **☎** *(03445) 243 60.* **FAX** *(03445) 24 36 66.*
This restaurant is housed in a former forge and serves fresh regional
food, including fish dishes.

QUEDLINBURG: *Theophano* €€
Markt 13–14, 06484. **Road map** D4. **☎** *(03946) 963 00.* **FAX** *(03946) 96 30 36.*
This restaurant, in one of the Romantik Hotels, is based in an almost
400-year-old renovated building. Tasty dishes are served in a beautiful
vaulted cellar. It is particularly worth trying the game dishes.
◑ *Sun.* **⚑**

STENDAL: *Altstadt-Hotel* €€
Breite Str. 60, 39576. **Road map** D3. **☎** *(03931) 698 90.* **FAX** *(03931) 69 89 39.*
Very pleasant, tastefully furnished hotel–restaurant, situated in the city
centre, serving regional and international dishes.

TANGERMÜNDE: *Kutscherstübchen* €
Lange Str. 52, 39590. **Road map** D3. **☎** *(039322) 23 91.* **FAX** *(039322) 36 42.*
Part of the Schwarzer Adler Hotel, this is a family-friendly restaurant. It
is pleasantly furnished, and serves generous portions. Try the
Altmärkische Hochzeitssuppe – wedding soup from the Altmark. Small
hotel bar. **&** **⚑**

WERNIGERODE: *Gothisches Haus* €€
Marktplatz 2, 38855. **Road map** D3. **☎** *(03943) 67 50.* **FAX** *(03943) 67 55 55.*
Restaurant and hotel are housed in the oldest building in town. The
selection of dishes is extensive, and the service friendly. Apart from the
restaurant there is also a café with conservatory, a wine bar and a small
country inn, serving tasty, inexpensive food. **&** **⚑** **♬**

WITTENBERG: *Luther-Schenke* €€€
Markt 2. **Road map** E3. **☎** *(03491) 40 65 92.* **FAX** *(03492) 02 03 11.*
Set in the vaulted basement of a 16th-century house, waiters dressed in
medieval costume serve traditional German and Saxonian dishes. **⚡**

SAXONY

AUGUSTUSBURG: *Waldhaus* €
Am Kurplatz 7, 09573. **Road map** E4. **☎** *(037291) 203 17.* **FAX** *(037291) 203 17.*
This restaurant, based in the hotel of the same name, has recently been
renovated. It is pleasant, albeit modest, and serves excellent German
food. **&** **⚑**

BAD MUSKAU: *Am Schlossbrunnen* €
Köbelner Str. 68, 02953 Bad Muskau. **Road map** F4. **☎** *(035771) 52 30.*
FAX *(035771) 523 50.*
Family-run restaurant on the edge of town with good views. Pleasing
interior. Regional and international food is served, specializing in fish
caught locally in the heathland lakes and steak dishes. It is worth trying
the excellent Fürst-Pückler ice-cream, a local speciality. **&**

BAUTZEN: *Residence* €
Wilthener Str. 32, 02625 Bautzen. **Road map** F4. **☎** *(03591) 35 57 00.*
FAX *(03591) 35 57 05.* **W** *www.residence.bautzen.de*
Situated close to the historic centre of the town, this new, tastefully
furnished hotel-restaurant offers good regional dishes as well as
international cuisine. There is also a large sun terrace.
P **⚡** **⚑**

CHEMNITZ: *Glashaus* €€
Salzstr. 56, 09113. **Road map** E4. **☎** *(0371) 334 10.* **FAX** *(0371) 334 17 77.*
Based in the Renaissance Hotel and surrounded by lush greenery, this
restaurant offers great views of the old town and the restaurant pond.
International dishes are served in this pleasant, modern venue, which
seems almost like a botanical garden. There is also an attractive terrace,
and various seasonal attractions are available to guests. **⚑**

For key to symbols *see back flap*

		CREDIT CARDS	GARDEN OR TERRACE	GERMAN WINES	VEGETARIAN DISHES

Prices of a three course meal without drinks, including cover charge, tax and service:

€ up to €20
€€ €21–€29
€€€ €30–€39
€€€€ €40–€49
€€€€€ over €49

CREDIT CARDS
Credit cards are accepted.
GARDEN OR TERRACE
Weather permitting, it is possible to eat *al fresco*.
GERMAN WINES
A good selection of German wines.
VEGETARIAN DISHES
The restaurant offers a good selection of meat free and vegetarian dishes.

	CREDIT CARDS	GARDEN OR TERRACE	GERMAN WINES	VEGETARIAN DISHES
DRESDEN: *Sophienkeller* €€	●			■

Taschenberg 3, 01067. **Road map** E4. ☎ *(0351) 49 72 60.* FAX *(0351) 497 26 11.*
This is one of the most popular and lively restaurants in town. The Sophienkeller recreates the rustic atmosphere of an 18th-century beer-cellar, serving authentic regional cuisine. 🍴 🔥

	CREDIT CARDS	GARDEN OR TERRACE	GERMAN WINES	VEGETARIAN DISHES
DRESDEN: *Intermezzo* €€€€	●	■	●	■

Taschenberg 3, 01067. **Road map** E4. ☎ *(0351) 491 27 12.* FAX *(0351) 491 27 16.*
Located in the Kempinski Taschenbergpalais (*see p478*), this elegant restaurant serves unconventional dishes with a touch of the Mediterranean. ♿

	CREDIT CARDS	GARDEN OR TERRACE	GERMAN WINES	VEGETARIAN DISHES
DRESDEN: *Das Caroussel* €€€€€	●	■	●	■

Rähnitzgasse 19, 01097. Dresden-Neustadt. **Road map** E4. ☎ *(0351) 800 30.*
FAX *(0351) 800 31 00.*
The hotel and restaurant are based within a recently restored Baroque palace in the historic city centre, dating from the 18th century. In culinary terms, this is one of the best addresses in Saxony. Only open in the evenings. French cuisine. ♿ 🔥

	CREDIT CARDS	GARDEN OR TERRACE	GERMAN WINES	VEGETARIAN DISHES
GÖRLITZ: *Am Goldenen Strauss* €	●		●	

Struvestr. 1, 02826. **Road map** F4. ☎ *(03581) 40 65 77.* FAX *(03581) 40 65 79.*
This restaurant is located in the Sorat Hotel, which is in a former merchant's house. It is decorated in a modern style and serves excellent food in a welcoming atmosphere.

	CREDIT CARDS	GARDEN OR TERRACE	GERMAN WINES	VEGETARIAN DISHES
KAMENZ: *Goldener Hirsch* €	●	■	●	■

Markt 10, 01719. **Road map** F4. ☎ *(03578) 30 12 21.* FAX *(03578) 30 44 97.*
A beautifully situated restaurant, part of a hotel right on the market square, with traditions dating back to the 16th century. The elegant establishment serves exquisite Italian dishes. The rustic Ratskeller, serving traditional German fare, is also recommended. 🔥

	CREDIT CARDS	GARDEN OR TERRACE	GERMAN WINES	VEGETARIAN DISHES
LEIPZIG: *Yamato* €€	●		●	■

Gerberstr. 15, 04105. **Road map** E4. ☎ *(0341) 21 11 068.* FAX *(0341) 128 11 15.*
A very popular Japanese restaurant in which the majority of dishes are prepared in front of diners. The service is courteous – guests are, for example, given small aprons and hot towels. Book in advance. ♿

	CREDIT CARDS	GARDEN OR TERRACE	GERMAN WINES	VEGETARIAN DISHES
LEIPZIG: *Kaiser Maximilian* €€€	●	■	●	■

Neumarkt 9–19, 04109. **Road map** E4. ☎ *(0341) 998 69 00.* FAX *(0341) 998 69 01.*
A bright restaurant, pleasantly decorated in well-chosen colours, with small recesses for the tables. There is a large selection of Italian dishes, and the menu changes every other week. ♿ 🔥 🎵

	CREDIT CARDS	GARDEN OR TERRACE	GERMAN WINES	VEGETARIAN DISHES
MEISSEN: *Mercure Grandhotel Meissen* €	●	■	●	■

Hafenstr. 27–31, 01662. **Road map** E4. ☎ *(03521) 722 50.* FAX *(03521) 72 29 04.*
This classy hotel–restaurant, based in a large Art Nouveau villa on the banks of the Elbe river, serves regional and international food, including a wide selection of fish dishes. Guests can also dine in the café, which has a terrace, or in the intimate hotel bar. 🅿 🔥

	CREDIT CARDS	GARDEN OR TERRACE	GERMAN WINES	VEGETARIAN DISHES
MORITZBURG: *Churfürstliche Waldschaenke* €	●	■	●	■

Große Fasanenstr., 01468. **Road map** E4. ☎ *(035207) 86 00.* FAX *(035207) 860 93.*
This restaurant, in the Waldschänke Hotel and near a former pheasantry, serves regional German and international food, with a good choice of game dishes. There is also a winebar and café with a terrace.
🅿 ♿ 🔥

	CREDIT CARDS	GARDEN OR TERRACE	GERMAN WINES	VEGETARIAN DISHES
PIRNA: *Deutsches Haus* €	●	■	●	■

Niedere Burgstr. 1, 01796. **Road map** E4. ☎ *(03501) 52 81 03.* FAX *(03501) 52 81 04.*
The restaurant, part of a hotel belonging to the chain of Romantik Hotels, is highly rated in the area. ♿ 🔥 🎵

TORGAU: *Central-Hotel* €
Friedrichplatz 8, 04860. **Road map** E4. 🄲 *(03421) 732 80.* 𝖥𝖠𝖷 *(03421) 732 850.*
Pleasant, modest hotel–restaurant, serving specialities from Baden.

ZWICKAU: *Restaurant Orangerie Holiday Inn* €
Kornmarkt 9, 08056. **Road map** E4. 🄲 *(0375) 279 20.* 𝖥𝖠𝖷 *(0375) 27 92 666.*
The Holiday Inn hotel, located within the centre of the old town, has
several restaurants, a small bistro, serving well-prepared, uncomplicated
and inexpensive fare, as well as a hotel bar and a café with terrace. The
service is friendly.

ZITTAU: *Riedel* €
Friedensstr. 23, 02763. **Road map** F4. 🄲 *(03583) 68 60.* 𝖥𝖠𝖷 *(03583) 68 61 00.*
The restaurant in the Riedel Hotel serves typical German food. There is
also a small Bavarian pub and a garden.

THURINGIA

ALTENBURG: *Altenburger Hof* €
Schmöllnsche Landstr. 8, 04600. **Road map** E4. 🄲 *(03447) 58 40.* 𝖥𝖠𝖷 *(03447) 58 44 99.*
The Altenburger Hof Hotel has a restaurant, a café and a day-time bar – in
Germany hotel bars often close at night. 🅑 🚻 🎵

EISENACH: *Eisenacherhof* €
Katharinenstr. 11–13, 99817. **Road map** D4. 🄲 *(03691) 293 90.* 𝖥𝖠𝖷 *(03691) 29 39 26.*
Modern restaurant and pizzeria in the Eisenacherhof Hotel, which
specializes in German regional dishes. A good selection of fish and pasta
dishes. There is also a pleasant hotel bar, a disco and a café with terrace.
🅑 🚻 🎵

ERFURT: *Zum alten Schwan* €
Gotthardtstr. 27, 99084. **Road map** D4. 🄲 *(0361) 674 00.* 𝖥𝖠𝖷 *(0361) 674 04 44.*
The restaurant is housed in the Sorat Hotel situated in a historic part of
the city. The cooking is of a very high standard, and there is a wide
selection of dishes on offer. 🅑 🚻

ERFURT: *Castell Feinschmecker Restaurant* €€€
Kleine Arche 4, 99084. **Road map** D4. 🄲 *(0361) 644 22 22.* 𝖥𝖠𝖷 *(0361) 644 22 22.*
Restaurant, wine bar and Baroque café belong to the same complex,
located in one of the most beautiful parts of the city. Sophisticated dishes
and a good selection of wines are served. 🅑 🚻

GERA: *Piazzetta* €€
Gutenbergstr. 2a, 07548. **Road map** D4. 🄲 *(0365) 290 94 14.* 𝖥𝖠𝖷 *(0365) 290 91 00.*
The restaurant is based in the well-located Marriot Courtyard Hotel. One
of its main attractions is that the diner can see the dishes being prepared
from start to finish. Foods in season are highlighted by special events,
such as "asparagus week" or "game week". The hotel also has a pleasant
pub, a bar and a garden restaurant. Pleasant and friendly service. 🅑 🚻

GOTHA: *Hotel am Schlosspark* €
Lindenauallee 20–24, 99867. **Road map** D4. 🄲 *(03621) 44 20.* 𝖥𝖠𝖷 *(03621) 44 24 52.*
A nice, sunny hotel restaurant, with a wealth of plants, offering both
international and local dishes. Pleasant hotel bar. The restaurant is
situated at the end of the castle park. 🅑 🚻

JENA: *Steigenberger Maxx Hotel Jena* €
Stauffenbergstr. 59, 07747 Jena-Lobeda. **Road map** D4. 🄲 *(03641) 30 00.*
𝖥𝖠𝖷 *(03641) 30 08 88.*
Part of the Steigenberger Maxx Hotel, this restaurant specializes in local
dishes. Restaurant and hotel are both themed and decorated to evoke the
style of America in the years 1930–50. There is a beer garden, a hotel bar
and a terrace. The restaurant is relatively inexpensive. 🎵 🅑 🚻

MÜHLHAUSEN: *Brauhaus Zum Löwen* €
Kornmarkt 3, 99974. **Road map** D4. 🄲 *(03601) 47 10.* 𝖥𝖠𝖷 *(03601) 47 12 22.*
A rustic hotel–restaurant and pub, serving beer that has been brewed on
the premises as well as traditional German food. 🅑 🚻 🎵

SAALFELD: *Obstgut Geblen* €€
Hohe Str. 1, 07318. **Road map** D4. 🄲 *(03671) 20 27* 𝖥𝖠𝖷 *(03671) 51 60 16.*
Restaurant and hotel are based in a beautiful Art Nouveau building,
located some distance outside the town. A range of dishes are prepared
in the intimate restaurant, including food from France and Germany's
regions. 🚻

For key to symbols *see back flap*

Prices of a three course meal without drinks, including cover charge, tax and service: €) up to €20 €)€) €21–€29 €)€)€) €30–€39 €)€)€)€) €40–€49 €)€)€)€)€) over €49	**CREDIT CARDS** Credit cards are accepted. **GARDEN OR TERRACE** Weather permitting, it is possible to eat *al fresco*. **GERMAN WINES** A good selection of German wines. **VEGETARIAN DISHES** The restaurant offers a good selection of meat free and vegetarian dishes.	**CREDIT CARDS** **GARDEN OR TERRACE** **GERMAN WINES** **VEGETARIAN DISHES**

WEIMAR: *Wolff's Art Hotel & Restaurant*   €)
Freiherr-vom-Stein-Allee 3a/b, 99425. **Road map** D4. ☑ *(03643) 540 60.*
FAX *(03643) 54 06 99.*
Both the Art Hotel and its restaurant are furnished in the style created by
the Bauhaus School. The menu includes international as well as German
dishes. ☒ ☒

CREDIT CARDS	GARDEN OR TERRACE	GERMAN WINES	VEGETARIAN DISHES
●	■		

WEIMAR: *Alt Weimar*   €)€)
Prellerstr. 2, 99423. **Road map** D4. ☑ *(03643) 861 90.* FAX *(03643) 86 19 10.*
For a hundred years this restaurant has been a popular meeting place for
actors from the nearby theatre. Its cooking, consisting mainly of Italian
dishes, is renowned throughout the region.

●	■		

WEIMAR: *Anna Amalia*   €)€)€)€)
Markt 19, 99423. **Road map** D4. ☑ *(03643) 80 20.* FAX *(03643) 80 26 10.*
This restaurant has a venerable tradition – famous celebrities, including
Richard Wagner and Thomas Mann, have dined here, and it has
remained very popular to this day. The finest Italian cooking in all of
Thuringia is served in the restaurant, with a new menu to choose from
every day. The interior is decorated in Art-Deco style. ☒ ☒

●	■	●	

MUNICH

Austernkeller   €)
Stollbergstr. 11, 80539. **Map** D7. ☑ *(089) 29 87 87.* FAX *(089) 22 31 66.*
This restaurant serves mainly dishes of the day. Seafood, including the
Austern (oysters) of its name, is a speciality. ☒

●			

Bistro Terrine   €)€)€)
Amalienstr. 89, 80799 München-Schwabing. **Map** D7. ☑ *(089) 28 17 80.*
FAX *(089) 280 93 16.*
The former chef of the Tantris, one of the best restaurants in Germany,
now cooks here, preparing delicious, low-calorie dishes, particularly with
lamb and fish. Try, for example, ray with artichokes or *zander* in a herb
sauce, and for dessert the exquisite crème brûlée. The restaurant has a
romantic ambience. ☒

●	■	●	■

Dallmayr   €)€)€)
Dienerstr. 14, 80331. **Map** D7. ☑ *(089) 213 51 00.* FAX *(089) 213 51 67.*
This exceptionally elegant restaurant is popular with locals and visitors
alike, just like the famous coffee of the same name. Traditional German
and international dishes are served here. ☒

●			

Käferschänke   €)€)€)€)€)
Prinzregentenstr. 73, 81675. **Map** D7. ☑ *(089) 416 82 47.* FAX *(089) 416 86 23.*
Serving French and Italian food, this restaurant is one of the finest in
Munich. Next door is a delicatessen counter run by the same company,
selling regional delicacies. ☒

●	■		■

Königshof   €)€)€)€)€)
Karlsplatz 25, 80335. **Map** D7. ☑ *(089) 55 13 60.* FAX *(089) 55 13 61 13.*
Elegantly furnished restaurant in the centre of the old town, very highly
esteemed by gourmets. Wine lovers will be astonished by the vast
selection: 1,000 different drinks are on offer.

●			■

Tantris   €)€)€)€)€)
Johann-Fichte-Str. 7, 80805 München-Schwabing. **Map** D7.
☑ *(089) 361 95 90.* FAX *(089) 36 19 59 22.*
One of the very best restaurants in Germany, the Tantris will satisfy even
the jaded palate of a seasoned gourmet. It is luxuriously furnished, and
the service is of a very high standard. Additional attractions include a
terrace and a garden that is large enough to cater for 100 people.
Reservation is recommended.

●	■	●	■

BAVARIA

ANSBACH: *Drechsels-Stuben* €€
Am Drechselsgarten 1, 91522. **Road map** D6. 📞 *(0981) 890 20.* 📠 *(0981) 890 26 05.*
This restaurant, in the Best Western Hotel Am Drechelsgarten, serves
French and international specialities. You can also while your time away
in the bar or the café which has a terrace. From the restaurant, the diner
will have magnificent views of the surrounding area. ♿

ASCHAFFENBURG: *Post* €€
Goldbacher Str. 19–21, 63739. **Road map** C5. 📞 *(06021) 33 40.*
📠 *(06021) 13 483.*
The smartly furnished restaurant, based in the Post Hotel, has received
several awards for its cooking. Diners praise the traditional Bavarian
dishes, including *Wiener Schnitzel.* Special dishes on request. ♿ 🌳

AUGSBURG: *Die Ecke* €€
Elias-Holl-Platz 2, 86150. **Road map** D6. 📞 *(0821) 51 06 00.* 📠 *(0821) 31 19 92.*
This restaurant, housed in a 16th-century building and traditionally
furnished, has an excellent atmosphere. Many celebrities have dined
here, including Brecht, Diesel and Mozart. One of the best restaurants in
town, it also has a beautiful garden. 🌳

AUGSBURG: *Wirthaus im Zuckerhof* €€
Pfärrle 18, 86152. **Road map** D6. 📞 *(0821) 34 58 394.* 📠 *(0821) 34 58 395.*
Modern and pleasant restaurant which has long been run by the same
family. The food is delicious and sophisticated – try the excellent trout
coated in sesame seeds or the vegetable dumplings with a herb sauce.
The restaurant is small, and reservation is recommended. 🌳

BAMBERG: *St Nepomuk* €€
Obere Mühlbrücke 9, 96049. **Road map** D5. 📞 *(0951) 98 42–0.* 📠 *(0951) 984 21 00.*
A good restaurant with beautiful views over the surrounding area,
specializing in fish and game dishes. ♿ 🌳

BAYREUTH: *Schlossgaststätte Eremitage* €
Eremitage 6, 95448. **Road map** D5. 📞 *(0921) 79 99 7–0.* 📠 *(0921) 799 97 30.*
Cosima Wagner, the composer's wife, used to dine in this beautifully
furnished restaurant, one of the finest gastronomic establishments in town.
The excellent cooking is Franconian and international.

BAYREUTH: *Schloss Thiergarten* €€
Oberthiergärtner Str. 36, 95448. **Road map** D5. 📞 *(09209) 98 40.*
📠 *(09209) 984 29.*
There are two restaurants in the castle, the elegantly furnished Schloss-
Restaurant, and the less expensive Jagdstübchen, in a former hunting
lodge, which specializes in game dishes. 🅿 🎵 ♿ 🌳

BURGHAUSEN: *Bayerische Alm* €€
Robert-Koch-Str. 211, 84489. **Road map** E7. 📞 *(08677) 98 20.* 📠 *(08677) 98 22 00.*
Traditional Bavarian hospitality rules in this restaurant, based in the hotel
of the same name. It serves regional specialities, and many are prepared
right in front of the diners. 🌳

COBURG: *Kräutergarten & Die Petersilie* €€
Rosenauer Str. 30c, 96450. **Road map** D5. 📞 *(09561) 42 60 80.*
📠 *(09561) 42 60 81.*
There are two restaurants in the Best Western Blankenburg Hotel, one
serving exquisite gourmet food, the other specializing in local Franconian
dishes. Elegant interiors and friendly service. 🌳

DINKELSBÜHL: *Zum kleinen Obristen* €
Martin-Luther-Str.1, 91550. **Road map** D6. 📞 *(09851) 577 00.* 📠 *(09851) 57 70 70.*
This connoisseurs' restaurant in the Eisenkrug Hotel is superbly furnished
and has a pleasant atmosphere. The menu includes the finest dishes from
the Franconian and Schwabian cuisines as well as international dishes.
The hotel also has a wine bar with a very attractive ceiling. Wine lovers
will enjoy the large selection of wines on offer.

EICHSTÄTT: *Klosterstuben* €
Pedettistr. 24–26, 85072. **Road map** D6. 📞 *(08421) 35 00.* 📠 *(08421) 39 00.*
This rustic restaurant in the Klosterstuben Hotel is situated in the old
town. The restaurant is small, and the chef prepares the food, mainly
Bavarian dishes, himself. 🌳

For key to symbols *see back flap*

Prices of a three course meal without drinks, including cover charge, tax and service:

€ up to €20
€€ €21–€29
€€€ €30–€39
€€€€ €40–€49
€€€€€ over €49

CREDIT CARDS
Credit cards are accepted.
GARDEN OR TERRACE
Weather permitting, it is possible to eat al fresco.
GERMAN WINES
A good selection of German wines.
VEGETARIAN DISHES
The restaurant offers a good selection of meat free and vegetarian dishes.

	CREDIT CARDS	GARDEN OR TERRACE	GERMAN WINES	VEGETARIAN DISHES

FREISING: *Zur alten Schießstätte* €€
Dr. von Daller Strasse 1–3, 85356. **Road map** D6. ((08161) 53 24 41.
FAX (08161) 53 21 00.
This restaurant, in the Dorint Hotel, serves superbly prepared international dishes, as well as Bavarian specialities. Its reputation for excellent cooking is well deserved.

FÜSSEN: *Geiger* €
Uferstr. 18, 87629 Füssen-Hopfen am See. **Road map** D7. ((08362) 70 74.
FAX (08362) 388 38.
An attractive restaurant with a beautiful view of the lake, based in the Geiger Hotel.

GARMISCH-PARTENKIRCHEN: *Reindl's Restaurant* €
Bahnhofstr. 15, 82467. **Road map** D7. ((08821) 94 38 70.
FAX (08821) 94 38 72 50.
The restaurant is part of the Reindl's Partenkirchner Hof Hotel. Its chef, who previously worked in other well-known establishments around Europe, has received many accolades for his cooking. The cuisine is international, mainly French, one of the specialities being crab cocktail. On request, the restaurant caters for guests who are on a special diet or wish to lose weight. A large selection of wines is available in the restaurant and the bar. **P & ♿**

INGOLSTADT: *Hummel* €€
Feldkirchener Str. 69, 85055. **Road map** D6. ((0841) 95 45 30. FAX (0841) 592 11.
Pleasant restaurant in the Domizil Hummel Hotel, serving German and Italian dishes. The hotel also has a café with a terrace, a bar and a pub.
& ♿

KEMPTEN: *Peterhof* €
Salzstr. 1, 87435. **Road map** C7. ((0831) 524 40. FAX (0831) 524 42 00.
Friendly restaurant in the Peterhof Hotel, serving international food, including Greek dishes, pizzas and regional specialities. **& ♿**

LANDSHUT: *Schloss Schönbrunn* €€
Schönbrunn 1, 84036. **Road map** E6. ((0871) 952 20.
FAX (0871) 952 22 22.
The restaurant, part of the Schloss Schönbrunn Hotel, is based in the castle. It is furnished in rustic style, and a friendly family atmosphere prevails. Bavarian and international food is served, including excellent poultry and game dishes. **& ♿**

LINDAU: *Bayerischer Hof* €€€
Seepromenade, 88131. **Road map** C7. ((08382) 91 50. FAX (08382) 91 55 91.
This restaurant, part of the Bayerischer Hof Hotel and situated right on the shores of Bodensee (Lake Constance), is renowned for its excellent service. A variety of fare, including much liked and highly prized trout dishes, is served in stylish surroundings. **& ♿**

NEU-ULM: *Landhof Meinl* €€
Marbacher Str. 4, 89233 Neu-Ulm–Reutti. **Road map** C6. ((0731) 705 20.
FAX (0731) 705 22 22.
This restaurant belongs to the Silence Hotels chain, a group of hotels situated in particularly quiet and tranquil surroundings. The elegant and rustic restaurant, 7 km (4 miles) south of Neu-Ulm, serves dishes prepared from historical recipes. **& ♿**

NEUBURG AN DER DONAU: *Zum Klosterbräu* €€
Kirchplatz 1, 86633 Neuburg an der Donau-Bergen. **Road map** D6.
((08431) 677 50. FAX (08431) 411 20.
A restaurant with a long family tradition, specializing in regional food, with a predominance of game and fish dishes. Friendly service. **& ♿**

NÜRNBERG (NUREMBERG): *Schelhorn* €€€
Am Schlosspark 2, 90475 Nürnberg-Fischbach. **Road map** D6. 🄲 *(0911) 83 24 24.*
FAX *(0911) 983 73 98.*
This elegant restaurant is popular in the area. Service is courteous and
professional. 🛉

NÜRNBERG (NUREMBERG): *Seewald* €€€
Weinmarkt 14, 90403 Nürnberg. **Road map** D6.
🄲 *(0911) 38 13 03.* FAX *(0911) 34 63 13.*
This restaurant has a cosy atmosphere. It is adorned with many pictures
and features a traditional tiled stove. Courteous staff serve appetizing
dishes, mainly Italian and German. 🄿 🕭 🛉 🎵

NÜRNBERG (NUREMBERG): *Essigbrätlein* €€€€€
Weinmarkt 3, 90403. **Road map** D6. 🄲 *and* FAX *(0911) 22 51 31.*
Small and cosy restaurant, excellent cooking and elegant table settings.
Booking is recommended. Lunch menu is considerably less expensive.

OBERAMMERGAU: *Böld* €
König-Ludwig-Str. 10, 82487. **Road map** D7. 🄲 *(08822) 91 20.* FAX *(08822) 71 02.*
The restaurant is part of the Böld Hotel, which also has a pub. In summer it is
possible to eat in the garden, which is set out in Bavarian style. 🎵 🕭 🛉

OBERSTDORF: *Exquisit* €€
Prinzenstr. 17, 87561. **Road map** C7. 🄲 *(08322) 963 30.* FAX *(08322) 96 33 60.*
The restaurant of the Exquisit Hotel provides excellent service, starting
from the moment you enter. The staff are concerned that guests should
feel happy throughout their stay. 🎵 🕭 🛉

PASSAU: *Heilig-Geist-Stift Schenke/Stiftskeller* €
Heiliggeistgasse 4, 94032. **Road map** E6. 🄲 *(0851) 26 07.* FAX *(0851) 353 87.*
Rustic restaurant and wine bar, specializing in Bavarian food, including
fish dishes and delicious Austrian cakes. Open until late. 🛉

PASSAU: *Wilder Mann* €€
Am Rathausplatz, 94032. **Road map** E6. 🄲 *(0851) 350 71.* FAX *(0851) 317 12.*
Situated in a good spot, right in the city centre, this restaurant draws
diners with its good cooking and stylish surroundings. 🕭 🛉

REGENSBURG: *Zum Neuen Gänsbauer* €€€
Kepler Str. 10, 93047. **Road map** D6. 🄲 *(0941) 578 58.* FAX *(0941) 56 53 71.*
A rustic restaurant with a charming courtyard. Try one of the many exotic
specials of the day, or one of the duck or fish dishes. 🕭 🛉

REGENSBURG: *David* €€€€
Watmarkt 5, 93047. **Road map** D6. 🄲 *(0941) 56 18 58.* FAX *(0941) 516 18.*
This restaurant, in an historical tower near the cathedral, offers quality
regional and international food. There are great views over the charming
old town from the large roof garden. 🕭 🛉

ROTHENBURG OB DER TAUBER: *Eisenhut* €€
Herrngasse 3–7, 91541. **Road map** C6. 🄲 *(09861) 70 50.* FAX *(09861) 705 45.*
The restaurant, in the hotel of the same name, has a pleasingly stylish
interior. Sophisticated dishes, friendly service. There is also a garden
restaurant, a café with terrace and a hotel bar. 🎵 🛉

WÜRZBURG: *Nikolaushof* €€€
Spittelbergweg, 97082. **Road map** C5. 🄲 *(0931) 79 75 00.* FAX *(0931) 797 50 22.*
This restaurant is situated on top of a hill, right next to the famous
Baroque chapel. It serves international and Franconian dishes.

WÜRZBURG: *Schloss Steinburg* €€€
Auf dem Steinberg, 97080 Würzburg-Unterdürrbach. **Road map** C5.
🄲 *(0931) 970 20.* FAX *(0931) 971 21.*
This restaurant, part of a hotel and based in a castle, boasts attractive and
exclusive furnishings. German cuisine is its speciality, and it is open late
at night. Excellent service. 🛉

BADEN-WÜRTTEMBERG

BADEN-BADEN: *Piemonte* €€
Hans-Bredow-Str. 20, 76530. **Road map** B6. 🄲 *(07221) 30 09 90.*
FAX *(07221) 300 99 51.*
This restaurant is located in the Tannenhof hotel and North Italian cuisine
is its speciality.

<table>
<tr><td colspan="2">

Prices of a three course meal without drinks, including cover charge, tax and service:

€ up to €20
€€ €21–€29
€€€ €30–€39
€€€€ €40–€49
€€€€€ over €49

</td></tr>
</table>

CREDIT CARDS
Credit cards are accepted.
GARDEN OR TERRACE
Weather permitting, it is possible to eat *al fresco.*
GERMAN WINES
A good selection of German wines.
VEGETARIAN DISHES
The restaurant offers a good selection of meat free and vegetarian dishes.

	Price	CREDIT CARDS	GARDEN OR TERRACE	GERMAN WINES	VEGETARIAN DISHES
BADEN-BADEN: *Rebstock* Schlossackerweg 3, 76534 Baden-Baden–Neuweier. **Road map** B6. (07223) 572 40. FAX (07223) 95 96 34. This restaurant made the French saying "it is better to eat well than to dress well" its motto. The decor is rustic, and the food includes both regional and classic dishes.	€€	●	■	●	■
BADEN-BADEN: *Stahlbad* Augustaplatz 2, 76530. **Road map** B6. (07221) 245 69. FAX (07221) 390 222. Elegant, romantic restaurant with a terrace, specializing in the most diverse range of casseroles, including many potato and fish dishes. Another attraction on the menu is the venison medallions served with chestnuts.	€€	●	■	●	■
BADEN-BADEN: *Zum Alde Gott* Weinstr. 10, 76534 Baden-Baden–Neuweier. **Road map** B6. (07223) 55 13. FAX (07223) 606 24. Beautifully located restaurant with a terrace, from where the diner has a magnificent view of the surrounding Baden vineyards. The family-run restaurant serves regional specialities – diners are particularly fond of the home-cooked goose and the selection of local fish and game dishes. The restaurant ranks as one of the best in Germany.	€€€	●	■	●	■
BRAUNSBACH: *Schloss Döttingen* Buchsteige 2, 74542 Braunsbach-Döttingen. **Road map** C6. (07906) 10 10. FAX (07906) 101 10. This restaurant, which is part of the Schloss Döttingen Hotel, is situated 16 km (10 miles) north of Schwäbisch Hall. Based in a former hunting lodge dating from the 12th century, it serves international cuisine. There is also a wine bar, a café with a terrace and a pleasant drawing room with an open fireplace.	€	●	■	●	■
FREIBURG IM BREISGAU: *Enoteca* Gerberau 21, 79098. **Road map** B7. (0761) 389 91 30. FAX (0761) 28 05 81. Modern, elegantly and stylishly furnished restaurant, located in the old town and beautifully set amid period buildings. The restaurant specializes in light Italian cuisine.	€€	●			
HEIDELBERG: *Schlossweinstube Schönmehls* Im Schlosshof, 69117. **Road map** B7. (06221) 979 70. FAX (06221) 16 79 69. Modern and elegantly furnished restaurant, housed in an old castle. When the weather permits, tables are set out on the terrace. Among the many dishes on the menu, the roast duck with all the trimmings is outstanding.	€€€	●	■	●	■
HEIDELBERG: *Simplicissimus* Ingrimstr. 16, 69117. **Road map** C6. (06221) 18 33 36. FAX (06221) 18 19 80. This friendly restaurant, in the old town, is as popular with tourists as with the locals. The service is excellent. French cuisine predominates; even the simplest dishes are very tasty. The selection of wines includes German as well as Portuguese and Italian wines. Booking is recommended.	€€	●	■	●	
HEILBRONN: *Grüner Kranz* Lohtorstr. 9, 74072 Heilbronn-Neckar. **Road map** C6. (07131) 96 17 77. FAX (07131) 96 17 55. This is a modern and elegant restaurant, which specializes in traditional beef dishes. It is worth trying, for example, the roast beef prepared with onion.	€	●		●	■

KARLSRUHE: *Ketterer* €€
Bahnhofplatz 14–16, 76137. **Road map** B6. ☏ *(0721) 371 50.* ℻ *(0721) 371 51 13.*
The restaurant is based in the Residenz Hotel, which is part of the
Ringhotel chain. The specialities include tripe in a soured sauce, served
with potatoes and salad, pork medallions with *Spätzle* (a type of small
dumpling) and trout. ☐ ☐

KARLSRUHE: *Oberländer Weinstube* €€€
Akademiestr. 7, 76133. **Road map** B6. ☏ *(0721) 250 66.* ℻ *(0721) 211 57.*
This restaurant has a beautiful interior, reminiscent of the 1920s, and a
courtyard in the garden. Huge selection of wines and dishes from around
the world. Excellent service; a pleasant time is usually had by all diners
and the food is excellent.

KARLSRUHE: *Zum Ochsen* €€€
Pfinzstr. 64, 76227 Karlsruhe-Durlach. **Road map** B6. ☏ *(0721) 94 38 60.*
℻ *(0721) 943 86 43.*
The very helpful staff will assist even the most indecisive person in
choosing the right meal and drink. The frequently changing menu is
dominated by French dishes. Try the green salad with oranges. One of
the longest wine lists in Germany. ☐ ☐

KONSTANZ: *Siber* €€€€
Seestr. 25, 78464. **Road map** C7. ☏ *(07531) 996 69 90.*
℻ *(07531) 996 69 933.*
Elegantly furnished restaurant, filled with flowers, based in the Seehotel.
Superb classic French cuisine, a good selection of wines and excellent
service. After the meal, the adjacent casinos may tempt diners. ☐ ☐

LUDWIGSBURG: *Stahl* €€
Dorfstr. 4–6, 71636 Ludwigsburg-Pflugfelden. **Road map** C6. ☏ *(07141) 441 10.*
℻ *(07141) 44 11 42.*
This stylishly furnished restaurant is based in a small hotel of the same
name. The menu is varied – the Schwabian dishes, particularly the roast
meat with onions, are especially worth trying. ☐ ☐

MANNHEIM: *Wartburg* €€
68 159 Mannheim, F4, 4–11. **Road map** B5. ☏ *(0621) 12 00 90.*
℻ *(0621) 12 00 94 44.*
This restaurant is located in a hotel of the same name, offering many
sophisticated dishes from around the world, and a large choice of fine
wines. Service is excellent, and the interior elegant.

MARBACH: *Schillerhöhe* €€
Schillerhöhe 12, 71672. **Road map** C6. ☏ *(07144) 855 90.*
℻ *(07144) 85 59 20.*
The restaurant, based in the Parkhotel, has an extensive menu which
offers dishes to suit every taste.

RAVENSBURG: *Goldene Uhr* €
Saarlandstr. 44, 88212. **Road map** C7. ☏ *(0751) 362 90.*
℻ *(0751) 36 29 256.*
A pleasant restaurant in the Goldene Uhr Hotel, specializing mainly in
fish and game dishes.

ROTTWEIL: *Haus zum Sternen* €€
Haupstr. 60, 78628. **Road map** C7. ☏ *(0741) 533 00.* ℻ *(0741) 53 30 30.*
This smart restaurant and historic winebar, in the Haus zum Sternen
Hotel, tries to satisfy all its customers' culinary desires, however
sophisticated. The menu, which changes every 2–3 weeks, includes a
good selection of vegetarian dishes. From the terrace diners have good
views of the Neckar valley. ☐

SALEM: *Reck* €
Bahnhofstr. 111, 88682. **Road map** C7. ☏ *(07553) 201.* ℻ *(07553) 202.*
A showcase restaurant in the hotel of the same name, serving very tasty
regional cuisine and offering a good choice of wines. During the summer
visitors can dine in the garden. ☐

SCHWÄBISCH GMÜND: *Gmünder Geigerle* €€
Türlensteg 9, 73525. **Road map** C6. ☏ *(07171) 35 90.* ℻ *(07171) 35 93 59.*
The restaurant is based in the Rühle City Hotel Pelikan in the old town.
The menu is characterized by dishes drawn from international cuisines.
☐ ☐

<table>
<tr><td colspan="2">

Prices of a three course meal without drinks, including cover charge, tax and service:

€ up to €20
€€ €21–€29
€€€ €30–€39
€€€€ €40–€49
€€€€€ over €49
</td><td colspan="4">

CREDIT CARDS
Credit cards are accepted.
GARDEN OR TERRACE
Weather permitting, it is possible to eat al fresco.
GERMAN WINES
A good selection of German wines.
VEGETARIAN DISHES
The restaurant offers a good selection of meat free and vegetarian dishes.
</td></tr>
</table>

	CREDIT CARDS	GARDEN OR TERRACE	GERMAN WINES	VEGETARIAN DISHES
STUTTGART: *Ecco* €€ Plieninger Str. 100, 70567. **Road map** C6. (*(0711) 900 72 72.* FAX *(0711) 900 72 73.* Bistro with modern decor. The speciality of this restaurant is international food; try for example the liver with spinach, highly rated by regulars. ♿ ♔	●		●	▪
STUTTGART: *Weber's Gourmet im Turm* €€€ Jahnstr. 120, 70597 Stuttgart-Degerloch. **Road map** C6. (*(0711) 24 89 96 10.* FAX *(0711) 24 89 96 27.* This restaurant is in a fantastic position, in a television tower, from where diners have stunning views over the town. The table settings are also exceptionally pretty and worth mentioning. All the dishes, mainly Italian and French cuisine, are tastefully prepared, and the service is highly professional. ♿	●	▪	●	
STUTTGART: *Schlossgastronomie Solitude* €€€€ Solitude, 70197 Stuttgart. **Road map** C6. (*(0711) 69 20 25.* FAX *(0711) 699 07 71.* The breathtakingly beautiful castle chambers and the regal cuisine ensure a culinary as well as an aesthetic experience. Receptions are held in the castle banqueting halls. **P** ♔	●	▪	●	▪
TÜBINGEN: *Carat* € Wöhrdstr. 7, 72072. **Road map** C6. (*(07071) 13 91 00.* FAX *(07071) 13 92 50.* This restaurant, in the Domizil Hotel, serves especially light veal, beef and fish dishes. There is also a wide selection of pasta dishes. ♿ ♔		▪	●	▪
WEINGARTEN: *Altdorfer Hof* € Burachstr. 12, 88250. **Road map** B6. (*(0751) 500 90.* FAX *(0751) 50 09 70.* The restaurant, in the Altdorfer Hotel, serves exquisite Schwabian specialities. ♔ ♫	●	▪	●	

RHINELAND–PALATINATE & SAARLAND

	CREDIT CARDS	GARDEN OR TERRACE	GERMAN WINES	VEGETARIAN DISHES
KOBLENZ: *Loup de mer* €€ Neustadt 12, 56068. **Road map** B5. (*(0261) 161 38.* FAX *(0261) 911 45 46.* This restaurant is one of the best in town, serving mainly seafood and fish dishes. ♔	●	▪	●	▪
MAINZ: *Bajazzo* €€€ Augustusstr. 6, 55131. **Road map** B5. (*(06131) 95 46 70.* FAX *(06131) 95 41 00.* This excellent restaurant is in the Dorint Hotel and offers international and regional dishes.	●	▪	●	▪
MAINZ: *Der Halbe Mond* €€€ In der Witz 12, 55252 Mainz-Kastel. **Road map** B5. (*(06134) 239 13.* FAX *(06146) 83 55 12.* The restaurant, located on the Hesse side of the Rhine, serves local specialities from the Rhineland–Palatine region. The venue is tastefully furnished, and the service is good.	●	▪	●	
MARIA LAACH: *Seehotel Maria Laach* €€€ Ortsteil Maria Laach, 56653 Glees-Maria Laach. **Road map** B5. (*(02652) 58 40.* FAX *(02652) 58 45 22.* This well-known restaurant, situated in quiet and tranquil surroundings right next to the famous Benedictine monastery, specializes in fish dishes. Its delicious eel and salmon are particularly highly recommended. There is also a café with a terrace. ♿ ♔	●	▪	●	▪

SAARBRÜCKEN: *Schloss Halberg* €€€
Am Halberg, 66121 Saarbrücken outskirts. **Road map** B6. **(** (0681) 631 81.
FAX (0681) 63 86 55.
Beautifully situated inside Halberg castle, from where there is an
excellent view of the park and surroundings. Elegant service, French
cuisine. **P**

SAARBRÜCKEN: *Villa Weismülleri Restaurant Quack* €€
Gersweilerstr. 43, 66117. **Road map** B6. **(** (0681) 521 53.
FAX (0681) 584 99 10.
This comfortably furnished restaurant is well known in the area. The
dishes are presented in a tasteful and stylish way. Try the goose prepared
in the French style. Very courteous service. **P** **&** **⌖** **♪**

SPEYER: *Zweierlei* €
Johannesstr. 1, 67346. **Road map** B6. **(** (06232) 611 10. **FAX** (06232) 611 29.
Modern restaurant serving good food, mainly German.

SPEYER: *Backmulde* €€
Karmeliterstr. 11–13, 67346. **Road map** B6. **(** (06232) 715 77. **FAX** (06232) 62 94 74.
Very cosy restaurant; tasty French-influenced food. **⌖**

TRIER: *Pfeffermühle* €€
Zurlaubener Ufer 76, 54292 Trier-Zurlauben. **Road map** A5. **(** (0651) 261 33.
FAX (0651) 991 09 04.
The restaurant is in a former fishermen's house dating from the 18th
century, beautifully situated on the banks of the Mosel River. Furnished
with numerous antiques and etchings. Classic and regional cuisine;
among the specialities are game, lamb and goose dishes. Booking is
recommended. **P** **⌖**

TRIER: *Römischer Kaiser-Taverne* €€
Porta-Nigra-Platz 6, 54292. **Road map** A5. **(** (0651) 977 00.
FAX (0651) 97 70 99.
A split-level restaurant, situated in Trier's main square, a fact that has
guaranteed a never-ending stream of diners for the past 100 years. A
romantic setting, stylish furniture and plenty of light wood in the decor.
The food is German and international. **P** **&** **⌖**

WORMS: *Rôtisserie Dubs* €€
Kirchstr. 6, 67550 Worms-Rheindürkheim. **Road map** B5.
((06242) 20 23. **FAX** (06242) 20 24.
Although situated in a less interesting area of Worms, it is well worth
visiting this very elegant and glamorously furnished restaurant, which
specializes in sophisticated dishes, revealing a French influence. The
manageress will be delighted to recommend a suitable wine. Booking is
advisable.

HESSE

ALSFELD: *Krone* €
Schellengasse 2, 36304. **Road map** C4. **(** (06631) 40 41–42.
FAX (06631) 40 43.
Both the restaurant and the Krone Hotel are known for their excellent
service. Among the house specialities are game dishes from its own
hunts. The menu features frequent variations. **&** **⌖**

BAD HOMBURG: *Charlys Bistro* €€
Kaiser-Friedrich-Promenade 69–75, 61348. **Road map** C5. **(** (06172) 18 10.
FAX (06172) 18 16 30.
In the romantic restaurant of the Steigenberger Bad Homburg Hotel,
diners are seated at beautifully set tables, and attended by professional
and courteous staff who serve delicacies originating from America as well
as international cuisine. Interesting combination of dishes. The wine list
comprises around 130 wines from all over the world. **&** **⌖**

DARMSTADT: *Bockshaut* €
Kirchstr. 7–9, 64283. **Road map** C5. **(** (06151) 996 70.
FAX (06151) 99 67 29.
Situated in the heart of Darmstadt, this restaurant has a long history going
back to 1795. Very popular and well known for its unique interior and
friendly atmosphere, Bockshaut (which means "skin of a goat") offers
rustic dishes, including specialities such as cooked ox breast, beef
roulade and roasted black pudding. **⌖**

For key to symbols *see back flap*

Prices of a three course meal without drinks, including cover charge, tax and service: € up to €20 €€ €21–€29 €€€ €30–€39 €€€€ €40–€49 €€€€€ over €49	**CREDIT CARDS** Credit cards are accepted. **GARDEN OR TERRACE** Weather permitting, it is possible to eat *al fresco.* **GERMAN WINES** A good selection of German wines. **VEGETARIAN DISHES** The restaurant offers a good selection of meat free and vegetarian dishes.		

	CREDIT CARDS	GARDEN OR TERRACE	GERMAN WINES	VEGETARIAN DISHES
ELTVILLE AM RHEIN: *Marcobrunn* €€€€€ Hauptstr. 43, 65346 Eltville-Erbach. **Road map** B5. ((06123) 67 60. FAX (06123) 67 64 00. The Schloss Reinhartshausen Hotel complex, surrounded by a park and beautifully situated at the foot of vineyards, has several restaurants. Marcobrunn, an elegant establishment for gourmets, serves international cuisine, including Austrian dishes. The Schlosskeller restaurant serves mainly regional food. The wine list includes many wines produced in the restaurant's vineyards. ⬤ 🏃 ♫	●	■	●	■
FRANKFURT AM MAIN: *Maaschanz* €€ Färberstr. 75, 60594 Frankfurt-Sachsenhausen. **Road map** C5. ((069) 62 28 86. FAX (069) 62 28 86. This restaurant, situated in one of the main tourist districts of Frankfurt, specializes in fish dishes. *Apfelwein,* the local cider, is available here as everywhere.	●	■	●	■
FRANKFURT AM MAIN: *Peninsula* €€ Konrad-Adenauer-str. 7, 60313. **Road map** C5. ((069) 298 10. FAX (069) 298 18 10. This elegant bistro, based in the Arabella Sheraton Grand Hotel, serves excellent Mediterranean food. The service and cuisine are of a high standard. **P**	●		●	■
FRANKFURT AM MAIN: *L'Artichoc* €€€ Bockenheimer Landstr. 89–91, 60325. **Road map** C5. ((069) 90 74 87 71. FAX (069) 90 74 87 72. This restaurant, located in the basement of the Palmenhof Hotel, is a popular tourist attraction just like the neighbouring botanical gardens. Traditional German and Asian food is served here. 🏃	●		●	■
FRANKFURT AM MAIN: *Zum Schwarzen Stern* €€€ Römerberg 6, 60311. **Road map** C5. ((069) 29 19 79. FAX (069) 28 05 01. Modern, elegant restaurant in the old town, conveniently located right next to the cathedral. Regional cuisine of a high standard. ⬤ 🏃	●	■	●	■
FRANKFURT AM MAIN: *Alte-Kanzlei* €€€€ Niedenau 50, 60325. **Road map** C5. ((069) 72 14 24. FAX (069) 17 38 54. A distinguished Italian restaurant located in an historic building close to the Frankfurt exhibition centre and not far from the city centre. It serves classic Mediterranean cuisine, and the fish dishes are recommended with the fish fresh from the market each day. 🏃	●	■	●	■
FRANKFURT AM MAIN: *Tigerpalast* €€€€€ Heiligenkreuzgasse 16–20, 60313. **Road map** C5. ((069) 92 00 22 25. FAX (069) 92 00 22 17. This venue is unusual among German restaurants, presenting a variety show in an elegant restaurant. It is easy to spend a pleasant evening here while watching the excellent show, which includes circus artists and other performers. Excellent service. A large selection of wines and many interesting Italian dishes. 🏃	●		●	■
FULDA: *Dachsbau* €€€ Pfandhausstr. 8, 36037. **Road map** C5. ((0661) 741 12. FAX (0661) 741 10. Beautifully situated split-level restaurant, in a road known as "the street for the hungry", with unusual furniture and decor, such as a huge wine barrel. Excellent selection of dishes and wines.	●	■	●	
FULDA: *Zum Stiftskämmerer* €€€ Kämmerzeller Str. 10, 36041 Fulda-Kämmerzell. **Road map** C5. ((0661) 523 69. FAX (0661) 595 45. This cosy and comfortable restaurant with rustic decor offers a variety of delicious dishes such as leg of lamb with a herb crust.	●	■	●	■

GIESSEN: *Köhler*   € ● ■ ● ■
Westanlage 33–35, 35390. **Road map** C4. **[** *(0641) 97 99 90.* **FAX** *(0641) 979 99 77.*
The Köhler Hotel and restaurant have been run by the same family for
many years, and the atmosphere is relaxed throughout. The menu has a
large selection of dishes, including German, Italian, French and
occasionally Hungarian food, and there is also a pleasant wine bar. 🏃

KASSEL: *Zum Steinernen Schweinchen*   €€ ● ■ ●
Konrad-Adenauer-Str. 117, 34132 Kassel-Wilhelmshöhe. **Road map** C4.
[*(0561) 94 04 80.* **FAX** *(0561) 94 04 85 55.*
The complex comprises a restaurant, a hotel and a small brewery, which
can be visited. The dining room has an open fireplace and leads out to
the beer garden. The cooking is excellent. **P**

LIMBURG: *Wirtshaus Obermühle*   €€ ● ■ ● ■
Am Huttig 3, 65549. **Road map** B5. **[** *and* **FAX** *(06431) 279 27.*
This lovely restaurant, situated in the old town near the cathedral and
right by the Lahn river, is housed in a 12th-century mill, renovated in the
traditional style. They serve seasonal, regional and international food, and
there is a bar. 🖐

MARBURG: *Das kleine Restaurant*   € ● ■ ●
Barfüßertor 25, 35037. **Road map** C4. **[** *(06421) 222 93.* **FAX** *(06421) 514 95.*
This restaurant, furnished like a French boudoir, serves appetizing French
food.

MICHELSTADT: *Drei Hasen*   € ● ■ ●
Braunstr. 5, 64720. **Road map** C5. **[** *(06061) 710 17.* **FAX** *(06061) 725 96.*
This well-run restaurant, in the hotel of the same name, is situated right
on the historic market square. Rustic furnishings and cuisine to match,
majoring on game dishes. Beer garden.

RÜDESHEIM AM RHEIN: *Krone*   €€€ ● ■ ● ■
Rheinuferstr. 10, 65385 Rüdesheim-Assmannshausen. **Road map** B5.
[*(06722) 40 30.* **FAX** *(06722) 30 49.*
The traditions of this restaurant, in the Krone Hotel, go back 400 years.
The interior, with its beautiful wooden features, is like a small museum.
Exquisite fish and game dishes, such as lobster in a champagne sauce or
venison with nuts. Wide selection of wines. **P** 🏃 🎵

WEILBURG: *Alte Reitschule*   €€ ● ■ ● ■
Langgasse 25, 35781. **Road map** B5. **[** *(06471) 50 900.* **FAX** *(06471) 50 90 111.*
This restaurant, in the Schlosshotel, is based in former riding stables. The
pleasantly furnished venue serves international food – the lamb comes
highly recommended. The hotel also has a café with terrace.
P 🖐 🏃

WETZLAR: *Der Postreiter*   €€ ● ● ■
Parisergasse 20–22, 35578. **Road map** C5. **[** *(06441) 90 30.*
FAX *(06441) 90 31 00.*
There are several restaurants in the Bürgerhof Hotel, among them the
Jägerstübchen and the Königlich-Preußisches Grenz-Post-Amt (royal
Prussian border post office), where regional and international dishes are
on offer. Large selection of wines. Very friendly service. 🖐 🏃

WIESBADEN: *Domäne*   €€€ ● ■ ●
65205 Wiesbaden-Erbenheim outskirts. **Road map** B5. **[** *(0611) 73 74 60.*
FAX *(0611) 73 74 79.*
A vast complex, including a café, a restaurant, a patisserie, a wine bar
and more, situated on a farm a few kilometers from the centre of town.
The establishment is known throughout the region, in part because of its
excellent cuisine.

WIESBADEN: *Käfer's Bistro*   €€€ ● ■ ● ■
Kurhausplatz 1, 65189. **Road map** B5. **[** *(0611) 53 62 00.* **FAX** *(0611) 53 62 22.*
Pleasant bistro in a spa building with garden and all-day piano music.
The restaurant is open late. The food is traditional German, although the
furnishings are more reminiscent of a French bistro. 🖐 🏃 🎵

NORTH RHINE–WESTPHALIA

AACHEN: *Palm Bistro*   €€ ● ● ■
Monheimsallee 44, 52062. **Road map** A4. **[** *(0241) 18 08 700.* **FAX** *(0241) 18 08 703.*
This restaurant is located in a casino. The interior is modest and they
serve delicious regional and international dishes. 🖐 🏃

For key to symbols see back flap

Prices of a three course meal without drinks, including cover charge, tax and service:

€ up to €20
€€ €21–€29
€€€ €30–€39
€€€€ €40–€49
€€€€€ over €49

CREDIT CARDS
Credit cards are accepted.
GARDEN OR TERRACE
Weather permitting, it is possible to eat *al fresco*.
GERMAN WINES
A good selection of German wines.
VEGETARIAN DISHES
The restaurant offers a good selection of meat free and vegetarian dishes.

	CREDIT CARDS	GARDEN OR TERRACE	GERMAN WINES	VEGETARIAN DISHES
AACHEN: *St Benedikt* €€€	●		●	

Benediktusplatz 12, 52076. **Road map** A4. **(** (02408) 28 88. **FAX** (02408) 28 77.
Diners tend to feel at home in this restaurant, which has beautiful, romantic and antique furnishings, and offers impeccable service. The menu is changed twice a week. 🏃

AACHEN: *Schloss Schönau* €€€	●	■	●	■

Schönauer Allee 20, 52072 Aachen. **Road map** A4. **(** *and* **FAX** (0241) 17 35 77.
This excellent gourmet restaurant, about 5 km (3 miles) from the centre of Aachen, is based in an 11th-century castle. French nouvelle cuisine is served in a nostalgic and elegant ambience. There is also a bistro, with a more rustic atmosphere.

BAD HONNEF: *Alexanders Restaurant* €	●	■	●	■

Alexander-von-Humboldt-Str. 20, 53604. **Road map** B4. **(** (02224) 77 10.
FAX (02224) 77 15 55.
One of the restaurants in the Seminaris Hotel, situated 18 km (11 miles) southeast of Bonn. German and international food. **P**

BIELEFELD: *Westfälische Hofstube* €€	●	■	●	■

Niedernholz 2, 33699 Bielefeld-Oldentrup. **Road map** C3. **(** (0521) 209 00.
FAX (0521) 209 01 00.
The restaurant is part of the Oldentruper Hof Hotel which belongs to the Best Western hotel group. It is a favourite place in the town for meeting a friend. Stylish setting; delicious regional cooking. The Scheune restaurant is also part of the hotel.

BONN: *il Gambero Rosso* €€	●	■		■

Thomas Mann Str. 18, 53111. **Road map** B4. **(** (0228) 63 22 55. **FAX** (0228) 908 68 43.
Special lunch menu, extensive salad buffet, fish dishes. The cuisine is predominantly Italian, and Italian wines are also on offer.

BONN: *Zur Lindenwirtin Aennchen* €€€	●	■	●	■

Aennchenplatz 2, 53173 Bonn-Bad Godesberg. **Road map** B4.
((0228) 31 20 51. **FAX** (0228) 31 20 61.
Romantic restaurant with original furnishings, known throughout the entire Rhineland for its fantastic selections of wines from around the world. The chef often uses wine to cook his elaborate dishes, featuring both German and international recipes.

BONN: *Halbedel's Gasthaus* €€€€€	●	■	●	■

Rheinallee 47, 53173 Bonn-Bad Godesberg. **Road map** B4.
((0228) 35 42 53. **FAX** (0228) 35 25 34.
A favourite haunt of politicians, this restaurant is housed in a beautiful Art Nouveau villa in an elegant part of the town. Diners will undoubtedly take away fond memories of their meal. Specialities include rabbit in French pastry. Gallant service, stylish tableware. 🏃

BRÜHL: *Seerose* €	●	■	●	■

Römerstr. 1–7, 50321. **Road map** B4. **(** (02232) 20 40. **FAX** (02232) 20 45 23.
This restaurant, in the Treff-Hansa Hotel, located about half-way between Cologne and Bonn, is in a particularly pleasant spot, surrounded by extensive green spaces. The elegant establishment offers its diners the choice between a number of different cuisines, including American, French and Bavarian. The hotel also has a café with a garden and the Treff bar, which is a popular meeting place.

DETMOLD: *Speisekeller im Rosental* €€€	●	■	●	■

Am Schlossplatz 7, 32756. **Road map** C3. **(** (05231) 222 67. **FAX** (05231) 337 56.
This modern and comfortable restaurant, with its beautiful terrace, is situated directly on the Detmold palace park and opposite the theatre. The cook serves light vegetarian and Mediterranean dishes, with an emphasis on fresh ingredients from the market each day. ▤ 🏃

DÜSSELDORF: *Savini*   €€
Stromstr. 47, 40221 Düsseldorf-Hafen. **Road map** B4. (*(0211) 39 39 31.*
FAX *(0211) 39 17 19.*
This modern restaurant and terrace sets its tables in innovative ways.
There is also a long bar, reminiscent of film sets. Many celebrities have
visited this establishment, which is situated in an interesting spot in the
Rhine harbour district, opposite the TV building (WDR). The restaurant is
always well frequented, and advance booking is definitely recommended.
Charming service. The wine list includes an extensive selection of Italian
wines.

DÜSSELDORF: *Libanon Restaurant*   €€€
Berger Str. 19–21, 40213. **Road map** B4. (*(0211) 13 49 17.*
FAX *(0211) 13 49 97.*
This romantic and elegant restaurant offers diners the chance, from
Wednesday to Saturday, to watch belly dancing, which is very popular
with Middle Eastern guests. Food and wines are Lebanese.

DÜSSELDORF: *Canonicus*   €€€€
Neusser Tor 16, 40625 Düsseldorf-Gerresheim. **Road map** B4.
(*(0211) 28 96 44.* FAX *(0211) 28 35 03.*
The restaurant is on the first floor of a 400-year-old building. Although
small and compact, the venue is pleasant. The avant-garde cuisine serves
up numerous culinary surprises.

DÜSSELDORF: *Im Schiffchen*   €€€€€
Kaiserswerther Markt 9, 40489 Düsseldorf-Kaiserswerth. **Road map** B4.
(*(0211) 40 10 50.* FAX *(0211) 40 36 67.*
This restaurant has gained the highest accolades from restaurant critics in
Germany, and so it is essential to reserve a table. The talented master
chef, Jean Claude Bourgeuil, works here together with his wife. Diners
can choose from countless exquisite dishes as well as 600 different
wines.

ESSEN: *Résidence*   €€€€€
Auf der Forst 1, 45219 Essen-Kettwig. **Road map** B4. (*(02054) 89 11.*
FAX *(02054) 825 01.*
The Résidence Hotel, based in a beautiful villa, has two restaurants: one
specializing in classical German cuisine, and the second preparing light
French dishes. The service is very friendly, and staff will be happy to
help undecided diners to choose a meal and a suitable wine.

HAGEN: *Felsengarten*   €
Wasserloses Tal 4, 58093. **Road map** B4. (*(02331) 39 10.*
FAX *(02331) 39 11 53.*
This modern restaurant, part of the Hotel Mercure, serves a large number
of delicious dishes from around the world. Among some of the
specialities on the menu, the masterfully prepared goose is worth trying.
Pleasant and professional service.

HÖXTER: *Entenfang*   €€€
Godelheimer Str. 16, 37671. **Road map** C3. (*(05271) 970 80.*
FAX *(05271) 97 08 88.*
The restaurant in the Weserberghof Hotel is attractively situated, with
views of the Weser and Solling rivers. The restaurant has an intimate,
homely atmosphere. The chef of the stylish and elegant establishment
prepares classical international dishes, including Scandinavian specialities.
Set-price menus are available.

KAMP-LINTFORT: *Casino im Park*   €€
Friedrich-Heinrich-Allee 54, 47475. **Road map** A4. (*(02842) 963 40.*
FAX *(02842) 606 61.*
Pleasant restaurant with an open fireplace, based in the hotel of the same
name, serving delicious regional fare. The hotel also has a pub and a
small café.

KÖLN (COLOGNE): *Landhaus Kuckuck*   €€
Olympiaweg 2, 50933. **Road map** B4. (*(0221) 48 53 60.*
FAX *(0221) 485 36 36.*
The proprietor of the Landhaus Kuckuck is renowned for his good taste.
This shows in the restaurant which is elegant and refined, offering a calm
atmosphere and a menu specializing in poultry dishes, and serving
delicious liver and roast goose.

For key to symbols *see back flap*

<table>
<tr><td colspan="2">

Prices of a three course meal without drinks, including cover charge, tax and service:

€ up to €20
€€ €21–€29
€€€ €30–€39
€€€€ €40–€49
€€€€€ over €49

</td><td colspan="4">

CREDIT CARDS
Credit cards are accepted.
GARDEN OR TERRACE
Weather permitting, it is possible to eat *al fresco*.
GERMAN WINES
A good selection of German wines.
VEGETARIAN DISHES
The restaurant offers a good selection of meat free and vegetarian dishes.

</td></tr>
</table>

	CREDIT CARDS	GARDEN OR TERRACE	GERMAN WINES	VEGETARIAN DISHES
KÖLN (COLOGNE): *Restaurant Pöttgen* €€ Landmannstr.19, 50825. **Road map** B4. ☎ *(0221) 55 52 46.* FAX *(0221) 559 54 50.* This traditional restaurant, based in an Art Nouveau house with typical Rhineland interior, has been run by the same family for four generations. It serves specialities from Cologne and the Rhineland, fresh from the market. *Flammkuchen* is a house favourite. ♿	●	■	●	■
KÖLN (COLOGNE): *Fischers* €€€ Hohenstaufenring 53, 50674. **Road map** B4. ☎ *(0221) 310 84 70.* FAX *(0221) 31 08 47 89.* This restaurant doubles as a wine bar, and the landlady is a connoisseur and one of the greatest authorities on wine. Accordingly, there is a large selection of wines on offer, which is matched by the food, with the menu featuring specialities from around the world. The restaurant has a pleasant courtyard.	●	■	●	
KÖLN (COLOGNE): *Börsen-Restaurant Maître* €€€€ Unter Sachsenhausen 10–26, 50667. **Road map** B4. ☎ *(0221) 13 30 21.* FAX *(0221) 13 30 40.* The stylish and elegant Maître restaurant has a wonderful menu, consisting of the most ingenious French dishes. It is characterized by a pleasant atmosphere and courteous service. Diners also have the option of visiting the Börsenstube at the same establishment, which serves traditional food.	●	■	●	■
LEMGO: *Im Borke* €€ Salzufler-Str. 132, 32657 Lemgo-Kirchheide. **Road map** C3. ☎ *(05266) 16 91.* FAX *(05266) 12 31.* This rustic restaurant has a family atmosphere. The building is located in a small garden which resembles a park. ♿ 🍴 🅿	●	■	●	■
MONSCHAU: *Wiesenthal* € Laufenstr. 82, 52156. **Road map** A4. ☎ *(02472) 860.* FAX *(02472) 861 99.* Modern, recently built restaurant in the Carat Hotel, which will delight even the most demanding diners. In the evening, the Christofel-Bistro is a favourite meeting place. ♿ 🍴	●	■	●	■
MÜNSTER: *Landhaus Eggert* €€ Zur Haskenau 81, 48157 Münster-Handorf. **Road map** B3. ☎ *(0251) 32 80 40.* FAX *(0251) 328 04 59.* This hotel, restaurant and beer garden is set on a former gentleman's estate, amid charming meadows and forests. The large selection of dishes includes specialities from around the world. The professional staff will help diners to select one of the 100 wines on offer. There is live music on Tuesdays. ♿ 🍴 🎵	●	■	●	■
MÜNSTER: *Villa Medici* €€€ Ostmarktstr. 15, 48145. **Road map** B3. ☎ *(0251) 342 18.* FAX *(0251) 39 30 94.* This attractively furnished restaurant is the best place for Italian food. The chef is very attentive to his customers' needs, and he also offers a wine tour of Italy. 🍴	●			■
PADERBORN: *Balthasar* €€€€ Warburger Str. 28, 33098. **Road map** C3. ☎ *(05251) 244 48.* FAX *(05251) 244 58.* This modern and exclusive restaurant is a mecca for gourmets. The "wild" young chef serves everything that is "fun"; a changing menu of freshly prepared dishes, often in surprising combinations.	●	■	●	■
SIEGEN: *Kaisergarten* € Kampstr. 83, 57072. **Road map** B4. ☎ *(0271) 501 10.* FAX *(0271) 501 11 50.* Comfortably furnished restaurant in the Ramada Treff Hotel, serving interesting international and regional dishes. Courteous service. 🍴	●		●	■

SOEST: *Hansa Hotel* €
Siegmund-Schultze-Weg 100, 59494. **Road map** B4. ☎ *(02921) 709 00.*
FAX *(02921) 70 90 75.*
Modern hotel restaurant, located on the edge of town, serving dishes
drawn from an international repertoire. There is also a café with terrace
and a beer garden. 🅿 ⓰ 🛉

WINTERBERG: *Waldhaus* €€
Kiefernweg 12, 59955. **Road map** C4. ☎ *(02981) 20 42.*
FAX *(02981) 36 70.*
This restaurant, in the Waldhaus Hotel, is beautifully sited in the middle
of the forest, near a tobogganing run. Excellently chosen furnishings
recreate the interior of a castle. Fish dishes are the house speciality. 🛉

WUPPERTAL: *Scarpati* €€
Scheffelstr. 41, 42327 Wuppertal-Vohwinkel. **Road map** B4. ☎ *(0202) 78 40 74.*
FAX *(0202) 78 98 28.*
This restaurant, in the hotel of the same name, is somewhat hidden, yet it
is definitely worth seeking it out. The interior is furnished in a very
original style. The restaurant serves many excellent, classic Italian dishes
and a large choice of Italian wines. Pleasant terrace.

XANTEN: *Hotel van Bebber* €
Klever Str. 12, 46509 Xanten. **Road map** B4. ☎ *(02801) 66 23.*
FAX *(02801) 5914.*
This historical four-star restaurant, situated in the centre of the city, serves
excellent regional cuisine. Famous visitors have included Queen Victoria
and Winston Churchill. ⓰

LOWER SAXONY, HAMBURG & BREMEN

BRAUNSCHWEIG (BRUNSWICK): *Herrendorf* €
Am Magnitor 1, 38100. **Road map** D3. ☎ *(0531) 471 30.*
FAX *(0531) 471 34 99.*
Stylish restaurant in the Stadthotel Magnitor, serving classic dishes and
regional fare. There is also a pleasant hotel bar, the Teatro, and a café
with a small garden.

BREMEN: *Meierei* €€
Im Bürgerpark, 28209. **Road map** C2. ☎ *(0421) 340 86 19.*
FAX *(0421) 21 99 81.*
Smart restaurant with rustic furniture, beautifully situated in the middle of
a park. The restaurant's stone oven, used for baking bread and other
dishes, is a particularly interesting feature.

BREMEN: *Westfalia-Bierlachs* €€
Langemarckstr. 38–42, 28199. **Road map** C2. ☎ *(0421) 590 20.*
FAX *(0421) 50 74 57.*
This elegant restaurant specializes in exquisite fish dishes. ⓰ 🛉

BREMEN: *L'Orchidée* €€€€
Am Markt, 28195. **Road map** C2. ☎ *(0421) 305 98 88.*
FAX *(0421) 337 81 21.*
The interior of this modern restaurant, located in the centre of the city
near the main railway station, is elegant and luxurious. Excellent French
and regional cuisine; the hotel has a bar. ⓰

BÜCKEBURG: *Ambiente* €
Herminenstr. 11, 31675. **Road map** C3. ☎ *(05722) 96 70.* FAX *(05722) 96 74 44.*
The restaurant is based in a modern hotel building. Diners can also eat in
the grill room or the garden. Regional specialities. ⓰ 🛉

CELLE: *Entenfang* €€€€€
Hannoversche Str. 55–56, 29221. **Road map** C3. ☎ *(05141) 20 10.*
FAX *(05141) 20 11 20.*
Restaurant in the Fürstenhof Celle, housed in a 17th-century palace. This
is one of the best venues in Celle, where diners can enjoy an excellent
meal in a superb setting. The restaurant is adorned with many valuable
paintings and stylish furniture. Service is exemplary, and the standard of
the French dishes excellent. ⓰ 🛉

CLOPPENBURG: *Schäfers Hotel* €€
Lange Str. 66, 49661. **Road map** B2. ☎ *(04471) 24 84.* FAX *(04471) 94 77 14.*
Pleasant, romantic hotel–restaurant serving a variety of delicious dishes.

<table>
<tr><td colspan="2">

Prices of a three course meal without drinks, including cover charge, tax and service:

€ up to €20
€€ €21–€29
€€€ €30–€39
€€€€ €40–€49
€€€€€ over €49

</td><td>

CREDIT CARDS
Credit cards are accepted.
GARDEN OR TERRACE
Weather permitting, it is possible to eat *al fresco*.
GERMAN WINES
A good selection of German wines.
VEGETARIAN DISHES
The restaurant offers a good selection of meat free and vegetarian dishes.

</td></tr>
</table>

	CREDIT CARDS	GARDEN OR TERRACE	GERMAN WINES	VEGETARIAN DISHES
GÖTTINGEN: *Clarion Hotel* €	●	■	●	■

Kasseler Landstr. 45, 37081 Göttingen-Grone. **Road map** C4. **(**(0551) 90 20. FAX *(0551) 90 21 66.*
This attractively furnished restaurant is based in the hotel of the same name. The menu changes every 2–3 weeks, reflecting the seasons. The lamb and game dishes come highly recommended. ⛓ 🔏 🎵

	CREDIT CARDS	GARDEN OR TERRACE	GERMAN WINES	VEGETARIAN DISHES
HAMBURG: *Fischereihafen-Restaurant* €€	●	■	●	

Große Elbstr. 143, 22767 Hamburg-Altona. **Road map** C2. **(**(040) 38 18 16. FAX *(040) 389 30 21.*
The restaurant has elegant, modern furnishings. From the windows there are fantastic views of the harbour. Restaurant and bar have played host to many celebrities, and their autographs now adorn the walls of the restaurant. The service is of the "old school". The menu features international fare, including a large selection of fish dishes. German, Californian and Australian wines. ⛓ 🔏

	CREDIT CARDS	GARDEN OR TERRACE	GERMAN WINES	VEGETARIAN DISHES
HAMBURG: *Fischküche* €€	●	■	●	■

Kajen 12, 20459. **Road map** C2. **(**(040) 36 56 31. FAX *(040) 36 09 11 53.*
A very popular restaurant, serving fresh fish dishes. The decor has a maritime theme. ⛓ 🔏

	CREDIT CARDS	GARDEN OR TERRACE	GERMAN WINES	VEGETARIAN DISHES
HAMBURG: *Fischmarkt* €€	●	■		■

Ditmar-Koel-Str. 1, 20459. **Road map** C2. **(**(040) 36 38 09. FAX *(040) 36 21 91.*
This restaurant is situated right on the Fish Market, which is a popular destination for virtually every visitor to Hamburg.

	CREDIT CARDS	GARDEN OR TERRACE	GERMAN WINES	VEGETARIAN DISHES
HAMBURG: *La Fattoria* €€	●			■

Isestr. 16, 20144. **Road map** C2. **(**(040) 420 02 55. FAX *(040) 420 94 49.*
This nostalgically fitted restaurant not only serves excellent food, but also offers some of its furnishings for sale. Italian cuisine. ⛓ 🔏

	CREDIT CARDS	GARDEN OR TERRACE	GERMAN WINES	VEGETARIAN DISHES
HAMBURG: *La Mer* €€€	●	■	●	■

An der Alster 9, 20099. **Road map** C2. **(**(040) 24 83 40 40. FAX *(040) 28 03 851.*
The restaurant in the Prem Hotel is beautifully situated on the edge of the Alster river. In its pleasant setting the diner can enjoy imaginative dishes. Professional service. 🅿 ⛓ 🔏 🎵

	CREDIT CARDS	GARDEN OR TERRACE	GERMAN WINES	VEGETARIAN DISHES
HAMBURG: *L'Auberge Française* €€€	●	■		■

Rutschbahn 34, 20146. **Road map** C2. **(**(040) 410 25 32. FAX *(040) 450 50 15.*
Although the interior is modest, the French food is excellent. Try the goose liver or the lobster with lemon. 🔏

	CREDIT CARDS	GARDEN OR TERRACE	GERMAN WINES	VEGETARIAN DISHES
HAMBURG: *Jacobs Restaurant* €€€€	●	■	●	■

Elbchaussee 401–403, 22609 Hamburg-Nienstedten. **Road map** C2.
((040) 82 25 50. FAX *(040) 82 25 54 44.*
The Louis C. Jacob Hotel and its elegant restaurant are known well beyond Hamburg. The master chef is amazingly imaginative and very skilled in his craft. He serves light French cuisine with Italian accents as well as German dishes. The wine list has 900 different wines. ⛓ 🔏

	CREDIT CARDS	GARDEN OR TERRACE	GERMAN WINES	VEGETARIAN DISHES
HAMBURG: *Tafelhaus* €€€€	●	■	●	■

Holstenkamp 71, 22525 Hamburg-Bahrenfeld. **Road map** C2. **(**(040) 899 33 24.
Bistro-style restaurant with original furnishings. The handwritten menu features international fare. Courteous service. ⛓ 🔏

	CREDIT CARDS	GARDEN OR TERRACE	GERMAN WINES	VEGETARIAN DISHES
HANNOVER: *Gallo Nero* €€	●	■		■

Kirchweg 72b, 30655 Hannover–Groß-Buchholz. **Road map** C3.
((0511) 546 34 34. FAX *(0511) 54 82 83.*
The furnishings in the "black cockerel" are elegant, and the service excellent. The menu includes Italian dishes and there is a large selection of wines. 🅿 🔏

HANNOVER: *Die Insel*
€€€
Rudolf-von-Bennigsen-Ufer 81, 30519. **Road map** C3. **(** *(0511) 83 12 14*.
FAX *(0511) 83 13 22*.
Modern restaurant, bar and café are combined in one gastronomic
complex that attracts many guests. The restaurant windows give great
views of the Masch lake. The menu includes interesting Asian specialities
and game dishes; lunch is less expensive. **P** **&** **†**

HANNOVER: *Hindenburg Klassik*
€€€
Gneisenaustr. 55, 30175. **Road map** C3. **(** *(0511) 85 85 88*. FAX *(0511) 81 92 13*.
A classy restaurant, serving Italian food, including pasta. The menu
changes daily. The restaurant also has an art exhibition. **&**

HANNOVER: *Le Chalet*
€€€
Isernhagener Str. 21, 30161 Hannover-List. **Road map** C3.
(*(0511) 31 95 88*. FAX *(0511) 31 33 54*.
"Klein aber fein" (small but good) is an appropriate epithet for this restaurant specializing in French cuisine. **†**

HILDESHEIM: *Kupferschmiede*
€
Am Steinberg 6, 31139 Hildesheim-Ochtersum. **Road map** C3.
(*(05121) 26 30 25*. FAX *(05121) 26 30 70*.
Well hidden in the middle of a forest, this restaurant offers 48 different
types of champagne – the chef's favourite drink. Nouvelle cuisine is
served here as well as traditional German dishes; the prices reflect the
high quality of the cooking. Booking is advisable. **P** **&**

KÖNIGSLUTTER: *Merlin*
€
Braunschweigerstr. 21 A, 38154. **Road map** D3. **(** *(05353) 50 30*.
FAX *(05353) 50 32 44*.
There are several restaurants in the Königshof Hotel, and this one is a
basic restaurant offering a quick service, and appetizing dishes.
& **†**

OLDENBURG: *Kiebitz-Stube*
€
Europaplatz 4–6, 26123. **Road map** B2. **(** *(0441) 80 80*. FAX *(0441) 80 81 00*.
Within the City-Club-Hotel is the elegant restaurant Kiebitz-Stube, serving
international cuisine. **&** **†**

OSNABRÜCK: *Villa Real*
€€€€
Natruper-Tor-Wall 1, 49076. **Road map** B3. **(** *(0541) 60 96 27*.
FAX *(0541) 609 66 00*.
Pleasant restaurant in the Remarque Hotel, situated not far from the old
town, serving a large choice of Italian dishes. **&** **†** **♫**

STADTHAGEN: *Gasthaus Oelkrug*
€€
Waldstr. 2, 31655 Stadthagen-Obernwöhren. **Road map** C3. **(** *(05721) 80 25 25*.
FAX *(05721) 80 25 50*.
This restaurant, in an inn about 4 km (2 miles) south of Stadthagen,
offers an abundance of dishes on its menu; the trout is especially worth
trying. During the summer guests may dine in the garden. **&** **†**

WOLFENBÜTTEL: *Parkhotel Altes Kaffeehaus*
€
Harztorwall 18, 38300. **Road map** D3. **(** *(05331) 88 80*. FAX *(05331) 88 81 00*.
This hotel–restaurant is housed in a 19th-century building. The hotel is
elegantly furnished, serving traditional German specialities. The historic
grotto, which houses a wine bar, is also worth a visit. **&** **†**

WOLFSBURG: *La Fontaine*
€€€
Gifhorner Str. 25, 38442 Wolfsburg-Fallersleben. **Road map** D3.
(*(05362) 94 00*. FAX *(05362) 94 04 00*.
The restaurant, in the Ludwig im Park Hotel, is superbly furnished with
valuable pieces. It is acclaimed by gourmets and professional food critics
alike. Many sophisticated dishes drawn from traditional German cuisine
are served here, complemented by suitable wines. The terrace is open
during the summer. Booking is advisable, as the restaurant only has 10
tables and 36 covers.

SCHLESWIG-HOLSTEIN

BAD MALENTE: *Gartenhotel Weisser Hof*
€€
Vossstr. 45, 23714. **Road map** D1. **(** *(04523) 992 50*. FAX *(04523) 68 99*.
This hotel–restaurant is beautifully sited amid greenery. The stylishly
furnished restaurant has been run by the same family for many years.
Among its specialities are fish and game dishes.

For key to symbols see back flap

	Credit Cards	Garden or Terrace	German Wines	Vegetarian Dishes

Prices of a three course meal without drinks, including cover charge, tax and service in euros:

€ up to €20
€€ €21–€29
€€€ €30–€39
€€€€ €40–€49
€€€€€ over €49

CREDIT CARDS
Credit cards are accepted.
GARDEN OR TERRACE
Weather permitting, it is possible to eat *al fresco.*
GERMAN WINES
A good selection of German wines.
VEGETARIAN DISHES
The restaurant offers a good selection of meat free and vegetarian dishes.

FLENSBURG: *Rôtisserie* €
24955 Flensburg-Harrislee, Alte Zollstrasse 44, Kupfermühle Grenze.
Road map C1. 【 *(0461) 70 20.* FAX *(0461) 70 27 02.*
The restaurant is based in the Hotel des Nordens, which is right next to the German–Danish border. The pleasant venue, serving German and international dishes, affords beautiful views of the surroundings. The hotel also boasts a swimming pool and other recreational facilities. 🔥 🏃

| | ● | ■ | ● | ■ |

KIEL: *Im Park* €€
Niemannsweg 102, 24105. **Road map** C1. 【 *(0431) 881 10.* FAX *(0431) 881 11 35.*
The elegant restaurant of the Parkhotel Kieler Kaufmann is located in a villa that was formerly the home of a banker. Its beautiful location gives fantastic views of the sea. The food – imaginative regional and international dishes – is highly rated in the area. There is also a good selection of wines. Charming lounge with an open fireplace.

| | ● | ■ | ● | ■ |

LÜBECK: *Das kleine Restaurant* €€
An der Untertrave 39, 23552. **Road map** D2. 【 and FAX *(0451) 70 59 59.*
This unique little restaurant offers almost its entire repertoire, ten courses, at affordable prices. The portions are small enough to manage, and diners are sure to remember an evening here for a long time.

| | ● | | | ■ |

LÜBECK: *Haus der Schiffergesellschaft* €€
Breite Str. 2, 23552. **Road map** D2. 【 *(0451) 767 76.* FAX *(0451) 732 79.*
This well-known historic restaurant, dating from the 16th century, is adorned with mementoes of Lübeck's yachtsmen. Booking is advisable as the venue is very popular. Many fish dishes and excellent lamb. 🔥

| | ● | | ● | ■ |

LÜBECK: *Wullenwever* €€€€
Beckergrube 71, 23552. **Road map** D2. 【 *(0451) 70 43 33.* FAX *(0451) 706 36 07.*
A restaurant for connoisseurs, in a 16th-century building. Captivating decor and excellent service as well as cuisine. Large selection of wines. ● *Sun, Mon.* 🏃

| | ● | | | |

RATZEBURG: *Hansa Hotel* €
Schrangenstr. 25, 23909. **Road map** D2. 【 *(04541) 20 94.* FAX *(04541) 86 41 41.*
This restaurant, in a hotel picturesquely situated by a lake, has attractive decor. The menu includes regional and international dishes. The hotel bar is also open to diners. 🔥 🏃 🎵

| | ● | | ● | |

SCHLESWIG: *Strandhalle* €€
Strandweg 2, 24837. **Road map** C1. 【 *(04621) 90 90.* FAX *(04621) 90 91 00.*
This hotel–restaurant, in a charming location on the banks of the Schlei river, has for many years been run by the same family. Famous in the area, the cuisine is particularly renowned for its seafood dishes. Wine lovers will find a large choice of styles from different regions to choose from. There is a café with terrace, serving delicious iced coffee. 🏃

| | ● | ■ | ● | ■ |

SYLT: *Stadt Hamburg* €€€
Strandstr. 2, 25980 Westerland. **Road map** B1. 【 *(04651) 85 80.*
FAX *(04651) 85 82 20.*
The elegant restaurant for connoisseurs, in the Stadt Hamburg Hotel, is furnished with beautiful English furniture and floral decorations. The chef specializes in fish dishes, and there is a large selection of wines to accompany the meal. The bistro – also modern and elegantly furnished – offers light, tasty and significantly less expensive dishes. P 🔥 🏃

| | ● | ■ | ● | ■ |

SYLT: *Fährhaus* €€€€
Heefwai 1, 25980 Sylt–Ost-Munkmarsch. **Road map** B1. 【 *(04651) 939 70.*
FAX *(04651) 93 97 10.*
This gourmet restaurant, the best-known one on the island, has a beautiful view of the yachting marina. A large choice of fish and seafood. There is also a less expensive restaurant, the Käpt'n Selmer. P 🏃

| | ● | ■ | ● | ■ |

MECKLENBURG–LOWER POMERANIA

BAD DOBERAN: *Residenz* €€ ● ■ ● ■
Prof.-Dr.-Vogel-Str. 16–18, 18209 Heiligendamm. **Road map** D1.
[(038203) 46 20. **FAX** (038203) 46 248.
Comfortable restaurant in the Residenz Hotel, which is part of the chain
of Romantik hotels. The extensive menu includes dishes from regional
and international cuisine. Café with terrace. **🏠**

DARGUN: *Am Klostersee* € ● ■ ●
Am Klosterdamm, 17159. **Road map** E2. **[** (039959) 25 20. **FAX** (039959) 252 28.
The restaurant, in the Hotel Am Klostersee, is situated on the outskirts of
the town, on the shores of a lake, right by the edge of the forest. Simple
furnishings. Delicious regional food, including excellent fish and game
dishes. Lounge with an open fireplace and beer garden. **🏠**

GREIFSWALD: *Am Gorzberg* € ● ■ ●
Am Gorzberg, 17489. **Road map** E1. **[** (03834) 54 40. **FAX** (03834) 54 44 44.
The hotel, in which the restaurant is located, is an excellent starting point
for exploring the area, with excursions to the islands of Rügen and
Usedom. The elegant restaurant serves German cuisine. **&** **🏠**

GÜSTROW: *Nordik-hotel* € ● ■ ● ■
Markt 2–3, 18273 Güstrow. **Road map** D2. **[** (03843) 78 00. **FAX** (03843) 78 01 00.
The Stadt Güstrow Hotel, which has a long tradition, has several restaurants
and cafés, as well as a friendly bar. Regional fare. **&** **🏠**

NEUBRANDENBURG: *Sankt Georg* € ● ■ ● ■
Rostocker Str. 6, 17033. **Road map** E2. **[** (0395) 544 37 88. **FAX** (0395) 560 70 50.
The restaurant of the St Georg Hotel is conveniently situated on the edge
of town, towards Rostock, next to the Treptow gate. The visitor can
sample dishes from the region here. Beer garden. **&** **🏠**

ROSTOCK: *Il Ristorante Atlantic* €€ ● ●
Am Strom 107/108, 18119 Rostock-Warnemünde. **Road map** D1.
[(0381) 526 74. **FAX** (0381) 526 05.
This modern restaurant, in the part of town which functions as a summer
resort, affords great views. The food and service are of a high standard.
Steak and fish dishes are particularly worth trying. **&** **🏠**

RÜGEN: *Poseidon* € ● ■ ● ■
Lottumstr. 1, 18609 Binz. **Road map** E1. **[** (038393) 26 69. **FAX** (038393) 337 12.
This spacious restaurant with terrace serves delicious Italian and regional
dishes. **P** **&** **🏠**

RÜGEN: *Orangerie* €€ ● ■ ● ■
Zeppelinstr. 8, 18609 Binz. **Road map** E1. **[** (038393) 50444. **FAX** (038393) 504 30.
Small, elegant restaurant in the Hotel Vier Jahres-zeiten, specializing in
traditional fish dishes, served in varying styles. This is a popular venue,
and booking is advisable. **&** **🏠**

SCHWERIN: *Weinhaus Uhle* € ● ■ ● ■
Schusterstr. 13–15, 19055. **Road map** D2. **[** (0385) 56 29 56. **FAX** (0385) 557 40 93.
This traditional restaurant, the best in town, is situated near the castle,
theatre and cathedral. Excellent regional and French dishes are served in
the elegant restaurant, the knights' hall and the wine bar. The
Mecklenburger Zander (pike-perch) is worth trying. **&**

USEDOM: *Villa Auguste Viktoria* € ● ■ ● ■
Bismarckstr. 1–2, 17419 Ahlbeck. **Road map** E2. **[** (038378) 24 10. **FAX** (038378) 241 44.
The restaurant is based in a hotel, and reminds one of an orangery.
Pleasant service – the staff are happy to recommend one of the exquisite
fish dishes or other specials. **🏠**

USEDOM: *Kräuterstuben* €€ ● ■ ● ■
Puschkinstr. 10, 17424 Heringsdorf. **Road map** E2. **[** (038378) 26 50.
FAX (038378) 265 99.
The elegant restaurant is part of the Oasis Hotel, which also features a café
with terrace and a bistro. Beach chairs are for hire, too. **🏠**

WISMAR: *Stadt Hamburg* € ● ■ ● ■
Am Markt 24, 23966. **Road map** D2. **[** (03841) 23 90. **FAX** (03841) 23 92 39.
Hotel–restaurant conveniently located near the market square, serving
nourishing German dishes, as well as light Mediterranean food. The
terrace gives a beautiful view of the city. **&** **🏠**

For key to symbols *see back flap*

SURVIVAL
GUIDE

PRACTICAL INFORMATION

GERMANY IS A COUNTRY that is particularly well prepared to receive visitors. Every town, large and small, has a helpful tourist information centre that can offer help with finding accommodation and providing information about local restaurants, attractions and activities. Virtually all the larger cities also have Internet web sites where up-to-date information on hotels, restaurants, museums and historic monuments can be

Posters advertising future events

readily accessed. The country is served by an excellent public transport system and a first-rate network of roads and motorways, which makes getting around quick and easy. There is a plentiful supply of comfortable, affordable tourist accommodation in Germany, but it is worth bearing in mind that hotels can become booked up quickly during the festivals and fairs that occur throughout the year in different parts of the country.

WHEN TO VISIT

IN GERMANY, A PLEASANT and relaxing vacation can be enjoyed at any time of the year. When planning to visit cities and historic monuments, however, it is best to come in the spring or early autumn, particularly in the south of the country where it can be very warm. July and August are the ideal months for spending a restful holiday by the sea, in the lake districts or in the mountains. Arriving in Bavaria during the second half of September provides the opportunity to take part in the Oktoberfest. In December everybody is preoccupied with frantic Christmas shopping, while, in the winter, skiing is a popular pursuit in the Black Forest, the Alps and the Harz Mountains.

Increased traffic on the roads depends on the dates of school holidays, which are set independently in each

PALAIS PREYSING
FRANCOIS CUVILLÉS D.A.
1695 – 1768
ZUGESCHRIEBEN

ASAM-HAUS
von Egid Quirin Asam
1733 erstorben
erbaut bereits im 16. Jahrhundert
Reiche Fassadengestaltung
um 1711

Typical information plaques on historic buildings

state. It can also be quite busy at the start of the "long weekends" that occur at Easter, Whitsun and around other national public holidays.

VISA REGULATIONS

CITIZENS OF COUNTRIES that are members of the European Union, the US, Canada, Australia, and New Zealand do not require a visa to visit Germany, so long as their stay does not exceed three months duration. Visitors from South Africa will need a visa. In addition, citizens of many EU countries do not require a passport to enter Germany, though a national ID card is necessary.

CUSTOMS REGULATIONS

GERMAN REGULATIONS totally prohibit the importation of drugs, animals and exotic plants that are under special protection. There are also

regulations that restrict the importation of cigarettes. An adult may bring in 200 cigarettes or 100 cigars, and 250g (9oz) of tobacco, as well as one litre of spirits and two litres of wine. You can also import up to 5kg (11lb) of foodstuffs, but not animal products which are forbidden. Beyond these limits, goods must be cleared by Customs when entering the country.

Tourist information office in Rottweil, Baden-Wurttemberg

TOURIST INFORMATION

A VERY WELL-DEVELOPED network of tourist information centres exists in Germany. These are generally run by the city or regional tourist authorities, *Verkehrsamt*. They provide information on accommodation, addresses and opening hours of historic monuments and museums, cruises, organized excursions and city tours, as well as brochures covering the most important tourist information.

Tourists on an excursion with a guide

◁ **Beer tankards from Heidelberg**

They sell useful guide books, maps and postcards and may be able to find and book you a hotel room.

OPENING HOURS

OPENING HOURS of shops, offices and other businesses depend to a great extent on the size of the town. In larger cities, the usual office opening hours are from around 9am until 6pm. Banks operate much shorter hours *(see p536)*. In smaller towns, however, nothing tends to open until 10am, and many businesses close from 1–2pm for lunch. Visitors must also bear in mind that there is a compulsory and virtually total ban on trading on Saturday afternoons, Sundays and on public holidays. Restrictions also limit the opening hours of shops *(see p540)*.

MUSEUMS AND HISTORIC MONUMENTS

MUSEUMS IN GERMANY are generally open from 9am until 6pm, and in smaller places from 10am until 5pm or even 4pm. Some museums, however, do close at lunchtime. Once a week, usually on Wednesdays or Thursdays, some museums may be open somewhat longer, while on Mondays they may be closed. Larger churches in major cities are accessible to tourists throughout the whole day. In smaller places, visiting may only be possible after making prior arrangements. There may be a notice on the door of the church advising visitors whom to contact in order to obtain the key.

Publications providing information on cultural events

ADMISSION TICKET PRICES

THE PRICE OF admission to museums and historic monuments can be high. For example, entrance to a small regional museum may cost €1–€1.5, to a large state-run museum around €2.5–€3, while a private or residential venue may charge as much as €5. Admission to smaller churches is usually free but a fee may be charged in certain cathedrals and monastic churches. There may also be a fee to see the church treasury, where the most valuable exhibits are displayed.

High fees are charged at large entertainment complexes: for example, you may have to pay €10–€15 for a tour of a film studio.

EMBASSIES AND CONSULATES

THE EMBASSIES OF several countries, including the UK and US, are located in Berlin. Consulates are also based in other major German cities.

Illustrated admission tickets for tourist attractions

Practical Information

A kiosk selling newspapers and cigarettes

DISABLED VISITORS

GERMANY IS A COUNTRY that is relatively well prepared to receive disabled travellers. Large museums and important historic monuments have special ramps or lifts for people who are confined to wheelchairs. Offices and banks are also accessible to wheelchair users, and there are usually lifts at railway stations and larger underground stations. A large proportion of public transport vehicles have been adapted to take wheelchair passengers. Most hotels, especially the higher grades, offer suitably equipped bedrooms. For visitors who use wheelchairs, there are usually specially designed toilet facilities within public toilets in car parks, railway stations and airports. A handicapped person may, however, still have problems in gaining access to small museums, certain historic monuments and to toilets in restaurants, which are often located in the cellar. **Contact Touristik Union International (TUI)** for further useful information.

RELIGION

IN A COUNTRY WITH profound historical influences, the dominant religion varies from area to area and from state to state, depending on which faith was chosen by local rulers in the past. Today, the southern states are predominantly Catholic while, in the north, Protestantism is more common. However, with a migrating population, this historical division has begun to change. The 20th century brought a huge influx of people of other faiths: the Muslim population now numbers several millions. Where large communities of ethnic minorities exist, services are held in their languages, while in most large cities there are some churches where extra services are held in English and in French.

Sign for public toilets, including facilities for disabled visitors

EVERYDAY CUSTOMS

GERMANS, AND particularly the older generation, attach great importance to courteous behaviour. You constantly hear "*Guten Tag*" when entering a shop, and "*Auf Wiedersehen*" – or the more youthful "*Tschüss*" when leaving. Germans are also very punctual and consider even a small delay to be very impolite. Arriving somewhat earlier than arranged for an engagement is regarded as courteous.

It is also important to adapt to German regulations. It is a violation, for example, to cross the road when there is a red light showing, even if the road is clear, and can result in an official reprimand.

Among younger Germans, however, shifts in traditional ideas of politeness can be observed. Older people and women are no longer treated with such respect and are no longer automatically offered seats on public transport by younger passengers. Another notable change is the huge tolerance now shown towards even the most unruly children by parents and other adults.

LANGUAGE

ALTHOUGH ALL Germans do speak German, many of them use dialects that are virtually incomprehensible, even to those from neighbouring regions. The most difficult dialects to understand are often considered to be those of southern Germany, particularly Bavarian and Schwabian, but Frisian and Saxon dialects are also likely to cause severe communication problems for visitors.

Travellers can usually be understood in Germany by speaking English, particularly in larger cities and in places that are frequented by foreign tourists and holidaymakers.

NEWSPAPERS

PUBLICATIONS CAN be bought not only in kiosks, but also in automatic vending machines. In the evenings, papers are distributed in bars

Two of the most popular German newspapers

and restaurants by news-vendors. Current newspapers are usually available in cafés. Every state has its own titles. In Berlin the most popular newspapers are *Berliner Zeitung, Der Tagesspiegel* and *Die Tageszeitung.* In southern Germany it is *Süddeutsche Zeitung.* Highly respected throughout Germany is the *Frankfurter Allgemeine Zeitung,* while the most widely read is *Bild.*

Foreign language publications, such as *International Herald Tribune, The Guardian, Le Monde, El País, Neue Zürcher Eeitung* and *Corriere della Sera,* are available at kiosks, railway stations and airports, as well as in more expensive hotels.

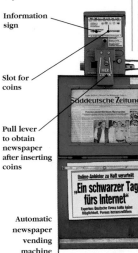

Information sign

Slot for coins

Pull lever to obtain newspaper after inserting coins

Automatic newspaper vending machine

TIME

GERMANY uses Central European Time (GMT plus one hour). Clocks move forward one hour on the last Sunday in March and back on the last Sunday in October.

WEIGHTS AND MEASURES

THE METRIC system of measurement is used in Germany. Note that half a kilogram is expressed by the word *pfund.* In contrast to UK usage, decimals are indicated by a comma and thousands by a point: thus 10,000.50 (UK) = 10.000,50.

ELECTRICITY

THE ELECTRICAL system in Germany provides 220V, 50 Hz AC, except in some hotel bathrooms where a lower current is provided as a standard safety measure. UK 220V appliances can be plugged into German sockets with an adaptor. However US 110V appliances will have to be used with a transformer.

WOMEN TRAVELLING ALONE

A WOMAN TRAVELLING on her own will not surprise anyone in Germany and only the usual safety precautions need be taken, particularly in large cities at night. However, it is best to avoid certain areas in towns where there is a lively nightlife – for example the *Reeperbahn* in Hamburg. Hitchhiking is quite popular in Germany, but a better option for single women may be to use the services of *Mitfahr-zentrale (see p549).*

TRAVELLING WITH CHILDREN

TRAVELLING WITH children is common in Germany and consequently their needs are well catered for. Restaurants can usually provide a high chair for a toddler and offer a special *Kinder-menu* with small portions. Public toilets at railway stations, airports and in motorway service stations, as well as in many museums and stores, usually offer a separate facility for mothers and babies. The majority of hotels and guest houses offer discounts for

Phantasialand, Brühl, a popular children's entertainment park

children *(see p473).* Discounts or even free travel for the youngest children are available on various forms of transport and there are similar concessions in most museums. In many German cities it is possible to purchase family tickets that provide substantial discounts on fares and admission fees.

An international student identity card, the ISIC card

INFORMATION FOR YOUNG PEOPLE

DURING A STAY in Germany it is worth carrying an International Student Identity Card (ISIC), which entitles holders to a 50 per cent discount in certain museums and reductions when buying some theatre tickets. It also allows students to get useful discounts on air tickets and certain urban public transport.

In the larger towns and cities there are special information bureaux for young people, where legal advice and support on such issues as education and employment is available.

Security and Health

Pharmacy sign

$\mathbf{A}$S IN OTHER COUNTRIES, visitors are far safer in small towns and villages in Germany than in big cities, where extra vigilance must be taken against pickpockets – particularly when travelling on public transport during rush hour. It is worth using a money belt or other means of concealing your money and documents. Taking out medical insurance cover is always advisable when travelling abroad, but for minor health problems that do not require the services of a doctor, pharmacists are a good and easily accessible source of assistance.

Characteristically coloured white and green police van

POLICE

$\mathbf{G}$REEN IS THE predominant colour of German police uniforms and signs. Motorized police units, *Verkehrspolizei*, which look after safety on the streets, roads and motorways, are distinguished by their white caps, while uniformed policemen patrolling city streets have a cap that is the same colour as their uniform. However, the police who are responsible for criminal offences, *Kriminalpolizei*, are generally dressed in plain clothes. They will produce their identification and insignia as necessary.

In towns, urban police in navy-blue uniforms are in evidence. Their role is, above all, to catch motorists who have parked illegally or have failed to pay the appropriate parking fee. Such traffic offences may incur on-the-spot fines and rigorous checking of documents.

PERSONAL PROPERTY

$\mathbf{T}$HE MOST SERIOUS threat for a tourist is always the pickpocket. This type of thief tends to prowl in crowded places, such as railway platforms, in the carriages of trains and on buses. They also frequent popular tourist sights and any events where large groups of people are likely to gather. When setting off on an excursion it is best to leave valuable items and documents in the hotel safe.

Policeman and policewoman

Police sign

Conceal valuable items, such as cameras and audio equipment, under clothing and carry cash in a money belt. Park your car in the hotel car park whenever possible and never leave valuable items in the vehicle, especially if it has to be left in the street overnight.

ACCIDENTS AND EMERGENCIES

$\mathbf{I}$F AN ACCIDENT or a serious breakdown occurs on the motorway, it is best to use one of the special telephones that are set out at regular intervals along the hard shoulder *(see p548)*. Throughout the whole of Germany there is a special emergency number, *112*, which will be answered by an operator who is an experienced member of a rescue team. Among their responsibilities are informing the appropriate emergency services. Every telephone, including mobile phones, will allow callers to connect free of charge to this number.

Thefts and burglaries must be reported immediately to the criminal police. If a crime is committed on the platform of the S-Bahn or the U-Bahn, the appropriate emergency alarm button can be used to summon assistance. Special alarm buttons, within small red boxes, also provide a direct connection with the fire brigade *(Feuerwehr)*. These alarm buttons are usually located in prominent positions on the streets and in large department stores.

In the case of more serious problems, such as loss of passport, visitors should turn to their Consulate *(see p531)*. Officials in a consulate are available to help travellers in case they need to acquire a replacement passport, obtain legal advice, hire the services of a translator or assistance in contacting their family. In some circumstances, they may even be able to arrange for financial loans to finance the purchase of a ticket home.

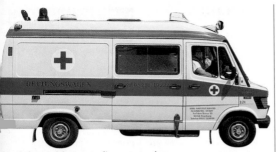
Ambulance of the paramedic rescue services

LOST AND STOLEN PROPERTY

BEFORE LEAVING home it is advisable to take out an insurance policy to cover property against loss or theft. Theft must be reported to the police immediately and a certificate obtained to confirm that the loss has been reported; this is needed if an insurance claim is submitted.

If property has been lost, it is worth asking at a lost property office (*Fundbüro*). These exist in every German city. The railway network has its own lost property offices – *Fundbüro der Deutschen Bahn AG* – as do the urban transport systems in individual towns.

Alarm button for the fire brigade

MEDICAL ASSISTANCE

CITIZENS OF COUNTRIES within the European Union do not have to take out medical insurance in order to obtain free medical care in Germany. In order to avail themselves

Entrance to a pharmacy in Heidelberg

of these reciprocal arrangements, however, visitors must obtain form E111 from a main post office before leaving home. However, it is still advisable to take out some form of health insurance. If plans include taking part in any sporting activities, particularly dangerous sports, make sure that the policy has a clause guaranteeing the refund of costs if rescue services are involved – for example mountain rescue services. This type of insurance is usually much more expensive.

In case of serious illness, it is necessary to call an ambulance who will take the patient to the nearest hospital out-patient clinic. In large hotels you can count on medical care being provided on the premises. For minor accidents it is best to turn for advice to a pharmacy (*Apotheke*).

HEALTH

GERMANY POSES NO health hazards for the traveller. The country is well served with hospitals and there are no prevalent diseases. No vaccinations are required when entering the country.

Visitors who require prescribed medication should ensure that they take enough to cover their stay, as it may not be available locally.

Throughout the whole of Germany, tap water is safe to drink. In department stores, pharmacies and large banks there are water tanks with plastic cups, which can be used free of charge.

PHARMACIES

PHARMACIES IN Germany are indicated by a stylized letter "A" (*Apotheke*) and are usually open from 8am–6pm; in small towns they may close from 1–3pm. In larger towns there is always a rota and this is displayed in the window of each pharmacy with a note of addresses. Information on rota pharmacies may also be obtained from tourist offices.

PUBLIC CONVENIENCES

IN LARGE CITIES, public toilets (often automatic cubicles) can usually be found without much difficulty. Instructions on how to use these facilities are given in several languages on the doors of the cubicles. Public toilets can also usually be found in museums, cafés, restaurants and department stores. Men's toilets are marked *Herren* and ladies' *Damen* or *Frauen*.

DIRECTORY

EMERGENCY SERVICES

Fire Brigade and Police
📞 110.

Ambulance
📞 19222.

Airborne Rescue Club (Deutsche Rettungsflugwacht)
📞 (0711) 70 10 70.

Emergency Poison Help Line
📞 (0761) 192 40.

LOST PROPERTY

Fundbüro der Deutschen Bahn AG
📞 (01805) 99 05 99.

Zentrales Fundbüro Berlin
Platz der Luftbrücke 6, Berlin.
📞 (030) 69 95.

Banks and Local Currency

Logo of the ReiseBank

U NTIL RECENTLY some credit cards, including Visa, were not quite as popular in Germany as in other countries. This has now changed, however, and tourists should have no problems. In cities and towns cash can be obtained from automatic cash points (ATMs) and foreign currency exchanged at a bank and currency exchange point.

Wechselstube – a currency exchange bureau in Berlin

CHANGING CURRENCY

T HERE ARE NO limits on the amount of foreign currency that can be brought into the country. Travellers generally use travellers' cheques or credit cards, both of which minimize problems in case of loss or theft.

Foreign currency can be exchanged in a bank or exchange bureau, *Wechselstube*. Both offer a similar rate of exchange, but they usually charge a commission. It is best to check this before undertaking a transaction in order to confirm how much you will have to pay. Most banks have quite inconvenient opening hours: they are open Monday–Friday, from 9am–3:30pm, with a break for lunch between noon and 1pm. Once a week (usually on a Thursday) they are open until 6pm. Opening hours may be a little longer in larger cities. It is advisable to take advantage of the services offered by a branch of the ReiseBank as soon as you arrive – these are

located in airports and railway stations. Currency exchange counters are usually located near railway stations or in places frequented by tourists. These have longer opening hours than banks, but may have less favourable exchange and commission rates.

Foreign currency can be exchanged at special automatic cash points, which can generally be found at larger airports, railway stations and in city centres that are visited by tourists. Cash can also always be exchanged at hotel reception desks, but check the exchange rate before going ahead as the rate may be quite low.

Automatic cash machine

TRAVELLERS' CHEQUES

T RAVELLERS' CHEQUES can be used to pay for goods and services, or to settle hotel bills, but it is often better to pay by cash. Cheques can be cashed in banks and currency exchange bureaux, but it should be remembered that

it is most advantageous to exchange them for local currency. It is a good idea to purchase travellers' cheques in Deutschmarks (DM) or Euro denominations.

✓ **Deutsche Bank**

Logo of Deutsche Bank, one of the biggest banks in Germany

CREDIT CARDS

C REDIT CARDS can be used to pay bills in most hotels and restaurants, in all department stores and in most shops – a fact that is always confirmed by a sticker with the credit card logo on the door or by the cash till. Sometimes, especially in restaurants and cafés, there is a compulsory minimum limit that can be paid by credit card. It is advisable, therefore, to check the situation before ordering just a drink or snack, since it may not be possible to pay for small amounts by credit card.

In busy parts of town and in commercial centres, it is easy to find a cash point that accepts credit cards, but note that some of these accept only EuroCard-

---

The Bayerische Vereinsbank in Munich

DIRECTORY

LOST CREDIT CARDS/ TRAVELLERS' CHEQUES

American Express
 (069) 97 97 10 00.

Diner's Club
 (05921) 86 12 34.

EC and Bank Cards
 (069) 74 09 87.

Euro-MasterCard
 (069) 79 33 19 10.

VISA
 (0800) 81 49 100.

Card. Lost credit cards or travellers' cheques should be reported immediately to a bank or the issuing organization.

CURRENCY

THE DEUTSCHMARK was the sole German currency until 2002. On 1 January 2002, the Euro, common currency of the European Union, was introduced into general circulation. Twelve countries have replaced their traditional currencies with the Euro: Austria, Belgium, Finland, France, Germany, Greece, Ireland, Italy, Luxembourg, Netherlands, Portugal and Spain chose to join the new currency; the UK, Denmark and Sweden stayed out, with an option to review their decision. All the old currencies were phased out by mid-2002.

Euro Bank Notes
Euro bank notes have seven denominations. The 5-euro note (grey in colour) is the smallest, followed by the 10-euro note (pink), 20-euro note (blue), 50-euro note (orange), 100-euro note (green), 200-euro note (yellow) and 500-euro note (purple). All notes show the 12 stars of the European Union.

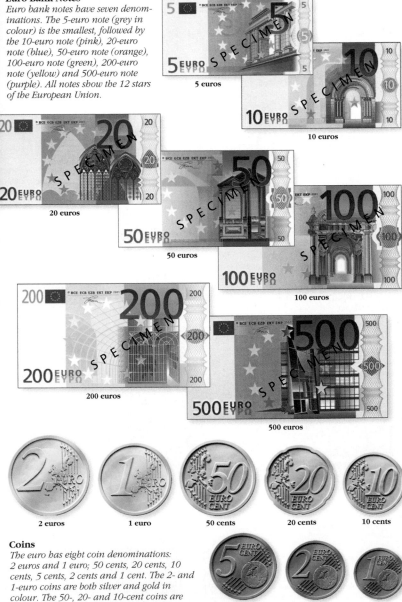

5 euros

10 euros

20 euros

50 euros

100 euros

200 euros

500 euros

2 euros   1 euro   50 cents   20 cents   10 cents

Coins
The euro has eight coin denominations: 2 euros and 1 euro; 50 cents, 20 cents, 10 cents, 5 cents, 2 cents and 1 cent. The 2- and 1-euro coins are both silver and gold in colour. The 50-, 20- and 10-cent coins are gold. The 5-, 2- and 1-cent coins are bronze.

5 cents   2 cents   1 cent

Communications

A rare, antique mail-box

THE POSTAL AND telecommunications services in Germany work very efficiently. Though it may be necessary to queue for a few minutes in the post office, letters and postcards are usually delivered within the country in 24 hours. There are no problems using the telephone. Call boxes can be found on every street corner, in U- and S-Bahn stations, and in virtually every restaurant and café. The distinctive yellow mail-boxes are also a common sight.

Every public phone should be equipped with a set of telephone directories, but these often go missing.

Telephone boxes marked with the word "*National*" can only be used to ring numbers with German dialling codes, but overseas calls can be made from other phones.

Telephone calls can be made from hotel rooms, but the cost of these will be much greater than those made from public telephone boxes. It is worth checking with your hotel first.

Telephone calls can also be made at post offices: there, calls are booked at a window marked "*Ferngespräche*".

USING THE TELEPHONE

GERMANY'S PUBLIC telephones are serviced by *Deutsche Telekom*. The oldest types are coin-operated and require a minimum deposit, which is the cost of a single local call. Smaller denomination coins are not accepted. Unused coins are returned, but no change is given. It is far more convenient to use a telephone card, which can be purchased at post offices, priced €3, 6 and 25.5. Alternatively, travellers may purchase an international phone card before leaving home. While using a phone card in a public phone, an illuminated display will show the amount of credit still remaining on the card. Card-operated public phones can be found in many busy areas of towns and cities. In order to use them it is necessary to dial in a personal pin number.

Deutsche Telekom sign

Many phone boxes have their own telephone number. This means that they can receive incoming calls, so that a caller can be called back if his money or card runs out.

TARIFFS

DEPENDING ON THE time and day, different tariffs apply to local telephone calls, as well as to intercity and international calls. The most expensive period to make a call is between 7am and 6pm. Calls cost less between 6pm and 9pm, and, later in the evening, they are even cheaper. Likewise, telephone calls are cheaper at weekends than on weekdays.

USING A COIN-OPERATED TELEPHONE

1 Lift the handset and wait for the dial tone.

2 Insert coins into the slot.

3 Dial number and wait to be connected.

4 Add more coins when signal is given.

5 When you have finished your call, replace the handset. For the return of unused coins, press the button above the slot where you inserted the coins.

Colourful chip telephone card (back and front)

USING A CARD-OPERATED TELEPHONE

1 Lift the handset and wait for the dial tone.

2 Choose the appropriate language.

3 Insert the card as instructed. The illuminated display will show the amount of credit remaining.

4 Dial the number and wait to be connected.

5 After finishing the call replace the handset. Withdraw the card by pressing the green button.

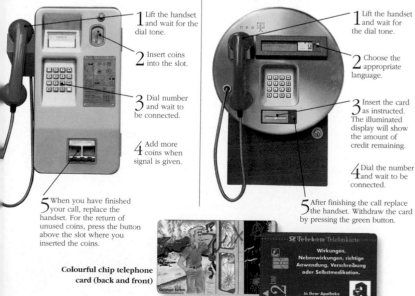

MOBILE TELEPHONES

A MOBILE (CELLULAR) telephone can prove invaluable on holiday, especially for phoning ahead to book hotel rooms or when taking part in mountain sports or travelling in remote areas. Before leaving home, travellers should discuss their requirements with their network provider, including which countries are to be visited. The different options can be explained and the most suitable tariff selected. Charges vary according to the facilities and coverage offered.

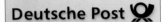

The logo of the German postal service

POSTAL SERVICES

J UST AS IN OTHER countries, registered mail, telegrams and parcels can be sent from post offices. As well as stamps, post offices also sell phone cards, postcards, envelopes and cartons in which to send items by post. Letters sent *Poste Restante* are usually issued from post offices near railway stations. Such correspondance should be marked with the words "*Postlagernde Briefe/Sendungen*". In order to collect mail, a passport or other form of identification will have to be produced.

SENDING A LETTER

S TAMPS FOR LETTERS and postcards can be bought at a post office, and sometimes they are sold along with postcards. Stamps can also be

bought from automatic stamp machines. Before posting a letter in a mail-box, check what is written on the box. Some mail-boxes have two slots – one marked for local post only, the other for all other destinations.

POST OFFICES

P OST OFFICES IN Germany are indicated by the word "*Post*", while mail-boxes and the official *Deutsche Post* logo are a distinctive yellow colour. In large towns, post offices are usually open from 8am until 6pm, and from 8am until noon on Saturdays. Branches with longer opening hours, and which are often also open on Sundays, can be found at most airports and large railway stations. In smaller towns, post offices are often located in local shops.

POSTAL ADDRESSES

I N GERMANY, THE postal code of five digits is an important part of the address, allowing a more precise location than simply the street name and house number. In cities, for example, different sections of long streets will have different

Entrance to one of the post offices in Bonn

postal codes. In multiple-occupancy buildings, the number of individual apartments is not given in the address. Instead, mail is delivered according to the name cards at the entrance to the building. Consequently, in order to send mail to a person who is staying in someone else's house, it is necessary to write at the top of the envelope the name of the main occupant, preceded by the letters "c/o" (care of).

THE INTERNET AND E-MAIL

T HE INTERNET AND e-mail have become increasingly popular and essential as a means of communication, and they can be especially useful for people who are abroad on holiday or business. As a result, many hotels now offer guests access to the Internet and e-mail facilities. Internet cafés, where online access can be obtained for a small fee, can be found in most towns and cities, while computers can often be hired by the hour in commercial centres.

Operating instructions

Buttons for different kinds of stamps

Slot for collecting stamps

Street vending machine selling postage stamps and telephone cards

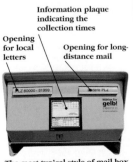

Information plaque indicating the collection times

Opening for local letters

Opening for long-distance mail

The most typical style of mail-box seen in Germany

USEFUL TELEPHONE NUMBERS

- Directory enquiries, national numbers: 11 833.
- Directory enquiries, international numbers: 11 834.
- International calls: Dial 00, wait for dialling tone, then dial country code, area code + number, omitting first 0.
- Country codes: UK 44; Eire 353; Canada and US 1; Australia 61; South Africa 27; New Zealand 64.

Shopping in Germany

Decorative herbal wreath

G ERMANS ARE RENOWNED for reliability and hard work, and manufactured goods produced here are of excellent quality. At the same time, the tradition of handicrafts and various types of folk art continue in different parts of the country. For elegantly produced, well-designed items, visitors should try one of the vast shopping centres that are to be found in every large city. However, visiting a market is an ideal opportunity to purchase a souvenir that is a regional speciality.

Souvenirs in the Wendt & Kühn shop in Meiningen

OPENING HOURS

D AYS AND OPENING hours of shops in Germany are governed by quite rigorous regulations. Apart from bakeries and pharmacies, which open on a rota system, very few shops are open on Sundays or in the evenings. From Monday to Friday shops are open from 9 or 10am and remain open until 7 or 8pm. However on Saturdays they cease trading at 3 or 4pm at the latest. On a Sunday the only shops open are those in petrol stations, railway stations or airports – but even then some of these shops close. Sunday- and late-night shopping is only really possible during December, when some department stores and shopping centres have extended opening hours.

MARKETS

A WEEKLY MARKET, known as *Wochenmarkt*, is held in many towns throughout Germany. In smaller towns, the stalls are set up in the market square, while in larger towns and cities the market is held in specially designated squares in different neighbourhoods. At these markets, fresh fruit and vegetables, cheeses, delicatessen items and cured meats, as well as many useful, everyday items, can be bought. Specialist fairs are often held at weekends – for example *Blumenmärkte*, at which flowers are sold, or *Kunstmärkte*, at which artists and craftsmen display their work for sale. Every large town also has its *Flohmarkt* (fleamarket). Christmas markets, held from the last week of November up to Christmas Eve, are hugely popular, selling traditional, handcrafted gifts in a truly enchanting atmosphere.

Black Forest cuckoo clock

VAT REFUNDS

E XCEPT FOR citizens of other EU countries, visitors to Germany are entitled to a VAT refund *(Mehrwertsteuer)* on any non-edible goods that are bought in German shops. Individual shops differ on the minimum taxable amount, but it is usually around €51. On entering a shop displaying a Tax-Free sign, visitors should ask for a special form or Tax-Free cheque. When going through Customs on leaving Germany, the form must be stamped. Visitors may be asked to show the goods, which must still be in their original packaging, unopened and unused. The tax is either refunded at the border or will be sent to the address on the envelope containing the cheque. Ensure that the correct information is given on the envelope, since chasing old VAT refund claims is a time-consuming amd often fruitless task.

SEASONAL DISCOUNTS

A LL SHOPS IN Germany hold vast sales *(Schlussverkauf)* twice a year. During the winter sales, *Winterschlussverkauf*, which begin in the last week of January, shops divest themselves of unsold autumn and winter clothing. The summer sale, *Sommerschlussverkauf*, begins in the final week of July.

During these huge shopping festivals, which last for two weeks, it is easy to come across great bargains, as the prices may be reduced by 30, 50 or even 70 per cent.

In addition to these major, twice-yearly events, there are usually other shopping offers or reductions throughout the year, but there are not many other genuine sales where customers can save such significant amounts of money.

Stall at a weekly market in Goslar

How to Pay

THE MOST POPULAR credit card in Germany, **Eurocard**, is accepted virtually everywhere, while somewhat less popular is **VISA**. This card can be used in department stores and in larger shops, but it is rather less useful when shopping in smaller shops, where cash is preferred. A sign on the door of restaurants and shops will tell you which cards are accepted.

Ceramics and Glass

THE FIRST porcelain factory in Europe was established in Saxony, following the discovery in the early 18th century of the formula for this fine china. Fragile artifacts produced by Meissen are among the most sought-after in the world. Factories in Berlin, Nymphenburg and elsewhere produce china of similarly exquisite quality.

German glass tableware is also renowned. Even now old glassworks in Saxony and Bavaria produce a range of artifacts made by traditional techniques: for example, beautifully cut and polished crystal tableware and ruby-coloured glassware.

Porcelain and glassware factories operate retail outlets in large towns. Visitors can arrange to have purchases sent to their home address.

A souvenir beer tankard

Regional Specialities

VIRTUALLY EVERY state in Germany produces its own regional speciality. For example, Lübeck is known for marzipan, while Nürnberg is synonymous with gingerbread. In the region of Spreewald, cucumbers are pickled in various ways, while excellent cherry jam and confiture are produced in the area of the Black Forest.

In the north, it is worth buying a jar of marinated herrings and some of the excellent cheeses produced, for example, in Friesland or Schleswig. Westphalian hams also have a well-deserved reputation, as do sausages from Brunswick, while equally delicious are the cured meats that are produced, for instance, in Regensburg or Nürnberg.

Alcoholic Drinks

RENOWNED GERMAN beers (*see pp32–3 and 503*) are best drunk straight from the barrel, but it is also worth trying a few bottles of beers that are rarely seen outside Germany. German wines are worth trying, especially those from vineyards in the Mosel and Rhine valleys. Excellent wines are produced in Bavaria and Baden-Wurttemberg, while wines from Saxony have recently regained popularity.

Local specialities providing souvenirs for gourmets

In Germany, there is large-scale production of various types of spirits, as well as herbal and root-flavoured liqueurs and bitters.

A unique souvenir from a holiday in Germany would be a bottle of a herbal infusion or liqueur produced at one of the country's monasteries according to their traditional centuries-old recipes.

Dolls in folk costumes

Handicrafts and Folk Art

DESPITE GERMANY'S high level of industrialization, local traditions have not vanished. Occasions such as holy days and festivals, which are held in the streets of towns in Bavaria and Schwarzwald, are still celebrated by men and women in folk costumes, while the shops stock folk costumes modelled on the local folklore. In mountain regions visitors can purchase items made from leather and wool. It is also worth looking at the traditional toys that are still crafted in some regions, such as miniature towns and dolls' houses together with their entire scaled-down furnishings. Nürnberg has a long tradition of toy manufacture, including colourful tin toys and wooden dolls.

A Berlin porcelain factory's retail outlet

Activity Holidays

GERMANY IS A COUNTRY that offers numerous opportunities for activity holidays. In the mountains visitors can climb and hike or go skiing in the winter, while the lake districts and coastal shores provide ideal conditions for sailing and water sports. Interesting areas for cycling tours can be found everywhere. Detailed information and advice on the availability of local sports activities and activity holidays can be obtained from regional tourist information offices.

A keen young hiker

LANGUAGE COURSES

A POPULAR WAY of spending a holiday in Germany and at the same time improving language skills is to take a summer language course. Popular with young people, these courses are often linked to the possibility of taking part in sporting activities. Many options are available, but courses organized by the **Goethe Institute** are of the very highest standard.

WALKING EXCURSIONS

HIKING IS virtually a national sport in Germany. Visitors can hike just about anywhere, but it is best in the mountains. The most demanding walkers can choose Alpine trails, but excursions in the Erzgebirge, Thuringian Forest, Harz Mountains, Franconian Switzerland or the ever-popular Schwarzwald are equally exhilarating.

Before setting off on an expedition it is worth getting maps showing walking trails in the chosen region. These are generally available from local tourist offices. More detailed information can be obtained from the **Verband Deutscher Gebirgs-und Wandervereine e.V.** For those who prefer to ramble through the Alps, the **Deutscher Alpenverein (DAV)** provides information on trails and hostels, as well as advice on safety and the protection of nature and wildlife. Guided walking excursions can also be organized through local tourist offices.

CYCLING TOURS

THE BICYCLE is a popular and environmentally friendly means of transport that allows visitors to combine the joys of sightseeing with a sporting activity. In larger towns and in particularly popular tourist areas bicycles can usually be hired for just a few days or for a week or more. A bike can easily be transported on the trains and on the U-Bahn or S-Bahn in towns. In most towns and also in large villages there are separate cycling lanes, and there are usually bicycle stands in front of offices, shops and cafés.

Well-earned relaxation after an arduous cycle ride

For visitors planning a cycle tour, **Bund Deutscher Radfahrer** can supply maps, guidebooks and advice.

GOLF AND TENNIS

MOST LARGE German towns have tennis courts that can be hired for a few hours. There are also many excellent golf courses throughout the country. For more information, or to make a booking, contact regional associations through the **Deutscher Tennis Bund** and the **Deutscher Golf Verband e.V.**

A relaxing afternoon sailing on the calm waters of a lake

WATER SPORTS

WATER SPORTS are very popular in Germany. Canoe trips can be undertaken on many rivers – from calm and picturesque stretches of water and the canals of the Spreewald to exhilarating adventures in rapidly flowing Alpine streams that demand professional skills. Windsurfing and waterskiing are also extremely popular. There are excellent conditions for sailing in the lake districts of Mecklenburg, the coastal region and Brandenburg, as well as by the sea.

Hikers on a bridge over a ravine in the mountains

CRUISING

Cruises are available from April to October on rivers and lakes in many parts of Germany. An interesting excursion, from Dresden to Saxonian Switzerland, can be made on the Elbe, while many trips can also be made on the Rhine and Danube.

From a cruise ship, visitors may enjoy a leisurely look at Berlin or marvel at the Frisian Islands, while a cruise around the Bodensee islands or on the Chiemsee (Bavaria's largest lake) is always popular.

HORSE RIDING

Germans love horses and riding and there are equestrian centres in many areas where visitors can ride under supervision or head off for a ride on their own. More information can be obtained from **Deutsche Reiterliche Vereinigung**.

SKIING

The most popular skiing centres are in the Alps, while the most renowned centre (having hosted the 1936 Winter Olympics) is Garmisch-Partenkirchen.

A beach volleyball match played on a square in Essen

However, it is also possible to ski in other regions – for example in Schwarzwald, in the Thuringian Forest or Erzgebirge. Throughout these areas are well-prepared skiing trails and an extensive network of ski-lifts and cable cars. Cross-country skiing is a popular winter sport in Germany, and there are many well-prepared and specially signed routes. Information and advice on this subject can be obtained from local tourist information offices. Visitors can also contact the **Freunde Des Skisports e.V.**

Deutscher Alpen-verein logo

MOUNTAIN SPORTS

The mountain regions of Germany provide ideal conditions for climbers. Interesting rock formations that provide memorable challenges are not only to be found in the Alps, but also in Franconian Switzer-land and in Saxony. Professional climbers who specialize in climbing without the use of safety harness undertake specialist training here.

Alpine mountain strips are excellent locations for taking off on flights in hang-gliders and para-gliders.

DIRECTORY

GENERAL INFORMATION

Deutscher Sportbund
Otto-Fleck-Schneise 12,
Frankfurt am Main.
[(069) 67 000.
FAX (069) 67 40 95.

LANGUAGE COURSES

Goethe-Institut e.V.
Dachauer Strasse 122,
80335 Munich.
[(089) 15 92 10.
FAX (089) 15 92 14 50.
W www.goethe.de

Goethe Institute
50 Princes Gate,
Exhibition Road,
London SW7 2PH.

[(020) 7596 4000.
FAX (020) 7594 0240.

HIKING TOURS

DAV Summit Club
Am Perlacher Forst 186
81545 München
[(089) 64 24 00.
FAX (089) 64 24 01 00.

Potsdamer Wanderbund e.V.
c/o Dietrich Kern,
Paul-Neumann-Str. 77
14482 Potsdam.
[(0331) 748 04 88.

Verband Deutscher Gebirgs- und Wandervereine e.V.
Wilhelmshöher Allee
157–159, 34121 Kassel.
[(0561) 93 87 30.
FAX (0561) 93 87 310.

CYCLING TOURS

Bund Deutscher Radfahrer
Otto-Fleck-Schneise 4,
60528 Frankfurt am Main.
[(069) 96 78 000.
FAX (069) 96 78 008.

GOLF & TENNIS

Deutscher Golf Verband e. V.
Viktoriastrasse 16,
65189 Wiesbaden.
[(0611) 99 02 00.
FAX (0611) 99 02 040.
W www.golf.de

Deutscher Tennis Bund
Hallerstrasse 89,
20149 Hamburg.
[(040) 41 17 80.
FAX (040) 41 17 82 22.
W www.dtb-tennis.de

WATER SPORTS

Deutscher Segler-Verband
Gründgensstraße 18,
22309 Hamburg.
[(040) 63 20 090.
FAX 040) 63 20 09 28.

HORSE RIDING

Deutsche Reiterliche Vereinigung
Frhr.-von-Langen-Str. 13,
48231 Warendorf.
[(02 581) 63 620.
FAX (02 581) 62 144.

SKIING

Haus des Ski
Im Deutschen
Skiverband.
[(089) 85 79 00.
W www.ski-online.de

TRAVEL INFORMATION

Travelling in Germany is very quick and easy. In every large city there is an airport, most of which offer international connections. The whole of Germany is linked by a dense network of motorways, while main roads are of a high standard and are well signposted. Rail travel throughout the country is comfortable

Lufthansa plane

and reliable; for longer journeys it is worth taking advantage of the fast connections offered by InterCity Express (ICE). Buses are also comfortable and efficient and are particularly useful in rural areas not served by rail. In German cities, trams, buses and sometimes underground rail systems provide useful services.

ARRIVING BY AIR

Germany's most important airports are Frankfurt am Main, Munich and Düsseldorf, from where connecting flights can be made to other German cities. The country's national carrier is Lufthansa, which operates regular, scheduled flights to most of the world's major destinations. British Airways also offers regular, scheduled flights to Germany from London (Heathrow and Gatwick) as well as from several regional airports in the United Kingdom.

The US is well served with flights to German cities, particularly to Berlin and to Frankfurt, which is Germany's largest airport and one of the busiest in Europe. Direct flights are usually available from major US cities, including New York (JFK), Washington DC, Boston, Chicago, San Francisco and Los Angeles.

Although Canada does not have many direct flights to Germany, AirCanada operates a regular flight from Toronto to Frankfurt while Canadian offers a direct flight from Vancouver to Frankfurt.

DOMESTIC FLIGHTS

In addition to Lufthansa, there are a number of other smaller carriers in Germany. These include Deutsche BA, which is a subsidiary of British Airways. These carriers often offer cheaper fares than Lufthansa on internal routes, as well as providing air links with small airports, such as Augsburg, Dortmund and Erfurt, that would not be economically viable for Lufthansa to operate.

AIR FARES

The cost of scheduled airfares can vary considerably, so it is always worth checking whether any carriers are offering special promotional fares. When buying a ticket it is worth finding out about any price reductions for children, young people and elderly passengers. Students and passengers under the age of 26 are often eligible for discounts. If the journey is going to be undertaken by a larger group, then it would be worth checking whether

Control tower at Munich's international airport

this qualifies for a group discount on the fare or a free ticket for the group leader.

It should also be borne in mind that fares vary depending on whether travellers are able to confirm their return date when buying the ticket. The cheapest scheduled ticket is an APEX, which requires booking well in advance, staying over a Saturday night,

Car park and airport building at Tegel airport, Berlin

View of runway and airport buildings at Frankfurt airport

and a fixed return date. Once booked, these tickets cannot be altered or cancelled, so it is wise to take out insurance to cover the loss if travel plans have to be changed.

The cheapest fares are often those offered by the new low-cost, no-frills airlines, or by discount agents. The latter are usually for seats on charter or scheduled flights.

INTERNATIONAL AIRPORTS

THE LARGEST German airports are Frankfurt am Main and Munich. The gigantic airport in Frankfurt comprises two huge terminals, which are connected by a fast over-ground railway. Both terminals are comprehensively equipped with everything that a traveller could possibly require. If you do have some free time it is worth watching the planes as they take off and land, and which form long queues at peak times.

The airport in Munich is somewhat smaller and less comfortable. The terminal extends along one axis, with the result that if you have to change planes, you have to take a long walk along a corridor to make the transfer.

Among the busiest airports are Düsseldorf, Cologne-Bonn and Berlin, which actually has three airports, Tempelhof, Tegel and Schönefeld.

AIRPORT	📞 INFORMATION	DISTANCE FROM CENTRE	JOURNEY TIME TO CENTRE BY TAXI	JOURNEY TIME TO CENTRE BY PUBLIC TRANSPORT
Berlin Tegel	(0180) 500 01 86	8 km (5 miles)	25 min	Bus: 25 min
Berlin Tempelhof	(0180) 500 01 86	5 km (3 miles)	20 min	U-Bahn: 15 min
Berlin Schönefeld	(0180) 500 01 86	20 km (12 miles)	45 min	S-Bahn: 35 min
Bremen-Neuenland	(0421) 559 50	3.5 km (2 miles)	15 min	Tram: 17 min
Dresden	(0351) 881 33 50	9 km (5.5miles)	25 min	Bus: 30 min
Düsseldorf	(0211) 42 10	8 km (5 miles)	25 min	S-Bahn: 13 min
Frankfurt am Main	(01805) 372 46 36	10 km (6 miles)	20 min	Train: 11 min S-Bahn: 10 min
Hamburg	(040) 507 50	13 km (8 miles)	30 min	Bus: 30 min
Hannover	(0511) 97 70	12 km (7.5 miles)	20 min	S-Bahn: 13 min
Cologne-Bonn	(02203) 400	Bonn: 28 km (17.5 miles) Cologne: 17 km (10.5 miles)	Bonn: 15 min Cologne: 20 min	Bus to Bonn: 35 min Bus to Cologne: 45 min
Leipzig	(0341) 224 11 55	18 km (11 miles)	30 min	Bus: 30 min
Munich	(089) 97 52 13 13	40 km (25 miles)	45 min	S-Bahn: 40 min Bus: 45 min
Nürnberg	(0911) 937 12 00	6 km (4 miles)	20 min	Bus: 45 min U-Bahn: 12 min
Stuttgart	(0711) 94 80	18 km (11 miles)	25 min	S-Bahn: 30 min

Travelling by Train, Ferry and Ship

Logo of German railways (Deutsche Bahn)

TRAVELLING AROUND Germany by train is not the cheapest form of transport, but it is undoubtedly one of the most comfortable. German trains are renowned for their punctuality, safety and cleanliness, though in high season visitors may feel that these are a little overrated. The fastest are InterCity-Express (ICE) trains. Germany is also well served by ports to which ferries and passenger ships operate.

Narrow-gauge tourist railway service in the Harz mountains

GETTING TO GERMANY BY TRAIN

TRAVELLING BY TRAIN from the UK generally costs more than flying, as well as taking longer. Main routes are via Dover to Ostend or Harwich to Hook of Holland. From either of these ports, connections to Berlin, Frankfurt and other German cities are made. An alternative is to travel to Brussels by Eurostar and make a connection there.

GERMAN TRAINS

THE FASTEST TRAINS, InterCity Express (ICE), are aerodynamically designed, painted white, with air-conditioning in coaches and airline-style seats. Unfortunately, there is not much room for luggage. They can travel at more than 200 kph (125 mph), which means that a journey from Hamburg to Munich takes only a few hours. ICE trains operate on just a few routes linking the country's largest cities. Somewhat slower and less expensive are the InterCity (IC) trains, which stop only at

certain stations, and offer an express service. When travelling over shorter distances it is best to take the Regional-Express (RE) trains.

Deutsche Bahn railway workers

TICKETS

TRAIN FARES are quite expensive in Germany and in express trains there is a compulsory surcharge, *Zuschlag*. It is not essential to reserve seats, but in the high season it is a good idea to do so and charges are not exorbitant. One way to travel more cheaply is to buy a *BahnCard*, which gives a 25 per cent discount. Alternatively, up to a 40 per cent discount is available if you book in advance.

When planning a lengthy stay in Germany and travelling around the country, it is worth acquiring an InterRail card, which is available to every European citizen, regardless of age. Every year the variety of discounted fares to which this card entitles the bearer is extended, so that it is worth checking out the full range. The price of the card depends on the age of the

traveller. Schoolchildren and students are entitled to a reduced rate. The cost also depends on which countries are to be visited. An InterRail card that is valid for travel in Germany is also valid for Austria, Switzerland and Denmark. InterRail cards can be obtained from Rail Europe or from some travel agents.

During the summer season in Germany, various discounts and special offers are introduced – for example, weekend tickets, family, group and so on, so it is worth making enquiries about these before setting off on a train journey.

RESERVATIONS

TRAIN TICKETS CAN be bought and reservations made in travel agents or at the railway station at the *Reisezentrum*, which at the same time acts as an information centre. Tickets can also be reserved by telephone or through the Internet, where a detailed timetable can be viewed. Using this facility, it is simple to plan the appropriate routes for your journey yourself.

RAILWAY STATIONS

IN GERMANY, many railway stations are magnificent, historic buildings with vast halls covering the platforms. Among the most beautiful is

The fastest and most comfortable German train – InterCity Express

TRAIN ROUTES IN GERMANY

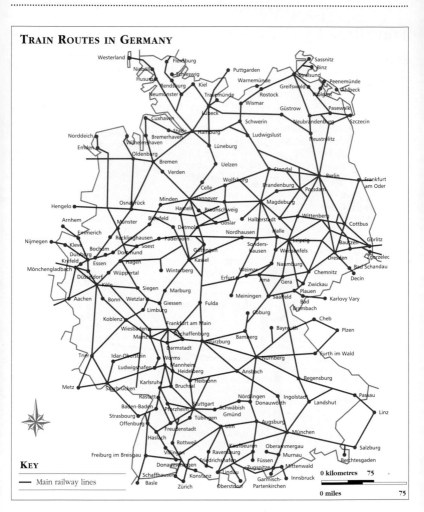

Westerland
Flensburg
Sassnitz
Niebüll
Schleswig
Puttgarden
Binz
Husum
Warnemünde
Stralsund
Rendsburg
Kiel
Peenemünde
Neumünster
Travemünde
Greifswald
Ahlbeck
Rostock
Wolgast
Wismar
Güstrow
Pasewalk
Cuxhaven
Lübeck
Schwerin
Neubrandenburg
Szczecin
Stade
Hamburg
Norddeich
Bremerhaven
Ludwigslust
Neustrelitz
Wilhelmshaven
Lüneburg
Emden
Oldenburg
Bremen
Stendal
Berlin
Verden
Frankfurt
Uelzen
am Oder
Hengelo
Osnabrück
Minden
Hannover
Wolfsburg
Brandenburg
Potsdam
Celle
Magdeburg
Arnhem
Münster
Bielefeld
Hameln
Braunschweig
Nijmegen
Emmerich
Recklinghausen
Detmold
Goslar
Halberstadt
Wittenberg
Cottbus
Kleve
Soest
Paderborn
Nordhausen
Halle
Görlitz
Bochum
Dortmund
Sonders-
Bauzen
Krefeld
Essen
Hagen
Kassel
hausen
Weissenfels
Dresden
Mönchengladbach
Düsseldorf
Wuppertal
Winterberg
Weimar
Naumburg
Bad Schandau
Köln
Siegen
Erfurt
Jena
Gera
Chemnitz
Decín
Aachen
Bonn
Wetzlar
Marburg
Fulda
Meiningen
Saalfeld
Zwickau
Plauen
Karlovy Vary
Koblenz
Giessen
Limburg
Coburg
Bad
Brambach
Wiesbaden
Frankfurt am Main
Cheb
Bayreuth
Plzen
Mainz
Aschaffenburg
Bamberg
Trier
Darmstadt
Würzburg
Idar-Oberstein
Worms
Nürnberg
Fürth im Wald
Ludwigshafen
Mannheim
Heidelberg
Ansbach
Regensburg
Metz
Karlsruhe
Bruchsal
Heilbronn
Saarbrücken
Rastatt
Nördlingen
Ingolstadt
Landshut
Passau
Baden-Baden
Pforzheim
Stuttgart
Donauwörth
Linz
Strasbourg
Tübingen
Schwäbisch
Augsburg
Offenburg
Gmünd
Ulm
Freudenstadt
München
Haslach
Rottweil
Kempten
Oberammergau
Salzburg
Freiburg im Breisgau
Villingen
Ravensburg
Murnau
Berchtesgaden
Donaueschingen
Friedrichshafen
Füssen
Zugspitze
Mittenwald
Schaffhausen
Konstanz
Lindau
Garmisch-
Innsbruck
Basle
Zürich
Oberstdorf
Partenkirchen

KEY

— Main railway lines

0 kilometres 75

0 miles 75

---

the main station in Leipzig. In large towns, railway stations are generally located in the centre. They include dozens of shops (often open on Sundays), car rental firms, hotel reservation bureaux, and other services, such as cash points, left luggage provision and public toilets with shower facilities.

TRAVELLING BY FERRY AND SHIP

VISITORS TRAVELLING TO Germany by car from the UK will have to decide which crossing to use (unless using the Channel Tunnel). This will depend to some extent on which part of Germany is to be visited. The crossings

from Dover to Ostend, in Belgium, or to Calais, in France, are the shortest, while the Harwich to Hook of Holland route is useful for those travelling from further north. There are also two ferry services to Hamburg, operated by Scandinavian Seaways – one from Harwich and one from North Shields, near Newcastle-upon-Tyne.

There are many links between German ports and other countries. Color Line from Oslo (Norway) to Kiel; Scandlines from Trelleborg, (Sweden) to Rostock and Trelleborg to Sassnitz, and also from Denmark: Gedser to Rostock, Rødby to Puttgarden and Rønne (Bornholm) to Sassnitz; DFDs Seaways operates from Harwich to Cuxhaven.

Ship taking passengers to Helgoland

Travelling by Car and Bus

Sign for parking ticket machine

THE FASTEST AND MOST comfortable way of travelling around Germany is to use the motorways. The excellent network of toll-free routes guarantees fast progress over longer distances, while a well-maintained system of main roads enables you to reach interesting places throughout the country. Motorways have the advantage of regularly sited service stations, where travellers can stop for fuel and something to eat. On lesser roads and in remote areas, petrol stations may be few and far between.

A selection of traffic signs on German roads

ARRIVING BY CAR

THERE ARE MANY border crossings into Germany and providing that you carry the necessary documents and your car does not look disreputable, you should experience a minimum of delay and formalities. EU citizens do not have to make a Customs declaration on arrival, but there are limits on the amount of duty-free goods that can be brought in *(see p530)*.

WHAT TO TAKE

VISITORS travelling by car in Germany must carry a valid driving licence as well as their vehicle's registration document and insurance policy. Before leaving home check with your insurance company whether your policy will cover you while you are in Germany. If may be necessary to obtain a Green Card to extend the cover for the duration of your stay.

The car must carry a plate indicating country of origin, and it must also be equipped with a red warning triangle for use in case of breakdown.

Seatbelts are compulsory and children under 12 must sit in the back, with babies and toddlers in child-seats.

ROADS AND MOTORWAYS

THE GERMAN motorway network is extensive. They are all toll-free and have regularly spaced petrol stations, as well as parking facilities with toilets, restaurants and motels. Ranging along the hard shoulder are yellow poles with emergency buttons, which can be used to call for help in the event of a breakdown or accident. An *Autobahn* (motorway) is indicated by the letter "A" followed by a number – some also have a letter "E" and a number, denoting that the road crosses the German border. A *Bundesstraße* (main road) is indicated by the letter "B" and a number.

Motorway telephone

ADDITIONAL ROAD SIGNS

IN ADDITION to internationally understood road signs on German roads, there are also written signs that clarify the meaning of the sign above.

On motorways, for example, a yellow triangular warning sign with a row of cars is a warning about the possibility of traffic jams, which may be accompanied by the word *"Stau"*. On mountain roads, a warning sign showing a car tyre wrapped in a chain will be accompanied by the word *"Schnee"*, which warns against driving without chains when there is snow.

A diversion is indicated by the colour yellow and the word *"Umleitung"*, while the diversion route is indicated by the letter "U" followed by the number of the road. A sign with the slogan *"Baustelle"* (meaning "refurbishment") always precedes the stretch that is being renovated.

A sign showing a horizontal blue arrow with the word *"Einbahnstrasse"* indicates a one-way street.

RULES OF THE ROAD

GERMANS on the whole drive in accordance with the regulations. They are generally courteous, but they can be a little aggressive, particularly on motorways. German drivers hurtle along the outside lane at very great speed and get very annoyed if they have to slow down because of other drivers. Visitors should be particularly careful when first starting to drive in Germany, especially if they are unused to driving on the right. Bear in mind that being caught exceeding the speed limit incurs a large fine.

In the event of an accident on the motorway, or if a traffic jam necessitates an abrupt reduction in speed, drivers should turn on their flashing emergency lights to warn drivers behind of the impending danger.

Petrol station at a motorway service area

Parking-ticket Machine

Automatic parking-ticket machines like this issue receipts that are placed on the inside of the windscreen. There are also parking meters with a timer, which allow parking for up to 2 hours.

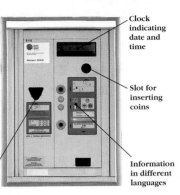

Clock indicating date and time

Slot for inserting coins

Information in different languages

Ticket is dispensed from here

DRIVING IN TOWNS

FINDING A PLACE in which to park is not easy: it is often best to use a multi-storey car park, which is indicated by "*Parkhaus*"; the word "*Frei*" indicates that parking spaces are available. It is never worth leaving your car in a prohibited area – a traffic warden will arrive immediately, impose a fine and arrange for the car to be towed away. Retrieving an impounded car is expensive and difficult.

Cars left in a controlled parking zone must either display a parking ticket or be parked validly at a meter.

ROAD TRAFFIC REGULATIONS

IN GERMANY, THE same road traffic regulations apply as in most European countries. For example, all passengers must wear a seat-belt and children under the age of 12 must travel in the back seats. Driving after drinking a small amount of alcohol is allowed, but if you cause an accident, the consequences will be more severe if a breathalyzer shows the presence of alcohol in your blood. In built-up areas the speed limit is 50 km/h (31 mph); beyond this it

is 100 km/h (62 mph), and on motorways there is no overall limit. Many drivers drive at speeds exceeding 200 km/h (125 mph). When travelling with a caravan or camping trailer outside built-up areas, drivers should not exceed 70 km/h (44 mph), and on motorways 100 km/h (62 mph). Road traffic police are strict about imposing fines for breaches of speed restrictions.

Drivers can incur fines for driving too close to the vehicle in front and for parking in prohibited areas as well as for breaking the speed limits.

HIRING A CAR

REPRESENTATIVES OF car-hire firms can be found at airports, railway stations and in more expensive hotels. In order to hire a car, drivers need to produce their passport and driving licence and to be over 18. In some cases, they may be required to have an international driving licence.

HITCH-HIKING

HITCH-HIKING IS A popular way of travelling, particularly among young people. A safer method of finding a lift or a travelling companion is

to make use of the services of Mitfahrzentralen, a contact agency for drivers who offer spare seats on a journey for an agreed fee. Check addresses and telephone numbers in local telephone directories.

ARRIVING BY COACH

TRAVELLING TO GERMANY by coach from the UK is not a very attractive option as the journey is long and fares are not particularly cheap. Routes are operated by Eurolines.

TRAVELLING BY COACH

THERE IS A GOOD network of inter-city coach services in Germany, though journeys are generally no cheaper than travelling by train. Most towns have a *Zentraler Omnibus Bahnhof* (ZOB) close to the train station. It is here that most bus services originate and where service timetables can be obtained and tickets purchased. Many local coach services also operate from the central bus station, although suburban areas have their own services to the centre of town. It is best to ask at the tourist information centre for information about getting to your destination.

DIRECTORY

CAR HIRE

Avis
((06171) 68 18 00.

Hertz
((01805) 33 35 35.

Sixt Rent-a-Car
((01805) 25 25 25.

ROADSIDE ASSISTANCE

Central Information ADAC
((01805) 10 11 12.

Road Assistance ADAC
((01802) 22 22 22.

ACE
((01802) 34 35 36.

AVD
((069) 660 60.

Comfortable, long-distance, double-decker coach

Transport in Cities

The S-Bahn logo

GETTING AROUND HUGE cities is not easy and the historic centres are best visited on foot. Large towns often suffer from traffic congestion and it can be difficult to find vacant parking places. It is advisable to leave your car in a car park on the outskirts and travel around using the fast railway (S-Bahn), underground (U-Bahn), trams or city buses. The latter operate frequent, timetabled services and can usually avoid traffic jams as they have the advantage of travelling along specially designated traffic lanes.

The city rail line, Schwebebahn, in Wuppertal

TAXIS

TAXIS OFFER A comfortable though expensive way of getting around towns and cities. If several people share a cab, however, this can work out cheaper than using the bus or train. Every taxi vehicle, regardless of make, is a cream colour and has a "TAXI" sign on the roof; this will be illuminated if the taxi is free. Cabs can be hailed on the street or booked by telephone. They can also be picked up at a taxi rank, though these are rare. If the rank is empty, a cab can be called for from the telephone there.

The fare for the journey is calculated by an illuminated meter on the dashboard. The same rates apply during the week, at weekends and at night, for journeys within the city limits.

Telephone at a taxi rank

TRAVELLING ON THE U-BAHN AND S-BAHN

ALL THE BIG German cities have a network of fast connections by underground railway (U-Bahn) and by rail (S-Bahn). The U-Bahn offers frequent services – in peak hours every 3–5 minutes – and individual stations are situated quite close to each other. The S-Bahn offers less frequent services, every 10 or 20 minutes, while the stations are quite markedly apart. Generally the S- and U-Bahn use the same tickets, as do buses and trams. Various

types of ticket can be bought from ticket machines located by the entrance to stations; the tickets must be punched in the red punching machine situated nearby. On German railway stations there are no regulatory measures, such as ticket-operated barriers, so it is easy for unscrupulous passengers to get onto a train without a ticket. However it is not worth trying to do this as trains are patrolled by ticket inspectors, often dressed in civilian clothes, who start checking tickets once a train has left the station. Fines for travelling without a ticket are very high.

U-Bahn stations are indicated by square signs with a white "U" on a dark blue background, while S-Bahn stations have round signs with a white "S" on a green background. On maps of the network, each line of the U- and S-Bahn is marked in a different colour and has its own number. The direction of

the route is indicated by the name of the station at which the route terminates. On every station platform a display shows the destination of the next incoming train. A white circle or oval on the map indicates an interchange station. On every station you will find town maps and maps of the transport network displayed in prominent positions. Maps are also displayed in carriages.

Carriage doors on U- and S-Bahn trains are operated manually, but they close automatically. At major stations a member of staff gives the signal for trains to leave the station. Passengers are not allowed to board the train after his cry of "*Zurück-bleiben!*" – which means that the doors are about to close. Throughout the journey, the names of the next stations are announced, while in modern trains these are usually also indicated on illuminated displays in the carriages.

Automatic Ticket Machine

To use this machine, select the appropriate ticket by pressing a button. Insert the amount of money indicated by the display. Your ticket and change will then be delivered.

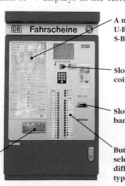

A map of the U-Bahn and S-Bahn system

Slot for coins

Slot for bank notes

Buttons for selecting different types of ticket

Opening, from which tickets and change are delivered

Tram and Bus Stop Sign

At every stop, a board displays the numbers and destinations of trams and buses that stop there. Timetables and maps of the public transport system are also displayed.

Tram stop stymbol: Haltestelle

Bus numbers and names of destinations

A map of the transport network

Timetable of individual routes

BUSES

Bus routes have individual timetables, which are displayed on boards at bus stops. Maps showing each stage of the route are also displayed there. As well as a route number, buses also have a sign indicating where their particular journey ends. This is useful as some buses operate on shorter routes outside peak hours.

During the journey, the bus driver generally announces the name of the bus stop that the bus is approaching. In the centre of town, this is not so important, as in heavy traffic the bus stops at every bus stop as a matter of course. However, further away from the city centre or in periods where the traffic is not so heavy, you have to listen out for these announcements.

At many bus stops, the driver will pull in only on request, so passengers must press the "Halt" button in plenty of time to warn the driver that they wish to alight.

TRAMS

Trams are a comfortable means of urban transport, with the advantage that they do not get stuck in traffic jams. The same tickets as for buses and S-Bahn can be used.

TICKETS

For the purpose of public transport charges, large cities are generally divided into zones, with the cost of a ticket depending on which zones are travelled through during a journey.

In many cities a single-use ticket is valid for two hours, and during this time you can use all the modes of transport available, including the S- and U-Bahn, even changing routes several times. However, using this type of ticket is the most expensive way to travel. In addition to these standard tickets *(Normltarif)*, there are also cheaper tickets available *(Kurzstrecke)*, which limit you to short distances. In many German cities you can also buy tickets in the form of a strip, which has to be punched according to the length of the journey.

Children who have not reached the age of 14 are eligible for a reduced rate *(Ermässigunstarif)*, while toddlers up to the age of six travel free. Children's push-chairs and dogs will often be carried on public transport without any extra charge.

A modern type of tram that operates in German cities

There are many other types of tickets and travelcards – for example a one-day ticket *(Tageskarte)*, a one-day group ticket *(Gruppentageskarte)*, and a weekly ticket *(7-Tage-Karte)*. Some towns issue a *WelcomeCard* that allows for three days' travel around town as well as giving many discounts in museums.

Bicycles parked near the entrance to the Hofgarten in Munich

BICYCLES

Bicycles are a popular form of transport in Germany. There are numerous cycle lanes and many junctions have special lights for cyclists. In front of virtually every office, bank and school there is a bicycle stand, although these should be used only for a short period and, of course, the bicycle still needs to be secured against theft. Bicycles can be transported on the S-Bahn, although owners will need to get on the train at the appropriate door and stand their vehicle in the designated place. Bicycles can be hired at the station or other hire places *(Fahrradverleih)*.

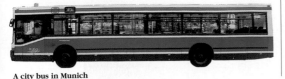

A city bus in Munich

Index

Page numbers in **bold** type refer to main entries

Acknowledgements

DORLING KINDERSLEY AND WIEDZA I ŻYCIE would like to thank
the following people for their help in preparing this guide:

ADDITIONAL TEXT
Michał Jaranowski, Barbara Sudnik-Wójcicka, Grażyna
Winiarska, Konrad Gruda, Bożena Steinborn

ADDITIONAL PHOTOGRAPHS
Maciej Bronarski, Demetrio Carrasco, Witold Danilkiewicz,
Grzegorz Kłosowski, Renata and Marek Kosińscy, Sergiusz
Michalski, Nils Meyer, Andrzej Zygmuntowicz and
Ireneusz Winnicki, Władysław Wisławski

PUBLISHING MANAGER
Helen Townsend

MANAGING ART EDITOR
Kate Poole

CONSULTANT
Gerhard Bruschke

FACTCHECKER
Barbara Sobeck, Jürgen Scheunemann

DIRECTOR OF PUBLISHING
Gillian Allan

EDITORIAL AND DESIGN ASSISTANCE
Sam Atkinson, Hilary Bird, Arwen Burnett, Lucinda Cooke,
Jo Cowen, Marcus Hardy, Lucinda Hawksley, Jacky Jackson,
Claire Marsden, Ferdie McDonald, Rebecca Milner,
Sam Merrell, Casper Morris, Dave Pugh, Simon Ryder,
Andrew Szudek, Karen Villabona, Stewart J. Wild

The publisher would also like to thank all the people and
institutions who allowed photographs belonging to them
to be reproduced, as well as granting permission to use
photographs from their archives:

Archäologische Staatssammlung in Munich; Arthothek
(Jürgen Hinrichsowi); Bavaria Filmstadt; Bayerisches
Nationalmuseum in Munich; Bildarchiv Preussischer
Kulturbesitz in Berlin (Heidrun Klein); Bildvorlagen
Römerschatz – Gäubodenmuseum Straubing (Dr. Prammer);
Bischöfliches Dom- und Diözesanmuseum Mainz
(Dr. Hansowi-Jurgenowi Kotzurowi); Brecht-Weigel-
Gedenkstätte in Berlin (Elke Pfeil); Bridgeman Art Library;
Bröhan-Museum in Berlin (Ingrid Jagr and Frau Betzker);
Brücke-Museum in Berlin; Brüder-Grimm-Museum in
Kassel, Corbis; Das Domkapitel (Gertraut Mockel, Büro Dr
Georg Minkenberg); Deutsches Apothekenmuseum in
Heidelberg; Deutsches Historisches Museum in Berlin (Kathi
Rumlow); Deutsche Press Agentur (dpa) in Berlin (Tanija
Teichmann); Deutsches Museum in Munich (Sigrid
Schneider and Marlene Schwarz); Deutsches
Schiffahrtsmuseum in Bremerhaven (Hansowi-Walterowi
Kewelohowi); Deutsches Tapetenmuseum Kassel (Sabine
Thümmler); Deutsches Technikmuseum Berlin (Renate
Förster); Diözesanmuseum in Bamberg (Birgit Kandora);
Dombauverwaltung des Metropolitankapitels Köln
(Birgit Lambert); Dresden Museum für Geschichte der
Stadt Dresden (Dr. Christel Wünsch); Flash Press Media
(Sylwii Wilgockiej); Forschungs- und Gedenkstätte
Normannenstraße (Stasi-Museum) in Berlin (Andrei
Holland-Moritz); Fürstlich Hohenzollernsche
Schlossverwaltung in Sigmaringen (Heldze Boban);
Gemäldegalerie Alte Meister (Steffi Reh);
Gemäldegalerie Neue Meister (Gisela Mehnert);
Germanisches Nationalmuseum in Nuremberg
(Hermanowi Maué); Hamburger Bahnhof in Berlin;
Hamburger Kunsthalle; Hessisches Landesmuseum Kassel;
Käthe-Kollwitz-Museum in Berlin (A. Ingrid Findell);
Komische Oper Berlin (Gaby Hofmann); Kunstmuseum
Düsseldorf (Anne-Marie Katins); Kunstsammlungen Paula
Modersohn in Bremen (Hubertusowi Morgenthalowi);
Kunstsammlungen zu Weimar (Angelice Goder);
Kunstverlag Maria Laach (Helmutowi Keipowi);
Kurdirektion des Berchtesgadener Landes (Vroni Aigner;

Birgit Tica); Landesmuseum Trier (Margot Redwanz); LBB
Photo Archives (Dyrektorowi Christophowi Kalischowi);
Linden-Museum Stuttgart, Staatliches Museum
für Völkerkunde (Dr. Doris Kurelli); Lutherstube in
Wittenberg (Jutcie Strehle); Markgräfliches Opernhaus in
Bayreuth; Mercedes-Benz-Museum in Stuttgart; Museum
am Ostwall in Dortmund; Museum der Bildenden Künste
in Leipzig (Roswitha Engel); Museum Folkwang in Essen,
Stadt Essen (Mr Hildebrandowi); Museum of the City of
Berlin; Porzellansammlung (Ulrike Maltschew); Rheinisches
Landesmuseum Bonn (Dr Gerhard Bauchhenß); Rüstkammer
(Yvonne Brandt); Schlösserverwaltung in Munich (Frau
Gerum); Seebul Ada and Emil Nolde (Dr Andreasowi
Fluckowi); Staatliche Graphische Sammlung in Munich
(Wiebke Tomaschek); Staatliche Kunstsammlungen
Dresden, Albertinum, Grünes Gewölbe; Staatliche
Porzellan-Manufaktur Meißen GMBH (Christine Mangold);
Staatliche Schlösser und Gärten, Pforzheim (Herr Braunowi);
Staatsarchiv Hamburg (Kathrin Berger); Staatsgalerie
Stuttgart (Frau Fönnauer); Städelsches Kunstinstitut in
Frankfurt am Main (Elisabeth Heinemann); Stadt Köln,
Wallraf-Richartz-Museum in Cologne (Dr Roswitha Neu-
Kock and Dr Mai); Stadtmuseum in Munich; Stiftung
Luthergedenkstätten in Sachsen-Anhalt; Stiftung Preussische
Schlösser und Gärten Berlin (Carli Kamarze); Superstock
Polska Sp. z.o.o. (Elżbiecie Gajewskiej); Von der Heydt-
Museum Wuppertal (Margarecie Janz); Wartburg-Stiftung
in Eisenach (Petrze Wilke); Zefa (Ewie Kozłowskiej)

The publisher would also like to thank the following for
their assistance on the guide:
Joanna Minz for coordinating information, Tamara and
Jacek Draber for their help with correspondence and
telephone contacts, Jürgen Christoffer of Deutscher
Wetterdienst for meteorological information.

Picture Credits
t = top; tl = top left; tlb = top left below; tc = top centre;
tcb = top centre below; tr = top right; tra = top right
above; trb = top right below; cl = centre left; cla = centre
left above; clb = centre left below; c = centre; ca = centre
above; cb = centre below; cr = centre right; cra = centre
right above; cbr = centre bottom right; crb = centre right
below; bl = bottom left; blb = bottom left below; bc =
bottom centre; br = bottom right; bra = bottom right
above; brb = bottom right below; b = bottom

Aachener Dom (Copyright: Domkapitel Aachen – photo.
Ann Münchow) 382t, 382ca, 382cb, 382t (Skarbiec), 383ca,
383cb, 383br, 383bl
Albertinum (Dresden) 162t
Amt fuer Stadtmarketing und Touristik, Limburg 348cla
Archäologische Staatssammlung (Munich) 209d
Artothek 26t, 26b, 27cla, 27blb, 50t, 166ca, 166cb, 166b,
167t, 167ca, 167cb, 167b, 165cb, 212cb, 247b, 422t, 422b,
423t, 423cb, 430t; Joachim Blauel 27bra, 46t, 212t, 212b,
213cb, 246t, 280cr; Blauel/Gnamm 208t, 212ca, 213t,
213ca, 245tr; Bayer d'Mitko 213d; Sophie-R. Gnamm 216;
Alexander Koch 27trb; Christoph Sandig 456d;
G. Westermann 418b, 423t

Bavaria Filmstadt 217t
Brecht-Weigel-Gedenkstätte (Berlin) 97c
Bridgeman Art Library 30br, 99t
Britstock 314–315
Bronarski Maciej 320t, 336t, 336c, 336b, 337t, 337ca,
337cb, 337b
Bröhan-Museum (Berlin) 92t
Brüder-Grimm-Museum (Kassel) 350tr, 354tr
(© Staatliche Museum Kassel)
Corbis 25tr, 25bra, 25blb, 162c (© Jack Fields/Corbis),
432–433 (©Bob Krist/Corbis), 440 (© Nilk
Wheeler/Corbis)
Danilkiewicz Witold 411b, 452, 460t
Deutsches Apothekenmuseum (Heidelberg) 284tr
Deutsches Techikmuseum Berlin 77b

Deutsches Historisches Museum Berlin (Zeughaus) 22b, 24c, 30ca, 30cla, 30clb, 30crb, 30br, 31cla, 31tlb, 31tr, 31clb, 31cb, 31crb, 31cbr (Holz & Kunststoff), 32 cla, 42, 48tl (R. Bemke), 48tr (Jurgen Liepe), 48c, 48b (A.C. Theil), 49t (R. Boemke), 50b, 51t, 51cla, 52cl, 56b, 57bl, 116tr, 116b, 117t
Deutsches Museum (Munich) 218–219 (all images)
Deutsches Schifffahrtsmuseum Bremerhaven 46d
Diözesanmuseum (Bamberg) 237t
dpa 22tra, 23tl, 23tr, 23cra, 23crb, 23br, 23bl, 24tl, 24tr, 31cla, 31cra, 31bl, 32tr, 39t, 56ca, 129t, 103t, 195tl, 279t, 447t; Jens Büttner 57t; Claus Felix 39b; Matthias Hiekel 36b; Peter Förster 36t; Wulf Hirschberger 37b; Ralf Hirschberger 34b; Peer Grimm 18tr; Frank Leonhardt 35t; Wolfgang Kluge 24b; Wolfgang Kumm 57br; Kay Nietfeld 34t, 35t; Frank Mächler 37t; Carsten Rehder 34t; Wulf Pfeiffer 37d; Martin Schutt 38t, 171d; Roland Scheidemann 39t; Ingo Wagner 57t; Heinz Wieseler 38b
Dresden Museum für Geschichte der Stadt Dresden 51crb

Eisenach-Wartburg 176t, 176tl, 176tr, 177t

Foto-Thueringen Barbara Neumann 112c

Gäubodenmuseum Straubing 43bl
Germanisches Nationalmuseum (Nuremberg) 246–247 (all images)
Grünes Gewölbe (Dresden) 162t

Hamburger Bahnhof (Berlin) 89bl
Hamburger Kunsthalle (Hamburg) 26cla, 422t
Hessisches Landesmuseum Kassel 350tl, 350b (© Staatliche Museum Kassel Deutsches Tapetenmuseum)

Käthe-Kollwitz-Museum (Berlin) 83t
Kłosowski Grzegorz 20cra
Kloster Maulbronn 288t, 288b, 289cla, 289crb, 289b
Kölner Dom 388tl, 388c, 388b, 389t, 389ca, 389cb, 389bl, 389br (© Dombauarchiv Köln, Matz und Schenk)
Komische Oper (Berlin) Rittershaus Monika 102b
Kosińscy, Renata and Marek 20clb, 20bra, 20blb, 21cla, 21tlb, 21blb, 194tl, 195ca, 195tr, 195cl, 195cr, 195br
Kunstmuseum Düsseldorf 26clb
Kunstsammlungen Paula Modersohn 419tl
Kunstverlag Maria Laach 320b, 344tl, 344tr, 344ca, 345t, 345ca, 345cb, 345b
Kurdirektion des Berchtesgadener Landes Storto, Leonberg 262b

Landesmuseum Trier Thomas Zühmer 328t
Linden Museum für Völkerkunde (Stuttgart) 296tlb
Ludwigsburg – Schloss 292ca, 292cb, 292b, 293t
Lutherstube (Wittenberg) 117t

Mainz – Dom 321b (© M. Hankel-Studio)
Mercedes-Benz-Museum (Stuttgart) 296tra
Meyer Nils 56cb
Michalski Sergiusz 16t
Mittelalterliches Museum (Rothenburg ob der Tauber) 248br
Museum der Bildenden Künste (Leipzig) 49t (MdbK, Gerstenberger 1994)
Museum Folkwang (Essen) 27t
Museum für Naturkunde (Berlin) 89br
Museum am Ostwall (Dortmund) 376t
Musikinstrumenten-Museum (Berlin) 81ca

Nationalmuseum (Munich) 209t

Opernhaus (Bayreuth) 238t

Philharmonie (Berlin) 81t
Presse- und Informationsamt des Landes Berlin BTM/Drewes 88bl; BTM/Koch 88cla

Rheinisches Landesmuseum Bonn 394t

Schauspielhaus (Konzerthaus Berlin) 68d
Schloss Sigmaringen 301b
Schlösserverwaltung (Munich) 232ca, 233t, 233ca, 233cb, 233b, 268t, 268ca, 268cb, 268b
Schneider Guenter 58–59
STA Travel 533tr
Staatsarchiv Hamburg 46–47
Staatliche Museen Preußischer Kulturbesitz (Berlin) 44c, 51br, 52–53, 53tl, 53br, 54t, 54cra, 54clb, 54b, 55t, 55bl, 55br, 56t, 60br, 61cra, 71t, 72ca, 73t, 85t, 86cb, 87clb, 87t, 87cra, 87d; Grammes 44br; Klaus Göken 52b, 55c, 72b, 73d; Erich Lessing 70clb, 72t, 73cb; Jurgen Liepe 71c, 72cb, 92d; Georg Niedermeister 73ca; Arne Psille 43br, 44tr, 44bl; Steinkopf 80tr
Staatliche Porzellan-Manufaktur Meißen GMBH 30cra, 114tr, 114cra, 114clb, 114b, 115t, 115bra Klaus Tänzer 115cra
Staatsgalerie Stuttgart 298tra, 298tlb, 298t, 298b, 299t, 299ca, 299cb, 299b
Städelsches Kunstinstitut (Frankfurt am Main) 364t, 364c, 364b, 365t, 365ca, 365cb, 365b
Stadtmuseum Berlin 65c, 67t; Hans-Joachim Bartsch 49bl
Stadtmuseum (Munich) 65c, 204tl; Hans-Joachim Bartsch 5t; Sudnik 21crb
Stasi-Museum (Berlin) 98b
Stiftung Preussische Schlösser und Gärten Berlin 50c, 94cl, 95ca, 95b, 95crb, 125cr, 126b, 129b
Superstock Polska Sp. zo.o. 310t

Tourist Office – Altötting 256t, 256b

Wallraf-Richartz-Museum (Cologne) 390t, 390ca, 390cb, 390b, 391t, 391c, 391br, 391bl (© Rheinisches Bildarchiv)

Zefa 21cl, 192–193c, 373b, 398–399, 408bra, 408t, 409b, 419b, 436t, 436c, 437tl, 437tr, 437b, 439b, 464t; Bloemendal 5t; Damm 17b, 384b, 274, 380b, 437tra, 453d; Eckstein 19b, 409tl, 409tr, 463b; Freytag 15b, 194tr, 313t; Haenel 1, 29tcb, 442b, 455t, 467t; Kehrer 21cr; Kinne 392t, 392b; Kohlhas 395t; Leidorf 11t, 11b; Rossenbach 4b, 7t, 308–309, 384c, 396b, 397t, 398–399, 445b, 456t; Rose 397t; Steeger 409t; Streichan 338–339, 349t, 369b; Svenja-Foto 380t, 389cra; Waldkirch 436t; M. Winkel 388tr
Zwinger (Dresden) 164t, 164cb, 165b Gemäldegalerie Alte Meister 166t

JACKET
Front - DK PICTURE LIBRARY: bc, bra; GETTY IMAGES: Josef Beck main image; Jorg Greuel bla. Back - DK PICTURE LIBRARY: t; GETTY IMAGES: Jorg Greuel b. Spine - GETTY IMAGES: Josef Beck.

All other images © Dorling Kindersley.
For further information see: www.dkimages.com

DORLING KINDERSLEY SPECIAL EDITIONS

Dorling Kindersley books can be purchased in bulk quantities at discounted prices for use in promotions or as premiums. We are also able to offer special editions and personalized jackets, corporate imprints, and excerpts from all of our books, tailored specifically to meet your own needs.

To find out more, please contact: (in the United Kingdom) – Sarah.Burgess@ dk.com OR SPECIAL SALES, DORLING KINDERSLEY LIMITED, 80 STRAND, LONDON WC2R 0RL. (in the United States) – SPECIAL MARKETS DEPARTMENT, DK PUBLISHING, INC., 375 HUDSON STREET, NEW YORK, NY 10014.

Phrasebook

IN AN EMERGENCY

Where is the telephone?	Wo ist das Telefon?	voh ist duss tel-e-fone?
Help!	Hilfe!	**hilf**-uh
Please call a doctor	Bitte rufen Sie einen Arzt	**bitt**-uh **roof** n zee ine-en artst
Please call the police	Bitte rufen Sie die Polizei	**bitt**-uh **roof** n zee dee poli-**tsy**
Please call the fire brigade	Bitte rufen Sie die Feuerwehr	**bitt**-uh roof n zee dee **foyer**-vayr
Stop!	Halt!	**hult**

COMMUNICATION ESSENTIALS

Yes	Ja	**yah**
No	Nein	**nine**
Please	Bitte	**bitt**-uh
Thank you	Danke	dunk-uh
Excuse me	Verzeihung	fair-**tsy**-hoong
Hello (good day)	Guten Tag	**goot**-en tahk
Goodbye	Auf Wiedersehen	owf-**veed**-er-zay-ern
Good evening	Guten Abend	goot'n **ahb**'nt
Good night	Gute Nacht	goot-uh **nukht**
Until tomorrow	Bis morgen	biss **morg**'n
See you	Tschüss	**chooss**
What is that?	Was ist das?	voss ist duss
Why?	Warum?	var-**room**
Where?	Wo?	**voh**
When?	Wann?	**vunn**
today	heute	**hoyt**-uh
tomorrow	morgen	**morg**'n
month	Monat	**mohn**-aht
night	Nacht	**nukht**
afternoon	Nachmittag	**nabkh**-mit-tahk
morning	Morgen	**morg**'n
year	Jahr	**yar**
there	dort	**dort**
here	hier	**hear**
week	Woche	**vokh**-uh
yesterday	gestern	**gest**'n
evening	Abend	**ahb**'nt

USEFUL PHRASES

How are you? (informal)	Wie geht's?	vee gayts
Fine, thanks	Danke, es geht mir gut	dunk-uh, es gayt meer goot
Until later	Bis später	biss **shpay**-ter
Where is/are?	Wo ist/sind...?	voh ist/sind
How far is it to...?	Wie weit ist es...?	vee **vite** ist ess
Do you speak English?	Sprechen Sie Englisch?	shpresh'n zee **eng**-glish
I don't understand	Ich verstehe nicht	ish fair-**shtay**-uh nisht
Could you speak more slowly?	Könnten Sie langsamer sprechen?	**kurnt**-en zee **lung**-zam-er shpresh'n

USEFUL WORDS

large	gross	**grohss**
small	klein	**kline**
hot	heiss	**hyce**
cold	kalt	**kult**
good	gut	**goot**
bad	böse/schlecht	**burss**-uh/**shlesht**
open	geöffnet	g'**urff**-nett
closed	geschlossen	g'**shloss**'n
left	links	**links**
right	rechts	**reshts**
straight ahead	geradeaus	g'**rah**-der-**owss**

MAKING A TELEPHONE CALL

I would like to make a phone call	Ich möchte telefonieren	ish mer-shtuh tel-e-fon-**eer**'n
I'll try again later	Ich versuche es später noch einmal	ish fair-zookh-uh es **shpay**-ter nokh ine-mull
Can I leave a message?	Kann ich eine Nachricht hinterlassen?	kan ish **ine**-uh nakh-risht hint-er-**lahss**-en
answer phone	Anrufbeantworter	an-roof-be-**ahnt**-vort-er
telephone card	Telefonkarte	tel-e-**fohn**-kart-uh
receiver	Hörer	**hur**-er
mobile	Handy	**han**-dee
engaged (busy)	besetzt	b'**zetst**
wrong number	Falsche Verbindung	falsh-uh fair-**bin**-doong

SIGHTSEEING

library	Bibliothek	bib-leo-**tek**
entrance ticket	Eintrittskarte	ine-tritz-**kart**-uh
cemetery	Friedhof	**freed**-hofe
train station	Bahnhof	**barn**-hofe
gallery	Galerie	**gall**-er-ree
information	Auskunft	**owss**-koonft
church	Kirche	**keersh**-uh
garden	Garten	**gart**'n
palace/castle	Palast/Schloss	pallast/shloss
place (square)	Platz	**plats**
bus stop	Haltestelle	**hal**-te-shtel-uh
national holiday	Nationalfeiertag	nats-yon-**ahl**-fire-tahk
theatre	Theater	tay-**aht**-er
free admission	Eintritt frei	ine-tritt fry

SHOPPING

Do you have/ Is there...?	Gibt es...?	geept ess
How much does it cost?	Was kostet das?	voss **kost**'t duss?
When do you open/ close?	Wann öffnen Sie? schliessen Sie?	vunn **off**'n zee **shlees**'n zee
this	das	duss
expensive	teuer	**toy**-er
cheap	preiswert	**price**-vurt
size	Grösse	**gruhs**-uh
number	Nummer	**noom**-er
colour	Farbe	**farb**-uh
brown	braun	brown
black	schwarz	**shvarts**
red	rot	**roht**
blue	blau	**blau**
green	grün	**groon**
yellow	gelb	**gelp**

TYPES OF SHOP

antique shop	Antiquariat	antik-**var**-yat
chemist (pharmacy)	Apotheke	appo-**tay**-kuh
bank	Bank	**bunk**
market	Markt	**markt**
travel agency	Reisebüro	rye-zer-boo-roe
department store	Warenhaus	**vahr**'n-hows
chemist's, drugstore	Drogerie	droog-er-**ree**
hairdresser	Friseur	freezz-**er**
newspaper kiosk	Zeitungskiosk	tsytoongs-kee-osk
bookshop	Buchhandlung	**bookh**-hant-loong

bakery	Bäckerei	beck-er-**eye**
post office	Post	posst
shop/store	Geschäft/Laden	gush-**eft**/**lard**'n
film processing shop	Photogeschäft	fo-to-gush-**eft**
self-service shop	Selbstbedienungsladen	selpst-bed-**ee**-nungs-lard'n
shoe shop	Schuhladen	shoo-lard'n
clothes shop	Kleiderladen, Boutique	klyder-lard'n boo-**teek**-uh
food shop	Lebensmittelgeschäft	lay-bens-mittel-gush-eft
glass, porcelain	Glas, Porzellan	**glars, Port-sellahn**

STAYING IN A HOTEL

Do you have any vacancies?	Haben Sie noch Zimmer frei?	harb'n zee nokh **tsimm**-er-fry
with twin beds?	mit zwei Betten?	mitt tsvy bett'n
with a double bed?	mit einem Doppelbett?	mitt ine'm **dopp**'l-bet
with a bath?	mit Bad?	mitt **bart**
with a shower?	mit Dusche?	mitt **doosh**-uh
I have a reservation	Ich habe eine Reservierung	ish **harb**-uh ine-uh rez-er-**veer**-oong
key	Schlüssel	shlooss'l
porter	Pförtner	**pfert**-ner

EATING OUT

Do you have a table for...?	Haben Sie einen Tisch für...?	harb'n zee tish foor
I would like to reserve a table	Ich möchte eine Reservierung machen	ish **mer**-shtuh ine-uh rezer-**veer**-oong makh'n
I'm a vegetarian	Ich bin Vegetarier	ish bin vegg-er-**tah**-ree-er
Waiter!	Herr Ober!	hair **oh**-bare!
The bill (check), please	Die Rechnung, bitte	dee **resh**-noong bitt-uh
breakfast	Frühstück	**froo**-shtock
lunch	Mittagessen	**mit**-targ-ess'n
dinner	Abendessen	**arb**'nt-ess'n
bottle	Flasche	**flush**-uh
dish of the day	Tagesgericht	**tahg**-es-gur-isht
main dish	Hauptgericht	**howpt**-gur-isht
dessert	Nachtisch	**nahkh**-tish
cup	Tasse	**tass**-uh
wine list	Weinkarte	vine-kart-uh
tankard	Krug	khroog
glass	Glas	**glars**
spoon	Löffel	**lerff'l**
teaspoon	Teelöffel	tay-lerff'l
tip	Trinkgeld	**trink**-gelt
knife	Messer	**mess**-er
starter (appetizer)	Vorspeise	**for**-shpize-uh
the bill	Rechnung	**resh**-noong
plate	Teller	**tell**-er
fork	Gabel	**gahb**'l

MENU DECODER

Aal	**arl**	eel
Apfel	**upf'l**	apple
Apfelschorle	**upf**'l-shoorl-uh	apple juice with sparkling mineral water
Apfelsine	**upf**'l-seen-uh	orange
Aprikose	upri-**kawz**-uh	apricot
Artischocke	arti-**shokh**-uh-	artichoke
Aubergine (eggplant)	or-ber-jeen-uh	aubergine
Banane	bar-**narn**-uh	banana
Beefsteack	**beef**-stayk	steak
Bier	beer	beer
Bockwurst	**bokh**-voorst	a type of sausage
Bohnensuppe	burn-en-zoop-uh	bean soup
Branntwein	brant-vine	spirits
Bratkartoffeln	brat-kar-toff'ln	fried potatoes
Bratwurst	brat-voorst	fried sausage
Brötchen	bret-tchen	bread roll
Brot	brot	bread
Brühe	bruh-uh	broth
Butter	**boot**-ter	butter
Champignon	**shum**-pin-yong	mushroom
Currywurst	**kha**-ree-voorst	sausage with curry sauce
Dill	**dill**	dill
Ei	**eye**	egg
Eis	**ice**	ice/ ice cream
Ente	**ent**-uh	duck
Erdbeeren	ayrt-**beer**'n	strawberries
Fisch	**fish**	fish
Forelle	for-**ell**-uh	trout
Frikadelle	Frika-dayl-uh	rissole/hamburger
Gans	ganns	goose
Garnele	**gar**-nayl-uh	prawn/shrimp
gebraten	g'**braat**'n	fried
gegrillt	g'**grilt**	grilled
gekocht	g'**kokht**	boiled
geräuchert	g'**rowk**-ert	smoked
Geflügel	g'**floog**'l	poultry
Gemüse	g'**mooz**-uh	vegetables
Grütze	**grurt**-ser	groats, gruel
Gulasch	**goo**-lush	goulash
Gurke	**goork**-uh	gherkin
Hammelbraten	hamm'l-**braat**'n	roast mutton
Hähnchen	haynsh'n	chicken
Hering	**hair**-ing	herring
Himbeeren	him-**beer**'n	raspberries
Honig	**hoe**-nikh	honey
Kaffee	kaf-**fay**	coffee
Kalbfleisch	kalp-flysh	veal
Kaninchen	ka-**neensh**'n	rabbit
Karpfen	**karpf**'n	carp
Kartoffelpüree	kar-toff'l-**poor**-ay	mashed potatoes
Käse	**kayz**-uh	cheese
Kaviar	**kar**-vee-ar	caviar
Knoblauch	k'**nob**-lowkh	garlic
Knödel	k'**nerd**'l	noodle
Kohl	**koal**	cabbage
Kopfsalat	**kopf**-zal-aat	lettuce
Krebs	**krayps**	crab
Kuchen	**kookh**'n	cake
Lachs	**lahkhs**	salmon
Leber	**lay**-ber	liver
mariniert	mari-neert	marinated
Marmelade	marmer-**lard**-uh	marmalade, jam
Meerrettich	may-re-tish	horseradish
Milch	**milsh**	milk
Mineralwasser	minn-er-**arl**-vuss-er	mineral water
Möhre	**mer**-uh	carrot
Nuss	**nooss**	nut
Öl	**erl**	oil
Olive	o-**leev**-uh	olive
Petersilie	payt-er-**zee**-li-uh	parsley
Pfeffer	**pfeff**-er	pepper
Pfirsich	**pfir**-zish	peach
Pflaumen	**pflow**-men	plum
Pommes frites	pomm-**fritt**	chips/ French fries
Quark	kvark	soft cheese
Radieschen	ra-**deesh**'n,	radish
Rinderbraten	**rind**-er-brat'n	joint of beef
Rinderroulade	**rind**-er-roo-lard-uh	beef olive
Rindfleisch	**rint**-flysh	beef
Rippchen	**rip**-sh'n	cured pork rib
Rotkohl	roht-koal	red cabbage
Rüben	rhoob'n	turnip
Rührei	**rhoo**-er-eye	scrambled eggs
Saft	**zuft**	juice
Salat	zal-aat	salad

Salz	**zults**	salt
Salzkartoffeln	zults-kar-toff'l	boiled potatoes
Sauerkirschen	zow-er-**keersh**'n	cherries
Sauerkraut	zow-er-krowt	sauerkraut
Sekt	**zekt**	sparkling wine
Senf	**zenf**	mustard
scharf	sharf	spicy
Schaschlik	shash-lik	kebab
Schlagsahne	shlahgg-zarn-uh	whipped cream
Schnittlauch	shnit-lowhkh	chives
Schnitzel	**shnitz**'l	veal or pork cutlet
Schweinefleisch	**shvine**-flysh	pork
Spargel	**shparg**'l	asparagus
Spiegelei	shpeeg'l-eye	fried egg
Spinat	shpin-art	spinach
Tee	**tay**	tea
Tomate	tom-art-uh	tomato
Wassermelone	vuss-er-me-lohn-uh	watermelon
Wein	**vine**	wine
Weintrauben	vine-trowb'n	grapes
Wiener Würstchen	veen-er voorst-sh'n	frankfurter
Zander	**tsan**-der	pike-perch
Zitrone	tsi-trohn-uh	lemon
Zucker	**tsook**-er	sugar
Zwieback	tsvee-bak	rusk
Zwiebel	**tsvee**b'l	onion

NUMBERS

0	null	**nool**
1	eins	**eye'ns**
2	zwei	**tsvy**
3	drei	**dry**
4	vier	**feer**
5	fünf	**foonf**
6	sechs	**zex**
7	sieben	**zeeb**'n
8	acht	**uhkht**
9	neun	**noyn**
10	zehn	**tsayn**
11	elf	**elf**
12	zwölf	**tserlf**
13	dreizehn	**dry**-tsayn
14	vierzehn	**feer**-tsayn
15	fünfzehn	**foonf**-tsayn
16	sechzehn	**zex**-tsayn

17	siebzehn	**zeep**-tsayn
18	achtzehn	**uhkht**-tsayn
19	neunzehn	**noyn**-tsayn
20	zwanzig	**tsvunn**-tsig
21	einundzwanzig	**ine**-oont-tsvunn-tsig
30	dreissig	**dry**-sig
40	vierzig	**feer**-sig
50	fünfzig	**foonf**-tsig
60	sechzig	**zex**-tsig
70	siebzig	**zeep**-tsig
80	achtzig	**uhkht**-tsig
90	neunzig	**noyn**-tsig
100	hundert	**hoond**'t
1000	tausend	**towz**'nt
1 000 000	eine Million	**ine**-uh **mill**-yon

TIME

one minute	eine Minute	**ine**-uh min-**oot**-uh
one hour	eine Stunde	**ine**-uh **shtoond**-uh
half an hour	eine halbe Stunde	**ine**-uh hullb-uh **shtoond**-uh
Monday	Montag	**mohn**-targ
Tuesday	Dienstag	**deens**-targ
Wednesday	Mittwoch	**mitt**-vokh
Thursday	Donnerstag	**donn**-ers-targ
Friday	Freitag	**fry**-targ
Saturday	Samstag/ Sonnabend	**zums**-targ zonn-ah-bent
Sunday	Sonntag	**zon**-targ
January	Januar	**yan**-ooar
February	Februar	**fay**-brooar
March	März	**mairts**
April	April	april
May	Mai	my
June	Juni	**yoo**-ni
July	Juli	**yoo**-lee
August	August	ow-**goost**
September	September	zep-**tem**-ber
October	Oktober	ok-toh-ber
November	November	no-**vem**-ber
December	Dezember	day-**tsem**-ber
spring	Frühling	**froo**-ling
summer	Sommer	**zomm**-er
autumn (fall)	Herbst	**hairpst**
winter	Winter	**vint**-er

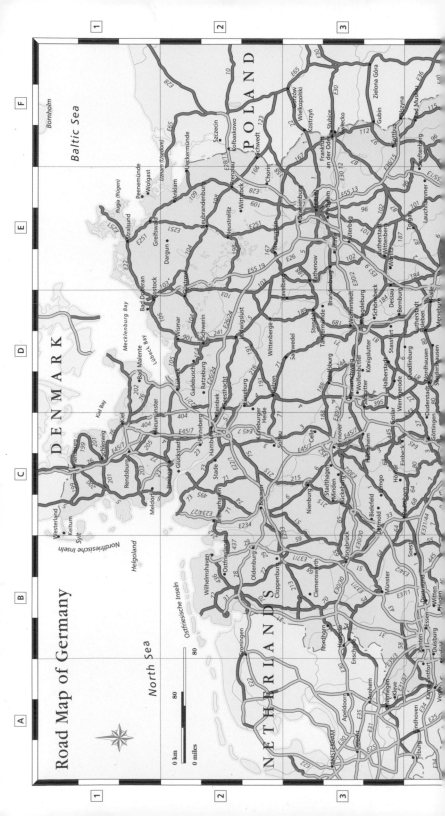

Road Map of Germany